Study Guide for

Organic Chemistry

Structure and Reactivity

Study Guide for

Organic Chemistry

Structure and Reactivity

Fourth Edition

Seyhan N. Eğe
The University of Michigan

Roberta W. Kleinman
Lock Haven University

Peggy Zitek

Houghton Mifflin Company   BOSTON   NEW YORK

Editor-in-Chief: Kathi Prancan
Senior Sponsoring Editor: Richard Stratton
Editorial Assistants: Sarah Gessner and Joy Park
Marketing Manager: Penelope Hoblyn

Cover image: Cover image of chromomycin dimer-DNA oligomer courtesy of Dr. D. J. Patel (X. Gao, P. Mirau, and D. J. Patel, *Journal of Molecular Biology,* **1992,** *223,* 259-279) Protein Data Bank (PDB) ID number ID83.

About the cover: Chromomycin belongs to a group of antibiotics that are effective antitumor agents against a variety of experimental and human tumors. It works by complexing to DNA as a dimeric structure containing a magnesium ion, inhibiting the synthesis of RNA, and, thus, the synthesis of proteins in the cell. The cover of this book shows a representation of the interaction of two molecules of chromomycin (the gold and magenta structures, held together by a green magnesium ion) with the minor grove of a segment of DNA (turquoise) consisting of eight nucleotides in each strand. The structure of the chromomycin-DNA complex was determined by Dr. Dinshaw J. Patel (then at Columbia University, now at Memorial Sloan-Kettering Cancer Center) and his colleagues using a combination of computer modeling and two-dimensional nuclear magnetic resonance spectroscopy. As a result of their work, scientists now have a picture of specific intermolecular interactions between the antitumor agent and DNA. These include coordination between oxygen atoms on the antibiotic and the positively-charged magnesium ion, hydrogen bonding between hydroxyl groups of the antibiotic and amino groups and nitrogen atoms of guanosine bases, and van der Waals interactions between hydrocarbon portions of chromomycin and the surface of the minor groove of the DNA. The researchers also were able to show that the DNA changes shape to accommodate the antibiotic.

An understanding of how a particular antitumor drug recognizes and interacts with a specific part of the double helix of DNA is important in enabling chemists to design better therapeutic agents. For example, Professor William Roush of the University of Michigan is using the Patel structure of the complex of the dimer of chromomycin with DNA to design simpler analogs with improved selectivity in their binding to DNA. Study of the complex of the dimer of chromomycin with DNA is also expected to shed light on the role of the carbohydrate units in stabilizing the DNA bound complex. Professor Daniel Kahne of Princeton University is especially interested in this latter question and is designing analogs of chromomycin in which the carbohydrate side chains are replaced by simpler oxygen-containing chains to investigate the role of the carbohydrate units in causing two chromomycin molecules to complex with one metal ion (D. J. Silva, D. Kahne, C. M. Kraml, *Journal of the American Chemical Society,* **1994,** *116,* 2641-2642).

Contents

To the Student

The *Study Guide* that accompanies your text has been prepared to help you study organic chemistry. The textbook contains many problems designed to assist you in reviewing the chemistry that you need to know. The *Study Guide* contains the answers to these problems worked out in great detail to help you to develop the patterns of thought and work that will enable you to complete a course in organic chemistry successfully. In addition, notes that clarify points that may give you difficulty are provided in many answers.

The *Study Guide* also contains *Workbook Exercises,* created by Professor Brian Coppola of the University of Michigan. These exercises are designed to help you review previous material and to introduce you to the problem-solving skills you will need for new material. They are found only in the *Study Guide,* and no answers are given for them. Many of the exercises can be explored with other students in your class.

Suggestions for the best way to study organic chemistry are given on pages 2 - 4 of the textbook and in the essay, "Learning Tips for Students of Organic Chemistry," immediately following this introduction. This essay was written by Professor Coppola as a way of sharing with you his long experience with helping students to learn. Before you work with the *Study Guide,* please review the essay as well as those pages in the text.

This *Study Guide* contains two features to help you to study more effectively. The sections on Problem-Solving Skills in the textbook show you how to analyze problems in a systematic way by asking yourself questions about the structural changes in and the reactivity of the reagents shown in the problem. These same questions are used in arriving at the answers shown in the *Study Guide* for some of the problems. If you follow the reasoning shown in these answers, you will review the thinking patterns that are useful in solving problems.

The *Study Guide* also contains concept maps, which are summaries of important ideas or patterns of reactivity presented in a two-dimensional outline form. The textbook has notes in the margins telling you when a concept map appears in the *Study Guide.* The concept maps are located among the answers to the problems. The Table of Contents of the *Study Guide* on pp. iii - vii will tell you where each concept map is. The concept maps will be the most useful to you if you use them as a guide to making your own. For example, when you review your lecture notes, you will learn the essential points much more easily if you attempt to summarize the contents of the lecture in the form of a concept map. At a later time you may want to combine the contents of several lectures into a different concept map. Your maps need not look like the ones in the *Study Guide.* What is important is that you use the format to try to see relationships among ideas, reactions, and functional groups in a variety of ways.

The *Study Guide* will be most helpful to you if you make every attempt to solve each problem completely before you look at the answer. Recognition of a correct answer is much easier than being able to produce one yourself, so if you simply look up answers in the book to see whether you "know how to do the problem" or "understand" a principle, you will probably decide that you do. In truth, however, you will not have gained the practice in writing structural formulas and making the step-by-step decisions about reactivity that you will need when faced by similar questions on examinations. Work out all answers in detail, writing correct, complete formulas for all reagents and products. Build molecular models to help you draw correct three-dimensional representations of molecules. Consult the models whenever you are puzzled by questions of stereochemistry.

If you do not understand the answer to a problem, study the relevant sections of the text again, and then try to do the problem once more. The problems will tell you what you need to spend most of your time studying. As you solve the many review problems that bring together material from different chapters, your knowledge of the important reactions of organic chemistry will solidify.

In addition to the answers to the problems in the textbook, the *Study Guide* also contains Supplemental Problems for most chapters. These are additional drill and thought questions for which answers will be available to you only through your instructor. These problems are excellent ways to review the material for a test.

We hope that the *Study Guide* will serve you as a model for the kind of disciplined care that you must take with your answers if you wish to train yourself to arrive at correct solutions to problems with consistency. We hope also that it will help you to develop confidence in your ability to master organic chemistry so that you enjoy your study of a subject that we find challenging and exciting.

Seyhan N. Eğe
Roberta W. Kleinman
Peggy Zitek

Learning Tips for Students of Organic Chemistry

by Brian P. Coppola
The University of Michigan

From the Outside Looking In...

Every year, I am more and more on the outside looking in when it comes to learning the subject of organic chemistry. The reason is simple: As a practicing organic chemist who has been an instructor of this subject for over fifteen years, I cannot see organic chemistry the way that a new student sees it. Students see this subject with the eyes of a fresh learner, with one new idea following another with few previous reference points. One of the things I value in my interactions with students is that they bring their unique perspectives as new learners to my course. The fresh eyes of my students are the greatest tool I have to improve my understanding of "learning organic chemistry", which greatly impacts my ability to help others learn it, too.

As a student, I was a chemistry major thinking about a career in science, so I was predisposed to take my chemistry courses seriously. Although most classmates in my own undergraduate courses were not prospective majors, I was still like many of them, as well as my own students today, in some other respects. One purpose (perhaps a motivation) for learning a subject was to get a good grade on exams. I wanted good grades because I took great pride in doing well in my academic studies. I also knew I needed good grades to get into graduate school. But there was something else. Only in retrospect did I realize that some of my college instructors were trying to get me to see learning from the broader perspective of improving myself through higher education. I think that understanding this lesson was difficult for two reasons. First, I did not have any reference points or experiences for this advice to make sense until much later in life (in fact, in some cases, not until I became an instructor myself). Second, as far as I can recall, these broad lessons in improvement never seemed to show up in my science classes, except maybe as a spoken line or two on the first day of class. These ideas never seemed to appear anywhere else. The book, the homework, the class time and the exams were all "just chemistry problems." Once I became responsible for organizing courses as a faculty member, I found myself wanting to address these two problems. As an instructor, I cannot do anything about the first difficulty. I cannot provide students with 10 years of experience in four months (although the students in my Honors course might disagree with that statement). Experience being what it is, generally, you have to get it in order to have it. One of the things that motivates me as an instructor, though, is the thought that I (and all instructors) can help out with the second difficulty, that of bringing evidence of a broader perspective to multiple aspects of a subject.

Although I may be on the outside looking in when it comes to learning organic chemistry for the first time, my knowledge continues to increase in two other areas. First, I understand better every year how the nuances of this subject fit together, often because of questions my students ask. Second, I continue to learn how students learn organic chemistry, which answers one of the most common questions students ask their instructors: How can teaching the same old thing year after year be interesting? For me, that is easy: I never do it the same way twice. There is always something new I learn about how students learn that makes me improve what I do the next time.

I wrote the phrase "bringing evidence of a broader perspective to multiple aspects of a subject" to describe an instructional goal. What does this mean?

In order to answer this, I have to start with a summary of all of my goals for students in my courses. Many times, when faced with the question of goals, faculty will drag out a copy of the syllabus and say "Here are my goals: On the first week of class we will cover chapter one, then chapter two...." If such statements are examples of goals, I find them unsatisfactory. Over the years, I have found it useful to categorize the goals that I have for student learning in my courses. I think there is an important hierarchy to goals that has been lost in higher education. At the most immediately obvious level are what I call "professional technical goals." These are the goals most directly related to the subject matter of the course: The factual understanding and operational skills you are supposed to develop in your studies, and on which examinations are generally based. In calculus this might be learning how to take a derivative; in French this might be learning how to construct the past participles of some regular verbs. In an organic chemistry course, one early goal is for students to be able to translate the drawings used to represent chemical structures into an inventory of the atoms involved and how they are connected to one other. The technical (subject matter) goals usually become more sophisticated as a course proceeds. The kind of skills you are supposed to develop are gauged by the type of problems that you are supposed to solve. An increasing number of individual skills are combined and balanced into ways for solving new problems. Later in a course, enough specific examples should have been assembled to allow students to make sense of broader categories and concepts. These larger categories and concepts are what define a discipline ("calculus," "French," "chemistry") and identify what I call "professional intellectual goals." These concepts and generalizations also allow me to understand new and unfamiliar information both by applying the larger ideas to any specific new situation and by creating analogies based on other factual information that I know. Indeed, I want my students to develop the skills that are used by a practicing chemist.

Courses and subjects are filled with professional technical goals. The professional intellectual goals are what keep a subject from becoming just an endless list of things that have to be remembered. There are professional intellectual goals that relate to chemistry, such as explaining and predicting everything from bonding to bonding changes (chemical reactions) on the basis of electrostatic interactions (the attraction between positive, or electron-poor atoms, and negative, or electron-rich atoms). There are also other professional intellectual goals that relate to science and scientific practice, such as understanding the role of reproducibility in experimental science or the significance of the Uncertainty Principle in understanding observations. It is my obligation to demonstrate consistently how and why the specifics of chemistry interact with larger ideas of both chemistry and science. It is my students' obligation to appreciate the validity and operational importance of these relationships. Finally, there are "general intellectual goals" that are, to a degree, the overriding purpose of an education. These are the skills acquired from the study of a subject that transcend the subject itself, especially new strategies, insights and experiences about the process of learning and understanding new things.

Learning Skills. Specific Strategies and Tactics

A few things we know (and a few we do not) about learning organic chemistry

You should expect that learning organic chemistry, for the reasons outlined above, may be different from other learning experiences that you have had. The myths that surround the subject of chemistry, and especially organic chemistry, do not help at all.

"Organic chemistry is the most difficult course at the University."

"Organic chemistry is the 'weeder' course for medical schools."

"Memorizing tons of information is the only way to get through."

"Look to your left in class, then look to your right. One of those people will not be there at the end of the term."

"Only students with previous college chemistry, a good AP background, and an organic chemistry prep course can do well."

"I just can't do science classes."

Is it any wonder that it is difficult to concentrate on the course with all of these anxieties lurking around? These statements are simply not true.

Structure and Reactivity is the large introductory course based on organic chemistry and taken by first-year students at the University of Michigan. Since 1989, the University of Michigan faculty have presumed that the precollege chemistry background of our students is adequate to the task of learning organic chemistry. One of the most gratifying aspects of teaching this course has been feedback that we are fulfilling one of the unstated expectations of new university students, that their academic program will be different and challenging and not a repeat of their high school experience (something that is certainly true in the non-academic portion of a student's experience in attending college).

We have looked carefully at what characterizes students who are successful in our *Structure and Reactivity* courses. Here is what we know:

(1) The amount and type of previous chemistry does not make a difference, but learning skills do.

• The fact that students did not take an AP Chemistry course does not matter. On average, the 35-40% of 1000-1200 students in our first-term Structure and Reactivity course who took AP Chemistry perform at the same level as the non-AP students do. We have strong indications that it is not the background in chemistry content that matters, but rather the learning skills of the student.

• A second thing that points to learning skills is the fact that the Math SAT score is the only other background factor that predicts anything significant about student performance in the first-term *Structure and Reactivity* course, even though the course is 100% narrative, or descriptive, and primarily non-mathematical in nature. Historically, the Math SAT score is thought to be representative of general learning skills.

• Students in *Structure and Reactivity* courses tend to develop their deeper learning skills more than their counterparts in a General Chemistry course, therefore the willingness to make these sorts of changes is an important characteristic of those who succeed in the course.

(2) Psychological motivation plays an important role.

• We also have observed that students' beliefs in their own abilities play as large a role in predicting success as the Math SAT score. A person who believes that he or she has developed a degree of control over learning (or over any task), tends to develop better understanding. Part of this is a feedback cycle, where those who do well to begin with get the message that what they were doing was the right thing. On the other hand, we also know from our course that the first exam does a relatively poor job of predicting course outcome. This means that many students who end up doing well develop their successful strategies later, after some less satisfactory experiences have motivated them to make a change. It is important for students to be patient and persistent, and not to let the first discouragement drag them down.

• Student responsibility is also significant. If students find themselves thinking "I did not learn because the instructor did not teach me well enough," then they are requiring far too much of the instructor and not enough of themselves. Similarly, if students conclude that "This course just did not match the way I learn," then they are missing the point about building new skills on the foundation of old ones. I think that becoming a more flexible learner has no down side. Why just reward the same old skills?

Learning skills

Learning skills include memorization , but memorization alone is not enough.

The subject matter of organic chemistry is particularly well-suited to encouraging students to develop deeper learning skills. This is because you spend an entire year with one specific subject that builds upon itself in a meaningful way. Many times, introductory courses are called surveys, where one topic follows another without much linkage. There can be advantages to this approach. For instance, each new topic becomes a fresh start without the immediate need to master a previous topic. On the other hand, you never spend long enough with any one topic to make deep connections that truly challenge your learning skills. Organic chemistry begins with a relatively few general principles for which you can develop a ever deepening understanding as the year goes on. At least, that's the plan! On the other hand, no one can force you to do anything, including learning differently. All an instructor can do is to create a situation where you will come to realize that your old skills are inadequate.

My instructional goal for students is to use chemistry as a way to encourage them to develop new learning skills. To accomplish this goal, students must be faced with learning situations where their old skills are inadequate but not abandoned. The skills with which students begin a course are their strengths, their point of reference. For the most part, students begin a course with what are called "surface skills." Surface skills include the ability to memorize, to organize, to recall and connect one set of symbols or representations with another. A concrete example of such skills is the multiplication tables. You can connect the symbols "2 × 2" with "4" without ever understanding the multiplication relationship. This is also your level of understanding when you learn to do multiplication with an electronic calculator. The multiplication tables or a calculator are just starting points. Your current understanding of multiplication has not replaced the times table or a calculator. Rather it has become broadened and deepened with alternative ways to think about multiplication. Notice that you have not abandoned your fluency with the multiplication tables or calculators because you now have a mastery of multiplication. Rather this fluency is inadequate when faced with a problem that is not on the table you have memorized. Without using a calculator to solve "345.8 × 45.5," a problem that you probably have not seen before but nonetheless can solve easily, you use your more general knowledge of multiplication as well as your specific recollection of the multiplication tables. Even when you use a calculator, your general understanding of multiplication combined with estimation skills would allow you to reject an answer such as "157.339" if it showed up on the display. The additional skills you need to combine with surface skills in order to solve this problem are called "deep processing skills." To solve this unfamiliar problem, the deeper skills interact with your surface skills in ways that allow you to judge whether you are adequately performing the task at hand.

Specific Strategies

Why should students develop new learning skills? I hope that the answer is self-evident: Such development is one of the objectives of higher education. In order to end up with an intellectually rewarding career, you have to be able to walk into a new and unfamiliar situation with the confidence that your skills will see you through. All people who are truly successful at what they do bring these kinds of skills to new problems, and new problems are the interesting ones! Experiences in (and out) of college classes are meant to model these situations. The behaviors and habits students develop during these years define their character for the future, long after the details of specific courses have faded away. I am deeply committed to the idea that we are all life-long learners, and that a necessary goal in education is to encourage the habits of the life-long learner. What does this mean? Mainly, it means that you become more and more responsible for your own education. Rather than having your interests defined by a course or curriculum, you begin to identify what you want to learn, including how to learn it, because it serves some greater, self-defined goal.

What does a deeper or higher order learning skill mean? The skills that more experienced learners bring to a task are complex, and vary from challenge to challenge. The process of making appropriate selections from a menu of existing strategies, or knowing when to invent new ones, is a skill unto itself, analogous to matching the right tool to a mechanical job. For an introductory course, I encourage students to master the following skills:

- **Restatement**
  Restatement is more than just putting it in your own words. It is the process of making new ideas make sense in terms of what you know. As you encounter a new concept, try to imagine having to give a short lesson to another beginning student to get them to understand it. Do not just rehearse the words of the text over and over, and do not just say them to yourself, in your head. If you have to, say your lesson out loud to yourself. If you can, find another classmate to talk to. More will be said on this in the section on "The role of teaching in learning."

- **Connections**
  One hallmark of the best learners I have known is their belief that everything is connected. What you learn in one place can help you understand something else. When I face new and unfamiliar information, one of my first reactions is to find an appropriate analogy. Rather than answering the question "What is this like...?" I start with the certainty of "This *is* like..."

• Review and reconnect

Connections are not enough. As you develop the map that is your understanding, it is also important to review what you once knew in terms of what you now know. New information should give you a new perspective on old information. Another version of this is the idea that your understanding should be sketched out rather than defined too specifically too early. When dealing with a new chapter in your text, for example, you can elect to move very linearly and deliberately through the book, one page at a time, digesting each adverb before you permit yourself to turn the page. Unfortunately, this approach minimizes opportunities to make connections. Another approach is to think of your understanding as a painting. First you start by making a sketch, which is a process filled with erasure and correction, a time when what once seemed right is now out of place, and a time to get a look at the whole canvas and try to see the big picture, even if it is a bit blurry. After this comes a time of refinement and elaboration, where self-consistency across the canvas allows the newly defined parts to complement one another.

• Self-constructed summaries and aids

As you build towards self-reliance, you must begin to solve problems with no information other than what will be available at your exams. Any amount of time you spend "getting little hints" or using anything other than the information in the problem to help solve it is wasted. If you tie your skills to an answer key, your notes, or where you are in the text, then you will be practicing skills that are useless for the exam. At some point, you must be willing to look at an unfamiliar problem and say "I don't know how to do that, yet." and move on to the things you can do with the knowledge you have. If you do construct aids, such as mnemonics, lists, or other associations, make sure they are the kinds of things you have actually used to solve problems.

• Self-constructed assessments

Whatever your course of study, the object of your study will be ideas and how people deal with information. One way to test your own proficiency is to create your own problems. This can be done many ways for many different subjects. In my chemistry courses, I usually recommend two things for everyone. First, take any general subject heading in the course ("resonance forms," "Brønsted acid-base reactions," and so on) and write it on a blank piece of paper. Now create (*do not* look up or recall) 10-20 examples of that phenomenon based on the general principle. One of the best uses students can make of their instructors is to share these creations. Other versions of this exercise might be to see if two or more of the general ideas can be combined, or to get together with others and use these problems as the basis for testing one another. The other advice I have is related to creating exam questions. Instead of creating examples under the topic heading, students can do what the faculty do: Go to chemistry journals. In my course, nearly all of the exam questions have a citation because it is very convenient to thumb through the journals and use simple sorting skills to look for specific examples of general phenomena. You can do this, too.

• Information and meaning

A theme that links the five skills listed above is the distinction between "information" and "meaning." When I write "cat" or "table," these words are just collections of symbols that are meant to represent the idea of a cat or a table. Without prior knowledge about these symbols, it is not possible to extract the meaning of "cat" from the letters c-a-t. The word "cat" is not a cat! Similarly, the symbolic representation "H_2O" is not water, but it is meant to represent all that water is and how it behaves and interacts. One of the things that make organic chemistry so interesting is that once you learn the basics of the structure/reactivity relationships, you will be able to predict the behavior of substances the structures of which you have never seen before, much the way a very complete knowledge of Greek, Latin, and word origins might allow you to understand words you had never seen. Information collects all of the surface features, while meaning gathers all of the inferences. One of the common mistakes made by instructors is to advise students that learning organic chemistry is like learning a foreign language; not so. When you learn any second (or third, etc.) language, you do so with an idea of what the objects that need to be described are. In other words, there is a great deal of translation. If you already know what a cat is, and you have a word for it in your first language ("cat"), then learning that "chat" is how this idea is represented in French benefits from your preconception of what a cat is. Now imagine that some other animal (or maybe you are not even sure it is an animal; it is like nothing you have ever seen before, actually) is not only named in a language with which you are unfamiliar, but that the descriptions of this thing are also only available in this unfamiliar language. Learning organic chemistry is not like learning a second language at all; it is more like learning your first language.

• Diagnosis and treatment

Diagnosis. Solving problems follows a medical metaphor quite well. There are two parts to the problem-solving process: Diagnosis and treatment. Diagnosis is the part where general classifications are made, and perhaps a general strategy is developed. On a chemistry exam, it simply means deciding which of 6 or 7 major ideas is represented by the problem. If you have created such a list before the exam, and practiced using it, then you can use it as a guide while taking the exam. The exam problems must represent the ideas from the chapters in question. This raises an interesting idea to keep in mind about textbooks. Textbooks themselves can allow you to underdevelop or avoid using your skills in diagnosis. For example:

(1) *Problems within the chapter are diagnosed for you before you get there!* Not surprisingly, the problems relate to the preceding section. One way to demonstrate that diagnosis is a real skill is to take photocopies of the in-chapter problems after you have done them, cut them apart from identifying markers, randomize them, and then try to answer the question, "What kind of problem is this?" The same problems that were *so easy* before are now difficult. Ready to learn diagnosis?

(2) *Problems at the end of chapters are still mostly associated with the chapter,* and are sometimes drill-like (Problem 23 had parts a, b, c, d...w). Once you struggle with 23a and 23b, all of a sudden 23c is easy. You are not actually getting any better at diagnosis because you can do 23c; you are just anticipating what the problem is about. It is being done for you. Any time you know what a problem is about before you have read any part of the problem, you probably should not do it. Skip it and come back later and see if you can still tell what it is about.

(3) *Keep book-reading and note-reading time separate from problem-solving time.* Try the problems in a new chapter before you read the chapter, just to see that you cannot do any of them. Even by reviewing the problems, you may begin to get a sense of the ideas that you will need to pay attention to. If something is unclear after a respectable effort, move on. Try to treat chapters as whole entities, as stories where all the parts are interwoven. As you make your initial fast pass through the text, see if any of the problems make more sense. If so, try them out. If you can't solve them, you will come back to them again. If you recognize that you do not know how to do a problem with the understanding that you have at that point, that is an important thing to know. Concentrate your efforts on learning what you *can* do with what you know, and work from there as you reread (and reread and reread). If you do not spend overly long with parts of the chapter that are not clicking, you will free up time for future readings. No knowledge can be presented so linearly that you can't learn from page 54 without getting page 53. And many times, what you learn on page 54 can help you understand page 53. Give yourself permission to turn the page!

The bottom line in learning to do diagnosis correctly is quite compelling: If you don't get this part right, it doesn't matter how well you do the next part, because it will be wrong. The correct answer to the wrong question never gets any points. After all, a physician may know how to treat two different diseases perfectly well, so the most important thing is first to make the diagnosis correctly! A physician does not get "partial credit" for prescribing the right medication for the wrong disease.

Treatments The following suggestions are, by definition, incomplete. These ideas are meant to inspire you to think about learning in ways you might not have before.

(1) *Practice useful skills.* Always ask yourself, "Am I doing this work honestly? Am I just rationalizing someone else's answer in the *Study Guide*? Am I using a resource that I will not have at an exam? Did I know what this problem was about before I did it?" You can learn how to do the wrong thing very well. It feels as though you are making progress, but it is in the wrong direction, or simply allowing you to generate incorrect answers more efficiently. It is fine to get the advice that you must spend a little time studying the subject every day, but this is the beginning of the story, not the end. How you spend your time

matters too. Many high school and beginning university students equate time spent with effort when what is needed is productive effort. The only way to know whether what you are doing is productive is to examine it honestly. Can you do problems when they are out of context, can you explain your ideas in writing, and can you explain them out loud?

(2) *Concentrate on your strengths.* Build on what you know and learn to identify the problems you can do with what you know. Learn to admit when you do not know something as well as when you do. Sketch out your understanding by trying to keep the broad arguments in mind when you are concentrating on the details. Work back and forth as you master new ideas, asking, "How does this fit into the overall picture?"

(3) *On an exam, you are the teacher.* Like it or not, instructors demand performance of one kind or another. If you always keep in mind that you need to express your ideas as well as learn them, you will be ahead of the game. You do not necessarily need to work with another person, but it is generally easier to develop such skills if you do. Self-examination and quizzing your study partners is a chance to practice those skills before the exam. During the examination, your role is that of the instructor, and your instructor is the student to whom you are explaining the ideas. If you have practiced this skill before the exam, you will not be forced to learn it there.

(4) *Constant, daily building of ideas.* If you play catch-up, you will be caught. Listen and think in class. Respond to questions. Create your own tools for solving problems, and do not wait until just before the exam. If you are allowed an index card of information, it should be created and refined throughout your study of the chapter. Even if you are not allowed to bring it to the exam, you can still think about developing a card's worth of information that is useful for solving problems. Look at the general statements and topic headings and conclusions from the lecture and ask yourself, "Do I believe these? Do I believe that the examples support the ideas?" Even if you wait until the last minute, at least give yourself a few days for the longer-term connections to begin to form. If your exam is Tuesday night, then pretend it is really on Saturday or Sunday and use the intervening days to review and allow the ideas to percolate. Whatever your time frame for study, push it back a few days, even if all you intend to do is cram for the exam.

(5) *Exams transmit expectations.* More than anything, the exam is where you really learn what the course is about. You must pick up your graded exam and analyze why you made errors. The "correct answer" simply does not count for that much compared with correcting the process by which you made the error. If you think an exam question was written poorly, then one thing to do is try to rewrite it yourself. Write out in words the thought process you used to create an answer and look for where you went wrong. Having this process written out also is a good way to engage your instructor. Avoid avoidance; when the exam is taken and graded, pick it up and look at it. If you do not pick it up, you are only making things worse, not better. The old exam is a place where you can inspect your real errors, the ones pertaining to how you were learning.

The role of teaching in learning

Learning to be a critical listener

I started with a discussion of how teaching impacts my learning. A phrase familiar to all instructors is based on their first teaching experiences: "I never really learned this subject until I had to teach it." Most instructors understand that the most important advice to give is that students should work together in their learning. The reason for this is that you develop teaching skills when you work with others. Developing teaching skills is relevant to all students who take exams, write papers and give presentations, which includes everyone. All of these events are fundamentally teaching events, that is, situations that call for explanations to be given. When a learner is consciously aware as a goal of the need to explain things to others (in other words, teaching), then learning is improved.

One useful teaching skill is to become a critical listener. When you work with others, don't decide only whether what they are saying is right or wrong according to your rules and ideas. Try to understand the rules and ideas being used by the other person in what they say or do. Let me use a specific example outside of chemistry. If you were helping a grade school student to learn multiplication, asking him or her to *create* 10 or 20 new problems, and their solutions, would be a good idea. Your expertise at multiplication would allow you to scan all 20 problems in a very short amount of time, and give that student some valuable feedback. The interesting thing is that understanding is hardly ever completely correct or completely incorrect. Usually, understanding is incomplete, adequate in some places, inadequate in others. The challenge in monitoring your own learning is to put yourself in situations where you can distinguish between adequate and inadequate understanding. For example, this young learner might come to you with 20 examples, and the first few you see are:

(a) $1.1 \times 11 = 12.1$ (b) $2 \times 2 = 4$ (c) $3.5 \times 1.4 = 4.9$ (d) $2 \times 4 = 6$

As an instructor, you can react in many ways to these examples. The worst thing to do is to say: "Letter (d) is wrong, you need to study more." In my experience, I have always noticed that I can learn about the way students understand something by assuming that what I see is the result of a consistent application of some set of rules. This is an example of critical listening. I am less concerned about only getting across my perspective and more concerned about understanding the perspective of the person I am with. The reason that I like the multiplication example is that it demonstrates something I see often; a student's inadequate rules and my generally more adequate rules can overlap. This means that we can both come to the same factual conclusion for different reasons. If I want to probe the deeper understanding of my students, so that I can better know that they are using the correct *process* to obtain their answers, then I must try to push the edge of understanding. By learning only how to produce (and evaluate) answers with surface strategies, students can end up learning how to do the wrong thing very well; that is, they master inadequate rules that just happen to produce the same answer as the better rules do. It is easy to make this mistake in teaching: Just because another person's interpretation or answer looks correct does not mean it was obtained by the same pathway as yours or that it means the same thing as it does to you. I do not mean to imply that multiple interpretations are not possible; I mean that better communication depends on double checking that I understand the connection between the process and the product of a student's effort before I build what I do on incorrect assumptions. For example, the cases of "multiplication" presented by your student were in fact created by the consistent application of the rules of addition, instead of those of multiplication. To tell the student that he or she was doing something inconsistently would have been very bad advice.

There are a number of different ways to practice your teaching skills as a way to improve your learning. The one prerequisite is that you learn how to open yourself up for interactions with other students: Good communication (speaking and listening) skills, mutual trust, and a willingness to be publicly incorrect and to be corrected are all necessary. You must examine the conditions under which an answer is provided in addition to the answer itself, and you need problems that are both difficult and for which you cannot easily obtain solutions. Better learning through teaching is a fact. It has worked for me, as I described at the beginning of this essay, and it can work for you, too.

Working with others is more than a social occasion

There are additional good reasons for having conversations about things you are trying to learn. Sitting by yourself alone somewhere, you can convince yourself of just about anything. Time on your own is a good beginning, but sooner or later you need to see if you can share what you know. Certainly, as discussed earlier, this is what happens at an exam! When you have the opportunity to say what you are learning out loud, you must consider organizing the ideas for someone else. In fact, when you know you are going to be in the situation of describing what you understand to someone else, you actually learn it differently. If you naturally learn by having discussions, that is fortunate. It probably means you are thinking appropriately about the exam situation. Anticipating the need to make explanations is at the core of this advice. A person does not necessarily have to work with someone else to achieve these benefits. On the other hand, in my experience, students do not seem to take this need enough into account. Editing your own ideas is a difficult task. An external editor, or proofreader, for your ideas, makes sense. Whether you like it or not, the exam will put you in the position of explaining ideas. If you wait until then to develop and practice that skill, you are overburdening the exam time with things that you could have practiced ahead of time.

Learning to use vocabulary actively and accurately

Ideas are represented by words and other symbols. In order to work with ideas, you must also work with words and symbols. As you test your ideas, speak out loud without the safety net of your books nearby. While you are walking across campus, talk chemistry with a friend. While you are out at dinner, get out a napkin and draw out chemical ideas. These are the only ways to build the proper confidence that you can actually communicate using chemistry. When I work with students, I am intolerant (in a nice way) about imprecise language. I will stop students who use phrases such as "that thing over there" or "you know, the one from class" and encourage them to think about the proper terminology and phraseology for communicating ideas in chemistry. These are important skills to practice before examinations. During your exams, you have no choice but to represent your ideas correctly. Your answers will be incorrect if the wrong symbols are used, or if a structure is drawn the wrong way, if the wrong words are used...even if you "knew it." Incorrect representation is an error. "I know I didn't write it that way, but I meant..." never ever works. Does the importance of vocabulary also apply to courses where multiple choice problems are used on examinations? Yes and, unfortunately, no. There are many strategies that rely on recognition and recall that can be used in preparing for these kinds of exams (which I have never given, by the way). This does not mean that students cannot develop a good idea about chemistry in courses with multiple choice exams, but I do think that there is less reason to do so. Learning strategies based only on memorization are familiar and well-practiced by students, so they feel quite comfortable with them. As you can probably tell by now, I think that this degree of comfort is exactly why moving away from those strategies is a good idea!

Examinations

Exams are the real curriculum, not the syllabus. Think about that one more time. Nothing I say about learning in this course matters if a student does not see clearly how it relates to the examinations. Like it or not, the structure and expectations of higher education include grading, and grading results, for the most part, from examinations. Students learn about my expectations at examinations, not from what I say in class. It is therefore quite important to ensure that there is *congruence* between (a) the stated goals in a course, (b) the instructional method, (c) the instructional tasks, and (d) the examinations and how they are evaluated.

I believe that nothing I say will matter, and that nothing I do in class will matter if the examinations do not fulfill the expectations created by the classwork. If I do not want memorization to be the only tool students develop, then my exams must ensure that this strategy alone will not work. In addition, I must think about instruction in a way that encourages the development of new learning strategies. To that end, nearly all of the examination questions in my course are derived from examples taken from current chemistry journals. There is no better way to demonstrate two important ideas. First, simply becoming familiar with the textbook examples cannot lead to success. Students must develop the skill to identify major ideas and themes and then use these concepts as their basis for drawing analogies. Second, we demonstrate that the subject is vital. The major ideas still appear and reappear in current research month after month. All the learning strategies previously discussed can apply to courses that use multiple choice exams. In my view, however, this style of exam does not obviously require this way of learning and can cause students to default to more familiar and comfortable strategies. Many educators debate whether a student's choice to use lower level learning skills should have any bearing on the decisions made by an instructor in choosing a testing strategy. After all, almost any exam will create a distribution of students in the class, and "good students" will probably learn well in any situation. This last sentence highlights my reason for giving the kind of course that I do: I do not see it as my professional responsibility to find the "good students" who are already sitting in my course on the first day of class. My responsibility is to provide an opportunity for improvement by all the students in my class (including me, by the way).

The course packs for the *Structure and Reactivity* courses at the University of Michigan have two parts: Essays such as this one, which constitute one way of transmitting the course goals to students, and actual pages from the last 4-5 years worth of old examinations, with no solutions provided. Sometimes no matter what I say or do, only an inspection of these exams will convince students that my words mean what they say.

Interestingly enough, every year all students think that their exam is more difficult than the one given the year before. This is just not true. There is also an aspect to taking examinations that is characteristic of any situation where performance is called for known as "performance anxiety" (or, in this case, "test anxiety"). Test anxiety is not attached to the subject, even though many students would like to think so. Test anxiety is like stage fright for acting or a musical recital, or like the tension at a sporting event when you are at the starting line for the race that counts. It does not matter how smoothly things have gone before. You are human, and human beings become anxious at the event that matters. There are many different strategies to use to combat this kind of anxiety, including what your teacher, mentor, or coach has to say to you prior to the event. What you need is confidence from two sources: Yourself and the people you respect. Clearly, the more practice you have that allows you to develop skills you can use during the event, the better off you are. An examination, at its core, is an event that requires you to make an explanation about things you have not necessarily thought about before. The more you have practiced this, the better off you will be. The more you have avoided it, the less prepared you will be.

We do not provide solutions to the old exams because we want students to work together. Although it is frustrating not to have an answer key, there are plenty of problems with solutions in the *Study Guide* associated with the textbook. In addition to encouraging students to work together, the old exams can help individuals to regulate their learning. Every day, after class or after studying, a student can go to this set of problems and use them to answer two questions:

> *(1) What can I do with the knowledge I have now?*

> *(2) Can I identify the kind of knowledge I need to solve the problems I cannot now do?*

One of the more sophisticated skills of the expert problem-solver is learning how to develop a sense about whether their solutions "seem reasonable" or "make sense." This is an intuition that only comes through solving problems in a way where problem-solvers are honest with themselves about the confidence they have in their abilities.

Getting the "A" grade

The techniques outlined in the section on specific learning strategies are meant to give you an alternative to simply "doing problems" and constantly re-working them. These techniques should become second nature to you. They will serve you in all courses, including organic chemistry. Working on these skills is like taking an art class. You must take some time to sketch out your ideas and practice your skills nearly every day. You need to show your creations to other people so that errors in your technique can be corrected. Learn how to share your chemistry ideas – especially your incomplete ones – with your peers and with your instructor. Remember, you cannot simply persist in old study practices if they are not working for you and expect to see different results no matter how much time you invest.

You want to get a good grade in your courses, and I want you to learn something about how to learn along with your mastery of chemistry. I want you to do well on your exams because I believe that if you do, there is a good chance you also will have done the following:

> 1. *You will have learned how to be successful at something very new to you.*

> 2. *You will understand that science operates as a narrative, where sophisticated stories are told by people just like you by using their common sense and reasoning skills.*

> 3. *You will realize that information or facts, alone, are not terribly interesting, but they can point to a fascinating understanding or meaning of the world.*

> 4. *Best of all, you will develop confidence that your new learning skills will be something you can carry into other parts of your academic life.*

For your part, I would like you to begin to attach a more meaningful value to getting good grades. Your introductory classes can be a valuable learning experience in being with a group of students who have been as successful in their previous work as you have, and in developing the kinds of skills you will need for more challenging courses in the future. "Getting an 'A'" is really not a goal; making sure you have learned how to do new things, including how to double-check yourself in those new abilities, is a goal. I am perfectly comfortable knowing that the majority of students who take chemistry classes will not become chemists who use the information from this course on a routine basis; therefore there must be some other value that goes beyond a grade for your transcript. I do hope students will exit a course like this understanding why some people find a career in chemistry an interesting place to spend their professional lives.

Study Guide for

Organic Chemistry
Structure and Reactivity

1

An Introduction to Structure and Bonding in Organic Compounds

Concept Map 1.1   Ionic compounds and ionic bonding.

Concept Map 1.2   Covalent compounds.

1.1   Note: The names of the compounds shown on the next page are given for information. You are not yet expected to know how to name the compounds, but an examination of the names to see if you recognize an emerging pattern is fun.

1.1 (cont)

$$H-\overset{\overset{\displaystyle H}{|}}{\underset{\underset{\displaystyle H}{|}}{C}}-\overset{\overset{\displaystyle H}{|}}{\underset{\underset{\displaystyle H}{|}}{C}}-\overset{\overset{\displaystyle H}{|}}{\underset{\underset{\displaystyle H}{|}}{C}}-\overset{\overset{\displaystyle H}{|}}{\underset{\underset{\displaystyle H}{|}}{C}}-\overset{\cdot\cdot}{\underset{\cdot\cdot}{O}}-H$$

$CH_3CH_2CH_2CH_2OH$

Lewis structure for 1-butanol   condensed formula for 1-butanol

connectivity: four carbon atoms in a row with the oxygen atom at the end of the row

$$H-\overset{\overset{\displaystyle H}{|}}{\underset{\underset{\displaystyle H}{|}}{C}}-\overset{\overset{\displaystyle H}{|}}{\underset{\underset{\displaystyle H}{|}}{C}}-\overset{\overset{\displaystyle H}{|}}{\underset{\underset{\displaystyle \overset{\cdot\cdot}{\underset{\cdot\cdot}{O}}-H}{|}}{C}}-\overset{\overset{\displaystyle H}{|}}{\underset{\underset{\displaystyle H}{|}}{C}}-H$$

$CH_3CH_2CHCH_3$ or $CH_3CH_2CHOHCH_3$
$\quad\quad\quad\;\; |$
$\quad\quad\quad OH$

Lewis structure for 2-butanol   condensed formula for 2-butanol

connectivity: four carbon atoms in a row with the oxygen atom on the second carbon atom of the row

$$H-\overset{\overset{\displaystyle H}{|}}{\underset{\underset{\displaystyle H}{|}}{C}}-\overset{\overset{\displaystyle H-\overset{\overset{\displaystyle H}{|}}{\underset{\underset{\displaystyle H}{|}}{C}}-H}{|}}{\underset{\underset{\displaystyle \overset{\cdot\cdot}{\underset{\cdot\cdot}{O}}-H}{|}}{C}}-\overset{\overset{\displaystyle H}{|}}{\underset{\underset{\displaystyle H}{|}}{C}}-H$$

CH_3
$|$
CH_3CCH_3 or $(CH_3)_3COH$
$|$
OH

Lewis structure for 2-methyl-2-propanol   condensed formula for 2-methyl-2-propanol

connectivity: three carbon atoms in a row with one carbon atom and one oxygen atom on the second carbon atom of the row

$$H-\overset{\overset{\displaystyle H}{|}}{\underset{\underset{\displaystyle H}{|}}{C}}-\overset{\cdot\cdot}{\underset{\cdot\cdot}{O}}-\overset{\overset{\displaystyle H-\overset{\overset{\displaystyle H}{|}}{\underset{\underset{\displaystyle H}{|}}{C}}-H}{|}}{\underset{\underset{\displaystyle H}{|}}{C}}-\overset{\overset{\displaystyle H}{|}}{\underset{\underset{\displaystyle H}{|}}{C}}-H$$

CH_3
$|$
CH_3OCHCH_3 or $CH_3OCH(CH_3)_2$

Lewis structure for methyl isopropyl ether   condensed formula for methyl isopropyl ether

connectivity: one carbon atom bonded to an oxygen that is bonded to two more carbon atoms in a row, with a third carbon atom attached to the first of these carbons

$$H-\overset{\overset{\displaystyle H}{|}}{\underset{\underset{\displaystyle H}{|}}{C}}-\overset{\overset{\displaystyle H}{|}}{\underset{\underset{\displaystyle H}{|}}{C}}-\overset{\cdot\cdot}{\underset{\cdot\cdot}{O}}-\overset{\overset{\displaystyle H}{|}}{\underset{\underset{\displaystyle H}{|}}{C}}-\overset{\overset{\displaystyle H}{|}}{\underset{\underset{\displaystyle H}{|}}{C}}-H$$

$CH_3CH_2OCH_2CH_3$

Lewis structure for diethyl ether   condensed formula for diethyl ether

connectivity: two carbon atoms in a row bonded to an oxygen atom that is bonded to two other carbon atoms in a row

1.2   The names (and the connectivities) of the compounds in this problem are related to some of those in Problem 1.1. See if you can find the pattern.

1.2 (cont)

$$\underset{\substack{| \\ H}}{H-}\overset{\substack{H \\ |}}{\underset{\substack{| \\ H}}{C}}-\overset{\substack{H \\ |}}{\underset{\substack{| \\ H}}{C}}-\overset{\substack{H \\ |}}{\underset{\substack{| \\ H}}{C}}-\overset{\substack{H \\ |}}{\underset{\substack{| \\ H}}{C}}-\overset{\bullet\bullet}{\underset{\bullet\bullet}{Br}}:$$

$CH_3CH_2CH_2CH_2Br$

Lewis structure for 1-bromobutane   condensed formula for 1-bromobutane

connectivity: four carbon atoms in a row with the bromine atom at the end of the row

Lewis structure for 2-bromobutane

$CH_3CH_2CHCH_3$ or $CH_3CH_2CHBrCH_3$
$\quad\quad\quad\quad |$
$\quad\quad\quad\quad Br$

condensed formula for 2-bromobutane

connectivity: four carbon atoms in a row with the bromine atom on the second carbon atom of the row

Lewis structure for 2-bromo-2-methylpropane

$\quad\quad CH_3$
$\quad\quad |$
CH_3CCH_3 or $(CH_3)_3CBr$
$\quad\quad |$
$\quad\quad Br$

condensed formula for 2-bromo-2-methylpropane

connectivity: three carbon atoms in a row with the bromine atom and a carbon atom on the second carbon atom of the row

Lewis structure for 1-bromo-2-methylpropane

$\quad\quad CH_3$
$\quad\quad |$
CH_3CHCH_2Br or $(CH_3)_2CHCH_2Br$

condensed formula for 1-bromo-2-methylpropane

connectivity: three carbon atoms in a row with the bromine atom at the end of the row and a carbon atom on the second carbon atom of the row

1.3

Lewis structure for propylamine

$CH_3CH_2CH_2NH_2$

condensed formula for propylamine

connectivity: three carbon atoms in a row with the nitrogen atom at the end of the row

Lewis structure for isopropylamine

CH_3CHCH_3 or $(CH_3)_2CHNH_2$
$\quad |$
$\quad NH_2$

condensed formula for isopropylamine

connectivity: three carbon atoms in a row with the nitrogen atom on the second carbon atom

1.3   (cont)

$$\begin{array}{ccccc} H & H & & H \\ | & | & \overset{..}{} & | \\ H-C-C-N-C-H \\ | & | & | & | \\ H & H & H & H \end{array}$$

$CH_3CH_2NHCH_3$

Lewis structure for methylethylamine   condensed formula for methylethylamine

connectivity: two carbon atoms in a row attached to a nitrogen atom that is bonded to one other carbon atom

$$\begin{array}{c} H \\ | \\ H-C-H \\ H \quad | \quad H \\ | \quad | \quad | \\ H-C-N-C-H \\ | \quad \overset{..}{} \quad | \\ H \quad\quad H \end{array}$$

$$\begin{array}{c} CH_3 \\ | \\ CH_3NCH_3 \quad \text{or} \quad (CH_3)_3N \end{array}$$

Lewis structure for trimethylamine   condensed formula for trimethylamine

connectivity: a nitrogen atom with three single carbon atoms bonded to it

---

Workbook Exercises

In most chemical reactions, molecules undergo changes in the connectivity, that is, the bonding, of their atoms. Learning how to identify these changes rapidly is a skill you should master.

EXERCISE I.   Identify these features in the following chemical reactions:
- (1) bonds broken
- (2) bonds formed
- (3) redistribution of bonding and nonbonding electrons

EXAMPLE

$$Na^+ \; {}^-\!:C\equiv N\!: \quad + \quad CH_3CH_2CH_2-\overset{..}{\underset{..}{Br}}\!: \quad \longrightarrow \quad CH_3CH_2CH_2-C\equiv N\!: \quad + \quad Na^+ :\overset{..}{\underset{..}{Br}}\!:^-$$

SOLUTION

While you are becoming comfortable with molecular structures, it is a good idea to use complete Lewis structures to follow the changes in connectivity. You should also examine the formal charges and electron configurations of the atoms involved in those changes.

$$Na^+ \; {}^-\!:C\equiv N\!: \; + \; \begin{array}{ccc} H & H & H \\ | & | & | \\ H-C-C-C-\overset{..}{Br}\!: \\ | & | & | \\ H & H & H \end{array} \; \rightarrow \; \begin{array}{ccc} H & H & H \\ | & | & | \\ H-C-C-C-C\equiv N\!: \\ | & | & | \\ H & H & H \end{array} \; + \; Na^+ :\overset{..}{\underset{..}{Br}}\!:^-$$

One bond is broken: the 2-electron C—Br bond breaks, and this electron pair becomes the fourth nonbonding electron pair on the bromide ion that forms. One bond is formed: the nonbonding electron pair on the carbon atom of cyanide ion (CN $^-$) is used to form the new C—C bond.

EXERCISE I.   Identify the bonds broken, the bonds formed, and the way electrons have been redistributed in the processes of chemical change for the following reactions.

1. $(CH_3)_2CHCH_2\overset{..}{\underset{..}{O}}H \quad + \quad Na^+ H\!:^- \quad \longrightarrow \quad (CH_3)_2CHCH_2\overset{..}{\underset{..}{O}}\!:^- Na^+ \quad + \quad H-H$

2.

$$\begin{array}{c} H \\ | \\ H_{\diagdown}{}^{\textstyle C}{\diagup}{}^{\textstyle H} \\ {}^{\textstyle C}{=}{}^{\textstyle C} \\ H{-}C{\diagdown} \quad {\diagup}C{-}H \\ {}^{\textstyle N} \\ | \\ H \quad H \end{array} \quad + \quad CH_3{-}\overset{..}{\underset{..}{I}}\!: \quad \longrightarrow \quad \begin{array}{c} H \\ | \\ H_{\diagdown}{}^{\textstyle C}{\diagup}{}^{\textstyle H} \\ {}^{\textstyle C}{=}{}^{\textstyle C} \\ H{-}C{\diagdown} \quad {\diagup}C{-}H \\ {}^{\textstyle N^+} \\ | \\ H \quad CH_3 \end{array} \quad :\overset{..}{\underset{..}{I}}\!:^-$$

Workbook Exercises (cont)

3. $CH_3 - \overset{+}{\underset{..}{S}} - CH_3$ $: \overset{..}{\underset{..}{I}} :^-$ + $CH_3 - \overset{O}{\overset{||}{C}} - \overset{..}{\underset{..}{O}} :^- Na^+$ $\longrightarrow$ $CH_3 - \overset{O}{\overset{||}{C}} - \overset{..}{\underset{..}{O}} - CH_3$ + $CH_3 - \overset{..}{S} - CH_3$ + Na^+ $: \overset{..}{\underset{..}{I}} :^-$

The next two examples involve double bonds, introduced in Section 1.5 of the text. Can you also describe these changes?

4. $K^+ \, ^- : \overset{..}{\underset{..}{O}} - H$ + $H - \overset{H}{\underset{H}{\overset{|}{\underset{|}{C}}}} - \overset{\overset{..}{\underset{..}{Cl}:}}{\underset{CH_3}{\overset{|}{\underset{|}{C}}}} - CH_3$ $\longrightarrow$ $\underset{H}{\overset{H}{C}} = \underset{CH_3}{\overset{CH_3}{C}}$ + $H - \overset{..}{\underset{..}{O}} - H$ + $K^+ : \overset{..}{\underset{..}{Cl}} :^-$

5. $\underset{H}{\overset{H}{C}} = \underset{CH_3}{\overset{CH_3}{C}}$ + $H - \overset{+}{\underset{..}{O}} - H$ $: \overset{..}{\underset{..}{Cl}} :^-$ $\longrightarrow$ $H - \overset{H}{\underset{H}{\overset{|}{\underset{|}{C}}}} - \overset{+}{\underset{CH_3}{\overset{|}{C}}} - CH_3$ + $: \overset{..}{\underset{..}{Cl}} :^-$ + $H - \overset{..}{\underset{..}{O}} - H$

EXERCISE II.   Complete each of the equations by providing the structure of the molecule that will balance the chemical equation. In a balanced equation, there must be an equal number of each kind of atom on both sides of the equation. The overall charge must also be the same on both sides of a chemical reaction equation. All of the atoms in the compounds in these exercises have closed shell configurations.

EXAMPLE

$$Li^+ \, ^- : \overset{..}{\underset{..}{S}} H + (CH_3)_2 CH \overset{..}{\underset{..}{Cl}} : \longrightarrow A + Li^+ : \overset{..}{\underset{..}{Cl}} :^-$$

SOLUTION

As in Exercise I, we can identify some of the bonding changes. From this information, and the fact that the equation must balance, we determine the structure of the unknown substance **A**.

What we see: the C—Cl bond breaks, and the electron pair from the single bond becomes the fourth nonbonding electron pair of chloride ion on the right side of the equation. The unknown compound **A** must (a) incorporate the atoms from the left hand side of the equation that are not shown on the right, (b) have an overall neutral charge in order to keep the charges balanced, and (c) be comprised of atoms with closed shell configurations.

So, compound **A** needs to include (a) the SH atoms derived from the ionic compound LiSH, and (b) the atoms from $(CH_3)_2 CHCl$, except for chloride ion which appears as a product. The product ion, Cl^-, must come from the uncharged molecule $(CH_3)_2 CHCl$ because there is no other source of chlorine atoms on the left hand side of the equation. Although we cannot identify the structure of **A** with certainty at this point, we can account for the atoms from $(CH_3)_2 CHCl$ that remain when the chloride ion, Cl^-, is removed. Perhaps only temporarily, we can imagine the presence of a positively charged fragment, $CH_3 - \underset{+}{\overset{H}{\overset{|}{C}}} - CH_3$, that comes from removing Cl^- from the uncharged starting compound.

In our imagination, the fragments we can use to make **A** are the cation, $CH_3 - \underset{+}{\overset{H}{\overset{|}{C}}} - CH_3$, and the anion, $^- : \overset{..}{\underset{..}{S}} H$. There are two possible ways to create a compound from these fragments:

the first way gives us an ionic compound:

$$CH_3 - \underset{+}{\overset{H}{\overset{|}{C}}} - CH_3$$
$$^- : \overset{..}{\underset{..}{S}} H$$

the second way gives us a covalent compound:

$$CH_3 - \overset{H}{\underset{|}{\overset{|}{C}}} - CH_3$$
$$: \overset{..}{\underset{..}{S}} H$$

Is there a way to decide between these two possible structures for **A**? Or are they both acceptable answers? When solving an open-ended problem such as this one, either in the homework or on an examination, it is important to check the assumptions and information given in the problem. In this case, rereading the question tells us that "All of the atoms in these compounds have closed shell configurations." Therefore, the covalent structure is the only one that satisfies this criterion. In the ionic structure, the positively charged carbon has an open shell.

Workbook Exercises (cont)

EXERCISE III.　　Complete each of the following equations, as demonstrated in the example above.

1.　$CH_3CH_2\ddot{Br}:$ + **B** $\longrightarrow$ $CH_3CH_2\overset{+}{N}H_3$ + $:\ddot{Br}:^-$

2.　$CH_3\!-\!\overset{\displaystyle :O:}{\underset{}{\overset{\|}{C}}}\!-\!\ddot{Cl}:$ + Li^+ $^-:\ddot{O}\!-\!CH_3$ $\longrightarrow$ **C** + Li^+ $:\ddot{Cl}:^-$

3.　**D** + $CH_3\!-\!\ddot{O}\!-\!CH_3$ $\longrightarrow$ $CH_3\!-\!\overset{\displaystyle H}{\underset{}{\overset{|}{O^+}}}\!-\!CH_3$ + $:\ddot{F}:^-$

The next two examples in this exercise involve double bonds. What are the structures of E and F?

4.　**E** + $\underset{\overset{|}{H}\quad\overset{|}{H}}{\overset{\overset{H}{\diagdown}\quad\overset{CH_3}{\diagup}}{C\!=\!C}}$ $\longrightarrow$ $H\!-\!\overset{\overset{Br}{|}}{\underset{\underset{H}{|}}{C}}\!-\!\overset{\overset{Br}{|}}{\underset{\underset{H}{|}}{C}}\!-\!CH_3$

5.　Na^+ $^-:\ddot{O}\!-\!H$ + $H\!-\!\overset{\overset{:\ddot{Cl}:}{|}}{\underset{\underset{:\ddot{Cl}:}{|}}{C}}\!\!-\!\!\overset{\overset{:\ddot{Br}:}{|}}{\underset{\underset{:\ddot{Br}:}{|}}{C}}\!-\!\ddot{Br}:$ $\longrightarrow$ $H\!-\!\ddot{O}\!-\!H$ + **F** + Na^+ $:\ddot{Br}:^-$

1.4 The molecular formulas for the following compounds match the C_nH_{2n+2} rule, either right away or after hydrogen atoms are mentally substituted for halogen atoms.

(c)　$C_2HBrClF_3$ has 5 halogen atoms, therefore it is the equivalent of C_2H_6.

(e)　$C_{20}H_{42}$

(g)　$CHCl_3$ is the equivalent of CH_4

The structural formulas of these three compounds will contain only singly bonded atoms. None of them can have a ring structure.

1.5 Formal charge = number of valence electrons − number of nonbonding electrons − $1/2$ number of bonding electrons.

(a)　CCl_4　　　　$:\ddot{\underset{:\ddot{Cl}:}{\overset{:\ddot{Cl}:}{Cl}}}:\!\!\overset{}{C}\!\!:\ddot{Cl}:$　　　　$:\ddot{Cl}\!-\!\overset{\overset{:\ddot{Cl}:}{|}}{\underset{\underset{:\ddot{Cl}:}{|}}{C}}\!-\!\ddot{Cl}:$　　　Cl　　$7-6-\frac{1}{2}(2)=0$

　　　　　　　　　　　　　　　　　　　　　　　　　　　　　　　C　　$4-0-\frac{1}{2}(8)=0$

Each chlorine atom has 6 nonbonding electrons and 1 electron from a pair of bonding electrons. Therefore each chlorine atom has 7 valence electrons, the number it needs, and no formal charge. Carbon shares 8 bonding electrons. It effectively has 4 electrons around it, the number it needs to have no formal charge.

(b)　CH_3Br　　$\overset{\overset{H}{}}{\underset{\underset{H}{}}{H\!:\!\ddot{C}\!:\!\ddot{Br}:}}$　　　$H\!-\!\overset{\overset{H}{|}}{\underset{\underset{H}{|}}{C}}\!-\!\ddot{Br}:$　　　H　　$1-0-\frac{1}{2}(2)=0$

　　　　　　　　　　　　　　　　　　　　　　　　　　　C　　$4-0-\frac{1}{2}(8)=0$

　　　　　　　　　　　　　　　　　　　　　　　　　　　Br　　$7-6-\frac{1}{2}(2)=0$

(c)　$\overset{+}{CH_3OH_2}$　　$\overset{\overset{H}{}}{\underset{\underset{H}{}}{H\!:\!\ddot{C}\!:\!\overset{+}{\ddot{O}}\!:\!H}}$　　$H\!-\!\overset{\overset{H}{|}}{\underset{\underset{H}{|}}{C}}\!-\!\overset{\overset{H}{|}}{\underset{}{\overset{+}{O}}}\!-\!H$　　　H　　$1-0-\frac{1}{2}(2)=0$

　　　　　　　　　　　　　　　　　　　　　　　　　　　C　　$4-0-\frac{1}{2}(8)=0$

　　　　　　　　　　　　　　　　　　　　　　　　　　　O　　$6-2-\frac{1}{2}(6)=+1$

　　　　　　　　　　　　　　　　　　　　　　　　　　　(deficiency of one electron)

1.5

(d) $^-NH_2$ H : N : H   H—N—H   H $1 - 0 - \frac{1}{2}(2) = 0$

  N $5 - 4 - \frac{1}{2}(4) = -1$
  (excess of one electron)

Each hydrogen atom shares 2 bonding electrons and therefore effectively has 1 electron and no formal charge. The nitrogen atom has 4 nonbonding electrons, and shares 4 bonding electrons. It effectively has 6 electrons around it, one more than the 5 electrons it needs to be uncharged. Nitrogen therefore has a formal charge of −1.

(e) $CH_3NH_3^+$

  H : C : N : H

  H $1 - 0 - \frac{1}{2}(2) = 0$
  C $4 - 0 - \frac{1}{2}(8) = 0$
  N $5 - 0 - \frac{1}{2}(8) = +1$
  (deficiency of one electron)

(f) H_2NNH_2

  H : N : N : H

  H $1 - 0 - \frac{1}{2}(2) = 0$
  N $5 - 2 - \frac{1}{2}(6) = 0$

(g) PH_3

  H : P : H

  P $5 - 2 - \frac{1}{2}(6) = 0$
  H $1 - 0 - \frac{1}{2}(2) = 0$

(h) H_2S

  H : S : H

  H $1 - 0 - \frac{1}{2}(2) = 0$
  S $6 - 4 - \frac{1}{2}(4) = 0$

(i) CH_3CH_2OH

  H : C : C : O : H

  H $1 - 0 - \frac{1}{2}(2) = 0$
  C $4 - 0 - \frac{1}{2}(8) = 0$
  O $6 - 4 - \frac{1}{2}(4) = 0$

(j) $HOCH_2CH_2OH$

  H : O : C : C : O : H

  H $1 - 0 - \frac{1}{2}(2) = 0$
  C $4 - 0 - \frac{1}{2}(8) = 0$
  O $6 - 4 - \frac{1}{2}(4) = 0$

(k) $CH_3OCH_3^+$ / CH_3

  H : C : O : C : H

  H : C : H

  H $1 - 0 - \frac{1}{2}(2) = 0$
  C $4 - 0 - \frac{1}{2}(8) = 0$
  O $6 - 2 - \frac{1}{2}(6) = +1$
  (deficiency of one electron)

Each hydrogen atom shares 2 bonding electrons and therefore effectively has 1 electron and no formal charge. Each carbon atom shares 8 bonding electrons and thus effectively has 4 electrons and no formal charge. The oxygen atom has 2 nonbonding electrons and shares 6 bonding electrons. It effectively has 5 electrons, 1 fewer than the 6 electrons it needs to be uncharged, and therefore has a formal charge of +1.

$$
\begin{array}{c}
\qquad\qquad\overset{\displaystyle CH_3}{\underset{\displaystyle CH_3}{\overset{|}{\underset{|}{CH_3-\overset{+}{N}-CH_3}}}}
\end{array}
$$

1.6 (a)

N $5 - 0 - \frac{1}{2}(8) = +1$

Each hydrogen atom shares 2 bonding electrons, and therefore effectively has 1 electron and no formal charge. Each carbon atom shares 8 bonding electrons, and thus effectively has 4 electrons and no formal charge. The nitrogen atom shares 8 bonding electrons. It effectively has 4 electrons, 1 fewer than the 5 electrons it needs to be uncharged, and, therefore, has a formal charge of +1.

(b) :Br—C—Br:

C $4 - 2 - \frac{1}{2}(4) = 0$

Each bromine atom has 6 nonbonding electrons and shares 2 bonding electrons, and, therefore, effectively has 7 electrons and no formal charge. The carbon atom has 2 nonbonding electrons and shares 4 bonding electrons, and thus effectively has 4 electrons and no formal charge.

(c) $CH_3-\overset{\displaystyle \overset{H}{|}}{\underset{..}{\overset{+}{O}}}-CH_3$

O $6 - 2 - \frac{1}{2}(6) = +1$

(d) $CH_3-\overset{..}{\underset{..}{\overset{-}{N}}}-H$

N $5 - 4 - \frac{1}{2}(4) = -1$

(e) :Cl—C—Cl: (with :Cl: above)

C $4 - 2 - \frac{1}{2}(6) = -1$

(f) $CH_3-\overset{\displaystyle CH_3}{\overset{|}{\overset{+}{C}}}-CH_3$

C $4 - 0 - \frac{1}{2}(6) = +1$

Each chlorine atom has 6 nonbonding electrons and shares 2 bonding electrons, and, therefore, effectively has 7 electrons and no formal charge. The carbon atom has 2 nonbonding electrons and shares 6 bonding electrons. It effectively has 5 electrons around it, one more than the 4 electrons it needs to be uncharged, and, therefore, has a formal charge of −1.

1.7

$$
\overset{\displaystyle :\overset{..}{F}:\ H}{\underset{\displaystyle :\overset{..}{F}:\ H}{:\overset{..}{F}-\overset{-}{B}-\overset{+}{N}-H}}
$$

F $7 - 6 - \frac{1}{2}(2) = 0$

H $1 - 0 - \frac{1}{2}(2) = 0$

B $3 - 0 - \frac{1}{2}(8) = -1$ (excess of one electron)

N $5 - 0 - \frac{1}{2}(8) = +1$ (deficiency of one electron)

Each fluorine atom has 6 nonbonding electrons and shares 2 bonding electrons. Each fluorine atom therefore effectively has 7 electrons and no formal charge. Each hydrogen atom shares 2 bonding electrons and therefore effectively has 1 electron and no formal charge. The nitrogen atom shares 8 bonding electrons. It effectively has 4 electrons, 1 fewer than the 5 electrons it needs to be uncharged, and therefore has a formal charge of +1. The boron atom shares 8 bonding electrons. It effectively has 4 electrons around it, one more than the 3 electrons it needs to be uncharged, and, therefore, has a formal charge of −1.

1.8 BF_3 has room in its orbitals to accept a pair of electrons. We expect it to react with any uncharged or negatively charged species that has nonbonding electrons.

$$
:\overset{..}{F}-\overset{\displaystyle :\overset{..}{F}:}{\underset{\displaystyle :\overset{..}{F}:}{B}}\ +\ H-\overset{..}{O}-H\ \longrightarrow\ :\overset{..}{F}-\overset{\displaystyle :\overset{..}{F}:}{\underset{\displaystyle :\overset{..}{F}:}{\overset{-}{B}}}-\overset{H}{\overset{+}{O}}-H
$$

1.8 (cont)

Even though the hydronium ion has a pair of nonbonding electrons, the positive charge on the ion makes them unlikely to participate in further bonding. The electrons on any positively charged species are tightly held, and not easily donated to another atom. Exploring the result of the reaction of BF_3 with H_3O^+ is useful. The resulting species is quite unstable because of the double positive charge on the oxygen atom next to the negative charge on the boron.

unstable

1.9   Condensed Formula   Lewis Structures

(a) CH_3CCH_3 (with O double bonded)

(b) $CH_3C{\equiv}CH$

(c) $HCNH_2$ (with O double bonded)

(d) $HCOH$ (with O double bonded)

1.9 (e) $CH_3\overset{O}{\overset{\|}{C}}OCH_3$

H : C : C : O : C : H (with O above center, and H's around)   H—C—C—O—C—H (Lewis structures)

(f) HON=O

H : O : N :: O   or   H—O—N=O

H : O : N :: O :   or   H—O—N=O :

Note that the nonbonding electrons may be placed around a doubly bonded oxygen in two ways, as illustrated in the structural formulas above.

(g) $CH_3N=NCH_3$

H : C : N :: N : C : H   H—C—N=N—C—H

(h) $CH_2=CHCl$

H : C :: C : Cl :   H—C=C—Cl :

1.10 (a) C_2F_4 is the equivalent of C_2H_4. The saturated compound with 2 carbons would be C_2H_6. C_2H_4 is missing 2 hydrogens; therefore, tetrafluoroethene has 1 unit of unsaturation.

(b) $C_{14}H_9Cl_5$ is the equivalent of $C_{14}H_{14}$. The saturated compound with 14 carbons would be $C_{14}H_{30}$. $C_{14}H_{14}$, DDT, is missing $(30 - 14) = 16$ hydrogens; therefore, DDT has $16/2 = 8$ units of unsaturation.

(c) $C_2HBrClF_3$, halothane, has 0 units of unsaturation (see Problem 1.4).

(d) $C_{10}H_{16}$, adamantane, has 3 units of unsaturation ($C_{10}H_{22}$ is saturated).

(e) $C_{20}H_{42}$, icosane, is saturated (see Problem 1.4).

(f) C_2H_3Cl, vinyl chloride, is the equivalent of C_2H_4 [see part (a)].

(g) $CHCl_3$, chloroform, is saturated (see Problem 1.4).

(h) C_4H_7Cl, methallyl chloride, is the equivalent of C_4H_8. The saturated compound with 4 carbons is C_4H_{10}. Methallyl chloride therefore has 1 unit of unsaturation.

- -

Concept Map 1.3 (see p. 12)

- -

1.11 (a)

$$H-O-\overset{\overset{:O:}{\|}}{C}-O:^- \leftrightarrow H-O-\overset{:\overset{-}{O}:}{C}=O \leftrightarrow H-\overset{+}{O}=\overset{\overset{:\overset{-}{O}:}{|}}{C}-O:^- \leftrightarrow H-O-\overset{\overset{:\overset{-}{O}:}{|}}{\overset{+}{C}}-O:^-$$

① major and equivalent; no separation of charge; complete octets

② minor; separation of charge; complete octets

③ minor; separation of charge; carbon has sextet

(b)

$$H-\overset{\overset{:O:}{\|}}{C}-H \leftrightarrow H-\overset{\overset{:\overset{-}{O}:}{|}}{\overset{+}{C}}-H \leftrightarrow H-\overset{\overset{:\overset{+}{O}:}{|}}{\overset{..}{C}}-H$$

① major; no separation of charge; complete octets

② minor; separation of charge with negative charge on more electronegative element; carbon has sextet

③ very minor; separation of charge with negative charge on less electronegative element; carbon has sextet

Note that resonance contributor 2 may nevertheless be significant in the chemical reactivity of a species (see Problems 1.12 and 1.13 for examples). Resonance contributor 3 does not explain the known chemistry of this compound and is, therefore, not considered as a resonance contributor. It is shown only to complete the set. See (e) for another example of a very minor resonance contributor that is not useful in explaining the properties of the known species.

1.11   (c)

major and equivalent;
no separation of charge;
complete octets

minor;
separation of charge;
nitrogen has sextet

(d)

major;
no separation of charge;
complete octets;
negative charge on more
electronegative atom

minor;
no separation of charge
complete octets;
negative charge on less
electronegative atom

minor;
separation of charge;
carbon has sextet

(e)

major and equivalent resonance contributors;
complete octets;
no contributor with complete
octets that does not have
separation of charge can be written

minor;
complete octets;
large charge separation;
two adjacent
positive charges

very minor;
nitrogen has septet;
large charge separation;
doubly positive charge
on nitrogen

(f)

major and equivalent;
complete octets

minor and equivalent;
one oxygen has sextet

all contributors have separation of charge

(g)

major;
complete octets;
positive charge on less
electronegative atom

minor and equivalent;
one oxygen has sextet;
positive charge on more
electronegative atom

(h)

minor;
large separation of charge

major and equivalent;
less separation of charge;
more covalent bonds

Note that chlorine is in the third period of the periodic table and may, therefore, have more than eight electrons around it.

Concept Map 1.3   Covalent bonding.

- -

1.12   The boron atom in boron trifluoride has only six electrons and can accept an electron pair from the nitrogen atom in ammonia to complete the octet. The arrow pointing from the nonbonding pair on one molecule to the electron deficient site on the other molecule represents the flow of electrons in the reaction.

formation of covalent bond

Likewise the reaction between carbon dioxide and hydroxide ion is rationalized by looking at a resonance contributor in which the carbon in carbon dioxide has only six electrons and can accept an electron pair from the oxygen atom of the hydroxide ion to complete the octet. The arrow pointing from the nonbonding pair on one molecule to the electron deficient site on the other molecule again represents the flow of electrons in the reaction.

formation of covalent bond

1.13 Ammonia will react with formaldehyde. In the minor resonance contributor of formaldehyde (Problem 1.11b), the carbon atom has a sextet and can accept an electron pair from the nitrogen atom in ammonia to complete the octet. The arrow pointing from the nonbonding pair on one molecule to the electron deficient site on the other molecule represents the flow of electrons in this reaction.

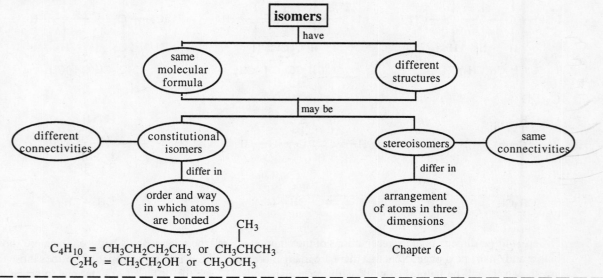

formation of covalent bond

Concept Map 1.4   Isomers.

isomers

have

same molecular formula   different structures

may be

different connectivities   constitutional isomers   stereoisomers   same connectivities

differ in   differ in

order and way in which atoms are bonded   arrangement of atoms in three dimensions

$C_4H_{10} = CH_3CH_2CH_2CH_3$ or CH_3CHCH_3 (with CH_3)

$C_2H_6 = CH_3CH_2OH$ or CH_3OCH_3

Chapter 6

1.14 C_3H_7Cl

$CH_3CH_2CH_2Cl$ $CH_3CHClCH_3$

C_3H_8O

$CH_3CH_2CH_2OH$ $CH_3CHOHCH_3$ $CH_3OCH_2CH_3$

$C_4H_8Cl_2$

$ClCH_2CH_2CH_2CH_2Cl$ $ClCH_2CH_2CHClCH_3$ $ClCH_2CHClCH_2CH_3$

1.14 (cont)

CHCl$_2$CH$_2$CH$_2$CH$_3$ CH$_3$CH$_2$CCl$_2$CH$_3$ CH$_3$CHClCHClCH$_3$

ClCH$_2$CH(CH$_3$)CH$_2$Cl   ClCH$_2$CCl(CH$_3$)CH$_3$ CHCl$_2$CH(CH$_3$)CH$_3$

C$_2$H$_4$O

CH$_3$CH   CH$_2$=CHOH   (enol)   CH$_2$–CH$_2$

1.15   Different three-dimensional representations of the compounds and the relationships between them are shown below and on the next page. Note that there are many more possibilities for each compound besides those that are shown. It will be helpful to work with molecular models to see the different orientations in space that molecules and parts of molecules may have.

(a)   109.5°

This is the same structure as

The formula representing the molecule has been rotated around an axis through the top chlorine atom and the carbon atom.

(b)   ~109.5° 1.09Å ~109.5°

This is the same structure as

The formula representing the molecule has been rotated in the plane of the paper.

(c)   ~109.5° 1.09Å ~109.5°

This is the same structure as

The formula representing the molecule was first rotated around an axis going through the top hydrogen atom and the carbon atom and then rotated in the plane of the paper.

1.15

(d)

This is the same structure as

The formula representing the molecule was rotated around an axis perpendicular to the carbon-carbon bond.

(e)

This is the same structure as

The formula representing the molecule was changed by rotating the O—H bond around an axis going through the carbon atom and the oxygen atom without rotating the carbon atom. This type of transformation will be discussed in greater detail in Chapter 5.

(f)

This is the same structure as

The formula representing the molecule was rotated around an axis going through the carbon atom and the nitrogen atom.

(g)

This is the same structure as

The formula representing the molecule was changed by rotating the CH_3 (methyl) group on the right about an axis through the carbon-oxygen bond on the left.

(h)

This is the same structure as

The formula representing the molecule was changed by rotating the CH_3 (methyl) group on the right about an axis through the carbon-sulfur bond on the left.

1.16

(a)

molecule perpendicular
to plane of paper

molecule in plane of paper

(b)

Bond angles and bond
lengths in this CH₃ are
the same as in the other one. →

(c)

This bond is expected
to be less than 1.54Å

(d)

molecule perpendicular
to plane of paper

molecule in plane of paper

(e)

Chlorine atoms are both on
the same side of the paper

Chlorine atoms are on the
opposite side of the paper.

1.17   (a)   (b)   (c)   (d)

(e)   (f)   (g)

Concept Map 1.5   Polarity of covalent molecules.

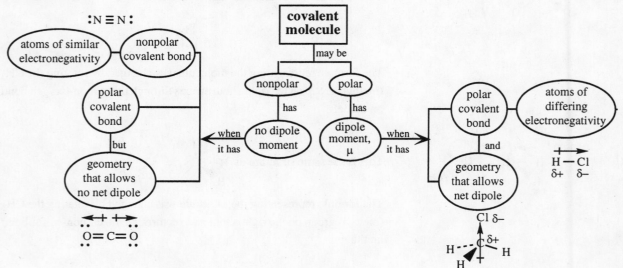

1.18   The molecular dipole is the **vector sum** of the individual bond dipoles in a molecule. A bond dipole is a **vector** quantity which by definition has both **magnitude** and **direction**. An arrow generally is used to represent a vector. The length of the arrow represents the magnitude of the charge separation and the direction of the arrow points toward the negative end of the dipole. When two vectors are added together, the direction of the dipole must be considered as well as the magnitude. Thus two vectors of equal magnitude and direction will yield a **resultant** vector pointing in the same direction with twice the magnitude as the original vectors, but two vectors of equal magnitude and opposite direction will exactly cancel out. For example, carbon dioxide is a linear molecule that has no dipole moment because it has equal bond dipoles that point in opposite directions.

$$O = C = O$$

vectors of individual bond dipoles exactly
cancel because the angle between them is 180°

Water is a bent molecule that has two equal bond dipoles pointing toward the oxygen atom away from the hydrogen atoms. The angle between the two bond dipoles is 104°. The resultant vector, the dipole moment, points toward the oxygen atom and bisects the angle between the two hydrogen atoms. The magnitude of the dipole moment is more than that of each individual bond dipole but less than the sum.

vectors of individual bond dipoles at
an angle result in a vector sum

(a)   (b)   (c) $I — Cl$ (d)

(e)   (f)   (g)   (h)

No dipole moment is shown for (e) because ions have full charges, either positive or negative, and thus do not have dipole moments, which are partial positive and negative charges separated within the same molecule.

1.19   (a) $CH_3CH_2CH_2CH_2OH$ has the highest boiling point because of hydrogen bonding.

$CH_3CH_2CH_2CH_2$

$CH_3CH_2CH_2CH_2$ $CH_2CH_2CH_2CH_3$

(b) CH_3OH has the highest boiling point because of hydrogen bonding.

CH_3

CH_3 CH_3

(c) CH_3OH has the highest boiling point [see(b)]. The hydrogen bonding in CH_3SH is not significant (see Section 1.10C in the text).

1.20   (a) CH_3CH_2OH

(b) $CH_3CH_2CH_2OH$

see (a) above and substitute $CH_3CH_2CH_2$— for CH_3CH_2—

(c) $HOCH_2CH_2CH_2CH_2CH_2OH$

$CH_3CH_2CH_2CH_2CH_2OH$ has one half as many hydrogen bonds as $HOCH_2CH_2CH_2CH_2CH_2OH$ since it has only one —OH group. Note that the hydrocarbon (nonpolar) portions are the same length.

(d) $CH_3CH_2\overset{\overset{O}{\|}}{C}OH$

$CH_3\overset{\overset{O}{\|}}{C}OCH_3$ is only a hydrogen bond acceptor.

(e) $CH_3CH_2CH_2NH_2$

$CH_3CH_2CH_2Cl$ does not participate in hydrogen bonding to any significant extent and has little solubility in water.

Concept Map 1.6   Nonbonding interactions between molecules.

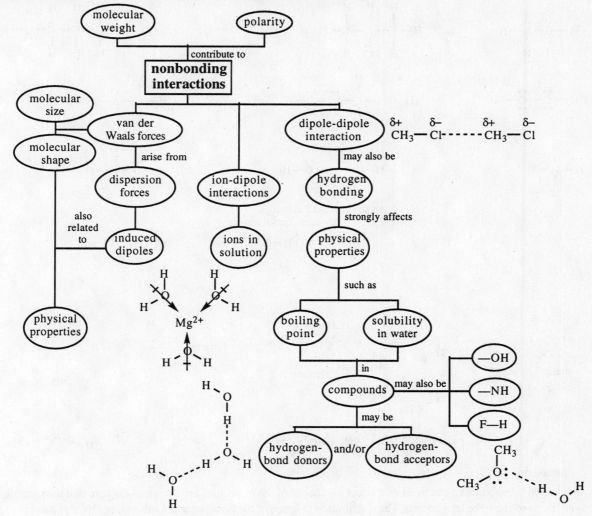

- -

1.21   (a) MgF_2, ionic   (b) SiF_4, covalent   (c) NaH, ionic
                                                   Si—F, polar bond   (the anion is $H\!:\!^-$)

         (d) ClF, covalent   (e) SCl_2, covalent   (f) OF_2, covalent
               polar bond   S—Cl, polar bond   O—F, polar bond

         (g) SiH_4, covalent   (h) PH_3, covalent   (i) $NaOCH_3$, ionic
               Si—H, polar bond   (the anion, CH_3—$\ddot{\underset{..}{O}}\!:^-$,
                                                                             contains covalent bonds)

         (j) CH_3Na, ionic   (k) Na_2CO_3, ionic   (l) BrCN, covalent
               (the anion, $^-\!:\!CH_3$,   (the anion, CO_3^{-2},   Br—C and C≡N,
               contains covalent bonds)   contains covalent bonds)   polar bonds)

1.22

(a) $:\!\ddot{F}\!—\!\ddot{N}\!—\!\ddot{F}\!:$ (b) $:\!\ddot{Cl}\!—\!Al\!—\!\ddot{Cl}\!:$ (c) $H\!—\!\underset{H}{\overset{H}{C}}\!—\!\ddot{S}\!—\!\underset{H}{\overset{H}{C}}\!—\!H$

         $:\!\ddot{F}\!:$ $:\!\ddot{Cl}\!:$

1.22

(d) H—C—N—H structure

(e) H—C—C—C—H structure

(f) $\overset{-}{:}\overset{..}{O}$—H

(g) H—C—C—C—$\overset{..}{O}$—H structure

(h) H—$\overset{..}{O}$—$\overset{..}{O}$—H

(i) H—C—N—$\overset{..}{O}$—H structure

(j) H—C—$\overset{..}{S}$—H structure

(k) H—$\overset{H}{\underset{H}{Si}}$—H

(l) H—$\overset{..}{O}$—$\overset{:O:}{\underset{:O:}{S}}$—$\overset{..}{O}$—H

Here sulfur has 12 electrons around it but a zero formal charge

$$S \qquad 6 - 0 - \frac{1}{2}(12) = 0$$

(m) H—$\overset{..}{O}$—$\overset{:O:}{\overset{+}{N}}$—$\overset{..}{O}$$\overset{-}{}$

1.23

(a) $\overset{..}{\underset{Cl \quad Cl}{S}}$
bent

(b) $\overset{..}{\underset{F \quad F}{O}}$
bent

(c) $\overset{CH_3 \quad H}{\underset{H \quad H}{C=C}}$
planar

(d) $CH_3—C\equiv N:$
linear

(e) $\overset{F}{\underset{F}{B}}$—F, F
tetrahedral

(f) $\overset{F}{\underset{Cl}{C}}$ Cl, Cl
tetrahedral

(g) $CH_3—\overset{CH_3}{\overset{+}{N}}$—CH₃, CH₃
tetrahedral

(h) H—$\overset{..}{P}$—H, H
pyramidal

(i) $CH_3—\overset{..+}{O}$—H, H
pyramidal

(j) $CH_3—\overset{..}{N}$—CH₃, CH₃
pyramidal

Note that only the nonbonding electrons that affect the shapes of the molecules are shown. Also note that the pyramidal shapes are derived from the tetrahedron. The distribution in space of the bonding and nonbonding electron pairs around these atoms is tetrahedral. The geometry around these atoms appears pyramidal because our experimental methods detect only the positions of the atoms and not the positions of the electrons.

1.24

(a) $\overset{H \quad H}{\underset{H \quad Cl}{C=C}}$

(b) structure with S

(c) structure
does not have a significant dipole moment

(d) $\overset{F}{\underset{Br}{C}}$ Br, Br
C—F bond dipole is much greater than C—Br bond dipoles

(e) structure with O

(f) H—C≡C—Cl

(g) $\overset{Cl \quad Cl}{\underset{Cl \quad Cl}{C=C}}$
individual bond dipoles cancel

1.25　(a) Hydrogen atoms are attached to carbon, not oxygen, nitrogen or fluorine. Hydrogen bonding is not important.

(b) There is a hydrogen atom attached to oxygen, so hydrogen bonding is important.

(c) No hydrogen atoms are on oxygen, nitrogen or fluorine, so no hydrogen bonding.

(d) There are hydrogen atoms attached to oxygen, so hydrogen bonding is important.

(e) Hydrogen atoms are attached to nitrogen, so hydrogen bonding does occur.

(f) Here, too, hydrogen bonding occurs because of presence of N—H bonds.

(g) The hydrogen attached to sulfur does not participate significantly in hydrogen bonding.

1.26

(a) Yes

(b) Yes

(c) Yes

(d) Yes

(e) Yes

(f) No　(g) Yes

(h) No　　(i) Yes

Sulfur is not a significant hydrogen bond acceptor

1.27　(a)

1.27 (b) Hydrogen bonding to water stabilizes 2,4-pentanedione and interferes with the intramolecular hydrogen bonding that stabilizes the enol.

ketone form   enol form

1.28

CH_3CH_2O—C—OCH_2CH_3

(second lowest) A
(lowest) B

D (highest electron density)
C (second highest)

1.29

The shorter-than-expected B—F bond lengths suggest that the compound has resonance contributors in which there is a double bond between the boron and each of the fluorine atoms. Such resonance contributors have the advantage of having an octet around each atom and additional bonding, even though they also put a positive charge on the electronegative fluorine atom.

1.30 (a)

Lewis structure

(b) CH_3— C≡N: dipole moment

(c) CH_3— C=N: Resonance contributor with separation of charge and negative formal charge on the more electronegative element. A separation of charge increases the dipole moment.

1.31 (a) NO has eleven electrons for bonding (5 from nitrogen and 6 from oxygen). It must, therefore, have one unpaired electron.

A   B   C D

(b) A is the major resonance contributor. It has the maximum number of covalent bonds, one atom (O) has an octet. and the contributor has no separation of charge. B is the next best. Even though it has separation of charge and a positive charge on the more electronegative atom, one atom (N) has an octet, and the contributor has more bonds than C or D.

(c) NO is highly reactive because it has an open shell on one of its atoms.

1.32 (a)

$:C{=}\ddot{O}$ $^{-}:C{\equiv}O:^{+}$ $^{+}:C{-}\ddot{\underset{..}{O}}:^{-}$

| carbon does not have octet | both atoms have octets but negative charge is on less electronegative atom | carbon does not have an octet but negative charge is on more electronegative atom |

(b) Fe^{2+} is an electron pair **acceptor.** The carbon atom of carbon monoxide bonds to iron; it must be an electron pair **donor.** Therefore, the resonance contributor in which carbon has a negative charge and each atom has a complete octet is more important than the other contributors. The resonance contributor with separation of charge and a positive charge on the carbon atom would lead to electrostatic repulsion between Fe^{2+} and the carbon atom and must, therefore, not make a significant contribution to the structure.

1.33 (a)

A   B

(b) A is the major resonance contributor because it has all closed shell atoms. The experimental evidence confirms that the C—O bond in protonated acetone is closer to a double bond in character than to a single bond.

1.34

①   ②   minor   ③

major
complete octets;
no separation of charge   complete octets; separation of charge
with negative charge on more electronegative atom   carbon has sextet;
separation of charge

1.35 SO_2 is an 18-electron molecule.

Note that this structure is possible because S is in the third period of the periodic table.

These resonance contributors would lead us to expect the bond lengths in SO_2 to be somewhere between 1.49 Å and 1.70 Å. The experimental bond length (1.43 Å) is shorter than expected. Chemists point to the polarity of the bonds (the strong attraction between the positive charge on sulfur and the negative charge on oxygen, for example) as a further factor in rationalizing such observations.

1.36 (a)

1.36 (b) Each has a resonance contributor in which the carbon atom marked *C has a positive charge. Thus each compound has a partial positive character at that carbon atom, making it reactive toward a negatively charged ion such as R$\ddot{\text{S}}$:$^-$.

Supplemental Problems

S1.1 Which compound in each pair do you expect to be more soluble in water?

(a) CH_3Cl or $NaCl$

(b) $\overset{\text{O}}{\overset{\|}{\text{HCOH}}}$ or $CH_3CH_2CH_2CH_2\overset{\text{O}}{\overset{\|}{\text{COH}}}$

(c) $\overset{\text{O}}{\overset{\|}{\text{HCOH}}}$ or $\overset{\text{O}}{\overset{\|}{\text{HCOCH}_2}}CH_2CH_2CH_2CH_3$

(d) $CH_3CH_2SCH_2CH_3$ or $CH_3CH_2OCH_2CH_3$

(e) $\overset{\text{O}}{\overset{\|}{\text{HOCCH}_2}}CH_2CH_3$ or $\overset{\text{O}}{\overset{\|}{\text{HOCCH}_2}}CH_2\overset{\text{O}}{\overset{\|}{\text{COH}}}$

S1.2 The boiling point of water (100 °C) is higher than the boiling point of hydrogen fluoride (19 °C) or ethanol (78 °C). Use drawings to explain this experimental observation.

S1.3 Draw resonance contributors for each of the following species. Be sure to show any formal charges. Decide which resonance contributors are major and which are minor.
  (a) Nitrous oxide, N_2O (a linear molecule in which the two nitrogen atoms are bonded to each other)
  (b) Sulfate anion, SO_4^{2-} (an ion in which all of the oxygens are equivalent)

  (c) Acetic acid, $CH_3\overset{\text{O}}{\overset{\|}{\text{COH}}}$

S1.4 The azide anion, N_3^-, is linear. The nitrogen-nitrogen bond lengths in the ion are all 1.15Å. Write resonance contributors for the azide anion that account for these experimental observations. (The typical nitrogen-nitrogen double bond length is 1.20Å; the typical nitrogen-nitrogen triple bond length is 1.10Å.)

S1.5 Methyl isothiocyanate has the following connectivity: CH_3NCS.
  (a) Draw a Lewis structure for the molecule in which all atoms have closed shells and no separation of charge.
  (b) Methyl isothiocyanate is highly reactive toward reagents with nonbonding electrons to share such as hydroxide ion (OH $^-$). Draw structural formulas other than the structure in part (a) for two resonance contributors for methyl isothiocyanate that may be used to rationalize this reactivity.
  (c) Methyl thiocyanate is a constitutional isomer of methyl isothiocyanate. It can be prepared from the thiocyanate ion, SCN $^-$, and methyl bromide, CH_3—Br, by a process called displacement. Draw a Lewis structure for this isomer, in which all atoms also have closed shells and no separation of charge.

S1.6 The anion derived from nitromethane is important in synthesizing new compounds. Chemists postulate that such an anion is easy to form because it is stabilized by resonance. The connectivity of the anion is $H_2CNO_2^-$.

    (a) There are three important resonance contributors in which all atoms have closed shells. Draw these three resonance structures, being sure to show all nonbonding electrons and formal charges. Identify the major resonance contributors and give the reasons for your choice.

    (b) The nitromethane anion reacts with positively charged species (such as the proton from an acid) to form a bond to the carbon atom. Which resonance contributor best rationalizes the reactivity described here?

S1.7 The concept of resonance is used to rationalize experimental properties of molecules or ions. Structural formulas for some species and experimental evidence about them are shown below. Draw resonance contributors for the structures that support the experimental evidence given.

the electrons on this nitrogen atom are not as available for bonding as are those on $CH_3-\overset{..}{N}-CH_3$, for example

this carbon atom is reactive toward reagents that are deficient in electrons such as protons in acids

this molecule reacts easily with electron-deficient reagents at the carbon atoms indicated by arrows

(a)

(b)

(c)

S1.8 A study of the mechanism of a certain reaction led to the conclusion that two piperidine molecules, shown below, form a strong intermolecular association as the first step of the process.

piperidine

What type of intermolecular interaction is most likely to be responsible for association between two molecules of piperidine? Draw a representation of the interaction and label it.

S1.9 There are many compounds with the molecular formula $C_5H_{12}O$. They fall into two categories, those with boiling points above $100\,°C$, and those with boiling points below $70\,°C$. Propose structural formulas for four of the constitutional isomers of $C_5H_{12}O$ and indicate whether you expect the boiling point of the compound that you have drawn to be higher than $100\,°C$ or lower than $70\,°C$. Your answer should include at least one compound of each category.

S1.10 Urea, H_2NCNH_2, is the compound used by mammals to excrete nitrogen.

    (a) What is the geometry of urea at the central carbon atom? Draw a structural formula that clearly illustrates this.

    (b) Even though urea has a low molecular weight, it is a solid that melts at $135\,°C$. Use structural formulas to propose a rationalization for its high melting point relative to its molecular weight and size.

    (c) Urea has high solubility in water. Draw structural formulas showing the factors responsible for its water solubility.

    (d) Urea easily loses a proton to a base to give an anion, H_2NCONH^-. This anion has two important resonance contributors, both of them closed shell species. What are they, and which one is the major one?

S1.11   Creatinine is an important end product in the metabolism of proteins. Blood tests for creatinine and urea are used to find out whether kidneys are functioning properly. A new and much more convenient blood test for creatinine has been reported recently. It depends on three precise intermolecular interactions between creatinine (called the guest molecule) and another molecule specifically designed to hold it (called the host molecule). The two molecules are shown below.

creatinine, the guest molecule

the host molecule

(a) What are the important intermolecular interactions between the host molecule and the guest molecule? Show these interactions pictorially using the structural formulas given above.

(b) In discussing the interactions between the host molecule and creatinine, the authors of the paper cited above drew the following three structural representations of species with the same molecular formula as creatinine, shown again in the middle below.

structure A   creatinine   structure B

What are the relationships between creatinine and structures A and B?

S1.12   Compounds with the molecular formula $C_5H_{10}O$ have one unit of unsaturation. Draw structural formulas for four possible constitutional isomers having this molecular formula, one containing a ring, one an alcohol function, one an ether, and one a carbonyl group. Other functional groups may also be present, depending on the structures you choose.

S1.13   About 20 years ago a new class of compounds was discovered in Munich (München in German), Germany, and named "munchnones". These compounds have a permanent separation of charge in a ring containing nitrogen and oxygen atoms and a carbonyl group. A munchnone has a much smaller dipole moment than would be expected for a compound with such a separation of charge. Chemists use the idea of delocalization of charge over the entire molecule by resonance to rationalize this experimental observation.

There are six resonance contributors to a munchnone (besides the one show below) that have closed shells around each of the atoms. Draw the four best (most important) ones of these six.

a munchnone

2

Covalent Bonding and Chemical Reactivity

Workbook Exercises

Simple geometrical relationships are an important part of chemistry. Some of these can be demonstrated with the two tetrahedral blocks that you can construct using the two large cardboard triangles at the back of the *Study Guide*. Fold each along the three dotted lines to bring the three darkened corners together, tuck the flaps inside, and then tape the sides together to make a tetrahedral block.

Hold the two tetrahedral blocks as indicated in the pictures below. Make special note of the spatial relationships between the vertices that are *not* touching.

   (1) Sharing a single vertex (touch A to A)

   (2) Sharing an edge (A to A and B to B)

   (3) Sharing a face (A to A, B to B, C to C)

the remaining 6 vertices can have many orientations, one of which is shown

the remaining 4 vertices are coplanar (What happens if you connect A to B and B to A instead?)

the remaining 2 vertices are colinear

There are many good sets of molecular models available commercially. You should develop the habit of using molecular models to help visualize the three-dimensional relationships of atoms in molecules. Using your set of molecular models, assemble 2 tetrahedral atoms and then join them together in a singly bonded connection. You will find that a vertex or bond of one tetrahedral atom will need to be connected directly to the other tetrahedral atom, rather than to a vertex of the other atom. Learn how to construct double and triple bonds with your model set and compare the geometry of the atoms in those constructions with those of the tetrahedral blocks. Keep the cardboard tetrahedra that you have constructed. You will need them for the exercises in later chapters.

2.1

	1s	2s	2p			3s	3p		
sodium	↑↓	↑↓	↑↓	↑↓	↑↓	↑			
magnesium	↑↓	↑↓	↑↓	↑↓	↑↓	↑↓			
aluminum	↑↓	↑↓	↑↓	↑↓	↑↓	↑↓	↑		
silicon	↑↓	↑↓	↑↓	↑↓	↑↓	↑↓	↑	↑	
phosphorus	↑↓	↑↓	↑↓	↑↓	↑↓	↑↓	↑	↑	↑
sulfur	↑↓	↑↓	↑↓	↑↓	↑↓	↑↓	↑↓	↑	↑
chlorine	↑↓	↑↓	↑↓	↑↓	↑↓	↑↓	↑↓	↑↓	↑
argon	↑↓	↑↓	↑↓	↑↓	↑↓	↑↓	↑↓	↑↓	↑↓

2.2

In the He_2^+ molecule-ion, there are only three electrons to be distributed, one from a neutral He atom and one from a positively charged He ion with only one electron and two protons. Two of the electrons go into the low energy bonding molecular orbital but only one into the high energy antibonding molecular orbital. The net result is a lowering of energy of the system, resulting in a bond.

2.3

2.4
- (a) No overlap possible; wrong orientation of *p* orbital in space. The *s* orbital is approaching the nodal plane of the *p* orbital where there is no electron density.
- (b) No overlap possible; wrong orientation of one *p* orbital in space.
- (c) No bonding will occur. The orbitals are out of phase, and only an antibonding interaction will occur.
- (d) Bonding will occur. The orbitals are in phase and are approaching each other so that overlap is possible.

2.5

overlap of 1s orbital on hydrogen and sp^3 hybrid orbital on carbon

overlap of 3p orbital on chlorine and sp^3 hybrid orbital on carbon

Concept Map 2.1   Molecular orbitals and covalent bonds.

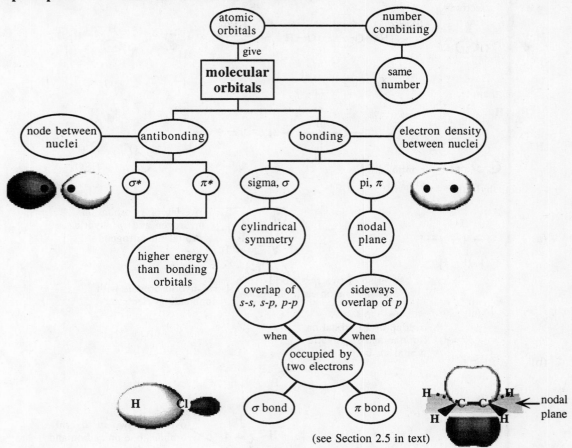

(see Section 2.5 in text)

- -

2.6

overlap of 1*s* orbital on
hydrogen and *sp*³ hybrid
orbital on carbon

overlap of two *sp*³ hybrid
orbitals, one on each carbon

overlap of 2*p* orbital on
fluorine and *sp*³ hybrid
orbital on carbon

2.7 The three 2*p* orbitals on nitrogen are 90° apart. Bonds formed by the overlap of these orbitals would have bond angles close to 90°. The actual bond angles in ammonia have been experimentally determined to be 107°.

2.8

nonbonding
electrons

+ HCl $\longrightarrow$

Cl⁻

2.9

2.10 (a)

(b) BF_4^-

(c) $CH_3-\overset{+}{\underset{CH_3}{\overset{CH_3}{N}}}-CH_3$

(d) $CH_3-\overset{+}{\underset{\cdot\cdot}{O}}-CH_3$
       $\quad\;\;CH_3$

2.11   (a) alcohol   (b) ether   (c) alkane   (d) amine   (e) alcohol   (f) amine

2.12   Reaction with H_2SO_4?   Reaction with H_2SO_4?

(a) $CH_3CH_2CH_2CH_2CH_2\overset{\cdot\cdot}{\underset{}{O}}H$ Yes   (b) $CH_3CH_2CH_2-\overset{\cdot\cdot}{\underset{}{O}}-CH_3$ Yes

2.12   Reaction with H_2SO_4?   Reaction with H_2SO_4?

(c)   No   (d)   Yes

(e)   Yes   (f)   Yes

2.13

σ bond backbone

π bond

2.14

The two pairs of nonbonding electrons on the tetrahedral oxygen are in sp^3 hybrid orbitals. The two pairs of nonbonding electrons on the oxygen of the carbonyl group are in sp^2 hybrid orbitals.

2.15   (a) alcohol   (b) alkene   (c) aldehyde   (d) ketone   (e) amine
           (f) alkane   (g) carboxylic acid   (h) ether   (i) ester

2.16   (a) alcohol and carboxylic acid   (b) amine and carboxylic acid   (c) ketone and carboxylic acid
           (d) alcohol and aldehyde   (e) alkene and carboxylic acid

2.17   (a)   CH₃—C—N—H
                      ‖ |
                     :O: H
                 ↑   ↑
                sp³ sp²
                      |
                      H

(b)   CH₃CH₂—C—O—C=C—H
                   ‖   ‥ | |
                  :O: :O: H H
              ↗   ↖
             sp³   sp²

(c)   CH₃—C—CH₃
              ‥
             :OCH₃
          ↗ | ↖
         sp³ :OCH₃

(d)   H—C=C—C—H
           | | |
           H H H
                  ↖
                 sp³
              ↑
             sp²

(e)   CH₃—N=C—CH₃
              ‥ |
                  CH₃
          ↑   ↖
         sp²   sp²

Concept Map 2.2   Hybrid orbitals.

2.18   (a) alkyne   (b) alkene   (c) ketone   (d) ester
           (e) nitrile   (f) aldehyde   (g) carboxylic acid (h) amine

2.19   (a)   H—C=O
                      |
                      H
                   3σ, 1π

(b)   H—C—C—O—H
            | |
            H   H
            | |
            H   H
              8σ

(c)   H—C≡C—C≡C—H

                5σ, 4π

2.19   (d)   H—C=C—C≡N   (e)   H—C—C—O—C—H   (f)   H—C—C—C—H

$6\sigma, 3\pi$ $10\sigma, 1\pi$ 10σ

Concept Map 2.3   Functional Groups.

---

overlap of 1s orbital
on hydrogen and *sp*
hybrid orbital on carbon

overlap of two *sp* hybrid
orbitals, one on carbon and
one on nitrogen

2.20

σ bond backbone

overlap of two sets of *p*
orbitals, two each on
nitrogen and carbon,
which are at angles of
90° to each other

π bonds

2.21

overlap of sp^3 hybrid orbital on one carbon and sp hybrid orbital on the other carbon

overlap of $1s$ orbital on hydrogen and sp hybrid orbital on carbon

overlap of two sets of p orbitals, two each on nitrogen and carbon, which are at angles of 90° to each other

overlap of two sp hybrid orbitals, one on each carbon

overlap of $1s$ orbital on hydrogen and sp^3 hybrid orbital on carbon

σ bond backbone

π bonds

2.22

E

$(\sigma \rightarrow \sigma^*)_{water}$ $(n \rightarrow \sigma^*)_{water}$

σ^*

n_1

σ

H_2O

$(\sigma \rightarrow \sigma^*)_{ammonia}$ $(n \rightarrow \sigma^*)_{ammonia}$

σ^*

n_1

σ

NH_3

The $\sigma \rightarrow \sigma^*$ and the $n \rightarrow \sigma^*$ transitions are higher energies (shorter wavelengths) for water than for ammonia.

2.23 The halogen with the highest electronegativity will have the highest energy (shortest wavelength) $n \rightarrow \sigma^*$ transition. Compound A (173 nm) is CH_3Cl, Compound B (204 nm) is CH_3Br, and Compound C (258 nm) is CH_3I.

2.24

overlap of two $2p$ orbitals to form π bond possible when orbitals are parallel

90° rotation around double bond

overlap of two $2p$ orbitals to form π bond not possible when orbitals are perpendicular

cylindrical symmetry of σ bond permits rotation

60° rotation around double bond

2.25

more electronegative oxygen,
higher energy, shorter
wavelength $n \rightarrow \pi^*$ transition

less electronegative sulfur,
lower energy, longer
wavelength $n \rightarrow \pi^*$ transition

Concept Map 2.4   Bond lengths and bond strengths.

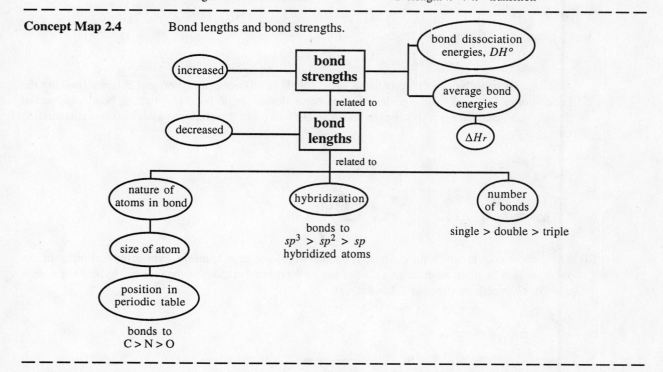

2.26

(a)   CH₃–§–H   +   Cl–§–Cl   ⟶   CH₃–§–Cl   +   H–§–Cl

Bond energies (kcal/mol)   99   58   81   103

$$\Delta H_r = (99 + 58) - (81 + 103) = -27 \text{ kcal/mol}$$

(b)   H₂C=§=O   +   H–§–C≡N   ⟶   H–§–O–§–CH₂–§–C≡N

Bond energies (kcal/mol)   176   99   111   86   83

$$\Delta H_r = (176 + 99) - (111 + 86 + 83) = -5 \text{ kcal/mol}$$

(Note that to calculate ΔH_r in a molecule in which a π bond is broken, both the π bond and the σ bond are broken and the σ bond is reformed in the product.)

(c)   H₂C=§=CH₂   +   H–§–Br   ⟶   H–§–CH₂–§–CH₂–§–Br

Bond energies (kcal/mol)   146   87   99   83   68

$$\Delta H_r = (146 + 87) - (99 + 83 + 68) = -17 \text{ kcal/mol}$$

(d)
$$\overset{83}{}$$

CH₃——CH–§–CH₂   ⟶   CH₃—CH=§=CH₂   +   H–§–O—H

86 〰 〰 99   146   111

HO   H

Bond energies (kcal/mol) $\Delta H_r = (86 + 83 + 99) - (146 + 111) = +11$ kcal/mol

2.27   (a)

chloroethane   chloroethene

(b)

A resonance contributor of chloroethene has a double bond between carbon and chlorine, making the bond shorter (1.72 Å) than expected for a carbon-chlorine single bond (1.78 Å). A bond with partial double bond character is also stronger than a single bond, and therefore has a higher bond dissociation energy.

(c)

(d)   The carbon atom to which the chlorine is bonded in chloroethene is an sp^2-hybridized carbon atom. An sp^2-hybridized carbon atom forms a shorter and stronger bond to chlorine than the sp^3-hybridized carbon atom of chloroethene (Section 2.8 in the text).

2.28   (a) $CH_3CH_2CH=CHCH_3$ + Br_2 $\xrightarrow[\substack{\text{carbon} \\ \text{tetrachloride} \\ \text{dark, 25 °C}}]{}$ $CH_3CH_2CH-CHCH_3$
                                                                                                       $\quad\quad\quad\quad\quad\;\; | \quad\; |$
                                                                                                       $\quad\quad\quad\quad\quad Br \; Br$

(b)

(c)

2.28   (d) $CH_3CH{=}CHCH_2CH{=}CHCH_3$ + 2 Br$_2$ $\xrightarrow[\text{dark, 25 °C}]{\text{carbon tetrachloride}}$

$$\begin{array}{c}\quad Br\quad Br\quad\quad Br\quad Br\\ \quad |\quad\ |\quad\quad\ |\quad\ |\\ CH_3CH{-}CHCH_2CH{-}CHCH_3\end{array}$$

Br$_2$

$$\begin{array}{c}Br\quad Br\\ |\quad\ |\\ CH_3CH{-}CHCH_2CH{=}CHCH_3\end{array}$$

Br$_2$

2.29

Alkanes: Tetrahedral carbon atoms bonded only to other tetrahedral carbon or hydrogen atoms

Alkenes: $-C{=}C-$

Alkynes: $-C{\equiv}C-$

Alkyl halides: $-C{-}X$

Alcohols: $-C{-}OH$

Ethers: $-C{-}O{-}C-$

Aldehydes: $-\overset{\overset{\textstyle O}{\|}}{C}H$

Ketones: $-\overset{\overset{\textstyle O}{\|}}{C}-$

Carboxylic acids: $-\overset{\overset{\textstyle O}{\|}}{C}{-}OH$

Esters: $-\overset{\overset{\textstyle O}{\|}}{C}{-}O{-}C-$

Amines: $-C{-}N-$

Nitriles: $-C{\equiv}N$

Aromatic hydrocarbons:

2.30

No delocalization of electrons in this structure.
We would expect the compound to behave like an alkene.

+ 2 Br$_2$ $\longrightarrow$

2.31   (a)   H:Be:H

sp, linear

(b)   :O::C::O:

sp, linear

(c)   H:C:H (with H above and + charge)

sp^2, trigonal planar

2.31

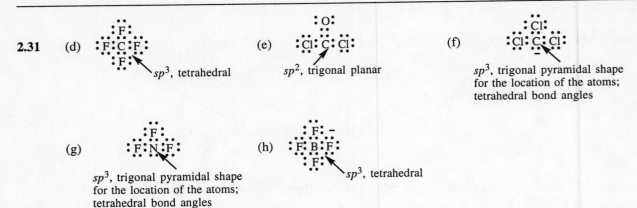

(d) sp^3, tetrahedral

(e) sp^2, trigonal planar

(f) sp^3, trigonal pyramidal shape for the location of the atoms; tetrahedral bond angles

(g) sp^3, trigonal pyramidal shape for the location of the atoms; tetrahedral bond angles

(h) sp^3, tetrahedral

2.32 (a) B_2H_6 cannot be adequately represented by a conventional Lewis structure. All twelve electrons contributed by the six hydrogen atoms and two boron atoms are needed to bond the hydrogen atoms to the boron atoms. There are no electrons left to hold the two boron atoms together.

$$H-B-H \qquad B-H$$

(b) $B_2H_6{}^{2-}$ is analogous to ethane, C_2H_6.

(c)

$$\left[\begin{array}{c}H\ H\\ |\ \ |\\ H-B-B-H\\ |\ \ |\\ H\ H\end{array}\right]^{2-} \quad \text{or} \quad H-B^--B^--H$$

This structure is more correct because it localizes formal charges.

(d)

2.33

(a) $CH_3C\equiv CH$ $H_2C=CHCH_3$ (benzene ring) $CH_3CH_2-CH_3$
     shortest   longest

(b) $H_2C=O$ $HC(=O)-OCH_3$ CH_3-OH
     shortest   longest

(c) $CH_3C\equiv N$ $H_2C=NCH_3$ CH_3-NH_2
     shortest   longest

2.34 (a)

(b)

2.34   (c)

alkyl halide   alcohol

alkyl halide   alkyl halide

(d)   ester   alkene

(e)   H alkene H   H alkene H

alkyne   carboxylic
acid

2.35

(a) $H_2C{=}O$

(b) CH_3NHOH

(c) $CH_3CH{=}CHCH_3$

one of two isomers

(d) $CH_3C{\equiv}CCH_3$

2.36   (a) The carbon and nitrogen atoms are sp^2-hybridized. The oxygen atom is sp^3 hybridized.

(b)

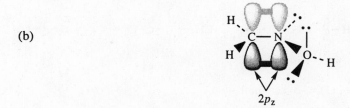

2.37

(a) $CH_3C\equiv N: + H-OSO_2H \rightarrow CH_3C\equiv \overset{+}{N}-H \quad HSO_4^-$

(b) $CH_3\overset{:O:}{\overset{\|}{C}}CH_3 + H-OSO_2H \rightarrow CH_3\overset{\overset{+}{O}-H}{\overset{\|}{C}}CH_3 \quad HSO_4^-$

(c) $CH_3\overset{CH_3}{\underset{\cdot\cdot}{C}}=NCH_3 + H-OSO_2H \rightarrow CH_3\overset{CH_3}{C}=\overset{+}{N}CH_3 \quad HSO_4^- $
(with H)

(d) $CH_3\overset{:O:}{\overset{\|}{C}}OCH_3 + H-OSO_2H \rightarrow CH_3\overset{\overset{+}{O}-H}{\overset{\|}{C}}OCH_3 \text{ or } CH_3C\overset{:O:}{O}-CH_3 \quad HSO_4^- \quad HSO_4^-$

2.38

(a) $CH_3CH=CHCH_3 + Br_2 \xrightarrow[\text{dark, 25 °C}]{\text{carbon tetrachloride}} CH_3\underset{Br}{CH}-\underset{Br}{CH}CH_3$

(b) $CH_3CH_2CH=CH_2 + H_2 \xrightarrow{\text{catalyst}} CH_3CH_2\underset{H}{CH}-\underset{H}{CH_2}$

(c) $CH_3CH_2CH_2CH_3 + Br_2 \xrightarrow[\text{dark, 25 °C}]{\text{carbon tetrachloride}}$ no reaction

(d) Ph$-CH=CH_2 + Br_2 \xrightarrow[\text{dark, 25 °C}]{\text{carbon tetrachloride}}$ Ph$-\underset{Br}{CH}-\underset{Br}{CH_2}$

(e) $CH_3C\equiv CH + Br_2 \text{ (excess)} \xrightarrow[\text{dark, 25 °C}]{\text{carbon tetrachloride}} CH_3\overset{Br}{\underset{Br}{C}}-\overset{Br}{\underset{Br}{CH}}$

(f) $CH_3C\equiv CH + H_2 \text{ (excess)} \xrightarrow{\text{catalyst}} CH_3\overset{H}{\underset{H}{C}}-\overset{H}{\underset{H}{CH}}$

2.39

(a) $H_2C=\overset{?}{}=CH_2 + Br-\overset{?}{}-Br \rightarrow Br-\overset{?}{}-CH_2-\overset{?}{}-CH_2-\overset{?}{}-Br$

Bond energies (kcal/mol)   146   46   68   83   68

$\Delta H_r = (146+46) - (68+83+68) = -27 \text{ kcal/mol}$

(b) $CH_3-\overset{CH_3}{\underset{CH_3}{C}}-\overset{?}{}-OH + H-\overset{?}{}-Cl \rightarrow CH_3-\overset{CH_3}{\underset{CH_3}{C}}-\overset{?}{}-Cl + H-\overset{?}{}-OH$

86   103   81   111

$\Delta H_r = (86+103) - (81+111) = -3 \text{ kcal/mol}$

2.39   (c)

$$\Delta H_r = (179 + 111) - (111 + 86 + 86) = +7 \text{ kcal/mol}$$

2.40

$$CH_2 = C = CH_2$$
$$sp^2 \quad sp \quad sp^2$$

In order to determine the sigma bond skeleton, we must first set up the pi bonds. When we do so, we can see that, in order for overlap to occur at the central carbon atom, the *p* orbitals on the two end carbon atoms must be perpendicular to each other. This causes the sp^2 hybrid orbitals on the end carbon atoms also to be perpendicular to each other.

σ bond backbone

2.41   (a)   120°   (b)

empty *p* orbital on boron overlaps
easily with nonbonding electrons
on oxygen in diethyl ether

(c)   Boron trifluoride etherate has a higher boiling point than either of the starting materials because the molecular weight of the etherate is higher and because the etherate is a more polar compound than either of the starting materials.

separation of charge in boron trifluoride etherate makes it polar;
dipole-dipole interactions between molecules leads to higher boiling point

2.42   (a)   H—C—N̈=N̈⁺=N̈⁻ ⟷ H—C—N̈⁻—N⁺≡N̈: ⟷ H—C—N≡N⁺—N̈:²⁻

This resonance contributor has the
greatest separation of charge and
makes the smallest contribution.

(b)   The N—N—N bond angle is 180° with *sp* hybridization for the central nitrogen atom.

the nonbonding electron pair is
delocalized over the three atom
pi system

2.43   (a) CH_3—C̈⁻=N⁺=CH_2 ⟷ CH_3—C≡N⁺—C̈H_2   (b)

2.44   (a)   O=C=C=C=O   (b)
                sp *sp* *sp*

2.45   (a)

(b)   The one in which the oxygen atom is sp^2-hybridized. The electron pair in the *p* orbital should have a
different energy than the electron pair in the sp^2 hybrid orbital. The model of water in which the oxgyen
atom is sp^3-hybridized has both pairs of nonbonding electrons in sp^3 hybrid orbitals. These electrons
should, therefore, be of the same energy. Experimentally we should not see them as occupying two
different energy levels.

(c)   Yes, lack of hybridization at the oxygen atom also results in two different energy levels for the two pairs
of nonbonding electrons.

overlap of a 1*s* orbital
on hydrogen with a 2*p*
orbital on oxygen

An sp^2-hybridized oxygen atom would be expected to have a H—O—H bond angle of 120°. If oxygen
were not hybridized, the H—O—H bond angle would be expected to be 90°. The experimentally determined value for the bond angle is 105°, between 120° and 90°.

2.45   (d) The oxygen atom would have *sp* hybridization.

overlap of a 2*s* orbital
on lithium with an *sp*
hybrid orbital on oxygen

overlap of a 1*s* orbital
on hydrogen with an *sp*
hybrid orbital on oxygen

Supplemental Problems

S2.1   Circle and name all the functional groups in each of the following molecules.

(a) $CH_3C \equiv CCCH_3$ (with CH_3 and OH substituents)

(b) $CH_3C = CHCCH_3$ (with CH_3 and O substituents)

(c) (benzene ring)$-CH_2NCH_3$ (with CH_3 substituent)

(d) $CH_3CH_2CHCH = CH_2$ (with Br substituent)

(e) $HOCCH_2CH_2COH$ (with two O substituents)

(f) $CH_3COCH_2CH_2OCH_3$ (with O substituent)

(g) (benzene ring)$-CH$ (with O substituent)

(h) CH_3CHCH_2CH (with O and OH substituents)

(i) (benzene ring)$-CH_2OH$

(j) $CH_3CH_2CH_2C \equiv N$

S2.2   Diazene, N_2H_2, has the following connectivity: HNNH. It is a good reducing agent, giving up hydrogen atoms easily to form the stable molecule, N_2.
(a) Draw a Lewis structure for diazene in which all the atoms have closed shells.
(b) The bonding in diazene may also be described using the model of orbital hybridization and molecular orbitals. What is the hybridization of the nitrogen atoms in diazene?
(c) Draw a three-dimensional picture of one isolated nitrogen atom in diazene showing the hybrid orbitals and any other orbitals around it with the electrons occupying those orbitals clearly shown.
(d) Draw a three-dimensional structural formula for diazene using lines (—), dashed lines (- - -), and wedges (◀) to indicate σ bonds, and show the actual orbitals involved in π bonds.

S2.3   Dicyanocarbene has the following Lewis structure

$$:N \equiv C - \ddot{C} - C \equiv N:$$

A carbene is a highly reactive neutral species because of the open shell on the central carbon atom.
(a) Predict the shape you would expect for dicyanocarbene from the structure given by drawing a three-dimensional representation, using lines, dashed lines, and wedges as needed. Nonbonding electrons may be shown in lobes

(⟁), or at the end of wedges (▶), or dashed lines (⋰) to indicate direction. Show the expected bond angle on your drawing.
(b) What is the hybridization of the central carbon atom in dicyanocarbene according to the picture you drew in part (a)?
(c) What is the hybridization of the carbon atoms bonded to nitrogen (the cyano groups) in dicyanocarbene?

S2.3

(d) Redraw the structure of dicyanocarbene using lines, wedges, or dashed lines for σ bonds and the location of nonbonding electrons, and show the p orbitals involved in any π bonding. You need to show the details of bonding for only *one* of the two cyano groups. Label the bonds and the orbitals so that it is clear how the bonding arises.

S2.4   The following two compounds are part of a synthesis of taxotere, a compound extracted from the bark of the Pacific yew tree and found to be useful in the treatment of ovarian cancer.

Compound A   Compound B

(a) What is the structural relationship, if any, of Compounds A and B? Some choices are (1) constitutional isomers, (2) stereoisomers, (3) resonance contributors, or (4) no structural relationship.

(b) Draw a structure for compounds that fit the descriptions given below.
   (1) A constitutional isomer of B that contains a triple bond.
   (2) A resonance contributor of B.
   (3) A constitutional isomer of B that contains a ring.
   (4) A constitutional isomer of B that has a different connectivity but no ring.

S2.5   An unusual structure, shown below, has been reported.

(a) What is the hybridization at each of the atoms in the compound?

(b) Draw a clear three-dimensional orbital picture of the π bonds in the compound. You may use CH_3 for the methyl groups, but do show how they, as well as the nonbonding electrons on phosphorus, point in space using wedges, dashes, or lines.

S2.6   Alkyl nitrile oxides (connectivity RCNO where R is a generic alkyl group) are a useful class of compounds for carrying out the preparation of more complex molecules. A relatively unimportant resonance contributor for methyl nitrile oxide is shown below.

Two other resonance contributors are more important because all atoms have closed shells and some have formal charges of -1 and $+1$. What are they? Of the two forms that you have drawn, which one is the more important?

3

Reactions of Organic Compounds as Acids and Bases

Workbook Exercises

Much of Chapter 3 is devoted to learning how to rank acidities. It is important for you to be able to draw and recognize, both quickly and accurately, the form of a molecule resulting from the loss of a proton. Such a reaction is called a deprotonation reaction.

The connectivity change that occurs in deprotonation may be imagined in the following way:

$$(A = any\ atom) \qquad A \text{—} H \longrightarrow A \text{:}^- \quad + \quad H^+$$

shared electron pair → (under A—H)

electron pair with A → (under A:⁻)

nucleus of a hydrogen atom; a proton (under H⁺)

EXERCISE I.   Draw all of the products that can result from a single deprotonation of the molecule shown below.

EXAMPLE

$$CH_3CHCH_2\ddot{O}H$$
$$|$$
$$CH_3$$

SOLUTION

(1)   Redraw the compound as a complete Lewis structure and then decide, based on connectivity, how many different types of hydrogen atoms there are.

(Note that regardless of how the molecule is drawn, the set of 6 hydrogens in circles are of the same type. That is, they are equally situated with respect to the other atoms in the molecule.)

There are 4 different types of hydrogen atoms.

(2)   There are 4 different deprotonations possible.

loss of ⟨H⁺⟩

loss of ☐H⁺

loss of △H⁺

loss of Ⓗ⁺

45

Workbook Exercises (cont)

PROBLEM I.   Draw all of the products that can result from a single deprotonation of the molecules shown below.

(a)

(b) $HOCCH_2CH_3$ (with carbonyl O)

(c) H_2

(d)

(e) $ClCH_2CN$

(f) $HC\equiv CCH_2CH$ (with carbonyl O)

(g) $H_2\overset{+}{O}CH_2CH_3$

(h) $(CH_3)_3S^{+ -}BF_4$

EXERCISE II.   The reverse of a deprotonation reaction is a protonation reaction. Protonation is the attaching of a proton, H⁺, to a molecule or ion. In order to form a bond with a proton, another atom must contribute both of the electrons to the bond (H⁺ has no electrons to contribute!). Nonbonding electron pairs from uncharged or negatively charged atoms are often the source of electrons for forming a new bond to a proton.

The connectivity change that occurs in protonation may be drawn in the following way:

(A = any atom)   uncharged $A\overset{\bullet\bullet}{:}$ + a proton (H⁺) source ⟶ $\overset{+}{A}$—H

anionic $A\overset{\bullet\bullet}{:}{}^{-}$ + a proton (H⁺) source ⟶ A—H

In both cases, the nonbonding electron pair
provides both electrons for the A—H bond.

Draw all of the products that can result from a single protonation of the molecules shown below. Locating the nonbonding electrons in each molecule is a good way to start.

(a) $CH_3CH_2CH_2O^- Na^+$

(b) $(CH_3)_2CHNHCH_2CH_2NH_2$

(c) CH_3OCNH_2 (with carbonyl O)

(d)

(e) $Li^+ {}^-C\equiv CCH_2CH_2O^- Li^+$

(f)

(g) $CH_3CCH_2CH_2CH_3$ with OCH₃ and OH substituents

(h) ^-OC—$CHCH_2OH$ (with carbonyl O and NH₂)

3.1   (a) $(CH_3)_2O$ $(CH_3)_2OH^+$

base

conjugate acid

(b) $H_2SO_4 = (HO)_2SO_2$ $HSO_4^- = HOSO_3^-$

acid

conjugate base
(one resonance contributor)

3.1   (c) $^-NH_2$ NH_3

$$H - \overset{\displaystyle\cdot\cdot}{\underset{\displaystyle\cdot\cdot}{N}} - H$$
base

$$H - \overset{\displaystyle H}{\underset{\displaystyle\cdot\cdot}{N}} - H$$
conjugate acid

(d) $CH_3OH_2{}^+$ CH_3OH

$$H - \overset{\displaystyle H}{\underset{\displaystyle H}{C}} - \overset{+}{\underset{\displaystyle\cdot\cdot}{O}} - H$$
acid

$$H - \overset{\displaystyle H}{\underset{\displaystyle H}{C}} - \overset{\displaystyle\cdot\cdot}{\underset{\displaystyle\cdot\cdot}{O}} - H$$
conjugate base

(e) $H_2C=O$ $H_2C=OH^+$

$$H - \overset{\displaystyle :\overset{\cdot\cdot}{O}:}{\underset{}{C}} - H$$
base

$$H - \overset{\displaystyle :\overset{+}{O} - H}{\underset{}{C}} - H$$
conjugate acid

(f) CH_3OH CH_3O^-

$$H - \overset{\displaystyle H}{\underset{\displaystyle H}{C}} - \overset{\displaystyle\cdot\cdot}{\underset{\displaystyle\cdot\cdot}{O}} - H$$
acid

$$H - \overset{\displaystyle H}{\underset{\displaystyle H}{C}} - \overset{\displaystyle\cdot\cdot}{\underset{\displaystyle\cdot\cdot}{O}}:^-$$
conjugate base

Concept Map 3.1   The Brønsted-Lowry theory of acids and bases.

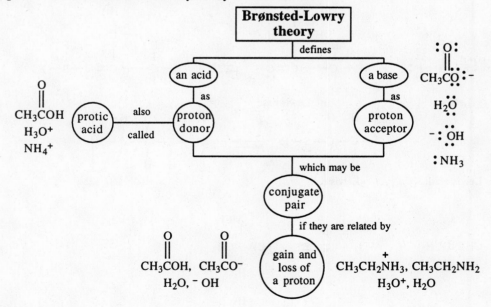

Concept Map 3.2   The Lewis theory of acids and bases.

- -

3.2 (a) Cu^{2+} +   4 H—N—H   ⇌   [structure of $[Cu(NH_3)_4]^{2+}$]
Lewis acid   Lewis base

(b) [isobutyl cation structure] + H—O—H ⇌ [protonated alcohol product structure]
Lewis acid   Lewis base

(c) [BF_3 structure] + [aldehyde structure] ⇌ [adduct structure]
Lewis acid   Lewis base

(d) Hg^{2+} + [thiol structure] ⇌ [Hg adduct structure]$^{2+}$
Lewis acid   Lewis base

3.3 (a) CH_3NHCH_3 + $AlCl_3$ ⇌ [product with $^-AlCl_3$ and $CH_3\overset{+}{N}CH_3$, H]

CH_3NHCH_3 + H_2SO_4 ⇌ [$CH_3\overset{+}{N}CH_3$ with H] + HSO_4^-

3.3   (b)

$$\underset{\text{HCH}}{\overset{\overset{\textstyle :O:}{\|}}{}} \;+\; AlCl_3 \;\rightleftharpoons\; \underset{\text{HCH}}{\overset{\overset{\textstyle :\overset{+}{O}-\overset{-}{}AlCl_3}{\|}}{}}$$

$$\underset{\text{HCH}}{\overset{\overset{\textstyle :O:}{\|}}{}} \;+\; H_2SO_4 \;\rightleftharpoons\; \underset{\text{HCH}}{\overset{\overset{\textstyle :\overset{+}{O}-H}{\|}}{}} \;+\; HSO_4^-$$

(c) $HC\!\equiv\!CH \;+\; AlCl_3 \;\rightleftharpoons\; HC\!\overset{+}{=}\!CH$ (with $\overset{-}{}AlCl_3$)

$HC\!\equiv\!CH \;+\; H_2SO_4 \;\rightleftharpoons\; HC\!\overset{+}{=}\!CH$ (with H) $\;+\; HSO_4^-$

(d)

$$CH_3CH_2\!-\!\underset{\underset{\textstyle ..}{|}}{\overset{\overset{\textstyle CH_2CH_3}{|}}{P}}\!-\!CH_2CH_3 \;+\; AlCl_3 \;\rightleftharpoons\; CH_3CH_2\!-\!\overset{\overset{\textstyle CH_2CH_3}{|}}{\underset{\underset{\textstyle AlCl_3}{\overset{-}{|}}}{\overset{+}{P}}}\!-\!CH_2CH_3$$

$$CH_3CH_2\!-\!\underset{\underset{\textstyle ..}{|}}{\overset{\overset{\textstyle CH_2CH_3}{|}}{P}}\!-\!CH_2CH_3 \;+\; H_2SO_4 \;\rightleftharpoons\; CH_3CH_2\!-\!\overset{\overset{\textstyle CH_2CH_3}{|}}{\underset{\underset{\textstyle H}{|}}{\overset{+}{P}}}\!-\!CH_2CH_3 \;+\; HSO_4^-$$

(e) $CH_3CH_2\!-\!\overset{..}{\underset{..}{O}}H \;+\; AlCl_3 \;\rightleftharpoons\; CH_3CH_2\!-\!\underset{\underset{\textstyle ..}{}}{\overset{+}{O}}H$ (with $\overset{-}{}AlCl_3$)

$CH_3CH_2\!-\!\overset{..}{\underset{..}{O}}H \;+\; H_2SO_4 \;\rightleftharpoons\; CH_3CH_2\!-\!\underset{\underset{\textstyle ..}{}}{\overset{+}{O}}H$ (with H) $\;+\; HSO_4^-$

(f) $CH_3CH_2\!-\!\overset{..}{\underset{..}{S}}\!-\!CH_2CH_3 \;+\; AlCl_3 \;\rightleftharpoons\; CH_3CH_2\!-\!\underset{\underset{\textstyle ..}{}}{\overset{+}{S}}\!-\!CH_2CH_3$ (with $\overset{-}{}AlCl_3$)

$CH_3CH_2\!-\!\overset{..}{\underset{..}{S}}\!-\!CH_2CH_3 \;+\; H_2SO_4 \;\rightleftharpoons\; CH_3CH_2\!-\!\underset{\underset{\textstyle ..}{}}{\overset{+}{S}}\!-\!CH_2CH_3 \;+\; HSO_4^-$ (with H)

3.4   (a)   ethyl acetate

$$H\!-\!\underset{\underset{\textstyle H}{|}}{\overset{\overset{\textstyle H}{|}}{C}}\!-\!\overset{\overset{\textstyle :O:}{\|}}{C}\!-\!\overset{..}{\underset{..}{O}}\!-\!\underset{\underset{\textstyle H}{|}}{\overset{\overset{\textstyle H}{|}}{C}}\!-\!\underset{\underset{\textstyle H}{|}}{\overset{\overset{\textstyle H}{|}}{C}}\!-\!H$$

$$CH_3\overset{\overset{\textstyle :O:}{\|}}{C}\!-\!\overset{..}{\underset{..}{O}}\!-\!CH_2CH_3 \;+\; H_2SO_4 \;\rightleftharpoons\; CH_3\overset{\overset{\textstyle :\overset{+}{O}-H}{\|}}{C}\!-\!\overset{..}{\underset{..}{O}}\!-\!CH_2CH_3 \;+\; HSO_4^-$$

$$CH_3\overset{\overset{\textstyle :O:}{\|}}{C}\!-\!\overset{..}{\underset{..}{O}}\!-\!CH_2CH_3 \;+\; H_2SO_4 \;\rightleftharpoons\; CH_3\overset{\overset{\textstyle :O:}{\|}}{C}\!-\!\underset{\underset{\textstyle H}{\overset{+}{|}}}{\overset{..}{O}}\!-\!CH_2CH_3 \;+\; HSO_4^-$$

3.4   (b)   2-(*N,N*-dimethylamino)ethanol

$$H-\overset{..}{\underset{..}{O}}-CH_2CH_2-\overset{CH_3}{\underset{..}{N}}-CH_3 \;+\; H_2SO_4 \;\rightleftharpoons\; H-\overset{..}{\underset{..}{O}}-CH_2CH_2-\overset{CH_3}{\underset{\overset{|}{H}}{\overset{+}{N}}}-CH_3 \;+\; HSO_4^-$$

$$H-\overset{..}{\underset{..}{O}}-CH_2CH_2-\overset{CH_3}{\underset{..}{N}}-CH_3 \;+\; H_2SO_4 \;\rightleftharpoons\; H-\overset{..}{\underset{\overset{+}{\underset{H}{|}}}{O}}-CH_2CH_2-\overset{CH_3}{\underset{..}{N}}-CH_3 \;+\; HSO_4^-$$

(c)   2-propen-1-ol

$$CH_2=CHCH_2-\overset{..}{\underset{..}{O}}-H \;+\; H_2SO_4 \;\rightleftharpoons\; CH_2=CHCH_2-\overset{..}{\underset{\overset{+}{\underset{H}{|}}}{O}}-H \;+\; HSO_4^-$$

$$CH_2=CHCH_2-\overset{..}{\underset{..}{O}}-H \;+\; H_2SO_4 \;\rightleftharpoons\; \overset{}{\underset{\underset{H}{|}}{CH_2}}-\overset{+}{C}HCH_2-\overset{..}{\underset{..}{O}}-H \;+\; HSO_4^-$$

(d)   methyl isocyanate

$$CH_3-\overset{..}{\underset{..}{N}}=C=\overset{..}{\underset{..}{O}} \;+\; H_2SO_4 \;\rightleftharpoons\; CH_3-\overset{+}{\underset{\underset{H}{|}}{N}}=C=\overset{..}{\underset{..}{O}} \;+\; HSO_4^-$$

$$CH_3-\overset{..}{\underset{..}{N}}=C=\overset{..}{\underset{..}{O}} \;+\; H_2SO_4 \;\rightleftharpoons\; CH_3-\overset{..}{\underset{..}{N}}=C=\overset{+}{\underset{..}{O}}-H \;+\; HSO_4^-$$

3.5   <u>base</u>   <u>conjugate acid</u>   <u>base</u>   <u>conjugate acid</u>

(a) $\underset{H}{\overset{CH_3CH_2}{C}}=\underset{CH_2CH_3}{\overset{H}{C}}$ $\underset{H}{\overset{CH_3CH_2}{\overset{+}{C}}}-\underset{CH_2CH_3}{\overset{H}{C}}-H$

(b) $CH_3CH_2-\overset{..}{\underset{..}{O}}-CH_2CH_3$ $CH_3CH_2-\overset{..}{\underset{\overset{+}{\underset{H}{|}}}{O}}-CH_2CH_3$ (c) $CH_3CH_2\overset{..}{\underset{\underset{H}{|}}{N}}CH_2CH_3$ $CH_3CH_2\overset{\overset{+}{\underset{H}{|}}}{\underset{\underset{H}{|}}{N}}CH_2CH_3$

(e) $CH_3CH_2\overset{\overset{\displaystyle :O:}{\|}}{C}H$ $CH_3CH_2\overset{\overset{\displaystyle :\overset{+}{O}-H}{\|}}{C}H$

(d) $CH_3CH_2CH_2-\overset{..}{\underset{..}{S}}-CH_3$ $CH_3CH_2CH_2-\overset{..}{\underset{\overset{+}{\underset{H}{|}}}{S}}-CH_3$

(f) $CH_3CH_2CH_2-\overset{..}{\underset{..}{O}}H$ $CH_3CH_2CH_2-\overset{..}{\underset{\overset{+}{|}}{O}}H$ (g) $CH_3CH_2\overset{\overset{\displaystyle :O:}{\|}}{C}CH_2CH_3$ $CH_3CH_2\overset{\overset{\displaystyle :\overset{+}{O}-H}{\|}}{C}CH_2CH_3$

3.6   Equations from Problem 3.3 rewritten:

(a)

$$CH_3\overset{\underset{\textstyle H}{|}}{\underset{}{N}}:\ \ + \ :\overset{..}{\underset{..}{Cl}}:\ \ \overset{\underset{\textstyle :Cl:}{|}}{\underset{\underset{\textstyle :Cl:}{|}}{Al}}-Cl:\ \longrightarrow\ CH_3\overset{\underset{\textstyle H}{|}}{\underset{}{\overset{+}{N}}}-\overset{-}{Al}Cl_3$$

$$CH_3\overset{\underset{\textstyle H}{|}}{\underset{}{N}}:\ \ H\overset{..}{\underset{..}{O}}-SO_3H\ \longrightarrow\ CH_3\overset{\underset{\textstyle H}{|}}{\underset{}{\overset{+}{N}}}-H\qquad ^-:\overset{..}{\underset{..}{O}}-SO_3H$$

(b)

$$\overset{:O:}{\underset{HCH}{\|}}\ \ \overset{\underset{\textstyle :Cl:}{|}}{\underset{\underset{\textstyle :Cl:}{|}}{Al}}-Cl:\ \longrightarrow\ \overset{:\overset{+}{O}-\overset{-}{Al}Cl_3}{\underset{HCH}{\|}}$$

$$\overset{:O:}{\underset{HCH}{\|}}\ \ H\overset{..}{\underset{\rightarrow}{O}}-SO_3H\ \longrightarrow\ \overset{:\overset{+}{O}-H}{\underset{HCH}{\|}}\qquad ^-:\overset{..}{\underset{..}{O}}-SO_3H$$

(c)

$$HC\equiv CH\ \ \overset{\underset{\textstyle :Cl:}{|}}{\underset{\underset{\textstyle :Cl:}{|}}{Al}}-Cl:\ \longrightarrow\ \overset{+}{H}C=\overset{\overset{\textstyle ^-AlCl_3}{|}}{CH}$$

$$HC\equiv CH\ \ H\overset{..}{\underset{\rightarrow}{O}}-SO_3H\ \longrightarrow\ \overset{+}{H}C=CH_2\qquad ^-:\overset{..}{\underset{..}{O}}-SO_3H$$

(d)

$$CH_3CH_2\overset{\underset{\textstyle CH_3CH_2}{|}}{\underset{\underset{\textstyle CH_3CH_2}{|}}{P}}:\ \ \overset{\underset{\textstyle :Cl:}{|}}{\underset{\underset{\textstyle :Cl:}{|}}{Al}}-Cl:\ \longrightarrow\ CH_3CH_2\overset{\underset{\textstyle CH_3CH_2}{|}}{\underset{\underset{\textstyle CH_3CH_2}{|}}{\overset{+}{P}}}-\overset{-}{Al}Cl_3$$

$$CH_3CH_2\overset{\underset{\textstyle CH_3CH_2}{|}}{\underset{\underset{\textstyle CH_3CH_2}{|}}{P}}:\ \ H\overset{..}{\underset{\rightarrow}{O}}-SO_3H\ \longrightarrow\ CH_3CH_2\overset{\underset{\textstyle CH_3CH_2}{|}}{\underset{\underset{\textstyle CH_3CH_2}{|}}{\overset{+}{P}}}-H\qquad ^-:\overset{..}{\underset{..}{O}}-SO_3H$$

(e)

$$CH_3CH_2-\overset{..}{\underset{..}{O}}H\ \ \overset{\underset{\textstyle :Cl:}{|}}{\underset{\underset{\textstyle :Cl:}{|}}{Al}}-\overset{..}{\underset{..}{Cl}}:\ \longrightarrow\ CH_3CH_2-\overset{\overset{\textstyle ^-AlCl_3}{|}}{\overset{+}{O}}\!\overset{..}{\underset{..}{H}}$$

$$CH_3CH_2-\overset{..}{\underset{..}{O}}H\ \ H\overset{..}{\underset{\rightarrow}{O}}-SO_3H\ \longrightarrow\ CH_3CH_2-\overset{\overset{\textstyle H}{|}}{\overset{+}{O}}\!\overset{..}{\underset{..}{H}}\qquad ^-:\overset{..}{\underset{..}{O}}-SO_3H$$

(f)

$$CH_3CH_2\overset{..}{\underset{..}{S}}-CH_2CH_3\ \ \overset{\underset{\textstyle :Cl:}{|}}{\underset{\underset{\textstyle :Cl:}{|}}{Al}}-\overset{..}{\underset{..}{Cl}}:\ \longrightarrow\ CH_3CH_2\overset{\overset{\textstyle ^-AlCl_3}{|}}{\overset{+}{S}}\!\!\!\underset{..}{}-CH_2CH_3$$

3.6 (f) (cont)

$$CH_3CH_2\ddot{S}-CH_2CH_3 \quad H\rightleftharpoons\ddot{O}-SO_3H \longrightarrow CH_3CH_2\overset{H}{\underset{\vert}{\overset{+}{S}}}-CH_2CH_3 \quad {}^-\!:\!\ddot{O}-SO_3H$$

Equations from Problem 3.4 rewritten:

(a)

$$CH_3\overset{:O:}{\underset{\Vert}{C}}-\ddot{O}-CH_2CH_3 \quad H\rightleftharpoons\ddot{O}-SO_3H \longrightarrow CH_3\overset{\overset{+}{O}-H}{\underset{\Vert}{C}}-\ddot{O}-CH_2CH_3 \quad {}^-\!:\!\ddot{O}-SO_3H$$

$$CH_3\overset{:O:}{\underset{\Vert}{C}}-\ddot{O}-CH_2CH_3 \longrightarrow CH_3\overset{:O:}{\underset{\Vert}{C}}-\overset{+}{\underset{\vert}{O}}-CH_2CH_3$$
$$H\rightleftharpoons\ddot{O}-SO_3H \qquad\qquad H \qquad {}^-\!:\!\ddot{O}-SO_3H$$

(b)

$$H-\ddot{O}-CH_2CH_2\overset{CH_3}{\underset{\underset{CH_3}{\vert}}{N}}: \quad H\rightleftharpoons\ddot{O}-SO_3H \longrightarrow H-\ddot{O}-CH_2CH_2\overset{CH_3}{\underset{\underset{CH_3}{\vert}}{\overset{+}{N}}}-H \quad {}^-\!:\!\ddot{O}-SO_3H$$

$$H-\ddot{O}-CH_2CH_2\overset{CH_3}{\underset{\vert}{N}}-CH_3 \longrightarrow H-\overset{+}{\underset{\underset{H}{\vert}}{O}}-CH_2CH_2\ddot{N}-CH_3$$
$$H\rightleftharpoons\ddot{O}-SO_3H \qquad\qquad\qquad {}^-\!:\!\ddot{O}-SO_3H$$

(c)

$$CH_2\!=\!CHCH_2-\ddot{O}-H \longrightarrow CH_2\!=\!CHCH_2-\overset{+}{\underset{\underset{H}{\vert}}{O}}-H$$
$$H\rightleftharpoons\ddot{O}-SO_3H \qquad\qquad\qquad {}^-\!:\!\ddot{O}-SO_3H$$

$$CH_2\!=\!CHCH_2-\ddot{O}-H \longrightarrow \overset{+}{CH_2}-\overset{\underset{H}{\vert}}{CH}CH_2-\ddot{O}-H$$
$$H\rightleftharpoons\ddot{O}-SO_3H \qquad\qquad\qquad {}^-\!:\!\ddot{O}-SO_3H$$

(d)

$$CH_3-\ddot{N}=C=\ddot{O} \longrightarrow CH_3-\overset{\underset{H}{\vert}}{\overset{+}{N}}=C=\ddot{O}$$
$$H\rightleftharpoons\ddot{O}-SO_3H \qquad\qquad\qquad {}^-\!:\!\ddot{O}-SO_3H$$

$$CH_3-\ddot{N}=C=\ddot{O} \quad H\rightleftharpoons\ddot{O}-SO_3H \longrightarrow CH_3-\ddot{N}=C=\overset{+}{\underset{\underset{H}{\vert}}{O}} \quad+\quad {}^-\!:\!\ddot{O}-SO_3H$$

3.7 (a)

$$\overset{CH_3CH_2}{\underset{H}{\overset{\vert}{:\!\ddot{O}\!:}}} \quad H\rightleftharpoons\ddot{I}: \longrightarrow CH_3CH_2-\overset{+}{\underset{\underset{H}{\vert}}{O}}-H \quad :\ddot{I}:{}^-$$

(b)

$$CH_3-\overset{CH_3}{\underset{\underset{CH_3}{\vert}}{N}}: \quad H\rightleftharpoons\ddot{Cl}: \longrightarrow CH_3-\overset{CH_3}{\underset{\underset{CH_3}{\vert}}{\overset{+}{N}}}-H \quad :\ddot{Cl}:{}^-$$

3.7 (c)

3.8   most basic   least basic
(a)   CH₃NHCH₃   >   CH₃OCH₃
            amine   ether
     (nonbonding electrons   (nonbonding electrons
        on nitrogen)   on oxygen)

(b)   CH₃⁻   >   NH₂⁻   >   OH⁻   >   F⁻
            methyl anion   amide ion   hydroxide ion   fluoride ion
            a carbanion   (nonbonding electrons on
         (nonbonding electrons   fluorine; EN 4.0)
            on carbon; EN 2.5)
            EN = electronegativity

(c)   CH₃ṄCH₃   >   CH₃O⁻
            amide anion   alkoxide anion

- -

Concept Map 3.3   Relationship of acidity to position of the central element in the periodic table.

the acidity of
a protic acid

depends on

position of
central atom in
periodic table

increases

left to right   down a
across a period   family

CH₄ < NH₃ < H₂O < HF   HF < HCl < HBr < HI
       NH₄⁺ < H₃O⁺   ─────────────────────►
CH₃CH₃ < CH₃NH₂ < CH₃OH   increasing acidity

increasing acidity

- -

3.9   H₂S is the stronger acid.

$$H_2S + HO^- \rightleftharpoons HS^- + H_2O$$

Hydrogen sulfide ionizes more readily than does water because the hydrogen sulfide anion is more stable relative to its conjugate acid than is hydroxide ion. The hydrogen sulfide anion is a weaker base than hydroxide anion for the same reason that methanethiolate anion is a weaker base than the hydroxide anion. The sulfur atom is larger than an oxygen atom. Therefore the negative charge on the hydrogen sulfide anion is more spread out. The anion is more stable relative to its conjugate acid than is hydroxide ion and less likely to be protonated.

3.10 $CH_3CH_2SH + CH_3O^- \rightleftarrows CH_3CH_2S^- + CH_3OH$

Ethanethiolate ion is a weaker base than methoxide ion because the negative charge is more spread out on the sulfur atom than on the oxygen atom. (See the answer to Problem 3.9.) In the reaction of ethanethiol and methoxide ion, the equilibrium lies far to the right.

3.11   (a)   One of the nonbonding electron pairs on the oxygen atom can react with the empty *p*-orbital of the carbocation.

an oxonium ion

(b)   The product formed is a protonated alcohol, an oxonium ion, which has a $pK_a \sim -2$. It will transfer a proton to the oxygen atom of water in an equilibrium reaction. With a large excess of water, equilibrium lies toward the right.

(excess)

3.12   (a)
least acidic				most acidic
$CH_3CH_2CH_3$	<	$CH_3CH_2NH_2$	<	CH_3CH_2OH	<	CH_3CH_2SH
alkene		amine		alcohol		thiol

(b)

CH_3OCH_3 < CH_3NHCH_3 <

(proton on   (proton on   (proton on the oxygen atom
a carbon atom)   a nitrogen atom)   of an oxonium ion)

(c) $CH_3CH_2CH_3$ <   <

alkane   ammonium ion   oxonium ion

3.13

acid	conjugate base	acid	conjugate base

(a)   (b)

(c)   (d)

3.13

3.14 $HO_3SO{-}H$ + H_2O $\rightleftharpoons$ HO_3SO^- + H_3O^+

sulfuric acid   water   hydrogen   hydronium
$K_a = 10^9$ sulfate anion   ion
                                               $K_a = 10^{1.7}$

energy →

$CH_3CO_2^-$ + H_3O^+
products

CH_3CO_2H + H_2O
starting materials

energy →

HO_3SOH + H_2O
starting materials

HO_3SO^- + H_3O^+
products

3.15   The acidity constant is

$$K_a = \frac{[H^+]\,[\colon\!B]}{[HB^+]}$$

where $\colon\!B$ and HB^+ are the conjugate base and conjugate acid forms respectively.

                pK_a is defined as $-\log K_a$

For formic acid pK_a $= -\log(1.99 \times 10^{-4})$
                           $= -(\log 1.99 + \log 10^{-4})$
                           $= -(0.299 - 4)$
           pK_a $= -(-3.701)$
           pK_a $= +3.701$

For acetic acid $pK_a = +4.76$

As the pK_a gets larger (more positive), K_a gets smaller and the amount of dissociation of the acid decreases. Formic acid has the smaller pK_a, and thus the larger K_a, and is a stronger acid than acetic acid.

3.16

base   conjugate acid
                (one resonance contributor)

$pK_a = -\log K_a$
$\log K_a = -7$
$K_a = 10^{-7}$

3.17 $ClCH_2COH$ + H_2O $\rightleftharpoons$ $ClCH_2CO^-$ + H_3O^+

$$K_{eq} = \frac{[ClCH_2CO_2^-]\,[H_3O^+]}{[ClCH_2CO_2H]\,[H_2O]}$$

$$K_{eq}\,[H_2O] = K_a = \frac{[ClCH_2CO_2^-]\,[H_3O^+]}{[ClCH_2CO_2H]}$$

3.17 (cont) $\overset{\overset{\displaystyle O}{\|}}{ClCH_2COH}$ + $\overset{\overset{\displaystyle O}{\|}}{CH_3CO^-}$ ⇌ $\overset{\overset{\displaystyle O}{\|}}{ClCH_2CO^-}$ + $\overset{\overset{\displaystyle O}{\|}}{CH_3COH}$

$$K_{eq} = \frac{[ClCH_2CO_2^-]\,[CH_3CO_2H]}{[ClCH_2CO_2H]\,[CH_3CO_2^-]}$$

$$K_{eq} = \frac{K_a \text{ of } ClCH_2CO_2H}{K_a \text{ of } CH_3CO_2H} = \frac{\dfrac{[ClCH_2CO_2^-]\,[H_3O^+]}{[ClCH_2CO_2H]}}{\dfrac{[CH_3CO_2^-]\,[H_3O^+]}{[CH_3CO_2H]}}$$

$$K_{eq} = \frac{[ClCH_2CO_2^-]\,\cancel{[H_3O^+]}\,[CH_3CO_2H]}{[ClCH_2CO_2H]\,[CH_3CO_2^-]\,\cancel{[H_3O^+]}}$$

$$K_{eq} = \frac{[ClCH_2CO_2^-]\,[CH_3CO_2H]}{[ClCH_2CO_2H]\,[CH_3CO_2^-]} = K_{eq} \text{ for the reaction of chloroacetic acid with acetate ion}$$

3.18 $\Delta G^\circ = -2.303\ RT \log K_{eq}$

$$-2.59 \text{ kcal/mol} = (-2.303)(1.987 \times 10^{-3} \text{ kcal/mol·K})(298 \text{ K})(\log K_{eq})$$

$$\log K_{eq} = 1.899$$

$$K_{eq} = 10^{1.899} = 79.3$$

$$K_{eq} = \frac{K_a \text{ of } ClCH_2CO_2H}{K_a \text{ of } CH_3CO_2H}$$

$$79.3 = \frac{K_a \text{ of } ClCH_2CO_2H}{(1.75 \times 10^{-5})}$$

$$K_a\,(ClCH_2CO_2H) = (79.3)(1.75 \times 10^{-5}) = 1.39 \times 10^{-3}$$

$$pK_a\,(ClCH_2CO_2H) = -\log K_a = -\log (1.39 \times 10^{-3})$$

$$pK_a = -(-3 + 0.143) = 2.86$$

This is very close to the value, 2.8, given in the front cover of the textbook for chloroacetic acid.

- -

Concept Map 3.4   The relationship of pK_a to energy and entropy factors.

$K_a = K_{eq}[H_2O]$

$\Delta G^\circ = -RT \ln K_{eq}$

$\Delta G^\circ = \Delta H^\circ - T\Delta S^\circ$

3.19

functional group	acid	pK_a
alkane	H—C—H (with H above and below)	47
amine	H—N̈—H (with H below)	36
alcohol	CH_3CH_2—Ö—H	17
thiol	CH_3CH_2—S̈—H	10.5
ammonium ion	CH_3—N̈⁺—H (with CH_3 above and CH_3 below)	9.8
carboxylic acid	Ph—C(=Ö)—Ö—H	4.2
oxonium ion	CH_3CH_2—O⁺—H (with H above)	−2.4

increasing
acidity

(Note that in this table acidity increases down the table, unlike the pK_a table inside the front cover of the textbook.)

3.20 (a) CH_3CH_2OH + K^+OH^- ⇌ $CH_3CH_2O^- K^+$ + H_2O
 pK_a 17 pK_a 15.7

(b) $CH_3CH_2\overset{+}{N}H_2$ Cl^- + Na^+OH^- → CH_3CH_2NH + H_2O + Na^+Cl^-
 CH_3CH_2 (below N) CH_3CH_2 (below N)
 pK_a 10 pK_a 15.7

(c) CH_2FCOH (C=O) + $Na^+HCO_3^-$ ⇌ $CH_2FCO^- Na^+$ (C=O) + H_2CO_3 [⇌ H_2O + CO_2↑]
 pK_a 2 pK_a 6.5

(d) CH_3—⟨benzene⟩—OH + $Na^+HCO_3^-$ ⇌ CH_3—⟨benzene⟩—$O^- Na^+$ + H_2CO_3
 pK_a 10 pK_a 6.5

(e) ⟨benzene⟩—NH_2 + HCl ⇌ ⟨benzene⟩—$\overset{+}{N}H_3$ Cl^-
 pK_a −7 pK_a 4.6

(f) $CH_3CH_2CH_2SH$ + $CH_3CH_2O^- Na^+$ ⇌ $CH_3CH_2CH_2S^- Na^+$ + CH_3CH_2OH
 pK_a 10.5 pK_a 17

(g) CH_3—⟨benzene⟩—COH (C=O) + Na^+CN^- ⇌ CH_3—⟨benzene⟩—$CO^- Na^+$ (C=O) + HCN
 pK_a 4 pK_a 9.1

3.20 (h) $\overset{\overset{O}{\|}}{CH_3C}CH_2\overset{\overset{O}{\|}}{C}CH_3$ + $CH_3O^- Na^+$ ⇌ $\overset{\overset{O}{\|}}{CH_3C}\overset{\cdot\cdot}{C}H\overset{\overset{O}{\|}}{C}CH_3$ + CH_3OH

         pK_a 9.0 Na^+ pK_a 15.5

3.21 $\Delta G° = -RT \ln K_{eq}$

         $= -2.303RT \log K_{eq}$

         $pK_{eq} = -\log K_{eq}$

         therefore $\Delta G° = 2.303RT\, pK_{eq}$

         At 298 K with $R = 1.987 \times 10^{-3}$ kcal/mol•K

         $\Delta G° = (2.303)(1.987 \times 10^{-3}$ kcal/mol•K$)(298$ K$)\, pK_{eq}$

         $\Delta G° = 1.36$ kcal/mol $\times pK_{eq}$

3.22 $pK_{eq} = (pK_a$ of starting acid$) - (pK_a$ of product acid$)$

<u>starting materials</u>   <u>products</u>

$CH_3CH_2^-$ + CH_3NH_2 CH_3CH_3 + CH_3NH^-

     pK_a ~36 pK_a ~49

$pK_{eq} = 36 - 49 = -13$; $\Delta G° = 1.4$ kcal/mol $\times (-13) = -18.2$ kcal/mol

There is a large decrease in free energy so the reaction goes essentially to completion as written.

CH_3NH^- + CH_3OH CH_3NH_2 + CH_3O^-

     pK_a 15.5 pK_a ~36

$pK_{eq} = 15.5 - 36 = -20.5$; $\Delta G° = 1.4$ kcal/mol $\times (-20.5) = -28.7$ kcal/mol

There is a large decrease in free energy so the reaction goes essentially to completion as written.

CH_3OH + OH^- CH_3O^- + H_2O

pK_a 15.5 pK_a 15.7

$pK_{eq} = 15.5 - 15.7 = -0.2$; $\Delta G° = 1.4$ kcal/mol $\times (-0.2) = -0.28$ kcal/mol

There is only a small decrease in free energy. Approximately equal amounts of both starting material and

products are present at equilibrium.

CH_3SH + OH^- CH_3S^- + H_2O

pK_a ~10.5 pK_a 15.7

$pK_{eq} = 10.5 - 15.7 = -5.2$; $\Delta G° = 1.4$ kcal/mol $\times (-5.2) = -7.3$ kcal/mol

There is a large decrease in free energy so the reaction goes essentially to completion as written.

$CH_3NH_3^+$ + OH^- CH_3NH_2 + H_2O

pK_a 10.6 pK_a 15.7

$pK_{eq} = 10.6 - 15.7 = -5.1$; $\Delta G° = 1.4$ kcal/mol $\times (-5.1) = -7.1$ kcal/mol

There is a large decrease in free energy so the reaction goes essentially to completion as written.

3.22 (cont)

$$CH_3OH_2^+ + H_2O \qquad\qquad CH_3OH + H_3O^+$$

$pK_a \sim -1.7$ $pK_a -1.7$

$pK_{eq} = -1.7 - (-1.7) = 0; \Delta G° = 1.4 \text{ kcal/mol} \times (0) = 0$

There is essentially no decrease in free energy. Approximately equal amounts of both starting material and products are present at equilibrium.

3.23 CF_3CH_2OH is more acidic than CH_3CH_2OH. CF_3CH_2OH ionizes more readily than CH_3CH_2OH because the $CF_3CH_2O^-$ ion is more stable relative to its conjugate acid than is the ethoxide ion. The electron-withdrawing effect (negative inductive effect) of the three fluorine atoms reduces the negative charge on the oxygen atom in 2,2,2-trifluoroethoxide ion relative to that in ethoxide ion. Withdrawal of negative charge from the oxygen atom stabilizes the anion.

<table>
<tr><td align="center">negative inductive effect of fluorine atoms reduces effective negative charge at the oxygen atom, stabilizing the anion</td><td align="center">no electron-withdrawing groups to stabilize this anion</td></tr>
</table>

3.24 $ClCH_2\overset{\displaystyle O}{\overset{\|}{C}}OH$ $Cl_2CH\overset{\displaystyle O}{\overset{\|}{C}}OH$ $CCl_3\overset{\displaystyle O}{\overset{\|}{C}}OH$

pK_a 2.86   1.30   0.64

$\longrightarrow$

increasing acidity

Inductive effects are additive. The more electron-withdrawing chlorine atoms there are in the molecule, the more stable its conjugate base will be relative to the acid, and, therefore, the more acidic the conjugate acid will be.

electron-withdrawing effect of one chlorine atom stabilizes the anion relative to acetate ion, making the conjugate acid more acidic than acetic acid (pK_a 4.8)

electron-withdrawing effect of two chlorine atoms leads to still further stabilization of the anion, and further strengthening of the conjugate acid

electron-withdrawing effect of three chlorine atoms makes this anion the most stable of the three compared here and, thus, its conjugate acid is the strongest

ΔG $ClCH_2CO_2^-$ $+ H_3O^+$

$ClCH_2CO_2H$ $+ H_2O$

large difference in energy between between acid and its conjugate base

ΔG $Cl_2CHCO_2^-$ $+ H_3O^+$

Cl_2CHCO_2H $+ H_2O$

ΔG $CCl_3CO_2^-$ $+ H_3O^+$

CCl_3CO_2H $+ H_2O$

much smaller difference in energy between acid and its conjugate base

3.25

$$:N \equiv C - \underset{\underset{H}{|}}{\overset{\overset{H}{|}}{C}} - \overset{\overset{:O:}{||}}{C} - \ddot{O} - H \ + \ H_2O \ \rightleftharpoons \ :N \equiv C - \underset{\underset{H}{|}}{\overset{\overset{H}{|}}{C}} - \overset{\overset{:O:}{||}}{C} - \ddot{O}:^- \ + \ H_3O^+$$

cyanoacetic acid   cyanoacetate anion

$$:N \equiv C - CH_2 - \overset{\overset{:O:}{||}}{C} - \ddot{O}:^- \longleftrightarrow \ ^-:\ddot{N} = C - CH_2 - \overset{\overset{:O:}{||}}{C} - \ddot{O}:^- \longleftrightarrow \ :N \equiv C - CH_2 - \overset{\overset{:\ddot{O}:^-}{|}}{C} = \ddot{O} \longleftrightarrow \ :N \equiv C - CH_2 - \underset{+}{\overset{\overset{:\ddot{O}:^-}{|}}{C}} - \ddot{O}:^-$$

Cyanoacetic acid is stronger than acetic acid because its conjugate base is a weaker base than acetate ion. The atom attached to the α-carbon atom has a positive charge in one important resonance contributor. The cyano group is therefore electron withdrawing, reducing electron density at the carboxylate ion by its inductive effect. The withdrawal of charge stabilizes the cyanoacetate ion relative to its acid, shifting the equilibrium toward greater ionization for cyanoacetic acid than for acetic acid.

$$^-:\underset{+}{\overset{\overset{:O:}{||}}{\ddot{O}}} - N - \underset{\underset{H}{|}}{\overset{\overset{H}{|}}{C}} - \overset{\overset{:O:}{||}}{C} - \ddot{O} - H \ + \ H_2O \ \rightleftharpoons \ ^-:\underset{+}{\overset{\overset{:O:}{||}}{\ddot{O}}} - N - \underset{\underset{H}{|}}{\overset{\overset{H}{|}}{C}} - \overset{\overset{:O:}{||}}{C} - \ddot{O}:^- \ + \ H_3O^+$$

nitroacetic acid   nitroacetate anion

$$^-:\underset{+}{\overset{\overset{:O:}{||}}{\ddot{O}}} - N - CH_2 - \overset{\overset{:O:}{||}}{C} - \ddot{O}:^- \longleftrightarrow \ \underset{+}{\overset{\overset{:\ddot{O}:^-}{|}}{O}} = N - CH_2 - \overset{\overset{:O:}{||}}{C} - \ddot{O}:^-$$

resonance involving the nitro group

$$^-:\underset{+}{\overset{\overset{:O:}{||}}{\ddot{O}}} - N - CH_2 - \overset{\overset{:O:}{||}}{C} - \ddot{O}:^- \longleftrightarrow \ ^-:\underset{+}{\overset{\overset{:O:}{||}}{\ddot{O}}} - N - CH_2 - \underset{+}{\overset{\overset{:\ddot{O}:^-}{|}}{C}} - \ddot{O}:^- \longleftrightarrow \ ^-:\underset{+}{\overset{\overset{:O:}{||}}{\ddot{O}}} - N - CH_2 - \overset{\overset{:\ddot{O}:^-}{|}}{C} = \ddot{O}$$

resonance involving the carboxylate group
(There are three more resonance contributors in which the nitro group
looks as it does in the resonance contributor at the upper right.)

Nitroacetic acid is a stronger acid than acetic acid because its anion is a weaker base than acetate ion. The nitrogen attached to the α–carbon atom is more electronegative than hydrogen and always has a formal positive charge. The nitro group, with one nitrogen atom and two oxygen atoms, is a strongly electron-withdrawing group. Nitroacetic acid is a stronger acid than cyanoacetic acid because the atom attached to the α-carbon atom in nitroacetic acid carries a full positive charge (all resonance contributors have a positively charged nitrogen atom). Only one resonance contributor in cyanoacetic acid has a positive carbon atom attached to the α-carbon atom.

3.26   In ethoxide anion, the basic oxygen atom is attached to an sp^3-hybridized carbon atom with no great polarity. In the acetate anion, the basic oxygen atom is attached to an sp^2-hybridized carbon atom which is more electronegative than an sp^3-hybridized carbon atom (see Section 2.8B in the text). In addition, this sp^2-hybridized carbon atom is attached to the still more electronegative oxygen atom, so it has considerable positive character. The positive nature of the carbon atom of the carbonyl group attracts electron density from the negatively charged oxygen atom of the acetate anion, resulting in stabilization of the anion.

sp^3-hybridized carbon atom; no stabilization of the negative charge

$$CH_3 - \underset{\underset{H}{|}}{\overset{\overset{H}{|}}{C}} - \ddot{O}:^-$$

sp^2-hybridized carbon atom with partial positive charge; attracts electron density from the negatively charged oxygen atom

$$CH_3 - \underset{\delta+}{\overset{\overset{:O:^{\delta-}}{||}}{C}} - \ddot{O}:^-$$

Concept Map 3.5   The effects of structural changes on acidity and basicity.

$$pK_a \sim 10.6 \qquad\qquad\qquad pK_a\ 15.7$$

$pK_{eq} = 10.6 - 15.7 = -5.1; \Delta G° = 1.4 \text{ kcal/mol} \times (-5.1) = -7.1 \text{ kcal/mol}$
There is a large decrease in free energy so the reaction goes essentially to completion as written.

(b) $H_2O + CH_3CH_2\overset{+}{O}CH_2CH_3 \rightleftharpoons CH_3CH_2OCH_2CH_3 + H_3O^+$
             |
             H

$$pK_a\ {-}3.6 \qquad\qquad\qquad\qquad pK_a\ {-}1.7$$

$pK_{eq} = -3.6 - (-1.7) = -1.9; \Delta G° = 1.4 \text{ kcal/mol} \times (-1.9) = -2.7 \text{ kcal/mol}$
There is a decrease in free energy. More product than starting material will be present at equilibrium.

(c) $CH_3\overset{O}{\overset{||}{C}}OH + CH_3CH_2S^- Na^+ \rightleftharpoons CH_3\overset{O}{\overset{||}{C}}O^- Na^+ + CH_3CH_2SH$

$$pK_a\ 4.8 \qquad\qquad\qquad\qquad pK_a\ 10.5$$

$pK_{eq} = 4.8 - 10.5 = -5.7; \Delta G° = 1.4 \text{ kcal/mol} \times (-5.7) = -8.0 \text{ kcal/mol}$
There is a large decrease in free energy so the reaction goes essentially to completion as written.

3.27   (d) $\overset{\overset{\displaystyle O}{\|}}{CCl_3COH}$ + $Na^+ HCO_3^-$ $\rightleftharpoons$ $\overset{\overset{\displaystyle O}{\|}}{CCl_3CO^- Na^+}$ + H_2CO_3 ($\rightleftharpoons$ H_2O + $CO_2\uparrow$)

     pK_a 0.6 pK_a 6.5

pK_{eq} = 0.6 − 6.5 = −5.9; $\Delta G°$ = 1.4 kcal/mol × (−5.9) = −8.3 kcal/mol
There is a large decrease in free energy so the reaction goes essentially to completion as written.

3.28   <u>least acidic</u>   <u>most acidic</u>

          NaH   < AlH_3 < H_2S <   HCl

The order of relative acidity of the hydrogen atoms increases as the electronegativity of the atom to which the hydrogen atom is attached increases. This is due to the increasing stability of the conjugate base as the electronegativity of the central atom increases.

3.29   <u>least acidic</u>   <u>most acidic</u>

(a) $\overset{\overset{\displaystyle O}{\|}}{CH_3COH}$ < $\overset{\overset{\displaystyle O}{\|}}{CCl_3COH}$ < $\overset{\overset{\displaystyle O}{\|}}{CF_3COH}$

(b) CH_3CH_2OH < $ClCH_2CH_2OH$ < FCH_2CH_2OH

(c) $CH_3CH_2NH_2$ < CH_3CH_2OH < CH_3CH_2SH

(d) $\overset{\overset{\displaystyle O}{\|}}{CH_3COCH_3}$ < $\overset{\overset{\displaystyle O}{\|}}{CH_3COH}$ < $\overset{\overset{\displaystyle \overset{+}{O}-H}{\|}}{CH_3COH}$

(e) $\overset{\overset{\displaystyle O}{\|}}{CH_3COCH_3}$ < $\overset{\overset{\displaystyle O}{\|}}{CH_3CNH_2}$ < $\overset{\overset{\displaystyle O}{\|}}{CH_3COH}$

3.30   <u>least basic</u>   <u>most basic</u>

(a) $CH_3\ddot{O}CH_3$ < $\underset{\underset{\displaystyle}{}}{\overset{\overset{\displaystyle CH_3}{|}}{CH_3\ddot{N}CH_3}}$ < $Cl_3C\!:^-$

(b) $:NF_3$ < $:NH_2\ddot{O}H$ < $:NH_3$

(c) $\overset{+}{NH_4}$ < $:NH_3$ < $^-:\ddot{N}H_2$

       (this cannot act as a base
       because there are no non-
       bonding or π electrons)

(d) $\underset{\underset{\displaystyle CH_3}{|}}{\overset{\overset{\displaystyle CH_3}{|}}{CH_3SiCH_3}}$ < $CH_3\ddot{S}CH_3$ < $\overset{\overset{\displaystyle CH_3}{|}}{CH_3\ddot{P}CH_3}$

       (no nonbonding or π electrons)

3.31   (a) F^- + BF_3 $\rightleftharpoons$ BF_4^- (b) Ag^+ + $2NH_3$ $\rightleftharpoons$ $Ag(NH_3)_2^+$

          Lewis base   Lewis acid   Lewis acid   Lewis base

      (c) $Al(H_2O)_6^{3+}$ + OH^- $\rightleftharpoons$ $Al(OH)(H_2O)_5^{2+}$ + H_2O

          Brønsted acid   Brønsted base   conjugate base   conjugate acid

3.31 (d)

$$CH_3CH_2\overset{O}{\overset{\|}{C}}OH + OH^- \rightleftharpoons CH_3CH_2\overset{O}{\overset{\|}{C}}O^- + H_2O$$

Brønsted acid   Brønsted base   conjugate base   conjugate acid

(e)

$$CH_3CH_2\overset{CH_2CH_3}{\overset{|}{N}}CH_2CH_3 + CF_3\overset{O}{\overset{\|}{C}}OH \rightleftharpoons CH_3CH_2\overset{CH_2CH_3}{\overset{|+}{\underset{|}{N}}}CH_2CH_3 + CF_3\overset{O}{\overset{\|}{C}}O^-$$
$$\overset{}{H}$$

Brønsted base   Brønsted acid   conjugate acid   conjugate base

3.32 Basicity is determined by the availability of the electron pair to the acid. $CH_3OCH_2CH_2CH_2NH_2$ is a weaker base than $CH_3CH_2CH_2CH_2NH_2$ because the electron-withdrawing oxygen atom of the methoxy group is pulling electron density away from the nitrogen atom. In $(CH_3O)_2CHCH_2NH_2$ there are two electron-withdrawing methoxy groups closer to the nitrogen atom than in the first case, which further reduce the availability of the electron pair. In $N\equiv CCH_2CH_2NH_2$ the cyano group is even more electron-withdrawing than the methoxy group because of the positive charge on the carbon atom of the cyano group in one resonance contributor (see Problem 3.25).

3.33

3.34

3.35 (a)

$$CHCl_2\overset{\overset{O}{\|}}{C}OH$$

$$pK_a = 1.3$$
$$K_a = 10^{-pK_a} = 10^{-1.3}$$
$$= 10^{+0.7} \times 10^{-2}$$
$$K_a = 5 \times 10^{-2}$$

(b)

$$CH_3\overset{+}{N}H_3$$

$$pK_a = 10.4$$
$$K_a = 10^{-pK_a} = 10^{-10.4}$$
$$= 10^{+0.6} \times 10^{-11}$$
$$K_a = 4 \times 10^{-11}$$

(c)

$$CCl_3CH_2OH$$

$$pK_a = 12.2$$
$$K_a = 10^{-pK_a} = 10^{-12.2}$$
$$= 10^{+0.8} \times 10^{-13}$$
$$K_a = 6 \times 10^{-13}$$

3.36 (a) CH_3CH_2OH

$$K_a = 10^{-17} \qquad = 10^{-pK_a}$$
$$pK_a = -\log K_a \qquad = +17$$

(b) CH_3CH_2SH

$$K_a = 3.16 \times 10^{-11}$$
$$pK_a = -\log (3.16 \times 10^{-11})$$
$$= -(\log 3.16 + \log 10^{-11})$$
$$= -(0.5 - 11) = -(-10.50)$$
$$pK_a = +10.50$$

(c)

$$CH_3CH_2\overset{H}{\underset{+}{O}}CH_2CH_3$$

$$K_a = 3.98 \times 10^{+3}$$

$$pK_a = -\log (3.98 \times 10^{+3})$$
$$= -(\log 3.98 + \log 10^{+3})$$
$$= -(0.60 + 3) = -(3.60)$$
$$pK_a = -3.60$$

3.37 (a) $H:^-$

(b) $Na^+ H^- + H_2O \longrightarrow Na^+ OH^- + H_2\uparrow$

(c) Hydride ion, H^-, is a base. Hydrogen, H_2, is its conjugate acid.

(d) $CH_3CH_2OH + Na^+ H^- \longrightarrow CH_3CH_2O^- Na^+ + H_2\uparrow$

3.38 (a)

3.38 (a) (cont)

ΔG

reactants

products

(b)

$$CH_3\overset{\overset{\textstyle :O:}{\|}}{C}-\overset{\overset{\textstyle :O:}{\|}}{\underset{\underset{\textstyle Na^+}{\cdot\cdot}}{C}}HCOCH_2CH_3 \;+\; CH_3CH_2\overset{\cdot\cdot}{\underset{\cdot\cdot}{O}}H \;\rightleftharpoons\; CH_3\overset{\overset{\textstyle :O:}{\|}}{C}CH_2\overset{\overset{\textstyle :O:}{\|}}{C}OCH_2CH_3 \;+\; CH_3CH_2\overset{\cdot\cdot}{\underset{\cdot\cdot}{O}}:^-\; Na^+$$

C
pK_a 17

D
pK_a 11.0

ΔG

products

reactants

(c) $[(CH_3)_3Si]_2\overset{\cdot\cdot}{N}H \;+\; CH_3CH_2CH_2\overset{\cdot\cdot}{C}H_2{}^-\; Li^+ \;\rightleftharpoons\; [(CH_3)_3Si]_2\overset{\cdot\cdot}{N}{}^-\; Li^+ \;+\; CH_3CH_2CH_2CH_3$

pK_a ~10

E

F
pK_a ~49

ΔG

reactants

products

(d) $CH_3CH_2-\overset{\overset{\textstyle :O:}{\|}}{\underset{\underset{\textstyle +}{}}{N}}-\overset{\cdot\cdot}{\underset{\cdot\cdot}{O}}:^- \;+\; (CH_3)_3C-\overset{\cdot\cdot}{\underset{\cdot\cdot}{O}}:^- \;\rightleftharpoons\; CH_3\overset{\cdot\cdot}{C}H-\overset{\overset{\textstyle :O:}{\|}}{\underset{\underset{\textstyle +}{}}{N}}-\overset{\cdot\cdot}{\underset{\cdot\cdot}{O}}:^- \;+\; (CH_3)_3C-\overset{\cdot\cdot}{\underset{\cdot\cdot}{O}}H$

pK_a ~10.2

G

H

pK_a 19

ΔG

reactants

products

(e) $CH_3\overset{\cdot\cdot}{\underset{\cdot\cdot}{O}}-\!\!\!\left\langle\!\!\bigcirc\!\!\right\rangle\!\!\!-\overset{\cdot\cdot}{\underset{\cdot\cdot}{O}}H \;+\; H:^- \;\rightleftharpoons\; CH_3\overset{\cdot\cdot}{\underset{\cdot\cdot}{O}}-\!\!\!\left\langle\!\!\bigcirc\!\!\right\rangle\!\!\!-\overset{\cdot\cdot}{\underset{\cdot\cdot}{O}}:^- \;+\; H_2$

pK_a ~10   I   J pK_a 35

ΔG

reactants

products

3.39 (a)

$$\overset{\displaystyle :\!\overset{..}{F}:^{\delta-}}{\overset{\displaystyle \uparrow}{\underset{\displaystyle \delta-\;:\overset{..}{F}:}{\overset{\delta-\;:\overset{..}{F}:\leftarrow\overset{..}{C}\leftarrow\overset{..}{O}-H}{}}}}\;^{\delta+}\qquad\qquad \overset{\displaystyle :\!\overset{..}{F}:}{\overset{\displaystyle \uparrow}{\underset{\displaystyle :\overset{..}{F}:}{:\overset{..}{F}:\leftarrow\overset{..}{C}\leftarrow\overset{..}{O}:^{-}}}}$$

acid   conjugate base

The inductive effect of the fluorines makes the proton on the hydroxyl group more acidic and the anion less basic. The inductive effect of the fluorines also reduces the availability of the electron pairs on the oxygen atom so they are not as readily involved in hydrogen bonding, decreasing the boiling point.

$$\overset{\displaystyle :\!\overset{..}{F}:}{\overset{\displaystyle \uparrow}{\underset{\displaystyle :\overset{..}{F}:\;\;H}{:\overset{..}{F}\leftarrow C\leftarrow N-H}}}$$

The basicity of the nitrogen atom is also decreased by the electron-withdrawing effect of the fluorines, which makes the electron pair on the nitrogen less available for protonation.

(b) $CF_3\overset{+}{N}H_3\;\;Cl^-\;\;+\;\;CH_3\underset{\underset{\displaystyle CH_3}{|}}{\overset{\overset{\displaystyle CH_3}{|}}{\overset{..}{N}}}:\;\;\rightleftharpoons\;\;CF_3\overset{..}{N}H_2\;\;+\;\;CH_3\underset{\underset{\displaystyle CH_3}{|}}{\overset{\overset{\displaystyle CH_3}{|}}{\overset{+}{N}}}-H\;\;Cl^-$

We would expect trimethylamine to be a stronger base than trifluoromethylamine [see part (a)], and to remove a proton from the trifluoromethylammonium ion.

3.40   When a strong acid such as H—Cl is added to water, the following reaction takes place.

$$\underset{pK_a\;-7}{H—Cl}\;+\;H_2O\;\longrightarrow\;Cl^-\;+\;\underset{pK_a\;-1.7}{H_3O^+}$$

The equilibrium constant for this reaction is greater than 10^{+5}, and the reaction proceeds essentially to completion. Similar reactions take place in water with other strong acids such as sulfuric, nitric, and phosphoric acids. A solution of strong acid in water thus consists of the hydronium ion, (the strongest acid which can exist in water) and the conjugate base of the strong acid.

When a strong base such as amide ion is added to water, a similar reaction takes place.

$$\underset{pK_a\;15.7}{NH_2^-}\;+\;H_2O\;\longrightarrow\;\underset{pK_a\;36}{NH_3}\;+\;OH^-$$

Again the equilibrium constant is very large ($>10^{+20}$), and the reaction proceeds essentially to completion. A solution of a strong base in water thus consists of the hydroxide ion (the strongest base that can exist in water) and the conjugate acid of the strong base.

3.41 $\overset{+}{H_3}N-CH_2\overset{\overset{\displaystyle O}{\|}}{C}O^-$ $H_2N-CH_2\overset{\overset{\displaystyle O}{\|}}{C}OH$

$pK_a\;\;R\overset{+}{N}H_3\;\sim\;10.6$ $pK_a\;\;R\overset{\overset{\displaystyle O}{\|}}{C}OH\;\sim\;4.0$

(a)   The carboxylate anion, $-\overset{\overset{\displaystyle O}{\|}}{C}O^-$, is a weaker base than the amino group, $-NH_2$. Therefore, a proton will be transferred from the carboxyl group to the amino group. Glycine is best represented as $\underset{+}{H_3N}CH_2\overset{\overset{\displaystyle O}{\|}}{C}O^-$.

(b)   The high melting point for a compound with such a low molecular weight is indicative of an ionic compound. The high water solubility is also indicative of strong electrostatic forces. Both observations are consistent with the charged structure, $\underset{+}{H_3N}CH_2\overset{\overset{\displaystyle O}{\|}}{C}O^-$, for glycine.

3.42   (a) $K_a = \dfrac{[A^-]\,[H_3O^+]}{[HA]}$

taking the log of both sides

$$\log K_a = \log\left(\dfrac{[A^-]\,[H_3O^+]}{[HA]}\right)$$

$$\log K_a = \log\,[H_3O^+] + \log\dfrac{[A^-]}{[HA]}$$

multiplying both sides by −1

$$-\log K_a = -\log\,[H_3O^+] - \log\dfrac{[A^-]}{[HA]}$$

rearranging the equation by adding $\log\dfrac{[A^-]}{[HA]}$ to both sides

$$-\log\,[H_3O^+] = -\log K_a + \log\dfrac{[A^-]}{[HA]}$$

substituting the following relationships

$$pK_a = -\log K_a$$

$$pH = -\log\,[H^+] = -\log\,[H_3O^+]$$

we get the Henderson-Hasselbalch equation

$$pH = pK_a + \log\dfrac{[A^-]}{[HA]}$$

(b)   when $pH = pK_a$, $\log\dfrac{[A^-]}{[HA]} = 0$ and $\dfrac{[A^-]}{[HA]} = 1$

or the concentrations of the acid and its conjugate base are equal.
$$[HA] = [A^-]$$

(c) $pH \cong 6.5$
$pK_a = 7$

$$pH = pK_a + \log\dfrac{[A^-]}{[HA]}$$

$$6.5 = 7 + \log\dfrac{[A^-]}{[HA]}$$

$$\log\dfrac{[A^-]}{[HA]} = -0.5$$

$$\dfrac{[A^-]}{[HA]} = 0.316$$

$$[A^-] = 0.316\,[HA]$$
$$\text{and } [HA] = {\sim}3\,[A^-]$$

There is more protonated than unprotonated imidazole present at pH 6.5.

Supplemental Problems

S3.1   Complete the following equations. Use the table of pK_a values to decide where the equilibrium will lie by determining K_{eq} and whether there is a decrease or increase in free energy for each reaction.

(a) $CH_3CH_2\overset{\overset{\displaystyle O}{\|}}{C}OH \; + \; NH_3 \longrightarrow$ (b) $CH_3NO_2 \; + \; CH_3CH_2O^- \, Na^+ \longrightarrow$

(c) $CH_3CH_2SH \; + \; NaNH_2 \longrightarrow$ (d) $HC\equiv CH \; + \; Na^+ HCO_3^- \longrightarrow$

S3.2   For each acid-base reaction given below, label acids, bases, conjugate acids, and conjugate bases, and tell whether Brønsted acids or Lewis acids are present.

(a) $CH_3CH_2SCH_2CH_3 \; + \; BF_3 \longrightarrow CH_3CH_2\overset{+}{\underset{}{S}}CH_2CH_3$ (with $^-BF_3$ on S)   (b) $H_2PO_4^- \; + \; OH^- \longrightarrow HPO_4^{2-} \; + \; H_2O$

(c) $ClCH_2\overset{\overset{\displaystyle O}{\|}}{C}OH \; + \; HCO_3^- \longrightarrow ClCH_2\overset{\overset{\displaystyle O}{\|}}{C}O^- \; + \; H_2CO_3$

(d) $CH_3CH_2CH_2SH \; + \; CH_3CH_2O^- \longrightarrow CH_3CH_2CH_2S^- \; + \; CH_3CH_2OH$

S3.3   Complete the following equations.

(a)

(b)

(c)

(d)

S3.4   1-Indanone has three different types of hydrogen atoms, labeled A, B, and C in the structure shown below.

1-indanone

(a)   Assign approximate pK_a values to the three different types of hydrogen atoms using exact values from analogous compounds in the pK_a table.

(b)   Removing the most acidic proton from 1-indanone leads to the formation of an anion that is stabilized by resonance. Draw structural formulas for the conjugate base corresponding to this deprotonation and for its major resonance contributor.

(c)   The conjugate base of 1-indanone can be protonated at two sites. One of these gives the 1-indanone structure; the other gives a new structure called the enol form of 1-indanone. What is the structure of the enol form of 1-indanone?

S3.5   The potency of an anesthetic has been found in recent research to be related to the extent to which it disrupts hydrogen bonding in nerve cell membranes. This capacity to disrupt hydrogen bonding is related to the *acidity of carbon-hydrogen bonds* and to the *basicity of oxygen atoms* in the compounds used as anesthetics. Three widely used anesthetics were examined. They are shown below.

$$CH_3CHClBr \qquad\qquad CH_3OCF_2CHCl_2 \qquad\qquad CHF_2OCF_2CHFCl$$

haloethane   methoxyflurane   enflurane

(a)   Haloethane has a pK_a of 23.8. What is the approximate pK_a that you would expect for ethane? Explain in a few words and with structural representations why the acidity of haloethane differs from that of ethane.

(b)   Methoxyflurane has two possible sites of deprotonation. The researchers found that only one site was deprotonated under the conditions of their reaction. Write a structural formula for the more stable of the two possible conjugate bases of methoxyflurane.

(c)   Methoxyflurane is ten times more potent than enflurane as an anesthetic even though both compounds have approximately the same pK_a, ~26. According to the criteria listed at the beginning of this problem, why should methoxyflurane be more potent than enflurane? Explain in a few words and with structural representations.

S3.6   Lithium diisopropylamide is a strong Brønsted base used in many organic reactions. It is prepared by combining diisopropylamine with one of the following reagents. Which one would work and why?

diisopropylamine   lithium diisopropylamide

Li$^+$ B$^-$ may be butyllithium ($CH_3CH_2CH_2CH_2Li$), lithium methoxide ($LiOCH_3$), or lithium chloride ($LiCl$).

S3.7   The following data show that the cyano group (CN) increases the acidity of the hydroxyl group on phenol. Discuss how inductive effects and resonance may be used to rationalize these observations.

phenol   3-cyanophenol   4-cyanophenol
pK_a = 10.0   pK_a = 8.8   pK_a = 7.95

S3.8   Photochromic processes are those where a compouind chanages color when exposed to light. The following compuond is photochromic. The curved arrow convention is used to show the changes in bonding that occur when the yellow compound on exposure to light turns orange. What is the structure of the orange species?

yellow

S3.9   The equation below shows a reaction known as a decarboxylation reaction, a reaction in which carbon dioxide, CO_2, is ejected from a molecule

(a) Provide a mechanism for this reaction using the curved arrow convention.

S3.9 (b) What is the product of the decarboxylation of the following compound? Is it more or less stable than the product of the reaction in part (a) and why?

$$H-\overset{\overset{\displaystyle H}{|}}{\underset{\underset{\displaystyle H}{|}}{C}}-\overset{\overset{\displaystyle H}{|}}{\underset{\underset{\displaystyle H}{|}}{C}}-\overset{\overset{\displaystyle F}{|}}{\underset{\underset{\displaystyle F}{|}}{C}}-\overset{\overset{\displaystyle :O:}{\|}}{C}-\ddot{O}:^{-}\longrightarrow \quad ?$$

S3.10 Vitamin C is a naturally occurring antioxidant. The interaction of some substances related to Vitamin C with oxygen have been studied.

(a) Using the curved arrow convention, show the mechanism for the transformation shown below.

(b) The next part of the transformation is represented by the mechanism shown below. What are the products implied by this mechanism?

Reaction Pathways

Workbook Exercises

EXERCISE I. A number of examples of connectivity changes were given as Workbook Exercises I and II in Chapter 1. Use the curved-arrow notation that was introduced for mechanisms in Chapter 3 to restate the bonding changes you have already described with words.

EXERCISE II. Draw the structures of the products implied by each of the following mechanisms.

(a)

(b)

(c)

(d)

(e)

(f)

(g)

(h)

- -

4.1 For those species in which more than one electrophilic or nucleophilic site is present, the stronger site is indicated. If a species contains both an electrophilic and nucleophilic site, the site that normally reacts is indicated.

(a) $CH_3 \!\!-\!\! \overset{..}{\underset{..}{O}}:^-$
nucleophile

(b) $:PH_3$
nucleophile

(c) Cu^{2+}
electrophile

(d) $\overset{\delta+}{H} \!\!-\!\! \overset{\delta-}{\overset{..}{\underset{..}{Br}}}:$
electrophile

(e) $\overset{\delta+}{CH_3} \!\!-\!\! \overset{\delta-}{\overset{..}{\underset{..}{Cl}}}:$
electrophile

(f) $CH_3\overset{..}{N}H_2$
nucleophile

(g) $H:^-$
nucleophile

(h) $(CH_3)_3B$
electrophile

(i) $H\overset{..}{\underset{..}{O}} \!\!-\!\! \overset{..}{N}H_2$
nucleophile

(j) $HC \!\!\equiv\!\! CH$
nucleophile

4.1 (cont)

(k)   AlCl₃   (l) electrophile   (m) nucleophile   (n) CH₃CH₂—S⁻   (o)   Hg²⁺

electrophile   nucleophile   electrophile

- -

Concept Map 4.1   The factors that determine whether a chemical reaction between a given set of reagents is
                           likely.

- -

4.2   (a)   electrophile - - ▸ CH₃ ⇌ Br: ⟶   CH₃—ÖH   :Br:⁻

nucleophile - - ▸ ⁻:Ö–H

(b)   electrophile - - ▸ CH₃ ⇌ I: ⟶   CH₃—ÖH   :I:⁻

nucleophile - - ▸ ⁻:Ö–H

(c)   CH₃CH₂ ⇌ Cl: ⟶   CH₃CH₂—ÖH   :Cl:⁻

electrophile -

nucleophile - - ▸ ⁻:Ö–H

(d)   electrophile - - ▸ CH₃ ⇌ I: ⟶   CH₃—NH₃⁺   :I:⁻

nucleophile - - ▸ :NH₃

4.3   Sodium ion, Na+, has a complete valence shell (see Problem 2.1 for the electronic configuration of elemental sodium), and the energies of the empty orbitals in the $n=3$ shell are too high to be available for accepting an electron pair. Both the mercury(II), Hg^{2+}, and copper(II), Cu^{2+}, ions are transition metals that have lower energy empty orbitals available to accept an electron pair.

Concept Map 4.2   A nucleophilic substitution reaction.

4.4   (a)   Overall equation must be:

$$Cl_2 \ + \ NH_3 \ \longrightarrow \ H_3\overset{+}{N}\!\!-\!\!Cl \ + \ Cl^-$$

$$H_3\overset{+}{N}\!\!-\!\!Cl \ + \ Cl^- \ + \ Na^+OH^- \ \longrightarrow \ H_2N\!\!-\!\!Cl \ + \ Na^+Cl^- \ + \ H_2O$$

(b)   Mechanism

Concept Map 4.3   The factors that determine the equilibrium constant for a reaction.

$$\log K_{eq} = \frac{-\Delta G_r^{\circ}}{2.303 \ RT}$$

$$\Delta G_r^{\circ} \ = \ \Delta G_f^{\circ} \ (products) \ - \ \Delta G_f^{\circ} \ (reactants)$$

4.5   At 311 K, $k_r = 3.55 \times 10^{-5}$ L/mol·sec.
       Initial rate $= k_r[CH_3Cl][OH^-]$; when $[OH^-]$ 0.05 M.
       Initial rate $= (3.55 \times 10^{-5}$ L/mol·sec$)(0.003$ mol/L$)(0.05$ mol/L$)$.
                $= 5.33 \times 10^{-9}$ mol/L·sec, which is five times the original rate of 1.07×10^{-9} mol/L·sec.
       When $[CH_3Cl] = 0.001$ M, the rate will be one-third the rate when $[CH_3Cl] = 0.003$ M, or 3.55×10^{-10} mol/L·sec.

Concept Map 4.4   The factors that influence the rate of a reaction as they appear in the rate equation.

Concept Map 4.5   Some of the factors other than concentration that influence the rate of a reaction.

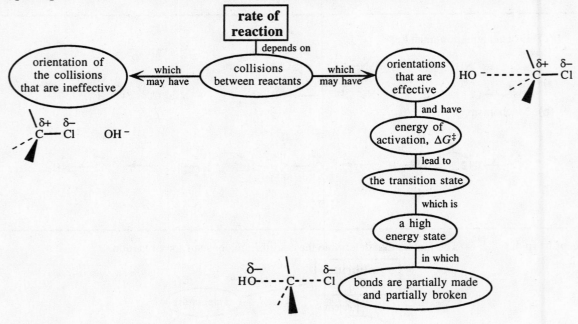

Concept Map 4.6   Factors that influence the rate of a reaction and the effect of temperature.

4.6   At 308 K, k_r = 5.3 × 10⁻⁴ L/mol·sec.
            Initial rate = (5.3 × 10⁻⁴ L/mol·sec)(0.001 mol/L)(0.01 mol/L)
                          = 5.3 × 10⁻⁹ mol/L·sec

Concept Map 4.7   An electrophilic addition reaction to an alkene.

4.7   The double bond in propene is another possible nucleophile in the reaction mixture.

Concept Map 4.8   Markovnikov's Rule.

4.8   (a) $CH_3\overset{\underset{|}{CH_3}}{C}=CH_2$ + HBr $\longrightarrow$ $CH_3\overset{\underset{|}{CH_3}}{\underset{\underset{Br}{|}}{C}}CH_3$

(b) $CH_3CH_2CH=CH_2$ +   HBr $\longrightarrow$ $CH_3CH_2\underset{\underset{Br}{|}}{C}HCH_3$

(c) $CH_3CH_2CH=CHCH_3$ + HBr $\longrightarrow$ $CH_3CH_2\underset{\underset{Br}{|}}{C}HCH_2CH_3$ + $CH_3CH_2CH_2\underset{\underset{Br}{|}}{C}HCH_3$

4.9   The methyl cation ($CH_3{}^+$) is less stable than the *n*-propyl cation ($CH_3CH_2CH_2{}^+$) because the methyl cation has no alkyl groups to stabilize the positive charge.

4.10   The *tert*-butyl cation is more stable than the isopropyl cation because the *tert*-butyl cation has three alkyl groups to stabilize the positive charge and the isopropyl group has only two.

tert-butyl cation $CH_3-\overset{\underset{|}{CH_3}}{\underset{\underset{CH_3}{|}}{C}}{}^+$ most stable

isopropyl cation $CH_3-\overset{\underset{|}{CH_3}}{\underset{\underset{H}{|}}{C}}{}^+$

n-propyl cation $CH_3CH_2-\overset{\underset{|}{H}}{\underset{\underset{H}{|}}{C}}{}^+$

methyl cation $H-\overset{\underset{|}{H}}{\underset{\underset{H}{|}}{C}}{}^+$ least stable

4.11 $\log K_{eq}$ $= -(\Delta G°/2.303\,RT)$
At 25 °C (298 K),
for 1-bromopropane
$\log K_{eq}$ $= -(-7.63\ \text{kcal/mol})/[(2.303)(1.99 \times 10^{-3}\ \text{kcal/mol·K})(298\ \text{K})]$
$\log K_{eq}$ $= 5.59$
$K_{eq} = 10^{5.59} = 10^{0.59} \times 10^5 = 3.89 \times 10^5$
for 2-bromopropane
$\log K_{eq}$ $= -(-8.77\ \text{kcal/mol})/[(2.303)(1.99 \times 10^{-3}\ \text{kcal/mol·K})(298\ \text{K})]$
$\log K_{eq}$ $= 6.42$
$K_{eq} = 10^{6.42} = 10^{0.42} \times 10^6 = 2.63 \times 10^6$

Note that the answers that you get may not correspond exactly to the numbers obtained here, depending on whether you round off to the correct number of significant figures at each stage of the calculation or carry all figures through and round off at the end of the calculation.

4.12   (a) $CH_3CH=CH_2$ (g)   +   HI (g) $\longrightarrow$ $CH_3\underset{\underset{I}{|}}{C}HCH_3$ (g)

(b)   Rate $= k\,[CH_3CH=CH_2][HI]$

Concept Map 4.9   Carbocations.

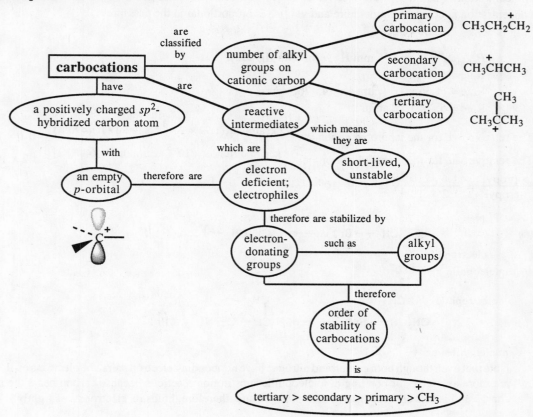

Concept Map 4.10   Energy diagrams.

4.13   Concentration is defined as the number of moles of a substance in a given volume. For an ideal gas, the concentration at constant temperature and volume is proportional to the pressure.

$$P = \frac{n}{V} RT$$

$P_{propene} = P_{HI} = (45 \text{ mm Hg})/(760 \text{ mm Hg/atm})$

Rate $= k \, (P_{propene})(P_{HI})$

Rate $= (1.66 \times 10^{-6}/\text{atm·sec})(45/760)^2 \text{atm}^2$

Rate $= 5.8 \times 10^{-9}$ atm/sec

4.14   The relative rate for the isopropyl cation $= e^{-22 \text{ kcal/mol}/[(1.99 \times 10^{-3} \text{ kcal/mol} \cdot \text{K})(490 \text{ K})]} = 1.6 \times 10^{-10}$

The relative rate for the *n*-propyl cation $= e^{-38 \text{ kcal/mol}/[(1.99 \times 10^{-3} \text{ kcal/mol} \cdot \text{K})(490 \text{ K})]} = 1.2 \times 10^{-17}$

$$\frac{\text{isopropyl}}{\text{\textit{n}-propyl}} = \frac{1.6 \times 10^{-10}}{1.2 \times 10^{-17}} = 1.3 \times 10^7$$

4.15   (a)

$$CH_3CH_2\text{—}\ddot{B}r: \longrightarrow CH_3CH_2\text{—}\ddot{I}: + :\ddot{B}r:^-$$

electrophile
nucleophile $\rightarrow :\ddot{I}:^-$

(b)

electrophile

$$CH_3\overset{\displaystyle CH_3}{\underset{}{C}}H\text{—}\ddot{B}r: \longrightarrow CH_3\overset{\displaystyle CH_3}{\underset{}{C}}H\text{—}C\equiv N: + :\ddot{B}r:^-$$

nucleophile $\rightarrow {}^-:C\equiv N:$

Note that even though both carbon and nitrogen have nonbonding electron pairs, the electrons on the carbon are more available for bonding in nucleophilic substitution reactions because carbon bears the negative charge and is less electronegative than nitrogen and, therefore, holds its electrons less tightly.

(c)

nucleophile   electrophile   H

$$CH_3CH_2CH\text{=}CH_2 \longrightarrow CH_3CH_2\overset{+}{C}H\text{—}CH_2 \longrightarrow CH_3CH_2CHCH_3$$

electrophile $\rightarrow H\text{—}\ddot{C}l:$ nucleophile $\rightarrow :\ddot{C}l:^-$ $:\ddot{C}l:$

(d)

electrophile CH_3 CH_3

$$CH_3CH_2\overset{\displaystyle CH_3}{\underset{}{C}}H\text{—}\ddot{B}r: \longrightarrow CH_3CH_2\overset{\displaystyle CH_3}{\underset{}{C}}H\text{—}\ddot{S}\text{—}CH_3 + :\ddot{B}r:^-$$

$CH_3\text{—}\ddot{S}:^- \leftarrow$ nucleophile

(e)

nucleophile   electrophile

$$CH_3CH\text{=}CH_2 + \overset{\delta+ \quad \delta-}{Cl\text{—}Cl} \longrightarrow CH_3\overset{\displaystyle}{\underset{\displaystyle Cl}{C}}HCH_2\text{—}Cl \quad \text{(see p. ~)}$$

4.16

reagent	type	reason for choice
(a) CH_3O^- Na^+	nucleophile	

The carbon atom bonded to the iodine atom in ethyl iodide is an electrophilic carbon and will react with a reagent that is a nucleophile. The reaction is a nucleophilic substitution. CH_3O^- is the nucleophile. The reagent is shown as also containing a sodium ion, because it is not possible to have a reagent with only anions in it. The sodium ions are called "spectator" ions. They do not participate directly in the reaction, but serve to neutralize the negative charges on the anions before and after the reaction takes place.

4.16 (a) (cont)

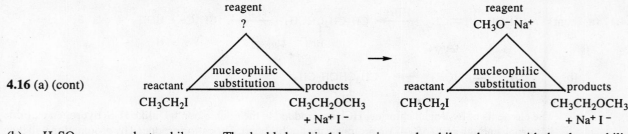

(b)   H₂SO₄   electrophile   The double bond in 1-butene is a nucleophile and reacts with the electrophilic proton in sulfuric acid. The carbocation produced in the first step of the reaction is an electrophile and will react with the conjugate base of sulfuric acid, a nucleophile, which is also produced in the first step of the reaction. The overall reaction is an electrophilic addition.

(c)   Br₂   electrophile   The nucleophilic double bond in 1-butene will react with the electrophile bromine (see Chapter 8 for the mechanism of the addition of bromine to alkenes). The overall reaction is an electrophilic addition.

(d)   NH₃   nucleophile   The carbon atom bonded to the bromine atom in *n*-propyl bromide is an electrophilic carbon and will react with a reagent that is a nucleophile. The reaction is a nucleophilic substitution.

4.17   (a) $CH_3CH_2CH{=}CH_2 \xrightarrow{?} CH_3CH_2\underset{\underset{SH}{|}}{C}HCH_3$

The elements of hydrogen sulfide, H₂S, have added to the double bond. The double bond is a nucleophile and is protonated by strong Brønsted acids. H₂S, with a pK_a ~10.5, is not sufficiently acidic (hydrogen sulfide is similar to ethanethiol, CH_3CH_2SH, and can be expected to have a similar pK_a); a hydrogen halide such as HBr (pK_a −8) is. In the product that is formed, the bromine atom will be attached to an electrophilic carbon atom and will leave when the hydrogen sulfide anion is used as a nucleophile.

4.17 (a) (cont) $CH_3CH_2CH=CH_2$ $\xrightarrow{HBr}$ $CH_3CH_2\overset{|}{\underset{Br}{C}}HCH_3$ $\xrightarrow{Na^+ SH^-}$ $CH_3CH_2\overset{|}{\underset{SH}{C}}HCH_3$ + Na^+Br^-

(b) $CH_3CH=CHCH_3$ $\xrightarrow{?}$ $CH_3\overset{|}{\underset{Cl}{C}}HCH_2CH_3$

The elements of hydrogen chloride, HCl, have added to the double bond. Unlike H_2S, hydrogen chloride is a strong enough acid (pK_a –7) to protonate the double bond. The cation produced by protonation will then react with the conjugate base of hydrogen chloride to give the desired product.

$CH_3CH=CHCH_3$ $\xrightarrow{HCl}$ $CH_3\overset{+}{\underset{H}{C}}H—CHCH_3$ + Cl^- $\longrightarrow$ $CH_3\overset{|}{\underset{Cl}{C}}HCH_2CH_3$

(c) $CH_2=CH_2$ $\xrightarrow{?}$ $CH_3CH_2\overset{+}{N}H_3$ I^-

The elements of the ammonium ion, NH_4^+, have added to the double bond. NH_4^+ is not sufficiently acidic (pK_a 9.4), but HI (pK_a –9) is. Ammonia can then be used as a nucleophile to react with the electrophilic carbon atom in ethyl iodide, the product of the first reaction.

$CH_2=CH_2$ $\xrightarrow{HI}$ CH_3CH_2I $\xrightarrow{NH_3}$ $CH_3CH_2\overset{+}{N}H_3$ I^-

(d) $CH_3\overset{|}{\underset{Br}{C}}HCH_2CH_2CH_3$ $\xrightarrow{?}$ $CH_3\overset{|}{\underset{CN}{C}}HCH_2CH_2CH_3$

Cyanide ion has substituted for bromide ion. This is a nucleophilic substitution reaction on 2-bromopentane, which requires only one species, NaCN.

$CH_3\overset{|}{\underset{Br}{C}}HCH_2CH_2CH_3$ $\xrightarrow{Na^+ CN^-}$ $CH_3\overset{|}{\underset{CN}{C}}HCH_2CH_2CH_3$ + Na^+Br^-

4.18 (a)

(b)

(c)

(d)

4.18 (e) $CH_3CH_2CH = CHCH_3 + Br_2 \longrightarrow \quad CH_3CH_2CH - CHCH_3$

nucleophile   electrophile   Br   Br

4.19   <u>reagent</u>   <u>type</u>   <u>reason for choice</u>

(a) $Na^+ SH^-$ nucleophile   The carbon atom bonded to the bromine atom in methyl bromide is an electrophilic carbon and will react with a reagent that is a nucleophile. The reaction is a nucleophilic substitution.

(b) $Na^+ CN^-$ nucleophile   The carbon atom bonded to the bromine atom in ethyl bromide is an electrophilic carbon and will react with a reagent that is a nucleophile. The reaction is a nucleophilic substitution.

(c) Cl_2 electrophile   The nucleophilic double bond in ethylene will react with the electrophile chlorine (see Chapter 8 for the mechanism of the addition of chlorine to alkenes). The reaction is an electrophilic addition.

(d) $CH_3CH_2O^- Na^+$ nucleophile   The carbon atom bonded to the bromine atom in *n*-propyl bromide is an electrophilic carbon and will react with a reagent that is a nucleophile. The reaction is a nucleophilic substitution.

(e)   HI   electrophile   The nucleophilic double bond in 1-butene will react with the electrophilic proton of hydrogen iodide, and the electrophilic carbocation that is produced will then react with the iodide ion. The reaction is an electrophilic addition.

(f) $Na^+ I^-$ nucleophile   The carbon atom bonded to the bromine atom in isopropyl bromide is an electrophilic carbon and will react with a reagent that is a nucleophile. The reaction is a nucleophilic substitution.

4.20 (a) $CH_2 = CH_2 \xrightarrow{\ ?\ } CH_3CH_2OCH_3$

The elements of methanol, CH_3OH, have added to the double bond. The double bond is a nucleophile and is protonated by strong Brønsted acids. Methanol is not sufficiently acidic (pK_a 15.5), but a hydrogen halide such as HBr (pK_a –8) is. In the product that is formed, the bromine atom will be attached to an electrophilic carbon atom and will leave when sodium methoxide is used as a nucleophile.

$$CH_2 = CH_2 \xrightarrow{HBr} CH_3CH_2Br \xrightarrow{CH_3O^- Na^+} CH_3CH_2OCH_3$$

(b) $CH_3CH = CH_2 \xrightarrow{\ ?\ } CH_3CHCH_3$

I

4.20 (b) (cont)

The elements of hydrogen iodide, HI, have added to the double bond. Hydrogen iodide is a strong enough acid (pK_a –9) to protonate the double bond. The cation produced by protonation will then react with iodide ion, the conjugate base of hydrogen iodide, to give the desired product.

$$CH_3CH{=}CH_2 \xrightarrow{\ HI\ } CH_3\underset{\underset{I}{|}}{C}HCH_3$$

(c) $$CH_3CH_2CH{=}CH_2 \xrightarrow{\ ?\ } CH_3CH_2\underset{\underset{OH}{|}}{C}HCH_3$$

The elements of water, H_2O, have added to the double bond. Water is not sufficiently acidic (pK_a 15.7), but the hydronium ion (pK_a –1.7), formed when a strong acid such as sulfuric acid is added to water, is (See Problem 3.43). The solvent, water, will then act as a nucleophile to react with the carbocation to give the final product.

$$CH_3CH_2CH{=}CH_2 \xrightarrow[\ H_2SO_4\ ]{\ H_2O\ } CH_3CH_2\underset{\underset{OH}{|}}{C}HCH_3$$

(d) $$CH_2{=}CH_2 \xrightarrow{\ ?\ } CH_3CH_2{-}\overset{\overset{H}{|}}{\underset{\underset{H}{|}}{\overset{+}{N}}}CH_3 \ Br^-$$

The elements of the methylammonium ion, $CH_3NH_3^+$, have added to the double bond. $CH_3NH_3^+$ is not sufficiently acidic (pK_a 10.6), but HBr (pK_a –8) is. Methylamine can then be used as a nucleophile to react with the electrophilic carbon atom in ethyl bromide, the product of the first reaction.

$$CH_2{=}CH_2 \xrightarrow{\ HBr\ } CH_3CH_2Br \xrightarrow{\ CH_3NH_2\ } CH_3CH_2{-}\overset{\overset{H}{|}}{\underset{\underset{H}{|}}{\overset{+}{N}}}CH_3 \ Br^-$$

4.21 (a)

electrophile ----▶CH_3⥂$\ddot{C}l{:}$ ⟶ $:\ddot{I}{-}CH_3$ $:\overset{..}{\underset{..}{C}l}:^-$

nucleophile ----▶$:\overset{..}{\underset{..}{I}}:^-$

(b)

(c)

(d)

4.21 (e)

(If excess $(CH_3)_2NH$ is used, it will act as a base in the second step of the reaction.)

(f)

(g)

4.22 Let us explore the two possible reactive intermediates for this reaction.

1° carbocation

2° carbocation destabilized by resonance

adjacent positive charges

In this case the 1° carbocation is more stable than the 2° carbocation and is on the path with the lower $\Delta G^{\ddagger}$. The 1° carbocation forms faster than the 2° carbocation and most of the product comes from that pathway.

4.23

$$pK_a \sim 10$$

$$+ \; Na^+ H \!:\!^- \longrightarrow$$

A

$$+ \; H_2$$

$$pK_a \sim 36$$

$$\xrightarrow[\substack{B \\ (\text{where } X= \\ Cl, Br, I)}]{CH_3X}$$

C

$$+ \; Na^+ X^-$$

4.24 No, the rate of reaction will decrease as the reaction progresses. The rate is a function of the concentration of starting material, and it decreases as starting material is converted into product.

4.25 At 308 K, $k = 5.3 \times 10^{-4}$ L/mol·sec. When the reaction is half over, the concentrations of hydroxide ion and methyl bromide will each be half the initial concentrations.

$$\begin{aligned}
\text{Rate} &= k\,[CH_3Br][OH^-] \\
&= k\,(0.5[CH_3Br]_{initial})(0.5[OH^-]_{initial}) \\
&= 0.25 \,(\text{initial rate}) = 0.25(5.3 \times 10^{-9} \text{ mol/L·sec}) \\
&= 1.3 \times 10^{-9} \text{ mol/L·sec}
\end{aligned}$$

4.26 When a reaction has gone to 99% completion, the final concentration of product will be 99% that of the initial starting material concentration.

$$[\text{product}]_{99\% \text{ completion}} = 0.99[\text{starting material}]_{initial}$$

and the concentration of starting material will be reduced to 1% of the initial concentration.

$$[\text{starting material}]_{99\% \text{ completion}} = 0.01[\text{starting material}]_{initial}$$

The reaction is over when it reaches equilibrium and

$$\begin{aligned}
K_{eq} &= [\text{product}]_{eq}/[\text{starting material}]_{eq} = 0.99[\text{starting material}]_{initial}/0.01[\text{starting material}]_{initial} \\
&= 0.99/0.01 = 99
\end{aligned}$$

$$\Delta G_r = -RT \ln K_{eq}$$

At 25 °C (298 K)

$$\begin{aligned}
\Delta G_r &= -(1.99 \times 10^{-3} \text{ kcal/mol·K})(298 \text{ K}) \ln 99 \\
&= -2.7 \text{ kcal/mol}
\end{aligned}$$

4.27 (a)

$$\underset{\substack{| \\ CH_3}}{CH_3C} \!\!=\!\! CH_2 \,(g) \;+\; H_2O \,(liq) \longrightarrow \underset{\substack{| \\ OH}}{\overset{\substack{CH_3 \\ |}}{CH_3CCH_3}}(liq)$$

$$\begin{aligned}
\Delta G_r^\circ &= \Delta H_r^\circ - T\Delta S_r^\circ \\
\Delta H_r^\circ &= -85.87 \text{ kcal/mol} - (-4.04 \text{ kcal/mol} - 68.32 \text{ kcal/mol}) = -13.51 \text{ kcal/mol} \\
\Delta S_r^\circ &= 46.30 \text{ cal/mol·K} - (16.72 \text{ cal/mol·K} + 70.17 \text{ cal/mol·K}) = -40.59 \text{ cal/mol·K} \\
&= -4.059 \times 10^{-2} \text{ kcal/mol·K} \\
\Delta G_r^\circ &= (-13.51 \text{ kcal/mol}) - (298 \text{ K})(-4.06 \times 10^{-2} \text{ kcal/mol·K}) \\
&= -1.41 \text{ kcal/mol}
\end{aligned}$$

$$\Delta G_r^\circ = -RT \ln K_{eq}$$

$$\ln K_{eq} = -\Delta G_r^\circ/RT$$

$$\begin{aligned}
K_{eq} &= \exp(-\Delta G_r^\circ/RT) = \exp[-(-1.41 \text{ kcal/mol})/(1.99 \times 10^{-3} \text{ kcal/mol·K})(298 \text{ K})] \\
&= 10.8
\end{aligned}$$

(b) When sulfuric acid is added to water, the proton is transferred completely to form the hydronium ion and the hydrogen sulfate anion.

$$H_2SO_4 + H_2O \longrightarrow H_3O^+ + HSO_4^-$$
$$pK_a\ -9 \qquad\qquad\qquad pK_a\ -1.7$$

In a dilute solution of H_2SO_4 in water, the electrophile is the hydronium ion, not sulfuric acid. The nucleophile is the double bond of the alkene, which requires a strong acid for protonation. H_2O (pK_a 15.7) is not strong enough, but H_3O^+ is. The hydronium ion is regenerated in the last step of the mechanism, so only a catalytic amount of sulfuric acid is necessary (see Section 8.4 for the mechanism).

4.28   (a)   HC≡C—C(=O)—Ö—H   ⁻:CH₂—N⁺≡N: → HC≡C—C(=O)—Ö:⁻   CH₃—N⁺≡N:

                                                             conjugate base   conjugate acid

(b)   HC≡C—C(=O)—Ö:⁻   CH₃—N⁺≡N: → HC≡C—C(=O)—Ö—CH₃   :N≡N:

(c)

HC≡C—C(=O)—O··C(δ−)···N≡N(δ+) activated complex [ ]‡

transition state

free energy →

free energy of activation, ΔG‡

HC≡CCO⁻
CH₃N⁺≡N
reagents

ΔG$_r$°

HC≡CCOCH₃
N≡N
products

reaction coordinate →

4.29   (a)

CH₃C(=CHCH₃) → CH₃C⁺(CH₃)—CCH₃(H) → CH₃C(CH₃)(H)—CCH₃(H)

CF₃CO(=O)—H → CF₃CO:⁻(=O) → CF₃CO:(=O)

(b)

CH₃C(CH₃)=CHCH₃   CH₃C(CH₂CH₃)=CH₂   CH₃CH(CH₃)CH=CH₂

    ↓ CF₃C(=O)OH   ↓ CF₃C(=O)OH   ↓ CF₃C(=O)OH

CH₃C⁺(CH₃)—CH₂CH₃   CH₃C⁺(CH₂CH₃)—CH₃   CH₃CH(CH₃)CH⁺—CH₃

3° carbocation   3° carbocation   2° carbocation

The 3° carbocations are more stable than the 2° carbocation. They form with a lower ΔG‡, and, therefore, at a faster rate than the 2° carbocation.

Supplemental Problems

S4.1   Supply a reagent that will give the chemical change shown in each of the equations below. Identify the reagents as electrophiles or nucleophiles and explain why you chose them. Constructing a concept triangle for each reaction may be helpful.

(a)   HOCH₂CH₂C≡CCH₂CH₂CH₂Cl —?→ HOCH₂CH₂C≡CCH₂CH₂CH₂CN

(b)   [cyclopentene with CH₃] —?→ [cyclopentane with CH₃ and Br]

(c)   CH₃CH₂OH —?→ CH₃CH₂O⁻ Na⁺ —?→ CH₃CH₂OCH₃

S4.2

(a)   Chloromethane reacts with water, as well as with hydroxide ion, to give methanol as the product. The rate constant given for the reaction of hydroxide ion with chloromethane (p. 120 in the text) was corrected for the reaction with water. Write an equation for the reaction of chloromethane with water. What is the nucleophile in the reaction? What are the other products of the reaction?

(b)   The mechanism for the reaction of chloromethane with water is essentially the same as the one for the reaction with hydroxide ion. Write out a detailed mechanism for the reaction of chloromethane with water.

(c)   Given the similarity of the mechanisms for the reactions of chloromethane with hydroxide ion and with water, what is the rate equation for the reaction with water?

(d)   When bubbled through water, chloromethane dissolves in it to the extent of about 0.003 mol/L. What is the concentration of water in such a solution? Under these conditions, is it possible to see a change in the concentration of water as the chloromethane reacts? What will the rate equation look like for this experiment?

S4.3   When cyclohexanol is heated in the presence of phosphoric acid, it loses water to become cyclohexene. This reaction is known as the dehydration of an alcohol. The acid serves as a catalyst and is regenerated in the reaction. The equation for the reaction and thermodynamic data for the compounds involved are as follows:

S_f^o (at 298 K)	78.32 cal/deg•mol	74.27 cal/deg•mol	45.11 cal/deg•mol
ΔH_f^o (at 298 K)	−70.40 kcal/mol	−1.28 kcal/mol	−57.80 kcal/mol

(a)   Does the entropy of the system increase or decrease during this reaction? How can you account for this result? What about the enthalpy of the system?

(b)   Calculate the equilibrium constant for this reaction at 298 K. Will products be formed from the starting material at that temperature?

(c)   The stages of the reaction (shown using simplified formulas, p. ~, for the cyclic compounds) are believed to be as follows:

4. H_3O^+ + $^-OPO_3H_2$ $\rightleftharpoons$ H_2O + $HOPO_3H_2$

When cyclohexanol is mixed with phosphoric acid at room temperature, heat is evolved. What does this say about the relative energy levels of all the species involved in the first step of the reaction?

(d)   No product is formed at room temperature. The reaction mixture must be heated for cyclohexene to be formed. Which step of this reaction do you think has the highest free energy of activation?

S4.4   Researchers from the University of North Carolina have reported that silica gel catalyzes the electrophilic addition reactions of hydrohalic acids (HCl, HBr, HI) to double and triple bonds.

(a)   For the following example, use the general concept of the electrophilic addition reaction to predict the structure of the major product that results from the addition of one HBr to the triple bond.

$$CH_3CH_2CH_2CH_2CH_2-C\equiv C-H \quad + \quad HBr \quad \xrightarrow[\substack{silica\ gel \\ 24\ h}]{H_2O}$$

1 equivalent

(b)   The addition of a hydrohalic acid in the presence of silica gel to an alkene is much faster than the addition to an alkyne. For example, the reaction with a simple alkene such as $CH_3CH_2CH_2CH_2CH_2CH=CH_2$ is complete in 1 hour in contrast to the 24 hours necessary for the alkyne shown above. The difference in rate between the reaction of an alkene and that of an alkyne is rationalized by considering the difference between reactive intermediates derived from the two starting materials.

1.   Draw structural formulas for the reactive intermediates involved in the rate-determining step for the addition reaction of the alkyne and of the alkene.

2.   How would you describe the difference between the two species shown in part 1, and why would this difference affect the relative rates of the two reactions?

S4.5   An electrophilic addition reaction is used in the preparation of ceralure, which is used to control the population of the Mediterranean fruit fly. The reaction shown below does not have high regioselectivity and gives two isomers. Draw their structural formulas, and explain why the two compounds are formed in roughly the same amounts.

$$+ \ HI \quad \longrightarrow \quad A \ + \ B$$

S4.6   When the following compound is treated with aqueous acid, a reaction product is observed, the formation of which is believed to begin with the electrophilic addition of water to the double bond.

A   B   C

+ H_3O^+ Cl^-

(a)   Using the curved arrow notation, draw a complete, stepwise mechanism for the transformation of A to B. (Note: strong bases, such as hydroxide ion, may not be used to describe the mechanism for reactions performed in acid, such as this one.)

(b)   Which of the following energy diagrams best describes the transformation of A to B?

(c)   On the energy diagram you selected in part (b), use an arrow to point to the transition state that corresponds to the rate-determining step.

Alkanes and Cycloalkanes

Workbook Exercises

EXERCISE I.   Insight into molecular structure comes from a detailed examination of the numbers and kinds of atoms in a molecular formula. For each of the following molecular formulas, determine the units of unsaturation (see Section 1.5).

      (a) $C_{10}H_{16}$, limonene from lemon oil

      (b) $C_{17}H_{21}NO_4$, cocaine, a local anesthetic

      (c) $C_{22}H_{37}NO_2$, anandiamide, a natural ligand for the receptor in the brain for tetrahydrocannabinol, the active ingredient of marijuana

      (d) $C_{23}H_{46}$, muscalure, an insect attractant

      (e) $C_5H_9NO_2$, proline, an amino acid

      (f) $C_4H_{12}N_2$, putrescine, found in decayed tissues

      (g) $C_6H_8O_6$, ascorbic acid

      (h) C_3H_6O, propylene oxide, a sterilant

      (i) $C_{43}H_{78}N_6O_{13}$, muroctasin, an immunostimulant

EXERCISE II.   What are some structural features that could account for the units of unsaturation in each of the compounds in Exercise I? Try to give up to three examples of such structural features for each. For example, proline [part (e)], has two units of unsaturation. These units could be represented by two rings, a ring and a carbon-oxygen double bond, or a carbon-nitrogen triple bond. Other structural features are also possible based on the information given.

EXERCISE III.   The structures for most of the compounds listed in Exercise I are found in chemistry textbooks. Find as many of these structures as you can, identify the units of unsaturation actually present, and compare this count to your answers to Exercise II.

- -

5.1   (a)

(b)

(c)

(d)

5.1   (e)

H---C with H, H and N (wedge) H, N–H ...   H–C(H)(H) with N below (N–H, N–H) ...   H–N(H) C–H (wedge) H   etc.

5.2 $C_2H_3Cl_3$:

CH₃CCl₃   ClCH₂CHCl₂

Lewis structures

three-dimensional
representations

$C_2H_2Cl_4$:

ClCH₂CCl₃   Cl₂CHCHCl₂

Lewis structures

three-dimensional
representations

5.3   The carbon nuclear magnetic resonance spectrum tells us that there are two different carbon atoms in the molecule. The proton magnetic resonance spectrum tells us that there are two sets of hydrogens, in a ratio of 2:1 (16 mm to 7 mm from the integration curves). The two isomers with the molecular formula $C_2H_3Cl_3$ are shown below.

CH₃CCl₃   ClCH₂CHCl₂
1,1,1-trichloroethane   1,1,2-trichloroethane

The hydrogens in 1,1,1-trichloroethane are equivalent and would give only one peak in its proton magnetic resonance spectrum. The three hydrogens in 1,1,2-trichloroethane consist of two sets in a ratio of 2:1. The compound is 1,1,2-trichloroethane.

5.4   The carbon nuclear magnetic resonance spectrum of Compound A has two peaks and thus two different carbon atoms and that of Compound B has one peak and only one type of carbon atom. Compound A must be 1,1,1,2-tetrachloroethane and Compound B must be 1,1,2,2-tetrachloroethane

ClCH₂CCl₃   Cl₂CHCHCl₂
1,1,1,2-tetrachloroethane   1,1,2,2-tetrachloroethane

The proton magnetic resonance spectra confirm these assignments. The hydrogen atoms in Compound A are bonded to a carbon atom that has one chlorine attached. These hydrogen atoms absorb further to the right (closer to the TMS standard) than the hydrogen atoms in Compound B, which are bonded to carbon atoms bearing two chlorine atoms each.

5.5   (a)   1-Bromopropane has three different carbon atoms and therefore will have three peaks in its carbon nuclear magnetic resonance spectrum. 2-Bromopropane has two sets of carbon atoms and therefore will have two peaks in its carbon spectrum.

$$CH_3CH_2CH_2Br \qquad\qquad CH_3CHBrCH_3$$
1-bromopropane   2-bromopropane

The top spectrum is that of 2-bromopropane and the bottom spectrum is that of 1-bromopropane.

(b)   1-Bromopropane has three sets of equivalent hydrogen atoms in a ratio of 2:2:3. The hydrogen atoms (c) on the carbon bonded to the bromine will be furthest to the left. The hydrogen atoms (b) on carbon 2 will be closer to the TMS standard, and the methyl hydrogen atoms (a) will be closest to the TMS standard.

(c)   2-Bromopropane has two sets of equivalent hydrogen atoms in a ratio of 6:1. The hydrogen atom on carbon 2 (b) will be further to the left than the methyl hydrogen atoms (a).

5.6 $C_3H_6Br_2$:

condensed formulas

(1) $CH_3CH_2CHBr_2$ (2) $CH_3CBr_2CH_3$

(3) $CH_3CHBrCH_2Br$ (4) $BrCH_2CH_2CH_2Br$

Lewis structures

5.6 (cont)

three-dimensional representations   (1)   (2)

(3)   (4)

5.7   (a) *sec*-butyl   (b isobutyl   (c) isopropyl
(d) propyl   (e) *tert*-butyl   (f) ethyl; butyl

5.8   (a) Constitutional isomers   (b) Not constitutional isomers; both formulas have the same connectivity.
(c) Constitutional isomers   (d) Constitutional isomers
(e) Constitutional isomers   (f) Constitutional isomers
(g) Not constitutional isomers; both formulas have the same connectivity.

Concept Map 5.1   **Determining connectivity.**

5.9   (a)   (b)

5.10 (a)

$$ClCH_2 - \overset{\overset{\displaystyle CH_3}{|}}{\underset{\underset{\displaystyle H}{|}}{C}} - CH_2Br \qquad CH_3 - \overset{\overset{\displaystyle CH_2Cl}{|}}{\underset{\underset{\displaystyle H}{|}}{C}} - CH_2Br \qquad CH_3 - \overset{\overset{\displaystyle CH_3}{|}}{\underset{\underset{\displaystyle Cl}{|}}{C}} - CH_2Br \qquad CH_3 - \overset{\overset{\displaystyle CH_3}{|}}{\underset{\underset{\displaystyle H \quad Cl}{|}}{C}} - CHBr$$

| four different carbon atoms, therefore four peaks | this structural formula has the same connectivity as the the one on the left, therefore four peaks | three different carbon atoms, therefore three peaks; the methyl groups are equivalent. | three different carbon atoms, therefore three peaks; the methyl groups are equivalent. |

(b)

$$ClCH_2 - \overset{\overset{\displaystyle CH_3}{|}}{\underset{\underset{\displaystyle H}{|}}{C}} - CH_2Br \qquad CH_3 - \overset{\overset{\displaystyle CH_2Cl}{|}}{\underset{\underset{\displaystyle H}{|}}{C}} - CH_2Br \qquad CH_3 - \overset{\overset{\displaystyle CH_3}{|}}{\underset{\underset{\displaystyle Cl}{|}}{C}} - CH_2Br \qquad CH_3 - \overset{\overset{\displaystyle CH_3}{|}}{\underset{\underset{\displaystyle H \quad Cl}{|}}{C}} - CHBr$$

| four different sets of hydrogen atoms, therefore four peaks | this structural formula has the same connectivity as the the one on the left, therefore four peaks | two different sets of hydrogen atoms, therefore two peaks; the methyl hydrogens are equivalent. | three different sets of hydrogen atoms, therefore three peaks; the methyl hydrogens are equivalent. |

5.11

Compound A
1-bromo-2,2-dimethylpropane

The hydrogen atoms belong in two groups, 9 in group *a* and two in group *b*. There are three groups of carbon atoms, those bonded to the *a*-hydrogen atoms, the one bonded to the *b*-hydrogen atoms, and the one labeled *c*, with no hydrogen atoms on it. There are no hydrogen atoms that are 3-bond neighbors of each other in this molecule.

Compound B
1-bromopentane

There are five groups of hydrogen atoms, labeled *a*-, *b*-, *c*-, *d*-, and *e*-hydrogen atoms. Each group of hydrogen atoms is bonded to the correspondingly labeled carbon atom. The *a*-hydrogen atoms are 3-bond neighbors to the *b*-hydrogen atoms. The *b*-hydrogen atoms are 3-bond neighbors to the *a*- and *c*-hydrogen atoms. The *c*-bond hydrogen atoms are 3-bond neighbors to the *b*- and *d*-hydrogen atoms. The *d*-hydrogen atoms are 3-bond neighbors to the *c*- and *e*-hydrogen atoms. The *e*-hydrogen atoms are 3-bond neighbors to the *d*-hydrogen atoms.

Compound C
3-bromopentane

There are three groups of hydrogen atoms and three groups of carbon atoms in the molecule, the *a*-hydrogen atoms (and carbon atoms), the *b*-hydrogen atoms (and carbon atoms), and the *c*-hydrogen atom (and the carbon atom to which it is bonded). The *a*-hydrogen atoms are 3-bond neighbors to the *b*-hydrogen atoms. The *b*-hydrogen atoms are 3-bond neighbors to the *a*- and *c*-hydrogen atoms. The *c*-hydrogen atom is a 3-bond neighbor to the *b*-hydrogen atoms.

5.12

perspective
formula

Newman
projection

staggered conformation

perspective
formula

Newman
projection

eclipsed conformation

Concept Map 5.2   **Conformation.**

5.13

anti A   eclipsed B   gauche C

eclipsed D   gauche E   eclipsed F

degree of rotation around the bond
between carbon 1 and carbon 2

5.14

no dipole moment
C—Cl bond dipoles cancel

dipole moment
C—Cl bond dipoles do not cancel

At room temperature in the liquid state, a significant portion of 1,2-dichloroethane molecules exist in the gauche conformation.

Even though the negative ends of the C—Cl bond dipoles are close enough in the gauche conformation to repel each other, considerable van der Waals attraction between the chlorine atoms also exists. There is no van der Waals attraction between the chlorine atoms in the anti conformation.

Concept Map 5.3   Representations of organic structures.

molecular formula

condensed   Lewis   line   perspective

CH₃CH₂Cl

Newman projection

5.15   (a)   (b)   (c)

(d)   (e)

5.16   (a) $CH_3CH_2CH_2CHCHCH_2OH$

≡ $CH_3CH_2CH_2CH(CH_3)CH(CH_3)CH_2OH$

(b)   ≡ $CH_3CH_2CH_2CH_2CH_2CHCl_2$

5.16 (c)

$$CH_3-CH_2-CH_2-\underset{O}{\overset{||}{C}}-\underset{Br}{\overset{|}{CH}}-CH_3 \equiv CH_3CH_2CH_2CH_2\underset{O}{\overset{||}{C}}CHBrCH_3$$

$$\equiv CH_3CH_2CH_2CH_2COCHBrCH_3$$

(d)

$$CH_3-CH_2-CH_2-\underset{\underset{CH_3}{|}}{CH}-\overset{\overset{O}{||}}{C}-OCH_3 \equiv CH_3CH_2CH_2CH_2\underset{\underset{CH_3}{|}}{CH}\overset{\overset{O}{||}}{C}OCH_3$$

$$\equiv CH_3CH_2CH_2CH_2CH(CH_3)COOCH_3$$

(e)

$$\begin{array}{c} CH_2 \\ CH_2 \quad\quad CH_3 \\ \quad\quad C \\ \quad\quad\quad F \\ CH_2-CH_2 \end{array}$$

5.17 (a) 2,2,6,7-tetramethyloctane   (b) 5-ethyl-2,6-dimethyloctane   (c) 2,3-dimethylpentane
(d) 4-*tert*-butylheptane   (e) 2,2,5-trimethyl-6-propyldecane   (f) 6-isopropyl-3-methylnonane

5.18 (a)

$$\underset{\underset{CH_3}{|}}{\overset{\overset{CH_3}{|}}{CH_3C}}CH_2CH_2CH_2CH_2CH_3$$

(b)

$$\underset{\underset{CH_3}{|}}{CH_3CH}CH_2CH_2CH_2\underset{\underset{CH_2CHCH_3}{|}}{\overset{\overset{CH_3}{|}}{CH}}CH_2CH_2CH_3$$

(c)

$$\underset{\underset{CH_3CHCH_3}{|}}{\overset{\overset{CH_3}{|}}{CH_3CH}}CH_2CH_2\overset{\overset{CH_3CHCH_3}{}}{C}CH_2CH_2\underset{}{\overset{\overset{CH_3}{|}}{CH}}CH_3$$

(d)

$$\underset{\underset{CH_3}{|}}{\overset{\overset{CH_3}{|}}{CH_3C}}CH_2\underset{}{\overset{\overset{CH_3}{|}}{CH}}CH\overset{\overset{CH_2CH_3}{|}}{CH}CH_2CH_2CH_2CH_2CH_3$$

5.19 Arrows connect equivalent carbon atoms. All hydrogen atoms on the same carbon atom are equivalent as are all hydrogen atoms on equivalent carbon atoms.

$$\underset{1° \quad 2° \quad 2° \quad 2° \quad 2° \quad 2° \quad 1°}{CH_3CH_2CH_2CH_2CH_2CH_2CH_3}$$
heptane

1° = primary carbon atom
2° = secondary carbon atom
3° = tertiary carbon atom
4° = quaternary carbon atom

$$\underset{1° \quad 3° \quad 2° \quad 2° \quad 2° \quad 1°}{CH_3\overset{\overset{1°\; CH_3}{|}}{CH}CH_2CH_2CH_2CH_3}$$
2-methylhexane

$$\underset{1° \quad 2° \quad 3° \quad 2° \quad 2° \quad 1°}{CH_3CH_2\overset{\overset{1°\; CH_3}{|}}{CH}CH_2CH_2CH_3}$$
3-methylhexane

$$\underset{1° \quad\quad\quad 2° \quad 2° \quad 1°}{1°\; CH_3\overset{\overset{1°\; CH_3 \;\; 4°}{|}}{\underset{\underset{1°\; CH_3}{|}}{C}}CH_2CH_2CH_3}$$
2,2-dimethylpentane

$$\underset{1° \quad 3° \quad\quad 3° \quad 2° \quad 1°}{CH_3\overset{\overset{1°\; CH_3}{|}}{CH}-\overset{\overset{1°\; CH_3}{|}}{CH}CH_2CH_3}$$
2,3-dimethylpentane

5.19 (cont)

$$1°$$
$$CH_3$$
$$4°$$
$$CH_3CH_2—C—CH_2CH_3$$
$$1°\ 2°\qquad 2°\ 1°$$
$$CH_3$$
$$1°$$

3,3-dimethylpentane

$$1°\qquad 1°$$
$$CH_3\qquad CH_3$$
$$CH_3CHCH_2CHCH_3$$
$$1°\ \ 3°\ 2°\ \ 3°\ 1°$$

2,4-dimethylpentane
all 1° C and H are equivalent
all 2° H are equivalent
all 3° C and H are equivalent

$$1°\qquad 1°$$
$$CH_3\qquad CH_3$$
$$CH_3C——CHCH_3$$
$$1°\ |4°\qquad 3°\ 1°$$
$$CH_3$$
$$1°$$

2,2,3-trimethylbutane

$$2°\ 1°$$
$$CH_2CH_3$$
$$CH_3CH_2CHCH_2CH_3$$
$$1°\ \ 2°\ \ 3°\ 2°\ \ 1°$$

3-ethylpentane
all 1° C and H are equivalent
all 2° C and H are equivalent

5.20   (a) 2-bromo-2,3-dimethylpentane   (b) 3-pentanol   (c) 4-chloro-3-hexanol
(d) 4,4-dichloro-2,2-dimethylhexane   (e) 2,3-dibromo-2,3-dimethylbutane   (f) 4-*tert*-butyl-3-nonanol

5.21   (a) $CH_3CHCH_2CH_2CH_2CH_2CH_2CH_3$
$$|$$
$$I$$

(b) $CH_3CH_2CHCH_2CH_2CH_3$
$$|$$
$$OH$$

(c) CF_3CH_2OH

(d) $ClCH_2CHCH_2CCH_3$
$$\ \ \ \ |\qquad |$$
$$\ \ \ OH\ \ \ CH_3$$
with CH_3 above the fourth carbon

(e) $HOCH_2CHCH_2OH$
$$|$$
$$OH$$

(f) $CH_3CH_2CH_2CH_2CH_2OH$

(g) $CH_3CHCCH_2CH_2CH_2CH_3$
with CH_2CH_3 above
$$\ \ \ |\ |$$
$$\ \ Cl\ Cl$$

5.22 $C_6H_{13}Cl$

$CH_3CH_2CH_2CH_2CH_2CH_2Cl$ 1°   1-chlorohexane

$CH_3CH_2CH_2CH_2CHCH_3$ 2°   2-chlorohexane
$$|$$
$$Cl$$

$CH_3CH_2CH_2CHCH_2CH_3$ 2°   3-chlorohexane
$$|$$
$$Cl$$

$CH_3CHCH_2CH_2CH_2Cl$ 1°   1-chloro-4-methylpentane
with CH_3 above first carbon

$CH_3CHCH_2CHCH_3$ 2°   2-chloro-4-methylpentane
with CH_3 above first carbon, Cl below fourth
$$\qquad\qquad |$$
$$\qquad\qquad Cl$$

$CH_3CHCHCH_2CH_3$ 2°   3-chloro-2-methylpentane
with CH_3 above first carbon, Cl below third
$$\qquad |$$
$$\qquad Cl$$

5.22 (cont)

$$
\begin{array}{l}
\quad\ \ \text{CH}_3 \\
\ \ \ | \\
\text{CH}_3\text{CCH}_2\text{CH}_2\text{CH}_3 \\
\ \ \ | \\
\quad\ \ \text{Cl}
\end{array}
\qquad 3° \quad \text{2-chloro-2-methylpentane}
$$

$$
\begin{array}{l}
\quad\quad\quad\ \ \text{CH}_3 \\
\quad\quad\quad\ \ | \\
\text{ClCH}_2\text{CHCH}_2\text{CH}_2\text{CH}_3 \\
\end{array}
\quad 1° \quad \text{1-chloro-2-methylpentane}
$$

$$
\begin{array}{l}
\quad\quad\ \ \text{CH}_3 \\
\quad\quad\ \ | \\
\text{CH}_3\text{CH}_2\text{CHCH}_2\text{CH}_2\text{Cl}
\end{array}
\quad 1° \quad \text{1-chloro-3-methylpentane}
$$

$$
\begin{array}{l}
\quad\quad\quad\ \ \text{CH}_3 \\
\quad\quad\quad\ \ | \\
\text{CH}_3\text{CH}_2\text{CHCHCH}_3 \\
\quad\quad\quad\quad\quad | \\
\quad\quad\quad\quad\ \ \text{Cl}
\end{array}
\quad 2° \quad \text{2-chloro-3-methylpentane}
$$

$$
\begin{array}{l}
\quad\quad\ \ \text{CH}_3 \\
\quad\quad\ \ | \\
\text{CH}_3\text{CH}_2\text{CCH}_2\text{CH}_3 \\
\quad\quad\ \ | \\
\quad\quad\ \ \text{Cl}
\end{array}
\quad 3° \quad \text{3-chloro-3-methylpentane}
$$

$$
\begin{array}{l}
\quad\quad\ \ \text{CH}_2\text{Cl} \\
\quad\quad\ \ | \\
\text{CH}_3\text{CH}_2\text{CHCH}_2\text{CH}_3
\end{array}
\quad 1° \quad
\begin{array}{l}
\text{3-(chloromethyl)pentane or} \\
\text{1-chloro-2-ethylbutane}
\end{array}
$$

$$
\begin{array}{l}
\quad\ \ \text{CH}_3 \\
\quad\ \ | \\
\text{CH}_3\text{CCH}_2\text{CH}_2\text{Cl} \\
\quad\ \ | \\
\quad\ \ \text{CH}_3
\end{array}
\quad 1° \quad \text{1-chloro-3,3-dimethylbutane}
$$

$$
\begin{array}{l}
\quad\ \ \text{CH}_3 \\
\quad\ \ | \\
\text{CH}_3\text{C}\!\!-\!\!-\!\!\text{CHCH}_3 \\
\quad\ \ | \quad\ \ | \\
\quad\ \ \text{CH}_3\ \text{Cl}
\end{array}
\quad 2° \quad \text{3-chloro-2,2-dimethylbutane}
$$

$$
\begin{array}{l}
\quad\ \ \text{CH}_2\text{Cl} \\
\quad\ \ | \\
\text{CH}_3\text{CCH}_2\text{CH}_3 \\
\quad\ \ | \\
\quad\ \ \text{CH}_3
\end{array}
\quad 1° \quad \text{1-chloro-2,2-dimethylbutane}
$$

$$
\begin{array}{l}
\quad\ \ \text{CH}_3 \\
\quad\ \ | \\
\text{CH}_3\text{CHCHCH}_2\text{Cl} \\
\quad\quad\ \ | \\
\quad\quad\ \ \text{CH}_3
\end{array}
\quad 1° \quad \text{1-chloro-2,3-dimethylbutane}
$$

$$
\begin{array}{l}
\quad\ \ \text{CH}_3\ \ \text{CH}_3 \\
\quad\ \ | \quad\quad | \\
\text{CH}_3\text{CH}\!\!-\!\!-\!\!\text{CCH}_3 \\
\quad\quad\quad\quad | \\
\quad\quad\quad\quad \text{Cl}
\end{array}
\quad 3° \quad \text{2-chloro-2,3-dimethylbutane}
$$

5.23 (1) 1,1-dichlorobutane   (2) 2,2-dichlorobutane   (3) 1,2-dichlorobutane
     (4) 1,3-dichlorobutane   (5) 2,3-dichlorobutane   (6) 1,4-dichlorobutane
     (7) 1,1-dichloro-2-methylpropane (8) 1,2-dichloro-2-methylpropane (9) 1,3-dichloro-2-methylpropane

5.24 (a) *sec*-butylbenzene   (b) isobutylbenzene   (c) isopropylbenzene
     (d) propylbenzene   (e) *tert*-butylbenzene   (f) 1-butyl-4-ethylbenzene
Note that if the substituent groups are simple alkyl groups, the compounds are named as alkylbenzenes. When the alkyl groups become large or are complicated by having other substituents on them (Problem 5.25), the benzene ring is treated as one of the substituents.

5.25 (a) 1-chloro-3-phenylpropane   (b) 3-iodo-3-phenylhexane   (c) 1-isopropyl-2-methylbenzene
     (d) 1,2-dichloro-1-phenylpropane (e) 2-methyl-2-phenylhexane (f) 3-phenyl-1-propanol

5.26 (a) CHCH₂CH₂CH₂CH₃ with OH

(b) CH₂CH₂CCH₃ with CH₃ and Br

5.26   (c)   CH₃CHCH₂CHCH₂CHCH₃

(d)   CH₃CHCH₂CHCH₂CH₂CH₂CH₃

5.27
(a) 1-methylcyclobutanol   (b) ethylcyclopropane   (c) 1-ethyl-1-methylcyclopentane   (d) iodocyclopentane

5.28   (a)   (b) ▷—OH   (c)

(d)   (e)

Concept Map 5.4   Conformation in cyclic compounds.

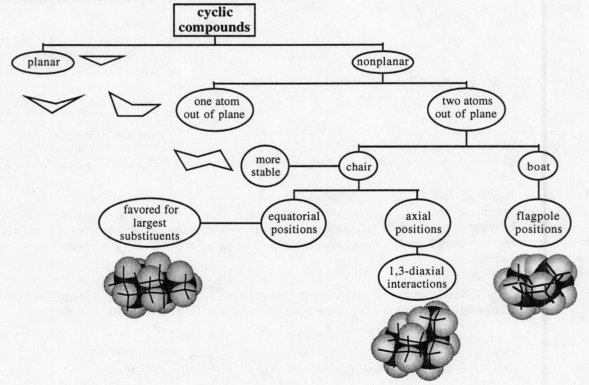

5.29

planar form

chair conformations
axial chlorine

equatorial chlorine

planar form

chair conformations
axial hydroxyl group

equatorial hydroxyl group

5.30

$$CH_3\overset{\overset{\displaystyle CH_3}{|}}{\underset{\underset{\displaystyle CH_3}{|}}{C}}\cdot \quad > \quad CH_3\overset{\overset{\displaystyle CH_3}{|}}{\underset{\underset{\displaystyle H}{|}}{C}}\cdot \quad > \quad CH_3\overset{\overset{\displaystyle H}{|}}{\underset{\underset{\displaystyle H}{|}}{C}}\cdot \quad > \quad H\overset{\overset{\displaystyle H}{|}}{\underset{\underset{\displaystyle H}{|}}{-C}}\cdot$$

5.31
(a) 1-bromo-1-methylcyclopropane   (b) 2,2,5,5-tetramethylhexane   (c) 1,1-dimethylcyclobutane
(d) 2-chloro-2-methylpentane   (e) isopropylcyclohexane or 2-cyclohexylpropane (f) 1-ethyl-1-cyclopentanol
(g) 1-chloro-1-ethylcyclohexane   (h) 3-bromo-3-ethyl-1-heptanol

5.32

$$\underset{\underset{\displaystyle Cl}{|}}{BrCHCF_3}$$

2-bromo-2-chloro-1,1,1-trifluoroethane

5.33   Beginning with this problem, if the benzene ring is not involved in a reaction or in resonance or is bonded to only one substituent, it will be represented by Ph, the symbol for the phenyl group (Section 5.10D) (see (g)).

(a) $CH_3\overset{\overset{\displaystyle CH_3}{|}}{\underset{\underset{\displaystyle OH}{|}}{C}}CH_2CH_2CH_2CH_3$

(b)

(c)

(d) $CH_3CH_2CH_2\overset{\overset{\displaystyle \overset{\displaystyle CH_3}{|}}{CH_3CCH_3}}{CH}CH_2CH_2CH_3$

(e) $CH_3CH_2CH_2CH_2CHCH_2CH_2CH_2CH_3$

(f)

(g) $CH_3CH_2\overset{\overset{\displaystyle Ph}{|}}{CH}CH_2CH_2CH_2CH_3$

(h)

(i) $CH_3\overset{\overset{\displaystyle CH_3}{|}}{\underset{\underset{\displaystyle Cl}{|}}{C}}CH_2CH_2CH_2\overset{\overset{\displaystyle CH_3}{|}}{\underset{\underset{\displaystyle OH}{|}}{C}}CH_3$

5.34   (a)

$$\underset{\underset{CH_3}{|}}{\overset{\overset{CH_3}{|}}{CH_3CH_2CCH_2CH_3}}$$

most spherical of the three constitutional isomers, least van der Waals attraction between the molecules

(b)

$$\underset{\underset{OH}{|}}{\overset{\overset{CH_3}{|}}{CH_3CCH_2CH_3}}$$

same as (a)

(c)

$$\underset{\underset{CH_3}{|}}{\overset{\overset{CH_3}{|}}{CH_3COCH_3}}$$

least polar (the other two are alcohols and form hydrogen bonds)

(d)

least polar

5.35   Isomers of $C_3H_8O_2$

$CH_3OCH_2OCH_3$	$CH_3OCH_2CH_2OH$	$HOCH_2CH_2CH_2OH$
two ether groups	ether, alcohol	2 hydroxyl groups
no hydrogen bonding	hydrogen bonding	more hydrogen bonding
bp 45 °C	bp 124 °C	bp 215 °C

5.36   (a) C_5H_9Br

Each halogen atom counts as a hydrogen atom in determining the units of unsaturation.

Units of unsaturation = $[(2 \times 5) + 2 - 10]/2 = (12-10)/2 = 1$

Some structural formulas are shown below:

alkenes: $CH_3CH_2CH = CHCH_2Br$ $\underset{\underset{Br}{|}}{CH_3CH_2CH = CCH_3}$ $\underset{\underset{Br}{|}}{\overset{\overset{CH_3}{|}}{CH_3C = CCH_3}}$

cyclic compounds:

(cyclopentyl)—Br   (cyclobutyl)$\overset{CH_3}{\underset{Br}{}}$ (cyclopropyl)—$\underset{\underset{Br}{|}}{CHCH_3}$ (cyclopropyl)—CH_2Br with CH_3

(b) $C_5H_{10}O$

Oxygen atoms do not affect the calculation

Units of unsaturation = $[(2 \times 5) + 2 - 10]/2 = (12-10)/2 = 1$

Some structural formulas are shown below:

aldehydes and ketones: $\underset{\underset{CH_3}{|}}{\overset{\overset{O}{\|}}{CH_3CH_2CHCH}}$ $\overset{\overset{O}{\|}}{CH_3CH_2CCH_2CH_3}$

unsaturated alcohols: $CH_2 = CHCH_2CH_2CH_2OH$ $\underset{\underset{OH}{|}}{CH_3CHCH = CHCH_3}$

unsaturated ethers: $CH_3OCH_2CH = CHCH_3$ $CH_2 = CCH_2OCH_3$ with CH_3 $\underset{\underset{OCH_3}{|}}{\overset{\overset{CH_3}{|}}{CH_3C = CHCH_3}}$

5.36 (b) (cont)

cyclic alcohols:

cyclic ethers:

ethers with
carbon rings:

(c) C_5H_8O

Units of unsaturation = $[(2 \times 5) + 2 - 8]/2 = (12-8)/2 = 2$
Some structural formulas are shown below:

unsaturated
aldehydes
and ketones:

unsaturated
alcohols
and ethers:

cyclic
compounds:

(d) Alkenes will react with bromine in carbon tetrachloride, therefore, the isomer cannot be an alkene. Cyclic
compounds that have rings with four or more carbon atoms will not react easily with bromine in carbon
tetrachloride. The ones with the molecular formula C_5H_9Br are:

(e) The hydrogenation data tells us that the original compound was an alkene with the carbon skeleton of 3-
methyl-1-butanol.

$$\underset{\displaystyle \quad CH_3}{CH_3CHCH_2CH_2OH}$$

The following structures are possible.

$$CH_3C=CHCH_2OH \qquad CH_2=CCH_2CH_2OH$$
(each with a CH_3 substituent)

5.37   (a)

fluorine in equatorial position
less crowded
lower in energy

(b)   The equilibrium constant, $K_{eq} = \dfrac{[axial]}{[equatorial]}$, is less than 1. The conformation with the fluorine in the equatorial position predominates.

(c)   The energy difference between the two conformations of bromocyclohexane would be expected to be larger than that for the fluoro compound. Bromine is considerably larger than fluorine and would experience even more crowding in the axial position than would fluorine.

5.38   Ph = ⟨benzene ring⟩ in these answers

(a) $CH_3CH_2NH_2$ +   HCl   ⟶ $CH_3CH_2NH_3^+$ Cl^-
       base   acid

(b) $CH_3CH_2C\equiv CH$ + $NaNH_2$ ⟶ $CH_3CH_2C\equiv C^- Na^+$ + NH_3
          acid   base

(c) $(CH_3CH_2CH_2)_2NH$ + CH_3CH_2Br ⟶ $(CH_3CH_2CH_2)_2\overset{+}{N}HCH_2CH_3$ Br^-
     nucleophile   electrophile

(d) $CH_3CH_2CH\!=\!CHCH_2CH_3$ +   HBr   ⟶ $CH_3CH_2CH_2CHBrCH_2CH_3$
       nucleophile   electrophile

(e) $CH_3CH_2CH_2SH$ +   NaOH   ⟶ $CH_3CH_2CH_2S^- Na^+$ + H_2O
       acid   base

(f) $Ph\overset{+}{N}H_2CH_3$ Cl^- +   NaOH   ⟶ $PhNHCH_3$ +   NaCl   + H_2O
       acid   base

(g) $CH_3CH_2CH\!=\!CHCH_3$ + Br_2 ⟶ $CH_3CH_2CHBrCHBrCH_3$
       nucleophile   electrophile

(h)   PhSNa   + $CH_3CH_2CH_2Br$ ⟶ $PhSCH_2CH_2CH_3$ +   NaBr
    nucleophile   electrophile

(i)   Br—⟨ring⟩—$\overset{\displaystyle O}{\overset{\|}{C}}OH$ + $NaHCO_3$ ⟶   Br—⟨ring⟩—$\overset{\displaystyle O}{\overset{\|}{C}}O^- Na^+$ + H_2O + $CO_2\uparrow$
     acid   base

5.38 (j) CH_3CH_3 + Cl_2 $\xrightarrow{hv}$ CH_3CH_2Cl + CH_3CHCl_2 + $ClCH_2CH_2Cl$ + HCl

  1 volume   1 volume

A pattern is not obvious for reaction (j).

electrophile with carbon
skeleton found in product

5.39 (a)   PhSH $\xrightarrow[H_2O]{NaOH}$ $PhS^-\ Na^+$ $\longrightarrow$ $PhSCH_2CH_2CHCH_3$

with $CH_3CHCH_2CH_2Br$ (with CH_3 substituent) and product $PhSCH_2CH_2CHCH_3$ (with CH_3 substituent)

lost in product
therefore need OH^-

nucleophile

nucleophile

(b) CH_3CH_2Br $\xrightarrow{CH_3NH_2}$ $CH_3CH_2\overset{+}{N}H_2CH_3\ Br^-$

this portion of the product comes from the nucleophile;
the rest must be from the electrophile with which it reacts

(c) $CH_2{=}CH_2$ $\xrightarrow{HBr}$ CH_3CH_2Br $\xrightarrow{CH_3O^-\ Na^+}$ $CH_3CH_2OCH_3$

nucleophile

looks as though CH_3OH has added; CH_3OH
is too weak an acid to add to double bond;
must use two consecutive reactions

(d) $CH_3CH_2CH_2CH_2NH_2$ $\xrightarrow{HCl}$ $CH_3CH_2CH_2CH_2\overset{+}{N}H_3\ Cl^-$

base   conjugate acid of base

(e) $CH_3CH_2C{\equiv}CH$ $\xrightarrow[\text{electrophile}]{2\ Br_2}$ $CH_3CH_2CBr_2CHBr_2$

nucleophile with carbon Br_2 added twice
skeleton of product;
triple bond will react two
times with Br_2

electrophile with carbon
skeleton found in product

(f) $CH_3CH_2CH_2CH_2OH$ $\xrightarrow{Na^+\ NH_2^-}$ $CH_3CH_2CH_2CH_2O^-$ $\xrightarrow{CH_3Br}$ $CH_3CH_2CH_2CH_2OCH_3$

nucleophile

proton lost in product,
therefore need base

5.39   (g) $CH_3CHCH_2CH=CH_2 \xrightarrow[PtO_2]{H_2} CH_3CHCH_2CH_2CH_3$
               | |
              OH   OH

has two more hydrogens than starting
material, therefore reagent is H_2

(h)

hydrogen substituted by halogen,
therefore need halogen with light

5.40   (a)

gauche   anti   gauche   anti
1,2-ethanediol   1,2-dimethoxyethane

Only one of the two gauche conformations is shown for each compound. The second gauche conformation
can be obtained by rotating the front carbon atom in the anti conformation 120° in a clockwise direction.

(b) Hydrogen bonding can take place in the gauche conformation of 1,2-ethanediol but not in the anti
conformation.

(c) The order of stability is A > C > B.

(d)

eclipsed

energy →

A   B

0   60   120
degree of rotation around
the bond between carbon
1 and carbon 2

5.41   (a) 1-chloro-1-methylcyclohexane

(b)

(c) The conformer in which the methyl group is axial must have larger 1,3-diaxial interactions between the axial group and the two axial hydrogens on the same side of the ring. The methyl group is effectively larger than the chlorine atom.

smaller 1,3-diaxial interactions

5.42

Linear shape of ethynyl group minimizes 1,3-diaxial interactions in axial conformation, therefore there is not as much difference in energy between the two forms.

1,3-Diaxial interactions in the axial conformer makes it less stable relative to the equatorial conformer.

5.43   The three other isomers with molecular formula C_4H_9Br are given below:

$CH_3CH_2CH_2CH_2Br$ $CH_3CH_2CHBrCH_3$

$$CH_3\overset{\displaystyle CH_3}{\underset{\displaystyle CH_3}{\overset{|}{\underset{|}{C}}}Br}$$

1-bromobutane	2-bromobutane	2-bromo-2-methylpropane
(*n*-butyl bromide)	(*sec*-butyl bromide)	(*tert*-butyl bromide)
four sets of hydrogen atoms	four sets of hydrogen atoms	one set of hydrogen atoms
in a ratio of 2:2:2:3	in a ratio of 1:2:3:3	and two sets of carbon atoms
and four different carbon atoms	and four different carbon atoms	

5.43 (cont) The rough proton spectra are:

The rough carbon spectra are:

2-bromo-2-methylpropane

5.43 (cont)

Supplemental Problems

S5.1 Name the following compounds.

(a) ClĊCH$_2$CH$_2$CH$_3$ (with Cl above and Cl below the first carbon)

(b) CH$_3$CH$_2$CHCH$_2$CH$_2$CH$_2$CH$_2$CH$_3$ (with I below)

(c) ⬡—CH$_2$CH$_2$CH$_2$—⬡

(d) ⬡—CHCH$_2$CHCH$_3$ (with CH$_3$ above second carbon and Cl below first carbon)

(e) △—Br

(f) cyclohexane with OH and phenyl at top carbon

(g) CH$_3$CH$_2$CHCH$_2$CH$_2$CHCHCH$_3$ (with CH$_3$ĊCH$_3$ and CH$_3$ group above, Cl Cl below)

(h) ⬡—CH$_2$CH$_2$CHCH$_3$ (with CH$_3$ above)

(i) ☐—OH

S5.2 Draw structural formulas for the following compounds
(a) 4-*tert*-butyl-3-ethyloctane (b) 1,2-ethanediol   (c) 4-bromo-3,3-dimethylheptane
(d) 2-bromo-3-ethylhexane   (e) 2-phenyl-1-ethanol (f) chlorocyclopentane (g) 2-cyclopentyloctane
(h) 1,3-diphenylpropane   (i) 1-chloro-3-methyl-1-phenylbutane

S5.3 For each molecular formula, draw structural formulas of all possible constitutional isomers. Name each one.
(a) C$_5$H$_{12}$O (Ethers may be named for the two alkyl groups they contain: for example, CH$_3$OCH$_2$CH$_3$ is methyl ethyl ether.)
(b) C$_3$H$_5$Cl$_3$

S5.4

(a) A compound with the molecular formula C_7H_{12} has two units of unsaturation. Such a compound may contain one triple bond, two double bonds, a ring and a double bond, or two rings. For each of the four categories given as a possibility for the molecular formula C_7H_{12}, draw one structural formula.

(b) Adding hydrogen to the compound with the molecular formula C_7H_{12} gives a C_7H_{16} compound, which is identified as being 2-methylhexane. In light of this evidence, what structures are possible for the C_7H_{12} compound?

S5.5   The conformations of 1,1,1,4-tetrachlorobutane can be clearly depicted using Newman projections.

(a)   Draw the structure of 1,1,1,4-tetrachlorobutane in its most stable conformation (conformation A) using a perspective formula and a Newman projection looking down the bond between carbon 2 and carbon 3.

(b)   Show a gauche (conformation C) and one of the two more stable eclipsed forms (conformation B) of this molecule as Newman projections.

(c)   Draw a potential energy diagram showing the relative energies of conformations A, B, and C, as one is transformed into the other. Label the "hills" and "valleys" with letters indicating the conformations that correspond to them.

S5.6   The ratios of different chair conformations at equilibrium for a large number of monosubstituted cyclohexanes are known. Examples of three of these are given below.

A
ratio 1.4 : 1

B
ratio 2.5 : 1

C
ratio 35.0 : 1

(a)   Which of the three equilibria (A, B, or C) will have the largest free energy difference ($\Delta G°$) between the two conformations?

(b)   What is responsible for the difference in observed ratios at equilibrium *(be very specific about structural features)?*

(c)   What is the value of the equilibrium constant, K_{eq}, for the equilibrium you selected in part (a)? Your answer may be expressed as a fraction.

(d)   When the compound in example C is treated with methyl iodide, it is converted to a new compound. Write an equation for this reaction. Show the two chair conformations for this new constant. Will the equilibrium constant, $K_{eq} = \dfrac{[\text{axial}]}{[\text{equatorial}]}$, for the conformational change for this new compound be smaller or larger than it was for example C? Explain your decision.

S5.7   2-Amino-3,3-difluoropentanedioic acid has been synthesized at the University of Michigan for research into the toxicity of compounds used in cancer chemotherapy. A perspective formula of the compound is shown below.

(a)   Draw a Newman projection of the conformation of this compound by looking along the bond between carbon 2 and carbon 3.

(b)   Rotate the front carbon atom by 120° of the Newman projection that you drew in part (a), and redraw the *perspective formula* corresponding to this new conformer of the compound.

S5.8   Experimental measurements of dipole moments have shown that for 1,2-dichloroethane in carbon tetrachloride solution at 25 °C, 70% of the molecules are in the anti and 30% in the gauche conformation. For 1,2-dibromoethane under the same conditions, 89% of the molecules have the anti and 11% the gauche conformation. Offer a rationalization for the differences in the percentages of anti and gauche conformers for the 1,2-dichloro- and 1,2-dibromoethanes. Pictures as well as words will be helpful.

S5.9   For the following molecule, the equilibrium constant, $\dfrac{[\text{equatorial}]}{[\text{axial}]}$, is less than 1. Draw an accurate picture of the more stable chair form and briefly state the reason for its stability.

S5.10   If the oxygen atom in fluoromethanol is assumed to be sp^3-hybridized, the highest energy conformation for the compound when viewed along the O—C bond is shown below.

(a)   Draw a Newman projection for this conformation. Why is this conformation the least stable?
(b)   Draw a Newman projection for the most stable conformation.

S5.11   Researchers recently investigated the effect of different substituents at the 2-position of cyclohexanones on the equilibrium between the two chair conformers of the compounds. The equilibrium being investigated is shown below, with **X** representing the substituent at the 2-position on cyclohexanone. Some of the data obtained in this research are given in the table to the right of the equilibrium.

X	% of axial form at equilibrium
F	17
Cl	45
Br	71
I	88
CH_3O	28
CH_3S	85

(a)   Consider the equilibrium for 2-fluorocyclohexane. Will the equilibrium constant, $\dfrac{[\text{equatorial}]}{[\text{axial}]}$, for the conformational change shown above be greater than, equal to, or less than 1?
(b)   Draw an energy diagram showing the relative energies of the axial and the equatorial forms of 2-bromocyclohexanone.
(c)   Which 2-substituted cyclohexanone has the largest difference in free energy (ΔG) between its equatorial and axial forms?
(d)   According to the data given in the table, what factor or factors appear to be important in determining whether a 2-substituted cyclohexanone exists primarily in the equatorial or the axial form?

S5.12   The following represent chemical transformations showing pathways from starting materials to products. All of these equations use the types of reactions that you have learned involving electrophilic and nucleophilic species. Fill in the structural formulas for the starting materials, reagents, or products represented by the letters below, using changes in molecular connectivity as clues.

S5.12 (cont)

(a) $Al(CH_3)_3$ + [benzene ring]—CH_2NH_2 $\longrightarrow$ A   (b) B $\xrightarrow[\substack{\text{dichloromethane} \\ 0\,°C}]{Br_2 \text{ (1 equivalent)}}$ [dibenzocyclooctadiene with two Br]

(c) $CH_3\overset{\overset{\displaystyle CH_3}{|}}{\underset{\underset{\displaystyle CH_3}{|}}{C}}-\overset{\overset{\displaystyle CH_3}{|}}{\underset{\underset{\displaystyle CH_3}{|}}{Si}}-OCH_2CH_2CH_2Br$ $\xrightarrow[\substack{\text{dimethyl} \\ \text{sulfoxide}}]{C}$ $CH_3\overset{\overset{\displaystyle CH_3}{|}}{\underset{\underset{\displaystyle CH_3}{|}}{C}}-\overset{\overset{\displaystyle CH_3}{|}}{\underset{\underset{\displaystyle CH_3}{|}}{Si}}-OCH_2CH_2CH_2CN$ + NaBr

(d) O_2N—[benzene ring]—$CH_2\overset{\displaystyle |}{\underset{\displaystyle \underset{O}{\overset{||}{C}}OH}{C}}HNH_2$ $\xrightarrow{D}$ O_2N—[benzene ring]—$CH_2\overset{\displaystyle |}{\underset{\displaystyle \underset{O}{\overset{||}{C}}OH}{C}}H—\overset{\overset{\displaystyle H}{\underset{\displaystyle |}{}}}{\underset{\underset{\displaystyle H}{|}}{\overset{+}{N}}}—CH_2\overset{\overset{\displaystyle O}{||}}{C}CH_2CH_3$ Br^-

(e) [5-methyl-1-bromotetralin structure with CH_3 and Br] + $Na^{+-}SCH_2CH_3$ $\longrightarrow$ E + NaBr

(f) [1-methylcyclohexene with CH_3] $\xrightarrow{F}$ [cyclohexane with Cl, CH_3, H, SCH_3]

(Hint: a single reagent does this in one step. What must it be?)

(g) [cholesterol structure]   cholesterol $\xrightarrow{G}$ [sodium cholesterolate structure with $Na^{+-}O$] + H_2 $\xrightarrow{H}$ [benzyl ether of cholesterol structure with CH_2O] + NaBr

Stereochemistry

Workbook Exercises

Before you begin to learn about some of the three-dimensional relationships that can exist in molecules, you should realize that these relationships are not unique to molecules, but also exist in the macroscopic world of common objects. To get the most benefit from the following exercises, you will need the two cardboard tetrahedra you constructed for the workbook exercises in Chapter 2. Use your model set to construct two tetrahedra with four atoms of different colors attached to each center.

In earlier chapters you learned the symbolism used to represent a tetrahedral arrangement of atoms around a central atom, for example, methane, CH_4.

These are two-dimensional representations, called perspective drawings, of a three-dimensional object. Your study of stereochemistry in Chapter 6 will be easier if you become comfortable relating these two-dimensional pictures with the three-dimensional structures they represent.

EXERCISE I.

(a) Place one of the tetrahedra on the table so that the face with only letters on it is toward you, and one of the edges is parallel to an edge of the table.

(b) The overall arrangement of the three letters on the face of the cardboard tetrahedron pointed towards you should be

, if you use lines to point to each vertex from the center.

Add the letters A, B, and C
as they appear to you on the
face of the tetrahedron:

(c) You can also use lines, dashes, and wedges to draw the arrangement of the four vertices of your cardboard model. If you imagine a point at the center of the cardboard model and then lines originating from there to each of the four vertices, the picture would look as follows:

Workbook Exercises (cont)

The face defined by the numbers 1-2-3, , is still directed toward you.

Draw a representation of the cardboard model you have on the table using lines, dashes, and wedges, and add the A, B, C, and● labels as they appear to you on the model.

(d) If you let your eyes travel from number 1 to number 2 to number 3 on the front face of the tetrahedron drawn in part (c), your eyes would be moving the way the hands of a clock do, or "clockwise."

counterclockwise (clock) clockwise

Look at your own cardboard model and decide what direction your eyes must travel in going from A to B to C.

(e) Place your other cardboard model on the table with one of its edges parallel to the tabletop and with its A-B-C face toward you. How do your eyes travel in going from A to B to C? Draw the figure using the symbolism of lines, dashes, and wedges to indicate three dimensionality.

(f) Place a molecular model of a tetrahedron with four different attached atoms on the table so that two of the attached atoms line up with the edge of the tabletop in a way that is similar to the way the front edge of your cardboard model is situated on the table. The four atoms on the molecular model should correspond in space to the vertices of your cardboard model. Draw the molecular model using three-dimensional symbolism.

(g) Select one of your cardboard models. There are five other edges on the cardboard model besides the one parallel to the edge of the table. Reposition the model so that each edge, in turn, is parallel to the edge of the table. Draw a three-dimensional representation for each one. Note that all six pictures you will have drawn for the model represent the same object. For those with an A-B-C face toward you, is the A→B→C direction clockwise or counterclockwise?

(h) You now have six three-dimensional representations for one of your cardboard models and one representation for the second model. Are any of the six representations of one model an exact match for the second model?

EXERCISE II.   We will now arbitrarily assign a set of priorities to the four vertices on your cardboard models:

(1) = highest priority = B
(2) = second highest = A
(3) = third highest = ●
(4) = lowest priority = C

(a) With one of your hands, grasp the cardboard model by the lowest priority vertex (C). (Lightly pinch the vertex between your thumb, index and middle fingers.) Hold the model so that the B-A-● face that is opposite this vertex is facing you. On this face, do your eyes turn clockwise or counterclockwise in looking from (1) to (2) to (3) (or B→A→●)? Using the same set of priorities, answer the same question for your other cardboard model. Now assign a set of priorities to the four colored atoms on one of your molecular models. Assign a clockwise or counterclockwise direction in going from (1) to (2) to (3) by grasping the group with priority (4) and holding the model so that the 1-2-3 face is pointing toward you.

(b) Using the same molecular model from part (a), disconnect and reconnect any two of the atoms, exchanging their positions. Keeping the same priorities that you assigned in part (a), decide whether your eyes move clockwise or counterclockwise when you look from (1) to (2) to (3) when atom (4) is held away from you. Exchange any two other atoms and examine the (1) to (2) to (3) direction again. Repeat this exercise once more. What generalization can you make about the number of different arrangements possible for four different atoms in a tetrahedral arrangement?

EXERCISE III.   When you hold the molecular model so that atom (4) is towards you, what direction do your eyes move in looking from (1) to (2) to (3)?

EXERCISE IV.   Arbitrarily assign priorities to the following four symbols: P, β, Σ, and q.

(1) = highest priority = _____   (2) = second highest = _____
(3) = third highest   = _____   (4) = lowest priority = _____

Using your molecular models as a guide, decide whether your eyes turn clockwise or counterclockwise in going from (1) to (2) to (3) when the priority (4) symbol in the following representations is held away from you.

Workbook Exercises (cont)

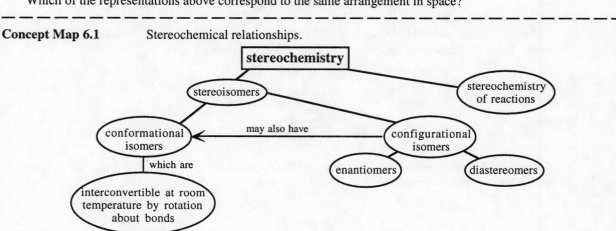

Which of the representations above correspond to the same arrangement in space?

Concept Map 6.1   Stereochemical relationships.

Concept Map 6.2   Chirality.

Concept Map 6.3   Definition of enantiomers.

6.1   (a)

If the mug had the word "MOTHER" written on one side, there would no longer be any planes of symmetry. The mug would now be chiral.

← plane of symmetry

If the mug had the word "MOM" instead of "MOTHER" written on one side, it would still be chiral. If the word "MOM" were written opposite the handle, it would be achiral.

(b)

Thread is helically wound around a spool. A helix has no planes of symmetry. A spool with helically wound thread has no plane of symmetry and is chiral.

(c)

← plane of symmetry

An empty spool has many planes of symmetry. One is shown.

6.2   (a)

helical thread; chiral

(b)

plane of symmetry

achiral

(c)

prongs equal length; achiral
prongs not equal length; chiral

mirror

(d)

plane of symmetry

achiral

(e)

plane of symmetry

socks are interchangeable; achiral

(f)

some mittens have a plane of symmetry; the mittens shown do not. Each mitten is chiral and is the mirror image isomer of the other mitten.

6.2   (g)   (h)   (i)

plane of
symmetry

achiral   Notice buttons and buttonholes; chiral   chiral

6.3   (a)   No

The molecule has a plane of symmetry.
The atoms that are behind the plane
are shown as gray letters

(b)   Yes

CH_2Cl CH_2Cl

H‐‐‐C‐‐CH₃   CH₃‐‐C‐‐‐H

HO   OH

(c)   Yes

CH_2Cl CH_2Cl

H‐‐‐C‐‐CH_2CH_3 CH_3CH_2‐‐C‐‐‐H

CH₃   CH₃

(d)   No

H
C‐‐H
H
H   H
H   Br
H   H
H
H   H
H   H

The molecule has a plane of symmetry.
[See part (a)]

(e)   Yes

CH_3 CH_3

$CH_3CH_2CH_2$‐‐C‐‐‐H   H‐‐‐C‐‐$CH_2CH_2CH_3$

Br   Br

(f)   Yes

CH_3 CH_3

CH_3CHCH_2‐‐C‐‐‐H   H‐‐‐C‐‐CH_2CHCH_3

CH₃   OH   HO   CH₃

Concept Map 6.4   Optical activity.

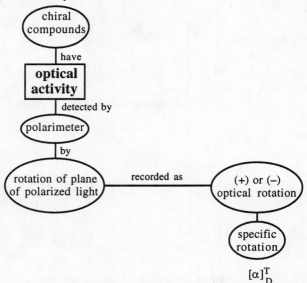

$$[\alpha]_D^T$$

6.4 $\dfrac{\text{optical rotation of unknown solution}}{\text{optical rotation of known concentration}} = \dfrac{+13.3°}{+53.2°} = \dfrac{1}{4}$

therefore the concentration of the unknown solution $= \dfrac{1}{4} \times$ the concentration of the original solution

$$= \dfrac{1}{4} \times (20 \text{ g}/100 \text{ mL}) = 5.0 \text{ g}/100 \text{ mL} = 0.05 \text{ g/mL}$$

6.5 $[\alpha]_D^{20°} = \dfrac{+2.46°}{(1.0 \text{ dm})(5 \text{ g}/100 \text{ mL})} = +49.2° \ (c \ 0.05, \text{ ethanol})$

6.6   The equation for specific rotation can be rearranged.

$$\alpha = [\alpha]_D^{20°} \ lc$$

The actual rotation, α, is directly proportional to the concentration. If the solution is diluted, for example, to twice the original volume, the concentration, and therefore the optical rotation, will be cut in half. Thus if the original specific rotation is $+90°$, the actual rotation for the diluted solution will be $45°$ in a clockwise direction. If the specific rotation is $-270°$, the actual rotation will be $-135°$, or $225°$ in a clockwise direction. In general, decreasing the concentration will cause a positive rotation to decrease in the clockwise direction and a negative rotation to increase in the clockwise direction.

6.7   (a)   enantiomeric excess $= \dfrac{\text{actual rotation}}{\text{rotation of pure enantiomer}} \times 100$

enantiomeric excess $= \dfrac{-14.70°}{-39.5°} \times 100 = 37.2\%$

(b)

(S)-(−)-2-bromobutanoic acid   (R)-(+)-2-bromobutanoic acid
               68.6%   31.4%

The mixture containing a 37.2% enantiomeric excess of the levorotatory compound is $100 - 37.2$ or 62.8% racemic. The racemic portion of the mixture contains equal amounts ($62.8/2 = 31.4\%$) of each enantiomer. Therefore the solution contains 31.4% of the dextrorotatory and $(31.4 + 37.2)\%$ or 68.6% of the levorotatory isomer.

Concept Map 6.5   Formation of racemic mixtures in chemical reactions.

- -

6.8   (a) (*S*)-3-hexanol   (b) (*S*)-2-bromopentane   (c) (*R*)-3-iodo-3-methylhexane

(d) (*R*)-1-bromo-1-chloropropane   (e) (*R*)-1,2-dichlorobutane   (f) (*S*)-4-chloro-2-methyl-1-butanol

(g) (*S*)-1-chloro-3,4-dimethylpentane   (h) (*R*)-4-bromo-2-butanol

6.9   (a)

6.10   (a)

(*R*)-3-methylhexane   (*S*)-3-methylhexane

These are enantiomers

(b)

(2*R*, 4*R*)-2-bromo-4-methylhexane   (2*S*, 4*S*)-2-bromo-4-methylhexane

These enantiomers are the diastereomers of the two enantiomers below.

(2*R*, 4*S*)-2-bromo-4-methylhexane   (2*S*, 4*R*)-2-bromo-4-methylhexane

These enantiomers are the diastereomers of the two enantiomers above.

6.10   (c)

(2*R*, 3*R*)-2,3-dibromopentane   (2*S*, 3*S*)-2,3-dibromopentane

These enantiomers are the diastereomers of the two enantiomers below.

(2*R*, 3*S*)-2,3-dibromopentane   (2*S*, 3*R*)-2,3-dibromopentane

These enantiomers are the diastereomers of the two enantiomers above.

6.11   3-bromo-2-butanol

(2*R*, 3*R*)-3-bromo-2-butanol   (2*S*, 3*S*)-3-bromo-2-butanol

These enantiomers are the diastereomers of the two enantiomers below.

(2*R*, 3*S*)-3-bromo-2-butanol   (2*S*, 3*R*)-3-bromo-2-butanol

These enantiomers are the diastereomers of the two enantiomers above.

2-chloro-3-methylheptane

(2*R*, 3*R*)-2-chloro-3-methylheptane   (2*S*, 3*S*)-2-chloro-3-methylheptane

These enantiomers are the diastereomers of the two enantiomers below.

(2*R*, 3*S*)-2-chloro-3-methylheptane   (2*S*, 3*R*)-2-chloro-3-methylheptane

These enantiomers are the diastereomers of the two enantiomers above.

6.12   2,3-butanediol

plane of symmetry

(2*R*, 3*R*)-   (2*S*, 3*S*)-   (2*R*, 3*S*)-
2,3-butanediol   2,3-butanediol   2,3-butanediol

These enantiomers are the diastereomers of the meso compound.   meso compound

6.12 (cont)

2,3-pentanediol

(2*R*, 3*R*)-2,3-pentanediol   (2*S*, 3*S*)-2,3-pentanediol

These enantiomers are the diastereomers of the two enantiomers below.

(2*R*, 3*S*)-2,3-pentanediol   (2*S*, 3*R*)-2,3-pentanediol

These enantiomers are the diastereomers of the two enantiomers above.

2,4-pentanediol

(2*R*, 4*R*)-2,4-pentanediol   (2*S*, 4*S*)-2,4-pentanediol   (2*R*, 4*S*)-2,4-pentanediol
These enantiomers are the diastereomers of the meso compound.   meso compound

- -

Concept Map 6.6   Configurational isomers.

- -

6.13

Note that the lowest priority group on carbon 3, H, is on a bond coming out of the plane toward you, thus the clockwise rotation you see is actually counterclockwise, and the designation is *S*, not *R*.

6.14   For a compound with *n* stereocenters, there can be a maximum of 2^n stereoisomers. 2,3,4-Tribromohexane has
3 stereocenters and thus a maximum of 8 stereoisomers. The number of different isomers will be reduced if there
are meso compounds. The easiest way to draw a set of stereoisomers is to start with one in which all stereocenters
are the same and first reverse the designation of all the stereocenters to get the mirror image enantiomer. Then
change one stereocenter at a time to generate the rest of the stereoisomers.

(2R,3R,4R)-2,3,4-tribromohexane

(2S,3S,4S)-2,3,4-tribromohexane

These two compounds are enantiomers and are diastereomers of the other six stereoisomers

(2S,3R,4R)-2,3,4-tribromohexane

(2R,3S,4S)-2,3,4-tribromohexane

These two compounds are enantiomers and are diastereomers of the other six stereoisomers.

(2R,3S,4R)-2,3,4-tribromohexane

(2S,3R,4S)-2,3,4-tribromohexane

These two compounds are enantiomers and are diastereomers of the other six stereoisomers.

(2R,3R,4S)-2,3,4-tribromohexane

(2S,3S,4R)-2,3,4-tribromohexane

These two compounds are enantiomers and are diastereomers of the other six stereoisomers.

6.15   (a)

(2S, 3S)-3-methoxy-2-methyl-4-phenyl-1-butanol

(b)

(2R, 3S)-3-methoxy-2-methyl-4-phenyl-1-butanol

This is a diastereomer of the original
compound. The configuration at
carbon 2 was changed by reversing the
methyl group and the hydrogen atom.

We could also have (2R, 3R), the enantiomer of the original compound, and (2S, 3R), the enantiomer of the
structure shown above.

6.16

(1*R*, 3*S*)-1,3-dimethyl-
cyclopentane
cis-1,3-dimethylcyclopentane
a meso compound

(1*R*, 3*R*)-1,3-dimethyl-
cyclopentane
trans-1,3-dimethylcyclopentane
enantiomers

(1*S*, 3*S*)-1,3-dimethyl-
cyclopentane

diastereomers

Note that in the meso compound the stereocenters have opposite configurations. Also, once an assignment of configuration is carefully made for one of the stereoisomers, the configurations of stereocenters can be assigned by looking to see if they are the same, or opposite, in configuration. For example, once the stereocenters in *cis*-1,3-dimethylcyclopentane have been assigned (see explanation that follows), the other two stereoisomers are easy. The first trans isomer has the same configuration (methyl up) at carbon 1 and the opposite configuration (methyl down) at carbon 3 as the cis isomer. Therefore, it is the (1*R*, 3*R*) isomer.

6.17

CH₃   Br
(1*R*, 2*R*)-1-bromo-
2-methylcyclopentane
trans-1-bromo-2-methylcyclopentane
enantiomers

CH₃   Br
(1*S*, 2*S*)-1-bromo-
2-methylcyclopentane

CH₃   Br
(1*R*, 2*S*)-1-bromo-
2-methylcyclopentane
cis-1-bromo-2-methylcyclopentane
enantiomers

CH₃   Br
(1*S*, 2*R*)-1-bromo-
2-methylcyclopentane

diastereomers

6.18   1-bromo-2-methylcyclohexane

trans-1-bromo-2-methylcyclohexane

cis-1-bromo-2-methylcyclohexane

enantiomers   enantiomers

1-bromo-4-methylcyclohexane

CH₃----⟨   ⟩----Br   CH₃----⟨   ⟩----Br

trans-1-bromo-4-methylcyclohexane   *cis*-1-bromo-4-methylcyclohexane

Note that 1-bromo-4-methylcyclohexane has no stereocenters

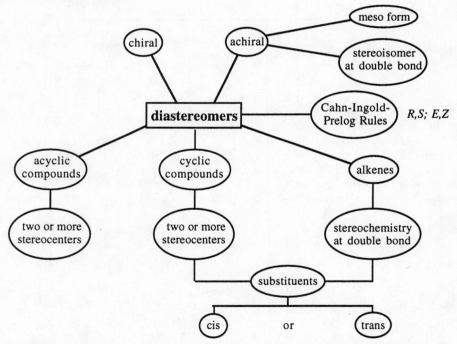

6.18 (cont)

6.19

Concept Map 6.7   Diastereomers.

6.20   (a)

(*E*)-3-methyl-3-hexene

(b)

(*Z*)-1,3-dibromo-1-chloro-
2- methylpropene

6.20 (c)

(Z)-5-chloro-3-ethyl-
2-pentenoic acid

(d)

(Z)-3-ethyl-3-hexen-1-yne

- -

Concept Map 6.8   The process of resolution.

racemic
mixtures

are

inseparable by normal
physical methods using
achiral techniques

separable

by

resolution

by treatment with
chiral reagents

diastereomers

- -

6.21

$\xrightarrow[\text{H}_2\text{O}]{\text{NaOH}}$

water-soluble salt   water-insoluble amine   water-soluble salt

6.22

+   +

(R)-(+)-1-amino-1-phenylethane   (S)-(−)-1-amino-1-phenylethane   (2R,3R)-(+)-tartaric acid

↓ methanol

6.22 (cont)

salt of (*R*)-(+)-1-amino-1-phenylethane
with (2*R*,3*R*)-(+)-tartaric acid; more
soluble in methanol; stays in solution

salt of (*S*)-(−)-1-amino-1-phenylethane
with (2*R*,3*R*)-(+)-tartaric acid; less
soluble in methanol; crystallizes out

NaOH
H₂O

NaOH
H₂O

distillation gives (*R*)-(+)-1-
amino-1-phenylethane

disodium tartrate
stays in solution

distillation gives (*S*)-(−)-1-
amino-1-phenylethane

disodium tartrate
stays in solution

6.23

(a) (*S*)-3-bromo-2-methylpentane   (b) (*S*)-1-phenyl-1-butanol   (c) butane
(d) (*S*)-1,2-dibromopentane   (e) (*R*)-3-methyl-3-hexanol   (f) (*S*)-3-methyl-3-hexanol
(g) (2*R*, 3*S*)-2,3-dibromobutane (*meso*-2,3-dibromobutane)   (h) (1*S*, 2*S*, 4*S*)-1,2-dibromo-4-methylcyclohexane

The assignment of configuration for (g) is easiest if the chair form is converted to the planar form using wedges and dashed lines to indicate the stereochemistry of the substituents. Assignment of configuration at carbon-2, for example, is shown below.

(1*S*, 2*S*, 4*S*)-1,2-dibromo-4-methylcyclohexane

The bromine is pointing down, therefore the group of lowest priority, the hydrogen, is pointing up. Our eye travels clockwise from priority 1 to priority 2 to priority 3, therefore the stereocenter *looks R*, but is really *S* because we are looking at it from the wrong face of the molecule.

6.24   b, c, e, h, and i have stereocenters.

(b)

CH_2Cl / CH_2Cl

$ClCH_2CH_2$ —C— H   H —C— CH_2CH_2Cl
        | |
        Cl   Cl

(c)

CH_3 / CH_3

—C— H   H —C—
  | |
  Br   Br
  H   H

(e)

CH_2OH / CH_2OH

CH_3CH_2 —C— CH_3 CH_3 —C— CH_2CH_3
        | |
        OH   HO

(h)

CH_3 / CH_3

CH_3COH CH_3COH

CH_3CH_2 —C— H   H —C— CH_2CH_3
        | |
        OH   HO

(i)

CH_2CH_3 / CH_2CH_3

Ph —C— H   H —C— Ph
  | |
  Cl   Cl

Ph— ≡ (benzene ring with methyl)

6.25
(a) enantiomers   (The molecule on the left has the *S* configuration, the one on the right, the *R* configuration.)

(b) identical   (c) identical   (d) identical

(e) enantiomers   (The molecule on the left has the *R* configuration; the other, the *S* configuration. Note also that the molecule on the right is not the mirror image of the molecule on the left but is a conformer of the mirror image.)

(f) constitutional isomers   [(*R*)-3-bromo-1-chlorobutane and (2*R*,3*S*)-2-bromo-3-chlorobutane]

(g) identical   (Both have the *R* configuration.)

(h) conformers   (The methyl group on carbon 2 is anti to the hydroxyl group on the left-hand molecule and gauche on the right.)

(i) constitutional isomers   [(*R*)-2-bromo-1-chlorobutane and (*S*)-3-bromo-1-chlorobutane]

(j) conformers   (The molecule on the left has an equatorial chlorine; the other has an axial chlorine.)

6.26

$CH=CH_2$
       |
HOC —C— CH_3
 ‖   C
 O   ‖‖
         C
         H

6.27

        O   O
        ‖   ‖
       COH   COH
        | |
   T —C— H   H —C— T
        | |
        D   D

   (*S*)-isomer   (*R*)-isomer

sp^2-hybridized, planar; Br^- can attack from front face (a) or back face (b) of carbocation

6.28

6.28 (cont)

(2R, 6S)-2,6-dibromoheptane;
meso compound; no optical activity

(2R, 6R)-2,6-dibromoheptane;
optically active

6.29 (a)

(R)-(−)-1-amino-2-propanol
hydrochloride

(S)-(+)-1-amino-2-propanol
hydrochloride

(b)   The S-enantiomer was recovered with higher optical purity (higher absolute specific rotation).

(c) $\dfrac{\text{enantiomeric excess}}{\text{for the } R\text{-isomer}} = \dfrac{-31.5°}{-35°} \times 100 = 90\%$

6.30 $\alpha = [\alpha]_D^{20°}\, lc$

$\alpha = (-92°)(0.5\text{ dm})(1\text{ g}/100\text{ mL})$

$\alpha = -0.46°$

6.31 $\text{enantiomeric excess} = \dfrac{\text{actual rotation}}{\text{rotation of pure enantiomer}} \times 100$

$[\alpha]_D^{20°}$ for pure (+) enantiomer = +13.90°, therefore $[\alpha]_D^{20°}$ for pure (−) enantiomer = −13.90°.

$\text{enantiomeric excess} = \dfrac{-3.5°}{-13.90°} \times 100 = 25\%$

The mixture contains a 25% enantiomeric excess of the levorotatory compound and is 100 − 25 or 75% racemic. The racemic portion of the mixture contains equal amounts (37.5%) of each enantiomer. Therefore the solution contains 37.5% of (+)-2-butanol and (37.5 + 25)% or 62.5% of (−)-2-butanol.

6.32

(R)-thalidomide

(S)-thalidomide

another representation of (R)-thalidomide

6.33

(2S, 3R)-4-dimethylamino-1,2-
diphenyl-3-methyl-2-butanol
medically useful form

(2R, 3S)-4-dimethylamino-1,2-
diphenyl-3-methyl-2-butanol

(2S, 3S)-4-dimethylamino-1,2-
diphenyl-3-methyl-2-butanol

(2R, 3R)-4-dimethylamino-1,2-
diphenyl-3-methyl-2-butanol

6.34

In *trans*-decalin, both of the methylene
groups on the ring junction are
equatorial in each case; more stable

In *cis*-decalin, one of the methylene
groups on the ring junction is
axial in each case; less stable

6.35

(a)

(b)

(R)-(Z)-2-methoxy-6-hexadecenoic acid

(c)

(S)-(Z)-2-methoxy-6-hexadecenoic acid

This is the enantiomer of the compound shown in (a). The *R*, *E* compound and the *S*, *E* compound would be
diastereomers of the compound shown in (a).

6.36   (a)   or

(b)   or

(c)

diequatorial conformer of *cis*-
1,3-dimethoxycyclohexane;
most stable conformer of the
four shown

diaxial conformer of *cis*-
1,3-dimethoxycyclohexane

both conformers of *trans*-1,3-dimethoxycyclohexane
have one axial and one equatorial methoxy group

6.37   (a)   Ph ≡

more stable conformer

chair conformations of Compound **A**

(b)   Compound **B** and Compound **C** are diastereomers.

(c)

(d)

the *S,S* stereoisomer, which is
a diastereomer of Compound **A**.
The *R,R* diastereomer, the enantiomer
of the compound above, is also a
stereoisomer of Compound **A**.

the enantiomer of Compound **A**

6.38

Supplemental Problems

S6.1   Pasteur isolated the stereoisomers of tartaric acid, and the compound was used to establish absolute configuration for the first time (Chapter 24). Tartaric acid has the formula

Its IUPAC name is 2,3-dihydroxybutanedioic acid. (+)-Tartaric acid is (2*R*, 3*R*)-2,3-dihydroxybutanedioic acid. Draw (+)-tartaric acid and any other possible stereoisomers for tartaric acid.

S6.2   (a)   In a stereoisomer of 2-isopropyl-5-methylcyclohexanol, the methyl group is cis to the hydroxyl group, and the isopropyl group is trans. Draw the two chair forms for the compound, and decide which conformer would be more stable.

   (b)   Draw the chair conformations of a stereoisomer of the compound described in part (a). There are several possible stereoisomers.

S6.3   Name the following compounds.

(a)

(b)

S6.4   Which of the following compounds have stereocenters? Draw three-dimensional pictures of any that does, showing any enantiomers and diastereomers.

(a) $CH_3CHCH_2CH_2Br$
       (with CH_3 above the second carbon)

(b) $CH_3CHCHCHCH_3$
       (with OH, OH, OH substituents)

S6.5   For each of the following pairs of structural formulas, tell whether the two represent identical molecular species, conformers of the same species, constitutional isomers, enantiomers, or diastereomers.

(a)

(b)

S6.6   Citronellol is a fragrant component of various plant oils, such as geranium oil and rose oil. A synthetic sample of (−)-citronellol with an enantiomeric excess of 88% has $[\alpha]_D^{20} = -4.1°$. What is the optical rotation of the pure enantiomer? (−)-Citronellol has the *S* configuration. The structure of citronellol is

$$CH_3C = CHCH_2CH_2CHCH_2CH_2OH$$

(with CH_3 groups on the indicated carbons)

Draw a stereochemically correct structural formula for (−)-citronellol.

S6.7   One method used to synthesize amino acids is a process known as reductive amination. This process, performed with 3-phenyl-2-oxopropanoic acid, results in a racemic mixture of the amino acid known as phenylalanine.

3-phenyl-2-oxopropanoic acid   racemic phenylalanine

Large quantities of stereochemically pure (S)-phenylalanine are required for the synthesis of the artificial sweetener, aspartame (NutraSweet). A Japanese firm is preparing (S)-phenylalanine by using an enzyme, phenylalanine dehydrogenase, from a bacterium, *Bacillus Sphaericus*, in the presence of a biological reducing agent, NADH.

3-phenyl-2-oxopropanoic acid   (S)-phenylalanine

(a) Draw a stereochemically unambiguous structural formula for (S)-phenylalanine.
(b) Is it possible to say whether the sign of optical rotation of the product of the reductive amination (H_2/catalyst) will be +, −, or 0?
(c) Is the product from the enzymatic reduction (NADH/enzyme) optically active? Can you tell what the sign of rotation of the product of this reaction will be?
(d) The structure of aspartame (not showing the stereochemistry of the phenylalanine unit) is drawn below. Find any other stereocenter(s) in the molecule, and assign configuration.

S6.8   Cyclic esters known as lactones are important components of natural products that have a wide range of antibiotic, antifungal, and antitumor activity. The biological activity of such compounds is dependent on their stereochemistry. Synthesis of such compounds must be designed in a way that gives the natural stereoisomer. One such synthesis starts with a racemic mixture of the methyllactone shown below and oxidizes its conjugate base with a chiral oxidizing agent. The major product of the oxidation is (2S, 3R)-(−)-2-hydroxy-3-methylpentanolide. The reactions are as shown.

racemic mixture of   conjugate base   2-hydroxy-3-
3-methylpentanolide   of 3-methylpentanolide   methylpentanolide

(a) What is the structure of the most stable conjugate base of 3-methylpentanolide? Use the pK_a table, and explore resonance contributors for each possible conjugate base before making your decision.
(b) How many stereoisomers are possible for 2-hydroxy-3-methylpentanolide? Draw structural formulas for all of them. Which one is the major product of the reaction?

S6.9   A number of recently found small peptides with the potential for being useful as medications all contain the unusual amino acid (3S, 4S)-4-amino-3-hydroxy-6-methylheptanoic acid (common name statine) or one of its analogs. How biologically active the peptides are depends mainly on which statine-like amino acid is found in the peptide. Heptanoic acid has seven carbon atoms in a chain with the first carbon atom being a carboxylic acid. What is the stereochemically correct structural formula of the amino acid statine?

S6.10   Cyclotheonamide A, isolated from marine sponges, is a potent inhibitor of thrombin, which plays an important role in the clotting of blood. The structure of cyclotheonamide A is shown below.

(a) How many stereocenters does cyclotheonamide A have?
(b) Does the compound contain any other source of stereoisomerism?
(c) Assign configuration to each source of stereoisomerism in the molecule.

S6.11   (a)   The following compound, Compound A, was synthesized in a study of carbohydrate chemistry. Identify each stereocenter in the compound and assign its configuration (*R* or *S*).

AcO— is shorthand for CH$_3$CO—

Compound **A**

(b)   Use the skeletal chair form given below to draw a structural formula for the most stable chair form of Compound **A.**

S6.12   A certain reaction produces the following two isomers, Compounds **B** and **C**, in almost equal amounts. The two isomers are observed to interconvert in an acidic solution to give an equilibrium mixture in which the major isomer is now 93% of the mixture.

Compound **B**   Compound **C**

S6.12 (cont)
  (a) Which is the major isomer at equilibrium and why?
  (b) Draw an energy diagram showing the relative positions of isomers **B** and **C**.

S6.13
(a) Draw an accurate three-dimensional representation for the other chair conformation of the molecule shown below.

CH_3— —H
HO CH_2Cl

(b) Is the equilibrium constant (K_{eq}) for this conformational change greater than, less than, or equal to 1? Why?
(c) When this molecule is treated with methyllithium, the following products are observed.

CH_3— —H $\xrightarrow{CH_3Li}$ CH_3— —H $+$ Li^+Cl^- $+$ CH_4
HO CH_2Cl O—CH_2

Use the curved arrow convention to draw out the mechanism of the Brønsted acid/base reaction that is proposed to be the first step, the structure of the deprotonated intermediate (the conjugate base), and the mechanism of its conversion to the observed product.

7

Nucleophilic Substitution and Elimination Reactions

Workbook Exercises

The structures in this text are comprised of single (σ), double ($\sigma + \pi$), and/or triple ($\sigma + 2\pi$) bonds. It is not surprising, then, that chemical reactions involve changes in σ and/or π bonding. In this chapter, you will be introduced to two important ways in which certain σ bonds can undergo changes. Many σ bonds to carbon are polar, or they are weak, meaning that they can be induced to break relatively easily. The ones shown below usually break heterolytically, in the same way that hydrogen chloride reacts with a base:

$$H_3N\colon \quad H - \ddot{C}l\colon \longrightarrow \quad H_3N - H \quad \colon \ddot{C}l\colon^-$$

base

TABLE 1   Examples of the direction of ionization of polar or weak σ bonds between carbon and elements of groups 15, 16, and 17 in the periodic table.

The carbon atoms shown in the table above are all losing a pair of electrons to the group, called the leaving group, that leaves when the bond breaks. In order to maintain or regain the closed shell configuration at these atoms, a new bond derived from an incoming electron pair is required. Two sources of such electron pairs are possible: (1) A nonbonding electron pair of some atom forms a new σ bond in a substitution reaction, and (2) the electrons from an adjacent C—H bond, which is deprotonated, give a new π bond in an elimination reaction.

For example, when trimethylamine is combined with 2-chloropentane, a mixture of products is observed:

2-chloropentane
(the C—Cl bond can break
to form a chloride ion)

trimethylamine
(the N atom electron pair can be used to
(1) form a new C—N bond or (2)
deprotonate a C—H adjacent to the C—Cl)

133

Workbook Exercises (cont)

the connectivity resulting from
substitution (because the carbon
atom attached to the nitrogen atom
is a stereocenter, stereoisomerism
is possible)

the connectivity resulting from **elimination**
(loss of the chloride ion as well as the proton from an adjacent
C—H to give a π bond. Sometimes stereoisomers are possible

EXERCISE I.   Predict the connectivities of the possible substitution and elimination product(s) derived from the following chemical reactions. Think about the possibility of the formation of stereoisomers, and show them when appropriate. Use Table 1 to help you decide which atoms or groups can be lost easily.

(a) [structure] + H_2O ⟶

(b) [cyclopentane structure] + $Na^+\ OH^-$ ⟶

(c) [structure] + $CH_3—C{\equiv}C^-\ Li^+$ ⟶

(d) [cyclopentane structure] + $Na^+\ ^-SCH_2CH_3$ ⟶

(e) [pyrrolidine structure] + [tosylate structure] ⟶

(f) $Na^+\ CN^-$ + [decalin structure] ⟶

Workbook Exercises (cont)
EXERCISE II.   Complete the following chemical equations based on the information provided. There may be more than one solution to each problem.

(a)   A + Na⁺ ⁻OCH₂CH₃ ⟶ [CH₃ / CH₃]C=C[H / H] + Na⁺ Cl⁻ + CH₃CH₂OH

(b)   [allyl]—SiCl₃ + 3 CH₃⁻ Li⁺ ⟶ B + 3 Li⁺ Cl⁻

(c)   C + CH₃CH₂CH₂I ⟶ CH₃—C(=O)—CH(CH₂CH₂CH₃)—C(=O)—OCH₃ + Na⁺ I⁻

(d)   Li⁺ ⁻SCH₃ + D ⟶ [cyclohexene ring with SCH₃] + Li⁺ ⁻O—S(=O)(=O)—⟨C₆H₄⟩—CH₃

([cyclohexadiene] + HSCH₃ + Li⁺ ⁻O—S(=O)(=O)—⟨C₆H₄⟩—CH₃)

(e)   CH₃O—C(=O)—C(CH₂Ph)(H)—⁺N≡N + E ⟶ CH₃O—C(=O)—C(CH₂Ph)(H)—⁺OH₂ + N≡N

+   F (a stereoisomer of the substitution product)   +   G and H (2 elimination products)

(f)   [bicyclic structure with CH₃, Br—O, H] + Na⁺ OH⁻ ⟶ I + H₂O + Na⁺ Br⁻

(Hint: This is an elimination reaction in which bromide ion is the leaving group.)

- -

7.1   (a)   CH₃CHCH₂CH₂—Ï: ⟶ CH₃CHCH₂CH₂——ÖPh   Ph— ≡ ⟨C₆H₅⟩—
                   |CH₃ |CH₃

                   Na⁺   ⁻:ÖPh   Na⁺   :Ï:⁻

(b)   [piperidine N—H with CH₃—Ï:] ⟶ [piperidinium H—N⁺—CH₃   :Ï:⁻]

first product;
acid with pKₐ ~ 10

7.1 (b) (cont)

is a base that has a conjugate acid with pK_a ~ 10. In the presence of excess base, the following

equilibrium will be established.

| base | acid | conjugate acid | conjugate base |
| in large excess | pK_a ~ 10 | pK_a ~ 10 | |

Because the two acids have roughly the same acidity, the relative amounts of the different species at equilibrium will be determined by the relative concentrations of the different reagents. Because there is a large excess of the amine used as a starting material in the reaction, the proton will spend most of its time with that amine and the product amine will be mostly in the unprotonated form.

(c) $CH_3CH_2CH_2$—$\overset{..}{\underset{..}{Br}}$: ⟶ $CH_3CH_2CH_2$—$\overset{..}{S}$—CH_3

         Na^+ $^-$: $\overset{..}{S}$—CH_3 Na^+ : $\overset{..}{\underset{..}{Br}}$: $^-$

7.2   The answers to part (b) analyze the problem as shown in the Problem-Solving Skills section of the chapter. The rest of the problems show only the equations, written so as to emphasize the necessity of reasoning backwards from the structure of the desired product to the structure of the starting material.

(a) $CH_3\underset{\underset{SCH_2CH_3}{|}}{CH}CH_3$ $\xleftarrow{\text{CH}_3\text{CH}_2\text{S}^-\ \text{Na}^+}$ $CH_3\underset{\underset{Br}{|}}{CH}CH_3$ $\xleftarrow{\text{HBr}}$ $CH_3CH=CH_2$

(b) $CH_3CH_2CH_2CH_2CH_2Br$ ⟶ $CH_3CH_2CH_2CH_2CH_2CH(\overset{\overset{O}{||}}{C}OCH_2CH_3)_2$

1.   What are the connectivities of the two compounds? How many carbon atoms does each contain? Are there any rings? What are the positions of branches and functional groups on the chains?
     The starting material has five carbon atoms in a row bonded to a bromine atom. In the product the bromine has been replaced by a carbon atom bearing two ester groups.
2.   How do the functional groups change in going from starting material to product? Does the starting material have a good leaving group?
     The bromine atom in the starting material is a good leaving group. The alkyl halide function in the starting material has been converted to an extra carbon with two ester functions on it.
3.   Is it possible to dissect the structures of the starting material and product to see which bonds must have been broken and which formed?

     $CH_3CH_2CH_2CH_2CH_2$—ξ—Br $CH_3CH_2CH_2CH_2CH_2$—ξ—$CH(\overset{\overset{O}{||}}{C}OCH_2CH_3)_2$

              bond broken   bond formed

7.2 (b) (cont)

4. New bonds are created when an electrophile reacts with a nucleophile. Do we recognize any part of the product molecule as coming from a good nucleophile or an electrophilic addition?

    Because the bromine atom is a good leaving group, and the carbon to which it is bonded is an electrophile, we suppose that the new fragment that bonds to it is a nucleophile. The pieces we need are:

$$CH_3CH_2CH_2CH_2\overset{\delta+}{C}H_2 \overset{\delta-}{\underline{\quad\quad}} Br \quad \text{and} \quad {}^-\!:\!CH(\overset{\overset{O}{\|}}{C}OCH_2CH_3)_2$$

electrophilic carbon   nucleophilic carbon

    We find the nucleophile in Table 7.1.

5. What type of compound would be a good precursor to the product?

    Displacement of the bromide ion by an incoming nucleophilic carbon atom will give us the product we want. We need a nucleophile with the structure shown above.

6. After this step, do we see how to get from starting material to product? If not, do we need to analyze the structure obtained in step 5 by applying questions 4 and 5 to it?

    We can now complete the synthesis.

$$CH_3CH_2CH_2CH_2CH_2CH(\overset{\overset{O}{\|}}{C}OCH_2CH_3)_2 \xleftarrow{\quad Na^+\, {}^-\!:\!CH(\overset{\overset{O}{\|}}{C}OCH_2CH_3)_2 \quad} CH_3CH_2CH_2CH_2CH_2Br$$

(c)

7.3   The initial rate of the reaction will be

rate = $k\,[CH_3CH_2Br]\,[OH^-]$

rate = $(1.7 \times 10^{-3}\ L/mol\cdot s)(0.05\ mol/L)(0.07\ mol/L)$

rate = $6 \times 10^{-6}\ mol/L\cdot s$

If the concentration of bromoethane is doubled (increased from 0.05 mol/L to 0.1 mol/L), the rate will double. The new rate would be ~ $1 \times 10^{-5}\ mol/L\cdot s$.

7.4   For the reaction

$$CH_3CH_2CH_2CH_2Br \ + \ K^+I^- \xrightarrow[\text{acetone}]{} \ CH_3CH_2CH_2CH_2I \ + \ K^+Br^-\!\downarrow$$

The rate at which *n*-butyl bromide is used up is:

rate = $k\,[CH_3CH_2CH_2CH_2Br]\,[I^-]$

rate = $(1.09 \times 10^{-1}\ L/mol\cdot min)(0.06\ mol/L)(0.02\ mol/L)$

rate = $1.3 \times 10^{-4}\ mol/L\cdot min$

7.5   For the reaction

rate = $k\,[\textit{tert}\text{-butyl chloride}]$

rate = $(0.145/h)(0.0824\ mol/L)$

rate = $1.19 \times 10^{-2}\ mol/L\cdot h$

7.5 (cont)

The units in which this rate is expressed are mol/L·h. The rate constant will remain the same, but the rate of the reaction will decrease as the *tert*-butyl chloride is used up in the reaction. When half of the *tert*-butyl chloride is gone, the rate of the reaction will be half of what it was initially or 5.95×10^{-3} mol/L·h.

7.6   The following species can act as bases (electron donors).

$$CH_3CH_2 - \overset{..}{\underset{..}{O}} - H \qquad CH_3\overset{\overset{CH_3}{|}}{\underset{\underset{CH_3}{|}}{C}} - \overset{..}{\underset{..}{O}} - CH_2CH_3 \qquad CH_3\overset{\overset{CH_3}{|}}{\underset{\underset{CH_3}{|}}{C}} - \overset{..}{\underset{..}{O}} - H$$

$$CH_3\overset{\overset{CH_3}{|}}{C} = CH_2 \qquad :\overset{..}{\underset{..}{Cl}}:^- \qquad H_2\overset{..}{\underset{..}{O}} \qquad {}^-:\overset{..}{\underset{..}{O}}H$$

7.7   (S)-(+)-2-Bromobutane will racemize by undergoing reversible bimolecular nucleophilic substitution reactions with inversion of configuration. The optical rotation will gradually decrease to 0° as the system reaches equilibrium.

Concept Map 7.1   A typical S_N2 reaction.

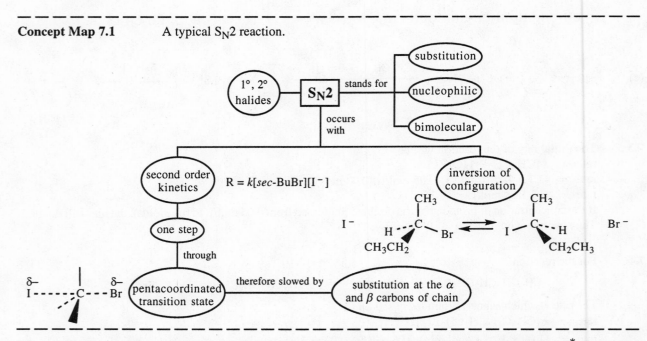

7.8   The fact that the rate of racemization is twice the rate of substitution of the radioactive iodine, I*, shows that every substitution occurs with inversion of configuration.

$$I - \overset{\overset{CH_3}{|}}{\underset{\underset{C_6H_{13}}{}}{C}} \cdots H \quad \overset{*}{I}{}^- \longrightarrow H \cdots \overset{\overset{CH_3}{|}}{\underset{\underset{C_6H_{13}}{}}{C}} \cdots \overset{*}{I} \quad I^-$$

(S)-(+)-2-iodooctane   (R)-(−)-2-iodooctane
                                                        inversion of configuration

Each S_N2 reaction incorporates *one* radioactive iodine atom into 2-iodooctane, but results in the loss of optical activity equal to that of two molecules of (S)-(+)-2-iodooctane: the one that had been converted to the (R)-isomer, and the other, the optical activity of which is cancelled by the presence of the (R)-isomer. Therefore the rate of racemization, the rate at which optical activity is lost, is *twice* the rate of the substitution reaction.

Concept Map 7.2   The S_N1 reaction.

- -

7.9

7.10 S_N1 mechanism

7.10 (cont)

S_N2 mechanism

7.11   (a)   [benzene]—S⁻ > [benzene]—O⁻

(Sulfur is more polarizable than oxygen.)

(b) OH^- > $\overset{\overset{\textstyle O}{\|}}{CH_3CO^-}$

(The hydroxide ion is more basic than the acetate ion. See Problem 7.12.)

(c) OH^- > NO_3^-

(The hydroxide ion is more basic than the nitrate ion. See Problem 7.12.)

7.12

Hydroxide ion is more basic than acetate ion. The pK_a of water, the conjugate acid of hydroxide ion, is 15.7. The pK_a of acetic acid, the conjugate acid of acetate ion, is 4.8. The greater basicity of the oxygen atom in hydroxide ion means that its electrons are more loosely held than those in acetate ion. Bonding between hydroxide ion and the carbon atom in methyl bromide starts more easily, and it requires less energy to get to the transition state.

7.13   The increase in the relative rates of the substitution reaction in this series of solvents is related to the decreasing ability of the solvent to hydrogen bond to the nucleophile, chloride ion, and to the steric hindrance of the positive end of the dipole of the carbonyl group.

CH_3OH $\overset{\overset{\textstyle O}{\|}}{HCNH_2}$ $\overset{\overset{\textstyle O}{\|}}{HCN(CH_3)_2}$ $\overset{\overset{\textstyle O}{\|}}{CH_3CN(CH_3)_2}$
methanol   formamide   *N,N*-dimethylformamide   *N,N*-dimethylacetamide

Methanol hydrogen bonds strongly and reduces the nucleophilicity of the chloride anion. Formamide has N—H bonds, so it also hydrogen bonds with chloride anion, but not as strongly as methanol does. Neither *N,N*-dimethylformamide nor *N,N*-dimethylacetamide can hydrogen bond at all, therefore the nucleophile behaves as a strong nucleophile in both solvents. The methyl substituent on the carbonyl group of *N,N*-dimethylacetamide prevents the chloride anion from getting as close to the positive end of the dipole as it can in *N,N*-dimethylformamide, making the chloride anion an even stronger nucleophile.

Concept Map 7.3   The factors that are important in determining nucleophilicity.

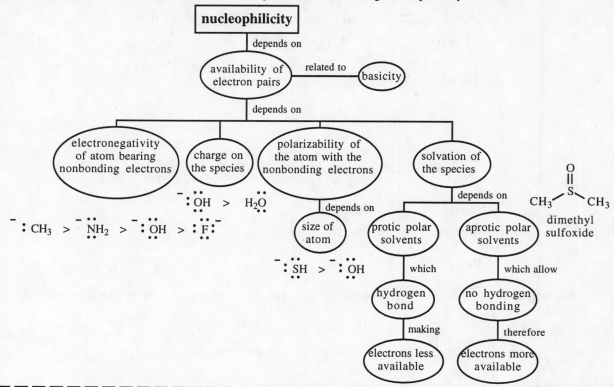

- -

7.14   **(a)** $H_2N-\overset{..}{\underset{..}{O}}H \xrightarrow{\text{H}\overset{..}{\underset{..}{Cl}}:} H_3\overset{+}{N}-\overset{..}{\underset{..}{O}}H \quad :\overset{..}{\underset{..}{Cl}}:^{-}$

$H_2N-\overset{..}{\underset{..}{O}}H \xrightarrow{CH_3\overset{..}{\underset{..}{I}}:} CH_3\overset{\overset{\displaystyle H}{|}}{\underset{\underset{\displaystyle H}{|}}{\overset{+}{N}}}-\overset{..}{\underset{..}{O}}H \quad :\overset{..}{\underset{..}{I}}:^{-}$

(b)   The pK_as of the oxonium ions are all less than zero while the pK_as of the ammonium ions are all between 4 and 11. The pK_a of the conjugate acid of hydroxylamine falls in the range of values for the ammonium ion.

$$pK_a \qquad \overset{+}{N}H_4 \qquad 9.4$$
$$pK_a \qquad H_3\overset{+}{N}OH \qquad 5.97$$

The presence of an electron-withdrawing oxygen atom on the nitrogen atom makes the nonbonding electrons on nitrogen less available. Hydroxylamine is therefore a weaker base than ammonia, and the conjugate acid of hydroxylamine is a stronger acid than ammonium ion.

7.15   The hydronium ion comes from protonation of the solvent, water, by the acid, HBr, that was added to the reaction mixture.

$$H_2O \quad + \quad HBr \quad \longrightarrow \quad H_3\overset{+}{O} \quad + \quad Br^{-}$$

7.16   The other nucleophiles that are present are the starting alcohol and water.
Two additional substitution reactions are possible. The carbocation can react with water to regenerate the starting alcohol or with another alcohol molecule to produce an ether.

7.16 (cont)

Nucleophiles are also bases and can remove a proton from the carbocation to give an alkene, the elimination product.

7.17 CH_3NH_2 + $CH_3CH_2CH_2CH_2O\overset{+}{-}H$ $\overset{H}{}$ $\rightleftharpoons$ $CH_3\overset{+}{N}H_3$ + $CH_3CH_2CH_2CH_2O-H$

      base   acid   acid   conjugate base

                           $pK_a \sim -2.4$ pK_a 10.6

7.18   All of the nucleophiles in Table 7.1 are too strongly basic to be used with oxonium ions formed by protonating an alcohol.

nucleophile	conjugate acid of nucleophile	pK_a of conjugate acid
HO^-	H_2O	15.7
RO^-	ROH	~16
ArO^-	$ArOH$	~10
HS^-	H_2S	~10
RS^-	RSH	~10.5
ArS^-	$ArSH$	~7.8
NH_3	NH_4^+	9.4
RNH_2	RNH_3^+	~10.6
N_3^-	HN_3	4.7
CN^-	HCN	9.1
$RC\equiv C^-$	$RC\equiv CH$	~26
$(CH_3CH_2O\overset{O}{\overset{\|}{C}})_2CH^-$	$(CH_3CH_2O\overset{O}{\overset{\|}{C}})_2CH_2$	~11

7.19

CH$_3$CH$_2$—O—H   *protonation of ethanol*   H—OSO$_3$H   →   CH$_3$CH$_2$—O$^+$—H $^-$:OSO$_3$H
   **ethyloxonium ion with
   a good leaving group**

CH$_3$CH$_2$—O$^+$—H   →   CH$_3$CH$_2$—O$^+$—CH$_2$CH$_3$:O—H
CH$_3$CH$_2$—O—H
*nucleophile displacing
leaving group*   **diethyloxonium ion**

:O—H   CH$_3$CH$_2$—O$^+$—CH$_2$CH$_3$ ⇌   CH$_3$CH$_2$—O—CH$_2$CH$_3$ H—O$^+$—H
*deprotonation of the
diethyloxonium ion*

7.20   CH$_3$CH$_2$—O—CH$_2$CH$_3$ H—I: →   CH$_3$CH$_2$—O$^+$—CH$_2$CH$_3$ →   CH$_3$CH$_2$—O—H   H—I:
*protonation of
diethyl ether*   :I:$^-$
                        *nucleophile displacing
                        good leaving group*

:I—CH$_2$CH$_3$
protonation of ethanol

CH$_3$CH$_2$—I: :O—H   ←   CH$_3$CH$_2$—O$^+$—H
:I:$^-$
*nucleophile displacing
good leaving group*

7.21   CH$_3$C≡C—C(H)(OH)—CH$_2$OH   TsCl
(1.2 equiv)
pyridine
dichloromethane
→   *primary carbon;
less hindered OH group;
reaction with TsCl favored* →   CH$_2$OTs
CH$_3$—C≡C—C(H)(OH)

*secondary carbon;
OH group more hindered
therefore slower to react with TsCl*

Concept Map 7.4   The factors that determine whether a substituent is a good leaving group.

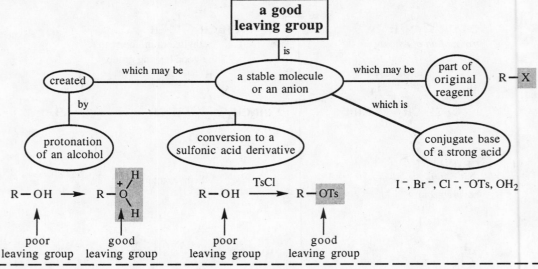

7.22

MsCl / pyridine → A → Na⁺ CN⁻ / dimethyl sulfoxide → B

7.23 (1) S_N2

(2) S_N1 slow

S_N1 fast

Note that attack of a nucleophile on the electrophilic carbocation can occur at either the front face (where the leaving group was attached) or at the back face. The next equation shows attack of a nucleophile at the back face.

S_N1 fast

E1 fast

7.23 (3)

7.24 Yes

(Z)-2-butene

The transition state for the formation of (E)-2-butene is less crowded, more favorable, and lower in energy than the transition state for the formation of (Z)-2-butene where the two methyl groups are close together.

7.25

(a) $CH_3CH_2CH_2CH_2CH_2Br \xrightarrow[\Delta]{\text{KOH} \atop \text{ethanol}} CH_3CH_2CH_2CH{=}CH_2 + H_2O + K^+Br^-$

(b)

$CH_3CHCH_2CH_2CH_3 \xrightarrow[\Delta]{\text{KOH} \atop \text{ethanol}} CH_3C{=}CHCH_2CH_3 + CH_3CHCH{=}CHCH_3 + H_2O + K^+Br^-$

major   minor

(c)

major   minor   very minor

(d)

found experimentally

7.26

(1R,2S)-1,2-dibromodi-phenylethane

(E)-1-bromo-1,2-diphenylethene

7.26 (cont)

(1R,2R)-1,2-dibromodiphenylethane

(Z)-1-bromo-1,2-diphenylethene

Concept Map 7.5   A comparison of E1 and E2 reactions.

Concept Map 7.6   (see p. 150)

7.27

(a) $CH_3CH_2CH_2CH_2Br \xrightarrow[\substack{\text{ethanol} \\ \Delta}]{\text{KOH}} CH_3CH_2CH=CH_2 + CH_3CH_2CH_2CH_2OH + H_2O + K^+Br^-$

major product with strong base at high temperature

(b) $CH_3CH_2CH_2CH_2Br \xrightarrow[\substack{50\% \text{ aqueous} \\ \text{ethanol}}]{\text{0.1 M NaOH}} CH_3CH_2CH_2CH_2OH + Na^+Br^-$

(c) $CH_3CH_2CH_2CH_2Br \xrightarrow{NH_3} CH_3CH_2CH_2CH_2\overset{+}{N}H_3 \; Br^- \xrightarrow{NH_3 \text{ (excess)}} CH_3CH_2CH_2CH_2NH_2 + NH_4^+ Br^-$

(d) $CH_3CH_2CH_2CH_2Br \xrightarrow{Na^+ N_3^-} CH_3CH_2CH_2CH_2N_3 + Na^+ Br^-$

(e) $CH_3CH_2CH_2CH_2Br \xrightarrow{Na^+ CN^-} CH_3CH_2CH_2CH_2CN + Na^+ Br^-$

7.27

(f) $CH_3CH_2CH_2CH_2Br \xrightarrow{CH_3CH_2S^- Na^+} CH_3CH_2CH_2CH_2SCH_2CH_3 + Na^+ Br^-$

(g) $CH_3CH_2CH_2CH_2Br \xrightarrow{CH_3\overset{O}{\overset{\|}{C}}O^- Na^+} CH_3CH_2CH_2CH_2O\overset{O}{\overset{\|}{C}}CH_3 + Na^+ Br^-$

(h) $CH_3CH_2CH_2CH_2Br \xrightarrow{CH_3CH_2C\equiv C^- Na^+} CH_3CH_2CH_2CH_2C\equiv CCH_2CH_3 + Na^+ Br^-$

(i) $CH_3CH_2CH_2CH_2Br \xrightarrow{Na^+ {}^-CH(\overset{O}{\overset{\|}{C}}OCH_2CH_3)_2} CH_3CH_2CH_2CH_2CH(\overset{O}{\overset{\|}{C}}OCH_2CH_3)_2 + Na^+ Br^-$

7.28

(a)
leaving group

$\bigcirc\!\!-CH_2CH_2CH_2OTs + Na^+ N_3^- \longrightarrow \bigcirc\!\!-CH_2CH_2CH_2N_3 + TsO^- Na^+$

nucleophile

(b)
leaving group   nucleophile

$PhCH_2CH_2Cl + Na^+ CN^- \longrightarrow PhCH_2CH_2CN + NaCl$

$^-:C\equiv N: \longleftrightarrow :C=\ddot{N}:^-$

more nucleophilic

(c)
leaving group   nucleophile

$CH_3CH_2CH_2CH_2Br + CH_3CH_2S^- Na^+ \longrightarrow CH_3CH_2CH_2CH_2SCH_2CH_3 + NaBr$

(d)
leaving group   nucleophile

$CH_3CH_2CH_2Cl + CH_3C\equiv C^- Na^+ \longrightarrow CH_3C\equiv CCH_2CH_2CH_3 + NaCl$

(e)
   CH_3 leaving group   nucleophile

$CH_3CHCH_2CH_2Br + NH_3$ (excess) $\longrightarrow$ $\overset{CH_3}{\underset{}{CH_3CHCH_2CH_2NH_2}} + NH_4Br$

(f)
$CH_3I + Na^+ {}^-CH(\overset{O}{\overset{\|}{C}}OCH_2CH_3)_2 \longrightarrow CH_3CH(\overset{O}{\overset{\|}{C}}OCH_2CH_3)_2 + NaI$

leaving group   nucleophile

7.29 (a) $SH^- > Cl^-$ (b) $(CH_3)_3P > (CH_3)_3B$
                                     (The boron atom has an empty orbital and is an electrophile;
                                     the phosphorus atom has nonbonding electrons.)

(c) $CH_3NH^- > CH_3NH_2$ (d) $CH_3SCH_3 > CH_3OCH_3$

7.30 (a) $\underset{\overset{|}{Br}}{PhCHCH_2CH_3} \xrightarrow[\Delta]{\underset{ethanol}{KOH}}$

$\underset{H}{\overset{Ph}{C}}=\underset{CH_3}{\overset{H}{C}}$ + $\underset{H}{\overset{Ph}{C}}=\underset{H}{\overset{CH_3}{C}}$

major   minor

7.30 (b) $CH_3CH_2\overset{\overset{\displaystyle CH_3}{|}}{\underset{\underset{\displaystyle Br}{|}}{C}}CH_2CH_2CH_3$ $\xrightarrow[\substack{\text{ethanol} \\ \Delta}]{\text{KOH}}$

$\underset{H}{\overset{CH_3}{C}}=\underset{CH_2CH_2CH_3}{\overset{CH_3}{C}}$ + $\underset{CH_3CH_2}{\overset{CH_3}{C}}=\underset{H}{\overset{CH_2CH_3}{C}}$

major

+ $\underset{H}{\overset{CH_3}{C}}=\underset{CH_3}{\overset{CH_2CH_2CH_3}{C}}$ + $\underset{CH_3CH_2}{\overset{CH_3}{C}}=\underset{CH_2CH_3}{\overset{H}{C}}$ + $CH_2=\underset{CH_2CH_3}{\overset{CH_2CH_2CH_3}{C}}$

minor

(c) [cyclohexane ring with CH₃ and Br] $\xrightarrow[\substack{\text{ethanol} \\ \Delta}]{\text{KOH}}$ [cyclohexene with CH₃] + [cyclohexane with =CH₂]

major   minor

(d) $CH_3CH_2CH_2\overset{\overset{\displaystyle O \\ \displaystyle \|}{}}{\underset{\underset{\displaystyle Br}{|}}{CH}}COH$ $\xrightarrow[\substack{\text{ethanol} \\ \Delta}]{\text{KOH}}$ $\underset{H}{\overset{CH_3CH_2}{C}}=\underset{\overset{\displaystyle CO^-K^+}{\|}}{\overset{H}{C}}$ + $\underset{H}{\overset{CH_3CH_2}{C}}=\underset{H}{\overset{\overset{\displaystyle O \\ \displaystyle \|}{CO^-K^+}}{C}}$

major O   minor

7.31 (a) $CH_3\underset{\underset{\displaystyle OH}{|}}{CH}CH_3$ $\xrightarrow[\text{pyridine}]{\text{TsCl}}$ $CH_3\underset{\underset{\displaystyle OTs}{|}}{CH}CH_3$ $\xrightarrow{\text{NaN}_3}$ $CH_3\underset{\underset{\displaystyle N_3}{|}}{CH}CH_3$
                                                                        A   B

(b) $CH_3\overset{\overset{\displaystyle CH_3}{|}}{CH}CH_2CH_2CH_2CH_2Br$ $\xrightarrow[\text{ethanol}]{\text{NaCN}}$ $CH_3\overset{\overset{\displaystyle CH_3}{|}}{CH}CH_2CH_2CH_2CH_2CN$
                                                                                                    C

(c) [cyclopentane-Br] $\xrightarrow[\substack{\text{ethanol} \\ \Delta}]{\text{KOH}}$ [cyclopentene]
                                                        D

(d) $CH_3CH_2CH_2C\overset{\overset{\displaystyle CH_3}{|}}{=}CHCH_2CH_2OH$ $\xrightarrow[\text{pyridine}]{\text{TsCl}}$

$CH_3CH_2CH_2C\overset{\overset{\displaystyle CH_3}{|}}{=}CHCH_2CH_2OTs$ $\xrightarrow[\text{acetone}]{\text{NaI}}$ $CH_3CH_2CH_2C\overset{\overset{\displaystyle CH_3}{|}}{=}CHCH_2CH_2I$
                        E   F

(e) [cyclohexane with H, H, CH₂CH₃, Cl substituents] $\xrightarrow[\substack{\text{ethanol} \\ \Delta}]{\text{KOH}}$ [cyclohexene with CH₂CH₃] $\xrightarrow{\text{HI}}$ [cyclohexane with CH₂CH₃, I, H]

major product
G

+

[cyclohexene with CH₂CH₃]

minor product

7.31 (f)

$$NCCH_2 \quad CH_2CH_2OH \xrightarrow[\text{pyridine}]{TsCl} NCCH_2 \quad CH_2CH_2OTs \xrightarrow[\substack{N,N\text{-dimethyl-}\\ \text{formamide}}]{NaCN} NCCH_2 \quad CH_2CH_2CN$$

I

J

7.32 (a)

$$\underset{CH_3}{\overset{CH_2CH_2CH_2OCH_3}{\underset{H}{\overset{|}{C}}}} \text{—Br} \xrightarrow[\text{ethanol}]{CH_3SNa} CH_3S \text{—} \underset{CH_3}{\overset{CH_2CH_2CH_2OCH_3}{\underset{}{\overset{|}{C}}}} \text{—H} \quad + \quad NaBr$$

A

(b)

$$\xrightarrow{NaN_3}$$

B   + NaOTs

(c)

$$\xrightarrow[\substack{\text{dimethyl}\\ \text{sulfoxide}\\ \Delta}]{CH_3\overset{CH_3}{\underset{CH_3}{\overset{|}{C}}}\text{—}O^-K^+}$$

C   + KI + $CH_3\overset{CH_3}{\underset{CH_3}{\overset{|}{C}}}$—OH

(d)

$$\xrightarrow[\substack{\text{dimethyl}\\ \text{sulfoxide}}]{NaI}$$

D   + NaOTs

(e)

$$\xrightarrow[\text{pyridine}]{TsCl} E \xrightarrow[\text{acetone}]{NaI} F$$

(f)

$$\xrightarrow[\text{pyridine}]{MsCl} G \xrightarrow{LiCl} H$$

7.33

(a) The reaction of the 1° alkyl halide, $CH_3CH_2CH_2Br$, will be faster than that of the 2° alkyl halide, $CH_3CHBrCH_3$. There is greater steric crowding in the transition state for the S_N2 reaction of the 2° alkyl halide with the good nucleophile, CN^-.

(b) The S_N2 reaction of the more nucleophilic CH_3S^- ion will be faster than that of the CH_3O^- ion.

(c) The *tert*-butyl bromide reacts faster in the S_N1 solvolysis reaction than *n*-butyl bromide because a 3° carbocation intermediate is much more stable than a 1° carbocation intermediate. We know that this is an S_N1 reaction because there is a good ionizing solvent (H_2O) and no strong nucleophile present.

(d) These reactions are electrophilic addition reactions, and go through carbocation intermediates. The second reaction, which gives a 3° carbocation intermediate, goes faster than the first reaction, which gives a 2° carbocation intermediate.

Concept Map 7.6   Overall view of nucleophilic substitution and elimination reactions

7.34

$Ph— \equiv$ (phenyl ring)

1.   What are the connectivities of the two compounds? How many carbon atoms does each contain? Are there any rings? What are the positions of branches and functional groups on the carbon skeletons?

There is one more carbon atom in the product. It has been added to carbon 1 of the starting material and is part of the cyano group. The starting material has two hydroxyl groups. One hydroxyl group is on a primary carbon atom and the other is on a tertiary carbon atom. The product contains a cyano group on the primary carbon atom and a hydroxyl group on the tertiary carbon atom.

2.   How do the functional groups change in going from starting material to product? Does the starting material have a good leaving group?

The primary hydroxyl group has been replaced by a cyano group. There is no good leaving group in the starting material but a hydroxyl group can be converted into one.

3.   Is it possible to dissect the structures of the starting material and product to see which bonds must be broken and which formed?

4.   New bonds are created when an electrophile reacts with a nucleophile. Do we recognize any part of the product molecule as coming from a good nucleophile or an electrophilic addition?

The cyano group, —CN, comes from CN⁻, a good nucleophile.

5.   What type of compound would be a good precursor to the product?

Something with a good leaving group where the hydroxyl group is, such as water, a halide, or a tosylate group, would be a good precursor. We cannot use strong acid to convert the hydroxyl group into a better leaving group because the cyanide anion is a better base than the alcohol and would deprotonate the oxonium ion.

6.   After this last step, do we see how to get from starting material to product? If not, we need to analyze the structure obtained in step 5 by applying questions 4 and 5 to it.

The precursor containing the tosylate group can easily be made from the starting material and tosyl chloride. A primary alcohol will react faster with tosyl chloride than a tertiary alcohol (see Problem 7.21). We can now complete the problem.

Complete correct answer:

7.35 The answers to parts (a), (c), and (d) analyze the problems as shown in the Problem-Solving Skills section of the chapter. The rest of the problems show only the equations, written so as to emphasize the necessity of reasoning backward from the structure of the desired product to the structure of the starting material. Ph is used to represent the benzene ring.

(a) $PhCH_2SCH_2CH_3$ $\xleftarrow{\text{?}}$ $PhCH_2OH$

1. What are the connectivities of the two compounds? How many carbon atoms does each contain? Are there any rings? What are the positions of branches and functional groups on the carbon skeletons?

    The product has two more carbon atoms than the starting material. These carbon atoms are on the sulfur atom. The thioether group in the product is on the same carbon atom to which the hydroxyl group was attached in the starting material.

2. How do the functional groups change in going from starting material to product? Does the starting material have a good leaving group?

    The hydroxyl group has been replaced by a thioether. The hydroxyl group is not a good leaving group but can be converted into one.

3. Is it possible to dissect the structures of the starting material and product to see which bonds must be broken and which formed?

$$PhCH_2-\overset{\displaystyle\frown}{\underset{\displaystyle\smile}{C}}-OH \xrightarrow{\text{?}} PhCH_2-\overset{\displaystyle\frown}{\underset{\displaystyle\smile}{C}}-SCH_2CH_3$$

                              bond broken   bond formed

4. New bonds are created when an electrophile reacts with a nucleophile. Do we recognize any part of the product molecule as coming from a good nucleophile or an electrophilic addition?

    The ethanethiolate anion, $CH_3CH_2S^-$, is a good nucleophile.

5. What type of compound would be a good precursor to the product?

    The displacement of a leaving group (halide or tosylate ion) by the nucleophile will give us the product we want.

$$PhCH_2-\boxed{X} \quad \text{or} \quad PhCH_2-\boxed{OTs}$$

6. After this last step, do we see how to get from starting material to product? If not, we need to analyze the structure obtained in step 5 by applying questions 4 and 5 to it.

    We now can complete the synthesis.

$$PhCH_2SCH_2CH_3 \xleftarrow{\;CH_3CH_2S^-\,Na^+\;} PhCH_2Br \xleftarrow[H_2O]{\;HBr\;} PhCH_2OH$$

The compound could also have been synthesized using an S_N1 reaction with ethanethiol in an ionizing solvent such as water, but the product of the reaction with the solvent would also form. When possible, it is better to use the S_N2 reaction for synthesis, instead of an S_N1 reaction, because there will be fewer competing side reactions to lower the yield of the desired product.

(b) $CH_3CH_2CH_2CH_2CH_2I \xleftarrow[\text{acetone}]{\;NaI\;} CH_3CH_2CH_2CH_2CH_2OTs \xleftarrow[\text{pyridine}]{\;TsCl\;} CH_3CH_2CH_2CH_2CH_2OH$

(c)

$$\underset{CH_3CH_2}{\overset{\displaystyle CH_3}{H\text{-}\text{-}\text{-}\underset{\displaystyle |}{C}\diagdown NH_2}} \xleftarrow{\text{?}} \underset{CH_2CH_3}{\overset{\displaystyle CH_3}{HO\text{-}\underset{\displaystyle |}{C}\text{-}\text{-}\text{-}H}}$$

1. What are the connectivities of the two compounds? How many carbon atoms does each contain? Are there any rings? What are the positions of branches and functional groups on the carbon skeletons?

    The carbon skeletons of the two compounds are the same. The compounds have opposite stereochemistry.

7.35 (c) (cont)

2. How do the functional groups change in going from starting material to product? Does the starting material have a good leaving group?

    A hydroxyl group has been replaced by an amino group. The hydroxyl group is not a good leaving group but can be converted into one.

3. Is it possible to dissect the structures of the starting material and product to see which bonds must be broken and which formed?

bond broken   bond formed

4. New bonds are created when an electrophile reacts with a nucleophile. Do we recognize any part of the product molecule as coming from a good nucleophile or an electrophilic addition?

    The amino group comes from ammonia, NH_3, a good nucleophile.

5. What type of compound would be a good precursor to the product?

    Displacement of a leaving group (halide or tosylate ion) by the nucleophile, NH_3, will give the product we want.

    This compound must have the same stereochemistry as the alcohol, so that an S_N2 reaction with ammonia gives the amine with the inverted configuration.

6. After this last step, do we see how to get from starting material to product? If not, we need to analyze the structure obtained in step 5 by applying questions 4 and 5 to it.

    We know how to convert a hydroxyl group into a leaving group with retention of configuration. We can now finish the synthesis.

(d) $PhCH_2CH_2CHCH_3$ $\xleftarrow{\ ?\ }$ $PhCH_2CH_2CH{=}CH_2$
                      |
                      N_3

1. What are the connectivities of the two compounds? How many carbon atoms does each contain? Are there any rings? What are the positions of branches and functional groups on the carbon skeleton?

    The carbon skeletons are identical in starting material and products. The azide functional group in the product is on the second carbon atom of the chain, carbon two of the double bond in the starting material.

2. How do the functional groups change in going from the starting material to the product? Does the starting material have a good leaving group?

    The double bond has disappeared. The product is an azide. There is no good leaving group in the starting material.

3. Is it possible to dissect the structure to see which bonds must be broken and which formed?

7.35 (d) (cont) $PhCH_2CH_2CH \overset{\mathclap{\zeta}}{=\!\!=} CH_2$

bond broken

$PhCH_2CH_2\overset{H}{\underset{N_3}{C}}HCH_2$

bonds formed

4. New bonds are created when an electrophile reacts with a nucleophile. Do we recognize any part of the product molecule as coming from a good nucleophile or an electrophilic addition?

The azide group, —N_3, comes from N_3^-, a good nucleophile.

5. What type of compound would be a good precursor to the product?

We need a compound that has a good leaving group where the azide group is in the product. Displacement of a leaving group (halide or tosylate ion) by the azide nucleophile will give us the product we want.

$$PhCH_2CH_2CHCH_3$$
$$\boxed{X}$$

6. After this last step, do we see how to get from starting material to product? If not, we need to analyze the structure obtained in step 5 by applying questions 4 and 5 to it.

Since the starting material does not have a leaving group, we need to repeat steps 4 and 5.

4. (again) New bonds are created when an electrophile reacts with a nucleophile. Do we recognize any part of the product molecule as coming from a good nucleophile or an electrophilic addition?

A good leaving group such as a halide can come from an electrophilic addition of a hydrogen halide to the double bond.

5. (again) What type of compound would be a good precursor to the product?

The electrophilic addition of a hydrogen halide such as hydrogen bromide to the double bond will give us the intermediate we need. We can now complete the problem.

7.36 (a) Rate = $k\,[CH_3CH_2CH_2CH_2Br]\,[NaOH]$

(b)

7.36 (c) The rate will be doubled.

(d) The rate will be halved.

(e) If some of the ethanol is replaced with water, there will be only a slight effect on the rate since there is only a slight build-up of positive charge in the transition state on the carbon atom undergoing the substitution.

7.37 (a) Rate $= k$ [PhCCH$_3$]

with Ph above and Br below the central carbon

(b)

reaction coordinate →

(c) The rate will double.

(d) Water is a better ionizing solvent than ethanol. The reaction involves the formation of a carbocation, resulting in the separation of charge in the rate-determining step, so an increase in the water content of the solvent will cause an increase in the rate of the reaction by stabilizing the activated complex at the transition state.

7.38   CH$_3$CH=CHCH$_2$—Cl: ⟶ [CH$_3$CH=CH—CH$_2^+$ ⟷ CH$_3$CH—CH=CH$_2^+$]   :Cl:$^-$

resonance-stabilized carbocation, an allylic cation, has partial positive character at carbon 1 and carbon 3

CH$_3$CH=CH—CH$_2^+$ ⟶ CH$_3$CH=CH—CH$_2$—O$^+$(H)(H) ⟶ CH$_3$CH=CHCH$_2$OH

7.38 (cont) $CH_3\overset{+}{C}H-CH=CH_2$ $\longrightarrow$ $CH_3CH-CH=CH_2$ $\longrightarrow$ $CH_3CH-CH=CH_2$

7.39

For *cis*-2-phenylcyclohexyl tosylate, the most stable product arises from a conformation of the cyclohexane ring that has the phenyl group in the equatorial position, and the leaving group, the tosyl group, in the axial position required for the E2 reaction to occur (see Section 7.6C).

no reaction

In *trans*-2-phenylcyclohexyl tosylate the bulky phenyl ring prevents the molecule from achieving the diaxial conformation required for elimination, and no reaction takes place.

7.40   (a)

(b)   The hydroxyl group on the 1° carbon atom is less hindered than the hydroxyl group on the 3° carbon atom and will react faster with tosyl chloride.

7.41 $^-:\overset{..}{\underset{..}{S}}-C\equiv N:$ $\longleftrightarrow$ $\overset{..}{\underset{..}{S}}=C=\overset{..}{N}:^-$ $R-\overset{..}{\underset{..}{S}}-C\equiv N:$
thiocyanate ion

$\overset{..}{\underset{..}{O}}=C=\overset{..}{N}:^-$ $\longleftrightarrow$ $^-:\overset{..}{\underset{..}{O}}-C\equiv N:$ $R-\overset{..}{N}=C=\overset{..}{\underset{..}{O}}$
cyanate ion

In the thiocyanate ion, the electrons on the sulfur are more polarizable than those on the nitrogen, and that end of the ion is the better nucleophile. In the cyanate ion, the electrons on the nitrogen are more polarizable than those on the oxygen, and the nitrogen is a better nucleophile.

7.42   (a)

(S)--2-bromopentane $\xrightarrow{\text{NaBr}}$ (R)--2-bromopentane
inversion of configuration

These compounds are enantiomers.

(b) The results of Experiment B, in which the reaction rate increases with an increase in the concentration of bromide ion, indicates that the reaction proceeds by an S_N2 reaction. The rate of an S_N2 reaction depends on the concentration of the nucleophile as well as on the concentration of the alkyl halide.

(c) The starting material is reversibly converted to product (Statement 3).

The starting material and the product are at the same level with respect to energy, therefore neither form is favored. The reaction proceeds randomly, converting each enantiomer to the other, until the mixture becomes optically inactive. The interconversion of the enantiomers continues, but can no longer be observed by a change in the optical activity of the solution.

7.43

(a) (–)-AZT   (b) (+)-AZT

(c) –56°

(d) The number of stereoisomers possible for a compound with n stereocenters is 2^n. There are 3 stereocenters so the total number of stereoisomers possible is 2^3 or 8.

(e) The reaction gives a mixture of stereoisomers at the stereocenter that undergoes substitution. This implies that the reaction went by way of a carbocation intermediate, an S_N1 reaction.

7.44   (a) Alkene **C** is the major product. It is the more highly substituted alkene. The transition state for its formation is of lower energy than the transition state for the formation of the other alkene.

(b)

7.44   (c)

7.45   Compound **X** forms 56% of the mixture. **X** and **Y** are not formed in equal amounts at equilibrium because they are diastereomers of each other. Enantiomers, which are of equal energy, form in equal amounts at equilibrium (see Problem 7.42). Diastereomers have different energies and form in different amounts.

7.46

(a)   The double bond has the *Z* configuration.

(b)

(c)

Supplemental Problems

S7.1   You can obtain experimental evidence for inversion of configuration by carefully working out the configurational relationships of different optically active compounds. One such cycle is outlined below. Look at all of the reactions, decide when bonds are being broken at a stereocenter and when not, and predict for each reaction whether it goes with inversion or retention of configuration. (Hint: You already know the answers for the first and third reactions.)

S7.1   (3) $CH_3(CH_2)_5CHCH_3$ $\xrightarrow{\underset{}{CH_3CO^-\,Na^+}}$ $CH_3(CH_2)_5CHCH_3$ + $TsO^-\,Na^+$
                          | |
                         OTs $OCCH_3$

(+)-2-octyl tosylate   (−)-2-octyl acetate

S7.2   The following equations represent some nucleophilic substitution reactions that are possible. Only primary alkyl groups are used, so the reactions will be S_N2, and competing elimination reactions will not be a problem. Complete the equations, showing the products that will form. In each case it will be helpful to label the leaving group and the incoming nucleophile.

(a) CH_3CH_2I + $P(CH_2CH_2CH_2CH_3)_3 \longrightarrow$ (b) $HOCH_2CH_2Cl$ + $CH_3S^-\,Na^+ \longrightarrow$

S7.3   The following incomplete reaction sequences give only a starting material and a product that can be prepared from it. Show the reagents that would be necessary to carry out each transformation and any major products that would be formed in the intermediate stages. There may be more than one correct way to complete a sequence. Ph is used to represent the benzene ring.

(a) $CH_3CH_2CH_2CH_2Br \longrightarrow CH_3CH_2CH_2CH_2C\equiv CH$ (b) $PhSH \longrightarrow PhSCH_2CH_2Ph$

S7.4   One of the classic experiments in which the stereochemistry of E2 reactions was explored involved menthyl chloride and neomenthyl chloride. These two compounds differ from each other only in the stereochemistry at the carbon atom to which the chlorine atom is attached. The following equations show the reactions they undergo without revealing their stereochemistry.

(a) Using the information given, assign relative stereochemistry to menthyl chloride and neomenthyl chloride. Menthyl chloride is derived from natural sources, and the substituents on the cyclohexane ring are in the most stable configuration.

(b) When the reaction with menthyl chloride is carried out in 80% aqueous ethanol with no added base, the following products are obtained. How do you explain these results?

S7.5   The following experimental observations were made. Even though the two reactions proceeded at very different rates, the relative amounts of the products obtained were practically identical.

The first reaction is 7.5 times faster than the second reaction.

(a) What do these data suggest about the mechanism of the reaction?

(b) Why are the rates of these two reactions different?

S7.6   Chromanones are compounds that are responsible for color in leaves and flowers. The following transformation was carried out as part of a recent synthesis of a chromanone.

(a) The first step is the deprotonation of the starting material, 2-hydroxyacetophenone. Examine the connectivities in the starting material and the product to identify where deprotonation has occurred. What is the base in the reaction? Use the pK_a table to assign an approximate pK_a value to the conjugate acid of this base.

(b) Which is the most acidic proton on the starting material and what is an approximate pK_a value for it? Draw a structural formula for the anion resulting from the first deprotonation of 2-hydroxyacetophenone.

(c) The second step of the synthesis involves reaction of the anion from the deprotonation of 2-hydroxyacetophenone with chlorotrimethylsilane. Silicon (Si) is just below carbon in the periodic table and resembles carbon in its ability to form covalent bonds. What general type of reaction has taken place in step 2 of the synthesis shown above? Write a mechanism using the curved-arrow symbolism to show how the anion formed in part (b) from 2-hydroxyacetophenone would react with chlorotrimethylsilane.

(d) Another deprotonation reaction takes place on the product of the reaction of the anion of 2-hydroxyacetophenone with chlorotrimethylsilane found in part (c). Use the pK_a table to determine the *second most acidic* proton in 2-hydroxyacetophenone. Resonance is important in stabilizing the anion that results from this second deprotonation. Draw a structural formula for this new anion and for its major resonance contributor.

S7.7   The metabolism of amino acids is often traced by synthesizing compounds that are labeled with isotopes of carbon or hydrogen at specific positions.

(a) Provide the product of the following reaction used to synthesize arginine labeled with ^{13}C.

S7.7 (cont)

(b) The following reactions were used in the synthesis of arginine labeled with deuterium, ^2H or D. Write structural formulas for compounds B and C, the intermediates in the synthesis.

S7.8   Many compounds that are toxic to cells act by alkylating DNA. One such compound is chlorambucil, which is used in the chemotherapy of cancer, especially for leukemia. The compound reacts with the nitrogen at position 7 of guanine, one of the four bases that are part of the genetic code in DNA. The reaction is helped by participation of the nonbonding electrons on the nitrogen at position 9 in guanine. Draw a mechanism for the reaction of guanine with chlorambucil. Only one of the leaving groups is lost in the reaction. In DNA, chlorambucil can react twice, linking different parts of the DNA helix together, thus stopping reproduction of the cell.

chlorambucil   guanine

S7.9   The following equations represent chemical reactions carried out in research into the synthesis of useful and interesting compounds. Fill in structural formulas for the missing starting materials, products, or reagents.

(a)   NaCN
                       dimethyl   A
                       sulfoxide   (Is the configuration
                                    of the product *R* or *S*?)

(b)   NaN₃
                                   B

(c) C   TsCl
          pyridine

                       NaCN
                       dimethyl   D
                       sulfoxide

(d)   TsCl
          pyridine   E   F

(e)   MsCl
                      triethylamine   G
                      4-dimethyl-
                      aminopyridine

Alkenes

Workbook Exercises

Addition to π bonds was first encountered in Chapter 4. Use the questions below to probe your understanding of the structural changes that occur in an addition reaction.

Q1. Under what experimental conditions does the addition occur?

Q2. What molecule is adding; what are the groups that add?

Q3. What is the regioselectivity (for example, the Markovnikov orientation)?

Q4. What is the stereochemistry? The two groups can add on the same side of the π bond (called **syn** addition), or on opposite sides of the π bond (called **anti** addition).

EXAMPLE

Using a familiar example:

$$CH_3CH_2 \overset{CH_3}{\underset{}{}} C=C \overset{D}{\underset{CH_3}{}} \xrightarrow[\substack{\text{diethyl ether} \\ 0\,°C}]{HCl} CH_3CH_2 - \overset{Cl}{\underset{CH_3}{C}} - \overset{D}{\underset{H}{C}} - CH_3$$

(D = deuterium, ^{2}H)   a mixture of stereoisomers

SOLUTION

Answers to Q1, Q2, and Q3: HCl adds H and Cl with the Markovnikov orientation.

Answer to Q4: Visualizing the changes is often easier if the alkene is represented as perpendicular to the plane of the paper.

a pair of enantiomers representing
syn (same side) addition

a pair of enantiomers representing
anti (opposite side) addition

An important skill for you to develop is to connect a written (and/or verbal) description of a structural change with a molecular representation of that transformation. The following example will help you develop this skill.

EXAMPLE

Draw the structure corresponding to the anti addition of bromine to cyclohexene (the six-membered hydrocarbon ring with one carbon-carbon double bond).

SOLUTION

Restatement of the verbal description in structural terms:

what you need to think about   what the product looks like

[Addition of Br₂ gives one
Br atom on each end of the
broken π bond; anti means
the Br atoms are on opposite
sides of the plane of the
molecule.]

and enantiomer

Workbook Exercises (cont)

EXERCISE I.   In each case, provide structural formulas for the starting materials, reagents, or products needed to complete the equation. Examine all of the information carefully.

(a)

syn addition of H$_2$

$\longrightarrow$ A + B

a pair of diastereomers
derived from the addition to
each face of the π bond

(b) C or D or E   Markovnikov addition of HBr $\longrightarrow$

and other isomers

(c) F   syn addition of an oxygen atom $\longrightarrow$

and enantiomer

EXERCISE II.   Give a complete description of the changes in connectivity that accompany each of the following reactions.

(a)

(b)

and enantiomer

(c)

- -

8.1   C$_5$H$_{10}$

(1) CH$_3$CH$_2$CH$_2$CH$=$CH$_2$

(2)

(3)

(4) CH$_3$CHCH$=$CH$_2$
            |
          CH$_3$

(5)

(6) CH$_2$$=CCH_2CH_3$
              |
            CH$_3$

8.2   (1) 1-pentene   (2) (*E*)-2-pentene   (3) (*Z*)-2-pentene
           (4) 3-methyl-1-butene   (5) 2-methyl-2-butene   (6) 2-methyl-1-butene

8.3   (a) [structure]   (b) [structure]   (c) [structure]

           (d) [structure]   (e) [structure]   (f) [structure]

8.4   No. Each carbon atom of the double bond must have two different substituents for this type of isomerism to be possible.

8.5

8.6   A concept triangle will be used to answer part (a). Only the equations will be shown for the rest of the problem.

(a)

The starting material is an alkene. The reagent is a mixture of water with a strong acid; therefore, the most abundant species in solution will be the hydronium ion, H_3O^+, an electrophile. The type of reaction is an electrophilic addition to the double bond. Because the electrophile in H_2O is H_3O^+, the overall addition is that of H—OH to the double bond.

8.6 (a) (cont)

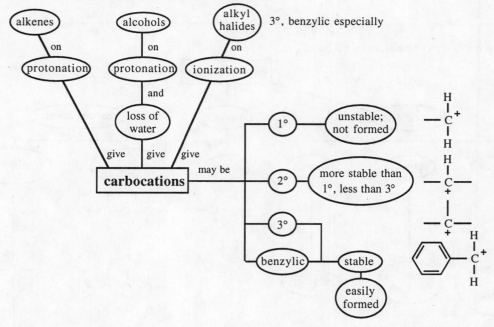

The alkene is symmetric, so we do not have to worry about regioselectivity in this case.

(b)

$$\xrightarrow[\text{H}_2\text{SO}_4]{\text{H}_2\text{O}}$$

(c) $\text{CH}_3\text{CH}_2\text{CH}_2\text{CH}_2\text{CH}=\text{CH}_2 \xrightarrow[\text{H}_2\text{SO}_4]{\text{H}_2\text{O}} \text{CH}_3\text{CH}_2\text{CH}_2\text{CH}_2\underset{\underset{\text{OH}}{|}}{\text{CH}}\text{CH}_3$

(d) $\text{CH}_3\underset{\underset{\text{OH}}{|}}{\text{C}}\text{CH}_3 \xrightarrow[\Delta]{\text{H}_3\text{PO}_4} \text{CH}_3\overset{\overset{\text{CH}_3}{|}}{\text{C}}=\text{CH}_2$ (e) $\text{CH}_3\overset{\overset{\text{CH}_3}{|}}{\text{C}}=\text{CHCH}_2\text{CH}_3 \xrightarrow[\text{H}_2\text{SO}_4]{\text{H}_2\text{O}} \text{CH}_3\underset{\underset{\text{OH}}{|}}{\overset{\overset{\text{CH}_3}{|}}{\text{C}}}\text{CH}_2\text{CH}_2\text{CH}_3$

(f)

$$\xrightarrow[\Delta]{\text{H}_3\text{PO}_4}$$

Concept Map 8.1   Reactions that form carbocations.

alkenes

alcohols

alkyl halides   3°, benzylic especially

on   on   on

protonation   protonation   ionization

and

loss of water

give   give   give

carbocations   may be

1°   unstable; not formed

2°   more stable than 1°, less than 3°

3°

benzylic   stable

easily formed

8.7

$$\text{CH}_3\overset{\overset{\text{CH}_3}{|}}{\text{C}}=\overset{\overset{\text{CH}_3}{|}}{\text{C}}\text{CH}_3 \longrightarrow \text{CH}_3\overset{\overset{\text{CH}_3}{|}}{\underset{+}{\text{C}}}-\underset{\underset{\text{H}}{|}}{\overset{\overset{\text{CH}_3}{|}}{\text{C}}}\text{CH}_3$$

$$\text{H}-\ddot{\text{O}}-\text{PO}_3\text{H}_2 \qquad\qquad {}^{-}:\ddot{\text{O}}-\text{PO}_3\text{H}_2$$

8.7 (cont)

Note that very little of this product is seen. It arises from a secondary cation, which is less stable than a tertiary cation.

Concept Map 8.2   Reactions of carbocations.

8.8

$$CH_3CCH_2-\overset{\underset{\displaystyle\cdot\cdot}{H}}{O}: \quad\longrightarrow\quad CH_3\overset{\underset{\displaystyle CH_3}{|}}{C}-CH_2-\overset{+}{O}\overset{H}{\underset{H}{|}} \qquad :\overset{\cdot\cdot}{\underset{\cdot\cdot}{Br}}:^-$$

(with CH_3 top left, CH_3 bottom left; H—$\overset{\cdot\cdot}{\underset{\cdot\cdot}{Br}}$:)

ionization with
1,2-methyl shift
(to avoid forming
a 1° cation)

$$CH_3\overset{\underset{\displaystyle :\overset{\cdot\cdot}{Br}:}{|}}{\overset{\displaystyle |}{C}}-CH_2CH_3 \quad\longleftarrow\quad CH_3\overset{\underset{\displaystyle :\overset{\cdot\cdot}{\underset{\cdot\cdot}{Br}}:^-}{|}}{\overset{+}{C}}-CH_2-CH_3 \qquad :\overset{H}{\underset{H}{O}}:$$

(with CH_3 at top of central carbon)

8.9

$$H:\overset{\overset{\displaystyle H}{\cdot\cdot}}{B}:H$$

shape is trigonal planar;
hybridization of the
boron atom is sp^2

empty p orbital

overlap of sp^2 hybrid
orbital on boron and
1 s orbital on hydrogen

8.10

cyclopentene $\xrightarrow{BH_3}$ tricyclopentylborane

$$CH_3(CH_2)_7CH=CH_2 \xrightarrow{BH_3} CH_3(CH_2)_7CH_2CH_2\overset{\overset{\displaystyle CH_2CH_2(CH_2)_7CH_3}{|}}{B}CH_2CH_2(CH_2)_7CH_3$$

$$CH_3\overset{\underset{\displaystyle CH_3}{|}}{\overset{\displaystyle |}{C}}-CH=CH_2 \xrightarrow{BH_3} CH_3\overset{\underset{\displaystyle CH_3}{|}}{\overset{\displaystyle |}{C}}CH_2CH_2-B-CH_2CH_2\overset{\underset{\displaystyle CH_3}{|}}{\overset{\displaystyle CH_3}{\overset{|}{C}}}CH_3$$

(with $CH_2CH_2\overset{CH_3}{\underset{CH_3}{C}}CH_3$ branch on B)

8.11 (a) $CH_3CH_2CH_2\overset{\underset{\displaystyle }{\overset{\displaystyle CH_3}{|}}}{C}=CH_2 \xrightarrow{\text{H-B}} CH_3CH_2CH_2\overset{\overset{\displaystyle CH_3}{|}}{CH}CH_2-B$

(b) $PhCH=CH_2 \xrightarrow{\text{H-B}} PhCH_2CH_2-B$

8.11   (c)

(d)

(e)

Concept Map 8.3   The hydroboration reaction.

8.12   (a)

cyclopentanol

(b) $CH_3(CH_2)_7CH_2CH_2BCH_2CH_2(CH_2)_7CH_3$ $\xrightarrow[\text{H}_2\text{O}]{\text{H}_2\text{O}_2,\ \text{NaOH}}$ $CH_3(CH_2)_8CH_2OH$
1-decanol

with $CH_2CH_2(CH_2)_7CH_3$ as the substituent on B.

8.12 (c)

$$
\begin{array}{c}
\hspace{3.5cm} CH_3 \\
\hspace{3.5cm} | \\
\hspace{2.2cm} CH_2CH_2CCH_3 \\
\hspace{3.5cm} | \\
CH_3 \hspace{3.0cm} CH_3 \;\; CH_3 \\
| \hspace{6.5cm} \\
CH_3CCH_2CH_2 - B - CH_2CH_2CCH_3 \\
| \hspace{6.5cm} | \\
CH_3 \hspace{4.3cm} CH_3
\end{array}
$$

$\xrightarrow[\text{H}_2\text{O}]{\text{H}_2\text{O}_2,\ \text{NaOH}}$

$$
\begin{array}{c}
CH_3 \\
| \\
CH_3CCH_2CH_2OH \\
| \\
CH_3
\end{array}
$$

3,3-dimethyl-1-butanol

(a')

$$
\begin{array}{c}
CH_3 \\
| \\
CH_3CH_2CH_2CHCH_2 - B
\end{array}
$$

$\xrightarrow[\text{H}_2\text{O}]{\text{H}_2\text{O}_2,\ \text{NaOH}}$

$$
\begin{array}{c}
CH_3 \\
| \\
CH_3CH_2CH_2CHCH_2OH
\end{array}
$$

2-methyl-1-pentanol

(b') $PhCH_2CH_2 - B$

$\xrightarrow[\text{H}_2\text{O}]{\text{H}_2\text{O}_2,\ \text{NaOH}}$ $PhCH_2CH_2OH$

2-phenylethanol

(c')

$$
\begin{array}{c}
CH_3 \\
| \\
CH_3C - CH_2 - CHCH_3 \\
| \hspace{3.3cm} | \\
CH_3 \hspace{1.9cm} B
\end{array}
$$

$\xrightarrow[\text{H}_2\text{O}]{\text{H}_2\text{O}_2,\ \text{NaOH}}$

$$
\begin{array}{c}
CH_3 \\
| \\
CH_3C - CH_2 - CHCH_3 \\
| \hspace{3.3cm} | \\
CH_3 \hspace{1.9cm} OH
\end{array}
$$

4,4-dimethyl-2-pentanol

(d')

$$
\begin{array}{c}
CH_3 \hspace{1.0cm} CH_3 \\
| \hspace{2.2cm} | \\
CH_3CH - CCH_3 \\
\hspace{1.6cm} | \\
\hspace{1.6cm} B
\end{array}
$$

$\xrightarrow[\text{H}_2\text{O}]{\text{H}_2\text{O}_2,\ \text{NaOH}}$

$$
\begin{array}{c}
CH_3 \hspace{1.0cm} CH_3 \\
| \hspace{2.2cm} | \\
CH_3CH - CCH_3 \\
\hspace{1.6cm} | \\
\hspace{1.6cm} OH
\end{array}
$$

2,3-dimethyl-2-butanol

(e')

$$
\begin{array}{c}
CH_3CH_2CH_2CHCH_2CH_3 \\
\hspace{2.0cm} | \\
\hspace{2.0cm} B
\end{array}
$$

$\xrightarrow[\text{H}_2\text{O}]{\text{H}_2\text{O}_2,\ \text{NaOH}}$

$$
\begin{array}{c}
CH_3CH_2CH_2CHCH_2CH_3 \\
\hspace{2.0cm} | \\
\hspace{2.0cm} OH
\end{array}
$$

3-hexanol

Concept Map 8.4   Catalytic hydrogenation reactions.

8.13

(a)

(b)

(c)

(d)

(e)

8.14   1.   Attack at carbon 3 of the enantiomeric bromonium ions derived from (*Z*)-2-pentene.

(2*S*, 3*S*)-2,3-dibromopentane
                                                                            (2*R*, 3*R*)-2,3-dibromopentane
         This is the same mixture as that obtained by attack at carbon 2 shown in the text.
      2.   Attack at carbon 2 of the enantiomeric bromonium ions derived from (*E*)-2-pentene.

(2*S*, 3*R*)-2,3-dibromopentane
                                                                            (2*R*, 3*S*)-2,3-dibromopentane

   Attack at carbon 3 of the enantiomeric bromonium ions derived from (*E*)-2-pentene.

(2*R*, 3*S*)-2,3-dibromopentane
                                                                            (2*S*, 3*R*)-2,3-dibromopentane
         This is the same mixture as that obtained by attack at carbon 2.

8.15   Part (a) will be analyzed in detail. Only the equations will be shown for the rest of the problem.

(a)

1.   To what functional group class do the reactants belong?

One reactant is an alkene. The double bond of the alkene is a nucleophile. The other reagent is a halogen, an electrophile.

8.15 (a) (cont)

2.   Does either reactant have a good leaving group?

Yes, Br⁻ from the bromine molecule is a good leaving group.

3.   Are any of the reactants good acids, bases, nucleophiles, or electrophiles? Is there an ionizing solvent present?

Bromine, above the arrow, is an electrophile. The solvent, carbon tetrachloride, is not an ionizing solvent.

4.   What is the most likely first step for the reaction? Most common reactions can be classified either as protonation-deprotonation, or as reactions of a nucleophile with an electrophile.

Attack by the nucleophilic double bond on the electrophilic bromine leading to the formation of a bromonium ion is the first step.

5.   What are the properties of the species present in the reaction mixture after the first step? Is any further reaction likely?

The species present in the reaction mixture are the bromonium ion, an electrophile, and bromide ion, a nucleophile. The bromonium ion will react with bromide ion to give the dibromide product.

6.   What is the stereochemistry of the reaction?

The opening of the bromonium ion by bromide leads to an overall anti addition and the creation of two stereocenters. The product, however, has a plane of symmetry and is therefore a meso compound.

Complete correct answer:

(3R,4S)-3,4-dibromohexane
meso-3,4-dibromohexane

(b)

racemic mixture

8.15

(c)

diastereomers

(d)

enantiomers

8.16   Formation of product from an unsymmetrical bromonium ion intermediate.

(1*S*, 2*R*)-2-bromo-1-phenyl-1-propanol

(1*R*, 2*S*)-2-bromo-1-phenyl-1-propanol

Formation of products from a carbocation.

attack from top

attack from bottom

8.16 (cont)

(1*S*, 2*S*)-2-bromo-1-
phenyl-1-propanol

(1*R*, 2*S*)-2-bromo-1-
phenyl-1-propanol

attack
from top

attack
from bottom

(1*S*, 2*R*)-2-bromo-1-
phenyl-1-propanol

(1*R*, 2*R*)-2-bromo-1-
phenyl-1-propanol

8.17   PhCH=CCH₃ $\xrightarrow[\text{dimethylsulfoxide}]{\text{NBS, H}_2\text{O}}$ PhCH—CCH₃   +   PhCH—CCH₃

mixture of enantiomers   mixture of enantiomers

Benzylic and tertiary carbocations are both relatively stable intermediates. Therefore, both the benzylic carbon atom and the tertiary carbon atom have about the same amount of partial charge in the bromonium ion. Attack by the nucleophile can occur at either carbon.

Concept Map 8.5   The addition of bromine to alkenes.

- -

8.18   (a) $CH_3\overset{\underset{\textstyle |}{CH_3}}{C}=CHCH_3$ $\xrightarrow{O_3}$ $\xrightarrow[H_2O]{Zn}$ $CH_3\overset{\overset{\textstyle O}{||}}{C}CH_3$ + $CH_3\overset{\overset{\textstyle O}{||}}{C}H$

(b) $CH_3\overset{\underset{\textstyle |}{CH_3}}{C}H\overset{\underset{\textstyle |}{CH_2CH_3}}{CH}=C CH_2CH_3$ $\xrightarrow{O_3,\ CH_3OH}$ $\xrightarrow{(CH_3)_2S}$ $CH_3\overset{\underset{\textstyle |}{CH_3}}{C}H-\overset{\overset{\textstyle O}{||}}{C}H$ + $CH_3CH_2\overset{\overset{\textstyle O}{||}}{C}CH_2CH_3$

(c) $CH_3\overset{\underset{\textstyle |}{CH_3}}{C}H\overset{\underset{\textstyle |}{CH_2CH_3}}{CH}=C CH_2CH_3$ $\xrightarrow[H_2O]{O_3}$ $\xrightarrow{H_2O_2,\ NaOH}$ $\xrightarrow{H_3O^+}$ $CH_3\overset{\underset{\textstyle |}{CH_3}}{C}H-\overset{\overset{\textstyle O}{||}}{C}OH$ + $CH_3CH_2\overset{\overset{\textstyle O}{||}}{C}CH_2CH_3$

(d)   (cyclohexene with CH_3) $\xrightarrow{O_3,\ CH_3OH}$ $\xrightarrow{(CH_3)_2S}$ $CH_3\overset{\overset{\textstyle O}{||}}{C}CH_2CH_2CH_2CH_2\overset{\overset{\textstyle O}{||}}{C}H$

(e)   (cyclic diene) $\xrightarrow[\substack{dichloromethane \\ 0\,°C}]{O_3}$ $\xrightarrow{H_2O_2,\ NaOH}$ $2\ Na^{+\ -}O\overset{\overset{\textstyle O}{||}}{C}CH_2CH_2CH_2CH_2\overset{\overset{\textstyle O}{||}}{C}O^-\ Na^+$

8.19 $CH_3CH=\overset{\underset{\textstyle |}{CH_3}}{C}\overset{\underset{\textstyle CH_3}{|}}{C}H_2CCH_3$ + $CH_3CH_2\overset{\underset{\textstyle |}{CH_3}}{C}=\overset{\underset{\textstyle CH_3}{|}}{C}HCCH_3$ $\xrightarrow{O_3}$ $\xrightarrow[H_2O]{Zn}$

$\overset{CH_3CH_2}{}$ $\overset{CH_3}{}$

90%   10%

$CH_3\overset{\overset{\textstyle O}{||}}{C}H$ + $CH_3CH_2\overset{\overset{\textstyle O}{||}}{C}\overset{\underset{\textstyle CH_3}{|}}{C}H_2\overset{\underset{\textstyle CH_3}{|}}{C}CH_3$ + $CH_3CH_2\overset{\overset{\textstyle O}{||}}{C}CH_2CH_3$ + $CH_3\overset{\underset{\textstyle CH_3}{|}}{C}-\overset{\overset{\textstyle O}{||}}{C}H$

~45%   ~45%   ~5%   ~5%

8.20 (a) CH₃CHCH=CH₂ — KMnO₄, KOH / H₂O / 0 °C → and enantiomer

(b) OsO₄, diethyl ether, pyridine → KOH, mannitol, H₂O →

(c) OsO₄, diethyl ether, pyridine → KOH, mannitol, H₂O →

Concept Map 8.6   The oxidation reactions of alkenes.

oxiranes (epoxides) — peroxyacids

cis-1,2-diols — permanganate anion or osmium tetroxide — syn addition

MnO₄⁻ or OsO₄

alkene

O₃ — ozone — ozonolysis reaction

H₂O₂ — oxidative workup — reductive workup — Zn, H₂O or CH₃SCH₃

acid   ketone   aldehyde

8.21 (a) CH₃C=CCH₂CH=CH₂ — 3-chloroperoxybenzoic acid (one molar equivalent) / chloroform / 25 °C → and enantiomer

8.21 (b)

Note that in parts (a) and (b), the more highly substituted double bond is more nucleophilic and therefore reacts faster with the peroxyacid than the less substituted double bond.

(c)

(d)

8.22

1. What are the connectivities of the two compounds? How many carbon atoms does each contain? Are there any rings? What are the positions of branches and functional groups on the carbon skeletons?

(*E*)-2-butene

(2*S*, 3*S*)-2,3-butanediol drawn in the eclipsed conformation. No plane of symmetry is present.

anti conformation of (2*S*, 3*S*)-2,3-butanediol

gauche conformation of (2*S*, 3*S*)-2,3-butanediol; more stable than anti because of hydrogen bonding

conformations of one of the enantiomeric products

The carbon skeletons of the two compounds are identical. Each contains four carbon atoms. The two carbon atoms that were doubly bonded in the starting material have hydroxyl groups on them in the product. The methyl groups in the starting alkene and in the eclipsed conformation of the product diol are on the opposite side of the two reacting carbon atoms.

2. How do the functional groups change in going from starting material to product? Does the starting material have a good leaving group?

The starting material is an alkene. It contains a double bond. The product is a diol with the two hydroxyl groups on adjacent carbon atoms. There is no leaving group present in the starting material.

8.22 (cont)

3. Is it possible to dissect the structures of the starting material and product to see which bonds must be broken and which formed?

bond broken   bonds formed

4. New bonds are created when an electrophile reacts with a nucleophile. Do we recognize any part of the product molecule as coming from a nucleophile or an electrophilic addition reaction?

    A double bond is converted to a diol by reaction with an oxidizing agent (an electrophile) such as permanganate ion or osmium tetroxide. The reaction of permanganate ion or osmium tetroxide is a syn addition so would give the stereochemistry we need to get from an alkene with methyl groups on opposite sides of the double bond to a diol, which also has methyl groups on the opposite sides of the molecule in its eclipsed conformation.

5. Do we see how to get from starting material to the product?

    The starting material can be converted directly to product.

    Complete correct answer:

    and enantiomer   and enantiomer   and enantiomer

8.23   (a) (*E*)-3-methyl-3-heptene   (b) 3-ethyl-2,5-dimethyl-2-hexene (c) (*E*)-3,4-dichloro-3-heptene
            (d) (*Z*)-3,4-dimethyl-3-heptene   (e) (*R*)-1,3-dichlorobutane   (f) (*Z*)-4-bromo-3-ethyl-2-pentene
            (g) 3-chloro-2-methyl-2-pentene   (h) *cis*-1,2-dibromocyclobutane
            (i) (2*R*, 3*S*)-2-bromo-3-chlorobutane

8.24   (a)   (b)   (c)

            (d) $CH_3CH_2CHC=CH_2$ (e)   (f)

8.25   (a)

            (b)

8.25   (c)

(d)

(e)

(f)

(g)

8.26   (Z)-6-dodecen-1-ol

8.27

(a)

(b)

(c)

(d)

(e)

and enantiomer

(f)

(g)

and enantiomer

8.27

(h)

$$CH_3COH + CH_3CCH_2CH_3$$

(i)

and enantiomer

(j)

and enantiomer   +   and enantiomer

8.28   (a)

and enantiomer

(b)

and enantiomer

(c)

+ HCH

(d)

dichloromethane

(e)

8.29   (a)

$$CH_3CH_2CCH_2CH_3$$

Note that (*E*)-3-methyl-2-pentene also gives 3-bromo-3-methylpentane [Prob. 8.27 (c)].

(b)

and enantiomer   +   and enantiomer

8.29 (c)

$CH_3CH_2CHCH_2CH_3$
|
OH

$\xrightarrow[\Delta]{H_3PO_4}$

major product

$+$

(d)

$\xrightarrow[\text{pyridine}]{OsO_4 \quad \text{tetrahydrofuran}}$

$\xrightarrow[\text{pyridine}]{NaHSO_3 \quad H_2O}$

(e)

$\xrightarrow[\text{(makes HOBr)}]{Ca(OBr)_2, \ CH_3COH}$

and enantiomer

8.30

(a)

$\xrightarrow[\text{dimethyl sulfoxide}]{N-Br, \ H_2O}$

and enantiomer
A

(b)

$\xrightarrow[Pt]{H_2}$

B

(c)

$\xrightarrow{CH_3(CH_2)_{10}COOH}$

C   +   D

(d)

$\xrightarrow[\substack{\text{(H}^- \text{ is a strong base.}\\ \text{See p. 455 in the text.)}}]{NaH}$

E

$\xrightarrow[\substack{\text{(Hint: I is a}\\ \text{good nucleophile)}}]{PhCH_2Br}$

F

(e)

$\xrightarrow{BD_3}$

$(CH_3COCH_2CH_2CH_2CHDCH)_3B$
G

$+ \ (CH_3COCH_2CH_2CH_2CH)_3B$
H

$\xrightarrow{H_2O_2, \ NaOH}$

$CH_3COCH_2CH_2CH_2CHDCH-OH$
I

$+ \ CH_3COCH_2CH_2CH_2CH-OH$
J

8.31

(a)

(b)

(c)

(d)

(e)

8.32

(a)

(b)

8.32

(c) $(CH_3)_3COC$ [benzene ring] $CH=CH_2$ $\xrightarrow[\text{tetrahydrofuran}]{\text{H-B}}$ $\xrightarrow[\text{H}_2\text{O}]{\text{H}_2\text{O}_2, \text{NaOH}}$ $(CH_3)_3COC$ [benzene ring] CH_2CH_2OH

C

(d) $\xrightarrow[\text{(D)}]{\text{OsO}_4 \text{ or KMnO}_4}$

(e) $\xrightarrow[\substack{\text{dichloromethane} \\ -78\,°C}]{\text{O}_3}$ $\xrightarrow[\text{H}_2\text{O}]{\text{H}_2\text{O}_2, \text{NaOH}}$ $+$ $\underset{F}{\overset{O}{\underset{}{HCOH}}}$

E

(f) $\xrightarrow[\substack{\text{carbon} \\ \text{tetrachloride}}]{\text{Br}_2}$ $+$ $\equiv$

G

(g) $CH_3(CH_2)_6CH=CH_2$ $\xrightarrow[\text{(H)}]{\text{HBr}}$ $CH_3(CH_2)_6\underset{\underset{Br}{|}}{C}HCH_3$

(h) $\xrightarrow[\text{dichloromethane}]{\text{Cl} \quad \text{COOH}}$ $+$

I

(i) $\xrightarrow{\text{O}_3, \text{CH}_3\text{OH}}$ $\xrightarrow{(CH_3)_2S}$ $+$ $\underset{}{\overset{O}{\underset{}{HCH}}}$

J

(j) $\xrightarrow[\text{pyridine}]{\text{OsO}_4 \\ \text{(K)}}$

8.33

1,2-shift of sigma bonding electrons of a ring carbon; another type of alkyl shift

8.34 (a)

A   B   C   D

(b) Both B and C have the positive charge on a carbon adjacent to oxygen, which allows for resonance stabilization of the cation.

8.35 Formation of pinacolone from pinacol

1,2-methyl shift; rearrangement to more stable cation

resonance-stabilized cation

pinacolone

8.36   (a)

$(CH_3)_2C=C(CH_3)_2$ $\xrightarrow[(CH_3CH_2)_4N^+OH^-]{(CH_3)_3COOH,\ OsO_4}$ $\xrightarrow[H_2O]{NaHSO_3}$ $CH_3\underset{OH}{\overset{CH_3}{C}}-\underset{OH}{\overset{CH_3}{C}}CH_3$

(b) $CH_3(CH_2)_7CH=CH_2$ $\xrightarrow[(CH_3CH_2)_4N^+OH^-]{(CH_3)_3COOH,\ OsO_4}$ $\xrightarrow[H_2O]{NaHSO_3}$

$CH_3(CH_2)_7\overset{CH_2OH}{\underset{OH}{C}}H$ and enantiomer

(c)

$\underset{H}{\overset{CH_3CH_2CH_2}{C}}=\underset{CH_2CH_2CH_3}{\overset{H}{C}}$ $\xrightarrow[(CH_3CH_2)_4N^+OH^-]{(CH_3)_3COOH,\ OsO_4}$ $\xrightarrow[H_2O]{NaHSO_3}$ $CH_3CH_2CH_2\underset{HO}{\overset{H}{C}}-\underset{CH_2CH_2CH_3}{\overset{OH}{C}}H$ and enantiomer

(d)

$\underset{H}{\overset{CH_3CH_2CH_2}{C}}=\underset{H}{\overset{CH_2CH_2CH_3}{C}}$ $\xrightarrow[(CH_3CH_2)_4N^+OH^-]{(CH_3)_3COOH,\ OsO_4}$ $\xrightarrow[H_2O]{NaHSO_3}$ $CH_3CH_2CH_2\underset{HO}{\overset{H}{C}}-\underset{H}{\overset{OH}{C}}CH_2CH_2CH_3$ meso compound

8.37

$CH_3\overset{O}{\overset{\|}{C}}CH=CHCH_2CH_2\overset{O}{\overset{\|}{C}}CH=CHCOCH_3$ $\xrightarrow[\substack{Pd/C\\ethanol}]{H_2}$ $CH_3\overset{O}{\overset{\|}{C}}CH_2CH_2CH_2CH_2\overset{O}{\overset{\|}{C}}CH_2CH_2COCH_3$

A
$C_{11}H_{14}O_4$

B
$C_{11}H_{18}O_4$
3 units of unsaturation

$\uparrow (CH_3)_2S$

[ring structure: cyclohexene with CH$_2$CH$_2$COCH$_3$ and CH$_3$ substituents] $\xrightarrow[dichloromethane]{O_3}$

C
$C_{11}H_{18}O_2$
3 units of unsaturation

8.38   (a)

[cyclohexane ring with HO and CH$_2$] $\xrightarrow{9\text{-}BBN\ \ H_2O_2,\ NaOH}$ A   +   B

Compound A, in which the large groups are trans to each other on the cyclohexane ring, is expected to be thermodynamically more stable. Compound B, however, is formed by way of a sterically less hindered transition state.

8.38   (b)

most stable conformer of A

8.39   The reaction causes a change in the connectivities of the carbon atoms. In the starting material the phenyl ring is attached to an unlabeled carbon atom. In the product, it is bonded to the C-14 labeled carbon atom. A rearrangement has taken place. Such rearrangements require carbocation intermediates.

2° carbocation

1,2-phenyl shift

3° carbocation

deprotonation

HOTs

8.40   (a)   (Z)-4-methyl-3-hexen-1-ol

(b)

(c)

desired product

unavoidable side reaction

8.40 (c) (cont)

It is important to remember that competing side reactions are unavoidable even if we use one equivalent of each reagent. The smallest quantity of material that we can experiment with contains billions of molecules of each reagent, randomly colliding with each other. The protonation of the hydroxyl group, especially, creates another acid, the oxonium ion, which is also strong enough to protonate the alkene, creating a carbocation that will react with the iodide ion. When a molecule contains more than one functional group, both may become involved in reactions unless we choose our reagents very carefully.

8.41   (a)   An anti-Markovnikov addition of H_2O appears to have taken place. It is a hydroboration-oxidation reaction.

(b)

The approach of the BH_3 from the side away from the substituents at the top of the ring is favored.

8.42   (a)

(*R*)-3-bromocyclohexene

(b)

Compound A
a meso form,
therefore optically inactive

Compound B
chiral,
therefore optically active

Both products are formed by anti addition of Br_2 to the double bond.

8.43   (a)

and enantiomer

(b)   *S* at each stereocenter
(1*S*, 2*S*)-2-bromo-1-fluoro-1-methylcyclohexane

(c)

bromonium ion

8.43 (c) (cont)

If a bromonium ion with little charge on the carbon atoms were the intermediate in the reaction, we would expect attack of fluoride ion at the less hindered carbon atom, which is not the regioselectivity observed. Therefore, the intermediate must be the partially open bromonium ion with cationic character at the 3° carbon atom.

8.44

8.45 (a)

(b) Methanol is a strong enough nucleophile to attack and open the strained three-membered ring with a positively charged nitrogen atom as the leaving group. Remember the reactions of the bromonium ion with water or alcohols. Methanol is not a strong enough base to deprotonate a carbon atom to form the alkene.

(c) The rate of the reaction increases as crowding at the carbon atom undergoing the S$_N$2 reaction decreases.

8.46   (a)

lower energy   higher energy

(b) The *tert*-butyl group in an axial position has severe 1,3-diaxial interactions with the axial hydrogen atoms on the same side of the ring, making that form higher in energy than the conformer in which the *tert*-butyl group is equatorial.

(c)

same cation whether
we start with *cis* or *trans*
isomer of starting material

Supplemental Problems

S8.1   A mixture of two primary alcohols obtained from natural sources, 3-methyl-1-butanol and 2-methyl-1-butanol, gives chiefly 2-methyl-2-butene when dehydrated with acid. 2-Methyl-2-butene is converted to 2-methyl-2-butanol with 90% yield by treatment with 50% aqueous sulfuric acid at 0°C. Write equations showing the details of the conversion of the mixture of primary alcohols into a single tertiary alcohol.

S8.2   Complete the following equations, predicting the starting material or products indicated by letter and showing stereochemistry wherever possible. If a racemic mixture is formed, show one enantiomer, and say "+ enantiomer."

(a)

(b) $CH_3\overset{\underset{\textstyle |}{CH_3}}{\underset{\underset{\textstyle OH}{|}}{C}}CH_2CH_3 \xrightarrow[\Delta]{H_2SO_4}$ B   +   C

S8.2

(c) Ph, CH₃ / C=C / H, CH₂CH₂CH₃ $\xrightarrow{O_3,\ CH_3OH}$ $\xrightarrow{(CH_3)_2S}$ D + E

(d) $\underset{\underset{CH_3}{|}}{CH_3C}=CCH_3$ (with CH₃ groups) $\xrightarrow[\text{diethyl ether}]{OsO_4}$ $\xrightarrow[\text{H}_2\text{O}]{KOH}$ F

(e) G $\xrightarrow[\text{H}_2\text{SO}_4]{\text{H}_2\text{O}}$ (1-methylcyclopentanol, CH₃ and OH)

(f) H $\xrightarrow{\text{I}}$ (trans-2-bromocyclopentanol, Br, OH) + (enantiomer, HO, Br)

(g) J $\xrightarrow[\text{tetra-hydrofuran}]{\text{9-BBN}}$ $\xrightarrow[\text{H}_2\text{O}]{\text{NaOH, H}_2\text{O}_2}$ $\underset{\underset{H}{|}}{CH_3C}\underset{\underset{OH}{|}}{CHCH_3}$ (with CH₃ group)

(h) K $\xrightarrow[\text{carbon tetrachloride}]{\text{Br}_2}$ CH₃CHCH₂—C(CH₂Br)(H)(Br) (with CH₃) + enantiomer

(i) L $\xrightarrow[\text{dichloromethane}]{\text{Cl—C}_6\text{H}_4\text{—COOH}}$ CH₃CH₂OCHCH—CH₂ (epoxide, CH₃CH₂O)

(j) $CH_3CH_2C=CH_2$ (with CH₃) $\xrightarrow[\text{H}_2\text{O}]{O_3,\ Zn}$ M + N

(k) $CH_3(CH_2)_{13}CH=CH_2$ $\xrightarrow[\text{H}_2\text{O}]{O_3}$ $\xrightarrow{\text{H}_2\text{O}_2,\ \text{NaOH}}$ $\xrightarrow{\text{H}_3\text{O}^+}$ O + P

(l) CH₃, H / C=C / H, CH₃ (cis) $\xrightarrow[\substack{\text{diethyl ether}\\ \text{pyridine}}]{OsO_4}$ Q $\xrightarrow[\substack{\text{mannitol}\\ \text{H}_2\text{O}}]{KOH}$ R

(m) CH₃CH₂CH₂, CH₃ / C=C / H, H $\xrightarrow[\substack{\text{H}_2\text{O}\\ 0\ °\text{C}}]{\text{KMnO}_4,\ \text{KOH}}$ S

(n) $CH_3CH_2CH_2CH=CH_2$ $\xrightarrow[\substack{\text{dichloromethane}\\ 25\ °\text{C}}]{\underset{\text{(one molar equivalent)}}{\text{Cl—C}_6\text{H}_4\text{—COOH}}}$ T

(o) $\underset{\underset{OH}{|}}{CH_3CHCH_3}$ $\xrightarrow[\Delta]{\text{H}_3\text{PO}_4}$ U

(p) $CH_2=CH_2$ $\xrightarrow[\text{H}_2\text{SO}_4]{\text{H}_2\text{O}}$ V

(q) $\underset{\underset{CH_3}{|}}{CH_3C}=CCH_3$ (with CH₃) $\xrightarrow[\text{Ni}]{\text{H}_2}$ W

(r) $\underset{\underset{CH_3}{|}}{CH_3CHC}=CH_2$ $\xrightarrow[\text{Ni}]{\text{H}_2}$ X

(s) $\underset{\underset{OH}{|}}{CH_3C}CH_2CH_2CH_3$ (with CH₃) $\xrightarrow[\Delta]{\text{H}_3\text{PO}_4}$ Y + Z $\xrightarrow[\text{Pt}]{\text{H}_2}$ AA

S8.3   A tertiary alcohol was dehydrated to give an alkene. Treatment of the alkene with ozone, then with water and zinc, gave equal amounts of 3-pentanone and acetaldehyde. What is the structure of the alcohol?

$$CH_3CH_2\overset{\overset{\displaystyle O}{\|}}{C}CH_2CH_3 \qquad\qquad CH_3\overset{\overset{\displaystyle O}{\|}}{C}H$$

3-pentanone   acetaldehyde

S8.4   Name each of the following compounds, assigning the correct configuration to any for which stereochemistry is shown.

(a)
$$\begin{array}{c} CH_3CH_2CH_2CH_2 \qquad H \\ C=C \\ CH_3 \qquad\qquad H \end{array}$$

(b)
$$\begin{array}{c} \overset{\displaystyle Cl}{\underset{|}{}} \\ CH_3CH \qquad CH_2CH_3 \\ C=C \\ CH_3CH_2 \qquad H \end{array}$$

(c)   (cyclohexene)—Br

S8.5   Propose a mechanism for the following reaction that accounts for the regioselectivity that is observed.

S8.6   Neopentyl bromide reacts in 50% aqueous ethanol at a high temperature (125 °C) in a first-order reaction. Under these conditions, the major products of the reaction are 2-ethoxy-2-methylbutane and 2-methyl-2-butene.

$$\begin{array}{c} \overset{\displaystyle CH_3}{\underset{|}{}} \\ CH_3\overset{|}{\underset{|}{C}}CH_2Br \\ \overset{|}{CH_3} \end{array} \xrightarrow[\substack{in\ H_2O \\ 125\ °C}]{50\%\ CH_3CH_2OH} \begin{array}{c} \overset{\displaystyle CH_3}{\underset{|}{}} \\ CH_3\overset{|}{\underset{|}{C}}CH_2CH_3 \\ \overset{|}{OCH_2CH_3} \end{array} + \begin{array}{c} \overset{\displaystyle CH_3}{\underset{|}{}} \\ CH_3C=CHCH_3 \end{array}$$

neopentyl bromide   125 °C   2-ethoxy-2-methylbutane   2-methyl-2-butene

Write a mechanism for the reaction that explains the observed products.

S8.7

(a) The structure of the following bicyclic compound was investigated by subjecting it to hydrogenation and ozonolysis. Give structural formulas for the products of the reactions shown.

(b) Another bicyclic compound, compound D, C_7H_{10}, also gives compound B after ozonolysis under the same conditions. What is the structure of compound D?

S8.8   Reactions of *cis*-4,5-dimethylcyclohexene and 3-*tert*-butylcyclohexene with *m*-chloroperbenzoic acid give predominantly one product in each case. Show the conformation of each starting alkene, and predict, by showing the reaction with the peroxyacid, what the structure of the expected product should be. (Hint: Using molecular models will help.)

S8.9   Recently pheromones (Problem 8.40) of both the Japanese beetle and the mosquito were synthesized in British Columbia.

(a) The structure of the pheromone of the Japanese beetle is shown below *without* any stereochemical information. To attract the beetle, the compound has to be the (*R*)-(–)-(*Z*)-isomer. As little as 5% of the (*S*)-isomer lowers the attractiveness of the compound to beetles. Draw a structural formula that clearly shows the correct stereochemistry for the (*R*)-(–)-(*Z*)-stereoisomer of this compound.

pheromone of the Japanese beetle

(b) The synthesis of this pheromone involved the preparation of a chiral alcohol from a ketone by the use of baker's yeast. The stereochemical structure of this chiral alcohol is shown below. Name the compound. (Hint: the name of a compound containing two hydroxyl groups ends in "diol".) Locate any sources of stereoisomerism in the compound, and assign configuration, *R* or *S*, *E* or *Z*, to those centers. What is the correct name for the compound, including its stereochemistry?

(c) In a later step of the synthesis, the double bond in the molecule had to be removed to create an aldehyde function. A partial equation for the reaction that was used is shown below. Fill in structural formulas for the reagents (A and B) that were used and for compound C, which is the other product of the reaction.

S8.10   The following reaction would be expected to produce the bromohydrin shown below on the left. However, the reaction actually gives the allylic bromide shown on the right.

(a) What are the structures for the two different bromonium ion intermediates that could result from the reaction of the alkene with bromine?

(b) Only one of these bromonium ions is proposed to form in this reaction. Which one is it, and what is wrong with the other one?

(c) Write a mechanism that rationalizes the formation of the allylic bromide from the bromonium ion that you selected as the one that forms in the reaction.

S8.11   Research into the reactions of alkenes substituted at the double bond with a good leaving group and with groups that stabilize carbocations show that they undergo S_N1 reactions. For example, the following reaction was observed.

vinyl mesylate A   ethyl vinyl ether B

ethyl vinyl ether C   ketone D

In aqueous ethanol, vinyl mesylate gives a mixture of stereoisomeric ethyl vinyl ethers B and C, and ketone D.

(a)   What is the configuration, *E* or *Z*, of ethyl vinyl ether B?

(b)   What is the structure of the carbocation that is the reactive intermediate in the reaction shown above? What is the hybridization of the carbon with the positive charge in this cation? What is the bond angle between the two nearest neighbors of the cationic carbon?

(c)   Using the curved arrow convention, draw the complete mechanism for the conversion of vinyl mesylate A to ketone D. Think carefully about the participation of the solvent in this reaction. A shorthand version of the structures for A and B are given below. You may use these to save time in writing your mechanism. You may also use HB^+ and B: as general acids and bases if you wish.

vinyl mesylate A   ketone D

S8.12   When the tosylate of 3-methyl-2-butanol is dissolved in trifluoroacetic acid, the major product is the trifluoroacetic acid ester of 2-methyl-2-butanol.

tosylate of   trifluoroacetic acid,   trifluoroacetate of   trifluoroacetate of   *p*-toluene-
3-methyl-2-butanol   also serves as solvent   2-methy-2-butanol   3-methy-2-butanol   sulfonic acid
                                               98.5%   1.5%

Using the curved arrow convention, write a complete mechanism that accounts for the formation of the major product as described in the equation above.

S8.13   The following transformation has been observed.

The reaction is catalyzed by trifluoromethylsulfonic acid, which is regenerated during the reaction.
(a) Propose an approximate pK_a for trifluoromethylsulfonic acid.
(b) Using the curved arrow convention, draw a mechanism for the conversion shown above.

S8.14   The following reactions are all used by chemists in the synthesis of natural products that display interesting biological effects. Supply structural formulas for the missing reagents or products indicated by letters. Show stereochemistry wherever it is known.

S8.15   The following solvolysis reactions were studied.
(a) Both are first-order reactions. Reaction B is ~10^4 times faster than reaction A. Draw a mechanism using the curved arrow convention for the rate-determining step of reaction A.

(b) Why is reaction B faster than reaction A? Use both words and pictures in your answer.

S8.16

(a) Professor Barry Sharpless recently reported that osmylation of compound A in the presence of the chiral catalyst B produced a single stereoisomer of compound C, (1*R*, 2*R*)-1-phenyl-1,2-propanediol. Provide structures for compounds A and C.

compound A $\xrightarrow[\text{Cl}]{\text{OsO}_4}$ (1*R*, 2*R*)-stereoisomer of compound C

catalyst B

(b) This reaction is said to be very stereospecific, since only one stereoisomer is formed in a reaction that could, in theory, give more than one stereoisomer. How many stereoisomers of compound C are possible?

(c) When the chiral catalyst B is left out of the reaction, (1*R*, 2*R*)-1-phenyl-1,2-propanediol is once again formed, and it is accompanied by one other stereoisomer. What are the configurational assignments of the stereocenters in this second isomer? What relative amounts of the (1*R*, 2*R*)-stereoisomer and this second isomer will be formed in this experiment?

S8.17   Vinyl acetate is the monomer used in the preparation of the polymer, poly(vinyl acetate). This polymer is the base material to which flavors and colors are added in manufacturing chewing gum.

vinyl acetate

Poly(vinyl acetate) forms an atactic (stereochemically nonregular) polymeric structure. Draw a representation of a poly(vinyl acetate) segment that includes at least six of the repeating units and shows the atactic nature of the structure.

9
Alkynes

Workbook Exercises

Your study of the structure and reactivity of organic compounds has included a number of different ways to represent a molecule based upon the type of information that is known or needed. One way of organizing this information is under the general heading of "isomerism," which can be viewed according to the hierarchy presented below.

(1) **Isomerism** (or, ways to represent molecules)

(2) A **molecular formula** provides the possibility of constitutional isomers that differ in their connectivity (see Chapter 1).

(3) A particular **connectivity** provides the possibility that there are stereoisomers that differ in the three-dimensional arrangement of bonded atoms (see Chapter 6).

(4) A particular **stereoisomer** (or a particular connectivity, if no stereoisomers are possible) may have conformational isomers that differ in nonbonded three-dimensional arrangements (see Chapter 5).

EXERCISE I.　　　For each of the three molecular formulas (a, b, and c) shown below,

   (a) $C_6H_{12}O_2$　　　　　　　　(b) C_7H_{10}　　　　　　　　(c) $C_5H_{11}NO$

1. Create 10 different constitutional isomers (for a total of 30 molecules). The molecules that you create should be comprised of uncharged, closed-shell atoms.

2. Decide how many stereoisomers are possible for each constitutional isomer that you create.

3. Choose five examples of single bonds between any 2 tetrahedral atoms in the isomers you create. Draw Newman projections for each example showing different possible conformations. For any cyclohexane or closely related six-membered ring, create the two appropriate chair forms.

(Note: This is an ideal problem to work with other students. You should also save your responses to part 1 of this exercise for the workbook exercise in Chapter 10.)

9.1　　(a) 6,6-dichloro-2-methyl-3-heptyne　　　　(b) 3,3-dimethyl-1-pentyne

     (c) 4-bromo-2-hexyne　　　　　　　　　　　　(d) 2,6-dimethyl-3-octyne

9.2　(a) $CH_3CH_2CH_2C\equiv CCCH_3$ with CH_3 above and Cl below　　(b) $CH_3C\equiv CCH_2CHCH_2CH_2CH_3$ with Ph below　　(c) $CH_3C\equiv C\equiv CCH_2CH_3$ with CH_3 above and CH_3 below

---

Concept Map 9.1　　　　Outline of the synthesis of a disubstituted alkyne from a terminal alkyne.

9.3   (a) $CH_3CH_2CH_2C \equiv CH$ $\xrightarrow[NH_3 \text{ (liq)}]{NaNH_2}$ $CH_3CH_2CH_2C \equiv C \colon^- Na^+$ $\xrightarrow{CH_3CH_2CH_2Br}$

$$CH_3CH_2CH_2C \equiv CCH_2CH_2CH_3$$
$$B$$

(b) $HC \equiv C \colon^- Na^+$ $\xrightarrow[NH_3 \text{ (liq)}]{\underset{D}{\overset{CH_3}{\underset{|}{CH_3CHCH_2CH_2Br}}}}$ $\underset{|}{\overset{CH_3}{\underset{}{CH_3CHCH_2CH_2C}}} \equiv CH$

     C

(c) $CH_3CH_2CH_2C \equiv CH$ $\xrightarrow[NH_3 \text{ (liq)}]{NaNH_2}$ $CH_3CH_2CH_2C \equiv C \colon^- Na^+$ $\xrightarrow{(CH_3)_2SO_4}$ $CH_3CH_2CH_2C \equiv CCH_3$

                                    E   F   G

The leaving group in dimethyl sulfate, $(CH_3)_2SO_4$, is the methyl sulfate anion, $^-OSO_3CH_3$.

9.4   (a) [cyclopentene with Cl] $\xrightarrow{HBr}$ [cyclopentane with Cl, Br]

(b) $CH_3C \equiv CCH_3$ $\xrightarrow{HBr \text{ (excess)}}$ $\underset{|}{\overset{Br}{\underset{Br}{CH_3CH_2CCH_3}}}$

(c) $CH_3CH_2CH_2CH = CH_2$ $\xrightarrow{HCl}$ $CH_3CH_2CH_2\underset{|}{\overset{}{\underset{Cl}{CHCH_3}}}$

(d) [cyclohexene with CH_3] $\xrightarrow{HI}$ [cyclohexane with CH_3, I]

9.5 $CH_3C \equiv C(CH_2)_7\overset{O}{\overset{\|}{C}}OH$ $\xrightarrow[H_2SO_4]{80\%}$ $CH_3\overset{O}{\overset{\|}{C}}CH_2(CH_2)_7\overset{O}{\overset{\|}{C}}OH$ + $CH_3CH_2\overset{O}{\overset{\|}{C}}(CH_2)_7\overset{O}{\overset{\|}{C}}OH$

- -

Concept Map 9.2   Electrophilic addition of acids to alkynes.

9.6

$CH_3CH_2C \equiv CCH_3 \longrightarrow CH_3CH_2\overset{+}{C}=CHCH_3 \longrightarrow CH_3CH_2C=CHCH_3 \longrightarrow CH_3CH_2C=CHCH_3$

$CH_3CH_2CCH_2CH_3 \longleftarrow \left[CH_3CH_2C-CH_2CH_3 \longleftrightarrow CH_3CH_2\overset{+}{C}-CH_2CH_3 \right]$

9.7

$HC \equiv CH \longrightarrow CH_2=\overset{+}{C}H \longrightarrow CH_2=CH \longrightarrow CH_2=CH$

$CH_3CH \longleftarrow \left[CH_3-CH \longleftrightarrow CH_3-\overset{+}{C}H \right]$

9.8

1. What are the connectivities of the starting material and the products? How many carbon atoms does each contain? Are there any rings? What are the positions of branches and functional groups on the carbon skeletons?

$$CH_3(CH_2)_{11}C \equiv CH \overset{?}{\longrightarrow} CH_3(CH_2)_{11}C \equiv CCH_2(CH_2)_7CH_3$$

1-tetradecyne   10-tricosyne

The starting material has a linear chain of 14 carbon atoms; the product has a linear chain of 23 carbon atoms. The starting material is a 1-alkyne, and the product is a 10-alkyne.

2. How do the functional groups change in going from starting material to product? Does the starting material have a good leaving group?
    A nonyl group in the product has replaced the terminal hydrogen in the starting material.

3. Is it possible to dissect the structures of the starting material and product to see which bonds must be broken and which formed?

9.8 (cont)

bond broken

$$CH_3(CH_2)_{11}C \equiv C - \} - H$$

bond formed

$$CH_3(CH_2)_{11}C \equiv C - \} - CH_2(CH_2)_7CH_3$$

Pieces that we need: $CH_3(CH_2)_{11}C \equiv C$——   and   ——$CH_2(CH_2)_7CH_3$

4.   New bonds are created when an electrophile reacts with a nucleophile. Do we recognize any part of the product molecule as coming from an electrophile or a nucleophile?
    The new carbon-carbon bond must have come from a nucleophilic substitution reaction. The terminal alkyne can be converted into a nucleophile. The alkyl group, attached to a leaving group, must supply the electrophile.

$$CH_3(CH_2)_{11}C \equiv C : ^- \xrightarrow{CH_3(CH_2)_7CH_2Br} CH_3(CH_2)_{11}C \equiv CCH_2(CH_2)_7CH_3$$

5.   After this last step, do we see how to get from starting material to product? If not, we need to analyze the structure obtained in step 4 by applying questions 3 and 4 to it.

Complete correct answer:

$$CH_3(CH_2)_{11}C \equiv CH \xrightarrow[NH_3 \ (liq)]{NaNH_2} CH_3(CH_2)_{11}C \equiv C : ^- Na^+ \xrightarrow{CH_3(CH_2)_7CH_2Br} CH_3(CH_2)_{11}C \equiv CCH_2(CH_2)_7CH_3$$

9.9 $CH_3(CH_2)_{11}C \equiv CCH_2(CH_2)_7CH_3 \xrightarrow[\substack{PtO_2 \\ hexane}]{H_2 \ (1 \ equivalent)}$

$$\underset{\text{alkene}}{\underset{H \quad\quad H}{\overset{CH_3(CH_2)_{11} \quad CH_2(CH_2)_7CH_3}{C=C}}} \quad + \quad \underset{\text{alkane}}{CH_3(CH_2)_{21}(CH_3)} \quad + \quad \underset{\text{alkyne}}{CH_3(CH_2)_{11}C \equiv CCH_2(CH_2)_7CH_3}$$

In the presence of one equivalent of hydrogen, the first product to form will be the alkene. As the concentration of alkene builds up in the reaction mixture, it will start to react with hydrogen to give the alkane. To the extent that this second reaction occurs, some of the alkyne will remain unchanged, because the system will run out of hydrogen before it runs out of alkyne.

- -

Concept Map 9.3   Reduction reactions of alkynes.

9.10

(a) $CH_3CH_2CH_2CH_2C \equiv CH$ $\xrightarrow[\text{quinoline}]{\text{H}_2 \atop \text{Pd/BaSO}_4}$ $CH_3CH_2CH_2CH_2CH = CH_2$

(b) $CH_3CH_2CH_2CH_2C \equiv CCH_3$ $\xrightarrow[\text{quinoline}]{\text{H}_2 \atop \text{Pd/BaSO}_4}$

$\begin{array}{ccc} CH_3CH_2CH_2CH_2 & & CH_3 \\ & C=C & \\ H & & H \end{array}$

(c) $CH_3CH_2CH_2CH_2C \equiv CCH_3$ $\xrightarrow[\text{NH}_3 \text{ (liq)}]{\text{Na}}$

$\begin{array}{ccc} CH_3CH_2CH_2CH_2 & & H \\ & C=C & \\ H & & CH_3 \end{array}$

(d) $CH_3CH_2CH_2CH_2C \equiv CCH_3$ $\xrightarrow[\text{acetic acid}]{\text{H}_2 \text{ (excess)} \atop \text{Pt}}$ $CH_3CH_2CH_2CH_2CH_2CH_2CH_3$

9.11 $CH_3C \equiv CCH_3$ $\xrightarrow[\text{Pd/Al}_2\text{O}_3]{\text{D}_2}$

$\begin{array}{ccc} CH_3 & & CH_3 \\ & C=C & \\ D & & D \end{array}$

9.12

(a) $\begin{array}{c} CH_3CH_2CH_2CHCH_3 \\ | \\ Br \end{array}$ $\xleftarrow{\text{HBr}}$ $CH_3CH_2CH_2CH = CH_2$ $\xleftarrow[\text{quinoline}]{\text{H}_2 \atop \text{Pd/BaSO}_4}$ $CH_3CH_2CH_2C \equiv CH$ $\xleftarrow{CH_3CH_2CH_2Br}$

$Na^{+-}:C \equiv CH$ $\xleftarrow[\text{NH}_3 \text{ (liq)}]{\text{NaNH}_2}$ $HC \equiv CH$

(b) $\begin{array}{c} O \\ \| \\ CH_3CH_2CH_2CCH_2CH_3 \end{array}$ $\xleftarrow[\text{H}_2\text{SO}_4]{\text{H}_2\text{O}}$ $CH_3CH_2C \equiv CCH_2CH_3$ $\xleftarrow{CH_3CH_2Br}$

$CH_3CH_2C \equiv C:^- Na^+$ $\xleftarrow[\text{NH}_3 \text{ (liq)}]{\text{NaNH}_2}$ $CH_3CH_2C \equiv CH$

(c) $\begin{array}{cc} HO_{\substack{\cdot\\\cdot}} \quad H \quad OH \\ C - C \\ CH_3CH_2CH_2 \quad ^{\substack{\cdot\\\cdot}} CH_2CH_3 \\ H \end{array}$ $\xleftarrow[\text{H}_2\text{O}]{\text{KMnO}_4, \text{ KOH}}$ $\begin{array}{ccc} CH_3CH_2CH_2 & & CH_2CH_3 \\ & C=C & \\ H & & H \end{array}$ $\xleftarrow[\text{quinoline}]{\text{H}_2 \atop \text{Pd/BaSO}_4}$

and enantiomer

$CH_3CH_2CH_2C \equiv CCH_2CH_3$ $\xleftarrow{CH_3CH_2Br}$ $CH_3CH_2CH_2C \equiv C:^- Na^+$ $\xleftarrow[\text{NH}_3 \text{ (liq)}]{\text{NaNH}_2}$ $CH_3CH_2CH_2C \equiv CH$

9.13   (a) (*R*)-2-chloro-4-octyne   (b) (*Z*)-3-methyl-3-heptene
         (c) 2-methyl-4-octyn-2-ol   (d) *trans*-1-methyl-2-vinylcyclohexane

9.14   (a)

$$CH_3CH_2\overset{\displaystyle CH_3}{\underset{\displaystyle Cl}{C}}\overset{\displaystyle}{\underset{\displaystyle H}{C}}=C\overset{\displaystyle H}{\underset{\displaystyle CH_2CH_2CH_3}{}}$$

(b)

$$H\text{-}\overset{\displaystyle CH_2CH_2CH_3}{\underset{\displaystyle Br}{C}}\text{-}CH_2C\equiv CH$$

(c)   HO⟍⟋CH_3

and enantiomer

(d) $CH_3CH_2C\equiv CCH_2CH_2OH$

9.15   (a) $CH_3CH_2C\equiv CCH_3$ $\xrightarrow[\substack{Pd/CaCO_3 \\ quinoline}]{H_2}$ $\underset{H}{\overset{CH_3CH_2}{}}C=C\underset{H}{\overset{CH_3}{}}$

(b) $CH_3CH_2C\equiv CCH_3$ $\xrightarrow[Pt]{H_2\ (excess)}$ $CH_3CH_2CH_2CH_2CH_3$

(c) $CH_3CH_2C\equiv CCH_3$ $\xrightarrow[NH_3\ (liq)]{Na}$ $\underset{H}{\overset{CH_3CH_2}{}}C=C\underset{CH_3}{\overset{H}{}}$

(d) $\underset{H}{\overset{CH_3CH_2}{}}C=C\underset{H}{\overset{CH_3}{}}$ $\xrightarrow[dichloromethane]{Cl-C_6H_4-COOH}$ $CH_3CH_2\overset{O}{\triangle}CH_3$ and enantiomer

(e) $\underset{H}{\overset{CH_3CH_2}{}}C=C\underset{CH_3}{\overset{H}{}}$ $\xrightarrow[dichloromethane]{Cl-C_6H_4-COOH}$ $CH_3CH_2\overset{O}{\triangle}H$ and enantiomer

(f) $CH_3CH_2C\equiv CCH_3$ $\xrightarrow{HBr\ (1\ molar\ equiv)}$ $\underset{H}{\overset{CH_3CH_2}{}}C=C\underset{CH_3}{\overset{Br}{}}$ + $\underset{Br}{\overset{CH_3CH_2}{}}C=C\underset{CH_3}{\overset{H}{}}$

major products

(g) $CH_3CH_2C\equiv CCH_3$ $\xrightarrow{HBr\ (2\ molar\ equiv)}$ $CH_3CH_2CBr_2CH_2CH_3$ + $CH_3CH_2CH_2CBr_2CH_3$

(h) $CH_3CH_2C\equiv CCH_3$ $\xrightarrow{Br_2\ (1\ molar\ equiv)}$ $\underset{Br}{\overset{CH_3CH_2}{}}C=C\underset{CH_3}{\overset{Br}{}}$

(i) $CH_3CH_2C\equiv CCH_3$ $\xrightarrow{Br_2\ (2\ molar\ equiv)}$ $CH_3CH_2CBr_2CBr_2CH_3$

(j) $CH_3CH_2C\equiv CCH_3$ $\xrightarrow[\substack{H_2SO_4 \\ HgSO_4}]{H_2O}$ $CH_3CH_2\overset{O}{\overset{\|}{C}}CH_2CH_3$ + $CH_3CH_2CH_2\overset{O}{\overset{\|}{C}}CH_3$

9.16 (a) $PhC \equiv CPh \xrightarrow[\text{quinoline}]{\underset{Pd/CaCO_3}{H_2}}$ A

(b) $CH_2 = CHBr \xrightarrow{HBr} CH_3CHBr_2$ B

(c) $CH_2 = CHCH_2Br \xrightarrow[\substack{\text{carbon} \\ \text{tetrachloride}}]{Br_2} BrCH_2CHBrCH_2Br$ C

(d) $PhC \equiv CCH_2CH_3 \xrightarrow[\text{NH}_3 \text{ (liq)}]{Na}$ D

(e) $\xrightarrow[\text{quinoline}]{\underset{Pd/CaCO_3}{H_2}}$ E

(f) $\xrightarrow[\text{quinoline}]{\underset{Pd/CaCO_3}{H_2}}$ F

(g) $\xrightarrow[\text{quinoline}]{\underset{Pd/BaSO_4}{H_2}}$ G

9.17 (a) $CH_3C \equiv CCH_3 \xrightarrow[\underset{A}{H_2SO_4}]{H_2O}$

(b) $HC \equiv CH \xrightarrow[B]{Na^+ NH_2^-} HC \equiv C:^- Na^+ \xrightarrow[D]{PhCH_2OCH_2CH_2Br} HC \equiv CCH_2CH_2OCH_2Ph$
C

(c) $CH_2 = CHCH_2CH_2Br \xrightarrow[\text{NH}_3 \text{ (liq)}]{HC \equiv C:^- Na^+} CH_2 = CHCH_2CH_2C \equiv CH$
E

(d) $CH_2 = CHCHCH_2CH_2OCH_2Ph \xrightarrow{O_3} \xrightarrow{(CH_3)_2S} O = CHCHCH_2CH_2OCH_2Ph$
          $|$ F   G $|$
         CH_3 CH_3

9.17 (e)

9.18

(a)

(b)

(c)

(d)

(e)

and enantiomer

An alternate synthesis is given on the next page..

9.18 (e) (cont)

(f)

9.19

9.20

(a)

(b)   The nucleophilic sites are the oxygen anion, $-\overset{\cdot\cdot}{\underset{\cdot\cdot}{O}}:^-$, and the carbon anion, $-C\equiv C:^-$. The reason for the regioselectivity of this reaction is that the carbon anion is much more nucleophilic than the oxygen anion because carbon is less electronegative than oxygen.

(c)   (*S*)-1-octyn-3-ol

9.21   (a) $HOCH_2(CH_2)_7C\equiv CH \xrightarrow[\text{NH}_3 \text{ (liq)}]{Na^+ NH_2^- \text{ (excess)}} Na^+{}^-OCH_2(CH_2)_7C\equiv C:^- Na^+ \xrightarrow{CH_3CH_2CH_2CH_2Br}$
D

$\xrightarrow{H_3O^+} HOCH_2(CH_2)_7C\equiv CCH_2CH_2CH_2CH_3 \xrightarrow[\text{poisoned catalyst}]{H_2}$

E
a carbon anion is more
nucleophilic than an oxygen anion

spodoptol
F

(b)

(c)

Aldehyde A   Aldehyde B

9.22

(a)

disparlure

$$CH_3(CH_2)_9C\!\equiv\!C(CH_2)_4CHCH_3 \xleftarrow{\;CH_3CH(CH_2)_3CH_2Br\;} CH_3(CH_2)_9C\!\equiv\!C\!:^- Na^+ \xleftarrow[NH_3\,(liq)]{NaNH_2} CH_3(CH_2)_9C\!\equiv\!CH$$

(b)

$$\xleftarrow[NH_3\,(liq)]{Na} CH_3(CH_2)_9C\!\equiv\!C(CH_2)_4CHCH_3$$

9.23

9.24

primary carbocation;
electron-withdrawing
group on α-carbon;
less stable; does not form

resonance stabilized secondary
carbocation; more stable

9.25 $CH_3C\!\!=\!\!CH_2$ (with CH_3 above) + HCl $\longrightarrow$ CH_3CCH_3 (with CH_3 above, Cl below)

In the reaction with 2-methylpropene, the intermediate is a tertiary carbocation that is stabilized by the electron-donating inductive effect of the three methyl groups.

tertiary carbocation; less stable than the resonance-stabilized carbocation from ethyl vinyl ether

$CH_3CH_2OCH\!\!=\!\!CH_2$ + HCl $\longrightarrow$ $CH_3CH_2OCHCH_3$ (with Cl below)

In the reaction with ethyl vinyl ether, the intermediate is a carbocation in which the positive charge can be delocalized over the carbon atom and the adjacent oxygen atom.

$$CH_3CH_2\ddot{O}\!-\!CH\!\!=\!\!CH_2 \longrightarrow \left[CH_3CH_2\ddot{O}\!-\!\overset{+}{C}HCH_3 \longleftrightarrow CH_3CH_2\overset{+}{\ddot{O}}\!\!=\!\!CHCH_3 \right] \quad :\!\ddot{C}l\!:^{-}$$

major contributor

delocalized carbocation; more stable

$$CH_3CH_2\ddot{O}\!-\!\overset{+}{C}HCH_3 \longrightarrow CH_3CH_2\ddot{O}\!-\!CHCH_3 \text{ (with } :\!\ddot{C}l\!: \text{ below)}$$

The reactive intermediate formed in this reaction is more highly stabilized, and therefore, closer in energy to the energy level of the starting materials than is the case for 2-methylpropene. The E_a for this reaction is therefore lower, and the reaction is faster.

9.26 (a)

Compound **X**

Compound **Y**
tetronic acid

(b)

Supplemental Problems

S9.1   The following equations represent chemical transformations showing pathways from starting materials to products. All of these use the types of reactions that you have learned involving electrophilic and nucleophilic species. Fill in the structural formulas for the starting materials, reagents, or products represented by the letters, using changes in molecular connectivity as clues. Be sure to show stereochemistry when it is known.

(a) $CH_3C{\equiv}CCH_2\overset{\overset{\displaystyle O}{\|}}{C}NH_2 \xrightarrow[\substack{Pd/BaSO_4 \\ quinoline}]{H_2}$ A

(b)

$C_6H_{13}C{\equiv}C{:}^-\ Li^+$
(2 equivalents)
$\xrightarrow[\substack{tetrahydrofuran \\ -78\ °C}]{}$ B

(c)

$\xrightarrow[\substack{(CH_3CH_2)_3N \\ dichloromethane}]{MsCl}$ C $\xrightarrow[acetone]{E}$

C $\xrightarrow[\substack{ethanol \\ H_2O,\ \Delta}]{K^+\ CN^-}$ D

(d)

$\xrightarrow[dichloromethane]{}$ F

Choose one of the following answers for F. It will be:
(a) a single compound   (b) a 1:1 mixture of enantiomers
(c) an unequal mixture of enantiomers
(d) a 1:1 mixture of diastereomers
(e) an unequal mixture of diastereomers

(e) $(CH_3)_3SiCH_2C{\equiv}CCH_2CH_2\underset{\underset{\displaystyle OH}{|}}{C}HPh \xrightarrow[\substack{Lindlar\ catalyst \\ (a\ poisoned\ Pd\ catalyst)}]{H_2}$ G

S9.1

(f)

Boc is a group used to protect the amino group.
It is unaffected by this reaction.

(g)

(h)

(i)

(j) $CH_3(CH_2)_4C \equiv CCH_2COCH_3$ $\xrightarrow{M}$

(k)

R is a large peptide chain and
is not changed in the reaction.

Which one of the oxirane
stereoisomers, O or P, would
you expect to be formed in
the larger amount and why?

(l) $HC \equiv CH$ $\xrightarrow{\text{HBr (excess)}}$ Q

(m) $PhCH_2CH == CH_2$ $\xrightarrow{\text{HBr}}$ R

(n) $PhC \equiv C - \overset{O}{\overset{\|}{C}}OCH_2CH_3$ $\xrightarrow[\substack{Pd/BaSO_4 \\ quinoline}]{H_2}$ S

S9.2   How would you carry out each of the following transformations? More than one step may be necessary.

(a)

(b) $CH_3\overset{CH_3}{\overset{|}{C}}HCH_2CH_2Br$ $\longrightarrow$ $CH_3\overset{CH_3}{\overset{|}{C}}HCH$ (with $== O$)

(c)

(d) CH_3CH_2Br $\longrightarrow$

S9.2

(e) $CH_3CH_2C\equiv CCH_2CH_3 \longrightarrow$

S9.3   Substitution of hydrogen with fluorine often causes significant changes in the chemical and physical properties of compounds while allowing them to be taken up by cells and to interact with key enzyme systems. For this reason, there is much interest in the synthesis of such compounds. Some steps from an investigation of trifluoromethyl compounds are shown below.

(a)   A racemic mixture of the following compound, compound A, was resolved by treatment with a mixture of vinyl acetate and an enzyme that converted the *S*-enantiomer to an acetate ester, and left the *R*-enantiomer untouched. The equation for this reaction is given below with no stereochemistry shown.

Draw a correct structural formula for the (*R*)-enantiomer of compound A, and show how it reacts with hydrogen in the presence of a poisoned palladium catalyst.

(b)   Fill in the structures of the ozonolysis products of compound C below, and draw a Newman projection for it looking down the bond indicated.

(c)   Compound B was shown in brackets in the equation in part (a) because it is not recovered from the mixture in the form written, but as acetaldehyde. What is the relationship between acetaldehyde and compound B?

(d)   Use the curved arrow convention to show how compound B is converted to acetaldehyde in the reaction mixture. Use HB$^+$ and B: as acids and bases as needed.

S9.4   Polyunsaturated fatty acids labeled with deuterium (D, also sometimes shown as ^{2}H, an isotope of hydrogen) are needed to study the metabolism of such acids. A compound used in the synthesis of such fatty acids is $HOCH_2C\equiv CCD_2CD_3$. 2-Propyn-1-ol (propargyl alcohol), $HOCH_2C\equiv CH$, is readily available as a starting material. Show below how you would convert 2-propyn-1-ol to the desired compound. The synthesis involves several steps. Pay special attention to the relative amounts of the reagents you need to use. Solvents may be ignored. Your pK_a table will be useful in choosing reagents and predicting the structures of reactive intermediates. You may assume that you can buy any necessary deuterated reagents.

S9.5   The following transformation is proposed to occur in a single, bimolecular step. Provide the curved arrows for the mechanism.

S9.6   Chemists are interested in how natural products are constructed in biological systems. In research into how some plant products are synthesized, the following reaction pathway was proposed. Use the curved arrow convention to show the electronic and bonding changes that occur as the starting material is converted to the final cation shown.

OPP is the diphosphate ion, nature's leaving group

What is the transformation shown in step 2 called?

10

Nuclear Magnetic Resonance Spectroscopy

Workbook Exercises

In Sections 5.4 and 5.7 of your text, encountered nuclear magnetic resonance (NMR) spectroscopy as a tool that allows us to observe the equivalence of atoms and groups in molecular structures, in other words, to detect symmetry in structures. You solved problems in which you used NMR spectra to make decisions about the connectivity of molecules. In this chapter, we will learn more about NMR and its uses in the determination of the structure of molecules.

A brief review of the ideas and terminology introduced in Sections 5.4 and 5.7
(You should re-examine those sections of the text for a more complete look at this topic.)

There are three structural descriptions for this molecule that relate to NMR spectroscopy:

I. **The number of sets of atoms and their relationships within a molecule**
   There are three distinct, nonequivalent sets, or groups, of hydrogen atoms (a, b and c) based on overall molecular symmetry (for example, the distance from the oxygen atom).

II. **The relative sizes of groups of atoms**
   The total of 10 hydrogen atoms that comprise sets a, b and c are in the ratio of 3:1:6, respectively.

III. **The environment of neighboring atoms as related by the number of intervening bonds**
   Any hydrogen atom in set c is related to hydrogen atom b by 3 intervening bonds (H_b—C—C—H_c). H_b is a 3-bond neighbor for any of the H_c atoms.

As you begin to study Chapter 10, remember that NMR spectroscopy simply provides graphical information that can be interpreted in terms of:

1. the number of groups of equivalent atoms and their connectivity relationships within a molecule.
2. the relative numbers of atoms within each of the groups.
3. the environment of groups of atoms based on the number of bonds intervening between them and other atoms.

The following two workbook exercises are extensions of problems from Chapter 5. They will focus your attention on structural ideas important to your study of NMR spectroscopy.

EXERCISE I. You created a number of molecules with different connectivities for part (1) of the workbook exercise in Chapter 9. Identify the number and relative size of the sets of equivalent hydrogen atoms for each of your molecules. Do the same for sets of carbon atoms.

EXERCISE II. In this problem, groups of equivalent atoms are ranked according to their proximity to an electronegative group in the molecule (for example, of groups a, b and c, group a is closest to the most electronegative group).

Molecules A, B, and C have the same molecular formula, $C_6H_{12}O_2$. Molecule A has a carbonyl group but no hydroxyl group. Molecule A has five sets of equivalent hydrogen atoms (a, b, c, d, and e) in the ratio of 3:2:2:2:3, respectively. Set a has no nonequivalent 3-bond hydrogen neighbors (hereafter referred to as "neighbors" unless a different description is required). Set b has two neighbors, set c has four, set d has 5, and set 3 has 2. Molecule A has six sets of carbon atoms.

Workbook Exercises (cont)

Molecule B has a carboxylic acid functional group. Molecule B has four groups of equivalent hydrogen atoms (a, b, c, and d) in the ratio of 1:2:6:3, respectively. Set a has no neighbors. Set b has three neighbors. Set c has no neighbors, and set d has two neighbors. There are five groups of carbon atoms in molecule B.

Molecule C has no alcohol, carbon-carbon double bond, or carbonyl functional groups. There are three groups of hydrogen atoms in molecule C (a,b, and c) in the ratio of 2:1:3 respectively. Set a has two neighbors. Set b has four neighbors. Set c has no neighbors. There are four groups of carbon atoms in molecule C.

Draw structural formulas for molecules A, B, and C that are compatible with the spectral data (and the molecular formula) that you have for them.

10.1   Replacement of any one of the *a* hydrogen atoms with a methyl group gives the same connectivity and, therefore, the same compound. Replacement of a *b* hydrogen atom gives a different connectivity.

10.2   Solid arrows point to chemical-shift equivalent hydrogen atoms; dashed arrows point to chemically equivalent carbon atoms. Hydrogen atoms on the same methyl group are always chemical-shift equivalent. Hydrogen atoms on the same methylene group are usually, but not always, chemical-shift equivalent. The carbon atoms to which the indicated hydrogen atoms are attached are also equivalent. In addition, there are two carbons with no hydrogen atoms on them, one in (c) and one in (e) that are different from the others.

10.2

10.3   The first compound has two sets of equivalent carbon atoms and, therefore, will have two chemical shifts in the ^{13}C nuclear magnetic resonance spectrum. The second compound has three sets of equivalent carbon atoms and, therefore, three chemical shifts in the ^{13}C nuclear magnetic resonance spectrum. The bottom spectrum is that of tetrahydrofuran, and the top spectrum is that of propanoic anhydride. The chemical shift assignments are given below.

10.4   (a) $^{28}_{14}$Si   even atomic and mass number; no nuclear magnetic moment

      (b) $^{15}_{7}$N   odd mass and atomic number; has nuclear magnetic moment

      (c) $^{19}_{9}$F   odd mass and atomic number; has nuclear magnetic moment

      (d) $^{31}_{15}$P   odd mass and atomic number; has nuclear magnetic moment

      (e) $^{11}_{5}$B   odd mass and atomic number; has nuclear magnetic moment

      (f) $^{32}_{16}$S   even atomic and mass number; no nuclear magnetic moment

10.5

$$CH_3-\overset{\overset{\displaystyle CH_3}{|}}{CH}-CH_2-CH_2-CH_3$$

2-methylpentane;
five sets of equivalent carbon atoms, therefore five chemical shifts; isomer 3

$$CH_3-CH_2-\overset{\overset{\displaystyle CH_3}{|}}{CH}-CH_2-CH_3$$

3-methylpentane;
four sets of equivalent carbon atoms, therefore four chemical shifts; isomer 2

$$CH_3-\overset{\overset{\displaystyle CH_3}{|}}{CH}-\overset{\overset{\displaystyle CH_3}{|}}{CH}-CH_3$$

2,3-dimethylbutane;
two sets of equivalent carbon atoms, therefore two chemical shifts; isomer 1

10.6

2-cyclohexenone;
six different carbon atoms, therefore six chemical shifts; bottom spectrum

2-butanone (methyl ethyl ketone);
four different carbon atoms, therefore four chemical shifts; top spectrum

pyrrolidine;
two sets of equivalent carbon atoms, therefore two chemical shifts; middle spectrum

10.7   Compound A, C_5H_8O, has two units of unsaturation. The chemical shift at δ 219.6 is that of the carbon of a ketone, which uses up one unit of unsaturation. There are two more chemical shifts and four carbon atoms left. The molecule must be symmetric with two additional sets of two carbon atoms. There are no bands in the alkene region, therefore the other unit of unsaturation must be a ring. Only cyclopentanone fits the given ^{13}C data.

10.8   The band that moves progressively upfield as the solution of the alcohol is diluted is the band for the hydrogen atom of the hydroxyl group. As the alcohol is diluted, the amount of hydrogen bonding decreases.

Hydrogen bonding further deshields a hydrogen atom because the hydrogen atom involved in hydrogen bonding is partially bonded to another electronegative atom (O, N, or F) and has even less electron density around it than a hydrogen atom which is not involved in hydrogen bonding.

$$R-O-H \qquad\qquad\qquad R-O-H\cdots\cdots O-R$$
$$\hspace{8.5cm} \underset{H}{/}$$

dilute solution; no hydrogen bonding;
the hydrogen atom is less deshielded
and absorbs farther upfield

concentrated solution; hydrogen bonding;
the hydrogen atom is more deshielded
and absorbs farther downfield

10.9

The absorption bands between δ 1.0 and 3.0 in the spectrum of cyclohexene fall in the region for hydrogen atoms that are bonded to sp^3-hybridized carbon atoms. The four hydrogen atoms absorbing farther downfield (δ ~2) are the allylic hydrogen atoms on carbon atoms 3 and 6. These hydrogens are more deshielded than the hydrogens on carbon atoms 4 and 5 because they are closer to the double bond. The four hydrogen atoms farther upfield (δ ~1.6) are those on carbon atoms 4 and 5.

10.10   In this problem, in which we assign the structure of a compound from its molecular formula and spectral data, the proton magnetic resonance data are analyzed in two ways. The chemical shift values for groups of different hydrogen atoms are read off the spectrum, these values are compared with the chemical shift values given in Table 10.3 for different types of hydrogen atoms, and a tentative assignment of partial structure is made. The integration of the spectrum is examined by measuring the relative heights of the steps in the integration curves. The two types of information are summarized in the answers to these problems in the following way:

$$\delta\ 3.8 \qquad (6H, O-C\underline{H}_3)$$

chemical
shift

number of hydrogen
atoms giving rise to
the peak with that
chemical shift

assignment of the type of hydrogen
atom by comparing chemical shift
value to typical values given in Table 10.3;
the results of the integration also taken into
account here

Compound B, $C_8H_{10}O_2$, has four units of unsaturation. Integration of the spectrum gives a ratio of 11:7.5 or 3:2 for the relative areas under the peaks. The molecular formula tells us that there are ten hydrogen atoms that absorb so the actual ratio is 6:4. Therefore, we have six hydrogen atoms that absorb at δ 3.8 and four that absorb at δ 6.8. The results of this reasoning and of our inspection of Table 10.3 are summarized on the next page.

10.10 (cont) δ 3.8   (6H, —OC$\underline{H}_3$)

                    δ 6.8   (4H, Ar$\underline{H}$)

The compound is 1,4-dimethyoxybenzene.

Note that the symmetry of the structure of the compound is reflected in the simplicity of the spectrum.

$$CH_3O - \langle \ \rangle - OCH_3$$

Compound C, C_7H_7Cl, has four units of unsaturation. (Each halogen atom counts as one hydrogen atom in determining units of unsaturation.) Integration of the spectrum gives a ratio of 10:22 or 2:5 (for a total of seven hydrogen atoms in C) for the relative areas under the peaks.

                δ 4.6   (2H, Y—C$\underline{H}_2$—X, where both X and Y deshield the methylene group)

                δ 7.4   (5H, Ar$\underline{H}$)

The compound is benzyl chloride.

$$\langle \ \rangle - CH_2Cl$$

Note that in using Table 10.3, we must realize that the values given will not match exactly the chemical shift values that we get from the spectra. We must put all the information together to make assignments of structure. In this problem, once we know that an aryl ring is present, we understand why the hydrogen atoms of the methylene group absorb at lower field than a typical RCH_2X group (δ 2.6 - 4.3 in Table 10.3).

Compound D, C_8H_8O, has five units of unsaturation. Integration of the spectrum gives a ratio of 9:15 or 3:5 (for a total of eight hydrogen atoms in D) for the relative areas under the peaks.

                                 $\overset{\displaystyle O}{\overset{\displaystyle \|}{}}$

              δ 2.6   (3H, — C$\underline{H}_3$)

            δ 7.4 – 8.0   (5H, Ar$\underline{H}$)

The compound is acetophenone (1-phenylethanone).

$$\langle \ \rangle - \overset{\displaystyle O}{\overset{\displaystyle \|}{C}} CH_3$$

The presence of the carbonyl group in the molecule was deduced from the chemical shift of the methyl group, the total number of carbon atoms in the molecule, and the one unit of unsaturation that had to be accounted for once the aromatic ring, with four units of unsaturation, was identified.

10.11   The spectrum of 1,1-dichloroethane has two groups of peaks with an integration giving a ratio of 30:10 or 3:1 for the relative areas under the groups of small peaks.

There are eight possible spin orientations of the three hydrogen atoms of the methyl group. Three orientations in the two middle sets are indistinguishable. The magnetic field sensed by the adjacent hydrogen atom varies slightly with a probability of 1:3:3:1, giving rise to similar relative intensities of the peaks in the quartet.

doublet,
peaks of equal
intensities
$J = 7$ Hz

10.11 (cont)

$J =$ $J =$ $J =$
7 Hz 7 Hz 7 Hz

δ 5.92

δ 2.05

The data from the spectrum may be summarized as follows:

δ 2.05   (3H, d, $J = 7$ Hz, C$\underline{H}_3$CHCl$_2$)

δ 5.92   (1H, q, $J = 7$ Hz, CH$_3$C$\underline{H}$Cl$_2$—)

(s = singlet, d = doublet, t = triplet, q = quartet)

10.12   C$_4$H$_{10}$O has no units of unsaturation. The proton decoupled spectrum tells us that four different carbon atoms are present. Three of the carbon atoms are alkyl carbons bonded to other carbon atoms (δ 10, 23, and 32). The fourth carbon atom (δ 69) is bonded to the oxygen atom.

The proton-coupled spectrum tells us how many hydrogen atoms are bonded to the carbon atoms. Two of the carbons are quartets (at δ 10 and 23), which tells us that these two carbon atoms are methyl carbons. The carbon atom at δ 32 is a triplet and thus has two hydrogens bonded to it. The carbon atom bonded to the oxygen (δ 69) is a doublet and has only one hydrogen bonded to it. The compound is 2-butanol.

$$CH_3 - \underset{\underset{OH}{|}}{CH} - CH_2 - CH_3$$

10.13

$$O_2N \overset{\overset{H_B \qquad H_A}{\bigcirc}}{\underset{H_C \qquad Br}{}} CH_3$$

$J_{AB} = 8.6$ Hz
$J_{BC} = 2.2$ Hz

H$_C$ H$_B$ H$_A$
δ 8.38 δ 8.04 δ 7.40

$J =$
8.6 Hz

$J =$ $J =$ $J =$ $J =$
2.2 Hz   2.2 Hz   2.2 Hz   8.6 Hz

10.14   CH$_3$CH$_2$CH$_2$Br
a   b   c
$J_{ab} = J_{bc} = 7$ Hz

The methylene hydrogen atoms are split into a quartet by the adjacent methyl hydrogen atoms.

10.14 (cont)

Each peak of the quartet is further split into a triplet by the other methylene hydrogen atoms. If the coupling constants for the two types of interactions are the same, the triplets overlap to give a sextet.

10.15

CH_3—⟨benzene ring⟩—$C≡N$
six sets of carbon atoms

⟨benzene ring with CH_3⟩—$C≡N$
eight sets of carbon atoms

⟨benzene ring with CH_3⟩—$C≡N$
eight sets of carbon atoms

The spectrum is that of 4-methylbenzonitrile. The symmetrical splitting pattern for the hydrogen atoms on the aromatic ring, similar in appearance to a doublet of doublets, is typical of an aromatic ring that is substituted in the para positions with two substituents of differing electronegativity.

10.16   Compounds F and G, C_4H_9Br, have no units of unsaturation. Integration of the spectrum of Compound F gives a ratio of 37:7:12 or 6:1:2 for the relative area under the peaks. The molecular formula tells us that there are nine hydrogen atoms that absorb so we have accounted for all the hydrogen atoms. The chemical shifts and coupling information are summarized below.

$δ$ 1.0   (6H, d, —CH($C\underline{H}_3$)₂)
$δ$ 1.95   (1H, multiplet, —C$\underline{H}$)
$δ$ 3.3   (2H, d, —CHC$\underline{H}_2$—Br)

Compound F is isobutyl bromide (1-bromo-2-methylpropane).

$$CH_3CHCH_2Br$$
with CH_3 branch

Integration of the spectrum of Compound G gives a ratio of 15:14:10:5 or 3:3:2:1 (for a total of nine hydrogen atoms in G) for the relative area under the peaks.

$δ$ 1.0   (3H, t, —CH₂C$\underline{H}_3$)
$δ$ 1.7   (3H, d, —CHC$\underline{H}_3$)
$δ$ 1.8   (2H, quintet, —CHC$\underline{H}_2$CH₃)
$δ$ 4.1   (1H, sextet, —CH₂C$\underline{H}$CH₃)

Compound G is *sec*-butyl bromide (2-bromobutane).

$$CH_3CHCH_2CH_3$$
with Br branch

10.17 $R—\ddot{O}\!:\!\curvearrow D—\ddot{\ddot{O}}\!:\!D$ ⇌ $R—\overset{+}{\ddot{O}}—D$ ⇌ $R—\ddot{O}\!:$ $:\ddot{O}—D$
         | | |
         H   H $\curvearrow :\ddot{O}—D$ H

10.18   Compound H, $C_4H_8O_2$, has one unit of unsaturation. Its proton magnetic resonance spectrum has bands at

δ 1.25	(3H, t, C$\underline{H}_3$CH$_2$)
δ 2.05	(3H, s, C$\underline{H}_3$C=O)
δ 4.15	(2H, q, CH$_3$C$\underline{H}_2$O)

The compound is ethyl acetate (ethyl ethanoate)

$$\underset{\displaystyle CH_3COCH_2CH_3}{\overset{\displaystyle O \atop \displaystyle \|}{}}$$

Note the characteristic triplet at ~δ 1 and quartet at ~δ 4 that are characteristic of an ethyl group bonded to an electronegative atom, in this case oxygen.

Compound I, $C_5H_8O_2$, has two units of unsaturation. The proton magnetic resonance spectrum has bands at

δ 1.9	(3H, s, C$\underline{H}_3$C=C)
δ 2.2	(3H, s, C$\underline{H}_3$C=O)
δ 5.7	(1H, s, C$\underline{H}$=C)
δ 12.1	(1H, broad s, $\underline{H}$OC=O)

The compound is 3-methyl-2-butenoic acid.

$$\begin{array}{ccc} CH_3 & & \overset{\displaystyle O \atop \displaystyle \|}{COH} \\ \diagdown & & \diagup \\ & C = C & \\ \diagup & & \diagdown \\ CH_3 & & H \end{array}$$

At first glance the two peaks around δ 2.0 appear to be a doublet, but since there are no other bands in the spectrum showing the same separation, the two peaks cannot have arisen because of coupling to another hydrogen atom. We assign the peaks to two nonequivalent methyl groups on a double bond.

Compound J, $C_7H_{12}O_3$, has two units of unsaturation. The proton magnetic resonance spectrum has bands at

δ 1.25	(3H, t, C$\underline{H}_3$CH$_2$)
δ 2.20	(3H, s, C$\underline{H}_3$C=O)
δ 2.55	(2H, t, CH$_2$C$\underline{H}_2$C=O)
δ 2.75	(2H, t, O=CC$\underline{H}_2$CH$_2$)
δ 4.15	(2H, q, CH$_3$C$\underline{H}_2$O)

Compound J has an isolated ethyl group bonded to oxygen and an isolated methyl group next to a carbonyl group. Each methylene group is also next to a carbonyl group. The compound is ethyl 4-oxopentanoate.

$$\underset{\displaystyle CH_3CH_2OCCH_2CH_2CCH_3}{\overset{\displaystyle O \qquad\quad O \atop \displaystyle \| \qquad\quad \|}{}}$$

Compound K, C_4H_8O, has one unit of unsaturation. The ^{13}C magnetic resonance spectrum has bands at

δ 26	(t, C$\underline{H}_2$)
δ 68	(t, C$\underline{H}_2$O)

Only two carbons are seen in the spectrum but Compound K has four carbon atoms. Each band must correspond to two equivalent carbon atoms. There are no peaks above 100 ppm, therefore the unit of unsaturation must be assigned to a ring and not a carbonyl group or an alkene. The splitting pattern tells us that each carbon atom is bonded to two hydrogen atoms. The compound is tetrahydrofuran.

10.19

$$\begin{matrix} & & b \\ & & CH_3 \\ e\left\{ \hspace{0.2em} \bigcirc \hspace{-1.8em} \text{—} \hspace{-0.5em} \underset{\underset{d\ \ c\ \ a}{}}{CHCH_2CH_3} \right. \end{matrix}$$

$\delta\,0.8$ (3H, t)

These are the methyl hydrogen atoms labeled a. They are split into a triplet by the two hydrogen atoms on the adjacent methylene group.

$\delta\,1.2$ (3H, d)

These are the methyl hydrogen atoms labeled b. They are split into a doublet by the hydrogen atom on the adjacent benzylic carbon atom.

$\delta\,1.6$ (2H, quintet, $J_{ac} = J_{cd}$)

These are the methylene hydrogen atoms labeled c. J_{ac} and J_{cd} are equal. The methylene hydrogens have four 3-bond neighbors and, therefore, are split into a quintet by the hydrogen atom on the adjacent benzylic carbon atom and the hydrogen atoms on the adjacent methyl group.

$\delta\,2.6$ (1H, sextet, $J_{bd} = J_{cd}$)

This is the benzylic hydrogen atom labeled d. J_{bd} and J_{cd} are equal, and the benzylic hydrogen, with five 3-bond neighbors, is split into a sextet by the hydrogen atoms on the adjacent methylene group and the hydrogen atoms on the adjacent methyl group.

$\delta\,7.2$ (5H, multiplet)

These are the aromatic hydrogen atoms labeled e. They are not chemical-shift equivalent and couple to each other in a complex pattern.

10.20

$$\begin{matrix} H_c & Br \\ Br\text{—}\bigcirc\text{—}NH_2 \\ H_b & H_a \end{matrix}$$

The bands are analyzed below:

$\delta\,4.10$ (2H, broad multiplet, —N$\underline{H}_2$)

$\delta\,6.65$ (1H, d, $J_{ab} = 8$ Hz, Ar$\underline{H}_a$)

$\delta\,7.20$ (1H, doublet of doublets, $J_{ab} = 8$ Hz, $J_{bc} = 2$ Hz, Ar$\underline{H}_b$)

$\delta\,7.55$ (1H, d, $J_{bc} = 2$ Hz, Ar$\underline{H}_c$)

H_a is the farthest upfield of the aryl hydrogen atoms because it is next to the amino group, which is strongly electron-donating (see Section 16.1C in the text) and distant from the electron-withdrawing bromine atoms. It is split into a doublet by H_b with $J = 8$ Hz.

H_b has the next highest chemical shift. It is next to only one bromine atom. A diagram showing the splitting pattern for H_b is shown below.

H_c is the most deshielded of the aryl hydrogen atoms because it is between two bromine atoms. It is also split into a doublet by H_b with $J = 2$ Hz.

10.21   The signal at δ 178 is that of a carbonyl carbon atom. It is split into a quartet, with a very small coupling constant, by three adjacent methyl hydrogen atoms that are three-bond neighbors of the carbonyl carbon atom. The signal of the methyl carbon at δ 20 is also split into a quartet, with a very large coupling constant, by the methyl hydrogen atoms that are one-bond neighbors to it.

10.22   The two peaks observed for the methyl groups cannot be due to spin-spin coupling because there are no other bands in the spectrum that also show splitting.

The two separate absorption bands for the two methyl groups tell us that there is partial double bond character between the carbon atom of the carbonyl group and the nitrogen atom, which prevents free rotation. If free rotation were possible, the two methyl groups would become chemically equivalent, and only one chemical shift would be observed for both. Because there is not free rotation, the two methyl groups are in different environments and thus have two different chemical shifts.

Resonance contributors for the amide group showing the existence of partial double bond character for the bond between the carbon atom of the carbonyl group and the nitrogen atom.

10.23   Compound L, $C_4H_8Cl_2$, has no units of unsaturation. We know that there are only two different types of carbon atoms in X because the ^{13}C magnetic resonance spectrum has only two bands. X must be 1,4-dichlorobutane.

$$ClCH_2CH_2CH_2CH_2Cl$$

δ 30.0
δ 44.1

2,3-Dichlorobutane also has the symmetry required for this spectrum, but we would expect the methyl groups to absorb at higher field than the chemical shift values observed (Table 10.2, p. 358 in the text).

Cl   Cl
$$CH_3CH—CHCH_3$$

δ >44
δ ~16

Also note that the carbon atoms bearing the chlorine atoms in this compound are even more highly substituted than in 1,4-dichlorobutane. We would expect them to absorb at lower field.

10.24   There are four possible isomers with the molecular formula C_4H_9Br.

		CH_3	CH_3
$CH_3CH_2CH_2CH_2Br$	$CH_3CH_2CHCH_3$	CH_3CHCH_2Br	CH_3CBr
	Br		CH_3
1-bromobutane	2-bromobutane	2-methyl-1-bromopropane	2-methyl-2-bromopropane
n-butyl bromide	*sec*-butyl bromide	isobutyl bromide	*tert*-butyl bromide

We know that there are four different types of carbon atoms in the two spectra shown because the ^{13}C magnetic resonance spectra each have four bands. That eliminates isobutyl bromide (3 sets of carbon atoms) and *tert*-butyl bromide (2 sets of carbon atoms) as possible structures.

10.24 (cont)

Tentative assignments can be made by looking at the carbon atom bonded to the bromine. The chemical shifts given in Table 10.2 (p. 358 in the text) show that the more highly substituted a carbon atom is, the further downfield it absorbs. Primary alkyl bromide carbon atoms, such as the one in *n*-butyl bromide absorb between 28 and 35 ppm and secondary alkyl bromine carbon atoms, such as in *sec*-butyl bromide will absorb farther downfield. We can assign the top spectrum to *n*-butyl bromide because it has no carbon atoms absorbing below 40 ppm. The bottom spectrum would be that of *sec*-butyl bromide, since it has one carbon atom at 54 ppm, suggesting that this carbon atom is more highly substituted.

Further confirmation could be made on the basis of the proton-coupled ^{13}C spectra. *n*-Butyl bromide would show three triplets and one quartet and *sec*-butyl bromide would show one doublet, one triplet, and two quartets. The proton magnetic resonance spectra can also be used for confirmation.

11

Ultraviolet-Visible and Infrared Spectroscopy. Mass Spectrometry

Concept Map 11.1   Visible and ultraviolet spectroscopy.

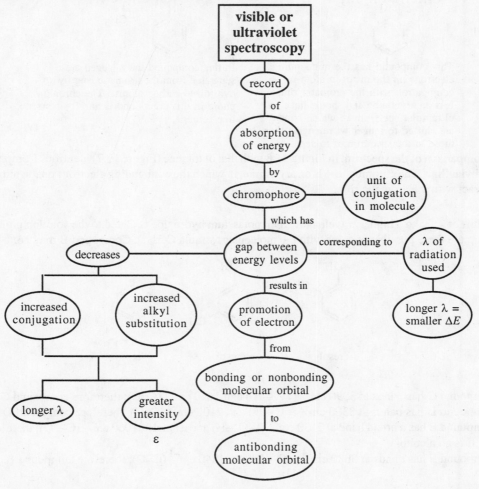

11.1   The compound with the most extended conjugation would be expected to absorb at the longest wavelength.

The compound above has the most extensive conjugation and would absorb at the longest wavelength.

11.2

1-Acetyl-2-methyl-1-cyclohexene has two absorption bands, $\lambda_{max}^{ethanol}$ 247 nm (ε 6000) and 305 nm (ε 100). The band at 247 nm corresponds to the $\pi \rightarrow \pi^*$ transition of the conjugated π system and the band at 305 nm, to the $n \rightarrow \pi^*$ transition of the carbonyl group.

11.3 $CH_3CH_2\ddot{N}CH_2CH_3$ $CH_2CH_2\ddot{N}CH_3$
                                                                           CH_3

This compound has the nonbonding electrons on the nitrogen atom in conjugation with the aromatic ring. It is an arylamine and should have an ultraviolet spectrum in which bands are shifted to longer wavelengths than those in the spectrum of toluene.   In this compound the nitrogen atom is separated from the aromatic ring by sp^3-hybridized carbon atoms. The chromophore in this compound is an alkylbenzene, like toluene.

A comparison of the spectrum in Figure 11.8 with that of toluene (Figure 11.7) identifies Compound A as *N,N*-diethylaniline. The chromophore is an arylamine, in which the nonbonding electrons on the nitrogen atom can interact with the aromatic ring.

11.4   A shift of λ_{max} to a higher wavelength when potassium hydroxide is added to the solution points to a phenol. There are three possible phenols with the molecular formula C_7H_8O. Compound B may be:

            o-cresol   *m*-cresol   *p*-cresol

11.5   Compound C has bands at 3090 cm^{-1} (=C—H) and 1650 cm^{-1} (C=C); therefore compound C is an alkene.
Compound D has bands at 3300 cm^{-1} ($\equiv$C—H) and 2100 cm^{-1} (C$\equiv$C); therefore compound D is an alkyne.
Compound E has a broad band at 3330 cm^{-1} (—O—H) and a band at 1060 cm^{-1} (C—O); therefore compound E is an alcohol.
Compound F has bands at 3080 cm^{-1} (=C—H) and 1640 cm^{-1} (C=C); therefore compound F is an alkene.

11.6   Compound G, $C_4H_{10}O$, has no units of unsaturation. It has bands at 3325 (broad) cm^{-1} (—O—H) and 1040 cm^{-1} (C—O); therefore it is an alcohol. Possible structures are:

                                             CH_3 CH_3

$CH_3CH_2CH_2CH_2OH$ $CH_3CH_2CHCH_3$ CH_3CHCH_2OH CH_3CCH_3
                                           OH   OH

Compound H, $C_6H_{12}O$, has one unit of unsaturation. It has bands at 3325 (broad) cm^{-1} (—O—H) and 1060 cm^{-1} (C—O); therefore it must be an alcohol. Since there is one unit of unsaturation and no alkene stretching frequency, it must be a cyclic alcohol. Possible structures are:

11.6 (cont)

Compound I, $C_6H_{12}O$, has one unit of unsaturation. It has a band at 1700 cm^{-1} (C=O). The unit of unsaturation corresponds to the carbonyl group; therefore, it cannot have a ring. There is no band at 2700 cm^{-1}; therefore it must be a ketone. Possible structures are:

Compound J, C_4H_8O, has one unit of unsaturation. It has a band at 2700 cm^{-1} (O=C—H); the band at 2900 cm^{-1} is hidden in the alkane band. In addition there is a band at 1740 cm^{-1} (C=O). Possible structures are:

11.7   Compound K, $C_5H_{10}O$, has one unit of unsaturation. It has bands at 1715 cm^{-1} (C=O). The absorption at 1715 cm^{-1} indicates that it has a carbonyl group. With only one unit of unsaturation, it cannot contain a ring. No absorption at ~2700 cm^{-1} indicates that it is not an aldehyde, but a ketone.
Possible structures are:

The proton nuclear magnetic resonance spectrum has bands at

δ 1.11   [6H, d, (C<u>H</u>₃)CH]
δ 2.15   [3H, s, C<u>H</u>₃C=O]
δ 2.60   [1H, septet, O=CC<u>H</u>(CH₃)₂] (The two outer peaks are very difficult to see.)

The ^{13}C nuclear magnetic resonance spectrum has bands at

δ 18.15   [CH(<u>C</u>H₃)₂]
δ 27.43   [<u>C</u>H₃C=O]
δ 41.65   [O=C<u>C</u>H(CH₃)₂]
δ 212.47   [CH₃<u>C</u>=O]

The nuclear magnetic resonance data allows us to assign the following structure to K:

11.8   The best approach to identifying which spectrum belongs to which compound is to first determine the functional groups that are present in each compound and then to look for the specific bands in the spectra that correspond to the functional groups.

There is only one alcohol, which should have a broad band at ~3350 cm^{-1} and no band in the carbonyl region. The only spectrum that fits is spectrum 4. Spectrum 4, therefore, must belong to 1-octanol.

3325 (broad) cm^{-1} (—O—H)
1060 cm^{-1} (C—O)

11.8 (cont)

One of the compounds is an acid and an alkene. Acids should have a broad band at ~3300–2400 cm^{-1} and a band in the carbonyl region. Alkenes should have a band at ~1600 cm^{-1}. Spectrum 5 has a band at 1645 cm^{-1}, as well as those corresponding to a carboxylic acid, therefore, spectrum 5 belongs to 3-butenoic acid.

3100–2500 (broad) cm^{-1}	(—O—H)
1715 cm^{-1}	(C=O)
1645 cm^{-1}	(C=C)

One of the compounds is an aldehyde, which should have a band in the carbonyl region and a band at 2700 cm^{-1}. Spectrum 2 has these two bands and must, therefore, belong to 10-undecenal, an unsaturated aldehyde. Spectrum 2 also has a band at ~1600 cm^{-1}, which confirms the presence of an alkene.

2715 cm^{-1}	(O=C—H)
1725 cm^{-1}	(C=O)
1640 cm^{-1}	(C=C)

Of the last two spectra to assign (1 and 3), one must belong to an ester (methyl pentanoate) and the other to a ketone (3-methylcyclohexanone). Both have bands in the carbonyl region, but spectrum 1 has broad bands between 1000-1300 cm^{-1}, suggesting that this spectrum belongs to an ester. Spectrum 3 must, therefore, belong to the ketone.

Spectrum 1 (methyl pentanoate)

1740 cm^{-1}	(C=O)
1260, 1175 cm^{-1}	(C—O)

Spectrum 3 (3-methylcyclohexanone)

1710 cm^{-1}	(C=O)

Concept Map 11.2   Infrared spectroscopy.

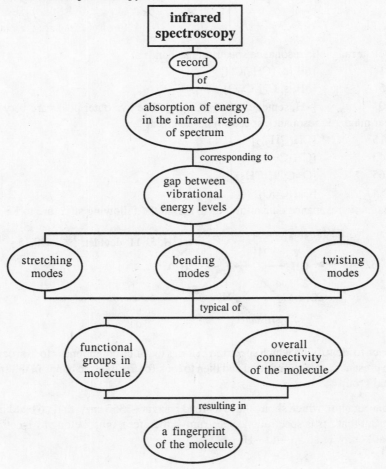

11.9   If we subtract the *m/z* value for the base peak from that for the peak of the molecular ion, we can determine the mass of the neutral fragment that is lost.

$$58 \quad - \quad 29 \quad = \quad 29$$

molecular   base   neutral
ion   peak   fragment

The fragment is most likely an ethyl radical, $CH_3\overset{\bullet}{C}H_2$, formed by homolytic cleavage of the bond between the carbon atom of the carbonyl group and the α-carbon atom. The fragment that is charged, with an *m/z* of 29, is a resonance-stabilized acylium ion, $HC{\equiv}O^+$. Putting these two fragments together gives us the identity of the unknown, propanal.

propanal

molecular ion
m/z 58

M⁺̇
m/z 58

ethyl radical
not seen in mass spectrum

an acylium ion
base peak *m/z* 29

11.10   A hydrogen atom is lost in going from the molecular ion at *m/z* 46 to the peak at *m/z* 45. The loss of a hydroxyl radical (*m/z* 17) from the molecular ion leads to the base peak at *m/z* 29. Both of these fragments come from homolytic cleavage of the two bonds to the carbonyl group. Putting these fragments together gives us the structure of the unknown acid, which is formic acid.

formic acid

molecular ion
m/z 46

M⁺̇
m/z 46

hydrogen
atom

an acylium ion
m/z 45

M⁺̇
m/z 46

hydroxyl
radical

another acylium ion
base peak *m/z* 29

11.11   Two possible cleavages of the molecular ion of 3-pentanone at the bonds to the α-carbon atom are shown below:

M⁺̇
m/z 86

$CH_3\overset{\bullet}{C}H_2$ + $CH_3CH_2C{\equiv}\overset{+}{O}$

m/z 57

11.11 (cont)

The expected cleavages of the molecular ion of 2-pentanone at the bonds to the two different α-carbon atoms are shown below:

The mass spectrum with base peaks at *m/z* 29 and *m/z* 57 is the spectrum of 3-pentanone. The mass spectrum with the base peak at *m/z* 43 and a small peak at *m/z* 71 is the spectrum of 2-pentanone.

11.12 The formation of the base peak in the spectrum of 2,2-dimethylpropanal from the molecular ion is shown below:

The equivalent fragmentation from the molecular ion of acetaldehyde is shown below:

The base peak in the fragmentation of the molecular ion of 2,2-dimethylpropanal is the stable tertiary cation, the *tert*-butyl cation. The comparable species in the fragmentation of the molecular ion of acetaldehyde would be the unstable methyl cation, *m/z* 15, which does not appear in the spectrum of acetaldehyde.

11.13

11.13 (cont)

$$CH_3 \text{—} {}^{37}\ddot{\underset{\cdot\cdot}{C}l}: \quad \xrightarrow{-e^-} \quad CH_3 \text{—} {}^{37}\ddot{\underset{\cdot\cdot}{C}l}\overset{+}{\cdot}$$

$$M\overset{+}{\cdot}$$
$$m/z \; 52$$

$$CH_3\text{—}{}^{37}\ddot{\underset{\cdot\cdot}{C}l}\overset{+}{\cdot} \quad \longrightarrow \quad \overset{+}{C}H_3 \; + \; {}^{37}\cdot \ddot{\underset{\cdot\cdot}{C}l}: \qquad\qquad CH_3\text{—}{}^{37}\ddot{\underset{\cdot\cdot}{C}l}\overset{+}{\cdot} \quad \longrightarrow \quad \cdot CH_3 \; + \; {}^{37}:\overset{\cdot\cdot}{\underset{\cdot\cdot}{C}l}{}^{+}$$
$$m/z \; 15 \qquad\qquad\qquad\qquad\qquad\qquad\qquad\qquad\qquad\qquad\qquad m/z \; 37$$
$$\qquad\qquad\qquad\qquad\qquad\qquad\qquad\qquad\qquad\qquad\qquad\qquad\qquad\text{not evident in}$$
$$\qquad\qquad\qquad\qquad\qquad\qquad\qquad\qquad\qquad\qquad\qquad\qquad\qquad\text{the spectrum}$$

- -

Concept Map 11.3   Mass spectrometry.

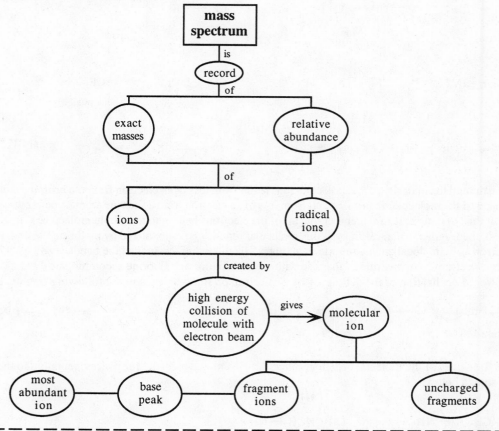

- -

11.14   The two ions with the highest *m/z* values appear in this spectrum at *m/z* 64 and *m/z* 66. The one at the higher mass is one-third the intensity of the other, suggesting that these are molecular ions for a compound containing chlorine.

$$M\overset{+}{\cdot} \qquad m/z \; 64 \quad ({}^{35}Cl) \qquad\qquad\qquad\qquad\qquad\qquad M\overset{+}{\cdot} \qquad m/z \; 66 \quad ({}^{37}Cl)$$

An important fragmentation of the molecular ion gives rise to the peak at *m/z* 29. This is the ethyl cation and results from loss of chlorine from the molecular ion. Putting these fragments together, we identify the haloalkane as ethyl chloride (chloroethane).

$$CH_3CH_2\text{—}{}^{35}\ddot{\underset{\cdot\cdot}{C}l}\overset{+}{\cdot} \; \longrightarrow \; CH_3\overset{+}{C}H_2 \; + \; {}^{35}\cdot\ddot{\underset{\cdot\cdot}{C}l}: \qquad CH_3CH_2\text{—}{}^{37}\ddot{\underset{\cdot\cdot}{C}l}\overset{+}{\cdot} \; \longrightarrow \; CH_3\overset{+}{C}H_2 \; + \; {}^{37}\cdot\ddot{\underset{\cdot\cdot}{C}l}:$$
$$M\overset{+}{\cdot} \qquad\qquad\qquad\qquad\qquad\qquad\qquad\qquad\qquad M\overset{+}{\cdot}$$
$$m/z \; 64 \qquad\qquad\quad m/z \; 29 \qquad\qquad\qquad\qquad m/z \; 66 \qquad\qquad\quad m/z \; 29$$

11.15 The high mass region of this mass spectrum has a pair of ions with equal intensity differing by 2 mass units (m/z 148, 150). This suggests that one of the two halogens in the unknown is bromine. The presence of bromine is confirmed by the two peaks of equal intensity at m/z 79 and 81.

The first fragmentation, m/z 148 to m/z 129, (or m/z 150 to m/z 131) is the loss of a species with a mass of 19, which corresponds to the atomic weight of fluorine. The base peak, which is at m/z 69, results from the loss of a bromine atom. The compound can have only one bromine atom, because the molecular weight is too low for more than one. Therefore, there must be three fluorine atoms. The compound is bromotrifluoromethane, CF_3Br.

The fragmentations are shown below. The molecular ion is shown as being formed by loss of a nonbonding electron from bromine. Because the electronegativity of bromine is lower than that of fluorine, and the bromine atom is much larger than a fluorine atom, it would be easier to lose the electron from bromine than from fluorine.

$$CF_3 - {}^{79}\ddot{B}r\!: \xrightarrow{-e^-} CF_3 - {}^{79}\overset{+}{\ddot{B}r}\cdot \qquad CF_3 - {}^{81}\ddot{B}r\!: \xrightarrow{-e^-} CF_3 - {}^{81}\overset{+}{\ddot{B}r}\cdot$$

$$\underset{m/z\ 148}{M^+} \qquad\qquad\qquad \underset{m/z\ 150}{M^+}$$

$$CF_3 - {}^{79}\overset{+}{\ddot{B}r}\cdot \longrightarrow \overset{+}{C}F_3 + {}^{79}\cdot\ddot{B}r\!: \qquad CF_3 - {}^{81}\overset{+}{\ddot{B}r}\cdot \longrightarrow \overset{+}{C}F_3 + {}^{81}\cdot\ddot{B}r\!:$$

$$\underset{\substack{\text{base peak}\\ m/z\ 69}}{} \qquad\qquad\qquad \underset{\substack{\text{base peak}\\ m/z\ 69}}{}$$

$$CF_3 - {}^{79}\overset{+}{\ddot{B}r}\cdot \longrightarrow \cdot CF_3 + {}^{79}\!:\!\overset{\cdot\,+}{\ddot{B}r} \qquad CF_3 - {}^{81}\overset{+}{\ddot{B}r}\cdot \longrightarrow \cdot CF_3 + {}^{81}\!:\!\overset{\cdot\,+}{\ddot{B}r}$$

$$\underset{m/z\ 79}{} \qquad\qquad\qquad\qquad \underset{m/z\ 81}{}$$

Even though the majority of the molecular ions result from loss of an electron from the bromine atom, a certain number of the molecular ions will result from loss of an electron from a fluorine atom. A better way of thinking about this, of course, is to remember that all of the electrons belong to the whole molecule. When an electron is lost, the fragments that result from this molecular ion may be rationalized by picturing the deficiency of the electron as being localized at one site or another. The relative intensities of the bands at m/z 69, 129, and 131 in the spectrum are a measure of the ease with which bromine and fluorine accommodate the deficiency of an electron. Localization of the deficiency of an electron on fluorine leads to the following fragmentations:

$$ {}^{79}\!:\!\ddot{B}r - CF_2 - \overset{+}{\ddot{F}}\cdot \longrightarrow {}^{79}\!:\!\ddot{B}r - \overset{+}{C}F_2 + \cdot\ddot{F}\!: \qquad {}^{81}\!:\!\ddot{B}r - CF_2 - \overset{+}{\ddot{F}}\cdot \longrightarrow {}^{81}\!:\!\ddot{B}r - \overset{+}{C}F_2 + \cdot\ddot{F}\!:$$

$$\underset{m/z\ 148}{} \qquad \underset{m/z\ 129}{} \qquad\qquad \underset{m/z\ 150}{} \qquad \underset{m/z\ 131}{}$$

11.16 The formation of the molecular ion for isobutylamine and the pathway for its fragmentation to the base peak are shown below:

$$\underset{\substack{}}{CH_3\overset{\displaystyle CH_3}{\underset{\displaystyle |}{C}}HCH_2 - \ddot{N}H_2} \xrightarrow{-e^-} CH_3\overset{\displaystyle CH_3}{\underset{\displaystyle |}{C}}HCH_2 - \overset{\cdot\,+}{N}H_2$$

$$\underset{m/z\ 73}{M^+}$$

$$CH_3\overset{\displaystyle CH_3}{\underset{\displaystyle |}{C}}H - CH_2 - \overset{\cdot\,+}{N}H_2 \longrightarrow CH_3\overset{\displaystyle CH_3}{\underset{\displaystyle |}{C}}H + \left[CH_2 = \overset{+}{N}H_2 \longleftrightarrow \overset{+}{C}H_2 - \ddot{N}H_2\right]$$

$$\underset{m/z\ 73}{M^+} \qquad\qquad\qquad\qquad \underset{\substack{\text{base peak}\\ m/z\ 30}}{}$$

The corresponding reaction for *sec*-butylamine is:

$$CH_3CH_2\overset{\displaystyle CH_3}{\underset{\displaystyle |}{C}}H - \ddot{N}H_2 \xrightarrow{-e^-} CH_3CH_2\overset{\displaystyle CH_3}{\underset{\displaystyle |}{C}}H - \overset{\cdot\,+}{N}H_2$$

$$\underset{m/z\ 73}{M^+}$$

11.16 (cont)

Similarly, for tert-butylamine:

The spectrum with the small molecular ion at m/z 73 and the base peak at m/z 30 is that of isobutylamine. The spectrum with the barely visible molecular ion at m/z 73 and the base peak at m/z 44 is that of *sec*-butylamine. The spectrum of *tert*-butylamine has a base peak of m/z 58. No molecular ion is seen in the spectrum of *tert*-butylamine.

11.17 $CH_3CH_2CH_2CH_2CH = CH_2 \xrightarrow{-e^-} CH_3CH_2CH_2CH_2CH \overset{\cdot +}{-} CH_2$
         1-hexene   M$^{+}_{\cdot}$
                                                   m/z 84

11.18   The expected fragmentations of the molecular ion from 2,2-dimethyl-1-phenylpropane are shown below:

The expected fragmentation of the molecular ion from 2-methyl-3-phenylbutane is shown below:

The spectrum with a peak at m/z 91 and the base peak at m/z 57 is that of 2,2-dimethyl-1-phenylpropane. The spectrum with the base peak at m/z 105 is that of 2-methyl-3-phenylbutane.

11.19

M⁺ m/z 100   rearranged M⁺ m/z 100   radical cation of lower mass m/z 72   ethylene

a carbene (See Section 27.6)   radical cation of lower mass m/z 56

$CH_3C\equiv\overset{+}{O}:$ $CH_3\overset{\cdot}{C}HCH_2CH_3$

M⁺ m/z 100   an acylium ion m/z 43

$\overset{+}{C}H_3CH_2$ $CH_3\overset{:O:}{\underset{}{C}}=CHCH_3 \longleftrightarrow CH_3\overset{:O:}{\underset{}{C}}\overset{\cdot}{C}HCH_3$

M⁺ m/z 100   ethyl cation m/z 29   radical stabilized by resonance

11.20   One possible rearrangement and fragmentation of the molecular ion from 1-hexene is shown below:

$CH_3\overset{+}{C}H-\overset{\cdot}{C}H_2$
a radical cation of lower mass m/z 42
+
$CH_3CH=CH_2$
propene

M⁺ m/z 84   a rearranged M⁺ m/z 84

Another possible rearrangement and fragmentation of the molecular ion from 1-hexene is shown below:

$\overset{+}{C}H_2CH_2CH_2\overset{\cdot}{C}H_2$
another radical cation of lower mass m/z 56
+
$CH_2=CH_2$
ethylene

M⁺ m/z 84   a rearranged M⁺ m/z 84

11.21   Compound L has bands at 3325 (broad) cm^{-1} (—O—H) and 1060 cm^{-1} (C—O). There is no carbonyl absorption; it is therefore an alcohol.

The ^{13}C spectrum shows that at least 5 carbon atoms are in the molecule. The bands at δ 14.05, 22.56, 28.02, and 32.47 belong to alkyl carbon atoms. The band at δ 62.76 is that of a carbon atom bonded to an oxygen atom.

The proton magnetic resonance has 5 sets of hydrogen atoms totaling 12 hydrogen atoms. Combining this information with the number of carbon atoms indicated by the ^{13}C nuclear magnetic resonance and the oxygen atom gives a molecular formula of $C_5H_{12}O$, which is the molecular formula of a saturated compound. Three sets of hydrogens can be assigned as follows:

$$\delta\ 0.90\ (3H,\ t) \qquad C\underline{H}_3CH_2-$$
$$\delta\ 2.90\ (1H,\ s) \qquad C-O\underline{H}$$
$$\delta\ 3.60\ (2H,\ multiplet) -C\underline{H}_2-OH$$

Adding up the numbers of atoms gives us C_3H_8O and subtracting these from the molecular formula leaves C_2H_4 to assign. This corresponds to a —CH_2CH_2— group. The rest of the hydrogens can be assigned as follows:

$$\delta\ 1.35\ (4H,\ multiplet) -C\underline{H}_2C\underline{H}_2-$$
$$\delta\ 1.55\ (2H,\ multiplet) -C\underline{H}_2CH_2-OH$$

We now have the following fragments:

$$C\underline{H}_3CH_2-$$
$$-C\underline{H}_2C\underline{H}_2- \qquad -C\underline{H}_2C\underline{H}_2-$$
$$-C\underline{H}_2OH$$

Since there are only 5 carbon atoms and 12 hydrogen atoms, some of the fragments must overlap. The molecule is 1-pentanol.

11.22   Compound M has 4 units of unsaturation. The infrared spectrum indicates the presence of an alcohol (3338 cm^{-1} is the O—H stretching frequency and 1031 cm^{-1} is the C—O stretching frequency).

The ^{13}C spectrum is analyzed below:

δ 32.02	(t, —$\underline{C}H_2$—)
δ 34.13	(t, —$\underline{C}H_2$—)
δ 61.95	(t, —$\underline{C}H_2OH$)
δ 125.74	(d, sp^2-$\underline{C}H$)
δ 128.29	(d, sp^2-$\underline{C}H$)
δ 128.33	(d, sp^2-$\underline{C}H$)
δ 141.78	(s, sp^2-$\underline{C}$)

The proton magnetic resonance spectrum is analyzed below:

δ 1.8	(2H, quintet, —$CH_2C\underline{H}_2CH_2$—)
δ 2.6	(1H, s, —O$\underline{H}$)
δ 2.8	(2H, t, ArC$\underline{H}_2CH_2$—)
δ 3.6	(2H, multiplet, —$CH_2C\underline{H}_2OH$) (see next page)
δ 7.2	(5H, multiplet, Ar$\underline{H}$)

The compound is 3-phenyl-1-propanol. The assignments are shown on the next page.

11.22 (cont)

δ 141.78
singlet

δ 61.95
triplet, split by two
hydrogen atoms

$CH_2CH_2CH_2OH$

δ 125.74, 128.29, 128.33
each split into a
doublet by one
hydrogen atom

δ 32.02, 34.13
each split into a
triplet by two
hydrogen atoms

^{13}C nuclear magnetic resonance

δ 2.8, triplet δ 3.6, multiplet

$CH_2CH_2CH_2OH$

δ 7.2, multiplet

δ 1.8,
quintet

δ 2.6, singlet
(see Section 10.5E
in the text)

proton magnetic resonance

A molecular formula of $C_9H_{12}O$ corresponds to a molecular weight of 136. The molecular ion in the mass spectrum is at *m/z* 136. The base peak (*m/z* 91) is the tropylium ion, which results from loss of a C_2H_5O unit and is the result of the following fragmentation:

$CH_2 \cdot\cdot\cdot CH_2CH_2\ddot{O}H \longrightarrow \cdot CH_2CH_2\ddot{O}H + \left[\langle \rangle = CH_2 \right]^{+} \longrightarrow$ tropylium ion

M $^{+}$
m/z 136

tropylium ion
m/z 91

11.23   Compound N has bands at 2720 cm^{-1} (O=C—H) and 1730 cm^{-1} (C=O). It is therefore an aldehyde.

Analysis of the proton magnetic resonance spectrum gives the following:

δ 0.95   [6H, d, $(C\underline{H}_3)_2CH$]
δ 2.20   [1H, multiplet, $(CH_3)_2C\underline{H}CH_2$]
δ 2.30   [2H, multiplet, $CHC\underline{H}_2CH=O$]
δ 9.75   [1H, t, $CH_2C\underline{H}=O$]

Analysis of the ^{13}C magnetic resonance spectrum is given below:

δ 22.57   [$(\underline{C}H_3)_2CH$]
δ 23.50   [$(CH_3)_2\underline{C}HCH_2$]
δ 52.59   [$\underline{C}H_2CH=O$]
δ 202.65   [$\underline{C}H=O$]

Compound N is 3-methylbutanal, $(CH_3)_2CHCH_2C\overset{\overset{O}{\|}}{H}$.

11.24

Compound P
λ_{max} 208 nm (ε 12,000)

Compound Q
λ_{max} 261 nm (ε 25,000)

Compound O
λ_{max} 302 nm (ε 36,000)

The wavelength of maximum absorption and the intensity of absorption increases with increasing conjugation.

11.25   (a)   A compound with a molecular formula of C_4H_6O has two units of unsaturation.

(b)   The observed λ_{max} 219 nm (e 16,600) is due to the $\pi \rightarrow \pi^*$ transition of a conjugated system, while λ_{max} 318 nm (ε 30) is due to the $n \rightarrow \pi^*$ transition of a carbonyl group. Only three structures fit both the molecular formula and the ultraviolet spectrum.

11.25   (c) Some other structures that are not compatible with the ultraviolet spectral data are:

11.26   (+)-17-Methyltestosterone

11.27   The absence of bands above 3000 cm^{-1} in the infrared spectrum eliminates both a phenol and an alcohol. The absence of bands in the region between 2000 and 1600 cm^{-1} eliminates a carbonyl compound such as an aldehyde or ketone. The ultraviolet spectrum is very similar to that of methoxybenzene (Figure 11.7), suggesting that Compound R is a substituted aromatic ether. Possible structures are:

o-bromomethoxy-benzene	*m*-bromomethoxy-benzene	*p*-bromomethoxy-benzene

11.28   Compound S, $C_{10}H_{12}O$, has five units of unsaturation. The infrared spectrum has bands at 1717 cm^{-1} (C=O). There are no bands in the infrared at about 2700 cm^{-1}; therefore, the compound must be a ketone and not an aldehyde.

The proton magnetic resonance spectrum has bands at

δ 2.13	(3H, s, C$\underline{H}_3$C=O)
δ 2.76	(2H, multiplet, —C$\underline{H}_2$CH$_2$—)
δ 2.90	(2H, multiplet, —CH$_2$C$\underline{H}_2$—)
δ 7.2	(5H, multiplet, Ar$\underline{H}$)

The compound is 4-phenyl-2-butanone,

11.29   The mass spectrum of Compound T has two molecular ions at m/z 60 and 62 having a ratio of intensities of 3:1. This ratio tells us that the halogen in Compound T is chlorine. If we subtract 35 from 60, we get a mass of 25, which corresponds to the molecular formula C_2H, and the structure HC≡C—. Compound B is chloroethyne, HC≡CCl.

11.30   Compound U has a band in its infrared spectrum at 1685 cm^{-1} (conjugated C=O). According to the infrared spectral information given, U is a ketone.

11.30 (cont)

The proton magnetic resonance spectrum has bands at

δ 1.20	(6H, d, $(CH_3)_2CH-$)
δ 3.57	(1H, septet, $(CH_3)_2CH-$)
δ 7.50	(3H, multiplet, Ar$\underline{H}$)
δ 7.95	(2H, multiplet, Ar$\underline{H}$)

The chemical shift of the methine hydrogen atom and the fact that the aryl hydrogen atoms are split indicate that the carbonyl group is between the aryl and the isopropyl groups. This is confirmed by the presence of a band for a conjugated carbonyl group in the infrared. The compound is 2-methyl-1-phenyl-1-propanone

(isobutyrophenone), with structure phenyl—$\overset{\overset{\displaystyle O}{\|}}{C}$$\underset{\underset{\displaystyle CH_3}{|}}{C}HCH_3$.

11.31 The two peaks of equal size in the mass spectrum of Compound V at m/z 79 and 81 tell us that bromine is present. The fact that the molecular ion fragments before it can be recorded suggests that the compound gives rise to a very stable cation, m/z 43. An acylium ion , $CH_3C\equiv O^+$, fits this description. Compound V is acetyl bromide.

$$CH_3\overset{\overset{\displaystyle O}{\|}}{C}Br$$

(Other possibilities that may come to mind are isopropyl or *n*-propyl bromide. Neither alkyl cation is as stable as the resonance-stabilized acylium ion, and we would therefore expect to see the molecular ion for either of these compounds.)

11.32 Compound W has bands at

3335 (broad) cm^{-1}	(—O—H)
3080 cm^{-1}	(C=C—H)
1650 cm^{-1}	(C=C)
1048 cm^{-1}	(C—O)

It is an alcohol and an alkene.

Compound X has bands at

2200 cm^{-1}	(C≡C)
1675 cm^{-1}	(C=O)

No band is seen at 3300 cm^{-1}; therefore, the compound is not a terminal alkyne. The low value for the carbonyl absorption suggests that the carbonyl group is conjugated with the multiple bond. The absence of a band at 2700 cm^{-1} indicates that it is a conjugated ketone and not a conjugated aldehyde.

Compound Y has bands at

3460 (broad) cm^{-1}	(—O—H)
1710 cm^{-1}	(C=O)

There is no band at 2700 cm^{-1}; therefore, the compound is a ketone and not an aldehyde. The other functional group in the compound is an alcohol.

Compound Z has bands at

3100 cm^{-1}	(C=C—H)
1740 cm^{-1}	(C=O, not conjugated with alkene)
1640 cm^{-1}	(C=C)
1240, 1040 cm^{-1}	(C—O)

The bands at 1240 and 1040 cm^{-1}, along with the presence of a carbonyl, indicate an ester. The other functional group is an alkene.

11.33   The absorption bands reported for the first compound are comparable to those for an alkylbenzene (compare with the spectrum of toluene, Figure 11.7). This suggests that the double bond in this compound is not conjugated with the aromatic ring. The first compound is 3-phenylpropene. In the spectrum of the second compound, the absorption bands are shifted to longer wavelengths and are also more intense, suggesting that this compound has a more extensive system of conjugation than the first one. The second compound is, therefore, 1-phenylpropene.

3-phenylpropene
no conjugation of the
double bond with the ring

1-phenylpropene
double bond in con-
jugation with the ring

11.34

M‡
m/z 86
small peak in spectrum

rearranged M‡

base peak
m/z 44

propene

11.35   The infrared spectral information tells us that Compound AA is a conjugated ketone (1676 cm^{-1} is the C=O stretching frequency for a conjugated carbonyl group). The proton magnetic resonance spectrum is analyzed below:

δ 2.57   (3H, s, C$\underline{H}_3$C=O)
δ 3.88   (3H, s, —OC$\underline{H}_3$)
δ 6.95, 7.95   (4H, para substitution pattern, Ar$\underline{H}$)

The fragments add up to $C_9H_{10}O_2$, which corresponds to a molecular weight of 150. The molecular ion of Compound AA is at *m/z* 150. Therefore, all atoms are accounted for. Compound AA is *p*-methoxyacetophenone.

The base peak, *m/z* 135, results from loss of a methyl radical from the molecular ion, leaving a resonance-stabilized acylium ion with *m/z* 135.

M‡
m/z 150

an acylium ion
m/z 135

11.36   The infrared spectral information tells us that Compound BB is an aldehyde (1703 cm^{-1} is the C=O stretching frequency, and 2730 cm^{-1} distinguishes an aldehyde group from a ketone group).

δ 2.45   (3H, s, ArC$\underline{H}_3$)
δ 7.32, 7.78   (4H, para substitution pattern, Ar$\underline{H}$)
δ 9.95   (1H, s, —C$\underline{H}$=O)

11.36 (cont)

These fragments add up to C_8H_8O corresponding to a molecular weight of 120, which is the *m/z* of the molecular ion of Compound BB. Putting the subunits from the proton magnetic resonance spectrum together gives us *p*-tolualdehyde. The first base peak, *m/z* 119, results from the loss of a hydrogen atom from the molecular ion, giving an acylium ion. The second base peak, *m/z* 91, is the tropylium ion, which most likely comes from a rearrangement of the methylphenyl cation formed by loss of carbon monoxide from the acylium ion.

The ^{13}C nuclear magnetic resonance is analyzed below:

Supplemental Problems

S11.1   Of the following three isomeric compounds, which one will absorb at the longest wavelength?

S11.2   Compound CC is an ester. It has a singlet in its proton magnetic resonance spectrum at δ 3.69. Identify the molecular ion from its mass spectrum, shown in Figure S11.1. Assign a structure to that ion and to the ions having an intensity greater than 50%.

S11.2 (cont)

FIGURE S11.1   (Adapted from Stenhagen et al. Reprinted by permission.)

S11.3   The mass spectra of two isomeric alcohols, compounds DD and EE, are given in Figure S11.2. The molecular ion shows up in the spectrum of one but not the other. Assign structures to the two alcohols, and write equations for the formation of the ion responsible for the base peak in each case.

(Adapted from Stenhagen et al. Reprinted by permission.)

FIGURE S11.2   (Adapted from Stenhagen et al. Reprinted by permission.)

S11.4   Compound FF has the proton magnetic resonance and mass spectra shown in Figure S11.3. There is a peak for the molecular ion in the mass spectrum. The ^{13}C nuclear magnetic resonance spectrum of the compound has bands at δ 33, 120, and 135. Tell which spectral bands belong to each carbon and each hydrogen atom in the compound. Write an equation for the formation of the ion responsible for the base peak in the mass spectrum.

Compound FF

(Adapted from Stenhagen et al. Reprinted by permission.)

FIGURE S11.3

12

Alcohols, Diols, and Ethers

12.1 1,2-Ethanediol (ethylene glycol) is a very polar compound and hydrogen bonds strongly to water. It is infinitely soluble in water. A solution of ethylene glycol in water depresses the freezing point of water so that the mixture does not freeze at temperatures usually seen in the winter time. This keeps pipes and radiators from bursting because of the expansion of the water as it forms ice. The high boiling point of ethylene glycol ensures that it will not boil out of the radiator of a car when the engine is hot.

12.2

Cholesterol is not very soluble in water even though it has a hydroxyl group because the rest of the molecule is nonpolar and is too large to be brought into solution by the small polar hydroxyl group (Section 1.10C).

12.3 Cholesterol is an alkene as well as an alcohol.

239

12.4 (a) The location of the hydroxyl group on the chain affects the solubility in water of the isomeric alcohols. *n*-Butyl alcohol has the polar hydroxyl group at one end of the molecule and a long hydrophobic chain stretching away from it. In *sec*-butyl alcohol all parts of the hydrocarbon portion of the molecule are closer to, and more under the influence of, the polar hydroxyl group. In *tert*-butyl alcohol there is no large hydrophobic chain that is far away from the polar, water-soluble portion of the molecule. The hydroxyl group is able to carry the rest of the molecule into solution with it.

(b) Hydrogen bonding of the alcohol is the most important factor in determining water solubility. The bromo compound is less soluble than the slightly more polar chloro compound. The dipole is weaker for the bromo compound, so even those interactions are not helpful for the bromo compound.

(c) Hydrogen bonding among molecules of the diol give it a very high boiling point. The alcohol also has hydrogen bonding, but with only one hydroxyl group to participate in the hydrogen bonding, it has a lower boiling point than the diol. The ether cannot have hydrogen bonding among its molecules, therefore it has the lowest boiling point of the three.

12.5 (a) 3-methyl-1-butanol   (b) (*E*)-4-hexen-3-ol   (c) 2-pentyn-1-ol
    (d) 4,5-dichloro-1-hexanol (e) 1-chloro-3-ethoxypropane (f) diphenyl ether (phenoxybenzene)
    (g) cyclohexanol   (h) (1*R*, 2*R*)-2-methylcyclopentanol (i) *cis*-4-*tert*-butylcyclohexanol
    (j) (*R*)-5-hexen-3-ol   (k) 1,3-dimethoxypropane   (l) 1,2-dimethoxybenzene

12.6 (a) $CH_3CHCH=CH_2$ $\xrightarrow{\text{Markovnikov addition}}$ $CH_3CHCHCH_3$
         with CH_3 and OH substituents

product not observed

(b) mechanism steps:

protonation → 1,2-hydride shift → reaction of the more stable tertiary carbocation with the nucleophilic solvent → deprotonation of the oxonium ion

12.7

protonation — 1,2-methyl shift — reaction of the more stable tertiary carbocation with the nucleophilic solvent — deprotonation of the oxonium ion

12.8 $CH_2=CHCH_2CH_2CH_2OH$ $\xrightarrow{H_3O^+}$ $CH_3CHCH_2CH_2CH_2OH$
         with OH substituent

Dehydration would also occur if the temperature were raised.

Concept Map 12.1   Conversion of alkenes to alcohols.

12.9

12.10

$$
\begin{array}{ccccc}
& CH_3 & & CH_3 & \\
& | & & | & \\
CH_3CCH_3 & \longrightarrow & CH_3CCH_3 & \longrightarrow & \cdots \\
& | & & | & \\
& \overset{..}{O}: & & \overset{+}{O}H & \\
\end{array}
$$

$$
\begin{array}{ccc}
CH_3 & & CH_3 \\
| & & | \\
CH_3\overset{+}{C}-CH_2 & \longrightarrow & CH_3C=CH_2 \\
\end{array}
$$

H—B$^+$

$$
\begin{array}{ccccc}
CH_3 & & CH_3 & & CH_3 \\
| & & | & & | \\
CH_3C=CH_2 & \longrightarrow & CH_3\overset{+}{C}CH_3 & \longrightarrow & CH_3CCH_3 \\
& & & & | \\
& & & & :\overset{..}{C}l: \\
\end{array}
$$

12.11 **(1)** With zinc chloride in concentrated hydrochloric acid, we have reaction conditions that allow for ionization of the alkyl halides that are formed as products and for equilibrium among different ionic species. As we saw in the *One Small Step*, p. 451 in the text, zinc chloride assists in the ionization of alkyl halides.

$$
\begin{array}{ccc}
CH_2CH_3 & & CH_2CH_3 \\
| & & | \\
CH_3CH_2CH-CH_2-\overset{..}{O}: & \longrightarrow & CH_3CH_2CH-CH_2-\overset{+}{O}: \longrightarrow \\
\end{array}
$$

1-chloro-2-ethylbutane

rearrangement of developing carbocation (postulated to avoid writing a primary carbocation as an intermediate)

Lewis acid assisting in the departure of chloride ion

$$ CH_3CH_2\overset{+}{C}HCH_2CH_2CH_3 \longrightarrow CH_3CH_2CHCH_2CH_2CH_3 $$

3-chlorohexane

rearrangement of developing carbocation

Lewis acid assisting in the departure of chloride ion

$$ CH_3CH_2\overset{+}{C}CH_3 \longrightarrow CH_3CH_2CCH_3 $$

3-chloro-3-methylpentane

$$ CH_3CH-\overset{+}{C}HCH_2CH_2CH_3 \to CH_3\overset{+}{C}HCH_2CH_2CH_2CH_3 \to CH_3CHCH_2CH_2CH_2CH_3 $$

rearrangement of one secondary carbocation into another one

2-chlorohexane

(2) With thionyl chloride in pyridine, an S$_N$2 reaction takes place. The alcohol is converted into the corresponding halide without rearrangement.

12.11 (2) (cont)

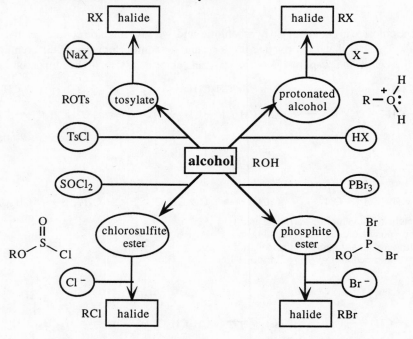

1-chloro-2-ethylbutane

Concept Map 12.2   Conversion of alcohols to alkyl halides.

12.12

nucleophilic substitution
on phosphorus

intermediate with a good leaving
group undergoing a nucleophilic
reaction at the chiral carbon atom
with inversion of configuration

12.13

12.14

(a)

cyclopentanol $\xrightarrow[\text{pyridine}]{\text{PBr}_3}$ cyclopentyl bromide

(b)

$\xrightarrow{\text{HCl (conc)}}$

(c) $CH_3(CH_2)_9CH_2OH \xrightarrow[\Delta]{SOCl_2} CH_3(CH_2)_9CH_2Cl$

(d) $CH_3(CH_2)_8CH_2OH \xrightarrow[\Delta]{HBr} CH_3(CH_2)_8CH_2Br$

(e) $CH_3SCH_2CH_2OH \xrightarrow[\text{chloroform}]{SOCl_2} CH_3SCH_2CH_2Cl$

(f) $CH_3CH_2OCH_2CH_2OH \xrightarrow[\text{pyridine}]{PBr_3} CH_3CH_2OCH_2CH_2Br$

(g)

$\xrightarrow[\text{0 °C}]{SOCl_2}$

12.15

(a) $CH_3\overset{\overset{\displaystyle CH_3}{|}}{C}HOH \xrightarrow{NaH} CH_3\overset{\overset{\displaystyle CH_3}{|}}{C}HO^-Na^+ \xrightarrow{CH_3CH_2CH_2Br} CH_3\overset{\overset{\displaystyle CH_3}{|}}{C}HOCH_2CH_2CH_3$

(b) $CH_3\overset{\overset{\displaystyle CH_3}{|}}{\underset{\underset{\displaystyle CH_3}{|}}{C}}OH \xrightarrow{NaH} CH_3\overset{\overset{\displaystyle CH_3}{|}}{\underset{\underset{\displaystyle CH_3}{|}}{C}}O^-Na^+ \xrightarrow{PhCH_2Br} CH_3\overset{\overset{\displaystyle CH_3}{|}}{\underset{\underset{\displaystyle CH_3}{|}}{C}}OCH_2Ph$

(c) $CH_3CH_2OH \xrightarrow{NaH} CH_3CH_2O^-Na^+ \xrightarrow{CH_2=CHCH_2Br} CH_3CH_2OCH_2CH=CH_2$

or $CH_2=CHCH_2OH \xrightarrow{NaH} CH_2=CHCH_2O^-Na^+ \xrightarrow{CH_3CH_2Br} CH_3CH_2OCH_2CH=CH_2$

(d) $CH_3CH_2CH_2CH_2OH \xrightarrow{NaH} CH_3CH_2CH_2CH_2O^-Na^+ \xrightarrow{CH_3I} CH_3CH_2CH_2CH_2OCH_3$

or $CH_3OH \xrightarrow{NaH} CH_3O^-Na^+ \xrightarrow{CH_3CH_2CH_2CH_2Br} CH_3CH_2CH_2CH_2OCH_3$

(e) $CH_3CH_2CH_2CH_2CH_2CH_2OH \xrightarrow{NaH} CH_3CH_2CH_2CH_2CH_2CH_2O^-Na^+ \xrightarrow{CH_3CH_2Br}$

$CH_3CH_2CH_2CH_2CH_2CH_2OCH_2CH_3$

or $CH_3CH_2OH \xrightarrow{NaH} CH_3CH_2O^-Na^+ \xrightarrow{CH_3CH_2CH_2CH_2CH_2CH_2Br}$

$CH_3CH_2CH_2CH_2CH_2CH_2OCH_2CH_3$

(f)

cyclohexanol $\xrightarrow{NaH}$ $\xrightarrow{CH_3CH_2Br}$

Concept Map 12.3   Preparation of ethers by nucleophilic substitution reactions.

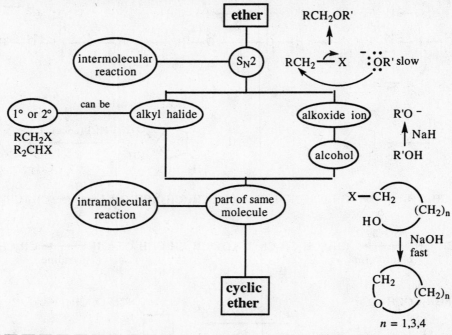

- -

12.16

trans, anti orientation of the
nucleophile and the leaving group
that is beginning to ionize from
a tertiary carbon atom

transition state for an intramolecular substitution reaction

one of two possible enantiomers

12.17   (a)

and enantiomer
A

B

12.17 (b) $CH_3CH_2CH_2\overset{\overset{\textstyle Cl}{|}}{C}H\underset{\overset{\textstyle |}{OH}}{C}HCH_2CH_2CH_3$ $\xrightarrow[\substack{H_2O \\ 25\,°C}]{NaOH}$ $CH_3CH_2CH_2CH\overset{\displaystyle -}{\underset{\underset{\textstyle C}{O}}{\diagup\diagdown}}CHCH_2CH_2CH_3$

(c) $ClCH_2\overset{\overset{\textstyle CH_3}{|}}{\underset{\underset{\textstyle OH}{|}}{C}}CH_2CH_2CH_2CH_3$ $\xrightarrow[\substack{H_2O \\ 25\,°C}]{NaOH}$ $CH_2\!\!-\!\!\overset{\overset{\textstyle CH_3}{|}}{\underset{\underset{\textstyle D}{O}}{C}}CH_2CH_2CH_2CH_3$

(d) $BrCH_2CH_2CH_2CH_2CH_2OH$ $\xrightarrow[\substack{H_2O \\ 25\,°C}]{NaOH}$ (ring structure) E

(e) (alkene) $+$ (phthalic acid) $\xrightarrow{\text{chloro-form}}$ F $+$ G

12.18

(1)

cis-2,3-dimethyloxirane
meso form

(2R, 3R)-2,3-butanediol

(2)

(2S, 3S)-2,3-butanediol

12.18 (cont)

(3)

trans-2,3-dimethyloxirane
(2*R*, 3*R*)-enantiomer

(2*R*, 3*S*)-2,3-butanediol
meso-2,3-butanediol

Note that attack at the other carbon atom also leads to the meso compound. (2S, 3S)-2,3-Dimethyloxirane, the enantiomer of the trans isomer shown above, also gives the same compound.

12.19

(2*R*, 3*R*)-2,3-
dimethyloxirane

attack at one carbon

(2*R*, 3*S*)-3-methoxy-
2-butanol

attack at the other carbon atom

(2*R*, 3*S*)-3-methoxy-
2-butanediol

12.20

$H\ddot{O}CH_2CH_2CH_2CH_2\ddot{C}l\colon$

protonation
of the ether

nucleophilic attack
on the oxonium ion

12.21 (a) CH_3C—$CHCH_2CH_3$ CH_3 +   → CH_3C—$CHCH_2CH_3$

12.21 (b)

$$\underset{\substack{\text{O}}}{\text{CH}_3\text{CH}-\text{CHCH}_3} + \text{NaN}_3 \xrightarrow[\text{CH}_3\text{CH}_2\text{OH}]{} \underset{\substack{\text{OH}\\ \\ \text{CH}_3\text{CHCHCH}_3\\ \\ \text{N}_3}}{}$$

(c)

$$\underset{\substack{\text{O}\\ \text{CH}_3\text{C}-\text{CH}_2\\ \\ \text{CH}_3}}{} + \text{Na}^{18}\text{OH} \xrightarrow[\text{H}_2{}^{18}\text{O}]{} \underset{\substack{\text{OH}\\ \\ \text{CH}_3\text{CCH}_2{}^{18}\text{OH}\\ \\ \text{CH}_3}}{}$$

(d)

$$\underset{\substack{\text{CH}_3 \quad\; \text{O}\\ \\ \text{CH}_3\text{CCH}_2\text{CH}-\text{CH}_2\\ \\ \text{CH}_3}}{} + \text{CH}_3\text{CH}_2\text{CH}_2\text{S}^-\,\text{Na}^+ \xrightarrow[\text{H}_2\text{O}]{} \underset{\substack{\text{CH}_3\; \text{OH}\\ \\ \text{CH}_3\text{CCH}_2\text{CHCH}_2\text{SCH}_2\text{CH}_2\text{CH}_3\\ \\ \text{CH}_3}}{}$$

(e)

$$\underset{\substack{\text{O}}}{\text{CH}_3\text{CH}-\text{CH}_2} + \text{HBr} \longrightarrow \underset{\substack{\text{OH}\\ \\ \text{CH}_3\text{CHCH}_2\text{Br}}}{} + \underset{\substack{\text{Br}\\ \\ \text{CH}_3\text{CHCH}_2\text{OH}}}{}$$

(f)

$$\underset{\substack{\text{O}}}{\text{CH}_2-\text{CH}_2} + \text{Na}^+{}^-{:}\text{C}\!\equiv\!\text{CCH}_2\text{CH}_3 \longrightarrow \text{Na}^+\,{}^-\text{OCH}_2\text{CH}_2\text{C}\!\equiv\!\text{CCH}_2\text{CH}_3 \xrightarrow{\text{H}_3\text{O}^+}$$

$$\text{HOCH}_2\text{CH}_2\text{C}\!\equiv\!\text{CCH}_2\text{CH}_3$$

Concept Map 12.4   Ring-opening reactions of oxiranes.

12.22 $\text{CH}_3\text{SH} + \text{CH}_3\text{CH}_2\text{O}^-\,\text{Na}^+ \longrightarrow \text{CH}_3\text{S}^-\,\text{Na}^+ + \text{CH}_3\text{CH}_2\text{OH}$

12.22 (cont)

12.23   (a)

and enantiomer
+

(b)

and enantiomer

1.   What are the connectivities of the two compounds? How many carbon atoms does each contain? Are there any rings? What are the positions of branches and functional groups on the carbon skeletons?

The carbon skeletons are the same. The alkene has two methyl groups cis to each other on the double bond. The methyl groups are also on the same side of the plane of the page which contains the hydroxyl groups, carbon-2, and carbon-3.

The two hydroxyl groups are anti to each other.

2.   How do the functional groups change in going from starting material to product? Does the starting material have a good leaving group?

The double bond of the alkene has disappeared. Two hydroxyl groups have been attached to the carbon atoms that were part of the double bond.

3.   Is it possible to dissect the structures of the starting material and product to see which bonds must be broken and which formed?

12.23 (b) (3) (cont)

bond broken   bonds formed

A π bond was broken; two carbon-oxygen bonds were formed anti to each other. The anti orientation of the two hydroxyl groups suggests the opening of an oxirane ring by hydroxide ion or water.

4. New bonds are created when an electrophile reacts with a nucleophile. Do we recognize any part of the product molecule as coming from a good nucleophile or an electrophilic addition?

An alkene can be converted into a compound containing one oxygen by oxidation with the electrophilic reagent, *m*-chloroperoxybenzoic acid. A hydroxyl group can come from water, a nucleophile.

5. What type of compound would be a good precursor to the product?

An oxirane can be converted to the 1,2-diol.

6. After this last step, do we see how to get from starting material to product? If not, we need to analyze the structure obtained in step 5 by applying questions 4 and 5 to it.

12.24   (1)

(2)

Concept Map 12.5   (see p. 253)

12.25   (a)

loss of two hydrogens and increase in oxidation number; oxidation; oxidizing agent

12.25 (b)

an increase in oxidation number at each carbon; oxidation; oxidizing agent

(c) $CH_3CH_2Br \longrightarrow CH_3CH_2NH_2$
$\qquad\quad -1 \qquad\qquad\qquad -1$

no change in oxidation state; not an oxidation-reduction reaction

(d)

gain of two oxygens and increase in oxidation number at each carbon; oxidation; oxidizing agent

(e)

no change in oxidation state; not an oxidation-reduction reaction

(f)

$$CH_3CH_2\overset{\displaystyle O}{\overset{\|}{C}}H \longrightarrow CH_3CH_2CH_2OH$$
$$\qquad\quad +1 \qquad\qquad\qquad\qquad -1$$

gain of two hydrogens and decrease in oxidation number; reduction; reducing agent

(g) $CH_3CH = CHCH_3 \longrightarrow CH_3CH - CHCH_3$
$\qquad\quad -1 \quad -1 \qquad\qquad\qquad |\qquad |$
$\qquad\qquad\qquad\qquad\qquad\qquad\qquad OH \quad OH$

increase in oxidation number at each carbon; oxidation; oxidizing agent

(h) $CH_3C \equiv CCH_2CH_3 \longrightarrow CH_3CH = CHCH_2CH_3$
$\qquad\quad\ 0 \quad\ 0 \qquad\qquad\qquad\qquad -1 \quad -1$

gain of two hydrogens and decrease in oxidation number at each carbon; reduction; reducing agent

(i) $CH_3C \equiv CCH_3 \longrightarrow CH_3C - CCH_3$
$\qquad\quad\ 0 \quad 0 \qquad\qquad\qquad +2 \ \ +2$

with the two carbonyl oxygens:

$$CH_3\overset{\displaystyle O}{\overset{\|}{C}} - \overset{\displaystyle O}{\overset{\|}{C}}CH_3$$

gain of two oxygens and increase in oxidation number; oxidation; oxidizing agent

(j)

$$CH_3\overset{\displaystyle O}{\overset{\|}{C}}H \longrightarrow CH_3 - \overset{\displaystyle OCH_3}{\underset{\displaystyle OCH_3}{C}} - H$$
$$\qquad\qquad\quad +1 \qquad\qquad\qquad\qquad +1$$

no change in oxidation state; not an oxidation-reduction reaction

Concept Map 12.5   Oxidation and reduction at carbon atoms.

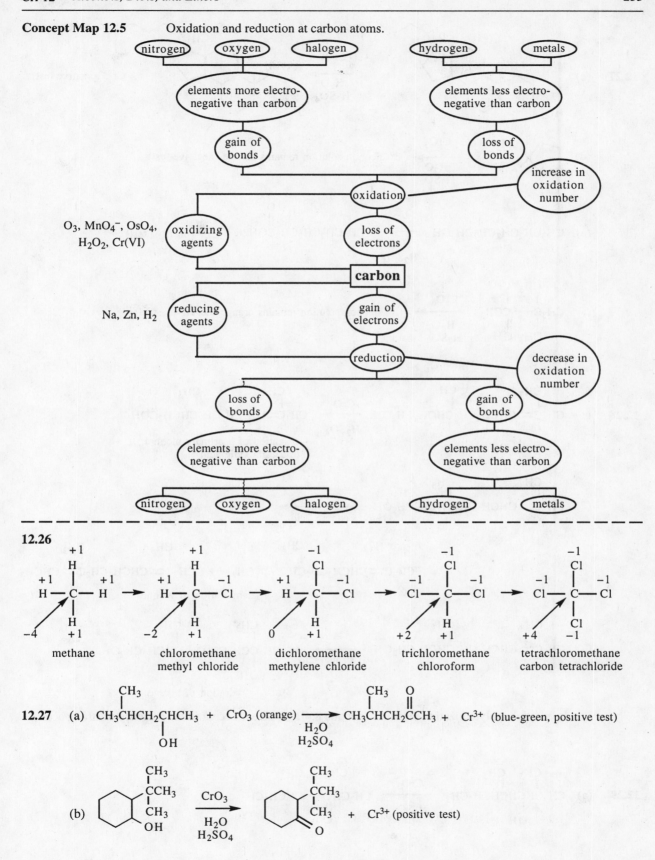

- -

12.26

methane → chloromethane methyl chloride → dichloromethane methylene chloride → trichloromethane chloroform → tetrachloromethane carbon tetrachloride

12.27 (a) CH₃CHCH₂CHCH₃ + CrO₃ (orange) $\xrightarrow[\text{H}_2\text{SO}_4]{\text{H}_2\text{O}}$ CH₃CHCH₂CCH₃ + Cr³⁺ (blue-green, positive test)

(b)

12.27 (c)

$+$ Cr^{3+} (positive test)

(d)

$3°$ alcohol, solution remains orange (negative test)

(e) $CH_3CH_2CH_2CH_2CH_2OH$ $\xrightarrow[\substack{H_2O \\ H_2SO_4}]{CrO_3}$ $CH_3CH_2CH_2CH_2\overset{\displaystyle O}{\overset{\|}{C}}OH$ $+$ Cr^{3+} (positive test)

(f)

$3°$ alcohol, solution remains orange (negative test)

12.28 (1)

oxidation of a primary alcohol to a carboxylic acid

(2)

dehydration of alcohol

(3)

hydration of alkene

In addition, polymerization reactions (Section 8.4B) of alkenes occur in the presence of strong acids.

12.29 (a)

12.29 (b), (c), (d), (e), (f)

Concept Map 12.6   Reactions of alcohols with oxidizing agents.

12.30 (a)

12.30 (b)

(c)

12.31

Experiment 1. The mechanism for the second stage of the Swern reaction has the base deprotonating the carbon atom next to the sulfur atom and not the one next to the oxygen atom. Dimethyl sulfoxide with deuterium substituting for hydrogen makes it possible to see the location of the deprotonation.

(a)

An alternative mechanism would have been the direct deprotonation of the carbon atom adjacent to the oxygen atom.

(b)

Such a mechanism results in the formation of dimethyl sulfide with six deuterium atoms, instead of the five actually observed.

Experiment 2. This experiment also supports the mechanism shown above. If there are no hydrogen atoms on the carbon atom attached to the sulfur atom, the carbonyl compound does not form, again demonstrating that pathway (b) shown above does not occur. The products observed come from an S_N2 reaction.

12.32 (a)

Note that this problem closely resembles the problem in Problem-Solving Skills Section 12.7F. Practice applying the same questions to it.

(b) $NH_4^+ Br^-$ + $CH_3CH_2CHCH_3$ $\longleftarrow$ $\overset{NH_3 \text{ (excess)}}{}$ $CH_3CH_2CHCH_3$ $\longleftarrow$ $\overset{HBr}{}$ $CH_3CH_2CH = CH_2$

with NH_2 below first structure and Br below second structure.

12.32   (c) $PhCH_2OH$ $\xrightarrow{\ ?\ }$ $PhCH_2C{\equiv}CCH_3$

1. What are the connectivities of the two compounds? How many carbon atoms does each contain? Are there any rings? What are the positions of branches and functional groups on the carbon skeletons?

    Both compounds contain an aromatic ring. The alcohol group on the benzylic carbon atom in the starting material has been replaced by a three-carbon chain containing a triple bond (a 1-propynyl group) in the product.

2. How do the functional groups change in going from starting material to product? Does the starting material have a good leaving group?

    The benzylic carbon atom is bonded to the first carbon atom of the triple bond. There is no good leaving group present in the starting material.

3. Is it possible to dissect the structures of the starting material and product to see which bonds must be broken and which formed?

$$PhCH_2{-}\!\!\left.\right\}{-}OH \qquad\qquad PhCH_2{-}\!\!\left.\right\}{-}C{\equiv}CCH_3$$

bond broken	bond formed

    A carbon-oxygen bond was broken. A carbon-carbon bond was formed.

4. New bonds are created when an electrophile reacts with a nucleophile. Do we recognize any part of the product molecule as coming from a good nucleophile or an electrophilic addition?

    The 1-propynyl group can come from an S_N2 reaction using an anion derived from an alkyne as the nucleophile.

$$PhCH_2C{\equiv}CCH_3 \xleftarrow{\ CH_3C{\equiv}C{:}^-Na^+\ } PhCH_2Br$$

5. What type of compound would be a good precursor to the product?

    A compound with a good leaving group, such as an alkyl halide or a tosylate, would be a good precursor to the product.

$$PhCH_2{-}\boxed{X}$$

    An alkyl bromide can easily be made from the starting material by reaction with concentrated hydrobromic acid.

$$PhCH_2Br \xleftarrow{\ HBr\ (conc)\ } PhCH_2OH$$

6. After this last step, do we see how to get from starting material to product? If not, we need to analyze the structure obtained in step 5 by applying questions 4 and 5 to it.

$$PhCH_2C{\equiv}CCH_3 \xleftarrow{\ CH_3C{\equiv}C{:}^-Na^+\ } PhCH_2Br \xleftarrow{\ \overset{HBr}{(conc)}\ } PhCH_2OH$$

12.33   (a) 1,3-propanediol   (b) 1,2-dimethoxyethane   (c) 3-ethoxy-2,2-dimethyl-1-propanol
            (d) 1-bromo-2-methoxyethane   (e) ethoxybenzene (ethyl phenyl ether)   (f) 2-ethoxyethanol
            (g) cyclobutanol   (h) (2*S*)(*E*)-5-methyl-4-hepten-2-ol   (i) (1*R*, 2*R*)-2-bromocyclopentanol
            (j) benzyloxyphenylmethane (dibenzyl ether)   (k) (1*S*, 2*S*)-2-methoxycyclohexanol
            (l) 1,1,1-triethoxyethane

12.34

(a) $CH_3CH_2OC{=}CH_2$ (b) $\underset{H}{\overset{CH_3CH_2CH_2O}{\diagdown}}C{=}C\underset{OCH_3}{\overset{H}{\diagup}}$ (c) $ClCH_2\underset{OH}{\overset{|}{C}}HCH_2Cl$ (d) ⬦$-CH_2OH$
      $\underset{Cl}{\overset{|}{}}$

12.34

(e)
$$CH_3\text{---}\overset{\displaystyle OH}{\underset{\displaystyle CH_3CH_2}{\overset{|}{C}}}\text{---}CH_2CH{=}CH_2$$

(f)
$$H\text{---}\overset{\displaystyle CH_2OH}{\underset{\displaystyle CH_3}{\overset{|}{C}}}\text{---}Cl$$

(g)
$$CH_3\text{---}\overset{\displaystyle \underset{\displaystyle \overset{|||}{C}}{\overset{\displaystyle H}{\underset{}{C}}}}{\underset{\displaystyle CH_3CH_2}{\overset{|}{C}}}\text{---}OH$$

(h) $O_2NCH_2CH_2OH$

(i)
$$H\text{---}\overset{\displaystyle OH}{\underset{\displaystyle CH_3CH_2}{\overset{|}{C}}}\text{---}CH_2\overset{\displaystyle CH_3}{\underset{\displaystyle CH_3}{\overset{|}{C}}}CH_2CH_3$$

(j)
$$\overset{\displaystyle CH_3CH_2}{\underset{\displaystyle HO}{C}}\text{---}\overset{\displaystyle CH_3}{\underset{\displaystyle CH_2CH_3}{C}}\text{---}H$$

Concept Map 12.7   Summary of the preparation and reactions of alcohols and ethers.

12.35   (a) $CH_3CH_2CH_2OH$ $\xrightarrow[\Delta]{HBr}$ $CH_3CH_2CH_2Br$ + H_2O

(b) $CH_3CH_2CH_2OH$ $\xrightarrow{PBr_3}$ $CH_3CH_2CH_2Br$ + H_3PO_3

(c) $CH_3CH_2CH_2OH$ $\xrightarrow[\text{pyridine}]{SOCl_2}$ $CH_3CH_2CH_2Cl$ + $SO_2\uparrow$ + Cl^-

(d) $CH_3CH_2CH_2OH$ $\xrightarrow{NaH}$ $CH_3CH_2CH_2O^-Na^+$ $\xrightarrow{CH_3CH_2CH_2CH_2Br}$

+ $H_2\uparrow$

$CH_3CH_2CH_2OCH_2CH_2CH_2CH_3$ + $NaBr$

(e) $CH_3CH_2CH_2OH$ $\xrightarrow[\text{cold}]{H_3O^+}$ $CH_3CH_2CH_2\overset{+}{O}H_2$ + H_2O

(f) $CH_3CH_2CH_2OH$ $\xrightarrow[\underset{\Delta}{H_2SO_4}]{}$ $CH_3CH=CH_2$ + H_2O

(g) $CH_3CH_2CH_2OH$ $\xrightarrow[H_2O]{CrO_3,\ H_3O^+}$ $CH_3CH_2\overset{O}{\overset{\|}{C}}OH$

(h) $CH_3CH_2CH_2OH$ $\xrightarrow[\text{dichloromethane}]{}$ $CH_3CH_2\overset{O}{\overset{\|}{C}}H$

(i) $CH_3CH_2CH_2OH$ $\xrightarrow{CH_3SCH_3,\ ClC-CCl}$ $\xrightarrow{(CH_3CH_2)_3N}$ $CH_3CH_2\overset{O}{\overset{\|}{C}}H$

12.36   (a) $CH_3CH_2CH_2CH_2\underset{\underset{OH}{|}}{C}HCH_3$ $\xrightarrow[\Delta]{HBr}$ $CH_3CH_2CH_2CH_2\underset{\underset{Br}{|}}{C}HCH_3$ + $CH_3CH_2CH_2\underset{\underset{Br}{|}}{C}HCH_2CH_3$

major

+ H_2O + some elimination products

(b) $CH_3CH_2CH_2CH_2\underset{\underset{OH}{|}}{C}HCH_3$ $\xrightarrow[\Delta]{PBr_3}$ $CH_3CH_2CH_2CH_2\underset{\underset{Br}{|}}{C}HCH_3$ + H_3PO_3

(c) $CH_3CH_2CH_2CH_2\underset{\underset{OH}{|}}{C}HCH_3$ $\xrightarrow[\text{pyridine}]{SOCl_2}$ $CH_3CH_2CH_2CH_2\underset{\underset{Cl}{|}}{C}HCH_3$ + $SO_2\uparrow$ + Cl^-

12.36 (d) $CH_3CH_2CH_2CH_2CHCH_3$ $\xrightarrow{NaH}$ $CH_3CH_2CH_2CH_2CHCH_3$ + $H_2\uparrow$
                  |
                  OH O^-Na^+

(e) $CH_3CH_2CH_2CH_2CHCH_3$ $\xrightarrow[ZnCl_2]{HCl}$ $CH_3CH_2CH_2CH_2CHCH_3$ + $CH_3CH_2CH_2CHCH_2CH_3$
                | | |
                OH   Cl   Cl

(f) $CH_3CH_2CH_2CH_2CHCH_3$ $\xrightarrow[\Delta]{H_2SO_4}$ $CH_3CH_2CH_2CH=CHCH_3$ +
                |
                OH

          $CH_3CH_2CH_2CH_2CH=CH_2$ + $CH_3CH_2CH=CHCH_2CH_3$ + H_2O

(g) $CH_3CH_2CH_2CH_2CHCH_3$ $\xrightarrow[H_2O]{CrO_3, H_3O^+}$ $CH_3CH_2CH_2CH_2\overset{\displaystyle O}{\overset{\|}{C}}CH_3$
                |
                OH

(h) $CH_3CH_2CH_2CH_2CHCH_3$ $\xrightarrow[\text{dichloromethane}]{}$ $CH_3CH_2CH_2CH_2\overset{\displaystyle O}{\overset{\|}{C}}CH_3$
                |
                OH

(above arrow: pyridinium CrO_3Cl^-)

(i) $CH_3CH_2CH_2CH_2CHCH_3$ $\xrightarrow{CH_3SCH_3,\ ClC-CCl}$ $\xrightarrow{(CH_3CH_2)_3N}$ $CH_3CH_2CH_2CH_2\overset{\displaystyle O}{\overset{\|}{C}}CH_3$
                |
                OH

(reagents: $CH_3\overset{\displaystyle O}{\overset{\|}{S}}CH_3$, $Cl\overset{\displaystyle O}{\overset{\|}{C}}-\overset{\displaystyle O}{\overset{\|}{C}}Cl$)

12.37 (a) cyclohexanol (C₆H₁₁–OH)
                                            2. H_2SO_4, cold, conc (heat evolved)
                                            4. CrO_3, H_2O, H_2SO_4 (color change)

(b) $\underset{H}{\overset{CH_3}{C}}=\underset{CH_2CH_3}{\overset{H}{C}}$
                                            2. H_2SO_4, cold, conc (heat evolved)
                                            3. Br_2, carbon tetrachloride (color change)

(c) $\underset{H}{\overset{CH_3}{C}}=\underset{CH_2Cl}{\overset{H}{C}}$
                                            2. H_2SO_4, cold, conc (heat evolved)
                                            3. Br_2, carbon tetrachloride (color change)
                                            5. $AgNO_3$, CH_3CH_2OH (ppt)
                                            6. NaI, acetone (ppt)

(d) 1-methylcyclopentanol (CH_3, OH)
                                            2. H_2SO_4, cold, conc (heat evolved)

(e) $PhCH_2Cl$
                                            5. $AgNO_3$, CH_3CH_2OH (ppt)
                                          6. NaI, acetone (ppt)

(f) $CH_3CH_2CH_2CH_2CH_2OH$
                                            2. H_2SO_4, cold, conc (heat evolved)
                                          4. CrO_3, H_2O, H_2SO_4 (color change)

(g) $CH_3C\equiv CCH_2CH_3$
                                            2. H_2SO_4, cold, conc (heat evolved)
                                          3. Br_2, carbon tetrachloride (color change)

12.37 (h) [cyclohexane ring]   none

(i) $HOCH_2CH_2OH$

1. H_2O, cold (dissolves)
2. H_2SO_4, cold, conc (heat evolved)
4. CrO_3, H_2O, H_2SO_4 (color change)

(j)
$$CH_3CH_2\overset{\overset{\displaystyle CH_3}{|}}{\underset{\underset{\displaystyle Br}{|}}{C}}CH_3$$

5. $AgNO_3$, CH_3CH_2OH (ppt)

(k)   [cyclopentane ring]—OCH_2CH_3 2. H_2SO_4, cold, conc (heat evolved)

(l) $CH_3CH_2CH_2CH_2CH_2CH_2Cl$ 6. NaI, acetone (ppt)

12.38 (a) The amino alcohol with two hydrogen bonding groups is most soluble in water. The alcohol, which can act as a donor as well as an acceptor of hydrogen bonds, is more soluble in water than the ester, which is only an acceptor of hydrogen bonds.

(b) The more stable the conjugate base (an anion in this example), the stronger is the acid (the alcohol). The *tert*-butoxide anion is destabilized by the bulk of the methyl groups, which interfere with solvation (and therefore stabilization) of the anion. The trifluoroethoxide anion, by contrast, is stabilized by the electron-withdrawing effect of the fluorine atoms.

12.38 (b) (cont)

(structures of hydrogen-bonded compounds with water)

CH$_3$CH$_2$CH$_2$CH$_2$—O ··· (with H bonds to O—H, H)

CH$_3$CH$_2$CH$_2$CH$_2$—S ··· (with H bonds to O—H, H)

(c) The compound that has the highest boiling point and the highest solubility in water is the one with two hydroxyl groups, which leads to increased hydrogen bonding, both between molecules of the same kind (giving rise to a higher boiling point) and between the compound and water (giving rise to higher solubility in water). Of the compounds with only one hydroxyl group, the one with the higher molecular weight and the longer carbon chain has the higher boiling point (from increased van der Waals attraction) and the lower solubility in water (because the hydrophobic part of the molecule is too large to be brought into solution by the polar hydroxyl group). See Sections 1.10B and 1.10C for review.

CH$_3$CH·CHCH$_2$CH$_2$CH$_3$

2,3-hexanediol   1-hexanol   1-butanol

(d) The hydroxyl group hydrogen bonds more strongly than the thiol group, and the alcohol is therefore more soluble than the corresponding sulfur compound.

CH$_3$CH$_2$CH$_2$CH$_2$—O ··· (with O—H, H)

CH$_3$CH$_2$CH$_2$CH$_2$—S (with O—H, H)

12.39 (a) CH$_3$CHCH$_2$OH $\xrightarrow[\text{pyridine}]{\text{SOCl}_2}$ CH$_3$CHCH$_2$Cl
      |CH$_3$ |CH$_3$

(b) CH$_3$CCH$_2$CH$_3$ $\xrightarrow{\text{HCl (conc)}}$ CH$_3$CCH$_2$CH$_3$
   with CH$_3$ and OH   with CH$_3$ and Cl

12.39 (c) $CH_3CH_2\underset{\underset{OH}{|}}{C}HCH_3$ $\xrightarrow{PBr_3}$ $CH_3CH_2\underset{\underset{Br}{|}}{C}HCH_3$

(d) $\xrightarrow[\text{diglyme}]{BH_3}$ $\xrightarrow[\text{H}_2\text{O}]{\text{H}_2\text{O}_2,\ \text{NaOH}}$

and enantiomer

(e) $HOCH_2(CH_2)_4CH_2OH$ $\xrightarrow[\text{(excess)}]{\text{HBr (g)}}$ $BrCH_2(CH_2)_4CH_2Br$ (f) $\xrightarrow{HI}$

(g) $\xrightarrow[\text{dichloromethane}]{}$

(h) $Ph\underset{\underset{OH}{|}}{C}HCH_3$ $\xrightarrow{CH_3SCH_3,\ ClC\!-\!CCl}$ $\xrightarrow{(CH_3CH_2)_3N}$ $Ph\underset{\underset{O}{||}}{C}CH_3$

12.40 (a) $\xrightarrow[\substack{\text{H}_2\text{SO}_4\\ \text{H}_2\text{O}\\ \text{acetone}}]{CrO_3}$

(b) $-CH_2CH_2CH_2CH_2OH$ $\xrightarrow[\text{pyridine}]{PBr_3}$ $-CH_2CH_2CH_2CH_2Br$

(c) $\xrightarrow[\substack{\text{H}_2\text{SO}_4\\ \text{H}_2\text{O}\\ \text{acetone}}]{CrO_3}$ (d) $\xrightarrow[\substack{\text{pyridine}\\ \Delta}]{SOCl_2}$

(e) $\xrightarrow[\text{dichloromethane}]{}$

two diastereomers

(f) $\xrightarrow[\text{ethanol}]{PhS^-\ Na^+}$ $CH_3\underset{\underset{OH}{|}}{C}HCH_2SPh$

12.41

(a) $PhCH_2CH_2CH{=}CH_2 \xrightarrow[\text{tetrahydrofuran}]{BH_3} \left(PhCH_2CH_2CH_2CH_2\right)_3B \xrightarrow[H_2O]{H_2O_2, NaOH}$

A

$PhCH_2CH_2CH_2CH_2OH \xrightarrow[\text{dichloromethane}]{} PhCH_2CH_2CH_2CH$

B   C

(b)

D
major isomers from less
hindered transition state

E
minor isomers

$D \xrightarrow[H_2O]{H_2O_2, NaOH}$

F
enantiomers

$E \xrightarrow[H_2O]{H_2O_2, NaOH}$

G
enantiomers

(c)

L

and enantiomer
H

and enantiomer
I

and enantiomer
J

and enantiomer
I

$\xrightarrow[\substack{H_2SO_4 \\ H_2O}]{CrO_3}$

and enantiomer
K

12.41

(d)

$$\text{cyclopentyl-CH}_2\text{CH}_2\text{Br} \xrightarrow[\text{NH}_3 \text{ (liq)}]{\text{HC}\equiv\text{C:}^-\text{Na}^+} \text{cyclopentyl-CH}_2\text{CH}_2\text{C}\equiv\text{CH} \xrightarrow[\substack{\text{H}_2\text{SO}_4 \\ \text{HgSO}_4}]{\text{H}_2\text{O}} \text{cyclopentyl-CH}_2\text{CH}_2\overset{\text{O}}{\text{C}}\text{CH}_3$$

M   N

$$\text{cyclopentyl-CH}_2\text{CH}_2\text{Br} \xrightarrow[\substack{\text{ethanol} \\ \Delta}]{\text{KOH (4 M)}} \text{cyclopentyl-CH}=\text{CH}_2 \xrightarrow[\substack{\text{carbon} \\ \text{tetrachloride}}]{\text{Br}_2} \text{cyclopentyl-CHCH}_2\text{Br}$$

O

Br
racemic mixture
P

$$\text{cyclopentyl-CH}=\text{CH}_2 \xrightarrow{\text{HBr}} \text{cyclopentyl-CHCH}_3 \xrightarrow[\text{ethanol}]{\text{NaCN}} \text{cyclopentyl-CHCH}_3$$

O   Br   CN
racemic mixture   racemic mixture
Q   R

(e)

$$\xrightarrow[\substack{\text{Pd/BaSO}_4 \\ \text{quinoline}}]{\text{H}_2}$$

S

12.42   (a)

$$\underset{\text{CH}_3}{\text{CH}_3\text{CHCH}_2}\overset{\text{O}}{\text{CCH}_3} \xleftarrow[\substack{\text{H}_2\text{SO}_4 \\ \text{H}_2\text{O}}]{\text{CrO}_3} \underset{\text{CH}_3}{\text{CH}_3\text{CHCH}_2}\underset{\text{OH}}{\text{CHCH}_3} \xleftarrow{\text{H}_3\text{O}^+} \underset{\text{CH}_3}{\text{CH}_3\text{CHCH}_2\text{CH}}=\text{CH}_2$$

(b)

$$\text{CH}_3(\text{CH}_2)_4\text{CH}_2\overset{\text{O}}{\text{CH}} \xleftarrow[\text{dichloromethane}]{\text{pyridinium chlorochromate}} \text{CH}_3(\text{CH}_2)_4\text{CH}_2\text{CH}_2\text{OH}$$

$$\xleftarrow[\text{H}_2\text{O}]{\text{H}_2\text{O}_2, \text{NaOH}} (\text{CH}_3(\text{CH}_2)_4\text{CH}_2\text{CH}_2)_3\text{B} \xleftarrow[\text{diglyme}]{\text{BH}_3} \text{CH}_3(\text{CH}_2)_4\text{CH}=\text{CH}_2$$

(c)

$$\text{PhCH}_2\text{CH}_2\text{CH}_2\text{CH}_2\text{OPh} \xleftarrow{\text{sodium phenoxide}} \text{PhCH}_2\text{CH}_2\text{CH}_2\text{CH}_2\text{Br}$$

$$\xleftarrow[\text{pyridine}]{\text{PBr}_3} \text{PhCH}_2\text{CH}_2\text{CH}_2\text{CH}_2\text{OH} \xleftarrow[\text{H}_2\text{O}]{\text{H}_2\text{O}_2, \text{NaOH}} \xleftarrow{\text{BH}_3} \text{PhCH}_2\text{CH}_2\text{CH}=\text{CH}_2$$

(d)

$$\xleftarrow[\text{H}_2\text{O}]{\text{H}_2\text{O}_2, \text{NaOH} \quad \text{BH}_3}$$

12.42 (e)

(f) PhCHCH$_2$N(CH$_3$)$_2$ $\xleftarrow{\text{(CH}_3\text{)}_2\text{NH}}$ PhCH$-$CH$_2$ $\xleftarrow[\text{dichloromethane}]{}$ PhCH$=$CH$_2$
            |
            OH

12.43

syn addition
of BH$_3$

migration of carbon
atom with retention
of configuration

preparation of tosylate
with retention of configuration

elimination of the tosylate
with hydrogen atom that
is trans and anti to it

12.44 (a)

(11*E*)-retinal

(b)

(11*Z*)-retinal

(c)

CrO$_3$Cl$^-$ in dichloromethane   or   CH$_3$SCH$_3$, ClC$-$CCl then (CH$_3$CH$_2$)$_3$N

12.45 (a)

A
C$_{10}$H$_{12}$O$_4$

12.45 **(b)**

(c)

(d)

12.46

12.47 $CH_3C \equiv CCH_2C \equiv CCH_2CH_2CH_2OH$ $\xrightarrow[\substack{NH_3 \text{ (liq)} \\ tert\text{-butyl alcohol} \\ \text{ammonium sulfate}}]{Li}$

12.48

12.48 (cont)

$$PhCH\!-\!CH_2 \xrightarrow[\text{CH}_3\text{OH}]{\text{CH}_3\text{O}^-\text{Na}^+} \underset{\text{OH}}{PhCHCH_2OCH_3}$$

(1)

(2)

12.49 (a)

(b)

(c)

12.49 (d)

F

12.50 (a)

(b)

leaving group
OTs
OH nucleophile

CHOH(CH₂)₄CH₃

This conformation will not give oxirane A because the hydroxyl group that will serve as the nucleophile in the displacement reaction is not anti to the leaving group, the tosylate.

(c) Potassium carbonate is a source of the base, carbonate ion, CO_3^{-2}. The pK_a of the conjugate acid of CO_3^{-2} is bicarbonate ion, HCO_3^{-}, pK_a 10.2. The carbonate ion does not completely deprotonate the hydroxyl group, $pK_a \sim 17$. Because the displacement reaction is intramolecular, and, therefore, very fast, it is sufficient to create only a low concentration of alkoxide ions, which are then rapidly converted into the oxirane.

(d)

note the inversion of configuration

12.51 $ClCH_2CH_2CH_2\overset{O}{\underset{\|}{C}}CH_3$ $\xrightarrow{\text{reduction}}$

(*S*)-5-chloro-2-pentanol

$\xrightarrow{\text{NaH}}$

(*S*)-2-methyltetrahydrofuran

12.52 (a) $HC\equiv CCH_2OH$ $\xrightarrow[\text{NH}_3 \text{ (liq)}]{\text{2 LiNH}_2}$ $Li^{+ -}:C\equiv CCH_2O^- Li^+$

A

$Li^{+ -}:C\equiv CCH_2O^- Li^+$ $\xrightarrow{CH_3(CH_2)_3CH_2Br}$ $\xrightarrow[H_2O]{H_3O^+}$ $CH_3(CH_2)_3CH_2C\equiv CCH_2OH$

A   2-octyn-1-ol

12.52   (b) $Li^+ {}^- : C \equiv CCH_2OCH_2(CH_2)_3CH_3$

(c)   An acetylide anion (charge on carbon) is more nucleophilic than an alkoxide ion (charge on oxygen) and will react faster with the electrophilic alkyl halide.

(d) $HC \equiv CCH_2O^- Li^+$

12.53

The unsymmetrical alkene can react with diborane by way of two different transition states.

The one with the partial positive charge next to the oxygen is more stable, because the charge can be delocalized to oxygen, shown by resonance contributors written as though an intermediate with a full positive charge forms.

has no additional stabilization

The reaction goes by way of the transition state of lower energy corresponding to the more stable of the two reaction intermediates.

12.54

(a)

racemic   dimethyl-   racemic   dichloromethane   and enantiomer   and enantiomer
mixture   formamide   mixture   B   C
                 100 °C   A

and enantiomer   and enantiomer   and enantiomer
B   D   (very minor product; bulky phenoxide
                                                                 group prevents the approach of amine to
                                                                 the carbon adjacent to the substituent)

12.54 (a) (cont)

and enantiomer
C

and enantiomer
E

and enantiomer
(minor product)

(b)   D and E are diastereomers. D is a racemic mixture.

12.55   (a)

(2*S*, 5*S*)-2,5-dimethyl-
1-boracyclopentane

looks *R* because we are looking at the stereocenter
from the side on which the group of lowest priority
comes up at us, therefore it is really *S*.

The numbers in the circles indicate priorities of groups on the left-hand stereocenter for the purpose
of assigning configuration; the numbers in the squares indicate priority of groups on the right-hand
stereocenter. Boron has a lower atomic number than carbon and so comes third in the order of priorities.

(b)

(*S*)-(+)-2-methyl-
cyclopentanone

or

(*R*)-(−)-2-methyl-
cyclopentanone

(c)

H_2O_2, NaOH

syn addition of H—OH to give
the *R* configuration at the carbon
atom bearing the methyl group

(*R*)-styrene oxide

(*R*)-1-phenylethane-1,2-diol

12.56   (a)

12.56   (b)

In this reaction (R)-1-phenylethane-1,2-diol must come from (S)-styrene oxide by inversion of configuration at the stereocenter.

12.57   (1)

(2)

cyclic ether

12.58   The following equation can be used to calculate the free energy of activation from the heat and entropy of activation.

$$\Delta G^{\ddagger} = \Delta H^{\ddagger} - T\Delta S^{\ddagger}$$

For the formation of oxirane

$$\Delta G^{\ddagger} = (23.2 \text{ kcal/mol} - (303 \text{ K})(9.9 \times 10^{-3} \text{ kcal/mol}\bullet\text{K})$$
$$\Delta G^{\ddagger} = 20.2 \text{ kcal/mol}$$

For the formation of tetrahydrofuran

$$\Delta G^{\ddagger} = (19.8 \text{ kcal/mol} - (303 \text{ K})(-5 \times 10^{-3} \text{ kcal/mol}\bullet\text{K})$$
$$\Delta G^{\ddagger} = 21.3 \text{ kcal/mol}$$

The formation of oxirane has the smaller free energy of activation and therefore the faster rate. Even though the heat of activation is smaller for the formation of tetrahydrofuran than for oxirane, the reaction giving rise to tetrahydrofuran has a negative (unfavorable) entropy of activation whereas the entropy of activation for the formation of oxirane is positive, contributing to a smaller overall free energy of activation for the reaction.

12.59   Compound A, $C_7H_{16}O$, has no units of unsaturation. The infrared spectrum shows the presence of an alcohol (3300 cm^{-1} for the O—H stretch and 1110 cm^{-1} for the C—O stretch).

Compound B, $C_7H_{14}O$, has one unit of unsaturation. The infrared spectrum shows the presence of an aldehyde (2700 cm^{-1} for the C—H stretch and 1725 cm^{-1} for the C=O stretch).

Analysis of the proton magnetic resonance spectrum of Compound A is shown below:

δ 0.9	(3H, t, C$\underline{H}_3$CH$_2$—)
δ 1.3	(10H, m, —(C$\underline{H}_2$)$_5$—)

(A linear chain of methylene groups that have similar chemical shifts and are at least one carbon away from electron-withdrawing atoms or π bonds will usually appear as a complex multiplet in this region.)

δ 2.2	(1H, s, —O$\underline{H}$)
δ 3.6	(2H, t, —CH$_2$C$\underline{H}_2$—O—)

12.59 (cont)

The ^{13}C magnetic resonance spectrum shows six alkyl carbon atoms (δ 14.2, 23.1, 26.4, 29.7, 32.4, and 33.2) suggesting a linear chain. The seventh carbon atom (δ 62.2) falls in the range of a carbon atom bonded to an oxygen atom. Compound A is 1-heptanol, $CH_3(CH_2)_5CH_2OH$. It must be oxidized by pyridinium chlorochromate to heptanal.

Analysis of the proton magnetic resonance spectrum of Compound B confirms that it is heptanal.

δ 0.9	(3H, t, C$\underline{H}_3$CH$_2$—)
δ 1.3	(8H, m, —(C$\underline{H}_2$)$_4$—)
δ 2.4	(2H, m, —C$\underline{H}_2$C=O)
δ 9.8	(1H, t, —CH$_2$C$\overset{\overset{\displaystyle O}{\|}}{H}$)

The ^{13}C magnetic resonance spectrum confirms the presence of an aldehyde functional group (δ 202.2).

$$CH_3(CH_2)_5CH_2OH \qquad\qquad CH_3(CH_2)_5\overset{\overset{\displaystyle O}{\|}}{C}H$$

$$\text{A} \qquad\qquad\qquad\qquad \text{B}$$

12.60   Compound C, $C_5H_{12}O$, has no units of unsaturation. The infrared spectrum shows the presence of an alcohol (3400 cm^{-1} for the O—H stretch). Compound C does not react with chromium trioxide so it must be a tertiary alcohol. Only one structural formula is possible for a five-carbon tertiary alcohol. Compound C must be 2-methyl-2-butanol (*tert*-amyl alcohol).

$$CH_3\overset{\overset{\displaystyle CH_3}{\|}}{\underset{\underset{\displaystyle OH}{\|}}{C}}CH_2CH_3 \xrightarrow[\substack{H_2SO_4 \\ H_2O}]{CrO_3} \text{solution remains orange}$$

$$\text{C}$$

Analysis of the magnetic resonance spectra of Compound C confirms the structure. The proton magnetic resonances are given below:

δ 0.9	(m, (C$\underline{H}_3$CH$_2$—)
δ 1.2	(s, (C$\underline{H}_3$)$_2$C—)
δ 1.5	(m, —C$\underline{H}_2$CH$_3$)

There are no bands for a hydrogen atom on a carbon bonded to an oxygen atom ($\delta \sim 4$), which also confirms that Compound C is a tertiary alcohol. The proton on the oxygen atom is hidden in one of the multiplets.

The ^{13}C magnetic resonance spectrum shows only four types of carbon atoms. Three of the types are alkyl carbon atoms (δ 8.8, 28.9, and 36.8) and one is a tertiary carbon atom bonded to an oxygen atom (δ 70.6).

Compound D, $C_5H_{12}O$, also has no units of unsaturation. The infrared spectrum again shows the presence of an alcohol (3400 cm^{-1} for the O—H stretch). A positive reaction with chromium trioxide points to a secondary or primary alcohol. The possible structures are shown below:

Primary alcohols:

$$CH_3CH_2CH_2CH_2CH_2OH \qquad CH_3\overset{\overset{\displaystyle CH_3}{\|}}{C}HCH_2CH_2OH \qquad CH_3CH_2\overset{\overset{\displaystyle CH_3}{\|}}{C}HCH_2OH \qquad CH_3\overset{\overset{\displaystyle CH_3}{\|}}{\underset{\underset{\displaystyle CH_3}{\|}}{C}}CH_2OH$$

Secondary alcohols:

$$CH_3CH_2CH_2\overset{\underset{\underset{\displaystyle OH}{\|}}{}}{C}HCH_3 \qquad CH_3CH_2\overset{\underset{\underset{\displaystyle OH}{\|}}{}}{C}HCH_2CH_3 \qquad CH_3\overset{\overset{\displaystyle CH_3}{\|}}{\underset{\underset{\displaystyle OH}{\|}}{C}}HCHCH_3$$

12.60 (cont)

The ^{13}C magnetic resonance spectrum shows five bands. The three alcohols that have five different types of carbon atoms are 1-pentanol, 2-pentanol, and 2-methyl-1-butanol. Of these, only 2-pentanol will have the observed doublet for the hydrogen atoms on carbon-1 and a multiplet for the hydrogen atom on the carbon atom bearing the hydroxyl group.

Analysis of the rest of the magnetic resonance spectra of Compound D confirms the structure. The proton magnetic resonances are given below:

δ 0.9-1.4   (complex multiplet, C$\underline{H}_3$C$\underline{H}_2$C$\underline{H}_2$—)
δ 1.2   (d, C$\underline{H}_3$CH—)
δ 3.7   (m, — CH$_2$C$\underline{H}$CH$_3$)
                                          |
                                         O—

$$CH_3CH_2CH_2\underset{\underset{D}{|}}{\underset{OH}{\overset{}{C}}}HCH_3 \xrightarrow[\substack{H_2SO_4 \\ H_2O}]{CrO_3} CH_3CH_2CH_2\overset{\overset{O}{\|}}{C}CH_3$$

Note that the hydrogen atom on the hydroxyl group is not seen as a separate band in the spectrum of either Compound C or Compound D.

Supplemental Problems

S12.1   Find the products or reagents corresponding to each of the capital letters. Show stereochemistry by appropriate conventions. When a racemic mixture forms, show the structure for one enantiomer and write "and enantiomer" below it.

(a)

(b)

(c)

(d)

(e)

(f)

S12.2   Supply the reagents that are necessary and the intermediate compounds that will form in the following transformations. There may be more than one good way to carry out each synthesis.

(a) $HOCH_2(CH_2)_6CH_2OH$ → $PhCH_2OCH_2(CH_2)_6\overset{\overset{O}{\|}}{C}H$

(b) $HOCH_2\underset{\overset{|}{\underset{NH_3}{+}} Br^-}{\overset{\overset{CH_2CH_3}{|}}{C}}CH_2OH$ → $BrCH_2\underset{\overset{|}{\underset{NH_3}{+}} Br^-}{\overset{\overset{CH_2CH_3}{|}}{C}}CH_2Br$

(c)   [structure: azetidine with CH_2CH_3 and OH, N–O_2N] → [structure: azetidine with CH_2CH_3 double bond, N–O_2N]

(d)   [bicyclic structure with CH_3–C=O, N] → [bicyclic structure with CH_3–C=O, N]

(e)   [bicyclic epoxide structure with H, O, CH_3, and CH_3–C=CH_2 groups] → [cyclohexane structure with CH_3–N, CH_3, OH, H, and CH_3–C=CH_2 groups]

(f)   [imidazole with $PhCH_2$–N and CH_2OH] → [imidazole with $PhCH_2$–N and CH_2CN]

(g) $CH_3(CH_2)_3CH{=}CH_2$ → $CH_3(CH_2)_4CH_2OCH_3$

S12.3   (a)   The following reactions were carried out in research leading to the synthesis of a compound isolated from the lichens of the Western Himalayas. Supply structures for the major products of the reactions shown below.

(1)   [cyclopentane structure with CH_3–CH–CH_3, H, CH_3, $HOCH_2$, CH_2Br groups] $\xrightarrow[\text{dichloromethane}]{\text{pyridinium } CrO_3Cl^-}$ A

(2)   [cyclopentene structure with CH_3–CH–CH_3, CH_3, CH_2O–Si(CH$_3$)$_2$–C(CH$_3$)$_3$] $\xrightarrow[\text{tetrahydrofuran}]{BH_3}$ $\xrightarrow{H_2O_2,\ NaOH}$ B + C

(3)   [cyclopentane structure with CH_3–CH–CH_3, H, CH_3, CH_2, CH_2OH] $\xrightarrow{O_3,\ CH_3OH}$ $\xrightarrow{CH_3SCH_3}$ D + E

(4)   [cyclopentene structure with CH_3–CH–CH_3, H, $CH_3OC(=O)$, CH_2Br] $\xrightarrow[\text{methanol}]{CH_3\overset{\overset{O}{\|}}{C}O^- K^+}$ F

S12.3   (b) The starting material for the first reaction above was found to be quite unstable and to lose HBr spontaneously to give a cyclic ether. Propose a structure for the ether and show, using the curved arrow representation, how it would form.

S12.4   In research into the stereochemistry of proton transfer reactions, researchers synthesized compounds in which the distances and the angles between basic sites and certain protons in the same molecules would be known. Some of the reactions that they used to synthesize the necessary compounds are shown below. Draw correct structural formulas for the starting materials, reagents, and products missing from the equations.

(a) $\xrightarrow{BH_3}$ $\xrightarrow{H_2O_2,\ NaOH}$ A   (b) $\xrightarrow[\text{dichloromethane}]{}$ B

(c)   A $\xrightarrow{C}$ $\xrightarrow[\text{acetone}]{NaI}$ D

S12.5   The following reaction was observed in the synthesis of chiral oxiranes.

$\xrightarrow[\substack{\text{dimethylformamide} \\ H_2O \\ 20\ °C,\ 6\ h}]{K_2CO_3}$

ethyl 2-chloro-3-hydroxy-
3-phenylpropanoate

85%
91% enantiomeric excess

(a)   What is the best analogy from the pK_a table for the pK_a of the most acidic proton in ethyl 2-chloro-3-hydroxy-3-phenylpropanoate?
(b)   Do you expect ethyl 2-chloro-3-hydroxy-3-phenylpropanoate to be a weaker or stronger acid than the compound you selected from the pK_a table? Explain the reasons for your prediction with a few words and a picture.
(c)   Draw the Newman projection looking down the bond between C-2 and C-3 for the conformer of ethyl 2-chloro-3-hydroxy-3-phenylpropanoate shown below *and* for the conformer that undergoes the intramolecular reaction giving rise to the oxirane product shown above.

S12.6   The following are examples of reactions used in the synthesis and study of natural products and their analogs. Supply precise formulas, including stereochemistry when it is known, for the reagents or major products as indicated by the capital letters.

(a) $HOCH_2CH_2CH_2CH_2CH = CH_2$ $\xrightarrow[\text{chloroform}]{}$ A

S12.6

(b) [phenanthrene epoxide structure with H, H, O] $\xrightarrow{\text{NH}_3 \text{ (excess)}}$ **B**

(c) [1,5-cyclooctadiene] $\xrightarrow[\substack{\text{chloroform} \\ -78\,°\text{C}}]{\substack{\text{Br}_2 \\ (1 \text{ equivalent})}}$ **C** $\xrightarrow[\text{tetrahydrofuran}]{\text{OsO}_4}$ $\xrightarrow{\text{H}_2\text{O}}$ **D**

(d) [cyclohexanone with CH₃, CH₃ and vinyl substituent structure] $\xrightarrow[\substack{\text{dichloromethane} \\ -78\,°\text{C}}]{\text{O}_3}$ $\xrightarrow[\substack{\text{(behaves like} \\ \text{CH}_3\text{SCH}_3)}]{\text{Ph}_3\text{P}}$ **E + F**

(e) CH_3O-[benzene ring]$-CH_2CH_2CH{=}CH_2$ $\xrightarrow{\quad}$ **G** $\xrightarrow{\quad}$ **H** $\quad CH_3O-$[benzene ring]$-CH_2CH_2CH_2CH_2OH$

(f) [divinyl cyclopentane–CH₂OTr structure] $\xrightarrow{\text{I}}$ $\xrightarrow{\text{J}}$ [cyclopentane structure with CH(OH) and –CH₂OTr]

$$Tr = \underset{\underset{Ph}{|}}{\overset{\overset{Ph}{|}}{C}}-Ph$$

a protecting
group for alcohols

[final step:] $\xrightarrow[\substack{\text{CH}_3\text{SCH}_3, \ \text{ClC}{-}\text{CCl} \\ (\text{with two C}{=}\text{O})}]{} \xrightarrow{(\text{CH}_3\text{CH}_2)_3\text{N}}$ **K**

S12.7   Provide structural formulas for the starting materials, reagents, or products indicated by capital letters.

(a) [structure: PhCH₂–C with CH₂OH, H, NHCOCH₂Ph] $\xrightarrow[\substack{\text{CH}_3\text{SCH}_3, \ \text{ClC}{-}\text{CCl}}]{} \xrightarrow{(\text{CH}_3\text{CH}_2)_3\text{N}}$ **A**

(b) [cyclopropane with D, D, H, H and C=CBr₂ structure] $\xrightarrow[\text{hexane}]{\text{CH}_3\text{CH}_2\text{CH}_2\text{CH}_2\text{Li}}$ **B**
product of an
E2 elimination

(c) [bicyclic structure with CH₂OH, H, H and dioxolane] $\xrightarrow[\text{Pd-C}]{\text{H}_2}$ **C** $\xrightarrow[\text{pyridine}]{\text{TsCl}}$ **D** $\xrightarrow{\text{NaBr}}$ **E** $\xrightarrow[\substack{\text{(a good source} \\ \text{of nucleophilic} \\ \text{hydride, H}{:}^-)}]{\text{NaBH}_3\text{CN}}$ **F**

S12.7

(d) $CH_2\!=\!CHCH_2CH_2\overset{\displaystyle O}{\overset{\|}{C}}\!-\!\overset{\displaystyle CH_3}{\underset{\displaystyle CH_3}{\overset{|}{C}}}\!-\!\overset{\displaystyle O}{\overset{\|}{C}}OCH_3 \xrightarrow{\;O_3\;} \xrightarrow{\;(CH_3)_2S\;} G\;+\;H$

(e) $CH_3CH_2C\!\equiv\!CCH_2CH_3 \xrightarrow{\;I\;} J \xrightarrow{\;K\;}$

(f)

$\xrightarrow[\substack{\text{dimethyl-}\\\text{formamide}}]{Na^+H\!:^-} L \xrightarrow[\substack{\text{dimethyl-}\\\text{formamide}}]{PhCH_2Br} M$

(g) $BrCH_2CH_2\!-\!\overset{\displaystyle CH_2CH_2Br}{\underset{\displaystyle CH_2CH_2Br}{\overset{|}{C}}}\!-\!CH_2CH_2Br \xrightarrow[\substack{\text{acetonitrile}\\\Delta}]{K^+CN^-\text{(excess)}} N$

S12.8   Provide structural formulas for the starting materials, reagents, or products indicated by capital letters.

(a)

(b)

$\xrightarrow[\text{pyridine}]{\substack{\text{TsCl}\\\text{(1 equivalent)}}} \xrightarrow{\;NaCN\;} C$

(c) $D \xrightarrow{\;CH_3COOH\;}$

$\xrightarrow{NaN_3} \xrightarrow{H_3O^+} E$

(d)

$\xrightarrow[\substack{H_2O,\ H_2SO_4\\\text{acetone}}]{CrO_3} F$

(e)

$\xrightarrow[\substack{Pd/BaSO_4\\\text{quinoline}}]{H_2} G \xrightarrow[\substack{KOH,\ H_2O}]{KMnO_4} H$

(f) $\underset{C_6H_8}{I} \xrightarrow{\;O_3\;} \xrightarrow{\;(CH_3)_2S\;} 2\ \overset{\displaystyle O}{\overset{\|}{H C}}CH_2\overset{\displaystyle O}{\overset{\|}{C H}}$

(g)

$\xrightarrow[\substack{Pt/C\\\text{ethyl acetate}}]{H_2} \substack{J\;+\;K\\\text{(stereoisomers}\\\text{of each other)}}$

PG is a protecting
group for the amine.
It does not participate
in this reaction.

S12.9   When *trans*-1-bromo-2-methoxycyclopentane is treated with a dilute solution of aqueous sodium hydroxide, only *cis*-2-methoxy-1-cyclopentanol is obtained. When *trans*-2-bromocyclopentanol is subjected to the same conditions, only *trans*-1,2-cyclopentanediol is formed. Draw mechanisms for these two reactions that account for the experimental observations described above.

S12.10   2,5-Dimethyl-1,5-hexadiene is converted to 2,2,5,5-tetramethyltetrahydrofuran when treated with aqueous sulfuric acid, as shown below.

Write a clear, rational mechanism for this transformation using the curved-arrow convention.

S12.11   In a key step in the synthesis of ciguatoxin, a neurotoxin responsible for occurrences of seafood poisonings, the following reactions were observed.

(a)   The base used in this reaction is shown over the arrow in the equation given above. It is the conjugate base of dimethyl sulfoxide, shown below the arrow. Use your pK_a table to assign an approximate pK_a value to dimethyl sulfoxide. To which compound in the pK_a table is it most analogous?

(b)   Write an equation for the reaction of compound A (abbreviated as ROH) with the conjugate base of dimethyl sulfoxide, and indicate by the relative lengths of the equilibrium arrows whether equilibrium will lie to the left or the right of the equation.

(c)   Choose *one* of the two cyclic ethers, B or C, shown at the beginning of this problem, and write a mechanism using the curved arrow convention that rationalizes its formation from alcohol A in the presence of base. You may use B: and HB⁺ to indicate bases and acids in the mechanism.

13

Aldehydes and Ketones. Addition Reactions at Electrophilic Carbon Atoms

Workbook Exercises

The reactions in the next set of chapters combine the mechanistic steps of substitution, addition, and elimination. If you feel unsure about your understanding of the general use of these terms, please take some time to review.

Like carbon-carbon π bonds, carbon-oxygen and carbon-nitrogen π bonds undergo addition reactions. Notice the similar changes in connectivity associated with the addition of methanol, under acidic conditions, to a $\diagdown C = C \diagup$, a $\diagdown C = N \diagup$,

and a $\diagdown C = O$ double bond.

The orientation (regioselectivity) of the addition reaction to π bonds where one of the atoms is nitrogen or oxygen is highly predictable in the direction shown above. The reaction is also reversible.

$$eN = NR, O \qquad Nu = NR_2, OR, SR$$

The simple addition reaction products shown above are generally not observed when the nucleophilic group is a nitrogen (RNH_2), an alcohol (ROH), or a thiol (RSH). Instead, the observed product, in many cases, can be understood in terms of an overall loss of water (H_2O) between the reactants:

Connectivity changes that show the overall stoichiometry:
For nucleophiles involving RNH_2:

Workbook Exercises (cont)

For nucleophiles involving ROH or RSH:

The ways of visualizing the reactions shown above are useful for quickly predicting structural relationships.

EXERCISE I.   Predict the product of the reaction, where water is also formed, when each of the compounds shown below is combined in separate reactions with (1) ethanol (CH_3CH_2OH), (2) methylamine (CH_3NH_2), (3) hydrazine (NH_2NH_2), and (4) ethanethiol (CH_3CH_2SH).

(a)   (b)   (c) $CH_3CH_2CCH_2CH_3$

EXERCISE II.   The reactions shown above are reversible when an excess of water is present. What are the structures of the carbonyl compounds (the compounds with a carbon-oxygen π bond) and the nucleophile(s) that result from re-introducing water into the compounds shown below?

(a)   (b)   (c)

(d)   (e)

The transformations shown above and on the preceding page may be seen in detail as the combination of two fundamental mechanistic steps. In the case of the RNH_2 nucleophiles, the formation of the carbon-nitrogen double bond is understood to be an addition to the carbon-oxygen π bond followed by the elimination of water. In the case of the ROH and RSH nucleophiles, the first step is also an addition to the carbon-oxygen π bond. This is followed by a substitution of the hydroxyl group, which, under acidic conditions, leaves as a molecule of water. The reverse reactions also have addition-elimination or substitution-elimination steps.

Workbook Exercises (cont)

EXERCISE III.   Redo Workbook Exercises I and II using the mechanistic scheme outlined on the previous page. Problem I (c), using ethanethiol, is solved for you here as an example.

SOLUTION

$$
CH_3CH_2\overset{\overset{\displaystyle O}{\|}}{C}CH_2CH_3 \quad \underset{\substack{\text{elimination of}\\CH_3CH_2SH}}{\overset{\substack{\text{addition of}\\CH_3CH_2SH}}{\rightleftharpoons}} \quad CH_3CH_2\underset{\underset{\displaystyle CH_3CH_2S}{|}}{\overset{\overset{\displaystyle O-H}{|}}{C}}CH_2CH_3 \quad \underset{\substack{\text{substitution by}\\H_2O}}{\overset{\substack{\text{substitution by}\\CH_3CH_2SH}}{\rightleftharpoons}} \quad CH_3CH_2\underset{\underset{\displaystyle CH_3CH_2S}{|}}{\overset{\overset{\displaystyle SCH_2CH_3}{|}}{C}}CH_2CH_3 \ + \ H_2O
$$

— —

13.1   2-Butanol is an alcohol and can serve as both a hydrogen bond donor and an acceptor. Strong hydrogen bonding among molecules of 2-butanol accounts for its high boiling point.

$$
\begin{array}{c}
\overset{\displaystyle ..}{\underset{\displaystyle |}{:O}}-CH_2CH_2CH_2CH_3 \\
H \\
CH_3CH_2CH_2CH_2-\overset{\displaystyle ..}{\underset{\displaystyle |}{O:}} \\
H \\
\overset{\displaystyle ..}{\underset{\displaystyle |}{:O}}-CH_2CH_2CH_2CH_3 \\
H
\end{array}
$$

There is no hydrogen bonding between molecules of 2-butanone or diethyl ether. They can serve only as hydrogen bond acceptors, not donors. Therefore, the intermolecular forces acting on the molecules of 2-butanone and diethyl ether are dipole-dipole interactions. The strong polarity of the carbonyl group results in stronger dipole-dipole interactions between molecules of 2-butanone than for molecules of diethyl ether.

$$
\underset{CH_3CH_2}{\overset{CH_3}{C}}=\ddot{O}: \qquad \underset{CH_3CH_2}{\overset{CH_3}{C}}=\ddot{O}: \qquad \underset{CH_3CH_2}{\overset{CH_3}{C}}=\ddot{O}:
$$

strong dipole-dipole interactions,
high boiling point

$$
\underset{CH_3CH_2}{\overset{CH_3CH_2}{\ddot{O}}}: \qquad \underset{CH_3CH_2}{\overset{CH_3CH_2}{\ddot{O}}}: \qquad \underset{CH_3CH_2}{\overset{CH_3CH_2}{\ddot{O}}}:
$$

weak dipole-dipole interactions,
low boiling point

13.2
(a) 3-hydroxy-2-methylpentanal   (b) 4-chlorobenzaldehyde   (c) 4-heptyn-3-one
(d) (*E*)-1,3-diphenyl-2-propen-1-one   (e) (*Z*)-6-methyl-5-nonen-2-one   (f) 2,2-dibromocyclohexanone
(g) 2,4-pentanedione   (h) trichloroethanal (trichloroacetaldehyde)   (i) *cis*-2-propylcyclopentanecarbaldehyde

13.3   (a) $CH_3-\square=O$ (b) $\underset{CH_3}{\overset{CH_3}{>}}\bigcirc=O$ (c) $PhC\overset{\overset{\displaystyle O}{\|}}{-}\pentagon$

13.3   (d)   (e) O_2N—⟨benzene⟩—$\overset{\overset{O}{\|}}{C}H$ (f) $CH_3CH_2CCH_2CH_2OH$ (with C=O)

(g) $\overset{\overset{O}{\|}}{H}CCH_2CH_2CH_2CH_2\overset{\overset{O}{\|}}{C}H$ (h) $Ph\overset{|}{C}HCPh$ (with C=O and OH below)   (i) O=⟨cyclohexane⟩=O

Concept Map 13.1   Some ways to prepare aldehydes and ketones.

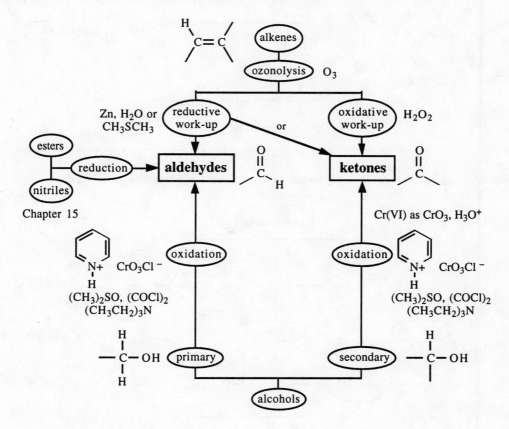

13.4

(a) $HC{\equiv}CCH_2CH_2CH{=}CHCH_2OH$ $\xrightarrow[\text{ClC—CCl}]{\overset{O}{\|}CH_3SCH_3 \;,\; \overset{O}{\|}\;\;\overset{O}{\|}}$ $\xrightarrow{(CH_3CH_2)_3N}$ $HC{\equiv}CCH_2CH_2CH{=}CHC\overset{\overset{O}{\|}}{}H$

A

13.4

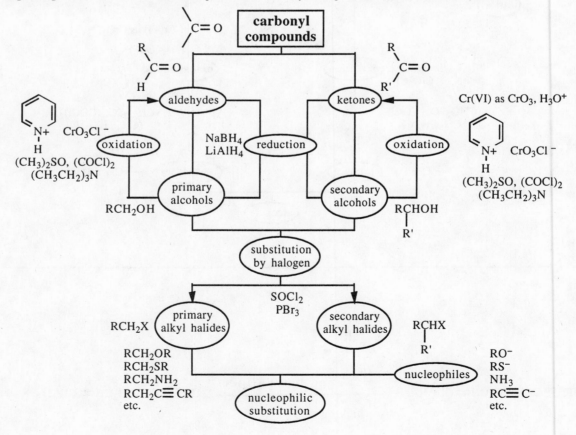

Concept Map 13.2   The relationship between carbonyl compounds, alcohols, and alkyl halides.

13.5 (a) $CH_3O-\langle\text{C}_6H_4\rangle-\overset{\overset{\displaystyle O}{\|}}{CH} \xrightarrow[\text{methanol}]{NaBH_4} CH_3O-\langle\text{C}_6H_4\rangle-CH_2OH$

(b) $CH_3(CH_2)_5\overset{\overset{\displaystyle CH_3}{|}}{CH}CH_2\overset{\overset{\displaystyle O}{\|}}{CH} \xrightarrow[\text{diethyl ether}]{LiAlH_4} \xrightarrow{H_3O^+} CH_3(CH_2)_5\overset{\overset{\displaystyle CH_3}{|}}{CH}CH_2CH_2OH$

(c) $PhCH_2\overset{\overset{\displaystyle O}{\|}}{C}CH_3 \xrightarrow[\text{diethyl ether}]{LiAlH_4} \xrightarrow{H_3O^+} PhCH_2\overset{\overset{\displaystyle}{|}}{\underset{\underset{\displaystyle OH}{|}}{C}}HCH_3$ (d) $Ph\overset{\overset{\displaystyle O}{\|}}{CH} \xrightarrow[\text{diethyl ether}]{LiAlH_4} \xrightarrow{H_3O^+} PhCH_2OH$

(e) $CH_3\overset{\overset{\displaystyle O}{\|}}{C}CH_2\overset{\overset{\displaystyle CH_3}{|}}{CH}CH_3 \xrightarrow[\text{diethyl ether}]{LiAlH_4} \xrightarrow{H_3O^+} CH_3\overset{\overset{\displaystyle}{|}}{\underset{\underset{\displaystyle OH}{|}}{C}}HCH_2\overset{\overset{\displaystyle CH_3}{|}}{CH}CH_3$

(f) $CH_3CH=CH\overset{\overset{\displaystyle O}{\|}}{C}CH_3 \xrightarrow[\substack{CeCl_3 \cdot 7 H_2O \\ \text{methanol}}]{NaBH_4} CH_3CH=CH\overset{\overset{\displaystyle}{|}}{\underset{\underset{\displaystyle OH}{|}}{C}}HCH_3$

13.6

attack by cyanide ion can occur at the top or the bottom of the carbonyl group

                                                                          R   *S*

                                                               racemic mixture

                                                                          ↓ HB⁺

(*R*)-lactic acid   (*S*)-lactic acid   *R*   *S*
        also racemic mixture   racemic mixture

Note that the hydrolysis of each nitrile proceeds with retention
of configuration, but hydrolysis of the racemic mixture of
nitriles gives rise to a racemic mixture of hydroxyacids

13.7 (a) $CH_3CH_2CH_2CH_2Br \xrightarrow[\text{tetrahydrofuran}]{Li} CH_3CH_2CH_2CH_2Li + Li^+Br^-$

(b) $PhCH_2CH_2Br \xrightarrow[\text{diethyl ether}]{Mg} PhCH_2CH_2MgBr$

(c) $CH_2=CHCl \xrightarrow[\substack{\text{tetrahydrofuran} \\ \Delta}]{Mg} CH_2=CHMgCl$

13.7 (d) $PhC \equiv CH \xrightarrow[\text{diethyl ether}]{CH_3CH_2MgBr} PhC \equiv CMgBr + CH_3CH_3 \uparrow$

(e) $PhCH_2Br \xrightarrow[\text{tetrahydrofuran}]{Li} PhCH_2Li + Li^+Br^-$

(f) $CH_3CH_2CH_2Li + NH_3 \longrightarrow CH_3CH_2CH_3 \uparrow + Li^+NH_2^-$

(g) $CH_3CH_2MgI + CH_3OH \longrightarrow CH_3CH_3 \uparrow + CH_3O^-Mg^{2+}I^-$

(h) $PhC \equiv CH \xrightarrow[\text{NH}_3 \text{ (liq)}]{Na^+NH_2^-} PhC \equiv C^- Na^+ + NH_3$

13.8 (a)

(b) $PhBr \xrightarrow[\substack{\text{diethyl} \\ \text{ether}}]{Mg} \underset{C}{PhMgBr} \xrightarrow{\overset{O}{\overset{/\backslash}{CH_2 - CH_2}}} \underset{D}{PhCH_2CH_2O^-Mg^{2+}Br^-} \xrightarrow{H_3O^+} \underset{E}{PhCH_2CH_2OH}$

(c) $PhBr \xrightarrow[\text{tetrahydrofuran}]{Li} \underset{F}{PhLi}$

(d) $CH_3CH_2C \equiv CH \xrightarrow[\text{NH}_3 \text{ (liq)}]{NaNH_2} \underset{I}{CH_3CH_2C \equiv C^- Na^+}$

Concept Maps 13.3 and 13.4   (see pp. 288 and 289)

13.9 (a) This is a tertiary alcohol. It can be prepared in three ways corresponding to the three dissections shown below. Each will lead to an organometallic reagent and a ketone. The ketone will be the fragment containing the oxygen.

13.9 (a) (cont)

Reagents for dissection 1:

$$CH_3C\!=\!CHMgBr \ \text{ or } \ CH_3C\!=\!CHLi \text{ (prepared from } CH_3C\!=\!CHBr \text{) and } CH_3CCH_2CH_2CH_2CH_3$$

(with CH_3 groups on the vinyl carbons and an O on the ketone carbonyl)

Reagents for dissection 2:

$$CH_3MgBr \ \text{ or } \ CH_3Li \text{ (from } CH_3Br \text{) and } CH_3C\!=\!CHCCH_2CH_2CH_2CH_3$$

Reagents for dissection 3:

$$CH_3CH_2CH_2CH_2MgBr \ \text{ or } \ CH_3CH_2CH_2CH_2Li \text{ (from } CH_3CH_2CH_2CH_2Br \text{) and } CH_3C\!=\!CHCCH_3$$

(b) This is a secondary alcohol. Two dissections are possible leading to an aldehyde and an organometallic reagent. A third dissection indicates that a reduction reaction, hydride addition, will also give this alcohol.

$$CH_3C\!=\!CHCH_2CH_2C\!=\!CHCH_2CH_2\!-\!\underset{①}{\{}\!-\!\underset{|}{\overset{H}{C}}\!-\!\underset{②}{\{}\!-\!C\!\equiv\!CH$$
$$O\!-\!\underset{③}{\{}\!-\!H$$

Reagents for dissection 1:

$$CH_3C\!=\!CHCH_2CH_2C\!=\!CHCH_2CH_2MgBr \ \text{ or } \ CH_3C\!=\!CHCH_2CH_2C\!=\!CHCH_2CH_2Li \text{ (prepared from }$$

$$CH_3C\!=\!CHCH_2CH_2C\!=\!CHCH_2CH_2Br \text{) and } HCC\!\equiv\!CH . \text{ This aldehyde may give problems depending on}$$

whether nucleophilic addition to the carbonyl group will compete with deprotonation of the alkyne.

Reagents for dissection 2:

$$HC\!\equiv\!CMgBr \ \text{ or } \ HC\!\equiv\!CNa \text{ (from } HC\!\equiv\!CH \text{) and } CH_3C\!=\!CHCH_2CH_2C\!=\!CHCH_2CH_2CH$$

This is the better choice for an aldehyde and an organometallic reagent.

Reagents for dissection 3:

$$NaBH_4 \ \text{ and } \ CH_3C\!=\!CHCH_2CH_2C\!=\!CHCH_2CH_2C\!-\!C\!\equiv\!CH$$

(c) This is a primary alcohol. A primary alcohol is prepared 1) by reduction of an aldehyde, 2) by addition of an organometallic reagent to formaldehyde or, sometimes, by addition of an organometallic reagent to oxirane. The dissections corresponding to these three routes are shown below.

$$\bigcirc\!\!-\!\underset{③}{\{}\!-\!CH_2\!-\!\underset{②}{\{}\!-\!\underset{\underset{H}{|}}{\overset{\overset{H}{|}\;①}{C}}\!-\!O\!-\!\underset{①}{\{}\!-\!H$$

Reagents for dissection 1:

$$NaBH_4 \ \text{ and } \ \bigcirc\!\!-\!CH_2CH \text{ (with } O \text{ on the carbonyl)}$$

13.9 (c) (cont)

Reagents for dissection 2:

⬡—CH₂MgBr or ⬡—CH₂Li (from ⬡—CH₂Br) and $\underset{\text{HCH}}{\overset{\text{O}}{\|}}$

Reagents for dissection 3:

⬡—MgBr or ⬡—Li (from ⬡—Br) and $\underset{\text{CH}_2-\text{CH}_2}{\overset{\text{O}}{\triangle}}$

Concept Map 13.3   Organometallic reagents and their reactions with compounds containing electrophilic carbon atoms.

Concept Map 13.4   Some ways to prepare alcohols.

- -

13.10

Two stereoisomeric hemiacetals are possible, resulting from the nucleophilic attack of the hydroxyl group at the bottom or the top of the planar carbonyl group. The two hemiacetals are enantiomers of each other.

13.11   Essentially all the ^{18}O will wind up in the oxygen of the carbonyl group.

13.11 (cont)

resonance-stabilized cation
lowers transition state energy
for the hydrolysis reaction

13.12 $CH_2=CH-\overset{..}{\underset{..}{O}}-CH_2CH_3 \longrightarrow \left[CH_3\overset{+}{C}H-\overset{..}{\underset{..}{O}}-CH_2CH_3 \longleftrightarrow CH_3CH=\overset{+}{\underset{..}{O}}-CH_2CH_3 \right]$

13.13   (a) $\underset{\overset{\|}{O}}{Ph\overset{}{C}H}$ + CH_3CH_2OH $\xrightarrow[\text{benzene, } \Delta]{\text{TsOH}}$ $\underset{OCH_2CH_3}{Ph\overset{|}{C}HOCH_2CH_3}$

(b) $CH_3CH_2CH_2\underset{\overset{\|}{O}}{\overset{}{C}H}$ + CH_3OH $\xrightarrow[\text{benzene, } \Delta]{\text{TsOH}}$ $CH_3CH_2CH_2\underset{OCH_3}{\overset{|}{C}HOCH_3}$

(c)   + $HOCH_2CH_2OH$ $\xrightarrow[\text{benzene, } \Delta]{\text{TsOH}}$

Concept Map 13.5   Hydrates, acetals, and ketals.

- -

13.14
$$CH_2\!-\!CH\!-\!CH_2 \; + \; CH_3\overset{O}{\overset{\|}{C}}CH_3 \; \longrightarrow \; C_6H_{12}O_3$$
$$\;\;\;|\;\;\;\;\;|\;\;\;\;\;|$$
$$OH \;\; OH \;\; OH$$

$$C_3H_8O_3 + C_3H_6O = C_6H_{14}O_4$$
$$C_6H_{14}O_4 - C_6H_{12}O_3 = H_2O$$

One molecule of water has been lost in the reaction.

$$HOCH_2CHCH_2OH \; + \; CH_3\overset{O}{\overset{\|}{C}}CH_3 \;\xrightarrow[\text{TsOH}]{}\;$$
$$\;\;\;\;\;\;\;\;\;\;|$$
$$\;\;\;\;\;\;\;\;\;OH$$

$$\begin{array}{c} CH_3 \\ \diagdown \\ C \\ \diagup \\ CH_3 \end{array}\!\! \begin{array}{c} O\!-\!CH_2 \\ \\ O\!-\!CHCH_2OH \end{array}$$

a cyclic ketal

13.15 (a)
$$\overset{CH_3}{\underset{|}{CH_3CHCH_2CH_2CH}}\overset{O}{\overset{\|}{}} \; + \; HO\overset{+}{N}H_3\;Cl^- \;\xrightarrow[\;]{\overset{O}{\overset{\|}{CH_3CO^-Na^+}}}\; \overset{CH_3}{\underset{|}{CH_3CHCH_2CH_2CH}}\!=\!NOH \; + \; H_2O$$

(b)
$$CH_3\overset{O}{\overset{\|}{C}}CH_2CH_2CH_3 \; + \; PhNHNH_2 \;\xrightarrow[\text{acetic acid}]{}\; \overset{CH_3}{\underset{}{CH_3CH_2CH_2C}}\!=\!NNHPh \; + \; H_2O$$

13.15 (c) cyclopentanone =O + CH₃—⟨benzene⟩—NH₂ —Δ→ cyclopentane =N—⟨benzene⟩—CH₃ + H_2O

(d) PhCH(=O) + O_2N—⟨benzene with NO₂⟩—NHNH₂ —H_2SO_4→ PhCH=NNH—⟨benzene with NO₂⟩—NO₂ + H_2O

(e) PhCH(=O) + CH₃CH₂CH₂NH₂ —benzene, Δ→ PhCH=NCH₂CH₂CH₃ + H_2O

Concept Map 13.6   Reactions of carbonyl compounds with compounds related to ammonia.

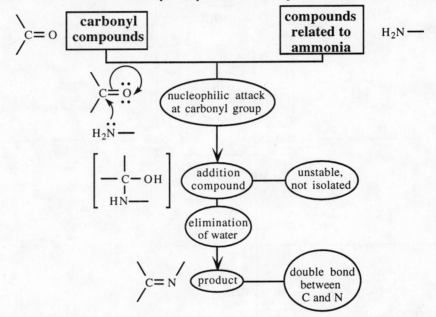

13.16

addition of nucleophilic nitrogen to electrophilic carbonyl group

deprotonation

protonation

protonation

loss of water

deprotonation

13.17

protonation   nucleophilic attack by water on   deprotonation
                               electrophilic carbon atom of
                               protonated imine

deprotonation   loss of amine   protonation

13.18   CH₃CCH₃

attack of the nucleophilic   deprotonation   protonation
amine on the electrophilic
protonated carbonyl group

loss of water

The catalytic amount of hydrochloric acid begins the reaction by protonating the oxygen of the carbonyl group. Sodium hydroxide is added at the end to neutralize the acid in order to prevent catalysis of the reverse reaction, the hydrolysis of the imine (Problem 13.16).

13.19

pyridoxamine-5'-phosphate   2-oxopropanoic acid

pyridoxal-5'-phosphate   alanine

In the presence of an enzyme, which is a chiral reagent, these reactions occur stereoselectively to give (*S*)-alanine.

Concept Map 13.7   Reduction of carbonyl groups to methylene groups.

13.20 (a)

$$\text{cyclohexanone} \xrightarrow[\substack{\text{diethylene glycol} \\ \Delta}]{\text{H}_2\text{NNH}_2,\ \text{NaOH}} \text{cyclohexane}$$

(b) PhCH=O $\xrightarrow[\substack{\text{diethylene glycol} \\ \Delta}]{\text{H}_2\text{NNH}_2,\ \text{NaOH}}$ PhCH$_3$

13.20 (c)

$$\xrightarrow[\substack{\text{diethylene glycol} \\ \Delta}]{\text{H}_2\text{NNH}_2, \text{KOH}}$$

(d)

$$\xrightarrow[\substack{\text{ZnCl}_2 \\ \text{Na}_2\text{SO}_4}]{2\ \text{CH}_3\text{CH}_2\text{SH}}$$

$$\xrightarrow[\substack{\text{dioxane} \\ \Delta}]{\text{Raney Ni}}$$

(e) $\text{CH}_3\text{CCH}_2\text{CH}_2\text{CH}_3$ $\xrightarrow[\substack{(\text{CH}_3\text{CH}_2)_2\text{OBF}_3}]{\text{HSCH}_2\text{CH}_2\text{SH}}$ $\text{CH}_3\text{CCH}_2\text{CH}_2\text{CH}_3$

(f)

$$\xrightarrow[\substack{\text{ZnCl}_2 \\ \text{Na}_2\text{SO}_4}]{2\ \text{CH}_3\text{CH}_2\text{SH}}$$

$$\xrightarrow[\substack{\text{dioxane} \\ \Delta}]{\text{Raney Ni}}$$

13.21

$$CH_3CCH_2CHC\equiv C\cdots \text{(dioxane ketal)} \xrightarrow{\;?\;} CH_3CCH_2CH \cdots C=C \cdots CHCH_2OH$$

1. What are the connectivities of the two compounds? How many carbon atoms does each contain? Are there any rings? What are the positions of branches and functional groups on the carbon skeletons?

   The atoms of the starting material and product molecules that are the same are shown below. The starting material has a triple bond, an alcohol, and two ketal functional groups; the product has a cis double bond, a ketone, and three alcohol functional groups. The rings that are present are cyclic ketals.

2. How do the functional groups change in going from starting material to product? Does the starting material have a good leaving group?

   The triple bond in the starting material has been converted to a cis double bond. One of the ketal groups in the starting material has been converted to a ketone; the other ketal group has been converted into two alcohol functional groups. There is no good leaving group in the starting material.

3. Is it possible to dissect the structures of the starting material and product to see which bonds must be broken and which formed?

   bonds broken

   bonds formed

4. New bonds are created when an electrophile reacts with a nucleophile. Do we recognize any part of the product molecule as coming from a good nucleophile or an electrophilic addition?

   No.

5. What type of compound would be a good precursor to the product?

   An alkyne that can be converted to a cis alkene by reduction with hydrogen and the appropriate catalyst.

   $$CH_3CCH_2CH\cdots C=C\cdots CHCH_2OH \xleftarrow[\substack{Pd/CaCO_3 \\ quinoline}]{H_2} CH_3CCH_2CHC\equiv CCHCH_2OH$$

   The ketal groups in the starting material can be removed by acid hydrolysis.

   $$CH_3CCH_2CHC\equiv CCHCH_2OH \xleftarrow{H_3O^+} CH_3CCH_2CHC\equiv C\cdots \text{(dioxane ketal)}$$

13.21 (cont)

6. After this last step, do we see how to get from starting material to product? If not, we need to analyze the structure obtained in step 5 by applying questions 4 and 5 to it.

The ketal groups are removed before reduction to prevent the acid-catalyzed addition of water to the alkene. Alkynes are less susceptible to hydration by dilute acid than alkenes (Section 9.4B).

13.22   A dissection of the starting material and the product shows that the aldehyde group in the starting material has been converted into an acetal, and a new carbon-carbon bond has formed to the aromatic ring at the position occupied by the bromine atom in the starting material.

bonds broken   bonds formed

The product is a tertiary alcohol so will form from the reaction of an organometallic reagent with a ketone. Another dissection shows us which two reagents we need for that step.

bonds formed   bonds broken

To make the organometallic reagent we need from the starting material we have, we must first protect the aldehyde. The complete synthesis is shown below:

Concept Map 13.8   Protecting groups.

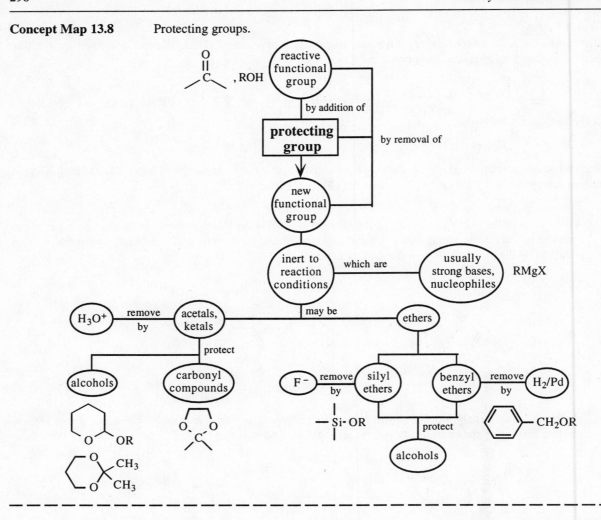

- -

13.23   The product has a protecting group on the alcohol function and a ketone at one of the carbon atoms of the double bond of the starting material. A ketone can be prepared by oxidizing a secondary alcohol, which must be why the original alcohol group was protected.

The alcohol can be prepared by anti-Markovnikov addition of H_2O to the double bond. The synthesis must be:

13.23 (cont)

$$CH_2=CCH_2CH_2OCH_2Ph \xrightarrow[\text{imidazole}]{} $$

13.24 $CH_2\!=\!CCH_2CH_2OCH_2Ph \xrightarrow{\ ?\ }$

1. What are the connectivities of the two compounds? How many carbon atoms does each contain? Are there any rings? What are the positions of branches and functional groups on the carbon skeletons?

    The starting material has a double bond and an ether functional group. The product has a double bond, an ether, and a secondary alcohol functional group. Carbon 2 of a four carbon segment has added to carbon 1 of the starting material (see structure in part 3).

2. How do the functional groups change in going from starting material to product? Does the starting material have a good leaving group?

    A four carbon segment has added to carbon 1 of the double bond. There is no good leaving group.

3. Is it possible to dissect the structures of the starting material and product to see which bonds must be broken and which formed?

    bonds broken   bonds formed

4. New bonds are created when an electrophile reacts with a nucleophile. Do we recognize any part of the product molecule as coming from a good nucleophile or an electrophilic addition?

    A Grignard reagent is a good nucleophile, which can add to the electrophilic carbon atom of an aldehyde to give a secondary alcohol.

5. What type of compound would be a good precursor to the product?

    An aldehyde would be a good precursor to the product we want.

6. After this last step, do we see how to get from starting material to product? If not, we need to analyze the structure obtained in step 5 by applying questions 4 and 5 to it.

    We need to prepare the aldehyde so we must apply questions 4 and 5 again.

4 (repeated). Do we recognize any part of the precursor molecule as coming from a good nucleophile or an electrophilic addition?

    No.

5 (repeated).   What type of compound would be a good precursor to the product?

13.24 (5) (repeated) (cont)

An aldehyde can be prepared by the oxidation of a primary alcohol.

A primary alcohol can be made by the electrophilic addition of diborane to the terminal double bond in the starting material, followed by oxidation of the alkylborane.

6 (repeated). After this last step, do we see how to get from starting material to product? If not, we need to analyze the structure obtained in step 5 by applying questions 4 and 5 to it.

The complete synthesis is shown below:

13.25

13.26

13.27

(a) cyclopentanecarbaldehyde   (b) cyclobutanone   (c) (*E*)-2-hexenal   (d) (*S*)-2-hydroxypropanal
(e) 2-methylcyclohexanone   (f) 5-methyl-2-hexanone   (g) 4-methoxybenzaldehyde (anisaldehyde)
(h) 3-methyl-2-cyclohexenone   (i) (4*S*, 5*S*)-4-chloro-5-methyl-2-heptanone

13.28

(a)   (b) $CH_3CH_2CH_2CH_2CCH_2Br$ (c)   (d)

(e) $CH_2=CHCH=CHCCH_3$ (f) $CH_3CH_2CH_2CHCH$ (g)   (h)

13.29 (a) $CH_3CH_2CH_2CH$ $\xrightarrow[H_2O]{NaBH_4}$ $CH_3CH_2CH_2CH_2OH$

(b) $CH_3CH_2CH_2CH$ $\xrightarrow[H_2SO_4]{}$ $CH_3CH_2CH_2CH=NNH$

(c) $CH_3CH_2CH_2CH$ $\xrightarrow{CH_3CH_2CH_2CH_2Li}$ $\xrightarrow{H_3O^+}$ $CH_3CH_2CH_2CHCH_2CH_2CH_2CH_3$
                                                                            OH

(d) $CH_3CH_2CH_2CH$ $\xrightarrow[\Delta]{PhNH_2}$ $CH_3CH_2CH_2CH=NPh$

(e) $CH_3CH_2CH_2CH$ $\xrightarrow[\substack{H_2O \\ H_2SO_4}]{NaCN}$ $CH_3CH_2CH_2CHCN$
                                                                   OH

(f) $CH_3CH_2CH_2CH$ $\xrightarrow[\substack{H_3O^+ \\ H_2O}]{CrO_3}$ $CH_3CH_2CH_2COH$ $+$ Cr^{+3}

(g) $CH_3CH_2CH_2CH$ $\xrightarrow[\underset{O}{CH_3CO^-Na^+}]{HONH_3^+Cl^-}$ $CH_3CH_2CH_2CH=NOH$

13.29 (h) $\underset{\displaystyle CH_3CH_2CH_2\overset{\displaystyle \overset{O}{\|}}{C}H}{} \xrightarrow[\text{diethyl ether}]{CH_3MgI} CH_3CH_2CH_2\underset{\displaystyle \underset{O^-\,Mg^{2+}\,I^-}{|}}{C}HCH_3 \xrightarrow{H_3O^+} CH_3CH_2CH_2\underset{\displaystyle \underset{OH}{|}}{C}HCH_3$

(i) $\underset{\displaystyle CH_3CH_2CH_2\overset{\displaystyle \overset{O}{\|}}{C}H}{} \xrightarrow[\text{diethyl ether}]{LiAlH_4 \quad H_3O^+} CH_3CH_2CH_2CH_2OH$

(j) $\underset{\displaystyle CH_3CH_2CH_2\overset{\displaystyle \overset{O}{\|}}{C}H}{} \xrightarrow[\substack{\text{diethylene glycol}\\ \Delta}]{H_2NNH_2,\ KOH} CH_3CH_2CH_2CH_3$

13.30 (a) $\underset{\displaystyle CH_3CH_2CH_2\overset{\displaystyle \overset{O}{\|}}{C}CH_3}{} \xrightarrow[H_2O]{NaBH_4} CH_3CH_2CH_2\underset{\displaystyle \underset{OH}{|}}{C}HCH_3$

(b) $CH_3CH_2CH_2\overset{\displaystyle \overset{O}{\|}}{C}CH_3 \xrightarrow[H_2SO_4]{} CH_3CH_2CH_2\overset{\displaystyle \overset{CH_3}{|}}{C}=NNH$—(2,4-dinitrophenyl)

(c) $CH_3CH_2CH_2\overset{\displaystyle \overset{O}{\|}}{C}CH_3 \xrightarrow[\Delta]{PhNH_2} CH_3CH_2CH_2\overset{\displaystyle \overset{CH_3}{|}}{C}=NPh$

(d) $CH_3CH_2CH_2\overset{\displaystyle \overset{O}{\|}}{C}CH_3 \xrightarrow[\text{tetrahydrofuran}]{PhLi} CH_3CH_2CH_2\underset{\displaystyle \underset{O^-Li^+}{\overset{\displaystyle \overset{CH_3}{|}}{C}}}{}Ph \xrightarrow[H_2O]{NH_4Cl} CH_3CH_2CH_2\underset{\displaystyle \underset{OH}{\overset{\displaystyle \overset{CH_3}{|}}{C}}}{}Ph$

(e) $CH_3CH_2CH_2\overset{\displaystyle \overset{O}{\|}}{C}CH_3 \xrightarrow[\substack{H_2O\\ H_2SO_4}]{NaCN} CH_3CH_2CH_2\underset{\displaystyle \underset{OH}{\overset{\displaystyle \overset{CH_3}{|}}{C}}}{}CN$

(f) $CH_3CH_2CH_2\overset{\displaystyle \overset{O}{\|}}{C}CH_3 \xrightarrow[\substack{CH_3\overset{\displaystyle \overset{O^-Na^+}{}}{}\ \\ CH_3\overset{O}{\underset{\displaystyle \|}{C}}O^-Na^+}]{HONH_3^+Cl^-} CH_3CH_2CH_2\overset{\displaystyle \overset{CH_3}{|}}{C}=NOH$

(g) $CH_3CH_2CH_2\overset{\displaystyle \overset{O}{\|}}{C}CH_3 \xrightarrow[\text{diethyl ether}]{CH_3CH_2MgI} CH_3CH_2CH_2\underset{\displaystyle \underset{O^-Mg^{2+}Br^-}{\overset{\displaystyle \overset{CH_3}{|}}{C}}}{}CH_2CH_3 \xrightarrow{H_3O^+} CH_3CH_2CH_2\underset{\displaystyle \underset{OH}{\overset{\displaystyle \overset{CH_3}{|}}{C}}}{}CH_2CH_3$

(h) $CH_3CH_2CH_2\overset{\displaystyle \overset{O}{\|}}{C}CH_3 \xrightarrow{CH_3C\equiv C^-\,Na^+} CH_3CH_2CH_2\underset{\displaystyle \underset{O^-Na^+}{\overset{\displaystyle \overset{CH_3}{|}}{C}}}{}C\equiv CCH_3 \xrightarrow[H_2O]{NH_4Cl} CH_3CH_2CH_2\underset{\displaystyle \underset{OH}{\overset{\displaystyle \overset{CH_3}{|}}{C}}}{}C\equiv CCH_3$

13.30   (i) $CH_3CH_2CH_2\overset{\overset{\displaystyle O}{\|}}{C}CH_3 \xrightarrow[\substack{\text{diethylene glycol} \\ \Delta}]{H_2NNH_2, \text{ KOH}} CH_3CH_2CH_2CH_2CH_3$

13.31   (a)   + PhNHNH₂ $\xrightarrow{\text{acetic acid}}$

(b) $\xrightarrow[\substack{\text{TsOH} \\ \text{benzene} \\ \Delta}]{\substack{HOCH_2CH_2OH \\ (1 \text{ equivalent})}}$

(c) $CH_2{=}CH\overset{\overset{\displaystyle O}{\|}}{C}H \xrightarrow[\text{diethyl ether}]{PhLi} \xrightarrow{H_3O^+} CH_2{=}CHCHPh$ with OH

(d) $\xrightarrow[\text{dichloromethane}]{\substack{\text{pyridinium} \\ CrO_3Cl^-}}$

(e)   + Br₂ $\xrightarrow[\substack{\text{carbon} \\ \text{tetrachloride}}]{}$

(f)   + KMnO₄ $\xrightarrow[H_2O]{NaOH}$

(g)   + $\xrightarrow[\substack{\text{dichloro-} \\ \text{methane}}]{}$

(h) $\xrightarrow{BH_3} \xrightarrow[H_2O]{H_2O_2, \text{ NaOH}}$

[See Problem 12.41(b)]   enantiomers   enantiomers

13.31 (i) $\underset{\text{PhCCH}_3}{\overset{\text{O}}{\|}}$ $\xrightarrow[\text{tetrahydrofuran}]{\text{CH}_3\text{CH}_2\text{CH}_2\text{CH}_2\text{Li}}$ $\xrightarrow[\text{H}_2\text{O}]{\text{NH}_4\text{Cl}}$ $\underset{\text{OH}}{\overset{\text{CH}_3}{\text{PhCCH}_2\text{CH}_2\text{CH}_2\text{CH}_3}}$

(j) cyclopentyl–CHO + O_2N–(2-NO$_2$ phenyl)–NHNH$_2$ $\xrightarrow[\text{ethanol}]{\text{H}_2\text{SO}_4}$ cyclopentyl–CH=NH–(2,4-dinitrophenyl)

13.32 (a) [bicyclic ketone with CH$_3$, CH$_3$, CH$_3$, H, H, CH$_3$ substituents] + HONH$_3^+$ Cl$^-$ $\xrightarrow{\text{CH}_3\text{CO}^- \text{Na}^+}$ [bicyclic oxime HO–N= with CH$_3$ substituents]

(b) furanyl–CHO + $\text{H}_2\text{N}-\underset{\text{Ph}}{\overset{\text{CH}_2\text{OH}}{\text{C}}}\text{-H}$ $\xrightarrow[\Delta]{\text{benzene}}$ $\underset{\text{Ph}}{\overset{\text{CH}_2\text{OH}}{\text{C}}}\text{-H}$, N=CH–furanyl

(c) $\text{CH}_3\text{CH}_2\text{CH}_2\text{C}\equiv\text{CH}$ + NaNH$_2$ $\xrightarrow{\text{NH}_3 \text{ (liq)}}$ $\text{CH}_3\text{CH}_2\text{CH}_2\text{C}\equiv\text{C}^- \text{Na}^+$ + NH$_3$

(d) $\text{CH}_3\text{CH}_2\text{CH}_2\text{C}\equiv\text{CH}$ + CH$_3$CH$_2$MgBr $\xrightarrow{\text{diethyl ether}}$ $\text{CH}_3\text{CH}_2\text{CH}_2\text{C}\equiv\text{CMgBr}$ + CH$_3$CH$_3\uparrow$

(e) cyclohexanone =O $\xrightarrow[\text{diethyl ether}]{\text{CH}_3\text{CH}_2\text{MgBr}}$ $\xrightarrow[\text{H}_2\text{O}]{\text{NH}_4\text{Cl}}$ cyclohexane with CH$_2$CH$_3$ and OH

(f) CH_3–(C$_6$H$_4$)–$\overset{\text{O}}{\overset{\|}{\text{C}}}CH_2CH_3$ + HOCH$_2$CH$_2$OH $\xrightarrow[\substack{\text{benzene}\\\Delta}]{\text{TsOH}}$ CH$_3$–(C$_6$H$_4$)–(1,3-dioxolane)CCH$_2$CH$_3$

(g) cyclohexanone =O + HSCH$_2$CH$_2$OH $\xrightarrow{(\text{CH}_3\text{CH}_2)_2\text{OBF}_3}$ [spiro oxathiolane with O and S]

(h) $\underset{}{\overset{\text{OTHP}}{\text{CH}_3\text{CH}_2\text{C}\equiv}}$ CCHCH$_2$CH$_2$CH=CH$\overset{\text{O}}{\overset{\|}{\text{C}}}CH_3$ $\xrightarrow[\text{base}]{\text{CH}_3\text{ONH}_3^+ \text{Cl}^-}$ $\underset{}{\overset{\text{OTHP}}{\text{CH}_3\text{CH}_2\text{C}\equiv}}$ CCHCH$_2$CH$_2$CH=CH$\overset{\text{NOCH}_3}{\overset{\|}{\text{C}}}CH_3$

(i) $\text{HOCH}_2\text{CH}_2\underset{\text{CH}_3}{\overset{\text{CH}_3}{\text{C}}}\text{CH}_2\text{CH}=\text{CH}\overset{\text{O}}{\overset{\|}{\text{C}}}\text{OCH}_3$ $\xrightarrow[\text{dichloromethane}]{\underset{\text{H}}{\overset{\text{N}^+}{\text{pyridinium}}} \text{CrO}_3\text{Cl}^-}$ $\text{HCCH}_2\underset{\text{CH}_3}{\overset{\text{CH}_3}{\text{C}}}\text{CH}_2\text{CH}=\text{CH}\overset{\text{O}}{\overset{\|}{\text{C}}}\text{OCH}_3$ with aldehyde $\overset{\text{O}}{\overset{\|}{\text{HC}}}$

13.33

(a)

$$PhCCH_2CH_2CH_2Cl \xrightarrow[\text{benzene, }\Delta]{\text{HOCH}_2\text{CH}_2\text{OH} \atop \text{TsOH}} PhCCH_2CH_2CH_2Cl \quad \mathbf{A} \xrightarrow[\Delta]{(PhCH_2)_2NH} PhCCH_2CH_2CH_2NCH_2Ph \quad \mathbf{B}$$

(b)

$$CH_3CH_2CH_2CCH_3 \xrightarrow[\text{H}_2\text{O}]{\text{NaBH}_4} CH_3CH_2CH_2CHCH_3 \atop OH \quad \mathbf{C} \xrightarrow[\text{pyridine}]{\text{TsCl}} CH_3CH_2CH_2CHCH_3 \atop OTs \quad \mathbf{D} \xrightarrow[\text{ethanol}]{\text{KOH (4 M)}}$$

$$CH_3CH_2CH=CHCH_3 \xrightarrow[\text{dichloromethane}]{\text{Cl—}C_6H_4\text{—COOH}} CH_3CH_2CH-CHCH_3 \atop \mathbf{F}$$

major product
E

(c)

$$\xrightarrow[\text{CH}_3\text{CCH}_3, \text{TsOH}]{\text{CH}_3\text{CCH}_3, \text{OCH}_3, \text{OCH}_3}$$

$$\mathbf{G} \xrightarrow[\text{dichloro-methane}]{\text{O}_3} \xrightarrow{\text{CH}_3\text{SCH}_3} HCH \quad \mathbf{H} \quad + \quad HCCH_2CH_2 \text{—} \mathbf{I}$$

(d)

$$\text{cyclopentyl-CH=O} \xrightarrow[\text{tetrahydrofuran}]{\text{PhLi}} \text{CHPh} \atop O^-Li^+ \quad \mathbf{J} \xrightarrow{H_3O^+} \text{CHPh} \atop OH \quad \mathbf{K} \xrightarrow[\text{acetone}]{\text{CrO}_3, H_3O^+}$$

$$\text{cyclopentyl-CPh} \quad \mathbf{L} \xrightarrow[\text{acetic acid}]{\text{PhNHNH}_2} \text{C=NNHPh} \atop Ph \quad \mathbf{M}$$

(e)

$$\xrightarrow{H_2NNH_2} \text{NNH}_2 \quad \mathbf{N} \xrightarrow[\text{diethylene glycol}]{\text{KOH}} \mathbf{O}$$

(f)

$$\text{—OH} \xrightarrow{\text{CH}_3\text{SCH}_3, \text{ClC—CCl}} \xrightarrow{(CH_3CH_2)_3N} \mathbf{P}$$

13.34

(a)
$$HC\equiv CCH_2CH_2OH \xrightarrow[\Delta]{\text{TsOH}} HC\equiv CCH_2CH_2OTHP \xrightarrow{CH_3CH_2MgBr}$$
A

$$BrMgC\equiv CCH_2CH_2OTHP \xrightarrow{CH_3(CH_2)_5\overset{O}{\overset{\|}{C}}H} CH_3(CH_2)_5CHC\equiv CCH_2CH_2OTHP \xrightarrow{H_3O^+}$$
B $O^- Mg^{2+} Br^-$ C

$$CH_3(CH_2)_5CHC\equiv CCH_2CH_2OH \xrightarrow[\substack{\text{quinoline} \\ \text{ethyl acetate}}]{H_2 \\ Pd/CaCO_3}$$
   OH   D

E

(b)
$$PhBr \xrightarrow[\substack{\text{diethyl} \\ \text{ether}}]{Mg} PhMgBr \xrightarrow{\triangle O} PhCH_2CH_2O^- Mg^{2+} Br^- \xrightarrow{H_3O^+} PhCH_2CH_2OH \xrightarrow[\text{dichloromethane}]{} PhCH_2\overset{O}{\overset{\|}{C}}H$$
F   G   H   I

(c)
$$CH_3\overset{CH_3}{\overset{|}{C}}=CHCH_2CH_2\overset{O}{\overset{\|}{C}}CH_3 \xrightarrow[\substack{\text{TsOH} \\ \text{benzene, }\Delta}]{HOCH_2CH_2OH} CH_3\overset{CH_3}{\overset{|}{C}}=CHCH_2CH_2\overset{O\diagup O}{C}CH_3 \xrightarrow[\text{tetrahydrofuran}]{BH_3}$$
J

$$CH_3\overset{CH_3}{\underset{BR_2}{\overset{|}{C}H}}CHCH_2CH_2CCH_3 \xrightarrow[\substack{H_2O}]{H_2O_2, NaOH} CH_3\overset{CH_3}{\overset{|}{C}H}CHCH_2CH_2CCH_3 \xrightarrow{H_3O^+}$$
K   OH   L

$$\left[CH_3\overset{CH_3}{\overset{|}{C}H}CHCH_2CH_2\overset{O}{\overset{\|}{C}}CH_3 \right] \rightleftharpoons$$
    OH

M

(d)
$$\xrightarrow[\substack{\text{tetrahydro-} \\ \text{furan}}]{PhLi} N \xrightarrow[H_2O]{NH_4Cl} O \xrightarrow[\text{cold}]{HCl (conc)} P \xrightarrow[\substack{\text{ethanol} \\ \Delta}]{KOH \\ (4 M)} Q$$

(e)
$$\xrightarrow[\substack{CeCl_3 \cdot 7 H_2O \\ \text{methanol}}]{NaBH_4} R$$

13.34

(f)

$$CH_3CH_2C\equiv CCHCH_2CH_2CH_2OTBDMS \xrightarrow{(CH_3CH_2CH_2CH_2)_4N^+F^-}$$

with OTHP above

$$CH_3CH_2C\equiv CCHCH_2CH_2CH_2OH \xrightarrow[\text{S}]{\underset{\text{(S)}}{\overset{\overset{O\ \ \ O\ \ \ O}{\parallel\ \ \parallel\ \ \parallel}}{CH_3SCH_3,\ ClC\!-\!CCl\ (CH_3CH_2)_3N}}} CH_3CH_2C\equiv CCHCH_2CH_2CH \ (T)$$

with OTHP groups

(g)

$$\xrightarrow[\text{acetic acid}]{HSCH_2CH_2SH \atop (CH_3CH_2)_2OBF_3} \quad U \quad \xrightarrow[\Delta]{\text{Raney Ni} \atop \text{ethanol}} \quad V$$

(h)

$$\underset{CH_3}{\overset{CH_3}{CH_3CHCH_2CH_2CCH_2CH_2COH}} \xrightarrow[\text{diethylene glycol} \atop \Delta]{H_2NNH_2,\ NaOH}$$

$$CH_3CHCH_2CH_2CH_2CH_2CH_2CO^-Na^+ \xrightarrow{H_3O^+} CH_3CHCH_2CH_2CH_2CH_2CH_2COH$$

W   X

13.35

(a)

$$\underset{\substack{| \\ H}}{\overset{\substack{CH_3CH_2 \quad CH_2CH_2OH \\ C=C}}{}} \xleftarrow[\text{Pd/CaCO}_3 \atop \text{quinoline}]{H_2} CH_3CH_2C\equiv CCH_2CH_2OH \xleftarrow{H_3O^+} CH_3CH_2C\equiv CCH_2CH_2O^-Mg^{2+}Br^-$$

$$\overset{O}{\triangle} \xleftarrow{} CH_3CH_2C\equiv CMgBr \xleftarrow{CH_3CH_2MgBr} CH_3CH_2C\equiv CH \xleftarrow{CH_3CH_2Br} Na^+\ {}^-C\equiv CH \xleftarrow[\text{NH}_3\text{ (liq)}]{NaNH_2} HC\equiv CH$$

(b)

$$\underset{}{\overset{O}{CH_3CH_2CH_2CCH_2CH_3}} \xleftarrow[\text{H}_3\text{O}^+]{CrO_3} \underset{OH}{CH_3CH_2CH_2CHCH_2CH_3} \xleftarrow{H_3O^+}$$

$$\underset{O^-Mg^{2+}Br^-}{CH_3CH_2CH_2CHCH_2CH_3} \xleftarrow{\overset{O}{CH_3CH_2CH}} CH_3CH_2CH_2MgBr \xleftarrow[\text{diethyl} \atop \text{ether}]{Mg} CH_3CH_2CH_2Br$$

13.35

(c)

$$CH_3C{=}CHCH_2CH_2CH_3 \xleftarrow[\Delta]{H_3PO_4} CH_3\overset{\displaystyle CH_3}{\underset{\displaystyle OH}{C}}CH_2CH_2CH_2CH_3 \xleftarrow{H_3O^+} CH_3\overset{\displaystyle CH_3}{\underset{\displaystyle O^-Mg^{2+}Br^-}{C}}CH_2CH_2CH_2CH_3 \xleftarrow{} CH_3\overset{O}{\overset{\|}{C}}CH_3$$

major product

$$CH_3CH_2CH_2CH_2MgBr \xleftarrow[\substack{\text{diethyl}\\\text{ether}}]{Mg} CH_3CH_2CH_2CH_2Br \xleftarrow[\text{pyridine}]{PBr_3} CH_3CH_2CH_2CH_2OH \xleftarrow{H_3O^+}$$

$$CH_3CH_2CH_2CH_2O^-Mg^{2+}Br^- \xleftarrow{} CH_3CH_2MgBr \xleftarrow[\substack{\text{diethyl}\\\text{ether}}]{Mg} CH_3CH_2Br$$

(d)

$$PhCH_2CH_2Br \xleftarrow[\text{pyridine}]{PBr_3} PhCH_2CH_2OH \xleftarrow{H_3O^+} PhCH_2CH_2O^- Mg^{2+} Br^- \xleftarrow{} PhMgBr \xleftarrow[\substack{\text{diethyl}\\\text{ether}}]{Mg} PhBr$$

(e)

$$\text{(stereochemical structure)} \xleftarrow[\substack{\text{carbon}\\\text{tetrachloride}}]{Br_2} \text{(alkene)} \xleftarrow[NH_3\ (liq)]{Na} CH_3CH_2CH_2C{\equiv}CCH_3 \xleftarrow{} CH_3I$$

and enantiomer

$$CH_3CH_2CH_2C{\equiv}C^-\ Na^+ \xleftarrow[NH_3\ (liq)]{NaNH_2} CH_3CH_2CH_2C{\equiv}CH \xleftarrow{CH_3CH_2CH_2Br} Na^{+\ -}C{\equiv}CH \xleftarrow[NH_3\ (liq)]{NaNH_2} HC{\equiv}CH$$

(f)

$$Ph\overset{O}{\overset{\|}{C}}CH_2CH_3 \xleftarrow[(CH_3CH_2)_3N,\ CH_3SCH_3,\ Cl\overset{O}{\overset{\|}{C}}{-}\overset{O}{\overset{\|}{C}}Cl]{} Ph\underset{OH}{C}HCH_2CH_3 \xleftarrow[H_2O]{NH_4Cl} CH_3CH_2\overset{O}{\overset{\|}{C}}H \xleftarrow{} PhMgBr \xleftarrow[\substack{\text{diethyl}\\\text{ether}}]{Mg} PhBr$$

(g)

and enantiomer   and enantiomer

$\uparrow H_3O^+$

and enantiomer

$\xleftarrow[\text{dichloromethane}]{Cl-\text{(benzene)}-COOH}$

$\xleftarrow[\substack{H_2O\\\text{cold, dilute}}]{KMnO_4}$

13.35 (g) (cont)

$$H_2C{=}C \quad (CH_3, H) \xleftarrow{\;\;Na\;\;/\;NH_3\,(liq)\;\;} \qquad \xrightarrow{\;\;H_2\;/\;Pd/CaCO_3\;/\;quinoline\;\;} (CH_3)C{=}C(CH_3)$$

$$CH_3C{\equiv}CCH_3 \xleftarrow[]{\;CH_3I\;}$$

$$Na^{+\,-}C{\equiv}CCH_3 \xleftarrow[\;NH_3\,(liq)\;]{\;NaNH_2\;} HC{\equiv}CCH_3$$

(h)
$$CH_3CHCH_2CH_2CHCH_3 \xleftarrow[]{\;H_3O^+\;\;CH_3CH{=}O\;} CH_3CHCH_2CH_2Li \xleftarrow[\text{diethyl ether}]{\;Li\;}$$
with CH₃ and OH substituents

$$CH_3CHCH_2CH_2Br \xleftarrow[\text{pyridine}]{\;PBr_3\;} CH_3CHCH_2CH_2OH \xleftarrow[]{\;H_3O^+\;\;\triangle O\;} CH_3CHCH_3 \xleftarrow[\substack{\text{diethyl}\\\text{ether}}]{\;Mg\;} CH_3CHCH_3$$
(MgBr and Br substituents, CH₃ groups)

(i)
$$PhCH_2CH_2CH_3 \xleftarrow[\substack{\text{diethylene glycol}\\\Delta}]{\;H_2NNH_2,\;NaOH\;} PhCCH_2CH_3 \xleftarrow[\text{dichloromethane}]{\;\text{(pyridinium}\;CrO_3Cl^-)\;}$$

$$PhCHCH_2CH_3 \xleftarrow[\;H_2O\;]{\;NH_4Cl\;\;CH_3CH_2CH{=}O\;} PhMgBr \xleftarrow[\substack{\text{diethyl}\\\text{ether}}]{\;Mg\;} PhBr$$
with OH substituent

(j)
$$(\text{epoxide: }H,\,O,\,Ph,\,Ph,\,H) \xleftarrow[\text{dichloromethane}]{\;Cl{-}C_6H_4{-}COOH\;} (Ph)(H)C{=}C(H)(Ph) \xleftarrow[\substack{H_2SO_4\\\Delta}]{} PhCH_2CHPh \xleftarrow[\text{diethyl ether}]{\;H_3O^+\;\;PhMgBr\;}$$
with OH substituent

$$PhCH_2CH{=}O \xleftarrow[\text{dichloromethane}]{\;\text{(pyridinium}\;CrO_3Cl^-)\;} PhCH_2CH_2OH \xleftarrow[]{\;H_3O^+\;\;\triangle O\;} PhMgBr \xleftarrow[\text{diethyl ether}]{\;Mg\;} PhBr$$

13.36

The reaction proceeds by a series of steps, each of which is an equilibrium. Removal by distillation of methanol, the lowest boiling component of the mixture, as it forms, will push the equilibrium towards the dibutoxypropane.

13.37

addition of nucleophile to electrophilic carbon of carbonyl group

protonation and deprotonation

protonation

elimination of water

deprotonation

13.38

Step 2 was necessary to protect the aldehyde group from oxidation during ozonolysis.

13.40

The large *tert*-butyl group occupies an equatorial position on the ring (Section 5.11C). Reduction takes place so that the major product has the hydroxyl group also in the equatorial position. This means that the hydride is delivered to the carbonyl group from the axial direction.

48%

52%

product from axial approach
of the borohydride anion

product from equatorial approach
of the borohydride anion

In 3,3,5-trimethylcyclohexanone, one of the methyl groups on carbon 3 is axial and hinders the approach of the borohydride anion from the axial direction. The major product is now the result of reduction of the carbonyl group from the less hindered side of the molecule.

13.41 $HC\equiv CCH_2OH$ + [dihydropyran] $\xrightarrow{HCl}$ $HC\equiv CCH_2O$—[tetrahydropyranyl] $\xrightarrow[\text{dimethyl sulfoxide}]{NaH}$ $Na^+ \ ^-C\equiv CCH_2O$—[tetrahydropyranyl]

A

B

$\xrightarrow{CH_2=CH(CH_2)_8CH_2OTs}$ $CH_2=CH(CH_2)_9C\equiv CCH_2O$—[tetrahydropyranyl] $\xrightarrow[\text{methanol}]{\begin{array}{c}H_2O\\HCl\end{array}}$ $CH_2=CH(CH_2)_9C\equiv CCH_2OH$

C

D

13.42 $BrCH_2CH_2CH_2OH$ $\xrightarrow[\text{dichloromethane}]{\text{pyridinium } CrO_3Cl^-}$ $BrCH_2CH_2CH_2CH \overset{O}{\parallel}$ $\xrightarrow[\text{benzene, }\Delta]{\begin{array}{c}HOCH_2CH_2OH\\TsOH\end{array}}$ $BrCH_2CH_2CH_2CH$[dioxolane] $\xrightarrow[\text{tetrahydro-furan}]{Mg}$

A

B

$BrMgCH_2CH_2CH_2CH$[dioxolane] $\xrightarrow{\begin{array}{c}CH_3 \ \ H\\ \backslash C=C /\\ H \ \ CH\\ \ \ \ \backslash O\end{array}}$

C

[structure with CH=C, CHCH₂CH₂CH₂CH dioxolane, O⁻Mg²⁺Br⁻] $\xrightarrow{H_3O^+}$

D

$\left[\begin{array}{c}\text{structure}\end{array}\right]$ $\longrightarrow$ [cyclic hemiacetal structure]

E
$C_8H_{14}O_2$
a stable, cyclic hemiacetal

$\xrightarrow[\text{dichloromethane}]{\text{pyridinium } CrO_3Cl^-}$ [lactone structure]

F
$C_8H_{12}O_2$
three units of unsaturation
(2 double bonds and a ring)

13.43 (a) [bicyclic structure with CH₃, H, OTBDMS, H, CH₃] $\xrightarrow{(CH_3CH_2CH_2CH_2)_4N^+ \ F^-}$

13.43 (a) (cont)

(b)

(c)

not isolated   stable cyclic hemiacetal

(d)

acetal, preferentially
hydrolyzed under
acidic conditions

note that the cyclic hemiacetal has not
hydrolyzed because it is favored in its
equilibrium with the open chain form

(e)

13.44   (a)

(b)

13.45   The benzylic carbon atom in the starting material that has a hydroxyl group on it is the carbon atom of a carbonyl group in the product. It is also bonded to another carbon atom. The formation of a carbon-carbon σ bond suggests the reaction of an organometallic reagent containing a nucleophilic center with the electrophilic carbon atom of a carbonyl compound. A ketone is formed by oxidation of a secondary alcohol. A secondary alcohol is formed by reaction of an organometallic reagent with an aldehyde. Therefore, we need an aldehyde function where the benzylic alcohol group is in the starting material.

this carbon is the same as the benzylic carbon with the hydroxyl group in the starting material shown below

this carbon is the same as the ketone carbon above

13.46 (a)

$$TsOCH_2CH-CH_2 \xrightarrow[\substack{CH_3\ CH_3 \\ CH_3C-SiCl \\ CH_3\ CH_3}]{\text{imidazole}} TsOCH_2CH-CH_2 \xrightarrow{HCCH=CHO^-\ ^+N(CH_2CH_2CH_2CH_3)_4}$$

with OH OH below first structure; TBDMSO OTBDMS below **A**

$$HCCH=CHOCH_2CH-CH_2$$

TBDMSO   OTBDMS

B

(b) $CH_3CH_2CH=CHCH=CHCHC\equiv CH \xrightarrow[\substack{\text{tetrahydrofuran} \\ -78\ ^\circ C}]{R_2N^-Li^+} CH_3CH_2CH=CHCH=CHCHC\equiv C^-\ Li^+$

with OTHP below; **C**   OTHP

(c) $HCCH=CHOCH_2CH-CH_2 + CH_3CH_2CH=CHCH=CHCHC\equiv C^-\ Li^+ \longrightarrow$

with TBDMSO   OTBDMS below; **B**   OTHP below; **C**

$CH_3CH_2CH=CHCH=CHCHC\equiv CCHCH=CHOCH_2CHCH_2OTBDMS \xrightarrow{\text{several steps}}$

OTHP   O^- Li^+   OTBDMS

D

$CH_3CH_2(CH=CH)_5OCH_2CHCH_2OTBDMS \xrightarrow{(CH_3CH_2CH_2CH_2)_4N^+ F^-} CH_3CH_2(CH=CH)_5OCH_2CHCH_2OH$

OTBDMS   OH

(±)-fecapentaene

13.47

(a) $CH_3C=CHCH_2CH_2CHCH_2CH_3 \xleftarrow{H_3O^+} \xleftarrow{CH_3CH_2CH\ (=O)} CH_3C=CHCH_2CH_2MgBr \xleftarrow{Mg} CH_3C=CHCH_2CH_2Br$

with CH_3 above and OH below middle structure

7-methyl-6-octen-3-ol

(b) $CH_3C=CHCH_2CH_2CHCH_2CH_3 \xrightarrow[\substack{CH_3C-SiCl \\ \text{imidazole} \\ \text{dimethylformamide}}]{} CH_3C=CHCH_2CH_2CHCH_2CH_3$

with CH_3 above, OH below left; CH_3 above, OTBDMS below right

13.47

(c)

The alcohol functional group is a nucleophile that can open the oxirane ring under acid catalysis (see Section 12.5A).

13.48

A

(See Problem 12.53 for an explanation of the regioselectivity.)

13.49

$$:\ddot{C}lMg-CH=CH_2$$

$$CH_2-CH_2 \qquad \qquad CH_2-CH_2 \qquad \qquad$$
$$:\ddot{C}l-CH_2 \qquad \underset{C}{\overset{CH_3}{\big|}} \qquad \longrightarrow \qquad :\ddot{C}l \quad CH_2 \qquad \underset{C}{\overset{CH=CH_2}{\big|}}_{CH_3} \qquad \longrightarrow \qquad$$

$$Mg^{2+} \quad :\ddot{C}l:^- \qquad \qquad :\ddot{C}l:^-$$

$$\xrightarrow[\text{H}_2\text{O}]{\text{BH}_3 \quad \text{H}_2\text{O}_2,\ \text{NaOH}} \qquad \xrightarrow[\text{pyridine}]{\text{PBr}_3}$$

$$\xrightarrow{\text{Na}^+\ ^-\text{CH(COCH}_2\text{CH}_3)_2}$$

13.50 (a) $HOCH_2CH_2CH_2CH_2Br$ $\xrightarrow[\text{dichloromethane}]{\text{TsOH}}$

$OCH_2CH_2CH_2CH_2Br$
A

(b) $HC\equiv CCH_2OH$ $\xrightarrow[\substack{\text{NH}_3\ \text{(liq)}\\-30\,°\text{C}}]{\text{LiNH}_2\ \text{(excess)}}$ $Li^+\ ^-:C\equiv CCH_2\ddot{O}:^-\ Li^+$
                                                                       B

(c) $OCH_2CH_2CH_2CH_2Br$ + $Li^+\ ^-:C\equiv CCH_2\ddot{O}:^-\ Li^+$ $\longrightarrow$
    A   **B**

$OCH_2CH_2CH_2CH_2C\equiv CCH_2\ddot{O}:^-\ Li^+$ $\xrightarrow{\text{protonation}}$ $OCH_2CH_2CH_2CH_2C\equiv CCH_2OH$
C   **D**

(d) $OCH_2CH_2CH_2CH_2C\equiv CCH_2OH$ $\xrightarrow{\text{CH}_3\text{CH}_2\text{CH}_2\text{CH}_2\text{Li}}$
    D

$OCH_2CH_2CH_2CH_2C\equiv CCH_2\ddot{O}:^-\ Li^+$ $\xrightarrow{\text{MsCl}}$ $OCH_2CH_2CH_2CH_2C\equiv CCH_2OMs$
E $\equiv$ **C**   **F**

$\xrightarrow[\text{acetone}]{\text{LiBr}}$ $OCH_2CH_2CH_2CH_2C\equiv CCH_2Br$
                                                                                       G

13.51   (a)

(b)   The only good leaving group in D is the tosylate group. It is the tosyl ester of a primary alcohol, so that must be the carbon atom being oxidized to the aldehyde group. Let RCH$_2$OTs stand for Compound D.

nucleophilic attack   deprotonation   decomposition

13.52

13.53

13.54   Compounds A and B, molecular formula $C_6H_{12}O$, each have one unit of unsaturation. The infrared spectra of the two compounds show the presence of a ketone (C=O at 1717 cm^{-1} and no bands at 2900 and 2700 cm^{-1}, which tells us that the compounds are not aldehydes). The presence of a ketone is confirmed by the ^{13}C magnetic resonance spectra in which the ketone carbon atom can be seen for A and B (A at δ 208.88 and B at 214.21). The carbonyl group of a ketone accounts for one unit of unsaturation, therefore neither A nor B can have a ring or a double bond. There are four ketones that have the molecular formula $C_6H_{12}O$.

The ^{13}C spectra tell us how many types of carbon atoms each compound has. Compound A has six different carbon atoms. Compound B has four sets of carbon atoms, and therefore must have three which are the same. 3,3-Dimethyl-2-butanone has four sets of carbon atoms and, therefore, must be Compound B. This is confirmed by the proton magnetic resonance spectrum. Both 2-hexanone and 3-hexanone have six different carbon atoms and could be Compound A. The proton magnetic resonance spectrum allows us to choose the correct structure for Compound A.

The structural formulas are shown below, along with the proton magnetic resonance data for each one.

Supplemental Problems

S13.1   Name the following compounds according to the IUPAC rules.

(a) $CH_3CCH_2CH_2CH_3$
$\overset{O}{\overset{\|}{}}$

(b)   [cyclohexane structure with CH_3, CH_3 groups and CHO group]

(c)   [cyclobutanone structure with CH_2CH_3 and CH_3 substituents]

(d)   [benzene ring]—$CH_2CH_2CH_2CH$ with O

S13.2   Complete the following equations.

(a)   [bicyclic diketone structure] $\xrightarrow[\substack{CeCl_3 \cdot 7\,H_2O \\ ethanol}]{NaBH_4\ (excess)}$ A

(b)   [cyclobutanone]=O $\xrightarrow[\substack{diethyl \\ ether}]{LiAlH_4}$ $\xrightarrow{H_3O^+}$ B

(c)   [dimethyl cyclohexenone structure with CH_3 CH_3] $\xrightarrow[\substack{diethyl \\ ether}]{CH_3Li}$ C $\xrightarrow{H_3O^+}$ D

(d) $PhCCH_2CH_2CH_3$ + H_2NNH_2 $\xrightarrow{\Delta}$ E
       with $\overset{O}{\overset{\|}{}}$

(e) $CH_3CCH_2CH_3$ + $CH_3CHCH_2NH_2$ $\xrightarrow[HCl]{}$ $\xrightarrow{NaOH}$ F
       with $\overset{O}{\overset{\|}{}}$ and $\overset{CH_3}{\overset{|}{}}$

(f) $CH_3CHCH_2CH_2CH$ + CH_3OH $\xrightarrow[\substack{TsOH \\ benzene \\ \Delta}]{}$ G
       with $\overset{CH_3}{\overset{|}{}}$ and $\overset{O}{\overset{\|}{}}$

(g) $CH_3CHCH_2CCH_2CHCH_3$ $\xrightarrow[\substack{diethylene\ glycol \\ \Delta}]{H_2NNH_2,\ NaOH}$ H
       with $\overset{CH_3}{\overset{|}{}}$, $\overset{O}{\overset{\|}{}}$, $\overset{CH_3}{\overset{|}{}}$

S13.3   A synthesis of talaromycin, a toxic metabolite of a fungus that grows on chicken litter, involved the transformation shown below. How would you carry it out?

[structure: $CH_3CHCC \equiv CCH_2OSi$—CCH_3 with CH_3 groups and CH_3 substituent] $\longrightarrow$ [structure with $HC \equiv CCH_2O$, CH_3CHCH, CH_2OSi—CCH_3, $CH_3\,C=C\,H$, H]

S13.4   Predict the structures of the products or intermediates designated by letters in the following equations. Show stereochemistry when it is known.

(a) $CH_3C = CHCH_3$ $\xrightarrow[\substack{tetrahydro- \\ furan}]{BH_3}$ A $\xrightarrow[H_2O]{H_2O_2,\ NaOH}$ B $\xrightarrow[\substack{H_2SO_4 \\ H_2O}]{CrO_3}$ C $\xrightarrow{NaCN}$ D $\xrightarrow{H_3O^+}$ E
       with $\overset{CH_3}{\overset{|}{}}$

S13.4

(b) $HC{\equiv}CH$ $\xrightarrow[\text{NH}_3 \text{ (liq)}]{\text{NaNH}_2}$ F $\xrightarrow[\text{diethyl ether}]{\text{PhCH}_2\text{Br}}$ G $\xrightarrow[\text{diethyl ether}]{\text{CH}_3\text{CH}_2\text{MgBr}}$ H $\longrightarrow$ I $\xrightarrow[\text{H}_2\text{O}]{\text{NH}_4\text{Cl}}$ J

(c) $\xrightarrow[\text{diethyl ether}]{\text{PhLi}}$ K $\xrightarrow{\text{H}_3\text{O}^+}$ L

(d) $CH_2{=}CHCH_2CH_2$– cyclohexanone $\xrightarrow[\text{chloroform}]{\text{Br}_2}$ M $\xrightarrow[\substack{\text{TsOH}\\ \text{benzene, }\Delta}]{\text{HOCH}_2\text{CH}_2\text{OH}}$ N

(e) $\xrightarrow[\substack{\text{diethyl}\\ \text{ether}}]{\text{CH}_3\text{Li}}$ O $\xrightarrow{\text{H}_3\text{O}^+}$ P

(f) $\xrightarrow[\text{H}_2\text{O}]{\substack{\text{HONH}_3{}^+ \text{ Cl}^-\text{, KOH}\\ \text{(2 equivalents)}}}$ Q

(g) $\xrightarrow[\text{CH}_3\text{OH}]{\text{R}}$ and enantiomer

(h) $\xrightarrow{(\text{CH}_3\text{CH}_2\text{CH}_2\text{CH}_2)_4\text{N}^+\text{ F}^-}$ pyridinium chlorochromate $\longrightarrow$ S

(i)   T + U $\longrightarrow$ V $\xrightarrow[\text{H}_2\text{O}]{\text{NH}_4\text{Cl}}$ and enantiomer

(j) $PhCCH_2CH_2CH_2Cl$ $\xrightarrow[\substack{\text{TsOH}\\ \text{benzene, }\Delta}]{\text{HOCH}_2\text{CH}_2\text{OH}}$ W $\xrightarrow[\Delta]{(\text{PhCH}_2)_2\text{NH}}$ X $\;C_{26}H_{30}ClNO_2$ $\xrightarrow[\text{H}_2\text{O}]{\text{HCl, H}_2\text{O}}$ $\xrightarrow[\text{H}_2\text{O}]{\text{NaOH}}$ Y $\;C_{24}H_{25}NO$

(k) $\xrightarrow[\text{H}_2\text{O}]{\text{NaBH}_4}$ Z   +   AA
                              major product   minor product

S13.5   Imines behave toward Grignard reagents in much the same way that carbonyl groups do. The following transformations were carried out. Supply the reagents that are necessary to carry out the reactions observed.

S13.6   Supply reagents for each of the following transformations. More than one step may be necessary for some.

14

Carboxylic Acids and Their Derivatives I. Acyl-Transfer Reactions

Workbook Exercises

There are two common classifications of functional groups that contain the carbonyl group ($-\overset{\overset{\text{O}}{\|}}{C}-$). These two classifications are based on an observed difference in reactivity. In the case of aldehydes and ketones (see Chapter 13), the fundamental reaction is addition. As demonstrated by the formation of imines and ketals, among others, the addition products of aldehydes and ketones can undergo further reactions. In Chapters 14 and 15, the second type of carbonyl chemistry is presented. In this case, groups other than simple alkyl or aryl groups (as in ketones) or hydrogen (as in aldehydes) are attached to the carbon atom of a carbonyl group. Instead, halogen, oxygen, nitrogen, or sulfur atoms (symbolized below as the generic electronegative group eN) are bonded to the carbonyl group. The overall reaction of these carbonyl compounds is not addition, as in the case of aldehydes and ketones, but rather substitution of the eN group.

$$R-\overset{\overset{\text{O}}{\|}}{C}-eN \quad \xrightarrow{\text{nucleophiles} \atop (\text{Nu})} \quad R-\overset{\overset{\text{O}}{\|}}{C}-Nu \;\; + \;\; eN$$

overall reaction = substitution at the sp^2-hybridized carbon atom

(eN = many O, N, S, and halogen groups, among others)

The functional unit symbolized by $R-\overset{\overset{\text{O}}{\|}}{C}-$ is called an **acyl group.** The S_N1 and S_N2 substitution reactions of alkyl halides by nucleophiles (R—LG → R—Nu) are called alkylations of the nucleophile, or alkyl transfer reactions. The substitution of the eN atom group of $R-\overset{\overset{\text{O}}{\|}}{C}-eN$ by a nucleophile to give $R-\overset{\overset{\text{O}}{\|}}{C}-Nu$ is called an **acylation** of the nucleophile, or an **acyl transfer reaction.**

A new term, such as acylation, is created in order to express a new idea. The process of acylation can be described as addition followed by elimination. The reference to ideas previously encountered is designed to make an unfamiliar process, such as acylation, more familiar to you. If the reference to addition and elimination reactions is not meaningful to you, your best strategy is to refamiliarize yourself with these previous types of reactions before attempting to master new ones. These types of analogies can be used in many ways to communicate meaning. When referring to the overall change in connectivity in an acylation, the term substitution is used to describe the transformation at the sp^2-hybridized carbon atom.

EXAMPLE
Compare the four examples of transformations using water as a nucleophile shown on the following page. Each one is accompanied by an equation describing the overall change in connectivity and the mechanistic rationalization of the change observed.

Workbook Exercises (cont)

EXERCISE I.   Complete the following acylation reactions.

(a) PhCOCH₂CH₃ + NH₃ ⟶   A + B   (b)   [lactone] O + CH₃OH ⟶ C

(c) HCNCH₃ + D ⟶ HCNCH₂CH₂CH₂CH₃ + E   (d)   F + G ⟶ CH₃COCCH₃ + NaCl
         | |
         CH₃   H

(e) [cyclopentane with CH₃ and CCCl₃] + NaOH ⟶ H* + I*

(*The trichloromethyl group, —CCl₃, behaves as a leaving group in this reaction. Under the aqueous base conditions of this reaction, the leaving group is protonated to give an uncharged product, while the acylated nucleophile is deprotonated to give its conjugate base.)

A MORE DETAILED LOOK AT THE ACYLATION MECHANISM

The overall transformation in an acylation reaction is viewed as the combination of two fundamental mechanistic steps: addition to the carbonyl group followed by an elimination. This is the same way that the reactions of the carbonyl group in Chapter 13 were characterized.

$$
\begin{array}{ccccc}
\text{O} & & \text{OH} & & \text{O} \\
\parallel & \xrightarrow{\text{addition of Nu-H}} & | & \xrightarrow{\text{elimination of H-eN}} & \parallel \\
\text{R} - \text{C} - \text{eN} & \underset{\text{elimination of Nu-H}}{\rightleftarrows} & \text{R} - \text{C} - \text{Nu} & \underset{\text{addition of H-eN}}{\rightleftarrows} & \text{R} - \text{C} - \text{Nu} \\
& & | & & \\
& & \text{eN} & & \\
\end{array}
$$

alcohol intermediate

Workbook Exercises (cont)

If the nucleophile is an anion, Nu⁻, the intermediate will be an alkoxide ion, $R - \overset{\overset{\displaystyle O^-}{|}}{\underset{\underset{\displaystyle eN}{|}}{C}} - Nu$, rather than an alcohol.

EXAMPLE

This scheme, applied to one of the molecules shown on the previous page, gives the following more detailed description.

previously shown: $\overset{\overset{\displaystyle O}{\|}}{CH_3CSPh}$ $\xrightarrow{H_2O}$ $\overset{\overset{\displaystyle O}{\|}}{CH_3COH}$ + HSPh

more detailed view: $CH_3 - \overset{\overset{\displaystyle O}{\|}}{C} - SPh$ $\underset{\substack{\text{elimination} \\ \text{of } H_2O}}{\overset{\substack{\text{addition} \\ \text{of } H_2O}}{\rightleftharpoons}}$ $CH_3 - \overset{\overset{\displaystyle OH}{|}}{\underset{\underset{\displaystyle SPh}{|}}{C}} - OH$ $\underset{\substack{\text{addition} \\ \text{of PhSH}}}{\overset{\substack{\text{elimination} \\ \text{of PhSH}}}{\rightleftharpoons}}$ $CH_3 - \overset{\overset{\displaystyle O}{\|}}{C} - OH$

EXERCISE II.   Redo Exercise I using the mechanistic scheme outlined above.

- -

14.1

progress of reaction for reaction
of aldehyde or ketone with amine

progress of reaction for reaction
of acid derivative with amine

The carbonyl group of an aldehyde or a ketone is not as highly stabilized as the carbonyl group of an ester is. The free energy of the aldehyde or ketone is thus higher than that of the ester. If we assume that the tetrahedral intermediates, in which we no longer have resonance, are approximately the same energy, then $\Delta G^{\ddagger}$ for an aldehyde or ketone is lower than for an ester. Therefore, an aldehyde or ketone reacts faster with the nucleophile than the ester does.

14.2   (a) $CH_3CH_2 - \overset{\overset{\displaystyle O}{\|}}{C} - OH$ $CH_3CH_2 - \overset{\overset{\displaystyle O}{\|}}{C} - \boxed{Cl}$ $CH_3CH_2 - \overset{\overset{\displaystyle O}{\|}}{C} - \boxed{O - \overset{\overset{\displaystyle O}{\|}}{C} - CH_2CH_3}$

$CH_3CH_2 - \overset{\overset{\displaystyle O}{\|}}{C} - OCH_2CH_3$ $CH_3CH_2 - \overset{\overset{\displaystyle O}{\|}}{C} - NH_2$

14.2 (b)

$$CH_3CH_2 - \overset{\overset{\displaystyle O}{\|}}{C} - \overset{+}{O}H_2 \quad HSO_4^- \underset{H_2SO_4}{\overset{\longrightarrow}{\longleftarrow}} \quad CH_3CH_2 - \overset{\overset{\displaystyle O}{\|}}{C} - OH \quad \underset{}{\overset{H_2SO_4}{\longleftrightarrow}} \quad CH_3CH_2 - \overset{\overset{\displaystyle \overset{+}{O} - H}{\|}}{C} - OH \quad HSO_4^-$$

major product

$$CH_3CH_2 - \overset{\overset{\displaystyle O}{\|}}{C} - \overset{\overset{\displaystyle +}{OCH_2CH_3}}{\underset{\displaystyle H}{|}} \quad HSO_4^- \underset{H_2SO_4}{\overset{\longrightarrow}{\longleftarrow}} \quad CH_3CH_2 - \overset{\overset{\displaystyle O}{\|}}{C} - OCH_2CH_3 \quad \underset{}{\overset{H_2SO_4}{\longleftrightarrow}} \quad CH_3CH_2 - \overset{\overset{\displaystyle \overset{+}{O} - H}{\|}}{C} - OCH_2CH_3 \quad HSO_4^-$$

major product

$$CH_3CH_2 - \overset{\overset{\displaystyle O}{\|}}{C} - \overset{+}{N}H_3 \quad HSO_4^- \underset{H_2SO_4}{\overset{\longrightarrow}{\longleftarrow}} \quad CH_3CH_2 - \overset{\overset{\displaystyle O}{\|}}{C} - NH_2 \quad \underset{}{\overset{H_2SO_4}{\longleftrightarrow}} \quad CH_3CH_2 - \overset{\overset{\displaystyle \overset{+}{O} - H}{\|}}{C} - NH_2 \quad HSO_4^-$$

major product

(c) The good leaving groups are shaded in the formulas shown in parts (a) and (b).

- -

Concept Map 14.1   Relative reactivities in nucleophilic substitutions.

14.3

$$CH_3CH_2\overset{\overset{\displaystyle :O:}{\|}}{C} - \overset{..}{\underset{..}{O}} - H \quad \longleftrightarrow \quad CH_3CH_2\overset{\overset{\displaystyle :\overset{..}{O}:^-}{|}}{C} - \overset{+}{\underset{..}{O}} - H \quad \longleftrightarrow \quad CH_3CH_2\overset{\overset{\displaystyle :\overset{..}{O}:^-}{|}}{C} = \overset{+}{\underset{..}{O}} - H$$

$$CH_3CH_2\overset{\overset{\displaystyle :O:}{\|}}{C} - \overset{..}{\underset{..}{Cl}}: \quad \longleftrightarrow \quad CH_3CH_2\overset{\overset{\displaystyle :\overset{..}{O}:^-}{|}}{C} - \overset{+}{\underset{..}{Cl}}: \quad \longleftrightarrow \quad CH_3CH_2\overset{\overset{\displaystyle :\overset{..}{O}:^-}{|}}{C} = \overset{+}{\underset{..}{Cl}}:$$

$$CH_3CH_2\overset{\overset{\displaystyle :O:}{\|}}{C} - \overset{..}{\underset{..}{O}} - \overset{\overset{\displaystyle :O:}{\|}}{C}CH_2CH_3 \longleftrightarrow CH_3CH_2\overset{\overset{\displaystyle :\overset{..}{O}:^-}{|}}{C} - \overset{+}{\underset{..}{O}} - \overset{\overset{\displaystyle :O:}{\|}}{C}CH_2CH_3 \longleftrightarrow CH_3CH_2\overset{\overset{\displaystyle :\overset{..}{O}:^-}{|}}{C} = \overset{+}{\underset{..}{O}} - \overset{\overset{\displaystyle :O:}{\|}}{C}CH_2CH_3 \longleftrightarrow$$

14.3 (cont)

$$CH_3CH_2\overset{\overset{\displaystyle :O:}{\|}}{C}-\overset{+}{\underset{\cdot\cdot}{O}}=\overset{\overset{\displaystyle :\overset{\cdot\cdot}{O}:^-}{|}}{C}CH_2CH_3 \longleftrightarrow CH_3CH_2\overset{\overset{\displaystyle :O:}{\|}}{C}-\overset{\cdot\cdot}{\underset{\cdot\cdot}{O}}-\overset{+}{\underset{}{C}}CH_2CH_3$$

$$CH_3CH_2\overset{\overset{\displaystyle :O:}{\|}}{C}-\overset{\cdot\cdot}{\underset{\cdot\cdot}{O}}CH_2CH_3 \longleftrightarrow CH_3CH_2\overset{\overset{\displaystyle :\overset{\cdot\cdot}{O}:^-}{|}}{C}-\overset{+}{\underset{\cdot\cdot}{O}}CH_2CH_3 \longleftrightarrow CH_3CH_2\overset{\overset{\displaystyle :\overset{\cdot\cdot}{O}:^-}{|}}{C}=\overset{+}{\underset{}{O}}CH_2CH_3$$

$$CH_3CH_2\overset{\overset{\displaystyle :O:}{\|}}{C}-\overset{\cdot\cdot}{\underset{}{N}}H_2 \longleftrightarrow CH_3CH_2\overset{\overset{\displaystyle :\overset{\cdot\cdot}{O}:^-}{|}}{C}-\overset{+}{\underset{\cdot\cdot}{N}}H_2 \longleftrightarrow CH_3CH_2\overset{\overset{\displaystyle :\overset{\cdot\cdot}{O}:^-}{|}}{C}=\overset{+}{\underset{}{N}}H_2$$

The resonance contributors shown above reduce the positive charge on the carbon atom of the carbonyl group. The carbon atom of the carbonyl group in acid derivatives is thus less electrophilic than the carbon atom of the carbonyl group in aldehydes and ketones. The compounds in which the resonance contributors involve oxygen or nitrogen are more stable than the one in which chlorine is involved. The orbitals of oxygen and nitrogen (second row elements of smaller size) overlap with those of carbon better than those of chlorine, therefore their resonance contributors are more important in the stabilization of the compounds. The amide is the most stable of all, because nitrogen is less electronegative than oxygen, and therefore bears a positive charge more easily than oxygen does.

14.4 Propanamide is much less basic than propylamine because the nitrogen atom in propanamide has a partial positive charge (see the resonance contributors for propanamide in Problem 14.3). This means that there is less electron density on the nitrogen atom in propanamide than in propylamine, and, therefore, lower basicity for the amide.

$$CH_3CH_2\overset{\overset{\displaystyle O^{\delta-}}{\|}}{\underset{\delta+\ \ \delta+}{C}}-\overset{\cdot\cdot}{N}H_2 \qquad\qquad CH_3CH_2CH_2-\overset{\cdot\cdot}{N}H_2$$

The electron pair on the nitrogen atom is less available; the amide nitrogen is less basic

The electron pair on the nitrogen atom is more available; the amine nitrogen is more basic

$$CH_3CH_2\overset{\overset{\displaystyle :O:}{\|}}{C}-\overset{\cdot\cdot}{\underset{\cdot\cdot}{N}}H \longleftrightarrow CH_3CH_2\overset{\overset{\displaystyle :\overset{\cdot\cdot}{O}:^-}{|}}{C}=\overset{\cdot\cdot}{N}H \qquad\qquad CH_3CH_2CH_2-\overset{\cdot\cdot}{\underset{\cdot\cdot}{N}}\bar{H}$$

delocalization of charge in conjugate base of propanamide; hence stabilization of base relative to its conjugate acid

no stabilization of negative charge; therefore strong base

14.5 $\xrightarrow{\qquad\qquad\text{decreasing solubility}\qquad\qquad}$

(a) $CH_3CH_2CH_2CH_2\overset{\overset{\displaystyle O}{\|}}{C}O^-Na^+ > CH_3CH_2CH_2CH_2\overset{\overset{\displaystyle O}{\|}}{C}OH > CH_3CH_2\overset{\overset{\displaystyle O}{\|}}{C}OCH_2CH_3$

ionic

covalent, but hydrogen bond donor as well as acceptor

only hydrogen bond acceptor

(b) $CH_3CH_2CH_2\overset{\overset{\displaystyle O}{\|}}{C}OH > CH_3CH_2CH_2CH_2OH > CH_3CH_2\overset{\overset{\displaystyle O}{\|}}{C}OCH_2CH_3$

can hydrogen bond at the carbonyl group as well as at the hydroxyl group

only one site for hydrogen bonding

only hydrogen bond acceptor

14.5   (c) $\underset{\substack{\text{hydrogen bond donor}\\\text{as well as acceptor}}}{CH_3CH_2CH_2\overset{\displaystyle O}{\overset{\|}{C}}NH_2}$ > $\underset{\substack{\text{hydrogen bond acceptor}}}{CH_3CH_2CH_2\overset{\displaystyle O}{\overset{\|}{C}}OCH_2CH_3}$ > $\underset{\substack{\text{hydrogen bond acceptor but}\\\text{nonpolar portion of the}\\\text{molecule now significantly}\\\text{larger than the polar part}}}{CH_3CH_2CH_2\overset{\displaystyle O}{\overset{\|}{C}}O(CH_2)_4CH_3}$

14.6

(R)-3-methylpentanoic acid

(S)-3-methylpentanoic acid

(S)-2-hydroxypropanoic acid

(R)-2-hydroxypropanoic acid

(S)-2-chlorohexanoic acid

(R)-2-chlorohexanoic acid

(R)-4-hydroxy-6-methylheptanoic acid

(S)-4-hydroxy-6-methylheptanoic acid

(S)-alanine

(R)-alanine

(2R, 3S)-tartaric acid
meso tartaric acid

(2S, 3S)-tartaric acid

(2R, 3R)-tartaric acid

14.6 (cont)

cis isomers   trans isomers

trans isomers

14.7   (a) undecanoic acid   (b) (*E*)-2-pentenoic acid   (c) (*S*)-2-hydroxybutanoic acid
           (d) *m*-bromobenzoic acid (e) 2-chloro-4-methylpentanoic acid (f) 3-hydroxyhexanedioic acid

14.8
(a) hexanoyl chloride   (b) butanoic anhydride   (c) methyl (*Z*)-4-hexenoate   (d) isobutyl *p*-chlorobenzoate

14.9   (a)   (b)   or   (c)

           (d) HOC(CH₂)₆COH   (e) CH₃OCCH₂COCH₃   (f) PhCOCPh

           (g) PhC—NCH₃   (h) ClC(CH₂)₃CCl   (i) Na⁺ ⁻OC—CO⁻ Na⁺   (j)

14.10   (a) ethyl 6-oxooctanoate   (b) decanoic acid   (c) *m*-bromobenzoyl chloride
            (d) sodium octadecanoate (sodium stearate)   (e) *N*-methylacetamide (f) *p*-methylbenzamide
            (g) (1*S*, 2*R*)-2-bromocyclopentanecarboxylic acid (h) (*E*)-2-butenoic acid (i) (*R*)-3-hydroxybutanoic acid
            (j) heptanenitrile   (k) 3-methylbutanoic anhydride   (l)   *N*-phenylbutanamide (butananilide)

Concept Map 14.2   Preparation of carboxylic acids.

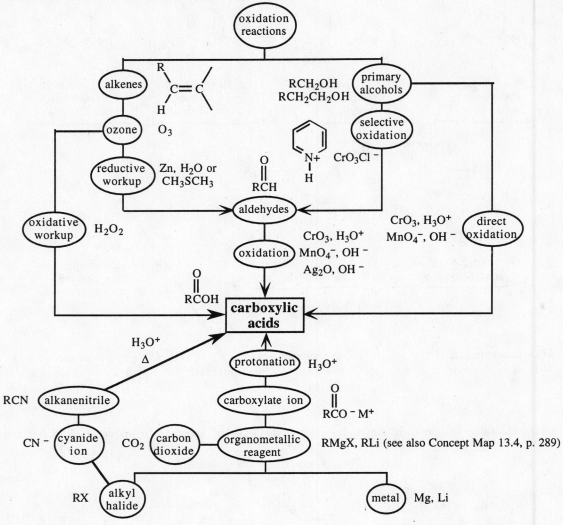

- -

14.11

(a) CH_3—⟨⟩—Br $\xrightarrow[\text{diethyl ether}]{Mg}$ CH_3—⟨⟩—$MgBr$ $\xrightarrow{CO_2}$

                      A

CH_3—⟨⟩—$\overset{\overset{\displaystyle O}{\|}}{C}O^-\ Mg^{2+}\ Br^-$ $\xrightarrow{H_3O^+}$ CH_3—⟨⟩—$\overset{\overset{\displaystyle O}{\|}}{C}OH$

            B   **C**

(b) $\overset{\displaystyle CH_3}{CH_3CH_2CH_2\overset{|}{C}HCH_2CH_2OH}$ $\xrightarrow[\substack{H_2O \\ \Delta}]{KMnO_4,\ NaOH}$ $CH_3CH_2CH_2\overset{\displaystyle CH_3}{\overset{|}{C}}HCH_2\overset{\overset{\displaystyle O}{\|}}{C}O^-\ Na^+$ $\xrightarrow{H_3O^+}$ $CH_3CH_2CH_2\overset{\displaystyle CH_3}{\overset{|}{C}}HCH_2\overset{\overset{\displaystyle O}{\|}}{C}OH$

                                                        D   **E**

14.11

(c)

$$\text{cyclohexene} \xrightarrow[\text{chloroform}]{O_3} \quad F \xrightarrow[\substack{H_2O \\ \Delta}]{Ag_2O,\ NaOH} \quad Na^+\ ^-OC(CH_2)_4CO^-\ Na^+ \xrightarrow{H_3O^+} HOC(CH_2)_4COH$$

F   G   H

(d)

$$PhCH_2CH_2CH \xrightarrow[\substack{H_2O \\ \Delta}]{Ag_2O,\ NaOH} PhCH_2CH_2CO^-\ Na^+ \xrightarrow{H_3O^+} PhCH_2CH_2COH$$

I   J

(e)

$$CH_3(CH_2)_9CH{=}CH_2 \xrightarrow[\text{chloroform}]{O_3} \xrightarrow{H_2O_2,\ NaOH} \xrightarrow{H_3O^+} CH_3(CH_2)_9COH + HCOH$$

K   L

14.12

(a) $PhCH_2CH_2COH \xrightarrow[\Delta]{SOCl_2} PhCH_2CH_2CCl$

(b) $CH_3CH_2CH_2COH \xrightarrow{PCl_3} CH_3CH_2CH_2CCl$

(c) $CH_3CH_2CH_2CCl\ +\ Na^+\ ^-OCCH_2CH_2CH_3 \longrightarrow CH_3CH_2CH_2COCCH_2CH_2CH_3$

(d) $HOCCH_2CH_2COH \xrightarrow{CH_3COCCH_3}$ succinic anhydride

(e) $CH_3CH_2COH \xrightarrow[\substack{clay \\ \Delta \\ 650\,°C}]{} CH_3CH_2COCCH_2CH_3$

(f) $HOC(CH_2)_5COH \xrightarrow[\Delta]{excess\ SOCl_2} ClC(CH_2)_5CCl$

14.13

(a) pyrrolidine $N{-}CCH_2CH_3 \longleftarrow NH + ClCCH_2CH_3$

(b) piperidine $N{-}CCH_2CH_3 \longleftarrow NH + ClCCH_2CH_3$

14.14

$$CH_3{-}\overset{\overset{\displaystyle :O:}{\|}}{C}{-}\ddot{\underset{..}{C}}l: \longrightarrow CH_3{-}\underset{\overset{+}{\underset{H}{O}}\overset{}{H}}{\overset{\overset{\displaystyle :\overset{..}{O}:^-}{|}}{C}}{-}\ddot{\underset{..}{C}}l: \longrightarrow CH_3{-}\underset{\overset{..}{O}{-}H}{\overset{\overset{\displaystyle :\overset{..}{O}:^-}{|}}{C}}{-}\ddot{\underset{..}{C}}l: \longrightarrow CH_3{-}\overset{\overset{\displaystyle :O:}{\|}}{C}{-}\ddot{O}H$$

$:\ddot{\underset{..}{C}}l:^-$

14.15

$$ClCH_2\overset{\overset{\displaystyle O}{\|}}{C}OH \quad + \quad {}^-C\equiv N \quad \longrightarrow \quad ClCH_2\overset{\overset{\displaystyle O}{\|}}{C}O^- \quad + \quad HC\equiv N$$

pK_a 2.8   pK_a 9.3

Chloroacetic acid is a much stronger acid than hydrogen cyanide. The cyanide anion will, therefore, be converted to hydrogen cyanide and will not be available to act as a nucleophile if chloroacetic acid is not first neutralized with base. In addition, even small amounts of hydrogen cyanide are lethal to humans.

14.16

14.17   The two oxygen atoms are equivalent and cannot be distinguished from each other (Section 1.6A).

14.18

Concept Map 14.3   Hydrolysis reactions of acid derivatives.

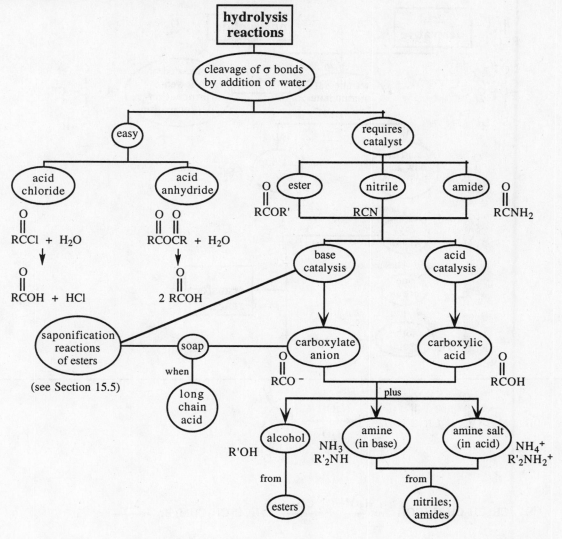

- -

14.19

For the carbon-nitrogen bond to break in the basic hydrolysis of acetamide, the leaving group must be the conjugate base of ammonia, amide anion. In basic solution, it is unlikely that protonation of the nitrogen in the tetrahedral intermediate will take place before the carbon-nitrogen bond begins to break. However, amide anion is such a strong base that it is improbable that it has any real existence in water. The mechanism accounts for this by showing the amide ion taking a proton from water as the tetrahedral intermediate breaks up.

Concept Map 14.4   Mechanism of acyl transfer reactions.

14.20   (a) Na^+ $^-OCCH_2CH_2CO^-$ Na^+ $\xleftarrow[\text{H}_2\text{O}]{\text{NaOH}}$

(b) $CH_3CH_2CH_2\underset{\underset{CH_3}{|}}{C}HCOOH$ $\xleftarrow{H_3O^+}$ $\xleftarrow{CO_2}$ $CH_3CH_2CH_2\underset{\underset{CH_3}{|}}{C}HMgBr$ $\xleftarrow{Mg}$

$CH_3CH_2CH_2\underset{\underset{CH_3}{|}}{C}HBr$ $\xleftarrow[\text{pyridine}]{PBr_3}$ $CH_3CH_2CH_2\underset{\underset{CH_3}{|}}{C}HOH$ $\xleftarrow{H_3O^+}$ $\xleftarrow{CH_3MgI}$ $CH_3CH_2CH_2CH$

14.21

1. How have connectivities been changed in going from reactant to product? How many carbon atoms does each contain? What bonds must be broken and formed to transform reactant into product?

$CH_3 — C \lessgtr\!N$

bonds broken

$CH_3C — N \lessgtr — H$

bonds formed

14.21 (cont)

The reactant and the product have the same number of carbon atoms. Two of the bonds between carbon and nitrogen have been broken. A carbon-oxygen double bond and two nitrogen-hydrogen single bonds have been formed.

2.   What reagents are present? Are they good acids, bases, nucleophiles, or electrophiles?

H_3O^+ is an acid, H_2O is a weak nucleophile. The carbon atom of the nitrile is electrophilic, and the nitrogen atom has nonbonding electrons on it.

3.   What is the most likely first step for the reaction: protonation or deprotonation, ionization, attack by a nucleophile, or attack by an electrophile?

An acid is present; therefore, protonation is the most likely first step. Water is a weak nucleophile and is unlikely to attack the unprotonated nitrile.

4.   What are the properties of the species present in the reaction mixture after the first step? What is likely to happen next?

The electrophilicity of the carbon bonded to nitrogen is greatly increased by the protonation of the nitrile; this carbon will now react with water.

4 (repeated).   What are the properties of the species present in the reaction mixture after this step? What is likely to happen next?

The oxonium ion resulting from the attack by water will be deprotonated by the solvent.

Comparing this new species to the desired product shows that it has a carbon-oxygen bond and a nitrogen-hydrogen bond in the right locations. To get to the product requires protonation at nitrogen and a shifting of the double bond.

This is a tautomerization.

14.21 (cont)

The complete mechanism is shown below:

14.22

14.23 $CH_3CH_2CH_2CH_2OH$ + $PhCCl$ $\xrightarrow[\text{H}_2\text{O}]{\text{10\% NaOH}}$ $PhCOCH_2CH_2CH_2CH_3$

The other organic product formed would be sodium benzoate.

$PhCCl$ $\xrightarrow[\text{H}_2\text{O}]{\text{10\% NaOH}}$ $PhCO^-\ Na^+$

14.24

(a)
$$CH_3\underset{\underset{CH_3}{|}}{\overset{\overset{CH_3}{|}}{C}}OH \;+\; CH_3\overset{O}{\overset{\|}{C}}O\overset{O}{\overset{\|}{C}}CH_3 \longrightarrow CH_3\overset{O}{\overset{\|}{C}}O\underset{\underset{CH_3}{|}}{\overset{\overset{CH_3}{|}}{C}}CH_3 \;+\; CH_3\overset{O}{\overset{\|}{C}}OH$$

(b)
$$Ph\overset{O}{\overset{\|}{C}}Cl \;+\; \langle\text{cyclohexyl}\rangle{-}OH \longrightarrow Ph\overset{O}{\overset{\|}{C}}O{-}\langle\text{cyclohexyl}\rangle$$

(c)
(maleic anhydride) $+\; CH_3CH_2OH$ (1 equivalent) $\longrightarrow$ $HO\overset{O}{\overset{\|}{C}}{-}C{=}C{-}\overset{O}{\overset{\|}{C}}OCH_2CH_3$ (with H's on the double bond carbons)

14.25

(a)
$$HO\overset{O}{\overset{\|}{C}}(CH_2)_9\overset{O}{\overset{\|}{C}}OH \xrightarrow[\substack{H_2SO_4 \\ \Delta}]{CH_3OH\ (\text{excess})} CH_3O\overset{O}{\overset{\|}{C}}(CH_2)_9\overset{O}{\overset{\|}{C}}OCH_3 \quad A$$

(b)
$$Ph\underset{\underset{OH}{|}}{CH}\overset{O}{\overset{\|}{C}}OH \xrightarrow[\substack{HCl\ (g) \\ \Delta}]{CH_3CH_2OH} Ph\underset{\underset{OH}{|}}{CH}\overset{O}{\overset{\|}{C}}OCH_2CH_3 \xrightarrow{SOCl_2} Ph\underset{\underset{Cl}{|}}{CH}\overset{O}{\overset{\|}{C}}OCH_2CH_3$$
$$\qquad\qquad\qquad\qquad\qquad\qquad\qquad B \qquad\qquad\qquad\qquad\qquad\qquad C$$

(c)
(cyclohexene anhydride) $\xrightarrow[\substack{TsOH \\ \Delta}]{CH_3CH_2OH\ (\text{excess})}$ (cyclohexene with two $\overset{O}{\overset{\|}{C}}OCH_2CH_3$ groups) $\quad D$

(d)
$$CH_3CH{=}CH\overset{O}{\overset{\|}{C}}OH \xrightarrow[\substack{H_2SO_4 \\ benzene \\ \Delta}]{\overset{\overset{CH_3CH_2CHCH_3}{|}}{OH}} CH_3CH{=}CH\overset{O}{\overset{\|}{C}}O\underset{\underset{CH_2CH_3}{}}{\overset{\overset{CH_3}{|}}{C}}H \quad E$$

14.26

(a)
$$Ph\overset{O}{\overset{\|}{C}}OH \;+\; CH_3OH \underset{H_2SO_4}{\overset{}{\rightleftharpoons}} Ph\overset{O}{\overset{\|}{C}}OCH_3 \;+\; H_2O$$

mp 121 °C	bp 66 °C	bp 198 °C
insoluble in water;	miscible with water;	insoluble in water;
soluble in	soluble in	soluble in
diethyl ether	diethyl ether	diethyl ether

(b) The reaction mixture consists of excess methanol, unreacted benzoic acid, sulfuric acid, and the products, water and methyl benzoate.

Step 1: Add more water to the reaction mixture; most of the methanol and the sulfuric acid will go into the water layer. Methyl benzoate is insoluble in water and will appear as an oily layer. Unreacted benzoic acid will remain dissolved in the ester. Add diethyl ether, bp 37 °C, d 0.7, to dissolve the organic compounds. Separate the organic layer from the water layer.

14.26 (b) (cont)

Step 2: Shake the organic layer (diethyl ether, methyl benzoate, benzoic acid) with saturated aqueous sodium bicarbonate.

$$H_2SO_4 \quad + \quad NaHCO_3 \longrightarrow CO_2\uparrow + H_2O + SO_4^{2-} + 2\,Na^+$$

(traces that   (excess)   soluble in water;
remain in the   insoluble in
methyl benzoate)   diethyl ether

$$\overset{\displaystyle O}{\overset{\|}{\text{PhC}}}\text{OH} \quad + \quad NaHCO_3 \longrightarrow \overset{\displaystyle O}{\overset{\|}{\text{PhC}}}\text{O}^-Na^+ \quad + \quad CO_2\uparrow \quad + \quad H_2O$$

insoluble in water;   soluble in water;
soluble in diethyl ether   insoluble in diethyl ether

The mixture will separate into two layers. The upper layer will be the ether solution containing methyl benzoate, some of the methanol, and small amounts of water. The lower layer will contain sodium sulfate (the salt formed by the reaction of the remaining sulfuric acid with the sodium bicarbonate), sodium benzoate (the salt from the reaction of benzoic acid with sodium bicarbonate), and some methanol.

Step 3: Separate the ether layer from the water layer. The ether and remaining methanol can be removed by distillation, leaving the higher boiling methyl benzoate behind. This is usually done after the ether layer is dried by adding a solid, anhydrous inorganic salt to it.

Concept Map 14.5   Reactions of acids and acid derivatives with alcohols.

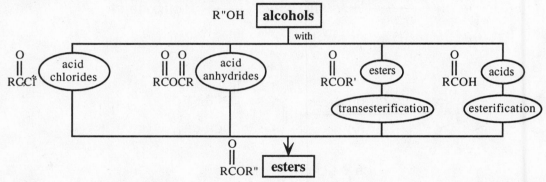

14.27   the acids may be in any order in the triglyceride

This is a transesterification reaction.

14.28   ethyl acetate   methanol

14.28 (cont)

The mechanism shows ethanol and methyl acetate reactions.

methyl acetate

14.29

H—SCoA   :B

14.30

$$HOCH_2C-CHCNHCH_2CH_2CO^- \quad Ca^{2+} \quad ^-OCCH_2CH_2NHCCH-CCH_2OH$$

with CH₃, O, O on left and O, O, CH₃ groups, OH and CH₃ substituents.

- -

Concept Map 14.6   Reactions of acids and acid derivatives with ammonia or amines.

14.31

An alkoxide ion is not a good leaving group in an S_N2 reaction, but does serve as a leaving group in acyl transfer reactions. The bond energy of the carbonyl group is so high (see Section 2.9 in the text) that the reaction forming the carbonyl group occurs even when the leaving group is not one usually recognized as such.

14.32

(a)

(b)

(c)

(d)

14.33   (a) 2,4-dichlorobenzoic acid   (b) 4-bromohexanoic acid
    (c) 2-methylbutanedioic anhydride (2-methylsuccinic anhydride)   (d) 2-methylpentanenitrile
    (e) ethyl (1*R*, 2*R*)-2-ethylcyclohexanecarboxylate   (f) *N*,*N*-dimethylpentanamide
    (g) (*R*)-2-hydroxypentanoic acid   (h) 2-chloropentanoyl chloride   (i) 4-ethylbenzanilide
    (j) ethyl 2-aminobenzoate   (k) (*E*)-4-octenoic acid   (l) (1*R*,2*R*)-cyclobutanedicarboxylic acid

14.34   (a)

(b)

or enantiomer

(c)

14.34   (d)

$$CH_3CH_2\underset{H}{\overset{\displaystyle |}{C}}=\underset{H}{\overset{\displaystyle |}{C}}CH_2COCH_2CH_3 \quad (\text{with } C=O)$$

(e) $CH_3CH_2CH_2CH_2CH_2CH_2C\equiv N$

(f) $CH_3CH_2CH_2CH_2CH_2\overset{\displaystyle O}{\overset{\|}{C}}\underset{\underset{\displaystyle CH_2CH_3}{|}}{N}CH_2CH_3$

(g) $CH_3CH_2O\overset{\displaystyle O}{\overset{\|}{C}}CH_2CH_2\underset{\underset{\displaystyle CH_3}{|}}{\overset{\overset{\displaystyle CH_3}{|}}{C}}\overset{\displaystyle O}{\overset{\|}{C}}OCH_2CH_3$

(h) $O_2N-\text{C}_6\text{H}_4-\overset{\displaystyle O}{\overset{\|}{C}}OCH_3$

(i) $Br-\text{C}_6\text{H}_4-\overset{\displaystyle O}{\overset{\|}{C}}O\overset{\displaystyle O}{\overset{\|}{C}}-\text{C}_6\text{H}_4-Br$

(j) $CH_3O-\text{C}_6\text{H}_4-\overset{\displaystyle O}{\overset{\|}{C}}CCl$

14.35

(a) $CH_3O-\text{C}_6\text{H}_4-NH_2 \xrightarrow[\substack{\text{acetic acid}\\ H_2O \\ 0\text{-}5\ ^\circ C}]{CH_3\overset{\displaystyle O}{\overset{\|}{C}}O\overset{\displaystyle O}{\overset{\|}{C}}CH_3} CH_3O-\text{C}_6\text{H}_4-NH\overset{\displaystyle O}{\overset{\|}{C}}CH_3 + CH_3\overset{\displaystyle O}{\overset{\|}{C}}OH$
A

(b) $Ph\overset{\displaystyle O}{\overset{\|}{C}}OH \xrightarrow[\Delta]{PBr_3} Ph\overset{\displaystyle O}{\overset{\|}{C}}Br$
B

(c)   (glutaric-type diacid) $\xrightarrow[\Delta]{CH_3\overset{O}{\overset{\|}{C}}O\overset{O}{\overset{\|}{C}}CH_3}$ C (cyclic anhydride) $+ CH_3\overset{\displaystyle O}{\overset{\|}{C}}OH$

(d) $Ph\overset{\displaystyle O}{\overset{\|}{C}}Cl \xrightarrow[H_2O]{NaOH} Ph\overset{\displaystyle O}{\overset{\|}{C}}O^- Na^+$
D

(e) $Ph\underset{\underset{\displaystyle CH_2CH_3}{|}}{CH}\overset{\displaystyle O}{\overset{\|}{C}}NH_2 \xrightarrow[\substack{H_2SO_4 \\ \Delta}]{H_2O} Ph\underset{\underset{\displaystyle CH_2CH_3}{|}}{CH}\overset{\displaystyle O}{\overset{\|}{C}}OH$
E

(f)   (2-methylbenzonitrile) $\xrightarrow[\substack{H_2SO_4 \\ \Delta \\ 5\ h}]{H_2O}$ F (2-methylbenzoic acid)

(g) $CH_3CH_2\overset{\displaystyle O}{\overset{\|}{C}}Cl \xrightarrow{NH_3\ (\text{excess})} CH_3CH_2\overset{\displaystyle O}{\overset{\|}{C}}NH_2$
G

(h) $Ph\overset{\displaystyle O}{\overset{\|}{C}}OCH_2CH_3 \xrightarrow{H_2NOH} Ph\overset{\displaystyle O}{\overset{\|}{C}}NHOH + CH_3CH_2OH$
H

14.36   (a) $CH_3\overset{\displaystyle O}{\overset{\|}{C}}OCH_2\underset{\underset{\displaystyle CH_3}{|}}{C}=CHCH_2NH\underset{\underset{\displaystyle CH=CH_2}{|}}{CH}CH_2OH \xrightarrow[\text{base}]{\underset{(\text{excess})}{Ph\overset{\displaystyle O}{\overset{\|}{C}}Cl}} CH_3\overset{\displaystyle O}{\overset{\|}{C}}OCH_2\underset{\underset{\displaystyle CH_3}{|}}{C}=CHCH_2\underset{\underset{\displaystyle PhC=O}{|}}{N}\underset{\underset{\displaystyle CH=CH_2}{|}}{CH}CH_2O\overset{\displaystyle O}{\overset{\|}{C}}Ph$
A

14.36 (b) $CH_3(CH_2)_{10}COCH_2(CH_2)_{10}CH_3$ + CH_3OH $\xrightarrow[\Delta]{H_2SO_4}$ $CH_3(CH_2)_{10}COCH_3$ + $CH_3(CH_2)_{10}CH_2OH$
                                                                                                    B   **C**

(c) $(CH_3)_3COCCH_2CH_2CH$ —⟨ring, I, OCH$_2$CH$_2$CH$_3$, OCH$_3$⟩ $\xrightarrow[\substack{H_2O \\ methanol \\ \Delta}]{KOH}$

with OH substituent

$K^+\ {}^-OCCH_2CH_2CH$ —⟨ring, I, OCH$_2$CH$_2$CH$_3$, OCH$_3$⟩ + $(CH_3)_3COH$
                         OH
                         D   **E**

(d) $HOC(CH_2)_4COH$ $\xrightarrow[\text{(excess)}]{SOCl_2}$ $ClC(CH_2)_4CCl$ $\xrightarrow[\substack{CH_3 \\ PhNCH_3}]{\substack{CH_3COH\ \text{(excess)}}}$ $CH_3CO—C(CH_2)_4C—OCCH_3$

F

G

(e) ⟨cyclohexene ring⟩—CH (=O) $\xrightarrow[H_2O]{Ag_2O}$ ⟨cyclohexene ring⟩—CO^-Ag^+ (=O) $\xrightarrow{H_3O^+}$ ⟨cyclohexene ring⟩—COH (=O)
                                                                 H   **I**

(f) ⟨ring with N—H, CH$_2$OH, CH$_2$Ph⟩ $\xrightarrow[\substack{NaHCO_3 \\ dichloromethane}]{\substack{PhCCl \\ (1\ equivalent)}}$ ⟨ring with N—CPh(=O), CH$_2$OH, CH$_2$Ph⟩ + ⟨ring with N—H, CH$_2$OCPh(=O), CH$_2$Ph⟩

J   **K**
major product   minor product

Nitrogen is more nucleophilic than oxygen, so the major product comes from acylation at the nitrogen atom.

(g) $CCl_3CH_2CH_2CH_2CH_2OH$ $\xrightarrow[\substack{H_2O \\ \Delta}]{KMnO_4}$ $CCl_3CH_2CH_2CH_2CO^-K^+$ $\xrightarrow{H_3O^+}$ $CCl_3CH_2CH_2CH_2COH$
                                                                        L   **M**

14.37 (a) ⟨furan⟩—Li $\xrightarrow{\substack{\text{epoxide with } CH_3, H}}$ ⟨furan⟩—$CH_2CHO^-Li^+$ $\xrightarrow{CH_3COCCH_3}$ ⟨furan⟩—$CH_2CHOCCH_3$
                                                         CH$_3$ CH$_3$
                                                   A   **B**
                                          nucleophilic attack at the
                                          less hindered carbon atom

14.37 (b)

$$CH_3CH(CH_2)_{10}CH_2OH \xrightarrow[\substack{(CH_3CH_2)_3N \\ \text{dichloromethane}}]{\overset{O}{\underset{O}{\overset{\|}{\underset{\|}{CH_3SCl}}}}} CH_3CH(CH_2)_{10}CH_2OSCH_3 \xrightarrow[\substack{\text{tetrahydrofuran} \\ \text{dimethyl sulfoxide}}]{K\,^{14}CN}$$

(with CH$_3$ branches shown on the left-hand carbons)

C

$$CH_3CH(CH_2)_{10}CH_2{}^{14}CN \xrightarrow[\substack{\text{ethanol} \\ \Delta}]{KOH,\ H_2O} CH_3CH(CH_2)_{10}CH_2{}^{14}CO^-\,K^+ \xrightarrow{H_3O^+} CH_3CH(CH_2)_{10}CH_2{}^{14}COH$$

D   E   F

(c)

(A double bond conjugated with a carbonyl
group is favored. See Section 17.5)

(d)

more nucleophilic site

K

(e)

L

(f)

$$CH_3C{=}CHCH_2Cl \xrightarrow[\text{dimethylformamide}]{NaCN} CH_3C{=}CHCH_2CN \xrightarrow[\substack{H_2O \\ \text{methanol} \\ \Delta}]{NaOH}$$

(with CH$_3$ on the terminal carbon)

M

$$CH_3C{=}CHCH_2CO^-\,Na^+ \xrightarrow{H_3O^+} CH_3C{=}CHCH_2COH$$

N   O

14.38

$$\underset{\text{PhCCF}_3}{\overset{\overset{\text{O}}{\|}}{}} \xrightarrow[\text{dimethoxyethane}]{\text{NaCN}} \underset{\underset{\text{CF}_3}{\overset{\text{O}^-\text{Na}^+}{\underset{|}{\text{PhCCN}}}}}{\overset{|}{}} \xrightarrow{(\text{CH}_3)_2\text{SO}_4} \underset{\underset{\text{CF}_3}{\overset{\text{OCH}_3}{\underset{|}{\text{PhCCN}}}}}{\overset{|}{}} \xrightarrow[\Delta]{\text{H}_3\text{O}^+} \underset{\underset{\text{CF}_3 \ \text{O}}{\overset{\text{OCH}_3}{\underset{|}{\text{PhC——COH}}}}}{\overset{|}{}}$$

A   B   C

14.39   HOCH$_2$C≡CH $\xrightarrow[\text{TsOH}]{}$ THPOCH$_2$C≡CH $\xrightarrow{\text{CH}_3\text{CH}_2\text{CH}_2\text{CH}_2\text{Li}}$ THPOCH$_2$C≡C$^-$Li$^+$

A   B

BrCH$_2$CH$_2$CH$_2$Cl $\longrightarrow$ THPOCH$_2$C≡CCH$_2$CH$_2$CH$_2$Cl $\xrightarrow[\text{dimethyl}]{\text{NaCN}}$ THPOCH$_2$C≡CCH$_2$CH$_2$CH$_2$CN $\xrightarrow[\text{ethanol}]{\text{NaOH, H}_2\text{O}}$

C   sulfoxide   D   Δ

(Bromide ion is a better leaving
group than choride ion.)

$\xrightarrow[\substack{0\,°C \\ 5\ \text{min}}]{\text{H}_3\text{O}^+}$ THPOCH$_2$C≡CCH$_2$CH$_2$CH$_2$C̈OH $\xrightarrow[\text{dimethyl-}]{\text{K}_2\text{CO}_3}$ THPOCH$_2$C≡CCH$_2$CH$_2$CH$_2$C̈O$^-$ K$^+$ $\xrightarrow{\text{CH}_3\text{I}}$

E   formamide   F

(The tetrahydropyranyl group is not
hydrolyzed under these conditions.)

THPOCH$_2$C≡CCH$_2$CH$_2$CH$_2$C̈OCH$_3$ $\xrightarrow[\substack{\text{PhSOH} \\ 3\ \text{h}}]{\text{CH}_3\text{OH}}$ HOCH$_2$C≡CCH$_2$CH$_2$CH$_2$C̈OCH$_3$ $\xrightarrow[\substack{\text{Pd/CaCO}_3 \\ \text{quinoline}}]{\text{H}_2}$

G   H

+

(tetrahydropyranyl ring with OCH$_3$)

$$\underset{\underset{\text{H} \quad \text{H}}{}}{\underset{\text{C=C}}{\overset{\text{HOCH}_2 \qquad \text{CH}_2\text{CH}_2\text{CH}_2\text{C̈OCH}_3}{}}} \xrightarrow[\substack{\text{pyridine} \\ \text{tetrahydro-} \\ \text{furan}}]{\text{CH}_3\text{C̈OC̈CH}_3} \underset{\underset{\text{H} \quad \text{H}}{\underset{\underset{\text{C}_{10}\text{H}_{16}\text{O}_4}{\text{J}}}{}}}{\underset{\text{C=C}}{\overset{\text{CH}_3\text{C̈OCH}_2 \qquad \text{CH}_2\text{CH}_2\text{CH}_2\text{C̈OCH}_3}{}}}$$

I

The infrared spectrum of Compound H shows the presence of an alcohol (3450 cm^{-1} for the O—H stretch) and an ester (1720 cm^{-1} for the C=O stretch). Analysis of the proton magnetic resonance spectrum of Compound H is shown below:

δ 1.6-2.0   (2H, m, —CH$_2$C$\underline{\text{H}}_2$—)

δ 2.2-2.6   (5H, m, —(≡CC$\underline{\text{H}}_2$CH$_2$C$\underline{\text{H}}_2$C=O and —O$\underline{\text{H}}$)

δ 3.68   (3H, s, —OC$\underline{\text{H}}_3$)

δ 4.2-4.3   (2H, m, —OC$\underline{\text{H}}_2$C≡)

Compound H is methyl 7-hydroxy-5-heptynoate

14.40 (a)

$$\underset{\text{Bu}_3\text{P:}}{\overset{\overset{:\ddot{\text{O}}:}{\|}}{\text{CH}_3\text{C—}\ddot{\text{O}}\text{—CCH}_3}} \longrightarrow \underset{\text{Bu}_3\text{P}^+}{\overset{:\ddot{\text{O}}:^-}{\text{CH}_3\text{C═}\ddot{\text{O}}\text{—CCH}_3}} \longrightarrow \underset{\text{new acyl transfer agent}}{\overset{:\text{O}:}{\text{CH}_3\text{C—PBu}_3}} \quad \overset{:\text{O}:}{:\ddot{\text{O}}\text{—CCH}_3}$$

The new acyl transfer agent is more reactive than acetic anhydride because it is less stabilized by resonance.

14.40 (a) (cont)

unfavorable

(b)

14.41   (a)

A

(b)

B

C

diethyl ether
(a source of hydride
ion, H:⁻, that reacts
with oxiranes as
a nucleophile)

racemic mixture
D

or

dichloromethane
E

14.42   (a)

A

14.42 (a) (cont)

$$\xrightarrow[\substack{H_2O \\ methanol}]{0.1\ M\ NaOH}$$

B (contains no nitrogen) + C (contains nitrogen)

B $\xrightarrow[\text{TsOH}]{\text{HOCH}_2\text{CH}_2\text{OH}}$ D $\xrightarrow{\text{several steps}}$ (+)-juvabione

(b)

E

14.43

$$\text{BrCH}_2-\underbrace{\xi}-\text{C}\equiv\text{CCH}_2\text{CH}_2\text{CH}_2\text{CH}_2\text{OTHP} \longleftarrow \text{H}-\underbrace{\xi}-\text{C}\equiv\text{CCH}_2\text{CH}_2\text{CH}_2\text{CH}_2\text{OTHP}$$

bond to be formed　　　　　　　　　　　　bond to be broken

We need to form a C—C bond; therefore we need an organometallic reagent and a carbonyl compound.

$$\text{BrCH}_2\text{C}\equiv\text{CCH}_2\text{CH}_2\text{CH}_2\text{CH}_2\text{OTHP} \xleftarrow{\text{PBr}_3} \text{HOCH}_2\text{C}\equiv\text{CCH}_2\text{CH}_2\text{CH}_2\text{CH}_2\text{OTHP}$$

LiBr or NaBr or KBr

$$\downarrow \substack{\text{TsCl} \\ \text{pyridine}}$$

$$\text{TsOCH}_2\text{C}\equiv\text{CCH}_2\text{CH}_2\text{CH}_2\text{CH}_2\text{OTHP}$$

$$\text{HOCH}_2\text{C}\equiv\text{CCH}_2\text{CH}_2\text{CH}_2\text{CH}_2\text{OTHP} \xleftarrow{\text{H}_3\text{O}^+} \text{Br}^-\text{Mg}^{2+}\ \text{or}\ \text{Na}^+\ \text{or}\ \text{Li}^+\ {}^-\text{OCH}_2\text{C}\equiv\text{CCH}_2\text{CH}_2\text{CH}_2\text{CH}_2\text{OTHP}$$

$$\overset{\text{O}}{\overset{\|}{\text{HCH}}}$$

$$\xleftarrow{} \text{Br}^-\text{Mg}^{2+}\ \text{or}\ \text{Na}^+\ \text{or}\ \text{Li}^+\ {}^-\text{C}\equiv\text{CCH}_2\text{CH}_2\text{CH}_2\text{CH}_2\text{OTHP} \xleftarrow[\substack{\text{NaNH}_2\ \text{or} \\ \text{CH}_3\text{CH}_2\text{MgBr}}]{\text{CH}_3\text{CH}_2\text{CH}_2\text{CH}_2\text{Li or}} \text{HC}\equiv\text{CCH}_2\text{CH}_2\text{CH}_2\text{CH}_2\text{OTHP}$$

14.44

$$\text{CH}_3(\text{CH}_2)_{14}\text{CH}_2\text{O} \quad \text{C} \quad \text{C} \quad \text{OTs} \xrightarrow[\text{(excess)}]{\text{H}_2\text{N}(\text{CH}_2)_4\text{OCH}_2\text{Ph}} \text{CH}_3(\text{CH}_2)_{14}\text{CH}_2\text{O} \quad \text{C} \quad \text{C} \quad \text{NH}(\text{CH}_2)_4\text{OCH}_2\text{Ph}$$

III

14.44 (cont)

14.45

14.45 (cont)

14.46   (a)   CH₃OCCH₂—C(HO)(H)—CH₂COCH₃   → [NH₃, lipase] →   CH₃OCCH₂—C(HO)(H)—CH₂CNH₂

achiral diester

(S)-enantiomer of monomethyl
ester - monoamide of
3-hydroxypentanedioic acid

(b)   (S)-enantiomer   +   (S)-enantiomer (CF₃, Ph, CH₃O, CCl, O)   →   (R, S)-enantiomer
only isomer formed, therefore
one signal for ¹⁹F in NMR

Note that the assignment of configuration at the stereocenter with the trifluoromethyl group changed when
the chlorine on the carbonyl group was replaced with an oxygen. In the acid chloride, the chloroacyl group
has a higher priority than the trifluoromethyl group; the priorities change when the ester is formed.

(S)-monoester - monoamide   +   (R)-monoester - monoamide

pair of diastereomers, therefore two signals for ¹⁹F in NMR

14.47   (a)

(b)

C
major product

D
minor product

diastereomers of each other

The transition state for the approach of BH_4^- to the face of the ring away from the large —OTBDMS substituent is more favored (less hindered) than the other possibility.

14.48   Compound A, $C_9H_{10}O_2$, has five units of unsaturation. When a compound has four or more units of unsaturation, we should look for an aromatic ring, which can be seen in both the proton and ^{13}C magnetic resonance spectra. The infrared spectrum shows the presence of an ester (1743 cm^{-1} for the C=O stretch and 1229 and 1118 cm^{-1} for the C—O stretch).

Analysis of the proton spectrum of Compound A is shown below:

δ 2.2   (3H, s, C$\underline{H}_3$C=O)
δ 5.2   (2H, s, ArC$\underline{H}_2$—O—)
δ 7.4   (5H, s, Ar$\underline{H}$)

The absence of splitting for the aromatic hydrogen atoms tells us that the group bonded to the aromatic ring does not differ significantly from the aryl carbon atoms in electronegativity and in magnetic anisotropy. A tetrahedral carbon atom meets this requirement.

The ^{13}C magnetic resonance spectrum shows two alkyl carbon atoms (δ 20.7 and 66.1). There are three types of aromatic carbon atoms (δ 128.1, 128.4, and 136.2) and one carbonyl carbon atom (δ 170.5). Compound A is benzyl acetate.

Note that the compound cannot be methyl phenylacetate because the band for the methyl singlet in the proton magnetic resonance spectrum of a methyl ester would be at ~δ 3.7.

Supplemental Problems

S14.1   Name the following compounds, including an indication of the stereochemistry where appropriate.

S14.1

(e) Cl—C₆H₄—COOC(=O)—C₆H₄—Cl   (f) C₆H₅—CO—CH₂CH₂CH₃   (g) CH₃CH₂C(=O)CH₂C(=O)OCH₂CH₃

(h) CH₃CHCH₂CHC(=O)OCH₃, with CH₃ on first carbon and Br on third carbon

(i) HOC(=O)CHCH₂CH₂CH₂COOH with =O branch

(j) (CH₃CH₂CH₂CH₂CH₂C)₂O

S14.2   Give structural formulas for all of the reagents, organic intermediates, and products indicated by letters in the following equations.

(a) $CH_3(CH_2)_{10}COOH \xrightarrow[\Delta]{SOCl_2} A$

(b) $CH_3CH_2CH_2CH_2OH + CH_3CH_2CH_2CCl(=O) \longrightarrow B$

(c) $HOOCC\equiv CCOOH \xrightarrow[\substack{H_2SO_4 \\ \Delta}]{CH_3OH\ (excess)} C$

(d) $BrCH_2COOH \xrightarrow[\substack{H_2SO_4 \\ \Delta}]{CH_3CH_2OH} D$

(e) $CH_3(CH_2)_4CHCOOH \xrightarrow[\Delta]{SOCl_2} E \xrightarrow[H_2O]{NH_3} F$ (with CH₂CH₃ substituent)

(f) $N\equiv CCH_2COCH_2CH_3 \xrightarrow[\substack{H_2O \\ 0\,°C}]{NH_3} G + CH_3CH_2OH$

(g) $CH_3(CH_2)_5CCl(=O) \xrightarrow{CH_3(CH_2)_5CO^-Na^+} H$

(h) phthalic-type ring with CH₂COOH and COOH(=O) groups $\xrightarrow[\Delta]{(CH_3C)_2O} I + 2\ CH_3COOH$

(i) steroid with OH group $\xrightarrow[\text{pyridine}]{CH_3COCCH_3\ (O,O)} J$

(j) $CH_3CCHCOCH_2CH_3 \xrightarrow[\substack{base, \\ toluene \\ \Delta}]{K}$ → product (menthyl ester type with CH₃CCHCO–, CH₃, and Ph/CH₃CCH₃, CH₃) $+ CH_3CH_2OH$

S14.3   The following transformation was observed. Propose a mechanism for it.

bicyclic structure with CH₂OCCH₃ group $\xrightarrow[\text{methanol}]{K_2CO_3}$ product with O—CH₂ ring, HO group

(H₃C CH₃, O, C, H₃C CH₃)

S14.4   Dimethyl (2*R*, 3*S*)-2-acetoxy-3-bromobutanedioate is converted into a chiral alcohol on treatment with methanol in the presence of a trace of hydrogen chloride. The chiral alcohol, in turn, reacts with potassium carbonate in acetone to give a chiral oxirane. Provide stereochemically correct structures for the ester, alcohol, and oxirane, and show how the transformations described occur.

S14.5   Compounds labeled with radioactive isotopes are needed for the medical imaging technique known as positron emission tomography (PET scanning). Such compounds have been synthesized to visualize the areas of the brain where cocaine (see section 23.8A in the text) is localized. A cocaine analog labeled with radioactive iodine on the aromatic ring was synthesized in the following way. Give structural formulas for compounds A and B.

S14.6   The following conversion was carried out. Work out the conditions for this transformation that requires several steps. There is more than one way to solve this problem.

15

Carboxylic Acids and Their Derivatives II. Synthetic Transformations and Compounds of Biological Interest

15.1

15.2

3-ethyl-3-pentanol-3-^{14}C

15.3 PhBr $\xrightarrow[\text{diethyl ether}]{\text{Mg}}$ PhMgBr $\xrightarrow{\overset{\text{O}}{\overset{\|}{\text{PhCPh}}}}$ Ph$_3$CO$^-$ Mg^{2+} Br$^-$ $\xrightarrow{\text{H}_3\text{O}^+}$ Ph$_3$COH

15.4

$$\text{PhCOH} + \text{SOCl}_2 \xrightarrow{\Delta} \text{PhCCl} + \text{SO}_2\uparrow + \text{HCl}\uparrow$$

$$\text{PhCCl} + \overset{+}{\text{CH}_3\text{NH}_2\text{OCH}_3}\ \text{Cl}^- + 2\ \text{pyridine} \longrightarrow \text{PhCNOCH}_3 + 2\ \text{pyridinium Cl}^-$$

pyridine or any
other tertiary amine

15.5 (a)

A

B   C

(b)

D

E   F

(c) PhBr $\xrightarrow[\text{diethyl ether}]{\text{Mg}}$ PhMgBr $\xrightarrow{\text{CH}_3\text{COCH}_2\text{CH}_3}$

G   H   I

Concept Map 15.1   (see p. 355)

15.6

15.6 (cont)

donation of other hydride ions by aluminum hydride reagent

15.7 (a)

(b)

(c) $CH_3CH=CHCH_2CH_2COCH_3$ $\xrightarrow[\text{diethyl ether}]{LiAlH_4}$ $\xrightarrow{H_3O^+}$ $CH_3CH=CHCH_2CH_2CH_2OH + CH_3OH$

(d)

15.8

15.8 (cont)

Compound A + CH$_3$CH$_2$OH, with pyridinium chlorochromate (C$_5$H$_5$NH$^+$ CrO$_3$Cl$^-$) in dichloromethane, gives B.

Concept Map 15.1   Reactions of organometallic reagents with acids and acid derivatives.

15.9 (1)

$$\text{cyclohexanol} \xrightarrow[\text{pyridine}]{PBr_3} \text{cyclohexyl bromide} \xrightarrow{NaCN}$$

$$\text{cyclohexyl-CN} \xrightarrow[\substack{\text{hexane}\\-70\ °C}]{(CH_3CHCH_2)_2AlH_2\ (1\ eq)} \xrightarrow{H_3O^+} \text{cyclohexyl-CHO}$$

with CH$_3$ substituent on the aluminum reagent.

15.9   (2)

Concept Map 15.2   Reduction of acids and acid derivatives.

15.10   (a) $CH_3CH_2OCH_2(CH_2)_5COCH_2CH_3$ $\xrightarrow[\substack{\text{hexane} \\ -70\,°C}]{\substack{CH_3 \\ (CH_3CHCH_2)_2AlH\ (1\ eq)}}$ $\xrightarrow{H_2O}$

$CH_3CH_2OCH_2(CH_2)_5CH$ + CH_3CH_2OH

15.10 (b)

$$PhCOH \xrightarrow[\substack{\text{benzene} \\ 45\,°C,\ 8\ h}]{\underset{CH_3}{(CH_3CHCH_2)_2AlH\ (3\ eq)}} \xrightarrow{CH_3OH,\ H_2O} PhCH_2OH$$

(one equivalent of the hydride is used
up in deprotonating the carboxylic acid)

(c)

$$\xrightarrow[\substack{\text{benzene} \\ 25\,°C}]{\underset{CH_3}{(CH_3CHCH_2)_2AlH\ (1\ eq)}} \xrightarrow{H_3O^+}$$

(d)

$$\xrightarrow[\text{tetrahydrofuran}]{\underset{CH_3}{(CH_3CHCH_2)_2AlH\ (excess)}} \xrightarrow{H_3O^+} \quad + \quad CH_3\overset{+}{N}H_2OCH_3$$

15.11 (a)

$$CH_3CHCHCH_2CH_2OCCH_3 \xleftarrow[\text{pyridine}]{\overset{O}{CH_3CCl}\ (excess)} CH_3CHCHCH_2CH_2OH \xleftarrow[\substack{\text{diethyl} \\ \text{ether}}]{H_3O^+\ \ LiAlH_4}$$

$$CH_3CHCHCH_2COCH_2CH_3 \xleftarrow[Pt]{H_2} CH_3C{=}CCH_2COCH_2CH_3$$

(b)

$$\xleftarrow[\substack{H_2O \\ \text{furan}}]{H_2O_2,\ NaOH \quad BH_3 \atop \text{tetrahydro-}} \qquad \xleftarrow[\substack{TsOH}]{CH_3CH_2OH} \qquad \xrightarrow[\substack{H_2O \\ \Delta}]{NaOH,\ CH_3CH_2OH}$$

$$\left(\quad + \quad CH_3\overset{O}{C}CH_2CH_3 \quad \right)$$

(c)

$$\xleftarrow[\text{acetone}]{NaI} \qquad \xleftarrow[\text{pyridine}]{TsCl}$$

$$\xleftarrow[\ ]{H_2O \quad LiAlH_4} \qquad \xleftarrow[TsOH]{}$$

15.12 (a) $\xrightarrow[\substack{H_2O \\ \Delta}]{NaOH}$ 2 HOCH$_2$CO$^-$ Na$^+$

(b) $CH_3\overset{O}{\underset{}{C}}CH_2CH_2CH_2COH$ $\xrightarrow[H_2O]{NaBH_4}$ $CH_3\underset{OH}{CH}CH_2CH_2CH_2CO^-$ Na$^+$ $\xrightarrow{H_3O^+}$

(c) $\xrightarrow[\substack{H_2O \\ \Delta}]{NaOH}$ $CH_3\overset{CH_3}{\underset{OH}{C}}CH_2CH_2CO^-Na^+$ (d) $\xrightarrow[H_2SO_4]{CrO_3}$

15.13 $\xrightarrow{CH_3OH}$ $\underset{A}{HOCH_2CH_2CH_2CH_2CH_2\overset{O}{\underset{}{C}}OCH_3}$ $\xrightarrow[\text{dichloromethane}]{}$ $\underset{B}{H\overset{O}{\underset{}{C}}CH_2CH_2CH_2CH_2\overset{O}{\underset{}{C}}OCH_3}$

15.14 $CH_3(CH_2)_4C\equiv CCH_2C\equiv C(CH_2)_7\overset{O}{\underset{}{C}}OH$ $\xrightarrow[\substack{Pd/BaSO_4 \\ quinoline}]{H_2}$

(9Z, 12Z)-9,12-octadecadienoic acid
(linoleic acid)

15.15 Compounds b, c, e, and f are surfactants.

15.16 (a) $\xrightarrow[\text{diethyl ether}]{LiAlH_4 \quad H_2O}$ + CH$_3$CH$_2$OH

(b) $\xrightarrow[\substack{Na_2CO_3 \\ H_2O \\ \Delta}]{TsCl}$ $\xrightarrow{H_3O^+}$

(c) $Ph\overset{O}{\underset{}{C}}\underset{OH}{CH}Ph$ $\xrightarrow{CH_3\overset{O}{\underset{}{C}}Cl}$ $Ph\overset{O}{\underset{}{C}}\underset{\underset{O}{O\overset{}{C}CH_3}}{CH}Ph$

E

15.16 (d)

Note: The cyclic acetal on the aromatic ring is stable and does not open during the protonation of the carboxylate anion.

(e)

(f)

15.17 (a)

(b)

(c)

(d)

15.17 (d) (cont) $\overset{\oplus}{\underset{H}{N}}$ is an acid with pK_a 5.2, close enough to the pK_a of the carboxylic acid (p$K_a \sim$ 4.8) to maintain

an equilibrium concentration of the acid. The carboxylic acid then forms the lactone under conditions in which water is removed from the reaction mixture.

(e)

(f)

15.18

(a) $CH_2{=}CHCH{=}CHCOH$ (with O double bond) $\xrightarrow[\text{diethyl ether}]{LiAlH_4}$ $\xrightarrow{H_2O}$

(b) $CH_3CH_2CH_2CH_2\overset{O}{\overset{\|}{C}}OCH_2CH_3$ $\xrightarrow[\text{diethyl ether}]{2\ CH_3CH_2MgBr}$ $CH_3CH_2CH_2CH_2\underset{\underset{O^-Mg^{2+}Br^-}{|}}{\overset{\overset{CH_2CH_3}{|}}{C}}CH_2CH_3$ $\xrightarrow[H_2O]{NH_4Cl}$ $CH_3CH_2CH_2CH_2\underset{\underset{OH}{|}}{\overset{\overset{CH_2CH_3}{|}}{C}}CH_2CH_3$

C   D

(c) $CH_3CH_2\overset{O}{\overset{\|}{C}}NHCH_2CH_3$ $\xrightarrow[\substack{\text{diethyl}\\\text{ether}}]{LiAlH_4}$ $\xrightarrow{H_2O}$ $CH_3CH_2CH_2NHCH_2CH_3$

E

(d) $CH_3CH{=}CHCH_2C{\equiv}CCH_2CH_2COH$ (with O double bond) $\xrightarrow[\substack{NH_3\ (liq)\\ethanol}]{Li}$ $\xrightarrow{H_3O^+}$

F

(e)

$\xrightarrow[\substack{\text{diethyl}\\\text{ether}}]{LiAlH_4}$ $\xrightarrow{H_3O^+}$

15.18 (e) (cont)

$$CH_3CH=CHCH_2 \quad \overset{H}{\underset{CH_2CH_2CH_2OH}{C=C}} \quad \xrightarrow[\text{dichloromethane}]{\overset{\oplus}{\underset{H}{N}}\ CrO_3Cl^-} \quad CH_3CH=CHCH_2 \quad \overset{H}{\underset{CH_2CH_2CH}{C=C}}\overset{O}{\parallel}$$

G

H

(f) $CH_3CH_2NH\overset{O}{\overset{\parallel}{C}}CH_2Ph \xrightarrow[\substack{H_2O \\ \Delta}]{NaOH} CH_3CH_2NH_2 + PhCH_2\overset{O}{\overset{\parallel}{C}}O^-\ Na^+$

I

J

(g) $CH_3O\overset{O}{\overset{\parallel}{C}}(CH_2)_3\overset{O}{\overset{\parallel}{C}}N\underset{CH_3}{\overset{|}{O}}CH_3 \xrightarrow[\text{tetrahydrofuran}]{\substack{PhMgBr \\ (6\ equivalents)}} \xrightarrow{H_3O^+} Ph_2\underset{OH}{\overset{|}{C}}(CH_2)_3\overset{O}{\overset{\parallel}{C}}Ph + CH_3\overset{+}{N}H_2OCH_3 + CH_3OH$

K   L   M

15.19

$$\underset{O=C{-}Cl}{\overset{CH_3 \quad CH_3}{[bicyclic]}} \xrightarrow[\text{diethyl ether}]{CH_3NH_2\ (2\ molar\ equiv)} \underset{O=C{-}NHCH_3}{\overset{CH_3 \quad CH_3}{[bicyclic]}} \xrightarrow[\substack{\text{diethyl} \\ \text{ether}}]{LiAlH_4 \quad H_2O} \underset{CH_2NHCH_3}{\overset{CH_3 \quad CH_3}{[bicyclic]}}$$

15.20

(a) $\underset{H}{\overset{CH_3}{C}}=\underset{CH_2CH_2Br}{\overset{H}{C}} \xleftarrow[\text{pyridine}]{PBr_3} \underset{H}{\overset{CH_3}{C}}=\underset{CH_2CH_2OH}{\overset{H}{C}} \xleftarrow{\overset{O}{\overset{\parallel}{HCH}}\ H_3O^+} \underset{H}{\overset{CH_3}{C}}=\underset{CH_2Li}{\overset{H}{C}} \xleftarrow[\substack{\text{diethyl} \\ \text{ether}}]{Li} \underset{H}{\overset{CH_3}{C}}=\underset{CH_2Cl}{\overset{H}{C}}$

(b) $\underset{H}{\overset{CH_3(CH_2)_3}{C}}=\underset{\overset{CH}{\overset{\parallel}{O}}}{\overset{H}{C}} \xleftarrow[\substack{\text{hexane} \\ -70\ ^\circ C}]{\overset{CH_3}{\overset{|}{(CH_3CHCH_2)_2AlH}}\ H_2O} \underset{H}{\overset{CH_3(CH_2)_3}{C}}=\underset{\overset{COCH_2CH_3}{\overset{\parallel}{O}}}{\overset{H}{C}}$

(c) $\underset{\underset{O}{\overset{|}{OCCH_3}}}{\overset{CH_3}{CH}}CHCH_2CH_2CH_2\overset{O}{\overset{\parallel}{CH}} \xleftarrow[\substack{\text{cold} \\ \text{short time}}]{H_3O^+} \underset{\underset{O}{\overset{|}{OCCH_3}}}{CH_3CH}CH_2CH_2CH_2\underset{OCH_3}{\overset{|}{CH}} \xleftarrow[\text{pyridine}]{(CH_3C)_2O} \underset{OH}{\overset{|}{CH_3CH}}CH_2CH_2CH_2\underset{OCH_3}{\overset{|}{CH}}$

(d) $CH_3(CH_2)_7\underset{OH}{\overset{|}{CH}}C\equiv C\overset{O}{\overset{\parallel}{C}}OCH_2CH_3 \xleftarrow[H_2O]{NH_4Cl} \xleftarrow{CH_3(CH_2)_7\overset{O}{\overset{\parallel}{CH}}} Na^+\ ^-C\equiv C\overset{O}{\overset{\parallel}{C}}OCH_2CH_3 \xleftarrow[NH_3\ (liq)]{NaNH_2} HC\equiv C\overset{O}{\overset{\parallel}{C}}OCH_2CH_3$

15.20

(e)

15.21

(a)

(b)

(c)

(d)

(e)

15.22 First reaction:

$$CH_3(CH_2)_4C \equiv N: \longrightarrow CH_3(CH_2)_4C = \overset{..}{N}{}^- \; Li^+$$

(with phenyllithium, C_6H_5–Li, adding)

Second reaction:

$$CH_3(CH_2)_4C = \overset{..}{N}{}^- \; Li^+ \longrightarrow CH_3(CH_2)_4C = \overset{..}{N}H \longrightarrow CH_3(CH_2)_4\overset{..}{C}-\overset{..}{N}H_2$$

$$CH_3(CH_2)_4\overset{+}{C} \longleftarrow CH_3(CH_2)_4\overset{+}{C}-\overset{+}{N}H_3 \longleftarrow CH_3(CH_2)_4\overset{..}{C}-NH_2$$

$$:NH_3$$

$$CH_3(CH_2)_4\overset{O}{C} \quad (\text{with } H_2\overset{+}{O}H \text{ and phenyl group})$$

15.23

$$CH_3CHC\overset{:O:}{O}CH_2CH_3 \longrightarrow CH_3CHCOCH_2CH_3 \longrightarrow CH_3CHCOCH_2CH_3 \xrightarrow{H_3O^+} CH_3CHCOCH_2CH_3$$

$$: \overset{..}{Br}: \quad :Zn$$

$$ZnBr:$$

$$Zn^{2+} \quad :\overset{..}{Br}:^-$$

Note the similarity of this reaction to reactions with Grignard and organolithium reagents. The organozinc reagent reacts selectively with the carbonyl group of the aldehyde function in the presence of the ester group.

15.24

$$HOCH_2(CH_2)_4COCH_2CH_3 \xrightarrow[\text{dichloromethane}]{\overset{\overset{\displaystyle \bigcirc}{N^+}}{\underset{H}{}} \; CrO_3Cl^-} \underset{A}{HC(CH_2)_4COCH_2CH_3} \xrightarrow{CH_2=CHMgBr}$$

15.24 (cont)

$$\xrightarrow[\text{H}_2\text{O}]{\text{NH}_4\text{Cl}} \quad \underset{\underset{\text{OH}}{|} \quad \text{B}}{\text{CH}_2=\text{CHCH(CH}_2)_4\text{COCH}_2\text{CH}_3} \quad \xrightarrow[\substack{\text{H}_2\text{O}\\\text{ethanol}}]{\text{KOH}} \quad \underset{\underset{\text{OH}}{|} \quad \text{C}}{\text{CH}_2=\text{CHCH(CH}_2)_4\text{CO}^-\text{K}^+} \quad \xrightarrow{\text{H}_3\text{O}^+}$$

$$\underset{\underset{\text{OH}}{|}}{\text{CH}_2=\text{CHCH(CH}_2)_4\text{COH}} \quad \xrightarrow[\text{pyridine}]{(\text{CH}_3\text{C})_2\text{O}} \quad \text{CH}_2=\text{CHCH(CH}_2)_4\text{COH}$$

$$\text{D} \hspace{8cm} \underset{\underset{\text{C}_{10}\text{H}_{16}\text{O}_4}{\text{E O}}}{}$$

The carbonyl group of the aldehyde is less stabilized by resonance than the carbonyl group of the ester and, therefore, is more reactive. (See Section 14.1A.)

15.25

15.26

15.27 (a) $HO(CH_2)_8OH$ $\xrightarrow[\text{H}_2\text{O}]{\text{HBr (48\%) (1 eq)}}$ $Br(CH_2)_8OH$ $\xrightarrow[\substack{\text{H}_2\text{SO}_4 \\ \text{acetone}}]{\text{CrO}_3, \text{H}_2\text{O}}$ $Br(CH_2)_7\overset{\overset{\displaystyle O}{\|}}{C}OH$

$\qquad\qquad\qquad\qquad\qquad\qquad\qquad\qquad$ A $\qquad\qquad\qquad\qquad\qquad\qquad\qquad$ B

(b) $HC\equiv C-\overset{\displaystyle \overset{H}{|}}{C}=\overset{\displaystyle \overset{|}{C}}{\underset{H}{|}}-CH_2OH$ $\xrightarrow[\substack{\text{NH}_3 \text{ (liq)} \\ \text{tetrahydrofuran}}]{\substack{\text{Li}^+\text{NH}_2^- \\ \text{(2 equiv)}}}$ $Li^+{}^-C\equiv C-\overset{\displaystyle \overset{H}{|}}{C}=\overset{\displaystyle \underset{H}{|}}{C}-CH_2O^-\,Li^+$

$\qquad\qquad\qquad\qquad\qquad\qquad\qquad\qquad\qquad\qquad\qquad\qquad\qquad\qquad\qquad\qquad\qquad\qquad\qquad$ C

(c) $Li^+{}^-C\equiv C-\overset{\displaystyle \overset{H}{|}}{C}=\overset{\displaystyle \underset{H}{|}}{C}-CH_2O^-\,Li^+$ $+$ $Br(CH_2)_7\overset{\overset{\displaystyle O}{\|}}{C}O^-\,Li^+$ $\rightarrow$ $Li^+{}^-\overset{\overset{\displaystyle O}{\|}}{O}C(CH_2)_7C\equiv C-\overset{\displaystyle \overset{H}{|}}{C}=\overset{\displaystyle \underset{H}{|}}{C}-CH_2O^-\,Li^+$ $\xrightarrow[\text{cold}]{\text{H}_3\text{O}^+}$

$\qquad$ C $\qquad\qquad\qquad\qquad\qquad\qquad\qquad\qquad$ B $\qquad\qquad\qquad\qquad\qquad\qquad\qquad\qquad$ D

$HOC(CH_2)_7C\equiv C-\overset{\displaystyle \overset{H}{|}}{C}=\overset{\displaystyle \underset{H}{|}}{C}-CH_2OH$ $\xrightarrow[\qquad\qquad\qquad]{\substack{\text{oxidizing agent} \\ \text{similar to}}}$ (pyridinium) CrO_3Cl^-

$\qquad\qquad\qquad$ E

$HOC(CH_2)_7C\equiv C-\overset{\displaystyle \overset{H}{|}}{C}=\overset{\displaystyle \underset{H}{|}}{C}-\overset{\overset{\displaystyle O}{\|}}{C}H$ $\xrightarrow[\substack{\text{diethyl ether} \\ \text{tetrahydrofuran}}]{\substack{\text{CH}_3(\text{CH}_2)_3\text{CH}_2\text{MgBr} \\ \text{(2 equivalents)}}}$ $\xrightarrow[\text{H}_2\text{O}]{\text{NH}_4\text{Cl}}$ $HOC(CH_2)_7C\equiv C-\overset{\displaystyle \overset{H}{|}}{C}=\overset{\displaystyle \underset{H}{|}}{C}-\underset{OH}{\overset{|}{C}}HCH_2(CH_2)_3CH_3$

$\qquad$ F $\qquad$ G

(d) $HOC(CH_2)_7C\equiv C-\overset{\displaystyle \overset{H}{|}}{C}=\overset{\displaystyle \underset{H}{|}}{C}-\underset{OH}{\overset{|}{C}}HCH_2(CH_2)_3CH_3$ $\xrightarrow[\substack{\text{Pd/BaSO}_4 \\ \text{quinoline} \\ \text{ethanol}}]{\text{H}_2}$ $H-\overset{\overset{H}{|}}{C}=\overset{\overset{H}{|}}{\underset{(CH_2)_7COH}{C}}... \overset{\overset{H}{|}}{C}=\overset{\overset{\underset{H}{|}}{|}}{C}-\underset{OH}{\overset{|}{C}}HCH_2(CH_2)_3CH_3$

$\qquad$ G $\qquad$ coriolic acid

15.28

15.29

15.30 $O={}^{13}C=O \xrightarrow{?} CH_3{}^{13}CH_2\overset{\overset{\displaystyle O}{\parallel}}{C}OH$

15.30 (cont)

$$CH_3{}^{13}CH_2CN \xleftarrow{\text{NaCN}} CH_3{}^{13}CH_2Br \xrightarrow[\text{diethyl ether}]{\text{Mg}} CH_3{}^{13}CH_2MgBr$$

$$\downarrow O=C=O$$

$$CH_3{}^{13}CH_2\overset{O}{\overset{\|}{C}}O^- Mg^{2+} Br^-$$

H₂O
H₂SO₄
Δ

$$\xrightarrow{H_3O^+}$$

$$CH_3{}^{13}CH_2\overset{O}{\overset{\|}{C}}OH$$

15.31

closes spontaneously
to the five-membered
ring lactone

trans orientation of
large groups preferred

15.32   Let $R\overset{..}{\underset{H}{N}}{-}H$ stand for the amine.

15.33 (a)

(b)

(c)

(d) CH_3CNHCH_2COH $\xrightarrow{SOCl_2}$ CH_3CNHCH_2CCl $\xrightarrow{CH_3CH_2SH}$ $CH_3CNHCH_2CSCH_2CH_3$

                                                          G   H

15.34 The structure shown has the molecular formula $C_{12}H_{20}O_2$ as established by mass spectrometry.

propanal

therefore two double bonds
or one triple bond in A

3644 cm^{-1} suggests an —OH group; 1737 cm^{-1} suggests $C{=}O$ in an aldehyde or ketone;

968 cm^{-1} suggests an $-C{=}C-H$

$C{=}O$ and —OH are compatible with a cyclic hemiacetal in equilibrium with open form.

15.34 (cont)

15.35   Compound C, $C_9H_{10}O_3$, has five units of unsaturation. The infrared spectrum shows the presence of a carboxylic acid (3300-2600 cm^{-1} for the O—H and 1719 cm^{-1} for the C=O stretching frequencies).

Analysis of the proton magnetic spectrum of Compound C is given below:

δ 3.56   (2H, s, —C$\underline{H}_2$—)
δ 3.78   (3H, s, C$\underline{H}_3$—O—)
δ 6.85   (2H, multiplet, Ar$\underline{H}$)
δ 7.18   (2H, multiplet, Ar$\underline{H}$)
δ 11.80   (1H, s, O=CO$\underline{H}$)

The splitting pattern in the aromatic region is typical of para substituted rings.
Compound C is (4-methoxyphenyl)acetic acid. Analysis of the ^{13}C nuclear magnetic spectrum of Compound C is shown below:

δ 114.00, 125.24
130.35, and 158.75

$$CH_3O-\!\!\langle \rangle\!\!-CH_2COH$$

δ 55.19 δ 40.14 δ 178.50

15.36   Compound D, $C_5H_8O_2$, has 2 units of unsaturation. The infrared spectrum shows the presence of an alkene (1635 cm^{-1} for the C=C stretching frequency and 989 cm^{-1} for a C=C—H bending frequency), and an ester (1731 cm^{-1} for the C=O and 1279, 1207, and 1069 cm^{-1} for the C—O stretching frequencies).

Analysis of the proton magnetic spectrum of Compound D is given below:

δ 1.95   (3H, multiplet, C$\underline{H}_3$C=CH)
δ 3.75   (3H, s, C$\underline{H}_3$O—)
δ 5.55   (1H, multiplet, C=C$\underline{H}$)
δ 6.20   (1H, multiplet, C=C$\underline{H}$)

Compound D is methyl 2-methylpropenoate (methyl methacrylate).
Analysis of the ^{13}C nuclear magnetic spectrum of Compound D is shown below:

δ 18.33

δ 125.33 CH$_3$ δ 51.77

$$CH_2 = CCOCH_3$$

δ 136.28   O δ 167.85

The allylic and vinyl hydrogen atoms are coupled to each other through the double bond.

15.37   Compound E, $C_8H_{14}O_4$, has 2 units of unsaturation. The infrared spectrum shows the presence of an ester (1736 cm^{-1} for the C=O, and 1160 and 1032 cm^{-1} for the C—O stretching frequencies).

The number of hydrogen atoms in the proton magnetic resonance spectrum of Compound E adds up to 7, or half the number of hydrogen atoms in the molecular formula. This points to symmetry in the molecule. This is confirmed by looking at the number of carbons (4) in the ^{13}C nuclear magnetic spectrum.

15.37 (cont)

Analysis of the proton magnetic spectrum of Compound E is given below:

δ 1.26   (6H, t, 2 C$\underline{H}_3$CH$_2$—)

δ 2.62   (4H, s, O=CC$\underline{H}_2$C$\underline{H}_2$C=O)

these hydrogen atoms are chemical shift equivalent and do not couple

δ 4.15   (4H, q, 2 CH$_3$C$\underline{H}_2$O—)

Compound E is diethyl butanedioate (diethyl succinate).

Analysis of the ^{13}C nuclear magnetic spectrum of Compound E is shown below:

15.38 (a) Let RMgBr stand for the Grignard reagent.

(b) ^{13}C nuclear magnetic resonance spectrum:

The other bands must be the CH$_2$ groups. It is not possible to assign them exactly with the information we have.

Proton magnetic resonance spectrum:

All the other protons absorb between d 1.0 – 2.4.

15.38   (c)

Side product at higher temperatures, formed when the Grignard reagent reacts with the carbonyl group that forms in the first part of the reaction [part (a)]

15.39   Compounds F and G show evidence for an ester functional group in the infrared spectra (C=O stretch at 1743 cm^{-1} for F and 1741 cm^{-1} for G and C—O stretch at 1243 and 1031 cm^{-1} for F and 1198 and 1097 cm^{-1} for G).

Analysis of the proton magnetic spectrum of Compound F is shown below:

δ 0.95   (3H, t, C$\underline{H}_3$CH$_2$—)
δ 1.40   (2H, sextet, CH$_3$C$\underline{H}_2$CH$_2$—)
δ 1.65   (2H, quintet, —CH$_2$C$\underline{H}_2$CH$_2$—)
δ 2.05   (3H, s, CH$_3$C=O)
δ 4.10   (2H, t, CH$_3$C$\underline{H}_2$—O—)

Compound F is butyl acetate. Analysis of the ^{13}C nuclear magnetic spectrum of Compound F is shown below:

δ 13.70, 19.19, and 20.95

Analysis of the proton magnetic spectrum of Compound G is shown below:

δ 1.00   [3H, t, C$\underline{H}_3$CH$_2$—]
δ 1.65   [2H, sextet, CH$_3$C$\underline{H}_2$CH$_2$—]
δ 2.30   [2H, t, (C$\underline{H}_2$CH$_2$C=O]
δ 3.70   (3H, s, C$\underline{H}_3$—O—)

Compound G is methyl butanoate (methyl butyrate). Analysis of the ^{13}C nuclear magnetic spectrum of Compound G is shown below:

Supplemental Problems

S15.1   Predict the major organic products of the following reactions.

(a)

S15.1

(b) $\text{(cyclohexyl)}\overset{O}{\overset{\|}{C}}N(OCH_3)(CH_3)$ $\xrightarrow[\text{tetrahydrofuran}]{\text{PhMgBr}}$ D $\xrightarrow{\text{H}_3\text{O}^+}$ E + F

(c) $CH_3CH_2O\overset{O}{\overset{\|}{C}}(CH_2)_4\overset{O}{\overset{\|}{C}}OCH_2CH_3$ $\xrightarrow[\text{diethyl ether}]{\text{LiAlH}_4}\xrightarrow{\text{H}_3\text{O}^+}$ G + H

(d) $CH_3CH_2\overset{O}{\overset{\|}{C}}NHCH_2CH_3$ $\xrightarrow[\text{diethyl ether}]{\text{LiAlH}_4}\xrightarrow{\text{H}_2\text{O}}$ I

(e) (seven-membered lactone) $\xrightarrow[\text{methanol}]{\text{CH}_3\text{O}^-\text{Na}^+}$ J

(f) (six-membered lactone) $\xrightarrow[\text{diethyl ether}]{\substack{\text{CH}_3\text{MgCl} \\ \text{(3 equiv)}}}\xrightarrow[\text{H}_2\text{O}]{\text{NH}_4\text{Cl}}$ K

S15.2   Give structural formulas for the intermediates and products indicated by letters in the following equations.

(a) $CH_3\overset{O}{\overset{\|}{C}}CH_2O\overset{O}{\overset{\|}{C}}H$ + CH_3OH $\xrightarrow[\Delta]{\text{KOH}}$ A + B

(b) $CH_3\overset{CH_3}{\overset{|}{C}}HCH_2\overset{O}{\overset{\|}{C}}O^-\,Na^+$ + $CH_3CH_2CH_2\overset{O}{\overset{\|}{C}}Cl$ → C

(c) $Ph\overset{O}{\overset{\|}{C}}Cl$ + $H_2N(CH_2)_5\overset{O}{\overset{\|}{C}}OH$ $\xrightarrow[\text{H}_2\text{O}]{\text{NaOH}}$ D $\xrightarrow{\text{H}_3\text{O}^+}$ E

(d) (N-methyl amide with 4-methylcyclohexenyl substituent) $\xrightarrow[\text{diethyl ether}]{\text{LiAlH}_4}\xrightarrow{\text{H}_2\text{O}}$ F

(e) (bicyclic ketone-lactam structure with CH₃ groups and N–CH(CH₃)(Ph)) $\xrightarrow[\substack{(CH_3CH_2)_2O\cdot BF_3 \\ \text{chloroform}}]{HSCH_2CH_2CH_2SH}$ G $\xrightarrow[\text{tetrahydrofuran}]{\text{LiAlH}_4}\xrightarrow{\text{H}_2\text{O}}$ H $\xrightarrow[\text{ethanol}]{\text{Raney Ni}}$ I

(f) $Ph\overset{O}{\overset{\|}{C}}N(OCH_3)(CH_3)$ $\xrightarrow[\substack{\text{tetrahydrofuran} \\ 20\,°C}]{PhC\equiv CLi}$ J $\xrightarrow{\text{H}_3\text{O}^+}$ K + L

S15.3   Suggest synthetic routes for the following transformations, showing all reagents and intermediate products.

(a) (spirocyclic lactone) → (cyclohexene with CH₂OH and OH-cyclohexyl)

(b) $CH_3\overset{HO\,\,H}{\overset{|}{\underset{}{C}}}\overset{O}{\overset{\|}{C}}OCH_2CH_3$ → $CH_3\overset{PhCH_2OCH_2O\,\,H}{\overset{|}{\underset{}{C}}}CH_2Br$

(c) (dioxolane-protected cyclopentanone with CH₂O-cyclohexyl and C≡N) → (cyclopentanone with =CH₂ and CNH₂ attached, amide O)

(d) $\underset{CH_3}{\overset{H}{\underset{}{}}}C=C\underset{H}{\overset{CH_2CH_2\overset{O}{\overset{\|}{C}}OCH_2CH_3}{}}$ → $\underset{CH_3}{\overset{H}{\underset{}{}}}C=C\underset{H}{\overset{CH_2CH_2CH_2O\overset{O}{\overset{\|}{C}}CH_3}{}}$

S15.4   The following reaction is observed. Offer an explanation for the selectivity of the reduction.

S15.5   The reactions used in the determination of the structure of musk ambrette (p. 599 in the text) serve as a review of the chemistry of alkenes, alcohols, aldehydes, and acid derivatives. Some of the reactions are given in the form of the incomplete equations below. Complete the equations, giving structures for all compounds indicated by Roman numerals.

(a)   musk ambrette $\xrightarrow[\substack{H_2O \\ \Delta}]{NaOH}$ $\xrightarrow{H_3O^+}$ I

(b)   I $\xrightarrow[\substack{Pt \\ ethanol}]{H_2}$ II $\xrightarrow{(CH_3C)_2O}$ III $(C_{18}H_{34}O_4)$

(c)   II $\xrightarrow[\substack{H_2SO_4 \\ acetic\ acid}]{CrO_3}$ IV $(C_{16}H_{30}O_4)$

(d)   I $\xrightarrow{O_3}$ $\xrightarrow{\substack{reductive \\ work\ up}}$ V + VI

(e)   VI $\xrightarrow[\substack{H_2O}]{KMnO_4}$ $\xrightarrow{H_3O^+}$ VII $(C_9H_{18}O_3)$

(f)   VII $\xrightarrow[\substack{H_2SO_4}]{CrO_3}$ VIII $(C_9H_{16}O_4)$

(g)   V $\xrightarrow[\substack{Na_2CO_3}]{HO\overset{+}{N}H_3\ Cl^-}$ IX $(C_7H_{13}NO_3)$

(h)   IX $\xrightarrow[\Delta]{(CH_3C)_2O}$ X $(C_7H_{11}NO_2)$

(i)   X $\xrightarrow[\substack{H_2O \\ \Delta}]{NaOH}$ $\xrightarrow{H_3O^+}$ heptanedioic acid

S15.6

(a)   Draw a mechanism for the following reaction showing each step and intermediate. You need not be concerned with the fate of the boron-containing products.

(b)   Which of the following describes the organic product of this reaction: achiral, racemic, optically active, or a mixture of diastereomers?

16

Structural Effects in Acidity and Basicity Revisited

16.1

anion of *ortho*-
nitrobenzoic acid

positive charge on the
carbon atom that is adjacent
to the carboxylate group;
stabilization of the anion

anion of *meta*-
nitrobenzoic acid

There is no resonance contributor of *meta*-nitrobenzoic acid in which there is a positive charge adjacent to the carboxylate group.

16.2 (a) Resonance contributors
1. *m*-nitrophenolate anion

The negative charge is stabilized by the inductive effect of the electron-withdrawing nitro group, so *m*-nitrophenol is a stronger acid than phenol.

16.2 (a) 2.   *p*-nitrophenolate anion

resonance contributor
in which the negative
charge is delocalized to
the oxygen atoms of the
nitro group

The negative charge of the *p*-nitrophenolate anion is stabilized not only by the inductive effect but also by a resonance effect. Additional delocalization of charge, beyond what is available in the phenolate anion and in the *m*-nitrophenolate anion, is possible for the *p*-nitrophenolate anion. This extra stabilization of the conjugate base is reflected in the greater acidity of *p*-nitrophenol.

(b)

Picric acid is a sufficiently strong acid to protonate the weak base bicarbonate anion. Although it is a phenol, the effect of the three nitro groups stabilizes the conjugate base of picric acid and thus increases the acidity of the compound so that it is more acidic than a simple carboxylic acid.

16.3   A carboxylic acid can usually be distinguished from a phenol by reaction with sodium bicarbonate, as long as the pK_a of the phenol is greater than that of carbonic acid. For example:

Aqueous sodium bicarbonate dissolves *p*-chlorobenzoic acid with the evolution of carbon dioxide gas. The carboxylic acid will be reprecipitated by strong acid. The phenol should not be soluble in sodium bicarbonate solution but should be soluble in a stronger base such as sodium hydroxide.

16.3 (cont)

insoluble in water   soluble in water   insoluble in water

16.4   (a) $K_{diss} = \dfrac{[R_3N\!:][BR'_3]}{[R_3N^+\!:^-BR'_3]}$

(b) The dissociation constants for the amine-borane complexes become smaller as the number of substituents on the nitrogen atom increases from none for ammonia to two for dimethylamine. When there are three substituents on the nitrogen atom, the dissociation constant is larger than it is for the other two complexes. The dissociation constant measures the strength of the bond between the atoms of the Lewis base, the amine, and the Lewis acid, the borane. The bond strength is influenced by two factors: (1) electronic factors, mainly the availability of the nonbonding electron pair on the nitrogen atom; and (2) steric factors. The values observed for the dissociation constants may be interpreted to mean that alkyl substitution on the nitrogen atom increases the availability of the nonbonding electrons on the nitrogen atom, but that the presence of three substituents on nitrogen leads to steric hindrance that interferes with bonding in the complex between trimethylamine and trimethylborane. The steric factor is more important in this case than in the reaction of the amine with a Brønsted-Lowry acid because trimethylborane is larger than a proton.

16.5   The acidity of a conjugate acid is related to the availability of the nonbonding electron pair on the base. The observed trend for the conjugate acids of the given amines is due to the decreasing availability of the electron pair on the nitrogen. This decreasing availability is caused by the electron-withdrawing ether and cyano substituents which pull electron density away by induction. The inductive effect is greatest when the electron-withdrawing group is closest to the amino group. The cyano group is more electron-withdrawing than the oxygen because resonance within the cyano group puts a partial positive charge on its carbon atom.

16.6

diethyl ether

solution of all three in the ether

10% NaOH in H₂O

H₂O layer   ether layer

16.6 (cont)

16.7   All of the cyanoanilines are weaker bases than aniline itself because the cyano group is an electron-withdrawing group. The effect of the cyano group is greatest when it is ortho, and smallest when it is meta, to the amino group. Resonance effects are important for the ortho- and para-substituted compounds, but only the inductive effect is important in *m*-cyanoaniline.

nonbonding electrons of the amino group are delocalized to the ring and to the cyano group

no resonance delocalization of the nonbonding electrons of the amino group to the cyano group; only the inductive effect

delocalization of the nonbonding electrons of the amino group to the ring and to the cyano group; inductive effect of the cyano group in the para position is weaker than when it is in the ortho position.

16.8

first ionization

16.8 (cont)

The carboxylic acid group on carbon 3 is likely to have the lowest pK_a value since it is closest to the electron withdrawing effect of the hydroxyl group.

16.9

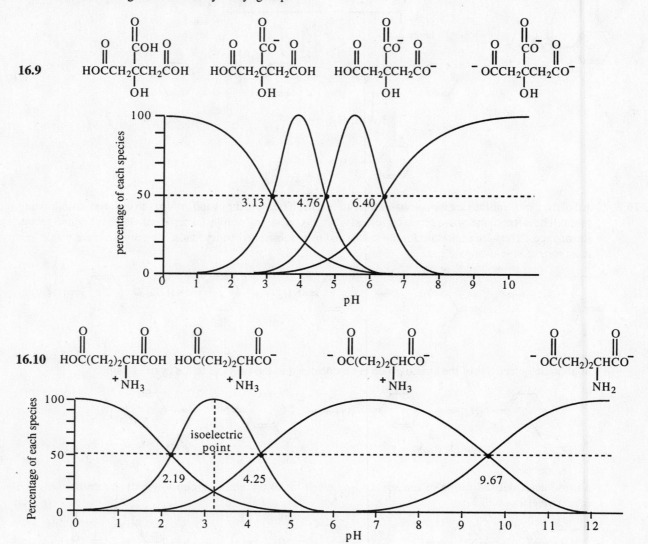

16.10

16.11   Triiodomethane (CHI_3) would be expected to be a weaker acid than trichloromethane ($CHCl_3$), because iodine is less electronegative than chlorine and cannot stabilize the conjugate base of triiodomethane as effectively as chlorine stabilizes the trichloromethyl anion.

The strongly electronegative (3.0) chlorine atoms withdraw electron density from the carbon atom, stabilizing the anion.

The iodine atoms have about the same electronegativity as carbon (2.4 vs. 2.5), and, therefore, do not really have a negative inductive effect. Any stabilization comes from the presence of atoms larger than hydrogen, which help to spread the charge away from the carbon and over the whole ion in a way that the small hydrogen cannot.

16.12   (a) $HO-CH_2-C(=O)-O-H$ $:O-H^-$ $\longrightarrow$ $\left[HO-CH_2-C(=O)-O:^- \longleftrightarrow HO-CH_2-C=O \right]$ $+ H_2O$

The anion produced by removal of the proton of the carboxyl group is stabilized by resonance. The anion that would be produced by removal of the proton on the hydroxyl group would not be stabilized by resonance.

(b) $CH_3CH_2CH-N^+(=O)-O:^-$ with H and $:O-H^-$ $\longrightarrow$ $\left[CH_3CH_2CH-N^+(=O)-O:^- \longleftrightarrow CH_3CH_2CH=N^+-O:^- \right]$ $+ H_2O$

The anion produced by the removal of the α-hydrogen atom is stabilized by resonance.

(c) $HOCH_2CH_2CH_2-S-H$ $:O-H^-$ $\longrightarrow$ $HOCH_2CH_2CH_2-S:^-$ $+$ H_2O

The removal of the proton from the thiol group is easier than the removal of a proton from the hydroxyl group. The larger size of the sulfur atom means that the negative charge is more spread out and, therefore, better stabilized than if it were on an oxygen atom.

(d) $:Br-C(Br)(H)(=O)-CCH_3$ $:O-H^-$ $\longrightarrow$ $\left[:Br-C(Br)(=O)-CCH_3 \longleftrightarrow :Br-C(Br)=C(O:^-)CH_3 \right]$ $+ H_2O$

The hydrogen atom on the α-carbon atom with the bromine atoms is more acidic than the hydrogen on the other α-carbon atom because the electron-withdrawing effect of the bromine atoms, as well as resonance, stabilizes the anion that results from its loss.

Concept Map 16.1   (see p. 381)

16.13   (a)   cyclohexadienone $\rightleftarrows$ phenol   tautomers   (b)   phenolate $\longleftrightarrow$ cyclohexadienone anion   resonance contributors

(c) $CH_2=N^+(O:^-)(O:^-)$ $\longleftrightarrow$ $:CH_2-N^+(=O)(O:^-)$ resonance contributors

(d) $H-C(H)-N^{2+}(O:^-)(O:^-)$ $\rightleftarrows$ $H-C=N^+(O-H)(O:^-)$ tautomers

16.14   (a)   ethyl acetate

$CH_3C(=O)OCH_2CH_3$ (with H and $:B$) $\rightleftarrows$ $\left[:CH_2-C(=O)-OCH_2CH_3 \longleftrightarrow CH_2=C(O:^-)-OCH_2CH_3 \right]$ $\rightleftarrows$ $CH_2=C(O-H)-OCH_2CH_3$

$H-B^+$

ethyl acetate
pK_a 23

16.14   (b) ethyl acetoacetate

an active
methylene group

ethyl acetoacetate
pK_a 11.0

(c) ethyl nitroacetate

an active
methylene group

ethyl nitroacetate
pK_a 5.8

(d) ethyl cyanoacetate

an active
methylene group

ethyl cyanoacetate
pK_a >9
(cannot be determined accurately
because the compound decomposes)

Concept Map 16.1   Enolization.

- -

16.15   (a) (active methylene)   (b) PhCCH$_2$CCH$_3$ active methylene   (c) CH$_3$COCH$_2$CH$_3$ (more electrophilic carbonyl carbon atom)   (d) CH$_3$OCCH$_2$COCH$_3$ (active methylene)

16.16

only one hydrogen on the
active methylene group

16.16 (cont)

enol form

16.17

(R)-1-phenyl-2-
methyl-1-butanone
chiral

planar enolate ion

attack
on top

(R)-2-deuterio-1-phenyl-2-
methyl-1-butanone

attack
on bottom

(S)-2-deuterio-1-phenyl-2-
methyl-1-butanone

16.18

(–)-iridomyrmecin

16.18 (cont)

(+)-isoiridomyrmecin

16.19 (a)

mannose

(b)

enediol intermediate
undergoing deprotonation at
the hydroxyl group at carbon 1
and protonation at carbon 2

mannose

16.20 (a)

glucose with
deuterium at C-2

The carbanion at C-2 reacts with D_2O to give a deuterium atom bonded to carbon at that position in glucose or mannose.

fructose with
deuterium at C-1

The carbanion at C-1 gives fructose with deuterium bonded to C-1.

(b) Fructose can pick up more than one deuterium atom because it can enolize again, losing a hydrogen atom from C-1. This enolate anion can be deuterated again at C-1.

16.20 (b) (cont)

The presence, on average, of more than one deuterium atom in mannose suggests that some of the mannose is coming from fructose. (In the answer to this problem we have ignored the fact that all of the protons on the hydroxyl groups very rapidly exchange with D_2O and become —OD groups. They are converted back in H_2O, but the deuterium atoms bonded to carbon are much slower to exchange. The deuterium atoms on carbon can be located upon analysis so we have been concentrating on them and ignoring the rapid exchange taking place at the oxygen atoms.)

$$ROH + D_2O \rightleftharpoons ROD + HOD$$

$$ROD + H_2O \rightleftharpoons ROH + HOD$$

16.21 (a) $CH_3\overset{O}{\overset{\|}{C}}CH_2\overset{O}{\overset{\|}{C}}CF_3 > CH_3\overset{O}{\overset{\|}{C}}CH_2\overset{O}{\overset{\|}{C}}CH_3$

(b)

(c) $CH_3\overset{O}{\overset{\|}{C}}CH_2\overset{O}{\overset{\|}{C}}OCH_2CH_3 > CH_3\overset{O}{\overset{\|}{C}}CH\overset{O}{\overset{\|}{C}}OCH_2CH_3$
with CH_2CH_3 branch

(d) $O_2NCH_2NO_2 > O_2NCH_2\overset{O}{\overset{\|}{C}}CH_3 > O_2NCH_2\overset{O}{\overset{\|}{C}}OCH_2CH_3$

(e) $HC\overset{O}{\overset{\|}{}}CH_2\overset{O}{\overset{\|}{C}}H > CH_3CH_2O\overset{O}{\overset{\|}{C}}CH_2\overset{O}{\overset{\|}{C}}OCH_2CH_3 > CH_3CH_2O\overset{O}{\overset{\|}{C}}CH\overset{O}{\overset{\|}{C}}OCH_2CH_3$
with CH_2CH_3 branch

16.22   The conjugate base of nitromethane is stabilized by resonance and by the positive charge next to the carbanion site. It is a much stronger acid than methane (pK_a 49), which has no additional stabilization of its conjugate base.

pK_a 10.2

Dinitromethane, $CH_2(NO_2)_2$, has two nitro groups to stabilize the carbanion and is, therefore, a stronger acid (more stable conjugate base) than nitromethane. Trinitromethane, $CH(NO_2)_3$, has three nitro groups to stabilize the carbanion and is an even stronger acid.

16.23   The conjugate bases of both diones are stabilized by resonance. The conjugate base of 1,1,1-trifluoro-2,4-pentanedione is also stabilized by the electron-withdrawing effect of the three fluorine atoms. Stabilization of the conjugate base increases the acidity of the corresponding acid.

16.24

tri(methylsulfonyl)methane
pK_a < 1

The negative charge formed by removal of the proton from the central carbon atom is stabilized by resonance with all three sulfonyl groups. Removal of a proton from the primary carbon atom is stabilized by resonance with only one sulfonyl group.

16.25

(a)

2-(phenylsulfonyl)ethanol

+   2 $CH_3CH_2CH_2CH_3$

16.25

(b)

16.26

forms racemic mixture

16.27 (a) *p*-Toluidine is a slightly stronger base than aniline. This is attributed to the electron-donating effect of the methyl group. 4-Aminobenzophenone is a weaker base than aniline because the carbonyl group is an electron-withdrawing group.

The carbonyl group decreases the availability of the nonbonding electrons on the amino group by the inductive effect and by resonance. In both series of compounds the trends can be rationalized by looking at the availability of the nonbonding electrons on the amino group in the conjugate base. The more available the electrons, the stronger the base, the weaker is the conjugate acid, and the larger the pK_a.

(b) The aromatic amine is less basic than the alkyl amines. The nonbonding electrons on the nitrogen atom are delocalized to the aromatic ring in *p*-toluidine; they are localized on the nitrogen atom in diethylamine and ethylamine.

The lower availability of electrons on the nitrogen atom of the aromatic amine compared to the alkyl amine is used to rationalize its lower basicity and the increased acidity of its conjugate acid. Diethylamine, with two alkyl groups on the nitrogen, is slightly more basic than ethylamine, which has only one alkyl group on the nitrogen.

16.27   (c)   The less positive (or more negative) a pK_a value is, the stronger is the acid, and the weaker is its conjugate base. In aniline, the nonbonding electrons of the nitrogen atom are delocalized to one aromatic ring. The conjugate acid of diphenylamine, with a pK_a of 0.8, is a strong acid, and diphenylamine is thus a weak base. The ability of a base to remove a proton from an acid depends on how available the electron pair of the base is, i.e., how much electron density is available. In diphenylamine, the electron pair on the nitrogen atom is delocalized into both phenyl rings, reducing the amount of electron density on the nitrogen atom even more than in aniline.

16.28   (a)

(b)   Arginine is more basic than lysine because the conjugate acid of arginine is stabilized by resonance. The positive charge is delocalized to three nitrogen atoms in arginine. In lysine it is localized on a single nitrogen atom.

16.29   (a)

$$pK_a \sim -1$$

(b)

Resonance delocalization of charge is possible.

16.29 (b) (cont)

If protonation occurs at the sulfur atom, resonance delocalization of charge is possible only with separation of charge.

No delocalization of charge is possible.

16.30 (a)

(b)

more stable because of resonance

16.31   At pH 4.15, the alkyl amine is fully protonated (pK_a of conjugate acid ~10), and is therefore not a nucleophile, while the aromatic amine (pK_a of conjugate acid ~4.5) is not, so it serves as the nucleophile in the reaction.

nucleophile at pH 4.15

At pH 11.25, the alkyl amine, as well as the aromatic amine, is free to serve as the nucleophile. The alkyl amine is more nucleophilic than the aromatic amine because of the resonance delocalization of the pair of electrons on the nitrogen to the aromatic ring.

nucleophile at pH 11.25

16.32   The left hand compound is more acidic than the right hand compound. Its conjugate base is better stabilized by resonance.

Delocalization of the negative charge onto the nitro group is not possible with the compound on the right.

16.33   (a)   Diisopropylamine has pK_a ~36, therefore only butyllithium, (2), will deprotonate it almost completely.

(b)

16.34

most
acidic
protons

16.35   Cytochrome c will have a net positive charge at pH 6.

16.36

pyridine ring
pK_a of conjugate
acid ~5

tertiary alkyl amine
pK_a of conjugate
acid ~10

At physiological pH, nicotine will be fully protonated at the alkyl amine site but not at the pyridine site.

16.37   (a) $\Delta G_r^\circ = E - A$
(b) $\Delta G_r^\circ < 0$
(c) $K_{eq} > 1$
(d) $\Delta G^\ddagger = B - A$
(e)   Protonation of the enolate ion at the oxygen atom is faster than protonation at carbon.
(f)   D
(g)   Step 2, conversion of the enolate ion to the ketone.

16.38

16.39 The increase in λ_{max} in the ultraviolet spectrum in basic solution compared with the spectrum in acidic solution tells us that Compound C is a phenol. The presence of the hydroxyl group is confirmed by the broad band in the infrared spectrum at 3400 cm^{-1}.

The proton magnetic resonance data are summarized below:

         $\delta\ 5.95$ (1H, s, ArO<u>H</u>)
         $\delta\ 6.80 - 7.20$ (4H, para substitution pattern, Ar<u>H</u>)

The data so far tell us that Compound C is a para-substituted phenol. The ^{13}C nuclear magnetic resonance spectrum has only four bands instead of six in the aromatic region, suggesting that the benzene ring is symmetrically substituted, such as in para substitution.

The mass spectrum has two molecular ions at m/z 128 and 130, with relative intensities of 3:1. These intensities suggest that Compound C contains chlorine. Putting together all the information gives us *p*-chlorophenol for the identity of Compound C.

The ^{13}C nuclear magnetic resonance spectrum is analyzed below:

129.7 ppm
(doublet, each split
by one hydrogen atom)

126.2 ppm
(singlet)

153.6 ppm
(singlet)

116.9 ppm
(doublet, each split
by one hydrogen atom)

p-chlorophenol

16.40 In aqueous sulfuric acid, the anilinium ion, the conjugate acid of aniline will be present in solution. At pH 8, aniline will be present and the nonbonding electrons on the nitrogen are in conjugation with the aromatic ring. Extended conjugation shifts the ultraviolet absorption to longer wavelength. The spectrum on the left is that of aniline and the one on the right is that of its conjugate acid, the anilinium ion.

no interaction of nonbonding
electrons with aromatic ring

interaction of nonbonding
electrons with aromatic ring;
absorption at longer λ_{max}

16.41 Integration of the bands in the proton magnetic resonance spectrum gives a ratio of 4:2:2:3. Disappearance of the broad band at δ 3.60 when Compound D is shaken with D_2O tells us that those hydrogens must be acidic protons attached to an oxygen or a nitrogen atom. The decrease in λ_{max} in the ultraviolet spectra in acid solution compared with basic solution tells us that Compound D is an aryl amine. The two bands in the infrared spectrum at 3480 and 3376 cm^{-1} point to the presence of a primary amine, and the band at 1621 cm^{-1} confirms the presence of the aromatic ring.

16.41 (cont)

The proton magnetic resonance data are summarized below:

δ 1.25	(3H, t, $J = 7$ Hz, —CH$_2$C$\underline{H}_3$)
δ 2.50	(2H, q, $J = 7$ Hz, ArC$\underline{H}_2$CH$_3$)
δ 3.60	(2H, broad s, —N$\underline{H}_2$)
δ 6.60 – 7.20	(4H, multiplet, Ar$\underline{H}$)

The data so far tell us that Compound D is an ethylaniline. The aromatic region in the proton magnetic resonance spectrum does not show the typical splitting pattern for para substitution. Therefore, Compound D must be either ortho- or meta-substituted. The carbon-13 nuclear magnetic resonance spectrum has eight bands, which also tells us that Compound D cannot be *p*-ethylaniline, which should have only six bands in the ^{13}C spectrum because of the symmetry of the molecule. The data, however, do not allow us to distinguish between *o*-ethylaniline and *m*-ethylaniline.

Supplemental Problems

S16.1   Arrange each of the following groups of compounds in order of decreasing acidity.

S16.2   The most acidic protons in the following compound have pK_a 13. Identify those protons, and show how you rationalize their acidity.

S16.3   2,3,3,4,4-Pentafluorocyclobutanone has been found to enolize completely in solvents such as acetonitrile, tetrahydrofuran, or diethyl ether. The keto form also is extremely hygroscopic, meaning that it spontaneously picks up moisture from the air to form a hydrate, which can be isolated as white crystals.

Draw structural formulas for the ketone, the hydrate, and the enol. Why is this ketone so reactive? Why is the enol form more stable than the keto form in the solvents given above?

S16.4

(a)   When Compound A is treated with a catalytic amount of sodium methoxide in methanol, Compound B is formed. This is an equilibrium process, where B is favored for steric reasons. Draw a complete mechanism, using the curved arrow convention, for the conversion of A to B.

(b)   If the reaction shown were carried out with a catalytic amount of sodium ethoxide in ethanol instead of the reagent given above, what would the product be?

(c)   What would be the product of the reaction of A with excess lithium aluminum hydride after work-up to give an uncharged product?

S16.5   The following reactions were carried out in the synthesis of vitamin D_3 derivatives that are deuterated. Provide structural formulas for the products obtained. In these products, all readily exchangeable hydrogen atoms have been substituted by deuterium.

S16.6   Research into compounds that prevent the clotting of blood involve the following reactions. Provide structural formulas for the missing compounds.

S16.7   Phosphorus-oxygen double bonds, $-\overset{|}{\underset{|}{P}}=O$, and sulfur-oxygen double bonds, $\diagdown S = O$, behave like

carbonyl groups (carbon-oxygen double bonds, $\diagdown C = O$) in stabilizing anions on carbons adjacent to them. Chemists

take advantage of this fact in the synthesis of interesting compounds.

(a)   Given this information, complete the following equation and predict whether the equilibrium will lie to the left or to the right by how you draw the equilibrium arrows. The pK_a table will be useful.

(b)   How do chemists rationalize the stability of the conjugate base of the phosphorus compound?

17

Enols and Enolate Anions as Nucleophiles I. Alkylation and Condensation Reactions

Workbook Exercises

The most efficient way for you to understand the subject matter in Chapter 17 is to seek out the appropriate analogies in your earlier work, as previously suggested. There are two fundamental ideas in this chapter that build on concepts from Chapter 16:

1. Carbon atoms connected to carbonyl groups, as well as to other electron-withdrawing groups, can behave as nucleophiles.

The carbon atom α to a carbonyl group can behave as a nucleophile in two ways:

as the uncharged tautomer;
the enol form

as the anionic conjugate base;
the enolate form

2. These carbon nucleophiles undergo the characteristic reactions that you already associate with nucleophiles: substitution, addition to carbonyl groups, and acylation. As before, reviewing these concepts from earlier chapters will benefit your learning.

EXAMPLE

the enolate anion behaves primarily
as a carbon nucleophile

Workbook Exercises (cont)

EXERCISE I.   For each of the following compounds, draw the structure of the enol and two resonance forms for the enolate anion . If there is more than one enol/enolate anion possible, show all of the possibilities.

(a) [structure: 2-methylcyclohexanone]   (b) $PhCCH_2CH_3$ (with O double bond)   (c) $CH_3CH_2COCH_3$ (with O double bond)

(d) [structure: 2,2-dimethylcyclopentanone]   (e) $PhCH_2CH$ (with O double bond)   (f) $CH_3CCH_2CCH_3$ (with two O double bonds)

EXERCISE II.   Use each of the enolate nucleophiles you created in Exercise I in substitution, addition, and acylation reactions with the three electrophiles shown in the example on the previous page ($CH_3CH_2CH_2CH_2I$, PhCHO, and $PhCO_2CH_3$). You have seen the mechanisms for each of these types of reactions in earlier chapters, so you should be able to draw mechanisms for the reactions you write.

— —

17.1   (a) [structure: $CH_3CCHCCH_3$ with CH_3 substituent] $\xrightarrow[H_2O]{Br_2}$ [structure: $CH_3C—C—CCH_3$ with CH_3 and Br substituents]

(b) 3-Methyl-2,4-pentanedione will enolize in water. This reaction is an equilibrium reaction, and after a day, the equilibrium concentration of enol is present. The reaction with bromine is fast because the electrophile reacts at the double bond of the enol until the equilibrium concentration of the enol is used up.

[structure: enol form] $\xrightarrow[fast]{Br_2}$ [structure: brominated diketone]

Once the enol has been used up, the rate of the overall reaction is determined by the rate at which the enol is formed. That is the slow, rate-determining step of this two-step process.

[structure: keto form] $\xrightarrow{slow}$ [structure: enol form] $\xrightarrow[fast]{Br_2}$ [structure: brominated product]

17.2   [mechanism: resonance structures of cyclohexanone enolate reacting with allyl bromide]

17.3   (a) [structure: cyclopentanone] + [structure: furfural] $\xrightarrow[\substack{H_2O \\ diethyl\ ether}]{NaOH}$ [structure: product A]

                                                                                A

17.3 (b)

B

(c)

C

Concept Map 17.1 Reactions of enols and enolates with electrophiles.

E^+ can be D_2O, X_2, RX, RCX, $RCOR'$, $RCOCR$

17.4 (a)

enolate ion   electrophile
(formed in base)

In excess D_2O (solvent) this process will repeat itself until all of the α-hydrogen atoms have been replaced by deuterium.

(b)

enol   electrophile
(formed in neutral
or acidic solution)

17.4   (c) $\overset{\overset{\displaystyle O^-}{|}}{CH_3CH_2C}=CHCH_3$ + Br_2 $\longrightarrow$ $CH_3CH_2\overset{\overset{\displaystyle O}{\|}}{C}\underset{\underset{\displaystyle Br}{|}}{C}HCH_3$

enolate ion   electrophile
(formed in base)

With a second equivalent of bromine, the process will repeat itself. The most acidic proton is the one on the carbon atom bearing the bromine atom.

$\overset{\overset{\displaystyle O^-}{|}}{CH_3CH_2C}=\underset{\underset{\displaystyle Br}{|}}{C}CH_3$ + Br_2 $\longrightarrow$ $CH_3CH_2\overset{\overset{\displaystyle O}{\|}}{C}\overset{\overset{\displaystyle Br}{|}}{\underset{\underset{\displaystyle Br}{|}}{C}}CH_3$

new enolate ion   electrophile

(d)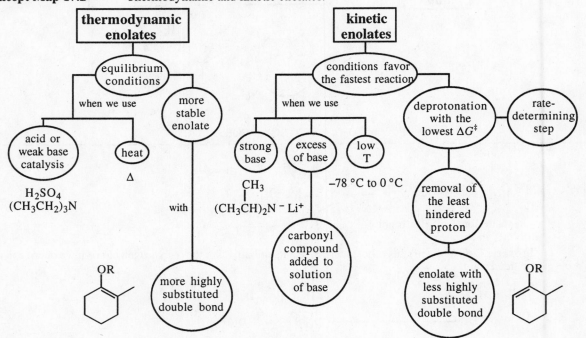

enol form   electrophile
(BF₃, a Lewis acid
replacing the proton)

(e) $\overset{\overset{\displaystyle O^-\,Li^+}{|}}{PhC}=CHCH_3$ +   PhSeCl $\longrightarrow$ $Ph\overset{\overset{\displaystyle O}{\|}}{C}\underset{\underset{\displaystyle SePh}{|}}{C}HCH_3$

enolate ion   electrophile

- -

Concept Map 17.2   Thermodynamic and kinetic enolates.

17.5   (a) $CH_3CH_2\overset{\overset{\displaystyle O}{\|}}{C}CH_3$ $\xrightarrow[\substack{\text{dimethylformamide} \\ \Delta}]{(CH_3)_3SiCl,\ (CH_3CH_2)_3N}$ $CH_3CH=\overset{\overset{\displaystyle OSi(CH_3)_3}{|}}{C}CH_3$

17.5 (b) $CH_3CH_2\overset{\displaystyle O}{\overset{\displaystyle \|}{C}}CH_3$ $\xrightarrow[\text{1,2-dimethoxyethane}]{(CH_3CH)_2N^-Li^+}$ $\xrightarrow{(CH_3)_3SiCl,\ (CH_3CH_2)_3N}$ $CH_3CH_2\overset{\displaystyle OSi(CH_3)_3}{\overset{\displaystyle |}{C}}=CH_2$

17.6 (a) A $\xrightarrow[\substack{-78\ °C \\ A}]{\overset{\displaystyle CH_3}{(CH_3CH)_2N^-Li^+} \\ \text{tetrahydrofuran}}$ B $\xrightarrow[\substack{\text{hexamethylphosphoric} \\ \text{triamide} \\ -78\ °C}]{HC\equiv CCH_2Br}$

(b) C $\xrightarrow[\substack{\text{hexane} \\ \text{diethyl ether} \\ -60\ °C}]{\overset{\displaystyle CH_3}{(CH_3CH)_2N^-Li^+}}$ [ ]

(c) $CH_3CH_2CH_2\overset{\displaystyle O}{\overset{\displaystyle \|}{C}}OCH_3$ $\xrightarrow[\substack{\text{tetrahydrofuran} \\ -78\ °C \\ D}]{\overset{\displaystyle CH_3}{(CH_3CH)_2N^-Li^+}}$ $CH_3CH_2CH=\overset{\displaystyle O^-Li^+}{\overset{\displaystyle |}{C}}OCH_3$ $\xrightarrow[\substack{\text{hexamethyl-} \\ \text{phosphoric triamide} \\ -78\ °C \\ F}]{ClCH_2OCH_3}$ $CH_3CH_2\overset{\displaystyle O}{\underset{\displaystyle CH_2OCH_3}{\overset{\displaystyle |}{C}H}}\overset{\displaystyle \|}{C}OCH_3$

E

Concept Map 17.3   Alkylation reactions.

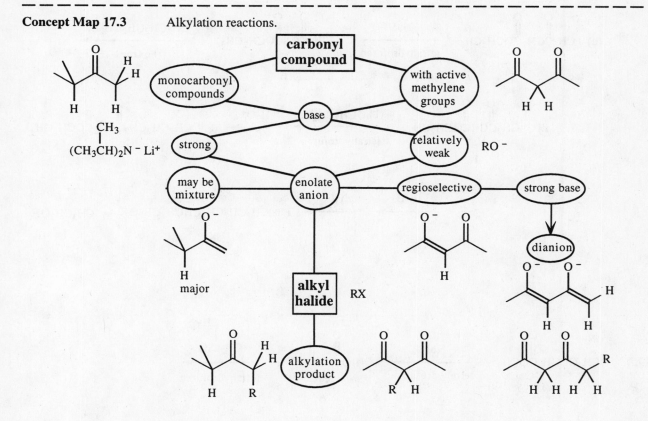

17.7   (a) $CH_2(COCH_2CH_3)_2$ $\xrightarrow[\text{ethanol}]{CH_3CH_2ONa}$ $Na^+ \ ^-CH(COCH_2CH_3)_2$ $\xrightarrow{CH_3CHCH_3 \ (Br)}$ $CH_3CHCH(COCH_2CH_3)_2 \ (CH_3)$
                                                                A   B

(b) $CH_3CH_2CH(COCH_2CH_3)_2$ $\xrightarrow[\substack{\textit{tert}\text{-butyl} \\ \text{alcohol}}]{(CH_3)_3CONa}$ $CH_3CH_2C(COCH_2CH_3)_2 \ Na^+$ $\xrightarrow{BrCH_2CH=CH_2}$
                                                                                C

$CH_2=CHCH_2C(COCH_2CH_3)_2$ with CH_2CH_3
                                                                D

(c) $CH_3CCH_2COCH_2CH_3$ $\xrightarrow[\text{ethanol}]{CH_3CH_2ONa}$ $CH_3CCHCOCH_2CH_3 \ Na^+$ $\xrightarrow{ClCH_2CH_2CH_2Br}$ $CH_3CCHCOCH_2CH_3$ with $CH_2CH_2CH_2Cl$
                                                                E   F
                                                                                (Br⁻ is a better leaving
                                                                                group than Cl⁻)

(d)   (epoxide) $+$ $Na^+ \ ^-CH(COCH_2CH_3)_2$ $\longrightarrow$ $Na^+ \ ^-OCH_2CH_2CH(COCH_2CH_3)_2$
                                                                                G

(e) $CH_3CCH_2COCH_2CH_3$ $\xrightarrow[\text{tetrahydrofuran}]{NaH}$ $CH_3CCHCOCH_2CH_3 \ Na^+$ $\xrightarrow[\text{hexane}]{CH_3CH_2CH_2CH_2Li}$
                                                                                H

$Li^+ \ ^-CH_2CCHCOCH_2CH_3 \ Na^+$ $\xrightarrow[\text{tetrahydrofuran}]{PhOCH_2CH_2Br}$ $\xrightarrow{H_3O^+}$ $PhOCH_2CH_2CH_2CCH_2COCH_2CH_3$
                        I   J

$\xrightarrow{LiAlH_4}$ $\xrightarrow{H_3O^+}$ $PhOCH_2CH_2CH_2CHCH_2CH_2OH \ (OH)$ $+$ CH_3CH_2OH
                                                                K   L

17.8 $CH_3OCCH_2COCH_3$ $\xrightarrow[\text{tetrahydrofuran}]{NaH}$ $CH_3OCCHCOCH_3 \ Na^+$ $\xrightarrow[\text{tetrahydrofuran}]{CH_3CHI \ (CH_3)}$
                                                                A

17.8 (cont)

$$CH_3OCCHCOCH_3 \xrightarrow[\text{tetrahydrofuran}]{LiAlH_4} \xrightarrow{H_2O} HOCH_2CHCH_2OH$$

with substituent CH_3CHCH_3 labeled **B**, and product labeled **C**

(0.3 equivalents) dihydropyran

pyridinium −OTs (a mild acid catalyst)

dichloromethane

$$THPOCH_2CHCH_2OH \xrightarrow[]{CH_3SCH_3, \; ClC—CCl} \xrightarrow{(CH_3CH_2)_3N} THPOCH_2CHCH$$

with CH_3CHCH_3 substituents, labeled **D** and **E**

17.9 **1.**

$$CH_3CHCH_2CH_2Br \xleftarrow{\text{conc HBr}} CH_3CHCH_2CH_2OH \xleftarrow{H_3O^+} \triangle \text{(epoxide)} \xleftarrow{} CH_3CHMgBr \xleftarrow[\substack{\text{diethyl} \\ \text{ether}}]{Mg} CH_3CHBr$$

(each bearing CH_3 group)

2.

barbituric-type ring structures with CH_2CH_3 and $CH_2CH_2CHCH_3$ / CH_3 substituents

$$\xleftarrow{H_3O^+} \quad Na^+ \; {}^-O \cdots \xleftarrow[\text{methanol}]{H_2NCNH_2, \; CH_3ONa}$$

$$CH_3CHCH_2CH_2C(COCH_2CH_3)_2 \quad (\text{with } CH_3, \; CH_2CH_3 \text{ substituents})$$

$$\xleftarrow{CH_3CHCH_2CH_2Br} CH_3CH_2C(COCH_2CH_3)_2 \; K^+ \xleftarrow[\substack{\textit{tert}\text{-butyl} \\ \text{alcohol}}]{(CH_3)_3COK}$$

$$CH_3CH_2CH(COCH_2CH_3)_2 \xleftarrow{CH_3CH_2Br} K^+ \; {}^-CH(COCH_2CH_3)_2 \xleftarrow[\substack{\textit{tert}\text{-butyl} \\ \text{alcohol}}]{(CH_3)_3COK} CH_2(COCH_2CH_3)_2$$

17.10

17.11 **(a)**

$$CH_3CCH_2COCH_2CH_3 \xrightarrow[\text{ethanol}]{CH_3CH_2ONa} CH_3C\overset{-}{C}HCOCH_2CH_3 \; Na^+ \xrightarrow[\Delta]{ClCH_2COCH_2CH_3}$$

labeled **A**

17.11 (a) (cont)

$$CH_3\overset{O}{\overset{\|}{C}}\overset{O}{\overset{\|}{CH}}COCH_2CH_3 \xrightarrow[\Delta]{H_3O^+} CH_3\overset{O}{\overset{\|}{C}}CH_2CH_2\overset{O}{\overset{\|}{C}}OH + CO_2\uparrow + 2\ CH_3CH_2OH$$

with $CH_2\overset{O}{\overset{\|}{C}}OCH_2CH_3$ branch labeled **B**, and **C** on the right product.

(b)

$$PhC\overset{O}{\overset{\|}{C}}CH_2\overset{O}{\overset{\|}{C}}OCH_2CH_3 \xrightarrow[ethanol]{CH_3CH_2ONa} Ph\overset{O}{\overset{\|}{C}}\overset{O}{\overset{\|}{CH}}COCH_2CH_3 \ Na^+ \xrightarrow[\Delta]{BrCH_2C\equiv CH}$$

D

$$PhC\overset{O}{\overset{\|}{C}}\overset{O}{\overset{\|}{CH}}COCH_2CH_3 \xrightarrow[\Delta]{H_3O^+} PhCCH_2CH_2C\equiv CH + CO_2\uparrow + CH_3CH_2OH$$

with $CH_2C\equiv CH$ branch labeled **E**, and **F** on the right product.

(c)

$$CH_2(\overset{O}{\overset{\|}{C}}OCH_2CH_3)_2 \xrightarrow[ethanol]{\overset{CH_3CH_2ONa}{(1\ molar\ equiv)}} Na^+\ ^-CH(\overset{O}{\overset{\|}{C}}OCH_2CH_3)_2 \xrightarrow{BrCH_2CH_2CH_2Cl}$$

G

$$ClCH_2CH_2CH_2CH(\overset{O}{\overset{\|}{C}}OCH_2CH_3)_2 \xrightarrow[ethanol]{\overset{CH_3CH_2ONa}{(1\ molar\ equiv)}} \left[ClCH_2CH_2CH_2\overset{Na^+}{\underset{-}{C}}(\overset{O}{\overset{\|}{C}}OCH_2CH_3)_2 \right] \longrightarrow$$

H

(Br $^-$ is a better leaving group than Cl $^-$)

cyclobutane ring with $\overset{O}{\overset{\|}{C}}OCH_2CH_3$ and $\overset{O}{\overset{\|}{C}}OCH_2CH_3$ substituents, labeled **I** $\xrightarrow[\Delta]{H_3O^+}$ cyclobutane ring with $\overset{O}{\overset{\|}{C}}OH$ and H substituents, labeled **J** $+ CO_2\uparrow + 2\ CH_3CH_2OH$

17.12 (a)

furan-2-carbaldehyde $+ CH_3\overset{O}{\overset{\|}{C}}CH_3 \xrightarrow[H_2O]{NaOH} \xrightarrow{H_3O^+}$ furan-2-yl$-CH=CH\overset{O}{\overset{\|}{C}}CH_3$

(b)

$$Ph\overset{O}{\overset{\|}{C}}H + CH_3\overset{O}{\overset{\|}{C}}CH_3 \xrightarrow[H_2O]{NaOH} \xrightarrow{H_3O^+} PhCH=CH\overset{O}{\overset{\|}{C}}CH=CHPh$$

(2 equiv)   (1 equiv)

(c)

$$Ph\overset{O}{\overset{\|}{C}}H + CH_3\overset{O}{\overset{\|}{C}}CH_2CH_3 \xrightarrow{HCl} PhCH=\overset{O}{\overset{\|}{C}}CCH_3$$

with CH_3 branch below.

(The more stable enol from
2-butanone has the more
highly substituted double bond)

17.12 (d) $\underset{\text{(2 equiv)}}{\text{PhCH}_2\overset{\displaystyle O}{\overset{\|}{\text{CH}}}}$ $\xrightarrow[\text{H}_2\text{O}]{\text{NaOH}}$ $\text{PhC}=\text{CHCH}_2\text{Ph}$ (with $\overset{\displaystyle O}{\overset{\|}{\text{CH}}}$ on the central carbon)

- -

Concept Map 17.4   The aldol condensation.

- -

17.13 (a)

$\text{CH}_3\text{O}-$(4-substituted benzene ring)$-\text{CH}=\text{C}-\text{CH}_3$ with $\overset{\displaystyle O}{\overset{\|}{\text{CH}}}$ $\longleftarrow$ $\text{CH}_3\text{O}-$(benzene ring)$-\overset{\displaystyle O}{\overset{\|}{\text{CH}}}$ + $\text{CH}_3\text{CH}_2\overset{\displaystyle O}{\overset{\|}{\text{CH}}}$

(b) $\text{CH}_3\text{CH}_2\text{CH}_2\text{CH}_2\underset{\displaystyle \text{HO}}{\overset{}{\text{CH}}}-\}-\underset{\displaystyle \text{CH}_2\text{CH}_2\text{CH}_3}{\text{CH}}\overset{\displaystyle O}{\overset{\|}{\text{CH}}}$ $\longleftarrow$ $2\ \text{CH}_3\text{CH}_2\text{CH}_2\text{CH}_2\overset{\displaystyle O}{\overset{\|}{\text{CH}}}$

(c) (cyclohexene ring with Ph)$-\overset{\displaystyle O}{\overset{\|}{\text{C}}}-\underset{\displaystyle \text{CH}_3}{\overset{\displaystyle \text{CH}_3}{\text{CCH}_3}}$ $\longleftarrow$ $\text{PhCCH}_2\text{CH}_2\text{CH}_2\text{CH}_2\text{CH}_2\text{C}-\underset{\displaystyle \text{CH}_3}{\overset{\displaystyle \text{CH}_3}{\text{CCH}_3}}$ (with $\overset{\displaystyle O}{\overset{\|}{}}$ on the two carbonyls)

17.13   (d)

17.14   The aldol condensation product must be reverting to an aldehyde and an enolate ion, which then reacts with the other aldehyde in the reaction mixture.

17.15

1.   How have connectivities changed in going from reactant to product? How many carbon atoms does each contain? What bonds must be broken and formed to transform starting material into product?

Both reactant and product have three carbon atoms. There is an alcohol function on carbon 1 and a ketone function on carbon 2 in the reactant. There is an aldehyde function on carbon 1 and an alcohol function on carbon 2 in the product. Both have a phosphate ester on carbon 3. The bonds to be broken and formed are shown below.

2.   What reagents are present? Are they good acids, bases, nucleophiles, or electrophiles? Is there an ionizing solvent present?

The enzyme, triosephosphate isomerase, can act as an acid and a base.

3.   What is the most likely first step for the reaction: protonation or deprotonation, ionization, attack by a nucleophile, or attack by an electrophile?

Protonation of the carbonyl group of the ester with later deprotonation of the α hydrogen on carbon 1 is the most likely first step.

17.15 (3) (cont)

4.   What are the properties of the species present in the reaction mixture after the first step? What is likely to happen next?

An enediol, which will tautomerize to the product, is formed.

17.16   (a) $HOCCH_2CH_2C-COH$

2-oxopentanedioic acid

(b)   We need to hydrolyze the triester and decarboxylate the resulting triacid.

intermediate triacid;
screened carboxylic acid group is β to screened
carbonyl group, so it is lost during the heating

17.17   (a)

(b)

(c)

17.18   (a)

(b)

(c)

17.19

17.20

This is the only enolate ion possible in this system. It does not form under the first set of reaction conditions because the base, ethoxide ion, is not strong enough to deprotonate that carbon atom (pK_a ~23). When the much stronger base, hydride ion, is used, deprotonation takes place to stabilize the product of the condensation reaction against the reverse reaction.

17.21

(a)

ethyl 1-methyl-2-oxo-
cyclohexanecarboxylate

nucleophilic attack of
ethoxide ion on the
electrophilic carbon
atom of the ketone

reversal of condensation;
formation of enolate anion

17.21 (a) (cont)

protonation of enolate
anion by solvent

(b)

ethyl 3-methyl-2-oxo-
cyclohexanecarboxylate

The product β-ketoesters in Claisen condensations are stabilized by deprotonation to the corresponding enolates. Ethyl 1-methyl-2-oxocyclohexanecarboxylate does not have a hydrogen atom on the carbon atom between the two carbonyl groups, and, therefore, cannot be stabilized this way. It undergoes reversal of the cyclization reaction. The product resulting from the other cyclization reaction, ethyl 3-methyl-2-oxocyclohexanecarboxylate, does have an active hydrogen. Under the conditions for the reaction, it is the thermodynamically more stable product.

17.22 (a)   PhCPh   + $\begin{array}{c}CH_2COCH_2CH_3\\|\\CH_2COCH_2CH_3\end{array}$ $\xrightarrow[\textit{tert}\text{-butyl alcohol}]{(CH_3)_3COK}$ $\begin{array}{c}Ph\\|\\PhC=CCH_2COCH_2CH_3\\|\\COCH_2CH_3\end{array}$ A

17.22   **(b)**

Concept Map 17.5   Acylation reactions of enolates.

17.23

1. What are the connectivities of the two compounds? How many carbon atoms does each contain? Are there any rings? What are the positions of branches and functional groups on the carbon skeletons?

The product has the same number of carbon atoms as the starting material. There are two five-membered rings in the reactant and three in the product. The carbonyl group of the side chain in the starting material has become an alcohol group in the product, and the side chain has been incorporated into the third ring. The new ring in the product is attached at the carbon atom of the carbonyl group in a ring of the starting material.

2. How do the functional groups change in going from starting material to product? Does the starting material have a good leaving group?

The carbonyl group of the side chain in the starting material has become an alcohol in the product. The carbonyl group that was on a ring has disappeared. There is no good leaving group in the starting material.

3. Is it possible to dissect the structures of the starting material and product to see which bonds must be broken and which formed?

bonds broken   bonds formed

The major transformation is the formation of a bond between one of the carbon atoms α to the carbonyl group of the side chain and the carbon atom of the ring carbonyl group.

4. New bonds are created when an electrophile reacts with a nucleophile. Do we recognize any part of the product molecule as coming from a good nucleophile or an electrophilic addition?

An enolate anion from a ketone is a good nucleophile and will react with the electrophilic carbon atom of a carbonyl group.

The enolate from the ketone of the side chain will react with the carbonyl group of the ring ketone in an intramolecular aldol condensation. The product will lose water to form an α,β-unsaturated ketone.

17.23 (cont)

5. What type of compound would be a good precursor to the product?

    A ketone that can be reduced to the alcohol.

The ketone that we need for step 5 is formed by the reduction of the α,β-unsaturated ketone we got in step 4.

6. After this last step, do we see how to get from starting material to product? If not, we need to analyze the structure obtained in step 5 by applying questions 4 and 5 to it.

17.24 (a)

(b)

17.24 (c)

(d)

(e)

17.25 (a)

(b)

(c)

(d)

17.25 (e)

17.26 (a)

(Z)-enolate

(b)

aldol product with
two stereocenters

17.27

The ester is hydrolyzed with base because long heating with acid would also remove the protecting group.

17.28 CO_3^{2-} + H_2O $\rightleftharpoons$ HCO_3^- + OH^-

17.29

17.30

17.30 (cont)

The top face of the ring system, which is on the same side as the hydrogen atoms and away from the bonds to the other ring, is more easily reached by the reagent.

17.31

17.32   (a)   lithium diisopropylamide

(b)

17.32 (b) (cont)

17.33   An examination of the major resonance contributors of the enolate anion from 1-phenyl-2-methyl-1-propanone reveals that there is double bond character to the carbon-carbon bond between carbons 1 and 2 in the structure in which the negative charge is localized on the oxygen atom. To the extent that there is such double bond character, free rotation around that bond is inhibited, and the two methyl groups are no longer chemical-shift equivalent (for example, one is trans and the other cis to the oxygen atom) and would be expected to have different chemical shifts.

The experimental observation that there are two chemical shifts for the methyl groups in the region δ 1.0–2.0 suggests that the resonance contributor with the negative charge on oxygen is the more important one. We would expect the positively charged lithium ion to be associated with the oxygen atom rather than with the carbon atom in the enolate anion.

17.34

enolate anion,
stable product of
ketolactone in base

17.35

stabilized carbanion

17.35 (cont)

17.36

B
(the most acidic hydrogen
is the one between the
two carbonyl groups)

C
(the most acidic hydrogens are the
ones α to the carbonyl group)

D
(the most nucleophilic
carbon is the one α to
only one carbonyl group)

E

F

G

H

dihydrojasmone

more stable enolate anion,
containing the more highly
substituted double bond

17.36 (cont)

less stable enolate anion,
with the less highly
substituted double bond

dihydrojasmone

this product does not form

17.37 (a)

(b)

17.38

17.38 (cont)

$$\xrightarrow[\text{dimethylformamide}]{\overset{\displaystyle O}{\overset{\|}{H_2NCH_2COCH_2CH_3}}} \xrightarrow{(CH_3CH_2)_3N \text{ (base)}}$$

1740 cm^{-1} 1670 cm^{-1}

$$CH_3CH_2OCCHCNHCH_2\!\!-\!\!\bigcirc\!\!-\!NO_2$$

$$CH_3CH_2OCCH_2NH$$

1740 cm^{-1}

B
$C_{16}H_{21}N_3O_7$

17.39

A
$C_{11}H_{14}O_2$

C
$C_{10}H_{18}O_3$

17.40 $TBDMSO(CH_2)_2CH_2Br \xrightarrow[\substack{\text{dimethyl} \\ \text{sulfoxide}}]{NaCN} TBDMSO(CH_2)_2CH_2CN \xrightarrow[\substack{\text{tetrahydrofuran} \\ -78\,°C}]{\overset{\displaystyle CH_3}{(CH_3CH)_2N^- Li^+}}$

A

$$\xrightarrow[]{\overset{\displaystyle O}{\overset{\|}{CH_3CH_2OCOCH_2CH_3}}} TBDMSO(CH_2)_2CHCN$$

$$O\!=\!C\!-\!OCH_2CH_3$$

B

17.41

17.41 (cont)

$$PhS:^-\ Li^+ \qquad \qquad \longleftarrow \qquad PhS:^-\ Li^+$$

Supplemental Problems

S17.1   Give structural formulas for all species symbolized by letters in the following equations.

(a) [2-acetylcyclohexanone with H] $+\ D_2O\ \longrightarrow\ A$

(b) $CH_2(COCH_2CH_3)_2 \xrightarrow[\text{ethanol}]{CH_3CH_2ONa} B \xrightarrow{\text{[benzyl-CH}_2\text{Cl]}} C$

(c) $CH_3\overset{O}{\underset{\|}{C}}CH_2\overset{O}{\underset{\|}{C}}OCH_2CH_3 \xrightarrow[\text{ethanol}]{CH_3CH_2ONa} D \xrightarrow{BrCH_2CH_2\overset{O}{\underset{\|}{C}}OCH_2CH_3} E$

(d) $CH_3\overset{O}{\underset{\|}{C}}CH_2\overset{O}{\underset{\|}{C}}OCH_2CH_3 \xrightarrow[\text{ethanol}]{CH_3CH_2ONa} F \xrightarrow{CH_2{=}CHCH_2CH_2Br} G \xrightarrow[\text{toluene}]{NaH} H \xrightarrow{\overset{I}{\underset{|}{CH_3CHCH_3}}} I$

(e) $CH_2(COCH_2CH_3)_2 \xrightarrow[\text{ethanol}]{CH_3CH_2ONa} J \xrightarrow{\text{[cyclopentenyl-Cl]}} K$

(f) [2-methoxybenzaldehyde] $+\ CH_3CH_2NO_2 \xrightarrow[\substack{\text{toluene} \\ \Delta}]{CH_3(CH_2)_3NH_2} L$

(g) $CH_3(CH_2)_4CH_2\overset{O}{\underset{\|}{C}}CH_2CH_2CH_2OH \xrightarrow[\text{dichloromethane}]{\text{[pyridinium CrO}_3\text{Cl}^-]} M \xrightarrow[\substack{H_2O \\ \text{tetrahydrofuran}}]{KOH} N$

S17.2   Write a mechanism for the decarboxylation of malonic acid, $HO\overset{O}{\underset{\|}{C}}CH_2\overset{O}{\underset{\|}{C}}OH$.

S17.3   The disubstituted malonic ester required for the synthesis of phenobarbital (p. 662 in the text) cannot be prepared by the usual route involving the enolate anion from diethyl malonate in a nucleophilic substitution reaction, because ordinary aryl halides do not undergo such substitution reactions. Work out a synthesis form diethyl ethylphenyl-malonate starting from phenylacetonitrile using condensation reactions and alkylation reactions of compounds containing active methylene groups.

[benzene ring]$-CH_2C{\equiv}N$

phenylacetonitrile

S17.4   Fill in structural formulas for the intermediates and products indicated by letters in the following sequence of reactions.

S17.5   Write mechanisms that rationalize the following experimental observations.

S17.6   When the ketolactone shown below is heated with concentrated hydrochloric acid, the product is 5-chloro-2-pentanone. Treatment of 5-chloro-2-pentanone with aqueous sodium hydroxide gives cyclopropyl methyl ketone in about 80% yield. How would you rationalize these experimental observations?

ketolactone used
as starting material

S17.7   Write a complete mechanism for the following reaction.

S17.8   Propose a mechanism that accounts for the product obtained in the following cyclization reaction.

S17.9   Compounds other than aldehydes and ketones may be used to provide components of aldol-type reactions. For example, the following reaction was observed.

Propose a mechanism for the reaction using the curved arrow convention. You may use HB$^+$ and B: to indicate acids and bases.

S17.10   Complete the following by providing structural formulas for the missing compounds.

(a)

(b)

(c)

(d)

(e)

S17.11   Synthesis of a subunit of the antibiotic ionomycin included the following reactions. Supply structural formulas for the missing reactive intermediate and product. How does the spectral data support your structure for the product?

IR: 3440, 1735 cm^{-1}
^{1}H NMR: δ 0.81 (d, 3H)

18

Polyenes

Concept Map 18.1   Different relationships between multiple bonds.

18.1   (a)   1,4-hexadiyne   (b)   4-hexen-2-yne (see note)   (c)   1,4-cyclohexadiene

(d)   1,5-cyclooctadiene   (e)   (*E*)-1-phenyl-1,4-pentadiene   (f)   1-chloro-2,4-heptadiyne

Note: the lower number goes to the group that is the end of the name. When an alkene and an alkyne functional group are present in a compound, the alkyne is the at the end of the name and thus gets the lower number.

18.2   (a) CH_2=$CHCH_2CH_2\overset{\overset{\displaystyle O}{\|}}{C}CH_3$ (b) HC≡CCH_2CH_2C≡CH (c) CH_2=$CHCH_2CH$=CH_2

(d) CH_3C≡CCH_2C≡CCH_3 (e) $\underset{H}{\overset{CH_3}{}}C=C\underset{CH_2\overset{\displaystyle |}{C}CH_2CH=CH_2}{\overset{H}{}}$ with CH_3 (f) HC≡CCH=$CHCH$=CH_2

Concept Map 18.2   A conjugated diene.

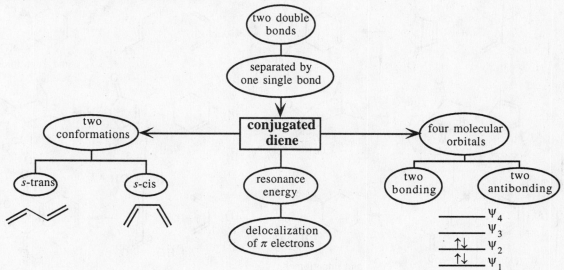

421

Concept Map 18.3   Addition to dienes.

18.5

red hot wire
absence of air

Concept Map 18.4   The Diels-Alder reaction.

dienophile **plus**   **conjugated diene**

EWG

EWG = { C=O
—NO₂
—CN, etc

cyclic — bicyclic compound — endo stereochemistry

s-cis conformation   acyclic

symmetrical — substituted cyclohexene — stereoselective

substituted

carbon 1   carbon 2

1,2-substituted cyclohexene   1,4-substituted cyclohexene

18.6

18.7

H₃PO₄
Δ

NH₄Cl
H₂O

CH₂=CHMgBr

major product

18.8

(a)

(b)

(c)

(d)

(e)

18.9

(a)

(b)

(c)

(d)

(e)

(f)

18.10

18.10 (cont)

enolate anion of ester (Section 16.1B); loss of
stereochemistry at the α-carbon atom of the ester

Generation of the carbanion from the methyl ester followed by reprotonation is an equilibrium reaction and gives the thermodynamically more stable trans stereoisomer. Compound D is different from Compound C, and Compound E is different from A. Therefore, the initial Diels-Alder product, Compound A, must have been the cis stereoisomer.

18.11 (a)

Note that the cis double bond, which is the less stable isomer, is introduced as late as possible in the synthesis to prevent isomerization by acidic reagents.

18.11   b)   To get the trans isomer, we would use sodium in liquid ammonia, instead of hydrogen and poisoned catalyst, in the reduction of the triple bond. The reduction in this case would be carried out at the alcohol stage to avoid reaction of the ester with ammonia. Because the trans double bond is the more stable of the two, it is not subject to isomerization as easily as the cis double bond is.

18.12

menthofuran
both are head to tail

bisabolol
both are head to tail

camphor

linaloöl

camphene

α-pinene

18.13

(a)

geraniol
(*E*)-double bond between
carbon 2 and carbon 3

nerol
(*Z*)-double bond between
carbon 2 and carbon 3

protonation of
the double bond

rotation around the
single bond between
carbon 2 and carbon 3

deprotonation

18.13

(b)

nerol

:B

:Ö—H
:O—H
H

terpin

α-terpineol

(c)

α-terpineol

limonene

terpin

α-terpineol

limonene

(d)

nerol

18.13 (d) (cont)

linalool

18.14

limonene

A Diels-Alder reaction between one isoprene unit and the less hindered double bond of the second one in a head-to-tail fashion gives limonene.

18.15

enzyme

farnesol

18.16

farnesyl pyrophosphate

enzyme →

geranylgeranyl pyrophosphate

H — B⁺

18.17

(a)

hexadecanoate ester of Vitamin A

(b)

$(CH_3C)_2O$
pyridine

18.18

monoperoxy-phthalic acid →

+

The most highly substituted double bonds are oxidized preferentially by the peroxyacid.

18.19

(a)

(b)

and enantiomer
B

(c)

HCl (1 mol)

major
C

+

D

(d)

and enantiomer
E

(e) $CH_3C{\equiv}CCH_2C{\equiv}CCH_2CH_3$ $\xrightarrow[\text{quinoline}]{\substack{H_2 \\ Pd/BaSO_4}}$

F

(f) CH_3COOH

and enantiomer
G

18.20 (a) $\xrightarrow{\Delta}$ 2

A

(b)

and enantiomer
B

18.20   (c)

(d)

(e)

(f)

(g)

18.21   (a)

(b)

18.21 (c)

(d)

18.22   σ bonds formed   σ bonds formed

(a)

(b)

(c)

(d)

(e)

(f)

18.23

(a)

18.23 (a) (cont)

(b)

protonated carbonyl compound
reacts easily with the nucleophile,
an alcohol

easy dehydration reaction to
give α,β-unsaturated carbonyl
compound after deprotonation

18.24 (a)

A
(more highly substituted
double bond is more
nucleophilic)

(b)

(c)

+ CH₃CH₂OH

(d)

E
C₉H₁₆O₂
(cyclic hemiacetal forms
whenever possible)

F
C₉H₁₄O₂

(e)

F

G

(+)-isoiridomyrmecin

no steric hindrance;
diene can achieve
s-cis conformation

steric hindrance;
difficult for diene to
achieve *s*-cis conformation

18.25

transition state for the addition
of 1,3-butadiene to maleic anhydride

transition state for the addition of 2,3-
di-*tert*-butyl-1,3-butadiene to maleic
anhydride. The bulkiness of the *tert*-butyl
groups prevents the diene from achieving
the *s*-cis conformation needed for the Diels-
Alder reaction. Good overlap of the π system
is also difficult, raising the energy of the
transition state to the point where the
reaction does not proceed.

18.26   (a)

$$\text{Cl} \quad \text{COOH} \atop \text{dichloromethane} \atop A$$

$$\xrightarrow{O_3} \quad B \quad \xrightarrow{(CH_3)_2S}$$

$$\text{Cl} \quad \text{COOH} \atop C$$

$$\xrightarrow{\text{Zn, NaI} \atop \text{acetic acid}}$$

(*R*)-(+)-acetate intermediate

(b)

$$\xrightarrow{LiAlH_4} \quad \xrightarrow{H_2O} \atop D \quad \text{OH}$$

$$\xrightarrow{TsCl \atop \text{pyridine}} \atop E \quad \text{OTs}$$

$$\xrightarrow{NaN_3 \atop N,N\text{-dimethyl-} \atop \text{formamide}} \atop N_3 \atop F$$

(c)

$$\xrightarrow{(CH_3CH_2CH_2CH_2)_4N^+ \ ^-OCCH_3 \atop N,N\text{-dimethylformamide}}$$

G
stereoisomer of the
(*R*)-(+)-acetate

18.27   (a)

(b)

(c)

(d)

(e)

18.28   (a)   Bisabolene has the molecular formula $C_{15}H_{24}$. The corresponding saturated alkane would have the formula $C_{15}H_{32}$. Bisabolene has four units of unsaturation. Hydrogenation of bisabolene gives Compound X, $C_{15}H_{30}$. Therefore, bisabolene contains one ring and three π bonds.

(b)

Compound Y
$C_{15}H_{28}$

6-methyl-2-
heptanone

4-methyl-
cyclohexanone

(c)

The third double
bond must be in
the ring. The exact
position is uncertain.

acetone

4-oxopentanoic acid

+ other cleavage products

18.28 (d)

nerolidol

: B

resonance-
stabilized cation

bisabolene;
location of third double
bond now known

(e)

bisabolol

(f)

bisabolol

bisabolene

18.28 (f) (cont)

Compound Z

18.29

$$HC{\equiv}CH \xrightarrow{\text{NaNH}_2} HC{\equiv}C^- Na^+ \xrightarrow[\text{B}]{\text{CH}_3(\text{CH}_2)_9\text{Br}} HC{\equiv}C(\text{CH}_2)_9\text{CH}_3 \xrightarrow[\text{diglyme}]{\text{CH}_3\text{CH}_2\text{CH}_2\text{CH}_2\text{Li}}$$

$$\underset{\text{C}}{\text{Li}^+ {}^- C{\equiv}C(\text{CH}_2)_9\text{CH}_3} \xrightarrow[\text{D}]{\overset{\text{CH}_3}{\overset{|}{\text{CH}_3\text{CH}(\text{CH}_2)_4\text{Br}}}} \text{CH}_3(\text{CH}_2)_9\text{C}{\equiv}\text{C}(\text{CH}_2)_4\overset{\overset{\text{CH}_3}{|}}{\text{CHCH}_3} \xrightarrow[\substack{\text{Pd/BaSO}_4\\\text{quinoline}\\\text{E}}]{\text{H}_2}$$

F

$$\xrightarrow[\text{dichloromethane}]{\overset{\text{Cl}}{\underset{\text{G}}{\bigcirc\!\!-\!\!\text{COOH}}}}$$

and enantiomer
disparlure

$$\overset{\overset{\text{CH}_3}{|}}{\text{CH}_3\text{CH}(\text{CH}_2)_4\text{OH}} \xrightarrow[\substack{\text{pyridine}\\\text{H}}]{\text{PBr}_3} \overset{\overset{\text{CH}_3}{|}}{\underset{\text{D}}{\text{CH}_3\text{CH}(\text{CH}_2)_4\text{Br}}}$$

18.30

and enantiomer
A

ν_{max} (cm^{-1})	
2844	C—H (aliphatic)
1658	C=C
1377	—NO$_2$
1178, 1166, 1117	C—O—C

and enantiomer
B

ν_{max} (cm^{-1})	
2844	C—H (aliphatic)
1722	C=O
1350	—NO$_2$
1117	C—O—C

18.31

R =

18.32

(a)

Bromine approaches the molecule from the less
hindered side, away from the methyl group.

trans-diaxial orientation of the bromine atoms
when the bromonium ion opens

(b)

The nucleophile and the leaving group are in a trans-diaxial orientation that is favored for an intramolecular S_N2
reaction.

18.32 (b) (cont)

The nucleophile and the leaving group are in a trans-diequatorial orientation, which is less favorable for an intramolecular S_N2 reaction. Because of the rigidity of the fused ring system, the two groups can have the trans-diaxial orientation to each other only when the cyclohexane ring is in a boat or twist conformation (Section 5.11C). Such a conformation is higher in energy than the chair conformation allowed for the reaction of Compound A, so the rate of reaction is much slower for B than for A.

18.33

Another product with two fused five-membered rings is theoretically possible. The structure shown for helenalin in the text indicates that the bonds joining the five-membered ring to the seven-membered ring are trans to each other. Such trans stereochemistry at the junction of two fused five-membered rings would create a lot of strain, but is all right at the junction of a five- and seven-membered ring. You may wish to prove this to yourself by building molecular models of both systems.

18.34

18.34 (cont)

18.35

18.36   (a) $(CH_3CH_2O)_2PCH_2CCH_2CH_3$

A

(b) $(CH_3CH_2O)_2P$

this one is more likely to form
because it has the more highly
substituted double bond

18.37 (a)

18.38 (a)

18.38 (a) (cont)

(b)

(−)-borjatriol

Supplemental Problems

S18.1   Assign structures to the major products designated by letters in the following reactions. Show the stereochemistry of the product when it can be predicted.

(a)

(b)

(c)

(d)

(e)

(f)

(g)

(h)

S18.2   What reagents would be required to obtain each Diels-Alder adduct shown below?

(a)

(b)

(c)

S18.3   Give the structural formulas, including the correct stereochemistry, for the major products represented by letters in the following synthetic sequence.

S18.4   The following reactions were carried out in the synthesis of the terpene neointermedeol. What are the structures of neointermedeol and the intermediates in its synthesis?

S18.5   An intermediate in the synthesis of quadrone, a sesquiterpene with possible antitumor activity, was prepared by the following reactions. Write structural formulas for the compounds represented by letters.

Hint: What happens to an enol ether in acid?

S18.6   Write structural formulas for the products and intermediates designated by letters in the following sequence of reactions.

19

Enols and Enolate Anions as Nucleophiles II. Conjugate Addition Reactions; Ylides

Concept Map 19.1   Electrophilic alkenes.

19.1

19.2   (a)

(b) CH_2=CHC≡N + NH_3 $\xrightarrow{\quad H_2O \quad}$ N≡$CCH_2CH_2NHCH_2CH_2C$≡N
      (2 equivalents)   C

19.2   (c)   PhSH + CH$_2$=CHCOCH$_3$ $\xrightarrow{\text{CH}_3\text{ONa}}$ PhSCH$_2$CH$_2$COCH$_3$
              D   E

(d)   PhC≡CCPh + CH$_3$CH$_2$NHCH$_2$CH$_3$ $\xrightarrow[\text{ether}]{\text{diethyl}}$ PhC=CHCPh
                            (1 equiv) |
                                                                      NCH$_2$CH$_3$
                                                                      |
                                                                      CH$_2$CH$_3$

                                                                      F

19.3

(E)--2-butenedioate
fumarate

attack at C-2   attack at C-2   attack at C-3   attack at C-3
from top   from bottom   from top   from bottom

(S)-(–)-malate   (R)-(+)-malate   (S)-(–)-malate   (R)-(+)-malate

If the reaction were taking place in an achiral environment, we would expect a racemic mixture as a result of all four of these processes occurring with equal probability.

19.4   (a)   CH$_3$CH$_2$CH$_2$CH$_2$Li + CuI $\xrightarrow[\text{0 °C}]{\text{diethyl ether}}$ (CH$_3$CH$_2$CH$_2$CH$_2$)$_2$CuLi

(b)   CH$_3$CH$_2$CH$_2$CH$_2$CH$_2$I $\xrightarrow[\substack{\text{diethyl ether} \\ \text{25 °C}}]{(\text{CH}_3)_2\text{CuLi}}$ CH$_3$CH$_2$CH$_2$CH$_2$CH$_2$CH$_3$

(c)   CH$_3$(CH$_2$)$_6$CH$_2$Cl $\xrightarrow[\substack{\text{hexamethylphosphoric} \\ \text{triamide} \\ \text{25 °C}}]{\left(\begin{smallmatrix} \text{CH}_3 & \text{H} \\ \text{C}=\text{C} \\ \text{H} & \end{smallmatrix}\right)_2\text{CuLi}}$

CH$_3$, H
  C=C
H   CH$_2$(CH$_2$)$_6$CH$_3$

19.4   (d)

$$\text{(cyclohexyl-I)} \xrightarrow[\substack{\text{diethyl ether} \\ 0\,^\circ\text{C}}]{(CH_3)_2CuLi} \text{(methylcyclohexane)}$$

19.5

$$\underset{\substack{\text{CH}_3\text{CH}_2 \\ \text{CH}_3}}{\overset{}{\text{C}}}=\underset{\substack{\text{H}}}{\overset{}{\text{C}}}\text{CH}_2\text{CH}_2\overset{\text{I}}{\text{C}}=\text{CHCH}_2\text{OH} \xrightarrow{(CH_3CH_2)_2CuLi} \underset{\substack{\text{CH}_3\text{CH}_2 \\ \text{CH}_3}}{\overset{}{\text{C}}}=\underset{\substack{\text{H}}}{\overset{}{\text{C}}}\text{CH}_2\text{CH}_2\overset{\text{CH}_2\text{CH}_3}{\text{C}}=\text{CHCH}_2\text{OH}$$

19.6

(a)

$$\text{(cyclohexenone)} \xrightarrow[\substack{\text{diethyl ether} \\ -78\,^\circ\text{C}}]{(CH_2=CHCH_2)_2CuLi} \underset{\text{A}}{\text{(enolate, }O^-Li^+\text{, }CH_2CH=CH_2)} \xrightarrow[\substack{H_2O}]{NH_4Cl,\ NH_3} \underset{\text{B}}{\text{(ketone, }CH_2CH=CH_2)}$$

(b)

$$\underset{\text{C}}{\text{(3-methylcyclohexenone)}} \xrightarrow[\substack{\text{diethyl ether} \\ -78\,^\circ\text{C}}]{(CH_3)_2CuLi} \underset{\text{D}}{\text{(enolate }O^-Li^+,\ CH_3,\ CH_3)} \xrightarrow[\substack{H_2O}]{NH_4Cl,\ NH_3} \text{(ketone, }CH_3,\ CH_3)$$

(c) $\text{PhLi} + \text{CuBr} \xrightarrow[\substack{\text{diethyl ether} \\ 0\,^\circ\text{C}}]{} \underset{\text{E}}{Ph_2CuLi} \xrightarrow[\substack{\text{diethyl ether} \\ 0\,^\circ\text{C}}]{} \underset{\text{F}}{\text{(enolate }O^-Li^+,\ CH_3,\ Ph)} \xrightarrow[\substack{H_2O}]{NH_4Cl,\ NH_3} \underset{\text{G}}{\text{(ketone, }CH_3,\ Ph)}$$

19.7

$$\text{(bicyclic, }CH_3,\ CH_3,\ Cl,\ O) \xrightarrow[\text{tetrahydrofuran}]{(CH_2=CHCH_2CH_2)_2CuLi}$$

$$\underset{\text{A}}{\text{(bicyclic, }CH_2=CHCH_2CH_2,\ CH_3,\ CH_3,\ Cl,\ O^-Li^+)} \xrightarrow{H_3O^+} \underset{\substack{\text{B} \\ C_{14}H_{21}ClO}}{\text{(bicyclic, }CH_2=CHCH_2CH_2,\ CH_3,\ CH_3,\ Cl,\ O)}$$

19.8 $\text{RSH} + \text{CH}_3(\text{CH}_2)_8\overset{\overset{\displaystyle O}{\|}}{\text{C}}\text{CH}=\text{CH}_2 \longrightarrow \text{CH}_3(\text{CH}_2)_8\overset{\overset{\displaystyle O}{\|}}{\text{C}}\text{CH}_2\text{CH}_2\text{SR}$

Concept Map 19.2   Reactions of electrophilic alkenes.

19.9

19.10

partial positive charge on β-carbon atom

19.11 (a)

(b)

19.11 (c)

NaNH₂   CH₂=CHC≡N

(The more highly substituted enolate anion and the one in which the double bond is conjugated with the aromatic ring is the more stable one.)

(d) CH_3NO_2 + $CH_3C{=}CHCCH_3$ $CH_3CH_2NHCH_2CH_3$ → $O_2NCH_2CCH_2CCH_3$

19.12   1.

The carbon atom of the carbonyl group in the carboxylate anion is much less electrophilic than the carbon atom of the ketone carbonyl.

2.

The same result can be obtained by hydrolyzing the enol ether (Problem 13.12) and then dehydrating the alcohol.

19.13

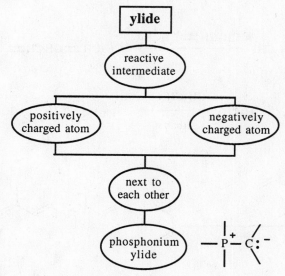

Concept Map 19.3   Ylides.

19.14   A carbon atom can be introduced by the reaction of an organometallic reagent such as a Grignard reagent with a carbonyl group (Section 13.6B). A double bond can be introduced via an E2 elimination (Section 7.6).

19.15   (a)

19.15 (b)

(c) Br^- $Ph_3\overset{+}{P}CH_2COCH_2CH_3$ $\xrightarrow[\text{ethanol}]{CH_3CH_2ONa}$

$Ph_3P{=}CHCOCH_2CH_3$ $\xrightarrow{CH_3CH{=}CHCH{=}O}$ $CH_3CH{=}CHCH{=}CHCOCH_2CH_3$ + $Ph_3P{=}O$

        E   F   G

(d) Br^-
      $Ph_3\overset{+}{P}CH_2$ ... $COCH_2CH_3$ $\xrightarrow[\text{ethanol}]{CH_3CH_2ONa}$ $Ph_3P{=}CH$ ... $COCH_2CH_3$

                                                                    H

19.16 (a) $CH_2{=}CHCH_2PPh_2$ $\xrightarrow[\substack{\text{tetrahydrofuran} \\ \text{hexamethylphos-} \\ \text{phoric triamide} \\ -78\,°C}]{CH_3CH_2CH_2CH_2Li}$ $CH_2{=}CHCHPPh_2$ $\xrightarrow{B}$

                                                                      A

(b) $(CH_3CH_2O)_2PCH_2COCH_2CH_3$ $\xrightarrow[\substack{\text{LiCl} \\ \text{acetonitrile}}]{\text{(good base)}}$

$(CH_3CH_2O)_2\overset{\parallel O}{P}\overset{-}{C}HCOCH_2CH_3$ $\xrightarrow{D}$

        C

Concept Map 19.4   The Wittig reaction.

19.18 (d) (cont)

CH₃CH₂CH₂CH₂Li

tetrahydrofuran
−20 °C

KOH

H₂O

HSCH₂CH₂CH₂SH

(CH₃CH₂)₂O•BF₃
acetic acid
chloroform

O
‖
HCH

Concept Map 19.5   Dithiane anions.

aldehyde carbonyl

electrophilic center

O δ−
‖
RCH
δ+

dithiane

deprotonation

inversion of polarity

dithiane anion

nucleophilic center

reacts with

acyl anion equivalent

$$\left[\begin{array}{c} RC\overset{..}{:}^- \\ \overset{\|}{O} \end{array} \right]$$

electrophiles

R'X   alkyl halides

O
‖
R'CH   carbonyl groups

oxiranes

then

hydrolysis

H₂O
HgCl₂
Δ

new carbonyl compounds

O
‖
RCR'

O
‖
RCCHR'
|
OH

O
‖
RCCH₂CHR'
|
OH

19.19

:O:
‖
CH₃S̈CH₃ + NaH →

:O:
‖
CH₃S̈—C̈H₂ Na⁺ + H₂↑

The anion formed from dimethyl sulfoxide is stabilized by delocalization of the negative charge to oxygen.

:O:
‖
CH₃S̈—C̈H₂   ⟷

:Ö:⁻
|
CH₃S̈=CH₂

The anion from dimethyl sulfoxide resembles an enolate anion.

:Ö:⁻
|
CH₃C=CH₂

enolate anion
from acetone

:Ö:⁻
|
CH₃S̈=CH₂

anion from
dimethyl sulfoxide

19.19 (cont)

$$CH_3\overset{\overset{\displaystyle O}{\|}}{\underset{\cdot\cdot}{S}}CH_2\ Na^+ \ + \ Ph\overset{\overset{\displaystyle O}{\|}}{C}Ph \ \longrightarrow \ Ph_2\overset{\overset{\displaystyle Na^+ \ ^-O}{|}}{C}-CH_2\overset{\overset{\displaystyle O}{\|}}{S}CH_3$$

$$CH_3\underset{\cdot\cdot}{S}CH_2\ Na^+ \ + \ \text{(cyclohexyl)}\overset{\overset{\displaystyle O}{\|}}{C}OCH_2CH_3 \ \longrightarrow \ \text{(cyclohexyl)}\overset{\overset{\displaystyle O}{\|}}{C}CH_2\overset{\overset{\displaystyle O}{\|}}{S}CH_3$$

19.20

(a) $CH_3\overset{\overset{\displaystyle O}{\|}}{C}CH=\overset{\overset{\displaystyle CH_3}{|}}{C}CH_3 \ + \ CH_2(COCH_3)_2 \ \xrightarrow[\text{methanol}]{CH_3ONa} \ CH_3\overset{\overset{\displaystyle O}{\|}}{C}CH_2\overset{\overset{CH_3}{|}}{\underset{\underset{\displaystyle CH_3}{|}}{C}}\overset{\overset{\displaystyle O}{\|}}{C}H(COCH_3)_2 \ \xrightarrow[\text{methanol}]{CH_3ONa}$

A

B (cyclohexanedione with CH₃, CH₃, COCH₃ substituents)

(b) (2,4-dimethylcyclopentanone) $+ \ CH_2=CHC\equiv N \ \xrightarrow{KOH}$ C

(c) $(C_6H_5)_3P=CHPh \ + \ \text{(cyclohexanone)} \ \xrightarrow[\text{24 h, 20 °C}]{\text{diethyl ether}} \ \text{(cyclohexylidene)}=CHPh \ + \ (C_6H_5)_3P=O$

D   E

(d) $PhCH=CH\overset{\overset{\displaystyle O}{\|}}{C}Ph \ + \ \text{(piperidine)NH} \ \xrightarrow[\Delta]{\text{ethanol}} \ N-\overset{\overset{\displaystyle |}{CH}}{\underset{\underset{\displaystyle Ph}{|}}{}}CH_2\overset{\overset{\displaystyle O}{\|}}{C}Ph$

F

(e) (cycloheptene) $\xrightarrow[\text{chloroform}]{O_3} \ \xrightarrow{CH_3SCH_3} \ $ G (dialdehyde) $\xrightarrow[H_2O]{NaOH} \ $ H (cyclohexene carbaldehyde)

(f) (pyrrolidine)$N-\overset{\overset{\displaystyle O}{\|}}{C}CH_2CH_2CH_2CH_2OCH_2Ph \ \xrightarrow[\substack{\text{tetrahydrofuran} \\ -78\ °C}]{(CH_3CH)_2N^-\ Li^+} \ (pyrrolidine)N-\overset{\overset{\displaystyle O^-\ Li^+}{|}}{C}=CHCH_2CH_2CH_2OCH_2Ph$

I

$CH_3O\overset{\overset{\displaystyle O}{\|}}{C}\text{(cyclopentene)} \ \xrightarrow{\text{tetrahydrofuran}}$ J

$\xrightarrow[\text{tetrahydrofuran}]{CH_3C=CHCH_2CH_2I}$ K

19.21   (a)

(b) Ph₃P + BrCH₂CH=CHCOCH₂CH₃ $\xrightarrow{\text{benzene}}$

(c)

(d)

(e)

19.21   (f)

19.22

(a)

(b)

(c)

(d)

19.22

(e) [cyclohexane ring with CCH_3 ketone and CH_2CH_2Br] $\xrightarrow[\text{hexane} \\ -60\,°C]{(CH_3CH)_2N^- Li^+ \;\; CH_3}$ [enolate J with O^-Li^+, $=CH_2$, CH_2CH_2Br] $\xrightarrow[\text{triamide} \\ 22\,°C]{\text{hexamethylphosphoric}}$

[decalone K] $\xrightarrow[\text{1,2-dimethoxyethane}]{(CH_3CH)_2N^- Li^+ \;\; CH_3}$ [enol L with O^-Li^+] $\xrightarrow[\text{1,2-dimethoxyethane}]{CH_3I}$ [methyl decalone M]

K   L   M

(f) $CH_3CH_2C\equiv CCHCH_2CH_2CH$ (with OTHP and O) $\xrightarrow{CH_3CCH_2P(OCH_3)_2, \text{ NaH}}$ $CH_3CH_2C\equiv CCHCH_2CH_2CH=CHCCH_3$ (with OTHP and O)

N

19.23 (a) $PhSCH_2CH_2C\equiv N \xleftarrow{\text{PhSH, NaOH}} CH_2=CHC\equiv N$

(b) [furan]$CH=CHCH$ (O) $\xleftarrow{\text{2-furaldehyde}}$ $\xleftarrow[\substack{\text{tetrahydrofuran} \\ -78\,°C}]{(CH_3CH)_2N \; Li \;\; CH_3}$ CH_3CH (O)

(c) $CH_3CH_2CH_2CH_2CH_2CH_2CH=CH_2 \xleftarrow{(CH_2=CHCH_2)_2CuLi} CH_3CH_2CH_2CH_2CH_2I$

(d) [bicyclic ketone with OH] $\xleftarrow{}$ $[Li^+ \; ^-O$ enolate $]$ $\xleftarrow[\text{diethyl ether}]{(CH_3)_2CuLi}$ [bicyclic diketone]

(e) $PhCHCOCH_2CH_3$ (with $C-COCH_2CH_3$, O O) $\xleftarrow{CH_3CH_2OC-COCH_2CH_3}$ $PhCH=COCH_2CH_3$ (with O^-Na^+) $\xleftarrow[\text{ethanol}]{CH_3CH_2ONa}$ $PhCH_2COCH_2CH_3$

19.24

$$CH_3C-CCH=CHCH_3 \;\;(\text{with } CH_3, O, CH_3)$$

$$CH_3CH_2CN(CH_3)_2 \rightarrow CH_3CH=CN(CH_3)_2 \xrightarrow[\text{hexen-3-one}]{\text{2,2-dimethyl-4-}} CH_3C-CCH_2CHCHCN(CH_3)_2$$

N,N-dimethylpropanamide   enolate ion from   product from the Michael reaction;
                N,N-dimethylpropanamide   2 stereocenters, therefore 4 stereoisomers

19.24 (cont)

one pair of enantiomers

second pair of enantiomers

19.25

resonance contributors for the carbanion from the sulfone

resonance contributors for the carbanion from the sulfoxide

The negative charge on the sulfone carbanion is delocalized to two oxygen atoms while that on the sulfoxide carbanion is delocalized to only one oxygen atom. The conjugate base of the sulfone is, for this reason, more highly stabilized relative to the acid, and is, therefore, a weaker base than is the conjugate base of the sulfoxide. Another way of rationalizing the difference in basicity is to say that the conjugate base of the sulfone has lower electron density at any one site than the conjugate base of the sulfoxide, and is, therefore, less readily protonated.

19.26

19.27

19.27 (cont)

$$\text{(cyclohexyl)OTBDMS}\cdots\text{CH}_2\text{C(CH}_3)=\text{CHCH}_2\text{OH} \xrightarrow[\text{pyridine}]{\text{PBr}_3} \text{(cyclohexyl)OTBDMS}\cdots\text{CH}_2\text{C(CH}_3)=\text{CHCH}_2\text{Br} \xrightarrow[\text{diethyl ether}]{\text{LiAlH}_4*}$$

$$\text{(cyclohexyl)OTBDMS}\cdots\text{CH}_2\text{C(CH}_3)=\text{CHCH}_3 \xrightarrow{(\text{CH}_3\text{CH}_2\text{CH}_2\text{CH}_2)_4\text{N}^+\text{F}^-} \text{(cyclohexyl)OH}\cdots\text{CH}_2\text{C(CH}_3)=\text{CHCH}_3$$

*Hydride ion is the nucleophile replacing the leaving group in this reaction.

19.28

$$\text{CH}_3\text{CH}_2\text{CHCH}_2\underbrace{}-(\text{CH}_2)_9-\underbrace{}\overset{O}{\overset{\|}{{}^{14}\text{C}}}\text{OH}$$
$$\qquad\quad |$$
$$\qquad\text{CH}_3$$

2-methyl-   9-bromo-   potassium
butanal   1-nonanol   cyanide
long chain fatty acid precursors

$$\text{CH}_3\text{CH}_2\text{CH(CH}_2)_9\text{CH}_2{}^{14}\text{COH} \xleftarrow[\Delta]{\text{H}_3\text{O}^+} \text{CH}_3\text{CH}_2\text{CH(CH}_2)_9\text{CH}_2{}^{14}\text{CN} \xleftarrow[\text{ethanol}]{\text{K}^{14}\text{CN}} \text{CH}_3\text{CH}_2\text{CH(CH}_2)_9\text{CH}_2\text{Br}$$
$$\qquad |\qquad\qquad\qquad\qquad\qquad\qquad |\qquad\qquad\qquad\qquad\qquad |$$
$$\qquad\text{CH}_3\qquad\qquad\qquad\qquad\qquad\qquad \text{CH}_3\qquad\qquad\qquad\qquad\qquad \text{CH}_3$$

12-methyltetradecanoic acid

$$\uparrow \text{PBr}_3$$
$$\quad\text{pyridine}$$

$$\text{CH}_3\text{CH}_2\text{CHCH}=\text{CH(CH}_2)_7\text{CH}_2\text{OTHP} \xrightarrow[\text{Pt}]{\text{H}_2} \text{CH}_3\text{CH}_2\text{CH(CH}_2)_9\text{CH}_2\text{OTHP} \xrightarrow[\text{methanol}]{\substack{\text{H}_2\text{O},\\\text{HClO}_4}} \text{CH}_3\text{CH}_2\text{CH(CH}_2)_9\text{CH}_2\text{OH}$$
$$\qquad |\qquad\qquad\qquad\qquad\qquad\qquad\qquad\qquad |\qquad\qquad\qquad\qquad\qquad\qquad |$$
$$\qquad\text{CH}_3\qquad\qquad\qquad\qquad\qquad\qquad\qquad\qquad \text{CH}_3\qquad\qquad\qquad\qquad\qquad\qquad \text{CH}_3$$

$$\uparrow$$

$$\text{CH}_3\text{CH}_2\text{CHCH}=\text{O}$$
$$\qquad |$$
$$\qquad\text{CH}_3$$
2-methylbutanal

$$(\text{C}_6\text{H}_5)_3\text{P}=\text{CH(CH}_2)_7\text{CH}_2\text{OTHP} \xleftarrow[\substack{\text{tetrahydrofuran}\\-20\,^\circ\text{C}}]{\text{CH}_3\text{CH}_2\text{CH}_2\text{CH}_2\text{Li}} \overset{\text{Br}^-}{(\text{C}_6\text{H}_5)_3\overset{+}{\text{P}}\text{CH}_2(\text{CH}_2)_7\text{CH}_2\text{OTHP}}$$

$$\uparrow (\text{C}_6\text{H}_5)_3\text{P}$$

$$\text{BrCH}_2(\text{CH}_2)_7\text{CH}_2\text{OH} \xrightarrow[\text{TsOH}]{} \text{BrCH}_2(\text{CH}_2)_7\text{CH}_2\text{OTHP}$$
9-bromo-1-nonanol

19.29 (a)

$$\text{CH}_3\text{CH}=\text{CHC}(=\text{O})\cdots\text{C(CH}_3)_3 \xleftarrow[\substack{\text{dichloromethane}\\\text{or}}]{\substack{\text{pyridinium}\\\text{CrO}_3\text{Cl}^-}} \text{CH}_3\text{CH}=\text{CHCH(OH)C(CH}_3)_3 \xleftarrow[\text{H}_2\text{O}]{\text{NH}_4\text{Cl}}$$

new carbon-
carbon bond

2° alcohol

$$\xleftarrow[\text{oxidation}]{(\text{CH}_3\text{CH}_2)_3\text{N} \quad \text{CH}_3\text{SCH}_3, \quad \text{ClC}(=\text{O})-\text{C}(=\text{O})\text{Cl}}$$

19.29 (a) (cont)

$$CH_3C \!-\! M$$ (with CH_3 groups)

(addition of organometallic
reagent to aldehyde;
M = MgBr or Li)

(b)

dehydration spontaneous
for aldol product

α,β-unsaturated ketone can be
product of aldol reaction

CH_3CH (with O)
carbonyl compound

aldol reaction

$(CH_3CH)_2N^- Li^+$ (with CH_3)

enolate

double bond where
starting material
has halogen; looks
like Wittig reaction

$CH_3CH_2O^- Na^+$
(base)

ethanol

Br^-
$+$
PPh_3

Ph_3P

(d)

H_2
$Pd/BaSO_4$
quinoline

cis double bond
comes from catalytic
hydrogenation of alkyne

19.29 (d) (cont)

19.30

(This is an example of equilibration. Enolization occurs at both sides of the carbonyl group. Protonation of the enolate anion gives the form that is thermodynamically more stable.)

19.31

19.31 (cont)

THPO—CH=CH—CH₂CH₂CO⁻K⁺ $\xrightarrow[\text{diethyl ether}]{\text{LiAlH}_4 \quad \text{H}_2\text{O}}$ THPO—CH=CH—CH₂CH₂CH₂OH $\xrightarrow[\text{pyridine}]{\text{CH}_3\text{SO}_2\text{Cl}}$

THPO—CH=CH—CH₂CH₂CH₂OSO₂CH₃ $\xrightarrow{\text{NaI}}$ THPO—CH=CH—CH₂CH₂CH₂I $\xrightarrow[\text{diethyl ether}]{\text{Mg}}$ HC(CH₂)₈COCH₃

THPO—CH=CH—CH₂—CH(OH)—(CH₂)₈COCH₃ $\xrightarrow[\text{dichloromethane}]{\text{pyridinium CrO}_3\text{Cl}^-}$ THPO—CH=CH—CH₂—CO—(CH₂)₈COCH₃

Mechanism of Step 2:

19.32

(0.3 equivalents)

MsCl
(CH₃CH₂)₃N

A

(Note that this molecule is symmetrical so it
does not matter which alcohol is protected)

NaBr or LiBr
C

Ph₃P
acetonitrile

CH₃CH₂CH₂CH₂Li

B   D

E   F   a sex pheromone of the cockroach

TsOH
methanol

19.33   HC≡CH + 2 CH₃CH₂MgBr $\xrightarrow{\text{diethyl ether toluene}}$ BrMgC≡CMgBr $\longrightarrow$

A

B

H₃O⁺

C

H₂
Pd/CaCO₃
quinoline

19.33 (cont)

$$\xrightarrow[-10\ ^\circ C]{HBr\ (48\%)}$$

$$\xrightarrow[benzene]{2Ph_3P}$$

E

Allylic carbocations are the intermediates in this reaction. The carbocations, stabilized by delocalization of charge by resonance, react with bromide ion to give the most highly conjugated system. The cis stereochemistry of the central double bond is lost in the conjugated triene, which has the most stable trans configuration at each double bond.

$$\xrightarrow[diethyl\ ether]{2\ \text{<phenyl>}-Li}$$

F

Wittig reagent

19.34 1.
$$CH_3CCH_2COCH_2CH_3 \xrightarrow[ethanol]{CH_3CH_2ONa} CH_3CCHCOCH_2CH_3 \xrightarrow[\substack{(1\ molar\ equiv)}]{Br(CH_2)_3Br}$$

(with O, O above the carbonyls; Na$^+$ below; labeled A)

$$\underset{B}{CH_3CCHCOCH_2CH_3} \xrightarrow[\Delta]{\substack{HBr \\ (48\%)}} \underset{C}{CH_3C(CH_2)_3CH_2Br} \xrightarrow[\substack{TsOH \\ benzene}]{HOCH_2CH_2OH} \underset{D}{CH_3 \diagdown (CH_2)_3CH_2Br} \xrightarrow[toluene]{Ph_3P}$$

(B has (CH$_2$)$_2$CH$_2$Br substituent)

$$\underset{E}{CH_3 \diagdown (CH_2)_3CH_2PPh_3^+ \ Br^-} \xrightarrow[benzene]{\text{<phenyl>}-Li} \underset{F}{CH_3 \diagdown (CH_2)_3CH=PPh_3} \xrightarrow[diethyl\ ether]{CH_3CH_2CH=O}$$

G

$$\xrightarrow[benzene]{Cl\text{-<benzoic acid>}-COOH}$$

and enantiomer   H   and enantiomer
(four stereoisomers)

$$\xrightarrow{H_3O^+}$$

19.34 (1) (cont)

and enantiomer   and enantiomer   and enantiomer   and enantiomer
               I   *endo*-brevicomin   *exo*-brevicomin

Removal of the protecting group from the carbonyl
group and opening of the oxirane ring in aqueous
acid gives I, which, under acidic conditions, forms
the stable cyclic ketal of the resulting ketone-diol.

2.

19.35

19.35 (cont)

19.36 The kinetic product of the reaction is the 1,2-addition product. It forms almost exclusively when the reaction is run for a short time at low temperatures. The 1,4-addition product is the thermodynamically more stable product. It is the major product when the reaction is run at higher temperatures and for a long period of time allowing for equilibrium to be established.

The reaction products must be formed reversibly, otherwise they could not equilibrate.

reversal of the
1,2-addition reaction

reversal of the
1,4-addition reaction

19.37 (a) 1.   Preparation of dianion from propanoic acid

19.37 (a) 1. (cont)

2.   Preparation of the Wittig reagent

Br⟶⟶⟶Br   +   Ph₃P   ⟶   Br⟶⟶⟶$\overset{+}{P}$Ph₃ Br⁻

Br⟶⟶⟶$\overset{+}{P}$Ph₃ Br⁻   +   (CH₃CH)₂N⁻ Li⁺   ⟶   ⟶⟶⟶$\overset{+}{P}$Ph₃ Br⁻   +   Li⁺Br⁻   +   (CH₃CH)₂NH

(b)   Li⁺ ⁻:O:⟶⟶⟶$\overset{+}{P}$Ph₃   ⟶   Li⁺ ⁻:O: ⟶⟶⟶PPh₃

nucleophilic attack of enolate
on phosphonium salt

Wittig reagent

19.38

(a)   12-oxo

19.38

(b)

[THPO(CH$_2$)$_8$]$_2$CuLi
A

$\xrightarrow{\text{H}_2\text{O}}$ TsOH CH$_3$OH
B

$\xrightarrow{\text{CrO}_3}$ H$_2$SO$_4$ H$_2$O acetone
C

(c)

This is a reversible reaction, therefore it is necessary to remove the cyclopentadiene that forms in order to shift the equilibrium toward the desired product, which is the free 12-oxophytodienoic acid.

other product
of the reaction

19.39

(a) S$_N$2 and conjugate addition of an amine to the α,β-unsaturated ester

(b)

R = CH$_2$—phenyl

19.40   (a)

R = CH$_3$(CH$_2$)$_7$—

19.40   (b) The electron-withdrawing effect of the fluorine atoms stabilizes the enolate ion intermediate, lowering the energy of activation for the reaction. It also increases the electrophilicity of the β-carbon atom, making it a more attractive target for a nucleophilic attack, more so than for —CH_3 ketone.

19.41

Each vinylic hydrogen atom is coupled only to the other vinylic hydrogen atom, and each appears as a doublet with $J \sim 14$ Hz.

The normal range for the chemical shift of vinylic hydrogen atoms is about δ 5–6. Both vinylic hydrogen atoms in ethyl (*E*)-3-phenyl propenoate are shifted farther downfield, indicating that they are being deshielded by something other than the carbon-carbon double bond. The higher field (δ 6.43) vinylic hydrogen atom is deshielded by the carbonyl group of the ester function. The lower field vinylic hydrogen atom (δ 7.68) is even more deshielded because it is β to the carbonyl group and adjacent to the phenyl ring.

The chemical shift of the hydrogen atom on the β-carbon atom reflects the lower electron density at this carbon, symbolized by the positive charge shown in the resonance contributor above.

19.42

Chemical shifts in ^{13}C magnetic resonance spectra have essentially the same kind of dependence on electron density as proton chemical shifts. A carbon atom attached to an electron-withdrawing group or atom will be shifted downfield (deshielded) relative to a carbon atom attached to an electron-donating group or atom. The carbon atom of the carboxylic acid group, attached to two oxygens, absorbs farthest downfield and the methyl group farthest upfield. Of the two carbon atoms of the double bond, carbon 3 absorbs farther downfield than carbon 2 because it is β to the carbonyl group.

19.42 (cont)

Supplemental Problems

S19.1   Give structural formulas for the reagents, intermediates, and products symbolized by letters in the following equations.

(a)

(b)

(c)

(d)

(e)

(f)

(g)

(h)

S19.1 (i) $CH_3\overset{O}{\overset{\|}{C}}H$ $\xrightarrow[\text{chloroform}]{\text{HSCH}_2\text{CH}_2\text{CH}_2\text{SH}}{\text{HCl (g)}}$ S $\xrightarrow[\substack{\text{tetrahydrofuran} \\ -20\,°C}]{\text{CH}_3\text{CH}_2\text{CH}_2\text{CH}_2\text{Li}}$ T $\xrightarrow{\overset{CH_3}{\underset{}{CH_3\overset{|}{C}HBr}}}$ U $\xrightarrow[\text{methanol}]{\text{HgCl}_2,\ \text{H}_2\text{O}}$ V

S19.2   Tell what reagents could be used to carry out the following transformations. More than one step may be required.

(a) $CH_2(COCH_2CH_3)_2 \longrightarrow CH_3\overset{O}{\overset{\|}{C}}CH_2\overset{CH_3}{\underset{CH_3}{\overset{|}{C}}}CH(\overset{O}{\overset{\|}{C}}OCH_2CH_3)_2$

(b) $CH_2=CHCH \longrightarrow$

(c) $\longrightarrow$

(d)

(e) $CH_3CH_2CH_2\overset{O}{\overset{\|}{C}}OCH_3 \longrightarrow CH_3CH_2\overset{O}{\underset{CH_2C\equiv CH}{\overset{\|}{C}H}}COCH_3$

(f) $\longrightarrow$

S19.3   Much current research is focused on the chemistry of vision. Compounds similar to rhodopsin (p. 714 in the text) have been synthesized for study. One such synthesis is outlined below. Supply the necessary reagents for the conversions shown.

S19.4   A synthesis of disparlure, the sex pheromone of the gypsy moth (p. 704 in the text) was carried out in the following way. Provide structural formulas for all compounds or intermediates that are designated by letters.

The Wittig reaction in hexamethylphoric triamide (p. 249 in the text) gives mostly the *Z* alkene.

20

The Chemistry of Aromatic Compounds. Aromatic Substitution Reactions

Workbook Exercises

Learning to represent resonance interactions between various functional groups attached to benzene and other benzene-like rings will help you to understand the topics in Chapter 20. There are two types of resonance interactions with a benzene ring: electron-donating or electron-withdrawing. By examining the nature of the atom(s) attached directly to the benzene ring, you can conclude whether the group is electron-donating or electron-withdrawing when resonance contributors are to be drawn.

(a)   The resonance interaction is electron-donating when the atom attached to the ring has a pair of nonbonding electrons. For example:

(b)   The resonance interaction is electron-withdrawing when the atom attached to the ring is involved with a multiple bond to an electronegative atom such as oxygen or nitrogen. For example:

EXERCISE I.   Draw resonance contributors that show the interaction between the benzene (or benzene-like) ring and the attached group in each of the following examples.

EXERCISE II.   Which of the following ions will be resonance-stabilized by one of the groups attached to the benzene ring?

20.1   The lone pair electrons that are counted in determining aromaticity are those that are in the plane of the conjugated cyclic π system and bring the total number of π electrons to $4n + 2$.

lone pair in sp^2 orbital
no overlap with p orbitals
on carbon

(a)
yes
planar π system,
6 π electrons;
one lone pair on
oxygen is needed

sp^2-hybridized oxygen;
lone pair in p orbital
overlaps with p orbitals
on carbon

(b)
no
π system not continuous

2 e in p orbital   empty p orbital

(c)
yes
planar π system,
6 π electrons;
all three lone pairs on
nitrogen are needed

6 p orbitals;
3 contain 2 electrons,
3 have room to
accept electrons

(d)
yes
planar π system, 6 π electrons;
the lone pair on oxygen is in
sp^2 hybrid orbital

(e)
yes; planar π system, 6 π electrons;
the lone pairs on the nitrogen in sp^2 hybrid orbitals,
do not overlap with π bonds

(f)
yes; planar π system, 6 π electrons;
the lone pair on the nitrogen bonded to the
hydrogen is in a p orbital and is part of the π system,
the lone pair on the other nitrogen is not.

20.2   The hydrogen atoms on the sp^2-hybridized carbon atoms in thiophene absorb at a much lower field than those bound to the sp^2-hybridized carbon atoms in methyl vinyl sulfide. The hydrogen atoms in thiophene are thus much more deshielded than the vinyl hydrogens in methyl vinyl sulfide. The chemical shifts of the thiophene hydrogen atoms fall in the region where hydrogen atoms on aromatic rings absorb, pointing to the presence of a ring current, which is one of the criteria for aromaticity.

thiophene
$(4n + 2)$ π electrons with $n = 1$, therefore
an aromatic system with delocalization
of electrons over the ring

$CH_3 — \overset{..}{\underset{..}{S}} — CH=CH_2$

methyl vinyl sulfide

20.3

Concept Map 20.1   Aromaticity.

20.4

σ bonds between the carbon atoms and
between the carbon and hydrogen atoms

20.5 (a) 1,3-dinitrobenzene   (b) 2-methylnaphthalene   (c) 3-ethylnitrobenzene
              m-dinitrobenzene   *β*-methylnaphthalene   *m*-ethylnitrobenzene
        (d) 4-chlorophenol   (e) 2,4-dichlorotoluene   (f) 4-*tert*-butylnitrobenzene
              p-chlorophenol   *p-tert*-butylnitrobenzene

20.6 (a)   (b)   (c)

        (d)   (e)   (f)

        (g)   (h)   (i)

20.7

Four of the five resonance contributors of phenanthrene have a double bond at the 9,10 position. That bond, therefore, has more localized double bond character than the other bonds in the molecule.

20.8

Phenol is much less likely to transfer a proton to acetic acid than it is to water. The water solution will contain a higher concentration of phenolate ion than will the acetic acid solution.

20.9

The reactive intermediate from the phenolate ion is better stabilized than the one from phenol. The phenolate ion gives rise to a reactive intermediate which has no separation of charge in its major resonance contributor, and hence is more stable than the reactive intermediate from phenol. A more stable reactive intermediate corresponds to a lower transition state and, therefore, to a faster reaction.

20.10   (a)

(b)

20.10 (c)

Concept Map 20.2   Electrophilic aromatic substitution.

Concept Map 20.3   Essential steps of an electrophilic aromatic substitution.

Concept Map 20.4   Reactivity and orientation in electrophilic aromatic substitution.

favorable   favorable   unfavorable   not good, not bad

20.11   If electrophilic substitution occurs at the para position of the ring, the intermediate will have the following resonance contributors:

In this resonance contributor
the positive charge on the ring
is next to the positively charged
nitrogen atom; unfavorable

A similar set of resonance contributors can be drawn for ortho substitution. If electrophilic substitution occurs at the meta position, the positive charge on the ring is separated from the positive charge on the nitrogen atom by at least one carbon atom in all resonance contributors.

The intermediate formed on electrophilic attack at the meta position is, therefore, of lower energy than the intermediate formed when reaction occurs at the ortho or para positions.

20.12

Amines are good Brønsted bases. Strong acid converts the amine into a substituted ammonium ion, which has a positively charged nitrogen atom directly attached to the ring, and is therefore meta directing. The last step of the reaction is the deprotonation of the aromatic ammonium ion by ammonia to generate the free amine.

20.13

The hydroxyl group hydrogen bonds to water and, therefore, undergoes rapid hydrogen-deuterium exchange. Exchange of the hydrogen atoms on the aromatic ring has a high energy of activation and requires strong acid catalysis because, for exchange to occur, the aromaticity of the ring must be disrupted by the formation of a cationic intermediate. In the absence of strong acid, such exchange is extremely slow.

20.14 (a)

(b)

(Note: reversing the order in which these reagents are used would give ortho- and para-substituted products.)

(c)

20.14 (d)

(e)

20.15 (a)

(b)

(c)

(d)

20.16

20.16 (cont)

The same process would take place with the other alcohol except that the point of attack of the chain would be different. Attack would be at carbon 1 of the ring instead of carbon 2.

20.17 $C_{60}Cl_n$ + n ⬡ $\xrightarrow{AlCl_3}$ C_{60}(⬡)$_n$ + n HCl

A Friedel-Crafts
reaction takes place

has aromatic hydrogens,
therefore band at δ 7.2 in the NMR

20.18 (a) 2 ⬡ + ClC(CH$_2$)$_3$CCl $\xrightarrow[\text{(excess)}]{AlCl_3}$ ⬡—C(CH$_2$)$_3$C—⬡

(b) ⬡—CH$_2$CCl + ⬡ $\xrightarrow{AlCl_3}$ ⬡—CH$_2$C—⬡

(c) ⬡(OCH$_3$) + (CH$_3$C)$_2$O $\xrightarrow{AlCl_3}$ (OCH$_3$)⬡(CCH$_3$) + (OCH$_3$)⬡(CCH$_3$)

20.19 (a) ⬡—CCH$_3$ $\xrightarrow[\Delta]{\text{H}_2\text{NNH}_2, \text{KOH} \atop \text{diethylene glycol}}$ ⬡—CH$_2$CH$_3$

(b) ⬡(CH)(CH$_3$O)(OCH$_3$)(OCH$_3$) $\xrightarrow[\Delta]{\text{H}_2\text{NNH}_2, \text{KOH} \atop \text{diethylene glycol}}$ ⬡(CH$_3$)(CH$_3$O)(OCH$_3$)(OCH$_3$)

(c) ⬡—CCH$_2$CH$_2$CH$_3$ $\xrightarrow[\Delta]{\text{HSCH}_2\text{CH}_2\text{SH} \atop \text{BF}_3}$ ⬡(S—S)CH$_2$CH$_2$CH$_3$ $\xrightarrow[\Delta]{\text{Raney Ni} \atop \text{ethanol}}$ ⬡—CH$_2$CH$_2$CH$_2$CH$_3$

Concept Map 20.5   Electrophiles in aromatic substitution reactions.

20.20 (a)

(b)

(c)

20.21 (a)

minor product because of
more steric interactions

(b)

(c)

20.22

(a)

(b) (1)

(2)

(c)

Concept Map 20.6   Nucleophilic aromatic substitution.

20.23 (a)

20.23 (d)

20.24

2,4-D

The phenolate anion is a stronger base and a better nucleophile than the chloroacetate anion. The oxygen atom of the phenolate anion will displace the chloride leaving group of the chloroacetate anion. Aromatic nucleophilic substitution reactions require strongly electron-withdrawing substituents on the benzene ring to stabilize the negative charge in the transition state. The chlorine atoms on the aromatic ring of the dichlorophenolate ion are not displaced in nucleophilic substitution reactions.

20.25 (a) 3,4-dimethylnitrobenzene (b) 4-methyl-1-phenylpentane (c) 2-chloro-6-ethylnaphthalene
(d) 2,4-dinitrotoluene (e) *m*-bromobenzoic acid (f) methyl 3,5-dimethylbenzoate
(g) 1-(4-methylphenyl)-1-butanone (h) *p*-bromobenzaldehyde (4-bromobenzaldehyde)

20.26 (a)

(b)

(c)

(d)

(e)

(f)

20.27

(a)

20.27

(b)

C   +   D

(c)

H₂NNH₂, KOH

ethylene glycol
Δ

E

(d)

Br₂

FeBr₃
Δ

F

(e)

CH₃CHCl

AlCl₃

G   +   H

(f)

HF

I   +   J

(g)

Δ
pressure

K

(h)

+ CH₃ONa

methanol

L

(i)

H₂SO₄

M

Pd/C
Δ
(no H₂)

N
C₂₆H₁₆

20.28

(a)

(b)

(c)

(d)

The location of the chlorine atom ortho to the nitro group is essential to the reaction. Chloride ion is a better leaving group than bromide ion for nucleophilic substitution reactions on aromatic rings (see Section 20.8A).

(e)

(f)

(g)

20.28 (g) (cont)

(h)

(i)

20.29

20.30 (a)

(b)

Only one possible isomer is shown for the reactions above.

20.30 (c)

(d)

20.31   (a)

(b)   The position attacked is para to the most highly activating, *o,p*-directing group, the hydroxyl group on the starting material, and meta to the *m*-directing carboxylic acid group. The carbocationic intermediate formed is stabilized by resonance.

(c)

benzylic carbocation

20.32

(a)

(b)

(c)

20.33

20.33 (cont)

NaOH H₃O⁺
H₂O   Δ
Δ

$+ \quad CO_2$

20.34 $CH_2 = CHCH_2 - \overset{..}{\underset{..}{O}} - H \longrightarrow CH_2 = CHCH_2 - \overset{+}{\underset{H}{\overset{..}{O}}} - H \longrightarrow CH_2 = CHCH_2 \quad \overset{..}{\underset{H}{O}} \overset{H}{\overset{}{}}$

3-phenyl-1-propene

1,2-diphenylpropane

20.35

Azulene has a planar π system with 10 π electrons, so we would expect the compound to have aromaticity. It has $4n + 2$ electrons with $n = 2$. One particularly interesting resonance contributor for azulene may be regarded as the juxtaposition of an aromatic tropylium ion with an aromatic cyclopentadienyl anion.

tropylium ion ⟶   ⟵ cyclopentadienyl anion

20.36

The reaction is a nucleophilic aromatic substitution reaction. The relative rates of reaction for the different nucleophiles reflect the relative nucleophilicities of the different species.

Methoxide and thiophenolate ions are the best nucleophiles. Methoxide ion is a good base, meaning that it is willing to share its electrons. The thiophenolate ion is a good nucleophile because of the polarizability of the sulfur atom. Aniline is the weakest nucleophile. It bears no negative charge, and its nonbonding electrons are delocalized to the aromatic ring by resonance and therefore not easily available for bond formation.

20.37

For Y: $-OCH_3$ > $-CH_3$ > $-H$ > $-Cl$ > $-NO_2$

fastest   slowest

The order of reactivity depends on the nucleophilicity of the nitrogen atom in the substituted aniline, which in turn is dependent on the availability of the nonbonding electrons. Electron-donating groups at the para position would increase the rate of the reaction, and electron-withdrawing groups would decrease the rate of the reaction.

The methoxyl group is strongly electron-donating by resonance.

The methyl group is weakly electron-donating by induction.

The chlorine is electron-withdrawing by induction.

The nitro group is strongly electron-withdrawing by resonance.

20.38 CH_3SCH_3 + NaH $\longrightarrow$ $Na^+ \; {}^-:CH_2SCH_3$ + $H_2\uparrow$

20.38 (cont)

cyclononatetraene $4n + 2 = 10$

$2K^+$

$4n + 2 = 10$

Both anions have $4n + 2 = 10$ π electrons delocalized in planar rings and are, therefore, aromatic species. They have aromatic stability just as the tropylium ion and the cyclopentadienyl anion do (Section 20.1D).

20.39

conjugate base of
fulvene-6,6-diol

resonance contributor
that has aromatic (cyclo-
pentadienyl anion-like)
character

20.40

Resonance contributors for heptafulvene have the positive charge delocalized over the seven-membered ring in what is a tropylium ion, but the negative charge is localized on a carbon atom. In the dicyano compound, the negative charge can be delocalized onto the two nitrogen atoms. The two electron-withdrawing cyano groups thus stabilize the negative character at the carbon atom outside the ring.

20.41

20.41 (cont)

20.42 (a)

(b)

hydrolysis product

tautomerization reaction

20.43

Brønsted acid

protonation
or deprotonation   1,2-alkyl
shift

1,2-alkyl
shift

protonation
or deprotonation

20.44

corannulene
$C_{20}H_{10}$

Corannulene has 3 double bonds in each six-membered ring.

20.45   (a) $C_{60} = 60 \times 12$ amu $= 720$ amu
1656 amu $-$ 720 amu $= 936$ amu
MW of benzene $= 78$ amu
936 amu/78 amu $= 12$ benzene units,
therefore MW 1656 corresponds to $C_{60}(C_6H_6)_{12}$.

   (b) The proton nuclear magnetic resonance spectrum shows that the hydrogen atoms on benzene have been converted into two kinds of hydrogens. Five of them remain as aromatic hydrogens; one has been converted into another type of hydrogen, perhaps more typical of alkene hydrogens.

   (c)

20.46   We get the following information from the spectral data:

Mass spectrum:	756 amu $-$ 720 amu $= 36$ amu, the gain in molecular weight of C_{60}. Therefore, 36 hydrogen atoms were added to C_{60}.
Proton NMR spectrum:	The new compound contains hydrogen atoms. The chemical shifts indicate that there are two types of hydrogens. The broad multiplets indicate that they are coupled.
IR spectrum:	The infrared spectrum confirms the presence of carbon-hydrogen bonds with bands at 2925 and 2855 cm^{-1}. Bands at 1620 and 675 cm^{-1} indicate the presence of double bonds.
UV spectrum:	The ultraviolet spectrum of C_{60} indicates that there is extensive conjugation of the double bonds. The new compound has lost that conjugation. The same conclusion can be drawn from the loss of the deep color of the C_{60} solution during the reaction.

All of the data suggest that 36 hydrogen atoms have added to C_{60}. They have done so in a way that breaks up the conjugation of the double bonds in C_{60}, leaving isolated double bonds in the compound, $C_{60}H_{36}$, that results. A look at the fragment of C_{60} shown on p. 767 in the text gives an idea of how this could happen.

20.47 The infrared spectrum tells us that Compound A is an alcohol (3329 cm^{-1} is the O—H stretching frequency, and 1046 cm^{-1} is the C—O stretching frequency), and Compound B is an ether (1245 and 1049 cm^{-1} are the C–O stretching frequencies). The proton magnetic resonance spectra are analyzed below:

Compound A:

δ 2.5	(2H, t, $J = 7$ Hz, —CH$_2$C$\underline{H}_2$—)
δ 3.4	(2H, t, $J = 7$ Hz, —OC$\underline{H}_2$CH$_2$—)
δ 3.7	(1H, s, —O$\underline{H}$)
δ 6.7	(5H, s, ArH)

Compound B:

δ 1.3	(3H, t, $J = 7$ Hz, —CH$_2$C$\underline{H}_3$)
δ 3.7	(2H, q, $J = 7$ Hz, —OC$\underline{H}_2$CH$_3$)
δ 6.3 – 7.0	(5H, m, Ar$\underline{H}$)

The fragments for both Compound A and Compound B add up to $C_8H_{10}O$, which corresponds to a molecular weight of 122, which is where the molecular ion of each compound appears in the mass spectrum. We thus have the molecular formulas for Compounds A and B. Compound A is 2-phenylethanol. The base peak for Compound A, m/z 91, is the tropylium ion, which results from the following fragmentation:

Compound A
2-phenylethanol

From the infrared spectrum we know that Compound B is an ether. The quartet at δ 3.7, and the triplet at δ 1.3 in the proton magnetic resonance spectrum tells us that there is an isolated ethyl group in which the methylene group is attached to an oxygen atom. Compound B is ethyl phenyl ether (ethoxybenzene). The base peak in Compound B, m/z 94, is 28 mass units less than the molecular ion and corresponds to a rearrangement in which ethylene, C_2H_4, is lost.

Compound B
ethyl phenyl ether
ethoxybenzene

Supplemental Problems

S20.1   Give structural formulas for all reagents, intermediates, and products designated by letters in the following equations.

(a)

$$\text{(naphthalene structure with OCH}_3\text{, CHOCH}_3\text{, CH=O substituents)} \xrightarrow[\text{methanol}]{\text{NaBH}_4} A \xrightarrow[\text{dioxane}]{\text{H}_3\text{O}^+} B$$

(Hint: Compound B does not show an absorption band for a carbonyl group in its infrared spectrum.)

(b)

$$\text{(structure)} \xrightarrow{\text{NaH} \quad \text{CH}_3\text{I}} C \xrightarrow[\substack{\text{tetrahydro-}\\\text{furan}}]{\text{BH}_3} \xrightarrow[\text{H}_2\text{O}]{\text{H}_2\text{O}_2,\ \text{NaOH}} D \xrightarrow[\substack{\text{H}_2\text{SO}_4\\\text{H}_2\text{O}\\\Delta}]{\text{CrO}_3} E \xrightarrow[\Delta]{\text{H}_3\text{PO}_4} F \xrightarrow[\substack{\text{diethyl}\\\text{ether}}]{\text{LiAlH}_4\ \ \text{H}_2\text{O}} G$$

(c)

$$\text{HOCCH}_2\text{CH}_2\text{—(benzene ring)—CH}_2\text{CH}_2\text{COH} \xrightarrow[\Delta]{\text{H}_3\text{PO}_4} H\ +\ I$$

(d)

$$\text{(structure with CH=O, OH, OCH}_3\text{)} \xrightarrow[\text{ethylene glycol}]{\text{H}_2\text{NNH}_2,\ \text{KOH}} J$$

(e)

$$\text{(structure with CH=O, OH, OCH}_3\text{)} \xrightarrow{\text{NaBH}_4} K \xrightarrow[\text{(2 equiv)}\ \ \text{(1 equiv)}]{\text{NaH} \quad \text{CH}_3\text{I}} \xrightarrow{\text{H}_3\text{O}^+} L$$

(f)

$$\text{(HO, COH, OH structure)} \xrightarrow{M} \text{(CH}_3\text{O, COCH}_3\text{, OCH}_3\text{)} \xrightarrow{N} \text{(CH}_3\text{O, CH}_2\text{OH, OCH}_3\text{)} \xrightarrow{O} \text{(CH}_3\text{O, Br, CH}_2\text{OH, OCH}_3\text{)}$$

(g)

$$\text{(benzoic acid, COH)} \xrightarrow[\text{Fe}]{\text{Br}_2} P$$

(h)

$$\text{(acetanilide, NHCCH}_3\text{)} \xrightarrow[\text{H}_2\text{SO}_4]{\text{HNO}_3} Q\ +\ R$$

S20.2   More practice in completing equations follows. Give structural formulas for all reagents, intermediates, and products designated by letters in the following equations.

(a)

$$\text{(phenol, OH)} + \text{CH}_3\text{CHCH}_2\text{OH (with CH}_3\text{)} \xrightarrow[\Delta]{\text{H}_2\text{SO}_4} A\ +\ B$$

(b)

$$\text{O}_2\text{N—(ring with NO}_2\text{, NO}_2\text{)—Cl} + \text{H}_2\text{N—N(phenyl)}_2 \xrightarrow{\text{chloroform}} C$$

S20.3   Propose syntheses for the following compounds starting with benzene, toluene, and any other organic compounds having no more than three carbon atoms. There may be more than one way to synthesize each compound; try to find the shortest route.

(a)   (b)   (c)   (d)

S20.4   Propose a complete, stepwise mechanism for the following transformation using the curved arrow convention.

S20.5   The reactions of several 2,4-dinitrochlorobenzenes with piperidine in ethanol as a solvent were studied. Structural formulas for the compounds and the relative rates of their reactions are shown below. What factor is influencing the rates in this series? How do you explain the effect? (Hint: A careful examination of the structural formula for the Meisenheimer complex on p. 793 in the text will furnish a clue.)

k_{rel} 956   267   16.2

S20.6   When 2-hydroxybenzoic acid is heated with isobutyl alcohol in the presence of sulfuric acid, compound A is formed. The same product is obtained when *tert*-butyl alcohol and sulfuric acid are used. What is the structure of compound A? Write a mechanism that accounts for these experimental facts.

S20.7   When 3,7-di-*tert*-butylnaphthalene is treated with two equivalents of bromine in the presence of ferric bromide, the major product has three sets of equivalent hydrogen atoms in its proton magnetic resonance spectrum in a ratio of 9:1:1. What is the most likely structure for this product? (Hint: Be sure to take steric factors into consideration in your answer.)

S20.8   The heterocyclic compounds pyrrole and indole, shown below, are not very basic. Pyrrole has pK_a ~15 and thus has considerable acidity. Explain why pyrrole is so much less basic (so much more acidic) than ammonia (pK_a ~36).

:NH₃

| ammonia | pyrrole | indole |
| ~36 | ~15 | ~15 |

pK_a

21

Free Radicals

Concept Map 21.1   Chain reactions.

- -

21.1   Propane has six primary hydrogen atoms and two secondary hydrogen atoms for a total of eight hydrogen atoms. If there were no difference in reactivity between primary and secondary hydrogen atoms, for every six primary hydrogen atoms that react, two secondary hydrogen atoms would react, and the product mixture would consist of 75% 1-chloropropane and 25% 2-chloropropane. When the difference in reactivity is considered, for every six primary hydrogen atoms that react, 2×2.5 or five secondary hydrogen atoms would react. The product mixture should thus consist of 55% 1-chloropropane and 45% 2-chloropropane.

$$\frac{6}{6+5} \times 100 = 55\%$$

$$\frac{5}{6+5} \times 100 = 45\%$$

2-Methylpropane has nine primary hydrogen atoms and one tertiary hydrogen atom. If there were no difference in reactivity between primary and tertiary hydrogen atoms, the product mixture would consist of 90% 1-chloro-2-methylpropane (isobutyl chloride) and 10% 2-chloro-2-methylpropane (*tert*-butyl chloride). When the difference in reactivity is considered, for every nine primary hydrogen atoms that react, 1×4 or four tertiary hydrogen atoms would react. The product mixture should thus consist of 69% 1-chloro-2-methylpropane and 31% 2-chloro-2-methylpropane.

$$\frac{9}{9+4} \times 100 = 69\%$$

$$\frac{4}{9+4} \times 100 = 31\%$$

21.2   The selectivity observed at 300 °C depends on small differences between energies of activation for the abstraction of primary, secondary, and tertiary hydrogen atoms. As the temperature increases, the average kinetic energy of chlorine atoms and alkane molecules increases. The number of collisions that have energies in excess of the energy of activation for the abstraction of the different kinds of hydrogen atoms also increases. Differences in energies of activation for different reactions become less and less relevant. We see a leveling off of the selectivity of the reactions. If the temperature is high enough, almost all molecules will have energy equal to or greater than the activation energies for any hydrogen to be abstracted, and the rates of reaction would be the same.

Concept Map 21.2   Halogenation of alkanes.

21.3   Neopentane (2,2-dimethylpropane) has only primary hydrogen atoms. The enthalpy for the abstraction of a primary hydrogen atom by a chlorine atom is -5 kcal/mol. The activation energy for this exothermic step is small (~ 1 kcal/mol), and the rate is correspondingly fast. The enthalpy for the abstraction of a primary hydrogen atom by a bromine atom, on the other hand, is $+12$ kcal/mol. The activation energy must be at least as large as the enthalpy, and the rate is correspondingly slow.

21.4   (a), (b)

This product is reported to form in 58% yield. Another possible product is the one in which the allylic hydrogen atom adjacent to the oxygen atom is replaced.

Usually an ether oxygen stabilizes a radical at an adjacent carbon atom. The following resonance contributors are written to explain the effect.

In this case, the electron-withdrawing carbonyl group attached to the oxygen atom reduces the electron density at the oxygen atom, making the corresponding resonance contributor unfavorable. The product, with two good leaving groups on the same allylic carbon atom, might also be too unstable to isolate.

21.5 $CH_3CH_2CH_2CH_2CH = CHCH_3 \xrightarrow{\text{NBS}} CH_3CH_2CH_2CHCH = CHCH_3$

with Br substituent; 60%

$CH_3CH_2CH_2CHCH = CHCH_3 \rightarrow CH_3CH_2CH_2\overset{\cdot}{C}HCH = CHCH_3 \longleftrightarrow CH_3CH_2CH_2CH = CH\overset{\cdot}{C}HCH_3$

$\downarrow Br_2 \qquad\qquad \downarrow Br_2$

$CH_3CH_2CH_2CHCH = CHCH_3$ (Br)   4-bromo-2-heptene

$CH_3CH_2CH_2CH = CHCHCH_3$ (Br)   2-bromo-3-heptene

$CH_3CH_2CH_2CH_2CH = CHCH_2 \rightarrow CH_3CH_2CH_2CH_2CH = CH\overset{\cdot}{C}H_2 \longleftrightarrow CH_3CH_2CH_2CH_2\overset{\cdot}{C}HCH = CH_2$

$\downarrow Br_2 \qquad\qquad \downarrow Br_2$

$CH_3CH_2CH_2CH_2CH = CHCH_2Br$ 1-bromo-2-heptene

$CH_3CH_2CH_2CH_2CHCH = CH_2$ (Br)   3-bromo-1-heptene

Concept Map 21.3   Selective free radical halogenations.

- -

21.6 (a) PhCH₂CH₃ $\xrightarrow[\Delta]{\overset{Cl_2}{h\nu}}$ PhCHCH₃

$\qquad\qquad$ | Cl

major product

(b) [indene] $\xrightarrow[\substack{\text{benzoyl peroxide}\\ \text{carbon tetrachloride}\\ \Delta}]{\text{NBS}}$ [1-bromoindene]

(c) [2-methylnaphthalene] $\xrightarrow[\substack{\text{carbon}\\ \text{tetrachloride}\\ \Delta}]{\text{NBS}}$ [2-(bromomethyl)naphthalene]

(d) PhCH₂CH₃ $\xrightarrow[h\nu]{Br_2}$ PhCHCH₃

$\qquad\qquad$ | Br

major product

21.7   The unpaired electron can be delocalized over three rings.

[resonance structures of the triphenylmethyl radical]

21.7 (cont)

21.8   1.

$$CH_3\overset{\cdot\cdot}{\underset{\cdot\cdot}{C}}O\!-\!\overset{:O:}{\overset{\|}{}}\!O\overset{:O:}{\overset{\|}{C}}CH_3 \xrightarrow{h\nu} 2\ CH_3\overset{:O:}{\overset{\|}{C}}O\cdot$$

$$CH_3\overset{:O:}{\overset{\|}{C}}O\cdot \quad :\!\overset{\cdot\cdot}{Br}\!-\!CCl_3 \longrightarrow CH_3\overset{:O:}{\overset{\|}{C}}O\overset{\cdot\cdot}{Br}: \quad \cdot CCl_3 \longrightarrow Cl_3CCH_2\overset{\cdot}{C}H(CH_2)_5CH_3 \longrightarrow$$

$$CH_2\!=\!CH(CH_2)_5CH_3$$

$$:\overset{\cdot\cdot}{Br}: \quad \cdot CCl_3$$

$$Cl_3CCH_2CH(CH_2)_5CH_3$$

2.

$$CH_3CH_2\overset{\cdot\cdot}{\underset{\cdot\cdot}{S}}\!-\!H \xrightarrow{\Delta} CH_3CH_2\overset{\cdot\cdot}{\underset{\cdot\cdot}{S}}\cdot \longrightarrow CH_3CH_2\overset{\cdot\cdot}{\underset{\cdot\cdot}{S}}CH_2\overset{\cdot}{C}CH_3 \longrightarrow CH_3CH_2\overset{\cdot\cdot}{\underset{\cdot\cdot}{S}}CH_2\overset{CH_3}{\overset{|}{C}HCH_3}$$

$$\cdot H$$

$$CH_2\!=\!\overset{CH_3}{\underset{|}{C}CH_3}$$

$$H\!-\!\overset{\cdot\cdot}{\underset{\cdot\cdot}{S}}CH_2CH_3$$

$$\cdot \overset{\cdot\cdot}{\underset{\cdot\cdot}{S}}CH_2CH_3$$

3.

$$CH_3\overset{:O:}{\overset{\|}{C}}O\!-\!O\overset{:O:}{\overset{\|}{C}}CH_3 \xrightarrow{h\nu} 2\ CH_3\overset{:O:}{\overset{\|}{C}}O\cdot$$

$$CH_3\overset{:O:}{\overset{\|}{C}}O\cdot \quad H\!-\!SiCl_3 \longrightarrow CH_3\overset{:O:}{\overset{\|}{C}}OH \quad \cdot SiCl_3 \longrightarrow Cl_3SiCH_2\overset{\cdot}{C}H(CH_2)_5CH_3 \longrightarrow$$

$$CH_2\!=\!CH(CH_2)_5CH_3$$

$$H\!-\!SiCl_3$$

$$\cdot SiCl_3$$

$$Cl_3SiCH_2CH_2(CH_2)_5CH_3$$

21.9   (a) (cyclohexene) + CH_3SH $\xrightarrow[\text{hv}]{\text{acetone}}$ (cyclohexane-SCH_3)

(b) Cl_3CBr + $CH_2\!=\!\underset{\underset{CH_2CH_3}{|}}{C}CH_2CH_3$ $\xrightarrow{\Delta}$ $Cl_3CCH_2\underset{\underset{Br}{|}}{\overset{\overset{CH_2CH_3}{|}}{C}}CH_2CH_3$

(c) $CH_3(CH_2)_4SiH_3$ + $CH_3(CH_2)_5CH\!=\!CH_2$ $\xrightarrow{\text{peroxides}}$ $CH_3(CH_2)_4SiH_2(CH_2)_7CH_3$

Concept Map 21.4   Free radical addition reactions of alkenes.

21.10

silphiperfol-6-ene

↑ H₂NNH₂, KOH
triethylene glycol

$(CH_3CH_2CH_2CH_2)_3SnH$

H₃O⁺

21.11

radical from
linoleic acid

other resonance
contributor of radical

(10*E*,12*Z*)-9-hydroperoxy-10,12-
octadecadienoic acid

21.12

(8*Z*,11*Z*,14*Z*)-8,11,14-icosatrienoic acid

$\xrightarrow[\text{enzyme}]{O_2}$

(8*Z*,11*Z*,13*E*)-15-hydroperoxy-8,11,13-icosatrienoic acid

21.12 (cont)

Note that while the opening of the ring in an unsymmetrical oxirane usually gives rise to a mixture of isomers, a reaction in biological systems gives rise to a single product. The mechanism shown above assumes that the reaction is taking place with a preferred orientation at the active site of an enzyme (see Section 25.5 for an example) and that, therefore, only one product is formed.

21.14   (a)   (b)

21.14 (c)

unstable, hydrolyzed in
water to *p*-napthoquinone

(d)

21.15 (a)

(b)

Both syntheses are Friedel-Crafts alkylation reactions. In (a) both the hydroxyl group and the methoxyl group are strong ortho,para directors, leading to attack at positions ortho to each. In (b) the hydroxyl group is a much stronger ortho,para director than the methyl group, and attack is at the two positions ortho to the hydroxyl group.

21.16

21.17

Concept Map 21.5 Oxidation reactions as free radical reactions.

21.18

An alternate synthesis is shown on the next page:

21.18 (cont)

21.19

(a) $CH_3CH=CHCH=CHCH_3$ $\xrightarrow[\substack{\text{carbon} \\ \text{tetrachloride}}]{\substack{Br_2 \\ \text{(1 molar equiv)}}}$ $CH_3CHBrCHBrCH=CHCH_3$ + $CH_3CHBrCH=CHCHBrCH_3$

(b)

(c)

(d) $CH_3CH_2CH_3$ $\xrightarrow[hv]{Cl_2}$ $CH_3CH_2CH_2Cl$ + $CH_3CHClCH_3$ + $CH_3CH_2CHCl_2$ + $CH_3CHClCH_2Cl$

major products   two of the possible minor products

(e)

(f)   (g)

(h)

(i)

21.19

(j)

PhO—CH₂CH₂—CH(Br)—CH₂CH₂CH=CH₂ + (CH₃CH₂CH₂CH₂)₃SnH

with AIBN initiator:

CH₃C(CN)(CH₃)—N=N—C(CN)(CH₃)CH₃   90 °C   →   PhO—CH₂CH₂—(cyclopentyl)

(k) $CH_3CH_2CH_2CH=CH_2$ + Cl_3SiH $\xrightarrow{280\ °C}$ $CH_3CH_2CH_2CH_2CH_2SiCl_3$

(l) $CH_3(CH_2)_5CH=CH_2$ + CCl_4 $\xrightarrow[\substack{CH_3COOCCH_3 \\ (O\ O) \\ h\nu}]{}$ $CH_3(CH_2)_5CHClCH_2CCl_3$

21.20

21.21   1.   Conditions for the formation of free radicals, such as heat, light, or peroxides, would be recommended for these reactions.

$$CH_3\overset{O}{\overset{\|}{C}}H \ + \ CH_3(CH_2)_5CH=CH_2 \xrightarrow{\text{peroxides}} CH_3\overset{O}{\overset{\|}{C}}(CH_2)_7CH_3$$

21.21 1. (cont)

2. *tert*-Butyl alcohol does not have a hydrogen atom attached to the carbon atom bonded to the hydroxyl group and would, therefore, not react with 1-octene under free radical conditions.

21.22

21.23 (a)

(b) PhCH=CHCH₂CH₃ ← $\xrightarrow{(CH_3)_2CuLi}$ ← PhCH=CHCH₂OTs

(c)

(d)

21.23   (e)

21.24   The final product in this series of reactions is a cyclic hemiketal that contains eleven carbon atoms. That is equal to the number of carbon atoms in the original starting material (except for the three carbon atoms of the protecting group on the diol) plus those of the nitrile and the Grignard reagent. Opening the hemiketal will give the structure of the last intermediate compound in the synthesis.

The first step of the reaction is a free-radical addition to the alkene.

In the next step the Grignard reagent must add to the nitrile.

The product of this step is the conjugate base of an imine, which will hydrolyze in dilute acid to a ketone.

21.24 (cont)

The cyclic ketal protecting group on the diol part of the molecule will be hydrolyzed by the same dilute acid solution that hydrolyzes the imine, giving the dihydroxyketone shown at the beginning of this answer. The hydroxyketone cyclizes spontaneously to the six-membered ring ketal.

21.25

21.26

21.26 (cont)

biological product

from Problem 21.11

21.27

21.27 (cont)

21.28 1.

2.

3.

4.

21.29

21.30

7-dehydrocholesteryl acetate

21.31

and diastereomer

radioactively labeled tamoxifen

21.32   (a)

A
two possible products;
the one actually isolated
is the one on the left

(b)

B

B   +   C

D

E

F

G

H   +   I

21.32 (b) (cont)

isopropyl group at this
stereocenter can be in the
plane or down; one is Compound
H, the other Compound I

Supplemental Problems

S21.1   When 3-phenyl-1-propene is treated with *N*-bromosuccinimide in the presence of benzoyl peroxide, 3-bromo-1-phenyl-1-propene (50%) and 3-bromo-3-phenyl-1-propene (10%) are formed. Write a mechanism for the reaction, and explain why the major product is 3-bromo-1-phenyl-1-propene.

S21.2   Complete the following equations, showing the product(s) you expect. If the stereochemistry is known for a reaction, make sure your answer shows it.

(a)

(b) $CH_3CH_2CH_2CH_3 \xrightarrow[hv]{Cl_2}$
       (excess)

(c) $CH_3CH_2SH + CH_2{=}CHOCH_2CH_3 \xrightarrow{\Delta}$

(d) $\xrightarrow[hv]{H_2S}$

(e) $\xrightarrow[\substack{carbon \\ tetrachloride \\ benzoyl\ peroxide \\ \Delta}]{NBS}$

S21.2

(f) + (CH₃CH₂CH₂CH₂)₃SnH $\xrightarrow{\qquad}$

$$(CH_3)_2\overset{\overset{\displaystyle CN}{|}}{C}-N=N-\overset{\overset{\displaystyle CN}{|}}{C}(CH_3)_2$$
$$\Delta$$

S21.3   The following reactions were carried out on the way to the synthesis of compounds for the study of free-radical reactions that form carbon–carbon bonds. Propose reagents for the transformations shown.

S21.4   In the same study described in Supplemental Problem S21.3, the following transformation was observed.

The product is the result of four successive free-radical carbon-carbon bond formation steps. Construct the final product from the two starting materials. Which carbon-carbon bond-forming reaction will be the first? Remember that if an intramolecular reaction is possible, it will occur more easily than an intermolecular reaction.

22

The Chemistry of Amines

22.1 (a) 2-methyl-1-propanamine (b) (1*R*, 2*S*)-2-ethyl-1-cyclopentanamine (c) *N,N*-diethylbutanamine
(isobutylamine) [(1*R*, 2*S*)-1-amino-2-ethylcyclopentane]

(d) 3-cyclopropyl-1-propanamine (e) 3-nitroaniline (*m*-nitroaniline) (f) 2,4-dibromoaniline
(3-cyclopropyl-1-propylamine)

22.2 (a)

$$CH_3CHCO^- + \overset{+}{N}H_4 \ Br^- \xleftarrow{\ NH_3 \ (excess)\ } CH_3CHCOH$$

with $\overset{+}{N}H_3$ below the left carbon and Br below the right carbon (O double bonds above both carbonyls)

(b)

$$PhNHCH_3 + Ph\overset{+}{N}H_3 \ I^- \xleftarrow[\text{(1 equiv)}]{CH_3I} PhNH_2$$
2 equiv

(c)

$$PhCH_2CH_2NH_2 \xleftarrow[]{\substack{NH_3 \\ (excess)}} PhCH_2CH_2Br \xleftarrow[\text{pyridine}]{PBr_3} PhCH_2CH_2OH \xleftarrow[]{H_3O^+} \triangle\!O$$

$$PhMgBr \xleftarrow[\substack{\text{diethyl} \\ \text{ether}}]{Mg} PhBr \xleftarrow[Fe]{Br_2} \bigcirc$$

22.3 4-Chlorobutanoic acid is a strong enough acid to protonate the phthalimidate anion, converting it to phthalimide. The nitrogen atom in phthalimide is not nucleophilic because the nonbonding electrons on nitrogen are delocalized to two carbonyl groups.

$$\text{(phthalimidate)} N^- K^+ + Cl(CH_2)_3COH \longrightarrow \text{(phthalimide)} NH + Cl(CH_2)_3CO^- K^+$$
$$pK_a \ 4.5 \qquad\qquad\qquad pK_a \ 7.4$$

22.4

$$ClCH_2CH_2CH_2C\equiv N \xleftarrow[\text{pyridine}]{SOCl_2} HOCH_2CH_2CH_2C\equiv N \xleftarrow[\text{ethanol}]{NaCN}$$
4-chlorobutanenitrile

$$HOCH_2CH_2CH_2Cl \xleftarrow[\text{pyridine}]{SOCl_2 \ (1 \ molar \ equiv)} HOCH_2CH_2CH_2OH$$

22.5

$$\overset{+}{H_3}NCH_2CH_2CH_2COH + CO_3^{2-} \rightleftharpoons \overset{+}{H_3}NCH_2CH_2CH_2CO^- + HCO_3^-$$
$$pK_a \sim 10.6 \qquad pK_a \sim 4.8 \qquad\qquad\qquad\qquad pK_a \ 10.2$$

The carboxylic acid group is more acidic than the conjugate acid of the amino group on the amino acid. As long as a large excess of carbonate ion is not used, the amino acid will be in the form shown.

22.6

$CH_3O\overset{O}{\underset{}{C}}$ ... $\xrightarrow[\substack{CH_3OH \\ H_2O}]{HCl}$ ... A $\xrightarrow[\substack{pyridine \\ methanol}]{HONH_2 \cdot HCl}$

B $\xrightarrow[\substack{PtO_2 \\ acetic\ acid}]{H_2}$ $\xrightarrow{HCl\ (g)}$ C

22.7

$\overset{HO}{}\ \overset{O}{\underset{}{C}}OCH_3$ ($+NH_3\ Cl^-$) $\underset{pH\ 8}{\overset{\longrightarrow}{\longleftarrow}}$ A (NH_2) $\xrightarrow[\substack{methanol \\ 30\ min}]{PhCH=O}$

B $\xrightarrow{NaBH_4}$ $\xrightarrow{HCl\ (g)}$ C ($Cl^-\ +NH_2CH_2Ph$) $\xrightarrow{NH_3}$ D ($NHCH_2Ph$)

22.8 (a) $PhCH_2CH_2NH_2 \xleftarrow[PtO_2]{H_2} PhCH=CHNO_2 \xleftarrow{CH_3NO_2,\ NaOH} PhCH=O \xleftarrow[dichloromethane]{\underset{H}{\overset{+}{N}}\ CrO_3Cl^-} PhCH_2OH$

(b) $CH_3CH_2CH_2\underset{NH_2}{CH}CH_2CH_3 \xleftarrow[Ni]{NH_3,\ H_2} CH_3CH_2CH_2CCH_2CH_3 \xleftarrow[acetone]{CrO_3} CH_3CH_2CH_2\underset{OH}{CH}CH_2CH_3$

$\xleftarrow[H_2O]{NH_4Cl} \xleftarrow[diethyl\ ether]{CH_3CH_2MgBr} CH_3CH_2CH_2CH=O \xleftarrow[dichloromethane]{\underset{H}{\overset{+}{N}}\ CrO_3Cl^-} CH_3CH_2CH_2CH_2OH$

(c) $\xleftarrow[\substack{diethyl \\ ether}]{H_2O\ \ LiAlH_4} \overset{O}{\underset{}{C}}NH_2 \xleftarrow{NH_3\ (excess)} \overset{O}{\underset{}{C}}Cl \xleftarrow[\Delta]{SOCl_2} \overset{O}{\underset{}{C}}OH$ ... CH_2NH_2

22.8 (d) Butadiene + maleonitrile → (via Diels-Alder) cyclohexene-dicarbonitrile $\xrightarrow[\text{diethyl ether}]{\text{LiAlH}_4}$ $\xrightarrow{\text{H}_2\text{O}}$ cyclohexene-bis(CH$_2$NH$_2$) $\xrightarrow[\text{PtO}_2]{\text{H}_2}$ cyclohexane-bis(CH$_2$NH$_2$)

22.9 (a) $\text{PhCH}=O + \text{NH}_3 \xrightarrow[\text{Raney Ni}]{\text{H}_2} \text{PhCH}_2\text{NH}_2$

(b) $\text{PhCH}_2\text{CH}_2\text{N}_3 \xrightarrow[\text{diethyl ether}]{\text{LiAlH}_4} \xrightarrow{\text{H}_2\text{O}} \text{PhCH}_2\text{CH}_2\text{NH}_2$

(c) O_2N—C$_6$H$_4$—CH_2COH (=O) $\xrightarrow[\text{Ni}]{\text{H}_2}$ H_2N—C$_6$H$_4$—CH_2COH (=O)

(d) cyclohexene oxide $\xrightarrow[\substack{\text{H}_2\text{O}\\ \text{dioxane}}]{\text{NaN}_3}$ trans-2-azidocyclohexanol (and enantiomer) $\xrightarrow[\text{PtO}_2]{\text{H}_2}$ trans-2-aminocyclohexanol (and enantiomer)

(e) cyclohexenyl-CH_2CN $\xrightarrow[\substack{\text{diethyl}\\\text{ether}}]{\text{LiAlH}_4}$ $\xrightarrow{\text{H}_2\text{O}}$ cyclohexenyl-$\text{CH}_2\text{CH}_2\text{NH}_2$

22.10 (a) cyclohexanone $\xrightarrow[\text{Ni}]{\text{NH}_3, \text{H}_2}$ cyclohexyl-NH_2 $\xrightarrow{2 \text{ CH}_3\text{I}}$ cyclohexyl-$\overset{+}{\text{N}}\text{H}(\text{CH}_3)_2$ I$^-$ ($\text{CH}_3\overset{+}{\text{N}}\text{HCH}_3$ I$^-$) $\xrightarrow[\text{H}_2\text{O}]{\text{NaOH}}$ cyclohexyl-$\text{N}(\text{CH}_3)_2$ (CH_3NCH_3)

(b) anisole (OCH$_3$) $\xrightarrow[\text{H}_2\text{SO}_4]{\text{HNO}_3}$ 4-nitroanisole (OCH$_3$, NO$_2$) $\xrightarrow[\text{H}_2\text{O}]{\text{Fe, HCl} \quad \text{NaOH}}$ 4-methoxyaniline (OCH$_3$, NH$_2$)

(c) $\text{CH}_3\text{CH}_2\text{CH}_2\text{CH}_2\text{Br}$ $\xrightarrow[\text{H}_2\text{O}]{\text{NaOH}}$ $\text{PhNCH}_2\text{CH}_2\text{CH}_2\text{CH}_3$ (with CH$_2$CH$_2$CH$_2$CH$_3$)

$\text{CH}_3\text{CH}_2\text{CH}_2\text{CH}=O$ $\xrightarrow{\text{PhNH}_2}$ $\text{PhN}=\text{CHCH}_2\text{CH}_2\text{CH}_3$ $\xrightarrow[\text{H}_2\text{O}]{\text{NaBH}_4}$ $\text{PhNHCH}_2\text{CH}_2\text{CH}_2\text{CH}_3$

(d) (1) $\text{CH}_3(\text{CH}_2)_6\text{CH}_2\text{Br}$ $\xrightarrow[\text{pyridine}]{\text{PBr}_3}$ ... $\xrightarrow{\text{NH}_3 \text{ (excess)}}$ $\text{CH}_3(\text{CH}_2)_6\text{CH}_2\text{NH}_2$

$\text{CH}_3(\text{CH}_2)_4\text{CH}_2\text{Br}$ $\xrightarrow[\text{pyridine}]{\text{PBr}_3}$ ... $\xrightarrow[\substack{\text{diethyl}\\\text{ether}}]{\text{Mg}}$ $\text{CH}_3(\text{CH}_2)_4\text{CH}_2\text{MgBr}$ $\xrightarrow{\text{ethylene oxide}}$ $\xrightarrow{\text{H}_3\text{O}^+}$ $\text{CH}_3(\text{CH}_2)_6\text{CH}_2\text{OH}$

22.10 (d) (1) (cont)

$$CH_3(CH_2)_4CH_2OH \xleftarrow{H_3O^+} \xleftarrow{\triangle O} CH_3CH_2CH_2CH_2MgBr \xleftarrow[\substack{\text{diethyl} \\ \text{ether}}]{Mg} CH_3CH_2CH_2CH_2Br$$

(2) $CH_3(CH_2)_6CH_2NH_2 \xleftarrow[\substack{Pd \\ \text{acetic acid}}]{H_2} CH_3(CH_2)_5CH=CHNO_2 \xleftarrow{CH_3NO_2,\ NaOH}$

$$CH_3(CH_2)_5\overset{O}{\overset{\|}{C}}H \xleftarrow[\substack{\text{dichloromethane} \\ \text{or}}]{\underset{H}{\overset{+N}{\bigcirc}}\ CrO_3Cl^-} CH_3(CH_2)_5CH_2OH \xleftarrow{H_3O^+} \xleftarrow{\square O} CH_3CH_2CH_2CH_2MgBr$$

[from (d) (1)]

$$(CH_3CH_2)_3N \leftarrow \xleftarrow{CH_3\overset{O}{\overset{\|}{S}}CH_3,\ Cl\overset{O}{\overset{\|}{C}}-\overset{O}{\overset{\|}{C}}Cl}$$

(3) $CH_3(CH_2)_6CH_2NH_2 \xleftarrow[Ni]{NH_3,\ H_2} CH_3(CH_2)_6\overset{O}{\overset{\|}{C}}H \xleftarrow[\text{dichloromethane}]{\underset{H}{\overset{+N}{\bigcirc}}\ CrO_3Cl^-} CH_3(CH_2)_6CH_2OH$

[from (d) (1)]

22.11

Procaine has two amine functions, an amino group on the aromatic ring and a tertiary alkyl amine function. The alkyl amine is much more basic (pK_a of a substituted ammonium ion, ~10) than an aryl amine (pK_a of the anilinium ion, 4.6). Therefore procaine hydrochloride has the structure shown above.

22.12 (a)

$$\xrightarrow[H_2SO_4]{CH_3OH,\ (CH_3O)_3CH} A \xrightarrow[\text{tetrahydrofuran}]{LiAlH_4} \xrightarrow{H_2O} B$$

$$\xrightarrow[\substack{(CH_3CH_2)_3N \\ \text{dichloromethane}}]{MsCl} C \xrightarrow[H_2O]{H_3O^+} D$$

$$E \xrightarrow[\text{acetone}]{NaI}$$

separated at this stage into cis and trans isomers, each as racemic mixture

22.12 (a) (cont)

$$ \xrightarrow[\substack{CH_3OH \\ F}]{NaBH_4} $$

and enantiomer   and enantiomer   +   and enantiomer

                                    major product   minor product

(b) The minor product can be converted into (+)-muscarine.

racemate   + $(CH_3)_2NH$ $\longrightarrow$ CH_3 ... $CH_2N(CH_3)_2$ $\xrightarrow{CH_3I}$ CH_3 ... $CH_2N(CH_3)_3^+$ I

            (excess)   racemate   (+)-muscarine

                                               +   and enantiomer

                                         + $(CH_3)_2NH_2$ I^-

---

Concept Map 22.1   Preparation of amines.

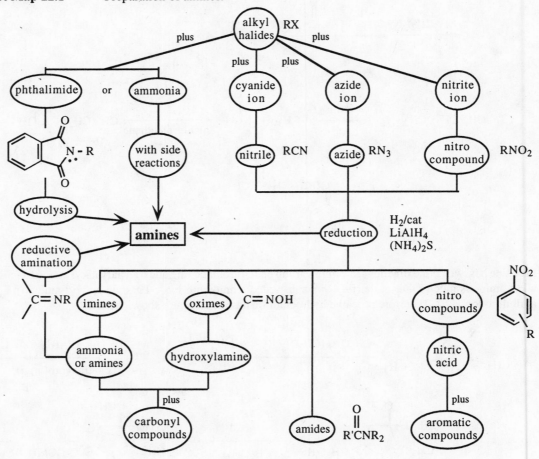

22.13 R_2NH + HCl $\longrightarrow$ $R_2NH_2^+$ Cl^-

                                             water soluble

22.13 (cont) R_2NH + HNO_2 $\xrightarrow[\text{HCl}]{}$ $R_2\overset{..}{N}-\overset{..}{N}=\overset{..}{\underset{..}{O}}$ $\longleftrightarrow$ $R_2\overset{+}{N}=\overset{..}{N}-\overset{..}{\underset{..}{O}}:^{-}$

The nonbonding electrons on the amine nitrogen atom are delocalized to the nitroso group. The nitrosamine is therefore much less basic than the original amine and will not form a salt. A nitrosamine resembles an amide in basicity.

Concept Map 22.2   Nitrosation reactions.

Chapter 20

22.14   (a)

22.14   (d) *[reaction scheme: anthranilic acid (2-aminobenzoic acid) + ICl, HCl (dilute), 0 °C → 5-iodo-2-aminobenzoic acid + NaNO₂, HCl, H₂O, 0–5 °C → diazonium salt]*

(e) *[reaction scheme: 2,6-diiodo-4-nitroaniline + NaNO₂, H₂SO₄, H₂O, 0–5 °C → diazonium hydrogen sulfate salt]*

Concept Map 22.3   Diazonium ions in synthesis.

22.15

(a)

separate from
the para isomer

(b)

separate from
the ortho isomer

(c)

22.16

(a)

(b)

separate from
the ortho isomer

(c)

[from (b)]

22.16 (c) (cont)

p-Bromotoluene can also be synthesized by treating toluene with bromine in the presence of ferric bromide, but it will be contaminated with o-bromotoluene. Separation of o-bromotoluene from p-bromotoluene is difficult because the two compounds differ by only 3° in boiling point. p-Nitrotoluene will also have the ortho isomer as a contaminant, but the two nitrotoluenes are easy to separate because the ortho isomer is a liquid at room temperature and the para isomer is a solid.

(d)

(e)

(f)

Concept Map 22.4   Reactions of diazonium ions.

Concept Map 22.3

22.17

Protonation of this nitrogen
atom gives a cation that has
no resonance stabilization.

Protonation of this nitrogen atom gives a cation that
is stabilized by resonance; the positive charge is
delocalized to the carbon atoms of an aromatic ring.

Protonation of this nitrogen atom gives a cation that is
stabilized by resonance; the positive charge is delocalized
to the carbon atoms of an aromatic ring and to the nitrogen
atom of the amino group. Therefore this is the most stable
cation of the three.

22.18

NaNO$_2$, HCl

H$_2$O
0 °C

22.19

NaNO$_2$
(2 molar equiv)
HCl

H$_2$O
10–15 °C

A

(2 molar equiv)

B

22.20   (a)   ClCCl + NH$_3$ (excess) ⟶ H$_2$NCNH$_2$

(b)   ClCCl   +   PhCH$_2$OH ⟶ PhCH$_2$OCCl
             (1 molar equiv)

22.20   (c) $PhN = C = O$ + $CH_3CH_2CH_2NH_2$ $\longrightarrow$ $PhNH\overset{\overset{\displaystyle O}{\|}}{C}NHCH_2CH_2CH_3$

(d) $CH_3CH_2O\overset{\overset{\displaystyle O}{\|}}{C}NH_2$ + H_2O $\xrightarrow[\Delta]{H_3O^+}$ CH_3CH_2OH + $CO_2\uparrow$ + $\overset{+}{N}H_4$

(e) $PhN = C = S$ + $PhNH_2$ $\longrightarrow$ $PhNH\overset{\overset{\displaystyle S}{\|}}{C}NHPh$

   phenyl isothiocyanate   a substituted thiourea

22.21   1.   Degradation in acid

H_2O + CO_2 $\longleftarrow$ H_2CO_3 + HB^+ $\longleftarrow$ [structure]   + H_2NCH_3 $\xrightarrow{HB^+}$ $\overset{+}{H_3}NCH_3$

22.21   2.   Degradation in base

22.22   (a)   (1*R*, 2*S*)-2-ethyl-1-(*N*-methylamino)cyclobutane   (b)   2-methylpyridine   (c)   triethylamine
(d)   2-amino-4-methylbenzoic acid   (e)   4-aminobutanoic acid   (f)   2,4,6-trichloroaniline
(g)   5-methyl-2-hexanamine (2-amino-5-methylhexane)   (h)   (1*R*, 2*S*)-2-aminocyclohexanol
(i)   *N,N*-diethyl-4-nitroaniline (*N,N*-diethyl-*p*-nitroaniline)

22.23   (a)

and enantiomer

(b)

(c)

(d)   CH₃O—

(e)

(f)   CH₃CH₂CH₂CHCH₂CH₂CHCH₃

(g)   CH₃CH₂CH₂CHCH₂CH₃

(h)

22.24   (a)   PhCH=NPh $\xrightarrow[\text{diethyl ether}]{\text{LiAlH}_4}$ $\xrightarrow{\text{H}_2\text{O}}$ PhCH₂NHPh

A

(b)

22.24 (c)

$$CH_3\underset{NO_2}{\underset{|}{C}}HCH_2CH_2\overset{O}{\overset{\|}{C}}OCH_3 \xrightarrow[\text{Ni}]{\text{H}_2 \atop \Delta} \left[CH_3\underset{NH_2}{\underset{|}{C}}HCH_2CH_2\overset{O}{\overset{\|}{C}}OCH_3 \right] \longrightarrow$$

(d)

$$H_2N\text{—}\bigcirc\text{—}SO_2NH_2 \xrightarrow[\text{Fe}]{\text{Br}_2} $$
D

(e)

$$CH_3\overset{O}{\overset{\|}{C}}(CH_2)_4CH_3 \xrightarrow[\text{Ni} \atop \Delta]{\text{NH}_3,\ \text{H}_2} CH_3\underset{NH_2}{\underset{|}{C}}H(CH_2)_4CH_3$$
E

(f)

$$CH_3CH_2CH_2NO_2 \xrightarrow{\overset{O}{\overset{\|}{\text{HCH}},\ \text{NaOH}}} CH_3CH_2\underset{NO_2}{\underset{|}{C}}HCH_2OH \xrightarrow[\text{Ni} \atop \Delta]{\text{H}_2} CH_3CH_2\underset{NH_2}{\underset{|}{C}}HCH_2OH$$
F   **G**

22.25 (a)

$$\xrightarrow[\text{pyridine} \atop \Delta]{\overset{+}{\text{HONH}_3}\ \text{Cl}^-} \mathbf{A} \xrightarrow[\text{diethyl} \atop \text{ether}]{\text{LiAlH}_4\ \text{H}_3\text{O}^+} \mathbf{B} \xrightarrow[\text{H}_2\text{O}]{\text{NaOH}} \mathbf{C}$$

(b)

$$^-O_3S\text{—}\bigcirc\text{—}\overset{+}{\text{N}}H_3 \xrightarrow[\text{H}_2\text{O}]{\text{Na}_2\text{CO}_3} \text{Na}^+\ ^-O_3S\text{—}\bigcirc\text{—}NH_2 \xrightarrow[\text{H}_2\text{O} \atop 0\text{–}5\,^\circ\text{C}]{\text{NaNO}_2,\ \text{HCl}} \ ^-O_3S\text{—}\bigcirc\text{—}\overset{+}{\text{N}}\equiv\text{N}$$
                         D   **E**

(c)

$$\xrightarrow[\text{diethyl} \atop \text{ether}]{\text{LiAlH}_4} \xrightarrow{\text{H}_2\text{O}} $$
F

(d)

$$\xrightarrow[\Delta,\ \text{pressure}]{\text{NH}_3,\ \text{H}_2 \atop \text{Ni}} $$
G

(e)

$$CH_3\overset{O}{\overset{\|}{C}}CH_3 \xrightarrow[\text{HCl (catalyst)}]{\bigcirc\text{—}NH_2} \mathbf{H} \xrightarrow{\text{NaOH}} \mathbf{I}$$

22.25   (f)

22.26

(a)

(b)

(c)

(d)

(e)

22.26

(f)

22.27

22.28

1.

2.

22.29

22.30

22.31

22.32

22.33

separate from
ortho isomer

22.34

22.35

$$HC{\equiv}CCH_2CH_2C(O\text{-}O)CH_3 \xrightarrow[\text{NH}_3 \text{ (liq)}]{\text{NaNH}_2} \xrightarrow{\text{CH}_3\text{I}} CH_3C{\equiv}CCH_2CH_2C(O\text{-}O)CH_3$$

$$\downarrow \begin{array}{c}\text{H}_3\text{O}^+\\ \text{cold}\end{array}$$

$$CH_3C{\equiv}CCH_2CH_2C{=}CHCOCH_2CH_3 \quad (\overset{\displaystyle CH_3}{|}) \xleftarrow{(C_6H_5)_3P{=}CHCOCH_2CH_3} CH_3C{\equiv}CCH_2CH_2CCH_3 \;(\text{O})$$

$$\downarrow \begin{array}{c}[(CH_3)_2CHCH_2]_2AlH\\ \text{(excess)}\end{array}$$

$$\downarrow \text{H}_3\text{O}^+$$

$$CH_3C{\equiv}CCH_2CH_2C{=}CHCH_2OH \;(\overset{CH_3}{|}) \xrightarrow{\;CH_3SCl\; (O,O)\;} CH_3C{\equiv}CCH_2CH_2C{=}CHCH_2OSCH_3 \;(\overset{CH_3}{|})\,(O,O)$$

$$\downarrow H_2NCH_2CH_2OH$$

$$CH_3C{\equiv}CCH_2CH_2C{=}CHCH_2N{=}NCH_2CH_2OH \;(\overset{CH_3}{|}) \xleftarrow[\begin{array}{c}\text{H}_2\text{O}\\ 0\,^\circ\text{C}\end{array}]{\text{NaNO}_2,\ \text{HCl}} CH_3C{\equiv}CCH_2CH_2C{=}CHCH_2NHCH_2CH_2OH \;(\overset{CH_3}{|})$$

22.36

22.37   (a)

(b)

22.38   (a)

22.38   (b)

This cyanohydrin forms at higher temperatures; therefore, it must be the thermodynamic product. The other one forms faster at lower temperatures, so it is the kinetic product. The formation of a cyanohydrin must be reversible for the equilibrium to occur at higher temperatures.

22.39   (a)

HBF$_4$, Δ ; NaNO$_2$, HCl, H$_2$O, 0 °C ; H$_2$, Ni ; HNO$_3$, H$_2$SO$_4$

(b)

Br$_2$, acetic acid ; H$_2$O, H$_2$SO$_4$; NaNO$_2$, HCl, H$_2$O, 0 °C ; H$_2$, Ni ; HNO$_3$, H$_2$SO$_4$; major product

(c)

H$_2$O, LiAlH$_4$, diethyl ether ; NH$_3$; SOCl$_2$; H$_3$O$^+$, Δ

CH$_3$CH$_2$Br, CH$_3$CH$_2$ONa, ethanol ; CH$_2$(COCH$_2$CH$_3$)$_2$, CH$_3$CH$_2$ONa, ethanol

22.39 **(d)**

(e)

22.40

used to model the
amino acid tyrosine

22.41 The proton magnetic resonance spectrum of Compound A, $C_{10}H_{15}N$, shows a typical ethyl splitting pattern (a triplet at δ 1.2 and a quartet at δ 3.4). The chemical shift of the quartet tells us that the ethyl group is bonded to the nitrogen atom. There are also protons absorbing in the aromatic region (δ 6.6 – δ 7.3). The integration is 5:4:6 and tells us that there must be two ethyl groups bonded to the nitrogen. Compound A is *N,N*-diethylaniline.

22.41 (cont)

$$CH_2CH_3$$
$$C_6H_5-NCH_2CH_3$$

The proton magnetic resonance spectrum is summarized below:

δ 1.2	(6H, t, J = 7 Hz, —CH$_2$C$\underline{H}_3$)
δ 3.4	(4H, q, J = 7 Hz, —NC$\underline{H}_2$CH$_3$)
δ 6.6 – 7.3	(5H, m, Ar$\underline{H}$)

22.42

$$\delta\ 22.8 \quad \overset{O}{\underset{\parallel}{}} \quad \delta\ 34.4$$
$$CH_3 - C - NHCH_2CH_3$$
$$\delta\ 171.0 \qquad \delta\ 14.6$$

22.43   Compound B, C_3H_9N, has no units of unsaturation. The appearance of only two bands in the ^{13}C nuclear magnetic resonance spectrum tells us that Compound B is symmetrical. Compound B is isopropylamine (2-aminopropane).

$$\delta\ 26.2$$
$$CH_3CHCH_3$$
$$\underset{NH_2}{} \quad \delta\ 42.8$$

22.44

butter yellow
λ_{max} 408 nm

acid →

λ_{max} 320 nm

Protonation of the nonbonding electrons on the amino group decreases the conjugation in the chromophore and, therefore, the wavelength of maximum absorption.

The chromophore in this species has quinoid character.

λ_{max} 510 nm

Supplemental Problems

S22.1   Write structural formulas for all products and intermediates designated by letters in the following equations.

(a)   [benzaldehyde structure] $\xrightarrow[\substack{H_2SO_4 \\ \Delta}]{HNO_3}$ A $\xrightarrow{\text{reduction}}$ B $\xrightarrow[\substack{H_2O \\ 0\text{--}5\,°C}]{NaNO_2,\ HCl}$ C $\xrightarrow[HCl]{CuCl}$ D

(b)   [3,5-dimethoxyaniline structure] $\xrightarrow[\substack{H_2O \\ 0\text{--}5\,°C}]{NaNO_2,\ H_2SO_4}$ E $\xrightarrow[H_2SO_4]{H_2O}$ F

(c)   [phenyl–CH$_2$C≡N] $\xrightarrow[\substack{Ni \\ NH_3}]{H_2}$ G

(d)   [2-aminobenzoic acid structure] $\xrightarrow[\substack{H_2O \\ 3\text{-}5\,°C}]{NaNO_2,\ HCl}$ H $\xrightarrow{\text{[C}_6\text{H}_5\text{N(CH}_3)_2]}$ I (methyl red)

(e)   [phenyl–CH$_2$Br] $\xrightarrow[\substack{\text{dimethyl-}\\\text{formamide}}]{NaNO_2}$ J

(f)   [4-nitro-2-hydroxyphenyl propyl ketone structure] $\xrightarrow[\substack{Ni \\ \text{ethyl} \\ \text{acetate}}]{H_2}$ K

(g)   [2-methyl-1,3-dinitrobenzene structure] $\xrightarrow[\substack{Ni \\ \text{ethanol}}]{H_2\ (1\ equiv)}$ L $\xrightarrow[\substack{H_2O \\ 0\text{--}5\,°C}]{NaNO_2,\ H_2SO_4}$ M $\xrightarrow[H_2SO_4]{H_2O}$ N

(h)   [4-nitro-1,2-dimethylbenzene structure] $\xrightarrow[Ni]{H_2}$ O $\xrightarrow[\substack{H_2O \\ 0\,°C}]{NaNO_2,\ H_2SO_4}$ P $\xrightarrow[\Delta]{CuCN}$ Q $\xrightarrow[\Delta]{H_3O^+}$ R

(i)   [4,4'-diamino-3,3'-dimethoxybiphenyl structure] $\xrightarrow[\substack{H_2O \\ 5\text{--}10\,°C}]{NaNO_2\ (excess),\ HCl}$ S $\xrightarrow[]{\substack{H_3PO_2 \\ (excess)}}$ T

S22.2   For still more practice in recognizing reactions, write structural formulas for all compounds symbolized by letters in the following equations.

(a) $CH_3\underset{\underset{Cl}{|}}{CH}COCH_2CH_3$ $\xrightarrow[\substack{\text{dimethyl} \\ \text{sulfoxide}}]{NaNO_2}$ A

(b)   [2-methylbenzonitrile structure] $\xrightarrow[\substack{\text{diethyl} \\ \text{ether}}]{LiAlH_4}$ $\xrightarrow{H_2O}$ B

S22.2

(c)

(d) $CH_3CH_2CHCH_2CH_2CH_3$ $\xrightarrow[\text{pyridine}]{\text{TsCl}}$ E $\xrightarrow{CH_3NHCH_3}$ $\xrightarrow{NaOH}$ F $\xrightarrow[\text{acetonitrile}]{CH_3I}$ G

(with OH substituent shown below the chain)

(e) PhNHCH$_3$ $\xrightarrow{CH_3OCC\equiv CCOCH_3}$ H (f) $\xrightarrow[\substack{\text{dimethyl}\\\text{sulfoxide}}]{NaNO_2}$ I (g)

S22.3 Show how you would carry out each of the following transformations. Some of them may require more than one step.

(a)

(b) $PhCH_2CH_2CCH_2CCH_3 \longrightarrow PhCH_2CH_2CHCH_2CHCH_3$

(two different methods)

(c) $HOCH_2CH_2CH_2OH \longrightarrow PhCH_2OCH_2CH_2CH_2NH_2$
(two different methods)

S22.4 Phthalimide is used to introduce an α-amino group in many syntheses of amino acids. These syntheses start with the reaction of diethyl bromomalonate with phthalimidate anion. They continue with alkylation (see Sections 17.4A and 17.4C) of the resulting substituted diethyl malonate with a suitable substituent and end with hydrolysis and decarboxylation steps. The amino acids methionine, phenylalanine, and aspartic acid were synthesized in this way. Show how these syntheses could be carried out.

methionine   phenylalanine   aspartic acid

23

The Chemistry of Heterocyclic Compounds

23.1 (a) 3-aminopyridine   (b) 2,5-dimethylthiophene   (c) ethyl 1-pyrrolecarboxylate

      (d) 4-ethylisoquinoline

      (e) 3-methyl-2-isoxazoline (Note that the number 2 defines the position of the double bond.)

      (f) 4,4-dimethylazetidinone   (g) 3-indolecarboxylic acid   (h) 3-methylfuran

      (i) 8-hydroxyquinoline   (j) 1,4-dimethylpyrazole   (k) 2,3-diphenyloxazole

23.2

Concept Map 23.1   Classification of cyclic compounds.

544

23.3

23.4

no resonance stabilization;
localized charge

delocalization of charge by resonance

23.5 (a) The basicity of an amine is determined by the availability of the nonbonding electrons on the nitrogen atom. The pK_a values for their conjugate acids indicate that 2-methylpyridine is a slightly stronger base than pyridine, and 3-nitropyridine is a much weaker base than pyridine. The methyl group is weakly electron-donating; the nitro group is strongly electron-withdrawing.

pK_a of
conjugate acid:

6.0
strongest base;
inductive effect of
the methyl group

5.2

0.8
weakest base;
inductive and
resonance effect of
the nitro group

(b) The arguments used in part (a) of this problem can be applied to the compounds in this series also.

pK_a
of conjugate acid:

2.0
strongest base;
inductive effect of
the methyl group

1.3

−0.68
weakest base;
inductive and
resonance effect of
the carbonyl group

23.6

$^+B\!\!=\!\!H$ Ph–C(=O)–CH(H)–CH$_2$CCH$_3$ $\rightarrow$ Ph–C=C–CH$_2$CCH$_3$ $\rightarrow$ (cyclic intermediate)

$^+B\!-\!H$ Ph–(furan ring)–CH$_3$ $\leftarrow$ $\leftarrow$

23.7   (a) $\underset{O}{\overset{O}{HCCH_2CH_2CH}}$ $\xrightarrow{HCl}$ (furan)

(b) $CH_3CCH_2CH_2CCH_3$ $\xrightarrow[\Delta]{CH_3NH_2}$ CH$_3$–(pyrrole, N–CH$_3$)–CH$_3$

23.8 $CH_3CCH_2CCH_3$; $H\!-\!N\!-\!N\!-\!H$ $\xrightarrow{}$ intermediate $\xrightarrow{}$ intermediate

CH$_3$–(pyrazole ring)–CH$_3$ $\leftarrow$ $\leftarrow$

$CH_3CCH_2CCH_3$; $H\!-\!N\!-\!O\!-\!H$ $\rightarrow$ intermediate $\rightarrow$ intermediate

23.8 (cont)

23.9   (a)

(b)

(c)

23.10

(a)

(b)

(c)

Concept Map 23.2   Synthesis of heterocycles from carbonyl compounds.

23.11   (a) $CH_3CCH_2COCH_2CH_3$ + H_2NCNH_2 $\xrightarrow[\text{ethanol}]{\text{HCl}}$

(b) $CH_3CCH_2CCH_3$ + $CH_3ONHCNH_2$ $\xrightarrow[\text{ethanol}]{\text{HCl}}$

(c) $PhCCH_2CCH_3$ + H_2NCNH_2 $\xrightarrow[\text{ethanol}]{\text{HCl}}$

23.12 (a)

(b)

(c)

(d)

(e)

(f)

(g)

23.13   Three possible intermediates can form:

from attack at carbon 5

23.13 (cont)

from attack at carbon 4

from attack at carbon 3

The intermediate of lowest energy is the one resulting from attack at the 4 position of the ring. In this intermediate the positive charge is delocalized to the nitrogen atom and no resonance contributor has a positive charge on the carbon atom bonded to the electron-withdrawing carbonyl group. Attack at carbon 5 is favored over attack at carbon 3 because there is greater delocalization of the positive charge in that intermediate.

major product

23.14

(a)

(b)

(c)

23.15

Concept Map 23.3   Substitution reactions of heterocycles.

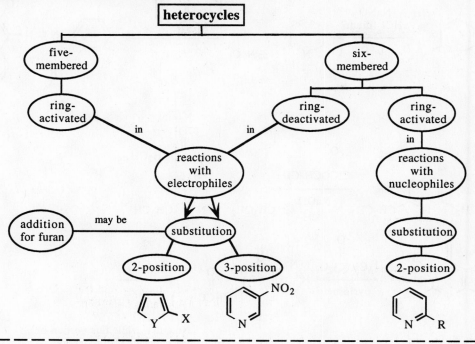

- -

23.16

The reaction starts with attack of the organolithium reagent (a very strong nucleophile) on the carbon adjacent to the nitrogen atom to give a resonance-stabilized intermediate (see Problem 23.15). The leaving group is hydride ion. The driving force for the loss of hydride ion in this reaction and in the reaction of amide ion with pyridine is the recovery of aromaticity of the pyridine ring.

23.17 (a)

(b)

(c)

(d)

23.17   (e)

23.18

(a)

(b)

Note that while this portion of the molecule also looks like an amide, it is, in fact, a tautomer of an aromatic system.

(c)

(d)

(e)

+ CH₃CH₂OH

(f)

23.19   The adenine-thymine pair is held together by two hydrogen bonds, and the guanine-cytosine pair is held together by three hydrogen bonds. It takes more energy to pull apart a guanine-cytosine pair than an adenine-thymine pair. Therefore, the more guanine and cytosine a particular form of DNA contains, the higher the temperature required before the DNA melts.

23.20   (a)

(b)

(c)

(d)

(e)

(f)

23.21

The heterocycles with three-membered rings are vulnerable to nucleophilic attack. The bases in DNA contain nucleophilic sites such as amino groups. Reaction of an amino group with an oxirane or an aziridine creates a new functionality at the sites in DNA that were previously involved in the hydrogen bonding so important to base pairing. Oxiranes and aziridines, therefore, disrupt the processes necessary for the transmission of genetic information and cause mutations.

23.22

(S)-ethanol-1-*d*

CH₃CD

(R)-ethanol-1-*d*

CH₃CH

23.23

hydrophobic site   hydrophilic site

ionic site

Nicotinamide fits the active site of the enzyme in this orientation.

hydrophobic site   hydrophilic site

ionic site

Nicotinamide does not fit the active site of the enzyme in this orientation.

The two orientations of the nicotinamide molecules as drawn are enantiomers of each other and are distinguished from each other by the enzyme.

23.24   (a)

$$CH_3-\underset{\underset{CH_3}{|}}{\overset{\overset{CH_3}{|}}{C}}-H$$

no enantiotopic hydrogens

(b)

CH₂−CH₃

↑

enantiotopic hydrogens

these two methyl groups are enantiotopic; replacement of one gives rise to a stereocenter on the adjacent carbon

CH₃
|
CH₃CH−CH₂−NH₂

↑

enantiotopic hydrogens

(c)

four sets of enantiotopic hydrogens; the two sets of cis hydrogens on carbons 2 and 5 and the two sets of cis hydrogens on carbons 3 and 4

(d)

23.25

One hydrogen atom from testosterone goes to the solvent, the other, to the back face of the nicotinamide group.

23.26

intermediate from the addition of
the ylid from thymine to pyruvic acid

Decarboxylation occurs easily because the carbanion that is formed is stabilized by delocalization of charge to the positively charged nitrogen atom of the ylid. (See Problem 23.27 for the resonance contributors of the decarboxylation product.)

23.27

decarboxylation product

23.27 (cont)

This resembles a retroaldol reaction.

23.28   (a)

S_N2

good leaving group

(b)

23.29

(–)-hyoscyamine   planar enolate ion; protonation   (+)-hyoscyamine
                                   on top or bottom equally likely

Atropine is a racemic hyoscyamine or the equilibrium mixture of the two enantiomers.

23.30

tropine   tropinone   ψ-tropine
                                                        a stereoisomer of tropine

23.31

α-ecgonine

23.32 (1)

(2)

Method 2 is better since it does not depend on an equilibrium process for yield.

23.33

(±)-lysergic acid

23.34

numbered around the isoquinoline
ring (*not* the numbering used in
naming the compound);
benzyl group on carbon 1

23.35

23.36 (a)

(b)

(c)

23.36   (d)

CrO$_3$ / H$_2$SO$_4$ → E

codeine

(e)

(CH$_3$CH)$_2$N$^-$ Li$^+$ (2 molar equiv)

tetrahydrofuran
−78 °C

BrCH$_2$COCH$_3$
(1 molar equiv)
−78 °C

H$_3$O$^+$

F   G

23.37   (a)   3-isoquinolinecarboxylic acid   (b)   3-chloropyridine   (c)   2-aminopyrimidine
(d)   3-phenylisoxazolidine   (e)   4-nitropyrazole   (f)   6-chloro-3-phenylquinoline
(g)   methyl 3-furancarboxylate   (h)   1,4-dimethylimidazole   (i)   3-indolecarboxamide
(j)   2-phenylthiazole   (k)   2-thiophenecarboxylic acid

23.38

(a)

+ (CH$_3$C)$_2$O

(CH$_3$CH$_2$)$_2$O•BF$_3$
Δ

A

(b)

+ H$_2$SO$_4$ →

B

(c)

LiAlH$_4$

diethyl
ether

H$_3$O$^+$

C
+ CH$_3$CH$_2$OH

(d)

+ H$_2$ Ni →

D

(e)

+ (CH$_3$CH$_2$CH$_2$C)$_2$O

BF$_3$
acetic acid

E

23.38

(f)

(g)

(h)

(i)

(j)

(k)

23.39

(a)

(b)

(c)

23.39

(d)

thebaine　→ (CH₃I) → D

(e)

morphine　→ (HCl, H₂O) → E

(f)

F

(g)

G

(h)

H　→ I　→ (PBr₃, pyridine) → J

K　→ (KOH, H₂O, Δ) → L　→ (H₃O⁺) → M

(i)

N　→ (H₂, Pt, methanol) → O

(j)

malic acid　→ (malic dehydrogenase, H₂O) → P　+　Q

23.40

two of four resonance contributors

A carbocation adjacent to the thiophene ring is like a benzylic cation in stability, so S$_N$1 and E1 reactions have been shown. S$_N$2 and E2 reactions are also a possibility.

23.41

A   B   C
(S)-ethanol-1-d   (R)-ethanol-1-d

23.41 (cont)

Alcohol A is converted to tosylate B with retention of configuration. The reaction of the tosylate B with hydroxide ion occurs by an S_N2 reaction with inversion of configuration. Thus an optically active alcohol is converted into its enantiomer. When the two alcohols, A and C, are oxidized with NAD^+, deuterium is removed from C and hydrogen is removed from A.

These reactions are the reverse of those used to prepare the alcohols by enzymatic reductions. Reduction of acetaldehyde-1-*d* by NADH gave Alcohol A, while that of acetaldehyde by NADD gave Alcohol C (see Section 23.6C in the text).

The enzymatic oxidation-reduction reactions are stereoselective, so the proof that the enantiomeric alcohols lose deuterium and hydrogen selectively in the experiments outlined above also proves that the original reduction reactions give rise to enantiomeric ethanol-1-*d* species.

23.42

9-benzyl-9-aza-bicyclo[4.2.1]nonane

23.43

23.43 (cont)

23.44

23.45

	4-methylimidazole	imidazole	benzimidazole	4-nitroimidazole
	least acidic			
pK_a values	7.5	7.0	5.5	−0.1

The acidity of each of these species is related to the basicity of the conjugate base, which, in turn, is related to the availability of nonbonding electrons on a nitrogen atom. In all of the imidazoles, basicity is derived from both nitrogen atoms in the ring because electrons from both are involved in stabilization of the conjugate acid by delocalization of charge. For example:

protonation   stabilization of the cation
at N-3   by electrons from N-1

23.45 (cont)

We expect 4-methylimidazole to be more basic than imidazole because the methyl group is electron-donating. In benzimidazole the nonbonding electrons are delocalized to the aromatic ring, making them less available at the nitrogen atoms.

In 4-nitroimidazole, the strong electron-withdrawing inductive effect of the nitro group combines with the resonance effect to greatly reduce electron density in the ring and at the nitrogen atoms.

23.46

Bao Gong Teng A

23.47 $PhNHNH_2$ + $CH_3CH=CHCOH$ →

product from nucleophilic addition to α,β-unsaturated compound

$C_{10}H_{12}N_2O$

23.47 (cont)

PhNHNH$_2$ + CH$_3$CCH$_2$COCH$_2$CH$_3$ →

$$\left[\begin{array}{c} \text{CH}_3\text{—C—CH}_2\text{COCH}_2\text{CH}_3 \\ \text{N}\diagdown\text{N—H} \\ \text{Ph} \end{array} \right]$$

product from nucleophilic
addition to carbonyl of ketone
followed by loss of water to
give a phenylhydrazone

→ (pyrazolone structure)

C$_{10}$H$_{10}$N$_2$O

23.48   (1)   The bicyclic ring must be formed.

base →

(2)   Carbonyl groups and the carbon-carbon double bond must be reduced.

$\xrightarrow[\text{catalyst}]{\text{H}_2}$

$\xrightarrow[\text{(CH}_3\text{CH}_2)_2\text{O•BF}_3]{\text{HSCH}_2\text{CH}_2\text{CH}_2\text{SH}}$

$\xrightarrow{\text{Raney Ni}}$

$\xrightarrow{\text{LiAlH}_4}$

(*R*)-δ-coniceine

23.49

$\xrightarrow{\text{CH}_3\text{SCH}_3, \text{ClC—CCl}}$ $\xrightarrow{\text{(CH}_3\text{CH}_2)_3\text{N}}$

A
C$_{17}$H$_{19}$NO$_4$

(CH$_3$CH$_2$O)$_2$PCH$_2$COCH$_2$CH$_3$

$$\begin{array}{c} \text{CH}_3 \\ | \\ \text{CH}_3\text{C—O}^- \text{ K}^+ \\ | \\ \text{CH}_3 \end{array}$$

tetrahydrofuran

23.49 (cont)

23.50   (a)   The highest wavelength of maximum absorption for vitamin B_6 shifts from 292 nm to 315 nm when the solution is made basic. This change suggests that the vitamin contains a phenolic hydroxyl group. When the acidic proton of the hydroxyl group is replaced by a methyl group, the compound no longer ionizes at high pH and the absorption spectrum does not change with pH.

     (b)   The structure of vitamin B_6 can be derived from its molecular formula, $C_8H_{11}NO_3$, and from the structures of the oxidation products of its methyl ether.

dicarboxylic acid
$C_9H_9NO_5$

precursor of
the lactone
$C_9H_{11}NO_4$

lactone

vitamin B_6
$C_8H_{11}NO_3$

methyl ether
of vitamin B_6
$C_9H_{13}NO_3$

23.50 (b) (cont)

The side chains that are oxidized are the ones already bearing a hydroxyl group. The equations outlining the transformation of vitamin B_6 are given on the previous page.

(c) Possible models for vitamin B_6 should have a pyridine ring with a hydroxyl substituent. Alkyl substituents at different positions on the ring would also be helpful. Ultraviolet spectra of the model compounds should be taken under both acidic and basic conditions. Structures of some possible models are:

Supplemental Problems

S23.1 For the following set of bases, discuss the trend observed for the pK_a values given, which are for the conjugate acids of the compounds shown.

pK_a –0.3 pK_a 1.5 pK_a 1.9

S23.2 Write structural formulas for all intermediates and products designated by letters in the following equations.

(a) $PhCCH_2CCH_3$ + $PhNHNH_2$ $\xrightarrow{\Delta}$ A

(Hint: Which carbonyl group is more likely to undergo nucleophilic attack first?)

(b) $PhCCH_2CCH_3$ $\xrightarrow[\Delta]{H_2NNH_3 \ HSO_4^-, \ NaOH}$ B

(c) $\xrightarrow[\substack{\text{acetic} \\ \text{anhydride} \\ -5\,°C}]{}$ + HNO_3 $\longrightarrow$ C

(d) + $(CH_3C)_2O$ $\xrightarrow[\substack{(CH_3CH_2)_2O \cdot BF_3 \\ 100\,°C}]{}$ D

(e) + HNO_3 $\xrightarrow[\substack{H_2SO_4 \\ \Delta}]{}$ E + F

(f) $\xrightarrow[\substack{H_2O \\ 0\,°C}]{NaNO_2, \ HI}$ G

S23.2   (g)

(h)

(i)

(j)

(k)

S23.3   Give structural formulas for all products and intermediates designated by letters in the following equations.

(a)

(b)

(c)

(d)

(e)

(f)

S23.3

(g)   PhCH=CHCH + O / HCl / Δ → I

(h)   NH₃ / Δ → J

(i)   NaNH₂ / toluene / Δ → K

(j)   H₂ / PtO₂ / ethanol / H₃O⁺ → L

(k)   (CH₃C)₂O / Δ → M

(l)   Cl₂ / 200 °C → N

(m)   (CH₃C)₂O (excess) → O   HNO₃ / H₂SO₄ → P

(n)   NBS / acetic acid / *hv* → Q

S23.4   Part of a synthesis of an analog of folic acid (p. 850 in the text) involves the following transformation. How would you carry it out?

S23.5   A synthesis of an analog of folic acid was carried forward by treatment of the amine synthesized in Supplemental Problem S23.4 with nitrous acid. The product of this reaction is the heterocycle shown below. Show by writing key intermediates and a mechanism how the heterocyclic ring came into being.

24 Carbohydrates

24.1 A is a ketotriose   B is an aldotriose   C is an aldotetraose   D is a ketopentose

- -

Concept Map 24.1   Classification of carbohydrates.

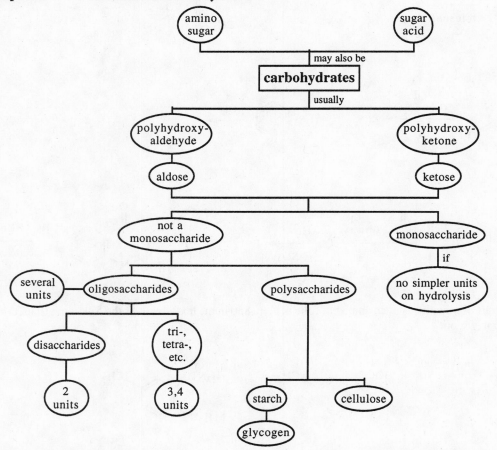

- -

24.2 From the known configuration of (R)-(−)-lactic acid, we can assign the R configuration to (−)-1-buten-3-ol and (−)-2-butanol, because the reactions used for the interconversions do not break bonds to the stereocenter.

24.3   (a)

$$\begin{array}{c} CH_3 \\ H\!\!-\!\!\!\!\underset{CH_2CH_3}{\overset{|}{}}\!\!\!\!-Br \end{array}$$

(S)-2-bromobutane

$$\begin{array}{c} Br \\ H\!\!-\!\!\!\!\underset{CH_2CH_3}{\overset{|}{}}\!\!\!\!-CH_3 \end{array}$$

(R)-2-bromobutane

enantiomers

(b)

$$\begin{array}{c} O \\ \| \\ COH \\ H\!\!-\!\!\!\!\overset{|}{}\!\!\!\!-OH \\ CH_3 \end{array}$$

$$\begin{array}{c} H \quad O \\ \quad\ \| \\ HO\!\!-\!\!\!\!\overset{|}{}\!\!\!\!-COH \\ CH_3 \end{array}$$

(R)-lactic acid
same

(c)

$$\begin{array}{c} CH_3 \\ H\!\!-\!\!\!\!\overset{|}{}\!\!\!\!-Br \\ H\!\!-\!\!\!\!\overset{|}{}\!\!\!\!-Br \\ CH_3 \end{array}$$

(2S, 3R)-2,3-
dibromobutane

$$\begin{array}{c} CH_3 \\ H\!\!-\!\!\!\!\overset{|}{}\!\!\!\!-Br \\ H\!\!-\!\!\!\!\overset{|}{}\!\!\!\!-CH_3 \\ Br \end{array}$$

(2S, 3S)-2,3-
dibromobutane

diastereomers

(d)

$$\begin{array}{c} O \\ \| \\ COH \\ H\!\!-\!\!\!\!\overset{|}{}\!\!\!\!-OH \\ HO\!\!-\!\!\!\!\overset{|}{}\!\!\!\!-H \\ COH \\ \| \\ O \end{array}$$

(2R, 3R)-2,3-
dihydroxy
butanedioic acid

$$\begin{array}{c} H \quad O \\ \quad\ \| \\ HO\!\!-\!\!\!\!\overset{|}{}\!\!\!\!-COH \\ HO\!\!-\!\!\!\!\overset{|}{}\!\!\!\!-COH \\ H \quad O \end{array}$$

(2R, 3S)-2,3-
dihydroxy
butanedioic acid

diastereomers

24.4   D-(+)-glyceraldehyde ≡ (R)-(+)-glyceraldehyde
D-(−)-lactic acid ≡ (R)-(−)-lactic acid
D-(−)-tartaric acid ≡ (2S, 3S)-(−)-2,3-dihydroxybutanedioic acid
D-(−)-ribose ≡ (2R, 3R, 4R)-(−)-2,3,4,5-tetrahydroxypentanal
D-(+)-glucose ≡ (2R, 3S, 4R, 5R)-(+)-2,3,4,5-pentahydroxyhexanal
D-(−)-fructose ≡ (3S, 4R, 5R)-(−)-1,3,4,5,6-pentahydroxy-2-hexanone
L-(−)-glyceraldehyde ≡ (S)-(−)-glyceraldehyde
L-(+)-lactic acid ≡ (S)-(+)-lactic acid
L-(+)-tartaric acid ≡ (2R, 3R)-(+)-2,3-dihydroxybutanedioic acid
L-(+)-alanine ≡ (S)-(+)-alanine
L-(+)-arabinose ≡ (2R, 3S, 4S)-(+)-2,3,4,5-tetrahydroxypentanal

24.5

$$\begin{array}{c} O \\ \| \\ CH \\ HO\!\!-\!\!\!\!\overset{|}{}\!\!\!\!-H \\ H\!\!-\!\!\!\!\overset{|}{}\!\!\!\!-OH \\ HO\!\!-\!\!\!\!\overset{|}{}\!\!\!\!-H \\ HO\!\!-\!\!\!\!\overset{|}{}\!\!\!\!-H \\ CH_2OH \end{array}$$

L-(−)-glucose

24.6   (a) D-*glycero*-D-*gluco*-heptose   (b) 4-deoxy-D-*glycero*-2-pentulose   (c) 3-deoxy-D-*ribo*-hexose

24.7   (a)

$$
\begin{array}{c}
\mathrm{CHO} \\
\mathrm{H} \!-\!\!-\! \mathrm{OH} \\
\mathrm{HO} \!-\!\!-\! \mathrm{H} \\
\mathrm{HO} \!-\!\!-\! \mathrm{H} \\
\mathrm{H} \!-\!\!-\! \mathrm{OH} \\
\mathrm{H} \!-\!\!-\! \mathrm{OH} \\
\mathrm{CH_2OH}
\end{array}
$$

(b)

$$
\begin{array}{c}
\mathrm{CHO} \\
\mathrm{HO} \!-\!\!-\! \mathrm{H} \\
\mathrm{H} \!-\!\!-\! \mathrm{H} \\
\mathrm{H} \!-\!\!-\! \mathrm{OH} \\
\mathrm{H} \!-\!\!-\! \mathrm{OH} \\
\mathrm{CH_3}
\end{array}
$$

(c)

$$
\begin{array}{c}
\mathrm{CHO} \\
\mathrm{H} \!-\!\!-\! \mathrm{OH} \\
\mathrm{HO} \!-\!\!-\! \mathrm{H} \\
\mathrm{H} \!-\!\!-\! \mathrm{NHCCH_3} \\
\mathrm{H} \!-\!\!-\! \mathrm{OH} \\
\mathrm{CH_3}
\end{array}
$$

24.8

$$
\begin{array}{c}
\mathrm{CH_2OH} \\
\mathrm{C}{=}\mathrm{O} \\
\mathrm{CHOH} \\
\mathrm{CHOH} \\
\mathrm{CHOH} \\
\mathrm{CH_2OH}
\end{array}
\xrightarrow[\mathrm{H_2O}]{\mathrm{HCN}}
\left[
\begin{array}{c}
\mathrm{CH_2OH} \\
\mathrm{HO}{-}\mathrm{C}{-}\mathrm{C}{\equiv}\mathrm{N} \\
\mathrm{CHOH} \\
\mathrm{CHOH} \\
\mathrm{CHOH} \\
\mathrm{CH_2OH}
\end{array}
\right]
\xrightarrow{\mathrm{H_2O}}
\begin{array}{c}
\mathrm{CH_2OH} \\
\mathrm{HO}{-}\mathrm{C}{-}\mathrm{COH} \\
\mathrm{CHOH} \\
\mathrm{CHOH} \\
\mathrm{CH_2OH}
\end{array}
\xrightarrow[\mathrm{P}]{\mathrm{HI}}
\begin{array}{c}
\mathrm{CH_3} \\
\mathrm{H}{-}\mathrm{C}{-}\mathrm{COH} \\
\mathrm{CH_2} \\
\mathrm{CH_2} \\
\mathrm{CH_2} \\
\mathrm{CH_3}
\end{array}
$$

fructose   no stereochemistry implied   2-methyl-
hexanoic acid

Because the addition of hydrogen cyanide to the carbonyl and the hydrolysis of the resulting nitrile give a seven-carbon carboxylic acid with branching at the second carbon atom, fructose must be a ketose with the ketone function on carbon 2.

24.9   (a)   The first step in the reduction is the protonation of the alcohol to give a good leaving group, followed by a nucleophilic substitution reaction (either S_N1 or S_N2, depending on the nature of the carbon atom) to form an alkyl halide.

$$\mathrm{R{-}OH} + \mathrm{HI} \longrightarrow \mathrm{R{-}I} + \mathrm{H_2O}$$

(b) $\mathrm{R{-}\overset{..}{O}{-}H} \rightarrow \mathrm{R{=}\overset{..}{O}{+}{-}H} \rightarrow \mathrm{R{-}\overset{..}{\underset{..}{I}}{:}} + \mathrm{H{-}\overset{..}{\underset{..}{O}}{-}H}$

The rest of the reaction must be a free radical chain reaction.

initiation step: $\mathrm{R{-}\overset{..}{\underset{..}{I}}{:}} \longrightarrow \mathrm{R{\cdot}} + {\cdot}\overset{..}{\underset{..}{I}}{:}$

propagation steps: $\mathrm{R{\cdot}} \quad \mathrm{H{-}\overset{..}{\underset{..}{I}}{:}} \longrightarrow \mathrm{R{-}H} + {\cdot}\overset{..}{\underset{..}{I}}{:}$

$\mathrm{R{-}\overset{..}{\underset{..}{I}}{:}} \quad {\cdot}\overset{..}{\underset{..}{I}}{:} \longrightarrow \mathrm{R{\cdot}} + {:}\overset{..}{\underset{..}{I}}{-}\overset{..}{\underset{..}{I}}{:}$

Concept Map 24.2   Structure of glucose.

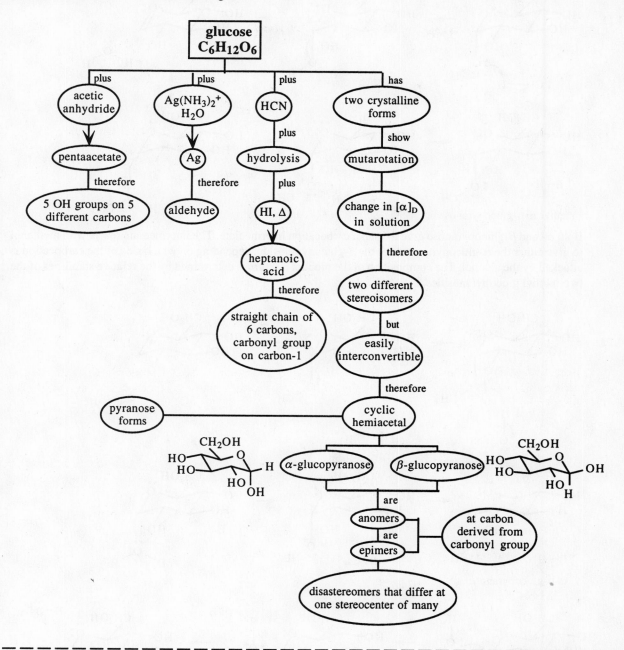

24.10

β-D-ribopyranose

24.11

methyl α-D-glucopyranose

Both α- and β-glucopyranose give the same carbocation intermediate. The intermediate reacts with methanol to give either the α-glucopyranoside or the β-glucopyranoside, depending on which side of the carbocation is attacked by the alcohol. The composition of the product mixture is determined by the relative stabilities of the two methyl glucopyranosides.

24.12

α-D-glucopyranose

β-D-glucopyranose

24.13

salicin   glucose   o-(hydroxymethyl)phenol

24.13 (cont)

salicylic acid

acetylsalicylic acid
aspirin

24.14

β-glucoside
cleaved by emulsin
arbutin

24.15

Hydrogen bonding to the solvent is more important for the β-pyranose, which has an anomeric hydroxyl group, than for the β-pyranoside, which has an anomeric methoxyl group. Hydrogen bonding counteracts the anomeric effect, stabilizing the equatorial hydroxyl group relative to the axial one, more than it affects the equilibrium between the forms with the equatorial and axial methoxyl groups.

24.16

D-(+)-galactose

24.17

α-D-mannopyranose

β-D-galactopyranose

24.18

24.18 (cont)

24.19

24.20   Acid hydrolysis would also cleave the glycosidic linkage between glucose and the phenol.

24.21

The reaction is an S_N2 reaction. It takes place with inversion of configuration.

24.22   Hydrolysis at C-1 gives a resonance-stabilized carbocation.

resonance-stabilized cation

Cleavage of the linkage at C-2 gives a secondary carbocation with no possibility of delocalization of charge.

secondary carbo-
cation at C-2; no
delocalization of
charge possible

24.23

D-allose

allaric acid

24.24   Excess sodium borohydride would reduce the aldose to the alcohol.

Concept Map 24.3   Reactions of monosaccharides.

24.25 (cont)

$$
\begin{array}{ccc}
& \overset{O}{\underset{\parallel}{C}}OH & \\
H & \!\!-\!\! & OH \\
H & \!\!-\!\! & OH \\
& \overset{}{\underset{\parallel}{C}}OH & \\
& O &
\end{array}
\qquad
\begin{array}{ccc}
& \overset{O}{\underset{\parallel}{C}}OH & \\
HO & \!\!-\!\! & H \\
H & \!\!-\!\! & OH \\
& \overset{}{\underset{\parallel}{C}}OH & \\
& O &
\end{array}
$$

meso-tartaric acid   D-(–)-tartaric acid

Concept Map 24.4   The Kiliani-Fischer synthesis.

24.26

24.26 (cont)

D-ribose

NaBH₄
reduction of
corresponding
lactone

↓ HNO₃

D-ribaric acid
meso form; no optical activity

D-arabinaric acid
optically active

NaBH₄
reduction of
corresponding
lactone

D-arabinose

↓ HNO₃

D-Ribose must have the OH groups on the right in the Fischer projection formula, while D-arabinose must be the epimer of D-ribose at the new stereocenter created in this synthesis.

24.27

D-glucose

NaBH₄

D-glucitol

rotate 180° in
plane of paper

L-sorbitol
(viewed in this way,
it is a member of
the L family)

L-sorbose

NaBH₄

another possible
reduction product
of L-sorbose

24.28

HO ⟶ OH + ═⟨OCH₃/CH₃⟩ ⟶(TsOH) ⟶ + CH₃OH

24.28 (cont)

24.29

A

B

C   D   E   (*R*)-epichlorohydrin

24.30

2,3,4,6-tetra-*O*-methyl-
D-glucopyranose
(therefore hydroxyl group
at C-1 in glycosidic linkage)

2,3,4-tri-*O*-methyl-
D-glucopyranose
(therefore hydroxyl group
at C-6 in glycosidic linkage;
anomeric carbon atom free because
gentiobiose is a reducing sugar)

β-glycosidic linkage
hydrolyzed by emulsin

methylation

methylated gentiobiose

O-*β*-D-glucopyranosyl-(1 → 6)-D-glucopyranose

24.31

portion of cellulose   portion of cellulose trinitrate

24.32

24.33

chitobiose

24.34

ascorbic acid

delocalization of charge to
oxygen atom of carbonyl group

no possible delocalization of
charge to another oxygen atom

24.35

cellobiose   digitoxigenin

24.36

(a)

(b)

(c)

(d)

(e)

(f)

(g)

(h)

(i)

24.37   (a)   *N*-acetyl-2-amino-2-deoxy-D-galactose
         2-acetamido-2-deoxy-D-galactose
   (c)   methyl β-D-2-deoxyribofuranoside
   (e)   L-galactose
   (g)   α-D-galactopyranose pentaacetate
   (i)   L-*gluco*-2-heptulose

   (b)   α-D-glucopyranose-1-phosphate
         (shown in ionized form)
   (d)   δ-galactonolactone
   (f)   *N*-(β-D-ribofuranosyl)dimethylamine
   (h)   methyl 2,3,5-tri-*O*-methyl-β-D-ribofuranoside

24.38   (a)

shown as β-D-arabinopyranose

mixture of methyl α- and
β-D-arabinopyranosides

   (b)

   (c)

   (d)

   (e)

   (f)

   (g)

24.38 **(h)**

(i)

Note: D-Arabinose will also be present in the equilibrium mixture.

(j)

(k)

(l)

gluconic acid   mannonic acid   δ-gluconolactone   γ-mannonolactone

D-glucose   D-mannose

24.39 (a)

and enantiomer
A

B

C
$C_{10}H_{16}O_3$

(b)

D

E

(c)

F

G

(d)

H

(e)

I

J

(f)

K

L

24.40 (a)

A

B

A and B are diastereomers

24.40 (b)

(c)

D and E are diastereomers

(d)

F

G   H   I

24.41

(+)-tartaric acid   A   B

24.41 (cont)

Note: Conversion of either hydroxyl group in (+)-tartaric acid to the chloro compound and reduction of the carbon-chlorine bond give (+)-malic acid.

compound obtained if the
lower hydroxyl group in
(+)-tartaric acid is replaced
by hydrogen

(+)-malic acid

24.42

24.43

(Arabinose is epimeric with ribose at
C-2, the 2' position in the sugar residue,
so the structure of Vira-A is easily
derived from that of adenosine.)

24.44

Exchange of oxygen atoms occurs at the anomeric carbon atom by way of the open-chain form of glucose.

24.45 (a)

(b)

24.45 (b) (cont)

24.46

In solution, fluoride ion exists hydrogen bonded to hydrogen fluoride as HF_2^- because of the strength of the hydrogen bond to fluorine.

24.47

24.47

24.48   (a)

xylose
β-D-xylopyranose

(b)   The glucose unit has the free hemiacetal function.

(c)

primeverose heptaacetate

primeverose

(d)

gaultherin

24.49

CH$_2$OH

HOCH$_2$CH$_2$

HO

CH$_2$OCH$_2$CH$_2$OH

HO

CH$_2$OH

HO

HO

HOCH$_2$CH$_2$O

CH$_2$

modified amylopectin   HO

HO

HOCH$_2$CH$_2$O

CH$_2$OCH$_2$CH$_2$OH

HO

HO

24.50   The reaction is an aldol condensation reaction between two glyceraldehyde molecules. The enediol intermediate that is necessary for the condensation reaction is formed faster from dihydroxyacetone (in which deprotonation occurs at an O—H bond) than from glyceraldehyde (in which deprotonation must occur at a C—H bond). The stereochemistry of the products is determined by the side of the carbonyl group that is attacked by the enediol. The reaction is shown as taking place with the polar and bulky hydroxyl group of the enediol pointing away from the oxygen atom of the carbonyl group undergoing nucleophilic attack.

D-glyceraldehyde   slow   endiol intermediate   fast   dihydroxyacetone

attack on one face of the carbonyl group of D-glyceraldehyde by the enediol intermediate; an aldol condensation   D-fructose

attack on the other face of the carbonyl group of D-glyceraldehyde by the enediol intermediate; an aldol condensation   D-sorbose

Supplemental Problems

S24.1   Write structural formulas for all compounds indicated by letters. Show the stereochemistry whenever it is known.

(a)

(b)

(c)

(d)

(e)

(f)

(g)

S24.2 α-D-Glucose reacts in its furanose form with 2 equivalents of acetone to give cyclic ketals with the hydroxyl groups at carbons 1 and 2 and carbons 5 and 6. Such cyclic ketals are known as isopropylidene derivatives of sugars. Draw the structural formula for the 1,2,5,6-di-*O*-isopropylidene-D-glucofuranose, and propose a mechanism for its formation.

S24.3   A cyanogenic glycoside called amygdalin has been substituted on the market for the compound originally patented as laetrile. Amygdalin has the same aglycon, (*R*)-(−)-mandelonitrile, as laetrile. The aglycon is linked by a β-glycosidic linkage to gentiobiose (Problem 24.30). What is the structure of amygdalin?

S24.4   The amygdalin that is marketed contains considerable amounts of the isomer in which the stereocenter in mandelonitrile has the *S* configuration. Natural amygdalin, (*R*)-amygdalin, is easily epimerized to (*S*)-amygdalin by treatment with base. Write a mechanism for this epimerization. Why does it happen so easily?

S24.5   Shikimic acid is an important intermediate in the biosynthesis of amino acids containing aromatic rings. Shikimic acid itself is synthesized in the body from phosphoenolpyruvic acid, which is the phosphate ester of the enol of pyruvic acid. Various steps of this synthesis are given below. Write mechanisms for the different transformations, supplying acid or base (HB$^+$ and B:) catalysts as necessary. The named intermediates are known; the unnamed one has not been proven.

phosphoenolpyruvic acid   erythrose 4-phosphate   III

5-dehydroquinic acid   3-deoxy-α-arabinoheptulosonic acid 7-phosphate

5-dehydroshikimic acid   enzymatic reduction   shikimic acid

no mechanism necessary

25

Amino Acids, Peptides, and Proteins

Concept Map 25.1   Amino acids, polypeptides, proteins.

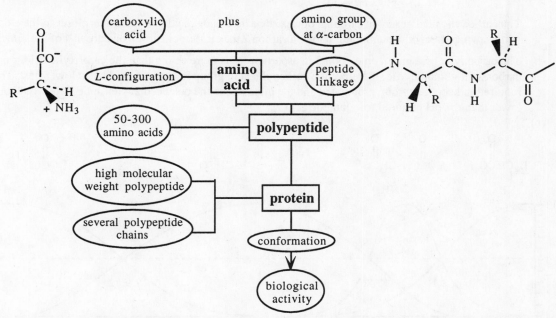

Concept Map 25.2   Acid-base properties of amino acids.

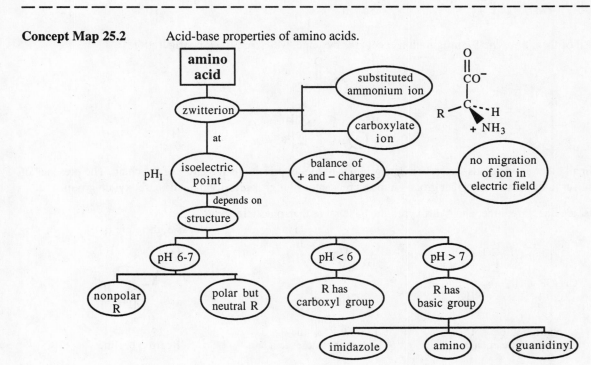

25.1   (a)

$$\text{HOCCH}_2\text{CHCO}^- \underset{\text{H}_3\text{O}^+}{\overset{\text{OH}^-}{\rightleftharpoons}} {}^-\text{OCCH}_2\text{CHCO}^-$$

aspartic acid

$$\text{HOCCH}_2\text{CH}_2\text{CHCO}^- \underset{\text{H}_3\text{O}^+}{\overset{\text{OH}^-}{\rightleftharpoons}} {}^-\text{OCCH}_2\text{CH}_2\text{CHCO}^-$$

glutamic acid

The carboxylic acid group on carbon 3 of aspartic acid is more acidic because it is closer to the electron-withdrawing effect of the ammonium ion on carbon 2 than is the acid group on carbon 4 of glutamic acid.

(b)   The carboxylic acid group on carbon 3 in aspartic acid is more acidic than the carboxylic acid group on carbon 4 in glutamic acid, therefore the carboxylic acid group in aspartic acid has a lower pK_a. The pH required to keep that group protonated and the molecule in the balanced zwitterionic state would also be lower than the pH required for glutamic acid.

(c)

25.2   All of them have the *S* configuration except for cysteine, which has the *R* configuration.

In all other amino acids the carboxylate group is of higher priority than the rest of the chain. The presence of sulfur in cysteine makes that group on the stereocenter of higher priority than the carboxylate group.

25.3   Isoleucine, threonine, and hydroxyproline have more than one stereocenter.

Ile
configuration not
specified at carbon 3

Thr
(2*S*, 3*R*)-2-amino-3-
hydroxybutanoic acid

looks *S*, therefore *R*

Hypro
(2*S*, 4*R*)-4-
hydroxyproline

25.4   (a)

$$\overset{\text{O}}{\overset{\|}{^-\text{OCCHCH}_2\text{CH}_2\text{CH}_2\text{CH}_2\ddot{\text{N}}\text{H}_2}} + \text{H}-\text{B}^+ \rightleftharpoons \overset{\text{O}}{\overset{\|}{^-\text{OCCHCH}_2\text{CH}_2\text{CH}_2\text{CH}_2\overset{+}{\text{N}}\text{H}_3}} + :\text{B}$$

with $^+\text{NH}_3$ below each, labeled lysine on the left.

When lysine is protonated at the ε-amino group, the resulting positive charge is localized at that nitrogen atom.

$$\overset{\text{O}}{\overset{\|}{^-\text{OCCHCH}_2\text{CH}_2\text{CH}_2\text{NHCNH}_2}} + \text{H}-\text{B}^+ \rightleftharpoons \overset{\text{O}}{\overset{\|}{^-\text{OCCHCH}_2\text{CH}_2\text{CH}_2\text{NHCNH}_2}} + :\text{B}$$

(with $\overset{\text{NH}}{\|}$ on the reactant C and $\overset{+\text{NH}_2}{\|}$ on the product C; $^+\text{NH}_3$ below, labeled arginine)

$$\overset{\text{O}}{\overset{\|}{^-\text{OCCHCH}_2\text{CH}_2\text{CH}_2\overset{+}{\text{N}}\text{H}=\text{CNH}_2}} \longleftrightarrow \overset{\text{O}}{\overset{\|}{^-\text{OCCHCH}_2\text{CH}_2\text{CH}_2\text{NHC}=\overset{+}{\text{N}}\text{H}_2}}$$

(with NH_2 on the C, $^+\text{NH}_3$ below each)

When the guanidinyl group in arginine is protonated, the resulting cation is stabilized by delocalization of the charge to three nitrogen atoms. The guanidinyl group is, therefore, more basic, more easily protonated, than an amino group. The conjugate acid of guanidine, with a pK_a of 12.5, is a weaker acid than the conjugate acid of a primary amine, p$K_a \sim 10.5$.

(b)

$$\overset{+\text{NH}_2}{\overset{\|}{\text{H}_2\text{NCNHCH}_2\text{CH}_2\text{CH}_2\text{CHCO}^-}} \qquad \overset{\text{NH}}{\overset{\|}{\text{H}_2\text{NCNHCH}_2\text{CH}_2\text{CH}_2\text{CHCO}^-}}$$
(with $\overset{\text{O}}{\|}$ and $^+\text{NH}_3$ below left; $\overset{\text{O}}{\|}$ and NH_2 below right)

$$\overset{+\text{NH}_2}{\overset{\|}{\text{H}_2\text{NCNHCH}_2\text{CH}_2\text{CH}_2\text{CHCOH}}} \qquad \overset{+\text{NH}_2}{\overset{\|}{\text{H}_2\text{NCNHCH}_2\text{CH}_2\text{CH}_2\text{CHCO}^-}}$$
(with $\overset{\text{O}}{\|}$ and $^+\text{NH}_3$ below left; $\overset{\text{O}}{\|}$ and NH_2 below right)

Graph: percentage of each species (y-axis, 0 to 100) vs pH (x-axis, 0 to 14). Curves cross at 50% at pH 2.1, 8.8, and 12.5. Dashed vertical line near pH 11 labeled "isoelectric point."

25.4   (c)

indole ring system

The nonbonding electrons on the nitrogen atom in the indole ring are part of an aromatic sextet and are therefore not available for protonation. Protonation of that nitrogen atom would lead to loss of aromaticity, so the difference in energy between indole and its conjugate acid would be very large.

25.5   (a)

(b)

(c)

(d)

(e)

25.5 (f)

$$CH_3CHCH_2\overset{CO^-}{\underset{+NH_3}{C}}H \xrightarrow{PhCH=O} CH_3CHCH_2\overset{COOH}{\underset{N=CHPh}{C}}H$$

(g)

$$H_3\overset{+}{N}CH_2CH_2CH_2CH_2\overset{CO^-}{\underset{+NH_3}{C}}H \xrightarrow{(CH_3C)_2O \text{ (excess)}} CH_3CNHCH_2CH_2CH_2CH_2\overset{COOH}{\underset{NHCCH_3}{C}}H$$

(h)

$$HO-\phi-CH_2\overset{CO^-}{\underset{+NH_3}{C}}H \xrightarrow{HNO_3} O_2N \text{—} HO \text{—} O_2N \text{—} CH_2\overset{COOH}{\underset{+NH_3}{C}}H \quad NO_3^-$$

25.6

25.7   One possible peptide is:

$$N\text{-terminal} \longrightarrow \text{Ala-Gly-Ser-Phe} \longleftarrow C\text{-terminal}$$
amino acid   amino acid

The other twenty-two, besides the one above and Ser-Ala-Phe-Gly, are:

Ala-Gly-Phe-Ser	Ser-Ala-Gly-Phe
Ala-Ser-Gly-Phe	Ser-Gly-Ala-Phe
Ala-Ser-Phe-Gly	Ser-Gly-Phe-Ala
Ala-Phe-Ser-Gly	Ser-Phe-Ala-Gly
Ala-Phe-Gly-Ser	Ser-Phe-Gly-Ala
Gly-Ala-Ser-Phe	Phe-Ala-Ser-Gly
Gly-Ala-Phe-Ser	Phe-Ala-Gly-Ser
Gly-Ser-Ala-Phe	Phe-Ser-Gly-Ala
Gly-Ser-Phe-Ala	Phe-Ser-Ala-Gly
Gly-Phe-Ala-Ser	Phe-Gly-Ser-Ala
Gly-Phe-Ser-Ala	Phe-Gly-Ala-Ser

N-terminal	*C*-terminal	*N*-terminal	*C*-terminal
amino acid	amino acid	amino acid	amino acid

25.8

The hydrolysis was done in strong acid. Therefore, all amino acids are shown in their fully protonated forms.

25.9   (a) Gly-Phe-Thr-Lys will have $pH_I > 6$; it will move to the negative pole in an electric field at pH 6.

   (b) Tyr-Ala-Val-Asn will have $pH_I \sim 6$; it will not move in an electric field at pH 6.

   (c) Trp-Glu-Leu will have $pH_I < 6$; it will move to the positive pole in an electric field at pH 6.

   (d) Pro-Hypro-Gly will have $pH_I \sim 6$; it will not move in an electric field at pH 6.

25.10

N-terminal lysine

The N-terminial lysine
will be doubly labeled.

Lys in middle of chain

The lysine from the middle of the chain
will have a single dinitrophenyl label.

25.11

25.11 (cont)

The carboxylic acid function of glycine, which was part of a peptide linkage, is labeled with ^{18}O.

No ^{18}O turns up in the carboxylic acid group of alanine, which was the *C*-terminal acid.

Note that glycine is shown with a protonated carboxylic acid function, and alanine has an unprotonated amino function. The final step in the reaction would be a proton transfer from glycine to alanine.

Concept Map 25.3   Proof of structure of peptides and proteins.

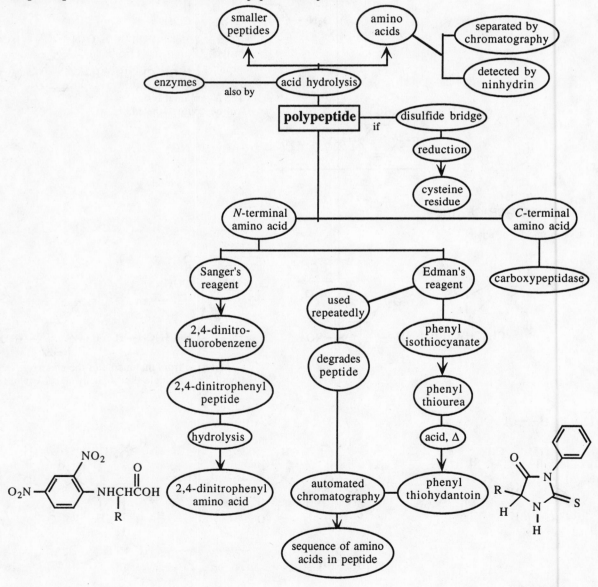

25.12   (a) The *N*-terminal amino acid is arginine.

(b) The fragments are shown lined up below:

Arg–Gly–Pro
               Pro–Pro
                    Pro–Phe–Ile–Val
                    Pro–Phe–Ile

Therefore, the structure of the peptide is: Arg–Gly–Pro–Pro–Phe–Ile–Val.

25.13   (a) Cysteine is the *N*-terminal amino acid.

        Glycinamide is the *C*-terminal amino acid.

        Arginine is the second amino acid from the *C*-terminal end.

        The peptide fragments are shown lined up below:

                                Cys–Pro–Arg–Gly (peptide of undetermined order*)
                        Asp–Cys
                 Glu–Asp–Cys
            Phe–Glu–Asp
            Phe–Glu
        Cys–Try–Phe

        *The information from the trypsin degradation gives the structure of the peptide of undetermined order.

           Cys–Try–Phe–Glu–Asp–Cys–Pro–Arg–Gly is the order of amino acids from the degradation work.

(b) The full structure of the peptide must show a disulfide bridge and three amide groups to account for the three moles of ammonia lost in the hydrolysis. There are three free carboxylic acid groups in the structure shown in part (a): Glu, Asp, and the *C*-terminal Gly.

arginine vasopressin

- -

Concept Map 25.4   Protection of functional groups in peptide synthesis.

Concept Map 25.5   Activation of the carboxyl group in peptide synthesis.

- -

25.14

(a)

25.14

(b)

(c)

(d)

25.15

25.16

Phe-Leu-Gly

Concept Map 25.6   Conformation and structure in proteins.

- -

25.17

25.17 (cont)

25.18 (a)

(shown at pH 6)

(b)

(c)

(d)

(e)

(f)

25.19 (a) *N*-2,4-dinitrophenylphenylalanine
(c) glycylcysteinylhistidine
(e) *p*-nitrophenyl alaninate

(b) methyl cysteinate
(d) *N*-benzoylglycine; hippuric acid
(f) *N-tert*-butoxycarbonylleucine

25.20 (a)

(b)

25.20 (c)

(d)

(e)

(f)

(g)

(h)

25.20 (h) (cont)

$$(CH_3)_3COCNH \quad \quad \quad OCH_3 \quad + \quad \text{cyclohexyl-NHCNH-cyclohexyl}$$

(i)

$$CH_3CH\underset{\overset{|}{+NH_3}}{\overset{CH_3}{C}}\,H \xrightarrow{\text{PhCH}} CH_3CH\underset{\overset{|}{N=CHPh}}{\overset{CH_3}{C}}\,H$$

25.21 (a)

$$HO-C_6H_4-CH_2-\underset{+NH_3}{C}-H \xrightarrow[H_2O]{Br_2} HO(Br)_2C_6H_2-CH_2-\underset{+NH_3}{C}-H \quad \textbf{A}$$

(b)

$$CH_3-\underset{+NH_3}{C}-H \xrightarrow{(CH_3C)_2O} CH_3-\underset{NHCCH_3}{C}-H \quad \textbf{B}$$

(c)

$$CH_3CHCH_2-\underset{+NH_3}{C}-H \xrightarrow{PhCCl} CH_3CHCH_2-\underset{NHCPh}{C}-H \quad \textbf{C}$$

(d)

$$HOCCH_2-\underset{+NH_3}{C}-H \xrightarrow{CH_3CH_2OH\,(excess),\,HCl} CH_3CH_2OCCH_2-\underset{+NH_3\;Cl^-}{C}-H \quad \textbf{D}$$

(e)

$$H_3^+N\cdots \xrightarrow[]{\substack{NO_2 \\ F-C_6H_3-NO_2}} O_2N-C_6H_3-NH\cdots \textbf{E}$$

25.21 (e) (cont)

$$\xrightarrow[\Delta]{\text{HCl, H}_2\text{O}}$$

25.22

(a)

$$\xrightarrow{\text{PhN}=\text{C}=\text{S}}$$

A

$$\xrightarrow[\substack{\text{nitromethane} \\ \Delta}]{\text{HCl}}$$

B   C

(b)

$$\xrightarrow[\substack{\text{Pd/C} \\ \text{methanol} \\ \text{HCl}}]{\text{H}_2}$$

$+ \; CO_2 + CH_3$—

D

(c)

$$\xrightarrow[\text{dioxane}]{\text{HCl}}$$

$+ \; CO_2 + CH_3C=CH_2$

E

(d)

$$\xrightarrow{\text{HO—N}\cdots, \text{DCC}}$$

F

25.22

(e)

G

H

25.23 (a)

pH 1

pH 6

pH 11

(b)

pH 1

pH 6

25.23 (b) (cont)

CH_3 ... structures

$CH_2CH_2CH_2CH_2NH_2$

pH 11

(c)

$CH_2CH(CH_3)_2$

pH 1

$CH_2CH(CH_3)_2$

pH 6

$CH_2CH(CH_3)_2$

pH 11

(d)

$CH_2CH_2SCH_3$

pH 1

$CH_2CH_2SCH_3$

pH 6

$CH_2CH_2SCH_3$

pH 11

25.24

Note that the configuration
at this stereocenter is reversed.

Tyr-D-Ala-Gly-Phe-Pro-NH$_2$

25.25

25.26

A

This functional group is like an anhydride in reactivity.

(The carboxylate anion is more nucleophilic than the hydroxyl group of the phenol.)

B

C

D

25.26 (cont)

$$
CH_2SCH_2Ph
$$

PhCH$_2$OCNH — ... — NH$_2$ $\xrightarrow[\text{acetic acid}]{\text{HBr}}$

E

F

C + F $\xrightarrow{\text{DCC}}$

$\xrightarrow[\text{NH}_3 \text{ (liq)}]{\text{Na}}$

Cys—Tyr—Phe—Gln—Asn—Cys—Pro—Lys—Gly—NH$_2$ $\xrightarrow[\text{oxidation}]{\text{air}}$

N-terminal end   *C*-terminal end

H

I

lysine vasopressin

25.27 (a) (1)

$$
\text{PhCHCH}_2\text{COCH}_2\text{CH}_3 \xleftarrow[\text{H}_2\text{O}]{\text{NH}_4\text{Cl}} \text{PhCHCH}_2\text{COCH}_2\text{CH}_3 \xleftarrow{} \text{CH}_2=\text{COCH}_2\text{CH}_3 \xleftarrow{} \text{CH}_3\text{COCH}_2\text{CH}_3
$$

OH

ethyl 3-hydroxy-3-
phenylpropanoate

25.27 (a) (2)

$$PhCHCH_2COCH_2CH_3 \xleftarrow[\text{ethanol}]{NaBH_4} PhCCH_2COCH_2CH_3 \xleftarrow{PhCCl} CH_2=COCH_2CH_3 \xleftarrow{(CH_3CH)_2N^-Li^+} CH_3COCH_2CH_3$$

(b)

$$\underset{S}{\overset{OH}{H-C-}}CH_2COCH_2CH_3 \quad + \quad CH_3CH_2OCCH_2\underset{R}{\overset{OH}{-C-H}}$$

Lipase PS-30
pH 7
phosphate buffer

separated *S* acid   ionic, soluble in buffer   covalent, can be extracted out with an organic solvent

$$\xrightarrow{H_3O^+}$$

separated *R* acid

25.28

R =

25.28 (cont)

pyrophosphate anion

acid phosphate linkage →

activated amino acid

25.29   Combining the fragments from trypsin and chymotrypsin digestion gives the following three segments:

A peptide containing 17 amino acids from the *N*-terminal end of viscotoxin A$_2$:
Lys–Ser–Cys–Cys–Pro–Asn–Thr–Thr–Gly–Arg–Asn–Ile–Tyr–Asn–Thr–Cys–Arg

A peptide containing 17 amino acids from the *C*-terminal end:
Ser–Gly–Cys–Lys–Ile–Ile–Ser–Ala–Ser–Thr–Cys–Pro–Ser–Tyr–Pro–Asp–Lys

A 12 amino acid peptide; no overlap with either of the *N*- or *C*-terminal fragments:
Phe–Gly–Gly–Gly–Ser–Arg–Glu–Val–Cys–Ala–Ser–Leu

The three peptides add up to 46 amino acids, the total number contained in viscotoxin A$_2$. The complete order of amino acids in viscotoxin A$_2$ is thus the order that exists in the sequence of the three peptide fragments.

Lys–Ser–Cys–Cys–Pro–Asn–Thr–Thr–Gly–Arg–Asn–Ile–Tyr–Asn–Thr
|

Ser–Leu–Ser–Ala–Cys–Val–Glu–Arg–Ser–Gly–Gly–Gly–Phe–Arg–Cys
|

Gly–Cys–Lys–Ile–Ile–Ser–Ala–Ser–Thr–Cys–Pro–Ser–Tyr–Pro–Asp–Lys

25.30

(a)

25.30 (a) (cont)

Schiff base at the active
site of the enzyme

glyceraldehyde
3-phosphate

(b)

Schiff base of dihydroxy-
acetone phosphate

25.30

(c)

$$HOCH_2-\overset{\overset{\displaystyle |}{C}}{\underset{\underset{\displaystyle H}{\overset{\displaystyle |}{N}}}{|}}-CH_2-O-\overset{\overset{\displaystyle O}{\|}}{\underset{\underset{\displaystyle O^-}{|}}{P}}-O^-$$

$\overset{\displaystyle (CH_2)_4}{|}$

$\xrightarrow[\displaystyle H_2O]{\displaystyle NaBH_4 \quad hydrolysis}$

$$CH_2OH$$
$$CHNHCH_2CH_2CH_2CH_2-\overset{\overset{\displaystyle O}{\|}}{\underset{\underset{+NH_3}{}}{C}}\overset{CO^-}{\underset{}{\cdots}}H$$
$$CH_2OH$$

lysine derivative of
dihydroxyacetone

25.31 Peptide P contains 11 amino acids:
Arg, Gln (2), Gly, Leu, Lys, Met, Phe (2), Pro (2)
Peptide A contains Arg, Gln (2), Lys, Phe, Pro (2). Therefore, Peptide B must contain Gly, Leu, Met, Phe.

Peptide P (and Peptide A) $\xrightarrow{\text{Edman's reagent}}$ phenylthiohydantoins of
Arg, Pro, Lys, Pro, in that order

Therefore, the *N*-terminal amino acid of Peptide P (and Peptide A) is Arg. Peptide A contains the amino acids from the *N*-terminal end of P, and Peptide B must contain the amino acids from the *C*-terminal end of P.

Peptide A $\xrightarrow[\text{carboxypeptidase}]{}$ first Phe and then Gln

Therefore, the *C*-terminal amino acid of A is Phe. Peptide A must have the structure Arg–Pro–Lys–Pro–Gln–Gln–Phe.

Peptide B $\xrightarrow{\text{Edman's reagent}}$ phenylthiohydantoins of
Phe, Gly, Leu, in that order

Therefore, Peptide B must have the structure Phe–Gly–Leu–Met.

Peptide P $\xrightarrow[\text{carboxypeptidase}]{}$ no amino acid

Therefore, the *C*-terminal amino acid of P does not have a free carboxylic acid group.

Peptide P $\xrightarrow[\substack{\text{(hydrolysis of} \\ \text{amide bonds)}}]{\text{HCl (0.03 M)}}$ Peptide C

Peptide C $\xrightarrow[\text{carboxypeptidase}]{}$ Gly, Met, Leu, Phe (order not determined)

Therefore, Peptide C has a *C*-terminal amino acid with a free carboxylic acid group. The same amino acids as those present in Peptides B and P are released to the solution, so Peptide C has the same sequence of amino acids as Peptide P. Both have Met as the *C*-terminal amino acid. In Peptide P, the *C*-terminal acid exists as the amide, Met—NH_2.
These conclusions can be summarized as answers to the subsections of the problem.

(a) The *N*-terminal amino acid of Peptide P is Arg.
(b) The *C*-terminal amino acid of Peptide P is Met.
(c) The sequence of amino acids in Peptide A is Arg–Pro–Lys–Pro–Gln–Gln–Phe.
(d) The sequence of amino acids in Peptide B is Phe–Gly–Leu–Met.
(e) The complete structure of Peptide B is Phe–Gly–Leu–Met—NH_2.
(f) The sequence of amino acids in Peptide C is Arg–Pro–Lys–Pro–Gln–Gln–Phe–Phe–Gly–Leu–Met.
(g) The complete structure of Peptide P is Arg–Pro–Lys–Pro–Gln–Gln–Phe–Phe–Gly–Leu–Met—NH_2.

25.32   The solid state synthesis of Peptide P:

(a)

(b)

(c)

25.32

(d)

$$\text{(CH}_3)_3\text{COCNH} \cdots \xrightarrow[\text{dioxane}]{\text{HCl}}$$

$$\cdots + \text{CH}_3\text{C}=\text{CH}_2 + \text{CO}_2\uparrow$$

$$\overset{CH_3}{}$$

(e)

$$\text{CH}_3\text{SCH}_2\text{CH}_2 \cdots \xrightarrow{\text{PhCH}_2\text{Cl}} \cdots$$

25.33

ADP

25.33 (cont)

25.34 (a)

(b)

(c)

25.35

N-benzoyl-3-phenylisoserine

25.36 (a) β–Carboxyaspartic acid is a malonic acid derivative. Malonic acid is stable when it is in basic solution, but it decarboxylates when it is heated with acid. β–Carboxyaspartic acid, therefore, survives basic hydrolysis of a peptide better than it survives acid-catalyzed hydrolysis. The decarboxylation product of β–carboxyaspartic acid is aspartic acid, which is then seen as the product of acid-catalyzed hydrolysis.

stable towards decarboxylation

β-carboxyaspartic acid (at low pH)

25.36 (a) (cont)

$$\text{peptide} \xrightarrow[\substack{H_3O^+ \\ \Delta}]{H_2O} \left[\underset{\underset{O}{\overset{\|}{HOC}}\ \ \overset{+}{NH_3}}{\overset{O \quad\quad O}{\overset{\|\quad\quad\ \|}{HOCCHCHCOH}}} \right] \longrightarrow CO_2\uparrow \ + \ \underset{\underset{+NH_3}{\quad}}{\overset{O \quad\quad O}{\overset{\|\quad\quad\ \|}{HOCCH_2CHCOH}}}$$

aspartic acid
(at low pH)

(b) $\underset{O}{\overset{O}{CH_2(COCH_3)_2}} \xrightarrow[\text{methanol}]{CH_3ONa} \underset{A}{Na^+{}^- CH(COCH_3)_2} \xrightarrow[\text{methanol}]{\overset{O}{\overset{\|}{ClCH_2COCH_3}}} \underset{B}{CH_3OCCH_2CH(COCH_3)_2}$

$\underset{B}{CH_3OCCH_2CH(COCH_3)_2} \xrightarrow[\substack{KOH \\ \Delta}]{PhCH_2OH} \underset{C}{PhCH_2OCCH_2CH(COCH_2Ph)_2} \xrightarrow[\substack{\text{carbon} \\ \text{tetrachloride} \\ \text{dark}}]{Br_2}$

$\underset{\underset{Br}{|}}{\underset{D}{PhCH_2OCCH_2C(COCH_2Ph)_2}} \xrightarrow[\text{diethyl ether}]{(CH_3CH_2)_3N} \underset{E}{PhCH_2OCCH=C(COCH_2Ph)_2}$

$\underset{E}{PhCH_2OCCH=C(COCH_2Ph)_2} \xrightarrow[\substack{\text{tetrahydro-} \\ \text{furan}}]{HN_3} \underset{\underset{N=N=N^-}{|}}{\underset{F}{PhCH_2OCCHCH(COCH_2Ph)_2}} \xrightarrow[\substack{Pd/C \\ \text{acetic acid} \\ \text{methanol} \\ 0\,°C}]{H_2}$

$\langle\text{Ph}\rangle{-}CH_2OH \ + \ N_2\uparrow \ + \ \underset{\underset{\underset{O}{\|}}{CH_3CO^-\ {}^+NH_3}}{\underset{G}{HOCCHCH(COH)_2}} \xrightarrow[\substack{H_2O}]{HCl} \underset{Cl^-\ {}^+NH_3}{HOCCHCH(COH)_2}$

(c) Free radical substitution of the benzylic hydrogen atoms of the benzyl ethers can occur with Br_2 in the presence of light.

(d) The ester groups on the carbon-carbon double bond are electron-withdrawing. The acid adds to give the more stable carbocation, the one with the positive charge on the carbon atom with only one ester group.

25.37

$\underset{\substack{N \\ | \\ H}}{\overset{H}{\underset{COH}{\diagdown}}} \xrightarrow[\substack{NaHCO_3 \\ \text{toluene}}]{PhCH_2OCCl} \underset{A}{\underset{\substack{N \\ | \\ PhCH_2OC}}{\overset{H}{\underset{COH}{\diagdown}}}} \xrightarrow{(CH_3CH_2)_3N} \underset{B}{\underset{\substack{N \\ | \\ PhCH_2OC}}{\overset{H}{\underset{CO^-}{\diagdown}}}} + HN(CH_2CH_3)_3 \xrightarrow{ClCOCH_2CH_3}$

(if 1 equiv of $NaHCO_3$ used)

25.37 (cont)

25.38

Supplemental Problems

S25.1   Complete the following equations:

S25.1 (cont)

(c) CH₃SCH₃, ClC—CCl   (CH₃CH₂)₃N   (d) TsCl / pyridine →

S25.2   Synthetic, racemic leucine is resolved using an enzyme, hog renal acylase, which is isolated from hog kidneys. Hog renal acylase catalyzes the hydrolysis of the amides of L-amino acids only. The reactions are

$$\text{D,L-leucine} \xrightarrow{(CH_3C)_2O} \textit{N}\text{-acetyl-D,L-leucine} \xrightarrow[\substack{\text{hog renal acylase}\\ H_2O,\ pH\ 7 \\ \text{maintained by buffer}}]{} \text{mixture}$$

Some useful information is that acetic acid has pK_a 4.8 and leucine has pI 6.0. Also, leucine and *N*-acetylleucine are crystalline solids when bearing no net charge.

(a) Write equations for the reactions described, being sure to show the correct stereochemistry for the species present at each step. What are the components of the mixture formed at the end of the enzymatic hydrolysis?

(b) How would you separate the components of the mixture that results from the enzymatic treatment? Write equations showing what you would have to do to recover the individual compounds. (Hint: What ionic species are present in the solution when the reaction is over?)

(c) Write equations to describe what you would have to do to recover pure D-leucine.

S25.3   The octapeptide xenopsin from the frog *Xenopus laevis* has a powerful contractile effect on muscles. The *N*-terminal amino acid of xenopsin is glutamic acid, which exists in the natural peptide as the cyclic amide pyroglutamic acid (p. 994 in the text). Carboxypeptidase releases leucine first. Trypsin digestion yields ⌐Glu‾Gly·Lys·Arg and

⌐Glu‾Gly·Lys·Arg·Pro·Trp . Chymotrypsin gives the same hexapeptide as is obtained with trypsin and Ile-Leu. What is the structure of xenopsin?

S25.4   The human growth hormone isolated from the pituitary gland has 188 amino acid residues and has been synthesized by a solid-state technique similar to that of Merrifield (p. 1004 in the text). The first five amino acids in the chain, starting from the *C*-terminal end, are phenylalanine, glycine, cysteine, serine, and glycine, in that order. Devise a solid-state synthesis of this portion of the chain. Assume that the amino acids cysteine and serine are available with benzyl groups protecting the thiol and the hydroxyl groups on their side chains. The benzyl group can be removed by reduction using sodium in ammonia.

S25.5   4-Hydroxy-L-proline (2*S*, 4*R*)-2-carboxy-4-hydroxypyrrolidine, is the starting material for a sequence of reactions that converts it to (2*R*, 4*S*)-2-carboxy-2-methyl-4-hydroxypyrrolidine as shown in a study of the synthesis of new antibacterial agents. The reactions are show below.

(a) Provide the reagents designated by letters.

S25.5 (a) (cont)

(b) An inversion of configuration takes place at the α-carbon of proline in the third step of the series of reactions shown above. How does this happen? Propose a mechanism.

26 Macromolecular Chemistry

Concept Map 26.1   Polymers.

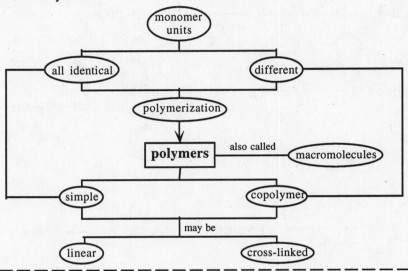

- -

26.1   (a) $HSCH_2\overset{\overset{\displaystyle O}{\|}}{C}OH$

(b) $PhCH{=}CH_2$

(c) $CH_2{=}CHCH_3$

(d) $O{=}C{=}N{-}\langle\ \rangle{-}N{=}C{=}O\ +\ HOCH_2CH_2OH$

        an isocyanate

(e) $CH_2{=}\overset{\overset{\displaystyle CH_3}{|}}{\underset{\underset{\displaystyle O}{\|}}{C}}COCH_3$

- -

Concept Map 26.2   Properties of polymers.

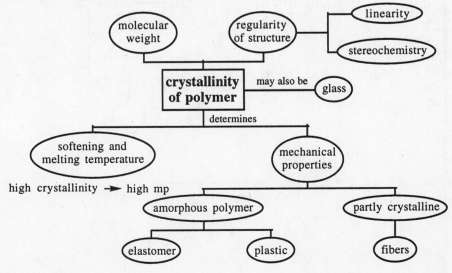

631

26.2

(a) $CH_2{=}\overset{Ph}{\underset{|}{C}}CH_3$ and $N{\equiv}C{-}CH{=}CH{-}C{\equiv}N$; a copolymer   (b) $CH_2{=}CCl_2$; a simple polymer

(c) $PhCH{=}CHPh$ and ; a copolymer   (d) $CH_2{=}\overset{CH_3}{\underset{|}{C}}Ph$ and $CH_2{=}\overset{CH_3}{\underset{|}{C}}{-}C{\equiv}N$; a copolymer

26.3

26.4   (a)

(b)

(c) $CH_2{=}CHCl$ + $CH_2{=}CHCOCH_3$ $\xrightarrow[\substack{\text{acetone}\\50\,°C}]{\text{benzoyl peroxide}}$

26.4 (c) (cont)

       → polymer

(d)

benzoyl peroxide
benzene
80 °C

→ polymer

(e) CH_3CH—CH_2 $\xrightarrow[\Delta]{KOH}$ $HOCH_2CHOCH_2CHO^- K^+$ → polymer

This is an S_N2 substitution reaction. The nucleophile reacts at the less hindered carbon atom of the oxirane.

26.5 CH_2=$CCOCH_3$ $\xrightarrow{}$

tetrahydrofuran
−80 °C

26.5 (cont)

A block copolymer can also be made by starting with isopropyl acrylate and then adding methyl methacrylate.

26.6 $AlCl_3$ + $CH_3C-Cl:$ $\longrightarrow$ $CH_3C\equiv O:^+$ + $^-AlCl_4$

initiation

propagation

polymer $\longleftarrow$

26.7   (a) $\longrightarrow$ (BF₃) $\longrightarrow$ $\longrightarrow$ polymer

(b) $\xrightarrow[\Delta,\ 2\ h]{0.1\ M\ HCl}$ $\longrightarrow$ $\longrightarrow$ polymer

(c) $\xrightarrow{acid}$ $HO(CH_2)_4C-Nu$ $\longrightarrow$ $HO(CH_2)_4CO(CH_2)_4C-Nu$ $\longrightarrow$ polymer

(Nu represents the conjugate base of the acid initiator.)

26.7   **(d)**   [cyclic lactone] $\xrightarrow[\text{base}]{}$ $^-O(CH_2)_4\overset{\displaystyle O}{\overset{\displaystyle \|}{C}}- B$ $\xrightarrow{\text{[lactone]}}$ $^-O(CH_2)_4\overset{\displaystyle O}{\overset{\displaystyle \|}{C}}O(CH_2)_4\overset{\displaystyle O}{\overset{\displaystyle \|}{C}}- B \longrightarrow$ polymer

(B represents the basic initiator.)

(e)   [cyclic diketone anhydride] $\xrightarrow[\substack{\text{(trace of acid} \\ \text{usually present)}}]{\text{solid state}}$ $HOCH_2CH_2O\overset{\displaystyle O}{\overset{\displaystyle \|}{C}}-\overset{\displaystyle O}{\overset{\displaystyle \|}{C}}OH \xrightarrow{\text{[ring]}}$

$HOCH_2CH_2O\overset{\displaystyle O}{\overset{\displaystyle \|}{C}}-\overset{\displaystyle O}{\overset{\displaystyle \|}{C}}OCH_2CH_2O\overset{\displaystyle O}{\overset{\displaystyle \|}{C}}-\overset{\displaystyle O}{\overset{\displaystyle \|}{C}}OH \longrightarrow \longrightarrow$ polymer

(f) $CH_3\overset{\displaystyle CH_3}{\overset{\displaystyle |}{C}}{=}CH_2 \xrightarrow[\substack{BF_3 \\ H_2O \text{ (trace)}}]{} CH_3\overset{\displaystyle CH_3}{\overset{\displaystyle |}{C}}CH_3^+ \xrightarrow{CH_3\overset{\displaystyle CH_3}{\overset{\displaystyle |}{C}}{=}CH_2} CH_3\overset{\displaystyle CH_3}{\overset{\displaystyle |}{C}}CH_2\overset{\displaystyle CH_3}{\overset{\displaystyle |}{\underset{\displaystyle CH_3}{C}}}CH_3^+ \longrightarrow$ polymer

26.8 $HO{-}\langle\text{ring}\rangle{-}CH_2CH_2{-}\langle\text{ring}\rangle{-}OH + BrCH_2(CH_2)_6CH_2Br \xrightarrow{NaOH}$

1,2-bis(4-hydroxyphenyl)ethane   1,8-dibromooctane

$\left[O{-}\langle\text{ring}\rangle{-}CH_2CH_2{-}\langle\text{ring}\rangle{-}OCH_2(CH_2)_6CH_2 \right]_n$

26.9

isotactic polystyrene   syndiotactic polystyrene   atactic polystyrene

fragment of the chain, showing only one
of several possible orientations of the
phenyl groups with respect to each other

26.10   In order for a polymer to be highly crystalline, it has to be highly ordered so it can pack easily into a crystal structure. Isotactic and syndiotactic polymers, with their very regular primary structures, have strong interactions between chains and form crystals. Atactic polymers, with their much less regular structures, do not have as good interactions between chains and are more amorphous.

26.11

atactic poly(methyl methacrylate)
fragment of chain showing one of several possible
arrangements of the ester groups on the chain

- -

Concept Map 26.3   Stereochemistry of polymers.

- -

26.12   (a) $CH_3CH_2\overset{\overset{\displaystyle CH_3}{|}}{C}HCH{=}CH_2$ $\xrightarrow[\substack{TiCl_4 \\ (CH_3CH_2)_2AlCl}]{CH_3CH_2OH}$

26.12 (b) $CH_2{=}CHOCH_3$ $\xrightarrow[\substack{VCl_3 \\ CH_3 \\ | \\ (CH_3CHCH_2)_3Al \\ heptane}]{}$ $\xrightarrow{CH_3CH_2OH}$

(structure of isotactic poly(methyl vinyl ether) with OCH₃ groups)

(c) $CH_2{=}CH_2$ $+$ (2-butene structure) $\xrightarrow[\substack{VCl_3 \\ CH_3 \\ | \\ (CH_3CHCH_2)_3Al \\ heptane \\ -30\,^\circ C}]{}$ $\xrightarrow{CH_3CH_2OH}$

(stereoregular alternating copolymer structure)

(d) $CH_2{=}\underset{\substack{| \\ O}}{\overset{\substack{CH_3 \\ |}}{C}}COCH_3$ $\xrightarrow[\substack{VCl_3 \\ CH_3 \\ | \\ (CH_3CHCH_2)_3Al \\ heptane}]{}$ $\xrightarrow{CH_3CH_2OH}$ $\left[CH_2\underset{\substack{| \\ COCH_3 \\ || \\ O}}{\overset{\substack{CH_3 \\ |}}{C}}\right]_n$

(e) $CH_3CH_2CH{=}CH_2$ $\xrightarrow[\substack{FeCl_3 \\ (CH_3CH_2)_2AlCl}]{}$ $\xrightarrow{CH_3CH_2OH}$ $\left[CH_2\underset{\substack{| \\ CH_2CH_3}}{CH}\right]_n$

26.13 $H_2N(CH_2)_{10}\overset{\substack{O \\ ||}}{C}OH$ $\xrightarrow{\Delta}$ $\left[NH(CH_2)_{10}\overset{\substack{O \\ ||}}{C}\right]_n$ $+$ $2n\ H_2O$

The commonly available lactams contain from four to seven atoms in the ring. The lactam of this monomer would contain twelve atoms in the ring and would not be readily available.

26.14 (5-aminoisophthalic acid structure) $+$ $PhC\overset{\substack{O \\ ||}}{H}$ $\xrightarrow[\substack{N,N\text{-dimethyl-} \\ formamide \\ \Delta}]{}$ (structure **A**, N=CHPh) $\xrightarrow[pyridine]{SOCl_2\ (excess)}$

(acid chloride **B**, N=CHPh) $+$ $H_2N{-}\langle\text{benzene}\rangle{-}CH_2{-}\langle\text{benzene}\rangle{-}NH_2$ $\xrightarrow{\hspace{2cm}}$ (polymer structure with N=CHPh)

26.15

$$HO{-}C_6H_4{-}\underset{CH_3}{\overset{CH_3}{C}}{-}C_6H_4{-}OH + CH_3O\overset{O}{\overset{\|}{C}}OCH_3 \xrightarrow[\text{temperature}]{\text{high}} \left[O{-}C_6H_4{-}\underset{CH_3}{\overset{CH_3}{C}}{-}C_6H_4{-}O\overset{O}{\overset{\|}{C}}\right]_n + 2n\ CH_3OH$$

$$CH_3O\overset{O}{\overset{\|}{C}}{-}C_6H_4{-}\overset{O}{\overset{\|}{C}}OCH_3 + HO(CH_2)_4OH \xrightarrow[\text{temperature}]{\text{high}} \left[O(CH_2)_4O\overset{O}{\overset{\|}{C}}{-}C_6H_4{-}\overset{O}{\overset{\|}{C}}\right]_n + 2n\ CH_3OH$$

26.16 (a)

$$ClCO(CH_2)_4OCCl + H_2N(CH_2)_6NH_2 \xrightarrow[\text{H}_2\text{O}]{\text{NaOH}} \left[NH(CH_2)_6NH\overset{O}{\overset{\|}{C}}O(CH_2)_4O\overset{O}{\overset{\|}{C}}\right]_n$$

(b)

$$O{=}C{=}N(CH_2)_6N{=}C{=}O + HO(CH_2)_4OH \xrightarrow{185-195\ ^\circ C} \left[O(CH_2)_4OCNH(CH_2)_6NHC\right]_n$$

(c)

$$\xrightarrow[\substack{\text{dimethyl}\\ \text{sulfoxide}\\ \text{4-methyl-}\\ \text{2-pentanone}\\ 115\ ^\circ C}]{} $$

26.17

beginning of polymer network

26.18

26.19

- -

Concept Map 26.4   Types of polymerization reactions.

```
                        ┌──────────────────┐
                        │  polymerization  │
                        │    reactions     │
                        └──────────────────┘
                   ┌───────────┴────────────┐
               ( chain-                 ( step-
                growth )                 growth )
           ┌───────┴────────┐
       ( free-          ( ionic )
        radical )
                      ┌──────┴──────┐
                  ( anionic )   ( cationic )
```

- -

26.20

26.21 $CH_3CH=CH_2$ $\xrightarrow[\Delta]{Cl_2\ (g)}$ $ClCH_2CH=CH_2$ $\xrightarrow[H_2O]{Cl_2}$ $ClCH_2\overset{\displaystyle Cl}{\underset{|}{C}}HCH_2OH$

free radical
chlorination
at the allylic
position

electrophilic addition
of chlorine to the
double bond with water
as the electrophile

$ClCH_2\overset{\displaystyle Cl}{\underset{|}{C}}HCH_2OH$ $\xrightarrow{Ca(OH)_2}$ $ClCH_2$—△

intramolecular
S_N2 attack by
alkoxide ion

26.22 $H_2NCH_2CH_2NH_2$ $\xrightarrow[\text{4 equivalents}]{CH_2=CHC\equiv N}$

$\xrightarrow{\text{reduction}}$

$\xrightarrow[\text{8 equivalents}]{CH_2=CHC\equiv N}$ $\xrightarrow{\text{reduction}}$

$\xrightarrow[\text{16 equivalents}]{CH_2=CHC\equiv N}$ $\xrightarrow{\text{reduction}}$

26.22 (cont)

26.23

O₃ → oxidation by atmospheric oxygen → $HOCCH_2CH_2CCH_3$

26.24 $CH_2=CHCH=CH_2$ → $TiBr_4$ / $(CH_3CH_2)_3Al$ →

26.25 $CH_3OCH=CHCH=CH_2$ →   free radical initiator   →

amorphous polymer;
cis double bonds

$CH_3OCH=CHCH=CH_2$ → VCl_3 / $(CH_3CHCH_2)_3Al$ (CH₃)   →

crystalline polymer;
trans double bonds

26.26

There are many different copolymers that can be written for these three monomers, depending on the order in which they are arranged and on whether 1,2- or 1,4-addition to 1,3-butadiene takes place. Two of the possibilities are shown.

26.27

(a)

(b)

(c)

(d)

(e)

(f)

26.27

(g)

$$CH_3\underset{CH_3}{\overset{|}{C}}=CH_2 \ + \ Cl-\langle \ \rangle-CH=CH_2 \xrightarrow[\substack{\text{nitrobenzene}\\ 0\,°C}]{SnCl_4} -\!\!\left[CH_2CHCH_2\underset{CH_3}{\overset{CH_3}{\underset{|}{\overset{|}{C}}}}\right]_n-$$

(h)

$$CH_2=CHOCH_2\underset{CH_3}{\overset{|}{C}}HCH_3 \xrightarrow{(CH_3CH_2)_2O\cdot BF_3} -\!\!\left[CH_2CH\right]_n-$$

(i)

$$CH_2=CHC\equiv N \xrightarrow[\substack{CaO\\ \text{dimethyl-}\\ \text{formamide}\\ 20\,°C}]{} \ ^-O\!\!\left[CH_2CH\right]_n\!\!CH_2\overset{..}{C}H \xrightarrow{HCl} HO\!\!\left[CH_2CH\right]_n\!\!CH_2CH_2$$

(j)

$$CH_2=CHOCHCH_3 \xrightarrow[\substack{VCl_3\\ CH_3\\ (CH_3CHCH_2)_3Al\\ \text{heptane}}]{CH_3CH_2OH}$$

26.28   Cyano and ester groups are electron-withdrawing and stabilize a carbanionic intermediate by their inductive effects and also by resonance.

$$R'\!-\!CH_2\overset{..}{\overset{-}{C}}HC\equiv N: \ \longleftrightarrow \ R'\!-\!CH_2CH=C=\overset{..}{\overset{-}{N}}:$$

$$R'\!-\!CH_2\overset{-}{\overset{..}{C}}H\overset{:O:}{\overset{||}{C}}\!-\!\overset{..}{\overset{..}{O}}R \ \longleftrightarrow \ R'\!-\!CH_2CH=\overset{:\overset{..}{O}:^-}{\overset{|}{C}}\!-\!\overset{..}{\overset{..}{O}}R$$

where R' is the initiator.

Radicals are also stabilized by groups such as the cyano group or carbonyl group.

$$R'\!-\!CH_2\overset{\bullet}{C}HC\equiv N: \ \longleftrightarrow \ R'\!-\!CH_2CH=C=\overset{\bullet}{N}:$$

$$R'\!-\!CH_2\overset{\bullet}{C}H\overset{:O:}{\overset{||}{C}}\!-\!\overset{..}{\overset{..}{O}}R \ \longleftrightarrow \ R'\!-\!CH_2CH=\overset{:\overset{\bullet}{O}:}{\overset{|}{C}}\!-\!\overset{..}{\overset{..}{O}}R$$

Reactions of these monomers that go through anionic or radical intermediates have low energies of activation and proceed easily.

26.28 (cont)

Cationic intermediates are destabilized by the electron-withdrawing cyano and ester groups. Any resonance contributors that are written for such species delocalize the positive charge from carbon to the more electronegative nitrogen or oxygen atom.

$$R' \!-\! CH_2\overset{+}{C}HC\!\equiv\! N \colon \quad\longleftrightarrow\quad R' \!-\! CH_2CH\!=\! C \!=\! \overset{+}{N}\colon$$

$$R' \!-\! CH_2\overset{+}{C}H\overset{\displaystyle\ddot{\overset{..}{O}}\colon}{\overset{\|}{C}}\!-\!\ddot{\overset{..}{O}}R \quad\longleftrightarrow\quad R' \!-\! CH_2CH\!=\! \overset{\overset{+}{\displaystyle\ddot{\overset{..}{O}}}\colon}{C}\!-\!\ddot{\overset{..}{O}}R$$

Such intermediates correspond to high-energy transition states and to high energies of activation for the reactions.

26.29   The rate of a reaction depends on the free energy of activation of the rate-determining step. The free energy of activation is the difference in energy between the reagents and the transition state. In rationalizing most relative rates, it is necessary only to look at the relative stabilization of the transition states. In general, the more stabilized the transition state is, the lower the free energy of activation and the faster the reaction. However, if the energy of a reagent is lowered even more by stabilization, the free energy of activation will be larger, and the rate correspondingly smaller.

In free radical polymerization the rate-determining step is the addition of an unstable radical to the alkene monomer. Substituents play an important role in stabilizing this radical, in which one species bears full radical character, and a less important role in stabilizing the transition state, in which radical character is distributed between two species. The consequences of this are illustrated graphically below.

The phenyl group stabilizes the reagent radical more strongly than does the chlorine atom. Even though the transition state for the reaction of the vinyl chloride may be higher in energy in absolute terms than the transition state for the reaction of styrene, the energy of activation for the reaction of vinyl chloride is smaller. The other three monomers fall in between vinyl chloride and styrene in terms of the relative stabilities of their free radicals. The relative rates of the polymerization reactions thus reflect the relative stabilization of radicals by the substituents on the double bond.

26.30   The first method would give a copolymer in which the amide bonds would be formed more or less randomly by the two different amines reacting with the acid chloride. There would be no pattern to the polymer. If we designate the siloxanediamine as $H_2N\!-\!\overbrace{Si}\!-\!NH_2$ and the aryldiamine as $H_2N\!-\!\overbrace{Ar}\!-\!NH_2$, the first method would give polymers such as

26.30 (cont)

a random copolymer

The second method would give a block copolymer. It would be formed from the polymerization of oligomer A and oligomer B, each of which is a simple polymer. Oligomer A is an amine because a deficiency of acid chloride molecules is used in making it. Oligomer B is an acid chloride.

oligomer A

+

oligomer B

In the block copolymer, stretches of the polymer chain have structural regularity. The amine is either the siloxanediamine or the aryldiamine for many repeating units before a change occurs.

26.31

small amount

26.31 (cont)

$$\xrightarrow[\Delta]{HCl,\ H_2O}$$

26.32   1.

$$\xrightarrow{\gamma\ \text{radiation}}$$

2.

β-alanine

26.33 1.

$$HOCH_2\underset{\underset{CH_3}{|}}{\overset{\overset{CH_3}{|}}{C}}-COOH \xrightarrow[HCl]{CH_3OH} HOCH_2\underset{\underset{CH_3}{|}}{\overset{\overset{CH_3}{|}}{C}}-\overset{O}{\overset{||}{C}}OCH_3 \xrightarrow{\Delta} \left[OCH_2\underset{\underset{CH_3}{|}}{\overset{\overset{CH_3}{|}}{C}}-\overset{O}{\overset{||}{C}}\right]_n + nCH_3OH$$

2.

$$CH_3\underset{\underset{}{}}{\overset{\overset{CH_3}{|}}{C}}\cdots \xrightarrow{acid} \left[OCH_2\underset{\underset{CH_3}{|}}{\overset{\overset{CH_3}{|}}{C}}-\overset{O}{\overset{||}{C}}\right]_n$$

26.34 1.

carbocation intermediate; chirality lost

26.35 1.

$$(CH_3CH_2CH_2CH_2)_3\overset{+}{N}CH_2-\overset{..}{\underset{..}{O}}CH_2\overset{..}{\underset{..}{O}}{}^- \longrightarrow \longrightarrow (CH_3CH_2CH_2CH_2)_3\overset{+}{N}CH_2\overset{..}{\underset{..}{O}}\left[CH_2\overset{..}{\underset{..}{O}}\right]_n$$

26.35 2.

26.36

26.37

(4 equivalents)

26.37 (cont)

$$H_2N-\overset{\overset{\displaystyle CH_2OH}{|}}{\underset{\underset{\displaystyle CH_2OH}{|}}{C}}-CH_2OH$$

(12 equivalents)

the other 11 amide
groups look like this

Supplemental Problems

S26.1   Predict the structures of the polymers that will result from the following reactions.

(a) $CH_3O-\langle\text{C}_6H_4\rangle-CH=CH_2$ + $\langle\text{C}_6H_5\rangle-CH=CH_2$ $\xrightarrow[\substack{\text{carbon tetrachloride} \\ \text{nitrobenzene} \\ 0\,°C}]{SnCl_4}$

(b) $CH_2=CHCl$ $\xrightarrow{\text{benzoyl peroxide}}$

(c) $CH_2=\overset{\overset{\displaystyle C\equiv N}{|}}{\underset{\underset{\displaystyle O}{\|}}{C}}COCH_3$ $\xrightarrow[\substack{H_2O \\ 20\,°C}]{\text{methanol}}$

(d) $HO-\langle\text{C}_6H_4\rangle-\overset{\overset{\displaystyle CH_3}{|}}{\underset{\underset{\displaystyle CH_3}{|}}{C}}-\langle\text{C}_6H_4\rangle-OH$ + $Cl\overset{\displaystyle O}{\overset{\|}{C}}Cl$ $\xrightarrow[\substack{H_2O}]{NaOH}$

(e) $CH_2=CH_2$ + $\langle\text{cyclopentene}\rangle$ $\xrightarrow[\substack{VCl_4 \\ (hexyl)_3Al \\ heptane}]{CH_3CH_2OH}$

(f) $CH_3CH_2OCH_2-\overset{\overset{\displaystyle CH_2OCH_2CH_3}{|}}{\underset{\underset{\displaystyle O}{\diagdown\diagup}}{}}$ $\xrightarrow[\substack{\text{methyl chloride}}]{(CH_3CH_2)_2O\cdot BF_3}$

(g) $\langle\text{phenyl azetidinone}\rangle$ $\langle\text{pyrrolidide}\rangle K^+$ $\xrightarrow[\substack{\text{dimethyl} \\ \text{sulfoxide}}]{}$

S26.2   The following reaction is used to anchor compounds onto the surface of a polymer. Draw the product of this reaction.

$$\boxed{\text{Polymer}} \sim\!\!\text{CH}_2\text{Cl} \;+\; \text{Na}^{+\,-}\text{OCH}_2 \diagdown \!\!\!\!\!\bigcirc\!\!\!\text{O} \xrightarrow[\substack{N,N\text{-dimethyl-}\\ \text{acetamide}\\ 25\,°\text{C, 16 h}}]{} \;?$$

S26.3

(a) The following polyimide has been used in a plastic film that retains its usefulness over a very wide range of temperatures. The repeating unit of the polymer is shown below. What monomeric units would you need to synthesize this polymer?

(b) The polymer shown above can be transformed into a more soluble polymer by reacting it with an amine. Write an equation predicting what will happen to the polymer if it is treated with 2-(N-methylamino)ethanol, $CH_3NHCH_2CH_2OH$.

27

Concerted Reactions

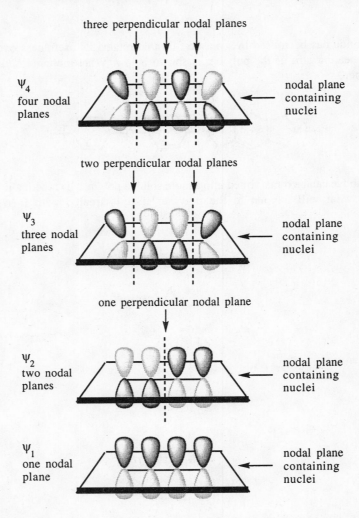

27.1

Ψ_4
four nodal
planes

three perpendicular nodal planes

nodal plane
containing
nuclei

Ψ_3
three nodal
planes

two perpendicular nodal planes

nodal plane
containing
nuclei

Ψ_2
two nodal
planes

one perpendicular nodal plane

nodal plane
containing
nuclei

Ψ_1
one nodal
plane

nodal plane
containing
nuclei

27.2 The symmetry of a molecular orbital can be determined by looking at the symmetry of the atomic *p*-orbitals from which it is constructed since the molecular orbital retains that symmetry.

Ψ_4 antisymmetric

Ψ_3 symmetric

27.2 (cont)

ψ_2 antisymmetric

ψ_1 symmetric

27.3

ground state of
1,3-butadiene

$\xrightarrow{hv}$

excited state of
1,3-butadiene

Note that electron spins remain paired in the excited state.

27.4

27.5

27.6 (a)

(b)

(c)

27.7 (a)

(b)   (c)

(d)

27.8

27.9

LUMO of diene

HOMO of dienophile

In this picture the lobes of the *p*-orbitals that are left over at carbons 2 and 3 of the diene will be bonding.

27.10

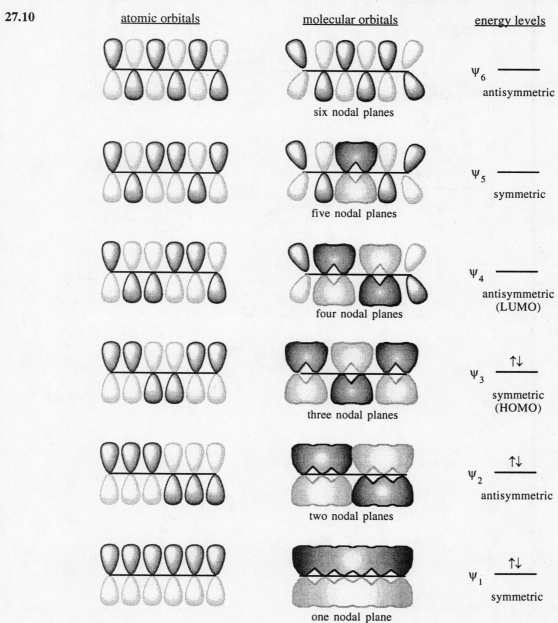

atomic orbitals	molecular orbitals	energy levels
	six nodal planes	ψ_6 ——— antisymmetric
	five nodal planes	ψ_5 ——— symmetric
	four nodal planes	ψ_4 ——— antisymmetric (LUMO)
	three nodal planes	ψ_3 ⇅ symmetric (HOMO)
	two nodal planes	ψ_2 ⇅ antisymmetric
	one nodal plane	ψ_1 ⇅ symmetric

The lower three molecular orbitals are bonding; the upper three are antibonding.

Concept Map 27.1   Cycloaddition reactions.

(Section 27.4)

LUMO of π bond interacting
with the HOMO of the σ bond

conrotatory
ring opening

ψ_2 of the diene   (2*E*, 4*E*)-2,4-hexadiene

27.11

LUMO of π bond interacting
with the HOMO of the σ bond

conrotatory
ring opening

ψ_2 of the diene   (2*Z*, 4*Z*)-2,4-hexadiene

steric crowding

This product is also possible from a conrotatory ring opening of trans-3,4-dimethylcyclobutene, but it is not formed because of steric crowding in the transition state.

27.12 The observed equilibrium involves two conrotatory electrocyclic reactions of a butadiene-cyclobutene system, one a ring closure and the other a ring opening.

Other possible stereoisomers:

27.13

butadiene system
disrotatory ring closure

hydrogen atoms on
same side of the ring

27.14

s-trans

s-cis

racemic mixture

Thermal process:

HOMO of the diene
in the ground state

conrotatory
ring closing

27.14 (cont)

Photochemical process:

HOMO of the diene in the excited state	disrotatory ring closing	

27.15

HOMO of the triene
in the ground state

(See Problem 27.10 for the molecular orbitals of the triene.)

27.16

HOMO of the triene
in the ground state;
thermal ring closure

same molecule as that
shown in Figure 27.11

HOMO of the triene
in the excited state;
photochemical ring closure

enantiomer of the molecule
shown in Figure 27.12

Concept Map 27.2   Electrocyclic reactions.

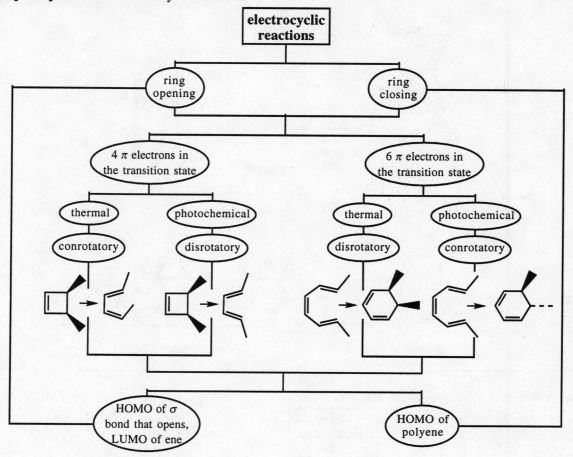

- -

27.17   HOMO of triene in the ground state:

precalciferol

→ outward disrotatory →

isopyrocalciferol

27.17 (cont)

precalciferol

inward
disrotatory

pyrocalciferol

27.18

allo-ocimene

hv
conrotatory

racemic mixture

- -

Concept Map 27.3   Woodward-Hoffmann rules.

27.19

$4n + 2$ electrocyclic reaction; $n = 1$; conrotatory in the excited state; the hydrogen atoms at the ring junctions in dihydrophenanthrene will be trans to each other.

27.20

and enantiomer

$4n$ electrocyclic reaction, $n = 1$; conrotatory in ground state; the methyl groups on the new five-membered ring will be trans to each other.

27.21

the dienophile is an allylic cation with two π electrons

Diels-Alder reaction;
$4n + 2$ electrons, $n = 1$,
in the transition state

- -

Concept Map 27.1   (see p. 656)

- -

27.22   (a)

(b)

(c)

27.22 (d)

and enantiomer

(e)

toluene
100 °C

27.23 (a) Ph—N=N=N⁻ + CH₃CH₂CH₂CH₂OCH=CH₂ ⟶

(b)

(c)

(d)

(e)

27.24

ψ_6 _____

ψ_5 _____

ψ_4 _____ LUMO

ψ_3 ↑↓ HOMO $\xrightarrow{h\nu}$

ψ_2 ↑↓

ψ_1 ↑↓

triene in the
ground state

ψ_6 _____

ψ_5 _____ LUMO

ψ_4 ↓   HOMO

ψ_3 ↑

ψ_2 ↑↓

ψ_1 ↑↓

triene in the
excited state

(See Problem 27.10 for pictures of the orbitals.)

27.24 (cont)

HOMO of triene
in the excited state

LUMO of a σ bond
in the ground state

new triene

27.25

(a) $CH_3CH_2O\underset{O}{\overset{O}{C}}$ ... $\xrightarrow{200\ °C}$ $CH_3CH_2O\underset{O}{\overset{O}{C}}$ ...

(b) Ph ... $\xrightarrow{180\ °C}$ Ph ...

(c) $CH_3CH_2O\underset{O}{\overset{N\equiv C}{C}}$ ... $\xrightarrow{160\ °C}$ $CH_3CH_2O\underset{O}{\overset{N\equiv C}{C}}$ ...

(d) ... $\xrightarrow{175\ °C}$ ...

27.26

two isoprene units   →   [desired product;
an unstable
intermediate] $\xrightarrow[\text{rearrangement}]{[3,3]\text{-sigmatropic}}$ ...

The Cope rearrangement occurs easily because of relief of ring strain in going from a cyclobutane to a cyclooctadiene system.

27.27 (a) $CH_2{=}CHOCH_2CH{=}CH_2$ $\equiv$ ... $\xrightarrow{255\ °C}$ ...

(b) ... $\xrightarrow{175\ °C}$ ...

27.27 (c)

Concept Map 27.4   Sigmatropic rearrangements.

27.28

LUMO of carbene →

antibonding interaction →

← HOMO of carbene

← bonding interaction

LUMO of alkene

Concept Map 27.5   Carbenes.

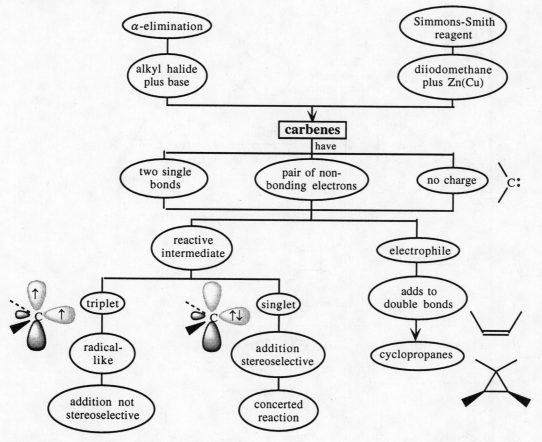

27.29 (a) CH_2I_2 $\xrightarrow[\text{diethyl ether}]{\text{Zn(Cu)}}$

and enantiomer

(b) $\begin{array}{c} CH_3 \\ \\ CH_3 \end{array} C=C \begin{array}{c} CH_3 \\ \\ CH_3 \end{array}$ + $CHCl_3$ + $(CH_3)_3CO^-\ K^+$ $\xrightarrow{-10\ °C}$

27.29 (c)

(d) $CH_2=CHOCH_2CH_3$ + $CHCl_3$ + $(CH_3)_3CO^-$ K^+ $\xrightarrow{-10\ °C}$

and enantiomer

(e) $CH_3(CH_2)_5CH=CH_2$ + CH_2I_2 $\xrightarrow[\substack{\text{diethyl} \\ \text{ether} \\ \Delta}]{Zn(Cu)}$

(f) + CH_2I_2 $\xrightarrow[\substack{\text{diethyl ether} \\ \Delta}]{Zn(Cu)}$ and enantiomer

(g) + CH_2I_2 $\xrightarrow[\substack{\text{diethyl ether} \\ \Delta}]{Zn(Cu)}$

and enantiomer

27.30

(a) + $CH_3C≡CCH_3$ $\xrightarrow{h\nu}$

and enantiomer

(b) + $CH_2=CHCH_2C≡N$ $\xrightarrow{\Delta}$

and enantiomer

(c) + $HC≡CCCH_3$ $\xrightarrow{130\ °C}$

(d) + $CH_2=CHC≡N$ $\xrightarrow{\Delta}$

(e) + $\xrightarrow{100\ °C}$

(f) + $CH_2=CHCCH_3$ $\xrightarrow[\Delta]{\text{benzene}}$

27.30

(g)

and enantiomer

(h)

and enantiomer

27.31   (a)

(b)

(c)

and enantiomer

27.32

(a)

(b)

(c)

(d)

(e)

27.33   (a)

$4n + 2$, conrotatory in the excited state

27.33 (b)

4n + 2,
conrotatory in
the excited state

(c)

4n + 2,
disrotatory in
the ground state

(d)

4n,
conrotatory in
the ground state

(e)

4n,
disrotatory in
the ground state

(f)

4n,
conrotatory in
the ground state

too hindered to form

27.34 (a)

and enantiomer

(b)

and enantiomer

(c)

(d)

27.35

the only possible isomerism
is stereoisomerism

The probable structures are shown on the next page. Each structure also has an enantiomer.

27.35 (cont)

The ones in which the hydrogens are trans on the cyclopentane ring are not considered because of the mechanism of the reaction. It is the excited state of the cyclohexenone that reacts with the ground state of cyclopentene. The double bond in cyclohexenone may become twisted in the excited state, giving rise to a trans fusion of the six- and four-membered rings. The trans-fused compounds will isomerize in base through enolization and reprotonation to give the more stable cis-fused ring system. For example,

This is the compound that is formed in the largest amount in the initial photochemical reaction.

27.36

B is (1Z, 3Z, 5E)-1,3,5-cyclononatriene.

A λ_{max} of 290 nm (ε 2050) in the ultraviolet spectrum points to the presence of a conjugated π system. The presence of bands in the infrared spectrum of B at 1645, 975, 960, and 670 cm^{-1} tells us that B has carbon-carbon double bonds. The band at 1645 cm^{-1} is the C=C stretching frequency. The bands at 975, 960 and 670 cm^{-1} are the bending frequencies for the C—H bonds on the double bonds.

The bands in the proton magnetic resonance spectrum of B correspond to the chemical shifts of vinyl hydrogen atoms (δ 4.7 – 6.2, 6H) and allylic and alkyl hydrogen atoms (δ 0.6 – 2.6, 6H).

27.37   The formation of *trans*-5,6-dichloro-5,6-difluorobicyclo[2.2.1]hept-2-ene is a thermally allowed [4n + 2] cycloaddition (a Diels-Alder) reaction, which occurs with high stereoselectivity.

27.37 (cont)

The concerted thermal cycloaddition reaction for a system with $4n$ electrons is forbidden. The formation of 6,7-dichloro-6,7-difluorobicyclo[3.2.0]hept-2-ene goes by a radical mechanism and gives mixtures of stereoisomers.

27.38

Diels-Alder reaction

27.39

an enol, which is unstable;
no stereochemistry implied

27.40

27.41 (a)

27.42

proton magnetic resonance assignments

^{13}C magnetic resonance assignments

A
product of a [2 + 2]
cycloaddition reaction

B
B is not the product of
a concerted reaction

C
product of the Cope
rearrangement of B

E
$C_8H_{10}O_4$

27.42 (cont)

The assignment of the structure of B is supported by the results of the ozonolysis reaction and by the proton magnetic resonance spectrum.

the bridgehead
hydrogen atoms,
δ 2.72 – 3.23

the vinyl
hydrogen atoms,
δ 4.69 – 6.17

the methylene
hydrogen atoms,
δ 1.33 – 2.22

$CH_3O-\overset{O}{\underset{}{C}}$

the hydrogen atoms
of the methoxy group,
δ 3.69

27.43 (a)

A
1,3-dipolar species

1,3-dipolar character

(b)

B is the structure that is related to Bao Gong Teng A.

27.44 (a)

toluene
Δ
15 h

CH_3
$(CH_3CH)_2N^-Li^+$
CH_3CH_2I

A

27.44 (a) (cont)

(b)   There are six electrons available for the reaction. The two nonbonding electrons on nitrogen participate. Conrotatory ring closure is expected.

A pair of 1,2-hydrogen shifts completes the reaction, restoring aromaticity in one of the rings.

27.45   (a)   PhC≡CPh +

(b)

27.46

Supplemental Problems

S27.1   Complete the following equations. Be sure to show stereochemistry if it can be predicted.

(a)

(b)

(c) $CH_3\overset{\underset{CH_3}{|}}{\underset{|}{C}}OCH_2CH=CH_2$ + CH_2I_2 $\xrightarrow[\substack{\text{diethyl} \\ \text{ether} \\ \Delta}]{Zn(Cu)}$

(d) $CH_3\overset{\underset{}{|}}{\underset{}{C}}=CH_2$ + $CHBr_3$ + $(CH_3)_3CO^- K^+$ $\xrightarrow[-10\,°C]{}$

(e)

(f)

(g)

(h)

(i) $Ph\overset{+}{N}=N=N^-$ + $CH_2=CHC\equiv N$ $\xrightarrow{\Delta}$

(j)

(k)

S27.1

(l)

(m)   + CH_2═$CHOCH_2CH_2CH_2CH_3$ $\xrightarrow{\Delta}$

S27.2   When (1Z, 3E)-1,3-cyclooctadiene is heated to 80 °C, it converts to bicyclo[4.2.0]oct-7-ene (shown below). (1Z, 3Z)-1,3-Cyclooctadiene undergoes a photochemical ring closure to give the same compound, with the same stereochemistry, but it does not give a cyclobutene product when heated. How do you explain these observations?

bicyclo[4.2.0]oct-7-ene

When bicyclo[4.2.0]oct-7-ene is heated above 300 °C, the cyclobutene ring opens and (1Z, 3Z)-1,3-cyclooctadiene is formed. Is this opening of the ring a concerted reaction?

S27.3   Of the two compounds shown below, one undergoes opening of the cyclobutene ring easily, whereas the other requires high temperatures. Predict which one reacts with ease, and explain why.